ISLANDS AND EXILES

The Creole Identities of Post/Colonial Literature

D1449836

Islands and Exiles

THE CREOLE IDENTITIES OF
POST/COLONIAL LITERATURE

Chris Bongie

STANFORD UNIVERSITY PRESS

STANFORD, CALIFORNIA

1998

Stanford University Press

Stanford, California

© 1998 by the Board of Trustees of the

Leland Stanford Junior University

Printed in the United States of America

CIP data appear at the end of the book

Acknowledgments

A great many people contributed, in one way or another, to the writing of this book. I would like to thank my colleagues at the College of William and Mary, and to acknowledge in particular the support of Chandos Michael Brown, Kirsten Silva Gruesz, Thomas Heacox, Richard S. Lowry, Robert P. Maccubbin, Terry Meyers, Eliza Nichols, Adam and Monica Potkay, Richard and Sally Price, Julia Walker, Walter Wenska, and Peter DeSa Wiggins. I am especially grateful to Régis Antoine, Anthony Appiah, Richard D. E. Burton, Christopher L. Miller, and Ralph Sarkonak for the interest they have taken in this project; to Kamau Brathwaite and Édouard Glissant for their encouragement and inspiration; and, belatedly, to René Girard, for the exertion of an influence about which I am no longer anxious. Thanks also to Maud Lavin and Nathan MacBrien at Stanford University Press for their careful editorial work, and to Helen Tartar, whose enthusiasm for and belief in this project has been a constant source of motivation for me over the course of the past five years. Above all, I would like to thank my students at William and Mary, who were the first to hear and comment on many of the ideas in *Islands and Exiles*.

My research trips to Paris would have been far more costly and much less amusing were it not for the copious hospitality of Chris Mooney and Clara Young. My sabbatical year in London was greatly enhanced by Paul Nelles and Laurie Setzer, who showed me the ropes and the croquet mallets, and by Alexander Samson and Stefan Simanowitz, who were good enough to share their lease with a Canuck from *outre-mer*. I also want to thank Jim English and Eileen Reeves for having me along on so many of their *tours de Jersey*, and Kim Bush for installing me in the various cities where she lives. Most of all, a special debt of gratitude is owed to Lorna Hemming for all those summers on Saltspring, and to Craig Moyes for the many years of Johnsonian (or was that Boswellian?) camaraderie.

A Harvard Junior Faculty Mellon Fellowship for 1993–94 provided me with the opportunity of getting this project well under way, and I remember with fondness and appreciation everybody who was involved in that program, especially its director, Richard Hunt, and the other Mellon fellows: Paige Baty, Jennifer Fleischner, Dagmar Herzog, Mary Jaeger, and Edward Wheatley. A William and Mary Faculty Research Assignment for 1996–97 allowed me to complete the book in London, where I also benefited from the support of the National Endowment for the Humanities (thanks to the directors of my summer seminar program, Reed Way Dasenbrock and Feroza Jussawalla) and from my association as a visiting scholar with the Department of African Languages and Cultures at the School of Oriental and African Studies (thanks to the director of the departmental seminar series, Nana Wilson-Tagoe).

Parts of Chapters 2, 4, 6, 7, and 8 have previously appeared in print: I am grateful to the editors of the collections *Asia/Pacific as Space of Cultural Production* and *(Un)writing Empire,* and of the journals *Callaloo, New West Indian Guide,* and *Modern Fiction Studies,* both for their encouragement and for their permission to use that material here. I am especially grateful to the board of *Modern Fiction Studies* for awarding me the 1993 Margaret Church Memorial Prize for my essay on Coetzee's *Foe.* Portions of my essay "Resisting Memories: The Creole Identities of Lafcadio Hearn and Edouard Glissant," originally published in *Sub/Stance* 84 (1997), appear here courtesy of the University of Wisconsin Press. I would also like to thank the Bibliothèque nationale in Paris for granting me permission to reproduce the portraits of Bissette and Schœlcher, as well as the Musée national d'art moderne in Paris and the estate of Wifredo Lam for their permission to use his *La réunion* on the cover.

Finally, I would like to dedicate this book to Laurence and Elizabeth Bongie: "There is a comfort in the strength of love; / 'Twill make a thing endurable, which else / Would overset the brain, or break the heart."

C.B.

Contents

Nous sommes tous solidaires les uns pour les autres.
—Bernardin de Saint-Pierre, *Études de la nature*

Car nous sommes, tous, réunis sur un seul rivage.
—Édouard Glissant, *Soleil de la conscience*

Part **1**

INTRODUCTION(S)

1   *Within the Shady Hold of Modernity*

A PREFACE TO CREOLIZATION

> The argument that I will be defending here is that *ours is a creolizing world*, which is to say that the cultures of the globe, placed in contact with one another in a sudden and now absolutely conscious manner, are in the process of changing through their exchange, in the face of irremissible conflicts and pitiless wars but also of advances in hope and awareness that give one leave to say—without being, or rather, by accepting to be, utopian—that people are today abandoning, with difficulty, something to which they had been stubbornly clinging for a long time: namely, the idea that one being's identity is only valid and recognizable if it excludes the identity of all other possible beings. And it is this painful mutation of human thought that I would like to trace out for you here.
>
> —Édouard Glissant, *Introduction à une Poétique du Divers*

In 1794, French forces led by Victor Hugues wrested back the Caribbean island of Guadeloupe from the British, who had briefly occupied it with the support of local plantation owners. As the newly appointed *Commissaire* of Guadeloupe, Hugues, who would soon earn the epithet "Robespierre of the Isles," immediately instituted the National Convention's decree of 16 Pluviose, Year II, which formally abolished slavery in the colonies (a decree that less than a decade later would be rescinded by Napoléon's law of 30 Floréal, Year X, and that in a number of the French colonies had, in any case, remained a dead letter). Revolutionary Guadeloupe experienced a profound if short-lived social transformation under Hugues's charismatic, if often ruthless, administration. Under pressure from the counterrevolutionary forces of the British and United States slavocracies, Hugues initiated the so-called war of the privateers soon after his successful restoration of French power, in an attempt at consolidating the political and economic stability of Guadeloupe and spreading the Revolution to neighboring islands. "Enormous fortunes were made," the novelist and historian Oruno Lara reports in his 1921 *La Guadeloupe dans l'histoire*, going on to assert that this period—when "wealth flowed into the country, thrown down in fistfuls, as in some tale of the Barbary Coast, by the black Corsairs of Guadeloupe"—was the most "brilliant" in his island's history.[1] In the brief and decidedly partial eclipse of the racially hierarchized world of the ancien régime that resulted from Hugues's governorship, a confirmed assimilationist like Lara might well have seen the prototype for that egalitarian relationship between France and its colonies to which he would always remain firmly committed, notwithstanding the sense of racial allegiance that led him to give voice in *La Guadeloupe dans l'histoire* to the un(der)represented world of his fellow "mulatto" and "black" islanders, thereby supplementing and tentatively challenging earlier histories of the island produced by members of its *béké* (native-born "white") elite. This revisionist gesture situates Lara's book in the vanguard of twentieth-century counterhistories of the Caribbean, of which the most famous example is, of course, C. L. R. James's 1938 paean to the Haitian Revolution, *The Black Jacobins*—in which the Frenchman Hugues also makes a brief appearance, albeit in the historically erroneous (if perhaps poetically just) guise of a "Mulatto Commander."[2]

It is on board one of Hugues's revolutionary pirate ships, *L'ami du peuple*, that the Cuban writer Alejo Carpentier places his protagonist Esteban toward the middle of *El siglo de las luces* (1962; translated as *Explosion in a Cathedral*), his epic account of the French Revolution and its transatlantic reverberations in the Caribbean. The nephew of a wealthy Havana merchant, Esteban had years before been roused out of his bourgeois slumbers by (a fictionalized) Hugues, and had accompanied the erstwhile Saint-Domingue merchant to France in 1791, where he bore witness to the alternately sublime and absurd unfolding of the Revolution. Now that Hugues is in charge of exporting this Revolution to the Americas, Esteban has become disillusioned with it, and his thoughts turn back with increasing intensity to the place of his birth. Having recrossed the Atlantic with Hugues, Esteban is prevented by various circumstances from returning to Cuba and finds himself employed on *L'ami du peuple* in the unlikely role of a "privateers' clerk" (*Escribano de Corsarios*). If, as the narrator puts it, "there was absurdity in the mere mention of such a profession,"[3] this is clearly because Esteban's bureaucratized identity involves an "absurd" conjunction of the rationalizing imperatives of capitalist bookkeeping and the swashbuckling heroism associated with a more archaic and spontaneous way of life. Moreover, Esteban's role as a mere scrivener is a mocking reminder of his earlier dreams of becoming a serious writer: reflecting upon the Revolution, for instance, he had earlier decided that "he would like to write, to discover, by means of writing and the disciplines which it imposes, the conclusions that were perhaps waiting to be drawn from what he had seen"

(p. 127). But such conclusions prove grievously hard to come by; instead, Esteban finds himself confronted with an inconclusive world in which the noble authorial project of which he once dreamt has been revealed as complicit, and perhaps interchangeable, with the degraded form of writing that engages him as an "Escribano de Corsarios." There is perhaps a certain autobiographical dimension to the depiction of Esteban here, for it was a similar degrading complicity that Carpentier had come to associate in the 1940s with the literary output of his European contemporaries and that had generated, by way of compensation, his influential vision of Latin America and the Caribbean as the privileged locus of "lo real maravilloso": a reality that marvelously transcended the absurdities and vagaries of a disenchanted, rationalized, Westernized writing from which, he had come to believe, nothing truly meaningful could be concluded. Indeed, during Esteban's voyages aboard *L'ami du peuple*, he is compensated for the absurdity of his situation by occasional glimpses of this marvelous reality in a series of epiphanies that disrupt the narrative progress of the story being told, momentarily suspending the Weberian progression (or, viewed from another perspective, the Spenglerian regression) of History and its successive and ultimately always unsuccessful revolutions.

These epiphanies of the Caribbean's marvelous reality take two apparently contradictory forms: the revelation, on the one hand, of America's still virginal *nature*, and, on the other, of its provocatively mixed *culture*. This double (and contradictory) identity—natural and cultural—of "lo real maravilloso" is evident in a passage from the preface to an earlier novel of Carpentier's about the Haitian Revolution, *El reino de este mundo* (1949; *The Kingdom of This World*). Here he notes that Latin America (and, by extension, the Caribbean) is "far from having exhausted its wealth of mythologies," a fact he ascribes to "its virginal landscape, its gestation, its ontology, the Faustic presence of Indians and blacks . . . the Revelation constituted by its recent discovery, [and] the fruitful racial mixtures that it favored."[4] The episode from Carpentier's *Explosion* that I am leading up to in these opening paragraphs occurs immediately after an extended meditation upon the first, *natural* manifestation of "lo real maravilloso," in which Esteban enthuses over the virginal landscape that has revealed itself to him during his travels and that has provided him with the means of escaping, if only temporarily, the iron cage of his bureaucratized identity. In the chapter that follows upon this ecstatic revelation of the primordial and naturally marvelous reality of the Caribbean, *L'ami du peuple* has chased down and boarded a Portuguese ship: in its holds (*calas*) the corsairs have discovered a full load of red, white, and Madeira wine, of which Esteban hastens to make an inventory before the thirstier members of the crew can get their hands on it. Finding himself "alone and safe from interference or competition in a shady hold that was more like a wine-cellar [*en una umbrosa bodega que lo era doblemente*], the clerk helped himself out of an ample mahogany bowl, in which the taste of the must was combined with the scent of the thick, cool wood, that had a fleshy feel against the lips" (pp. 182–83). This sensual encounter might well have produced a meditation similar to the one in the preceding chapter: it seems for a moment as if we are going to be asked to read this "shady hold" and the commodities it contains as quasi-natural products divorced from the historical negotiations that have made their presence in the Caribbean possible. This "shady hold" threatens, indeed, to be doubly cut off from that historical reality—a doubleness that results not just from the fact that "bodega" means both "wine-cellar" and "hold" in Spanish, but from the significant absence of other "shades," human ones, that might very well have been found in a ship's hold at the end of the eighteenth century. It is only in the absence of this other transatlantic cargo and this other history, one that itself doubles the more obvious absence of his emancipated black shipmates from the hold, that Esteban's solitary immersion in the realm of the senses could ever take place.

This particular encounter does not, however, simply generate the sort of ecstatic and ahistorical considerations of the preceding chapter: it does not give rise to an account of the natural marvels of the Caribbean but to a meditation on the entanglements of its history (though admittedly not that "other history" whose absence we have just remarked upon). These cultural entanglements turn out to be as constitutive of the New World's marvelous reality as its virginal nature. The narrator's commentary on the Madeira wine explicitly, and as we will see confusedly, raises the issue that will be central to *Islands and Exiles*: namely, "transculturation," the process of cultural mixing that has, in large part through the groundbreaking work of Carpentier and his fellow Cuban Fernando Ortiz, come to occupy the forefront of recent critical thinking about questions of (ethnic, racial, national) *identity*. Referred to by a variety of similar, though by no means entirely interchangeable, names such as *mestizaje, métissage*, hybridization, and (the term with which I will be chiefly concerned in this book) creolization, this process is at the heart of the passage from Carpentier's *Explosion* that I have been leading up to:

Esteban had learned in France to appreciate the noble juice of the vine, which had nourished the proud and turbulent civilisation of the Mediterranean, now spread into this Caribbean Mediterranean, where the blending of characteristics [*la Confusión de Rasgos*] had for many thousands of years been in progress within the ambit of the peoples of the sea. Here, after long being scattered, the descendants of the lost tribes had met again, to mingle their accents and their lineaments, to produce new strains, mixing and commixing, degenerating and regenerating, a temporary enlightenment followed by a leap backwards into the darkness [*mezclando acentos y cabelleras, entregados a renovadores mestizajes, . . . mezclados, entremezclados, despintados y vueltos a pintar, aclarados un días para anocherse en un salto atrás*], in an interminable proliferation of new profiles, new accents and proportions. In their turn they had been reached by the wine which had passed from the Phoenician ships, the warehouses of Cadiz, and the amphorae of Maarkos Sestos, into the caravels of the Discovery, along with the guitar and the glazed tile, and had landed on these shores so propitious to the transcendental encounter of the Olive with the Maize. (p. 183)

Ironically, this revelation of the mingling and migration of cultures immediately exacerbates Esteban's nostalgia for his lost island home: it has the effect of making him long for a return to the "old, patriarchal casks" stored in his relatives' warehouse in Havana, and for the closure of the original "family circle" that some five years earlier had been broken into by History, in the person of Victor Hugues and in the name of the linear progressions promised by the Revolution. Henceforth, Esteban's voyage on "the mighty ocean of Odysseys and Anabases" (p. 173) will be even more inseparable from his dream of a *nostos*—a dream that, as he discovers upon his eventual return to Cuba, is unrealizable in any but the most banal physical sense.

In this tremendously rich passage from *Explosion*, what most obviously sticks out is the emphasis on (racial, cultural, linguistic) mixing—an emphasis that is clearly meant to convey Carpentier's vision of the Americas as "a continent of symbioses, mutations, vibrations, mixings." The transcultural exchange of hitherto separated worlds that Carpentier here describes renders possible the "consciousness of being a new thing, a symbiosis," that he would elsewhere refer to as "creoleness" (*la criolledad*).[5] The identity of this "new thing" no longer seems dependent upon roots but upon migratory routes (to cite a distinction popularized by Iain Chambers).[6] The passage in question directs us toward not the consolidation of the One but what we might term the (con)fusion of the Many—a confusion that is always also, as the etymology suggests, a "fusing with"; indeed, in a revisionist gesture Carpentier demonstrates how this (con)fusion that took place on the propitious shores of the Americas was itself constitutive of "the proud and turbulent civilisation of the Mediterranean," envisioned here not in terms of a singular Greco-Roman filiation but of a diversity of origins. Clearly, on a first reading of this passage we are presented with a pioneering formulation of the "unceasing process of transformation" that the Martiniquan novelist Édouard Glissant, whose literary and cultural criticism will provide the central theoretical point of reference for me in this book, has valorized as "creolization": the entering into complex new relations of formerly isolated peoples under the sign of our ever more interdependent world economy—an entering into what Glissant defines, in terms whose opacity I will for now let stand, as "a completely new dimension that permits each and every one of us to be both here and elsewhere, rooted and exposed, lost in the mountains and at liberty under the sea, harmoniously at rest and restlessly wandering."[7]

I will be expanding upon Glissant's fluid definitions of creolization toward the end of the next chapter. Here, though, it is Carpentier's pioneering vision of this "new thing" that concerns us, and what is clear on a second reading of the passage from *Explosion* is that it is open to question in all sorts of ways. First, why does he feel compelled to describe this coming together as a *re*union of the lost tribes ("las Tribus Extraviadas"), thereby translating it back into the (biblical) terms of the Old World? Why should the new and unfamiliar be familiarized through an appeal to the diasporic *dispersión* of the world's peoples? The New World here seems to end up only confirming what came before, and the straight line forward into a creolized present thus circles back rather unexpectedly in the direction of a long lost past. Second, and even more glaringly, the Caribbean is further familiarized by being likened to the Mediterranean: what is the effect of reading the often violent cultural "mixing and commixing" that produced the (post-Conquest) Caribbean as simply a repetition of what went on in the ancient Mediterranean? Might not the likening of these two geographically distanced peoples of the sea ("los Pueblos del Mar"), whom Carpentier joins together in a series of colonial relays from the Phoenicians to Columbus, amount to nothing more than a superficially attractive but ultimately dangerous imitation of the discursive patternings of early works of exploration literature, in which "the familiar Mediterranean topoi of classical literature are used to gauge the novelty of Caribbean savagery"?[8] In both cases, Carpentier seems compelled, in order to convey the (marvelous) reality of *here*, to talk about it in other terms, in the language of *there*. He thus adopts an allegorical position, inseparable from categorizing and hierarchical perspectives, that may well be, as Stephen Slemon for one has argued, the single most distinguishing feature of colonial discourse: if, Slemon asserts, allegory involves "a process of signification in which an image in a literary text is interpreted against a pre-existing master code or typological system, [then] a similar process of interpreting signs has been used in imperial thinking to read the world and to legitimise the power relations it establishes within it."[9] Indeed, the disturbing presence of allegory in this passage, which a truly egalitarian thinking of cross-cultural relations ought surely to have transcended, is even more emphatic in the original Spanish, where Carpentier's extensive use of capital letters ("la Confusión de Rasgos," "los Pueblos del Mar," "las Tribus Extraviadas") has not been minimized by the tactfulness of his translator. This obtrusive use of capitals is, however, still visible in the final sentence of the passage: with this opposition between the Olive and the Maize, the complex "new thing," the baroque proliferation of forms and shades, that ought to be emerging from all this mestizaje is simplified into a "transcendental encounter" in which stable, abstract categories of identity that should have been dissolved through this meeting of cultures are in fact reinforced, as they are throughout Carpentier's novel (as when, to cite but one instance, the Carib-Spanish conflict is reduced to a struggle between "Totemic Man" and "Theological Man" [pp. 244–45]).

Clearly, this transformation of a process (back) into a product, which emerges on a second reading of the passage (that is to say, on a reading that has the luxury of basing itself on the many refinements of theories of transculturation put forward in the almost four decades since Carpentier wrote his novel), can be understood as an instance of the Cuban novelist's inability fully to grasp the hybridizing energies that are central to his "Mediterráneo Caribe" and that he is in the process of praising. What one recent proponent of creolization, Raphaël Confiant, has said of Carpentier's contemporary Gilbert Gratiant, a poet who consistently valorized the "racial cocktail" and the "kaleidoscope of types" that he associated with his native Martinique,[10] would seem equally applicable to the author of Explosion: "in the final analysis, he once again winds up with the One, with a new Caribbean being, the harmonious product of a double or a triple métissage."[11] This lingering attachment to the concept of a stable being (être), and a consequent inability fully to acknowledge the processual implications of what Homi Bhabha has termed the "third space" of cultural hybridity,[12] is just one of many other points of criticism that can, and certainly must, be identified with respect to Carpentier's position. For instance, does his positive assessment of mestizaje, which has an extensive genealogy in nineteenth-century Cuban thought, serve—despite its apparently egalitarian intentions—as a convenient excuse for avoiding the problem of social injustice? This, at least, is the criticism that Vera Kutzinski levels against the emphasis on transculturation in Carpentier and Ortiz: "the equality Ortiz casually implies, the same idea of equality that underlies popular notions of Cuba's mestizaje and Caribbean multiculturalism," is deceptive, she argues, not only because it overlooks the continued oppression of "blacks" by "whites" in Cuba, but because it submerges the often violent sexual relations that were, in the Caribbean context, one of the most prominent means by which such mixing was furthered.[13] Moreover, for those familiar with Carpentier's work as a whole, the absence of Africans in this particular "transcendental encounter" is rather troubling: why are they as absent in this passage as they are from the shady hold in which Esteban finds himself? Might this absence not point toward Carpentier's continued need—a need that is most visible in his early work on Afro-Cuban culture in the 1930s—to see them, and the people of the Maize as well, in primitivist terms that somehow escape the creolizing process? (One recalls the uneasy way in which the "Faustic" blacks and Indians fit in with his comments about the New World's marvelous reality, indeterminately situated as they are between the primary nature and hybridized culture that form the two antithetical poles of his revelation of the New World.) Is Carpentier, in other words, still partially engaged in a "foundational enterprise" that runs counter to the "translation sensibility" of a truly "critical criollism"[14]—or has he by this mature point in his career gone beyond the primitivism of his early modernist work and created, as his most astute critic has argued, a cross-culturalized world in which peoples of African descent are actually the carefully hidden motors of the (con)fusing experience that is being theorized (and thus, I will be suggesting, inevitably betrayed) in Esteban's shipboard encounter?[15]

These are all extremely valid points. Rather, though, than simply historicize and criticize such tendencies in Carpentier—rather than (only) read him as a flawed precursor of some more authentic poetics of creolization that is not haunted by the sort of gaps and abstractions I have pointed to in the preceding paragraphs—I believe a third reading of the passage from *Explosion* is not only possible but necessary as a supplement to the second. In this third reading, Carpentier's text suggests, at least to this reader, that no matter how refined our notion of transculturation, it will always fall short of what it points toward. A reliance upon, and a reversion to, fixed and ultimately fictional (ethnic, racial, national, and so on) identities is inescapable, notwithstanding our ever greater immersion in and sensitivity to a creolized and creolizing world. The (at times useful, at times obnoxious, and always in some way exclusionary) language of identity politics that our increasing awareness of the creolization process so rightly warns us against is not something we can simply, as it were, trans*cend*. In the spirit of this third reading, for instance, Carpentier's obtrusive use of capitalizations would constitute one strategy among many that he uses to emphasize this inescapable failure of (his) language to be anything but duplicitously allegorical in its approach to the transcultural mixing he describes and champions: it would be a way of self-consciously marking the distance of language, and the foundationalist biases that make all language possible, from the "new thing" that he is translating, with difficulty, into words.

It is, in any case, this type of third reading that will often be engaging me in *Islands and Exiles*, for whereas the primary critical intention of this book is quite simply to help further Glissant's argument that "ours is a creolizing world" (*ID*, pp. 15–16; "le monde se créolise") and to promote the ongoing critique of an essentializing, roots-oriented identity politics, another of its intentions, which (in what I hope is the best sense of the word) *hypocritically* supplements the first, is to pursue a counterargument generated out of both epistemological and ethical concerns. First, that no matter how much we would like to, we cannot simply do away with the sort of nonrelational, exclusionary thinking that is at the basis of conventional identity politics and its received wisdom: affirmations of fixed identity are inevitable, and every such affirmation—even that of a "creole identity"— necessarily betrays the "unceasing process of transformation" to which the passage from Carpentier's *Explosion* problematically attunes us. Second, that the laudable demystification of such identities, which is a necessary tactic of any postessentialist politics, is patently not a sufficient one: provisional affirmations of identity are often politically necessary, notwithstanding the fact that they are theoretically "unviable" (to echo Gayatri Spivak). Even, and perhaps especially, the most fervent demystifications of a stable identity end up repeating—be it strategically or unconsciously (or, most likely, an undecidable mixture of the two)—the same mystificatory act they critique: this is patently evident, to take but one example, in the case of such post- or anti-identitarian models as those of the "schizophrenic" or the "nomad" that Deleuze and Guattari (who are a frequent point of reference for Glissant, incidentally) offer up in the name of a pure "ethics of flow."[16] These epistemological and ethical concerns will temper my exploration of creolization in the following pages. Participating in and elaborating upon what is to my mind the most vibrant and persuasive insight into the workings of what I will be calling our post/colonial world, this book will thus also resist the very idea of creolization upon which it is founded. It will, at various critical junctures, put into question what that idea bravely signals: namely (to cite Confiant), "the emergence of a new model of identity that one might call 'multiple' or 'mosaic,' which is in the process of developing and making itself visible everywhere in the world, notably in the West's megalopoli" (*AC*, p. 266).

I will be elaborating upon the dynamics of this double-edged argument in the following chapter, first through a reading of the South African writer J. M. Coetzee's novel *Foe* (1986), and then through a more in-depth analysis of the concept of creolization that will be centered around the theoretical writings of Glissant and Kamau Brathwaite, who have produced two of the best known, but in many ways contrasting, accounts of what is meant by that word. Before doing so, however, I would like to make a few more preliminary comments about my own book, notably, regarding its historical parameters, the specific authors whom I will be discussing, and why, as my title suggests, I have chosen to concentrate much of my discussion on the etymologically related topoi of islands and exile.

I have taken Carpentier's novel as my point of departure, not only because *Explosion in a Cathedral* provides us with a very clear, though highly schematic and obviously problematic, description of transculturation, but also because it situates us at the beginnings of the two historical periods that I will be considering in tandem here: the late eighteenth century, which saw the consolidation of an "absolutely modern" colonialism, and the middle of the twentieth century, which marked the emergence of what has come to be known as post-colonialism. On the one hand, *Explosion* is a novel written *about* the (end of the) age of Enlightenment, a revolutionary period that witnessed, as Mary Louise Pratt has suggested, a definite shift in European "planetary consciousness," "a shift that coincides with . . . the consolidation of bourgeois forms of subjectivity and power, the inauguration of a new territorial phase of capitalism propelled by searches for raw materials, the attempt to extend coastal trade inland, and national imperatives to seize overseas territory in order to prevent its being seized by rival European powers."[17] As I have argued at some length in *Exotic Memories: Literature, Colonialism, and the Fin de Siècle*, it is from the late eighteenth century on, with the definitive mapping of the globe (a process that as far as marine exploration is concerned was essentially over with the South Seas voyages of Cook and La Pérouse and that in terms of inland exploration would be completed over the course of the following century), that the "second imperial phase" of European colonialism begins.[18] On the other hand, written *during* the golden age of the decolonization movement in Africa and the Caribbean, Carpentier's novel clearly provides a post-colonial reflection upon the origins of, and possible revolutionary responses to, this absolutely modern colonialism, although the publishing history of the novel can itself be read allegorically as a caution against mechanically segregating the colonial world from what comes after it. For the most part written in Venezuela in 1956–58, Carpentier revised the book—although the exact extent of this revision is not known—upon his return to Cuba after the fall of the Batista régime and Castro's accession to power, publishing it only in 1962.[19] Exactly where is *Explosion* situated historically and ideologically? On what side of the revolutionary divide? Might it not be most exact to locate it on neither side but in a "third space" that falls between the colonial (or, in Cuba's case, already a neocolonial) past and a truly post-colonial future, an intermediate location that participates in both while being neither one nor the other?

What we can read out of the ambivalent publishing history of *Explosion*, I would suggest, is the intimate (dis)connection of the colonial and the post-colonial, which are both, after all, the products of a fully global *modernity*—a "community-world," in Glissant's words (*FM*, p. 305)—in which the (con)fusing energies of creolization are an inescapable fact of life. It is this common, creolized and creolizing, culture that I am gesturing toward in the subtitle of this book with the neologism "post/colonial," in which two words and worlds appear uneasily as one, joined together and yet also divided in a relation of (dis)continuity. The slash mediates between them and urges us toward a grappling with the insight that, in Nicholas Thomas's words, "postcolonialism is distinguished, not by a clean leap into another discourse, but by its critical reaccentuation of colonial and anti-colonial languages."[20] My readings, which shuttle back and forth between the literatures of these two worlds, will thus be performed not (simply) in terms of opposition but (also) of epistemic complicity—a complicity that is specifically thematized in Coetzee's *Foe*, a rewriting of Defoe's *Robinson Crusoe* (1719) that remains errantly attached to the very thing from which it appears to be detaching itself. The "post/colonial," in short, will be distinguished throughout this book from other variants of the word, notably "postcolonial" and, more infrequently, "post-colonial." Postcolonial will be used simply as an historical marker, covering approximately the last half of this century and describing certain societies that have been or still are under the formal or informal control of another nation, as well as the cultural artifacts that these societies have produced; post-colonial will henceforth be limited to conveying the (purely ideological) hypothesis of a future that would be completely severed from colonialism—a fully liberated time that the "post/colonial" insistently puts into question.

The entangled condition that I am gesturing toward in the word "post/colonial" can be read in parallel with Lyotard's more recent uses of the word "postmodern," in which it signals not a "new age" following upon modernity (as was suggested in his earlier, and implicitly avant-gardist, formulations of the concept in the 1979 *La condition postmoderne*) but a self-reflective component of that modernity: "neither modernity nor the so-called postmodernity can be identified and defined as clear-cut historical entities," he asserts.[21] Rather, Lyotard's revised account of postmodernity makes it equivalent to what I would call post/modernity by defining it as simply an ongoing rewriting of modernity and its displacements, "the re-writing of some features modernity had tried or pretended to gain, particularly in founding its legitimation upon the purpose of the general emancipation of mankind." This critical rewriting, Lyotard continues, is something that may well have increased of late but "was for a long time active in modernity itself" (pp. 8–9). Our late-twentieth-century postmodern age, then, is one in which this "post/modern condition" becomes exceptionally apparent—a time in which the ostensible exhaustion and yet enigmatic survival of modernity and its projects confront us repeatedly and inescapably.

The application of Lyotard's argument to the terms colonial and postcolonial should be clear: the colonial project and its anticolonial double were founded upon certain legitimizing narratives—most notably, perhaps, authoritative narratives about progress that were indissociable from categorical and categorizing assertions of (racial, ethnic, national) identity; but these narratives were themselves subject to a rewriting made possible by the specifically hybrid conditions that the colonial enterprise inevitably promoted and that were always-already in the process of eroding its Manichean world view. In the postcolonial age, this hybridity, which is an inescapable consequence of a fully global(izing) modernity, has become increasingly apparent, and we are in a better position to valorize and analyze rather than demonize or ignore it. However, this positive appreciation, and the consequent move away from, say, an essentialist politics of identity or revolutionary calls for liberation, can never be final: we cannot help falling back into a (re)telling of the same old stories (the legitimizing narratives of our modernity) because, as Lyotard points out, "postmodernity [or what I would call post-modernity] is a promise with which modernity is pregnant definitely and endlessly" (p. 4). To live with(in) this promise is to continue to be haunted—be it to a lesser or a greater degree—by the desire for its eventual fulfillment: by the desire, that is, for the definitive termination of the compromised, hybridized and hybridizing, condition of post/coloniality that critics like Homi Bhabha and Gayatri Spivak have so ably insisted upon but that many neo-identitarian, and self-styled uprising or insurgent, critics predictably continue to reject, deriding it—from their self-proclaimed position "outside the postcolonial"—as a "trap," as "much like being stuck after coloniality in some 'hybrid space.'"[22] The rationale for this rejection is clear since, as Ella Shohat and Robert Stam succinctly put it, "'postcolonial' posits no clear domination and calls for no clear opposition," and the term's "structured ambivalence" thus makes it "a fragile instrument for critiquing the unequal distribution of global power and resources."[23]

Those more receptive to the ambivalences of inhabiting the post/modern and the post/colonial do not share this dissatisfaction with "fragile" instruments and "opaque" opposition. What they have in common is an awareness of being stuck in the so-called trap of an (endless) modernity that they have productively resigned themselves to working with(in). This modernity, as Glissant has suggested in his definition of the word, is inseparable from the colonial enterprise and its violent interruption or disruption of the past and its traditions: "there is modernity, perhaps, when a tradition at work in a certain time and place no longer assimilates the changes with which it is presented (either from within or without) as they come along but adapts to them under conditions of violence" (PR, p. 234). This violence does not always involve a rupture, he goes on to note, but "it is because the violence of change has accelerated and become generalized in our own time that we call it absolutely modern"; indeed, by virtue of its general diffusion, the category itself is losing much of its historical specificity ("the more modernity is on display, the less real it becomes; in this way, one might prognosticate successive futures without modernity, or infinite modernities without a future"). The violence of modernity is one to which the entire world has been *consciously subjected*,[24] but it is, ironically enough, only in the wake of this violence and as an unending supplement to it that the hybrid world of post/coloniality can emerge. As Stuart Hall has put it, "colonisation so refigured the terrain that, ever since, the very idea of a world of separate identities, of isolated or separable and self-sufficient cultures and economies, has been obliged to yield to a variety of paradigms designed to capture . . . different but related forms of relationship, interconnection and discontinuity."[25] This interconnected world of creolizing "relations" (to use a multivalent word that, as we will see, is central to Glissant's poetics) is the—unintended, to be sure—product of the colonial enterprise and the "planetary adventure" initiated by the European powers, as Glissant points out in his 1969 *L'intention poétique* (with a glaringly ironic recourse to the very concept of "race" that his advocacy of métissage intends to erase): "this active race has mapped out the sphere of the One and opened up the world of the Relative, which it does not want to live (in)" (p. 215). If "relationality leads us toward fruitful combinations" (p. 219; "la Relation porte l'univers au fécond métissage"), then colonialism and its literature repeatedly rejects this fecundity in the name of more categorical, less relative and relational, imperatives. In its absolute modernity, though, the colonial is nonetheless as marked as what comes after it by the "planetarization of thought" upon which the creolization process is founded; the colonial thus implicitly harbors what will become more explicit in and valuable to postcolonial theory and cultural practice. Both colonial and postcolonial literatures are forced, in their resembling-differing ways, to register (*consigner*) this planetary thought, to "acknowledge the completely new situation of man: in touch with himself—with his 'totality'—for the very first time, aware or unsettled by all the sides of himself that he had up until then been able—as a man of the West—to misjudge, remain oblivious to, or—as a non-westerner—remain oblivious or be subjected to" (*IP*, p. 27).

It is this double inscription, this mutual (con)signing, of what Glissant refers to as the "totalité-monde" that I am trying to give a sense of in *Islands and Exiles* through my juxtaposition of colonial and postcolonial literatures. To be sure, to have separated the one literature from the other is already to have bought into an historical narrative that takes us forward from the ideological limitations of the colonial to the manifold possibilities of the postcolonial—a predictable narrative, but one virtually impossible to avoid, as is certainly not the case, by contrast, with the distinction between the modern(ist) and the postmodern. Such a narrative can be read most easily in this book if one rearranges the central chapters that follow upon my

discussion of *Foe* and of postcolonial theory in Chapter 2. Thus, in Chapters 3, 5, and 6 I take us from the end of the Enlightenment to the age of
Romanticism and focus on a series of novels and political interventions that
are increasingly unable to avoid the problems posed by a fully globalized
and creolizing modernity toward which they are in part or wholly hostile:
Bernardin de Saint-Pierre's 1788 pastoral *Paul et Virginie* appears bent on
preserving the Indian Ocean territory of Île de France (present-day Mauritius) as the site of an uncorrupted, Rousseauesque nature free from the
conflicts and ambivalent negotiations of colonial culture (Chapter 3); Victor Hugo's reactionary rewriting of the Haitian Revolution, *Bug-Jargal*
(1820/1826), takes us forward to a time in which the egalitarian doctrines
of the Revolution are obligatory, if for the author regrettable, points of narrative reference (Chapter 5); the young Hugo's horrified vision of revolutionary change proves inseparable from a negative portrayal of interracial
relations—and of peoples of "mixed race," who most visibly embody those
relations—that also predominates in his close friend Louis Maynard's novel
Outre-mer (1835), a little-known work that I examine in tandem with the
groundbreaking writings of the "free colored" journalist and politician
Cyrille Bissette in the discussion of 1830s and 1840s Martiniquan literature
and politics that supplements my account of *Bug-Jargal* (Chapter 6).

Pursuing the thread of this colonial narrative would have led directly
into the fin de siècle territory mapped out in my *Exotic Memories*, where I
discussed the increasingly desperate attempts of late-nineteenth-century
writers like Pierre Loti at preserving an exotic "diversity" from the seemingly fatal threat posed it by the global hegemony of the New Imperialism,
as well as the self-consciously belated (re)inscription of this exoticist project
in the early-twentieth-century novelistic work of Victor Segalen and Joseph
Conrad, which forms a problematic bridge, an anxious relay, between the
worlds of colonial and postcolonial literatures (as demonstrated, for instance, by the importance of Segalen to Francophone novelists like Glissant
and Abdelkebir Khatibi, and of Conrad to Anglophone writers as diverse as
Wilson Harris and Edward Said). In contrast to my discussion of colonial
literature, my account of postcolonial literature in chapters 4 and 7 is more
synchronic, focusing most notably on Glissant's novel *Mahagony* (Chapter
4) and the Guadeloupe writer Daniel Maximin's *Soufrières* (Chapter 7),
both of which were published in 1987. These postcolonial novels will
be read as grappling in their different ways with issues of cultural mixing
and the effect that it has on a straightforward identity politics of the sort
that so evidently characterized not only colonial literature but much early
(anticolonial) postcolonial writing. Thus, undergirding my synchronic slice
of "mature" postcolonial literature from the 1980s will be a continuation
of the historical chronology mapped out in the chapters on colonial litera-

ture, taking us forward from the early- and mid-twentieth century, and from modernist authors committed to such now unpalatable essentialisms as Negritude, to the more flexible vision of creole identities that is currently being explored in the French Caribbean (which I will henceforth be referring to simply as the Antilles) by Glissant and the generation of younger writers that has been following his anti-essentialist lead.

That colonialism and its lack of enlightenment gives way to an enlightened postcolonialism, that nativist essentialisms give way to enlightened anti-essentialisms, are certainly among the (predictable) guiding narratives of *Islands and Exiles*. However, in line with Lyotard's cautionary assertion regarding the modern and the postmodern—namely, that we must always read the latter as "being next to the former" (p. 3), in a state of propinquity that I have called the post/modern condition—this book has not been structured in such a linear manner: I have chosen, rather, to shuttle back and forth between the colonial and the postcolonial, both from one chapter to the next and within individual chapters (as with the discussion of Lafcadio Hearn that begins the chapter on Glissant). Chapters 3 and 4, grouped together under the title "Irruptions: Bernardin de Saint-Pierre, Édouard Glissant, and the Double Time of Modernity," thus share a common concern with the Janus-faced figure of an intrusive modernity that compels its subjects simultaneously to look back toward an unattainable pre-modern, precolonial past and forward to an equally absent post-modern, post-colonial future: despite their obvious differences, Bernardin and Glissant share this vision of a lost nature that must be memorialized in the face of an alienating colonial history and in the name of a transfigured future that, for both authors, proves inseparable from the dynamics of creolization. The three chapters (5, 6, 7) brought together under the title "Eruptions: (Rewriting) Caribbean Romanticism" consider a variety of intertextually connected responses to the French and Haitian revolutions: twentieth-century metafictions like Faulkner's *Absalom, Absalom!* (discussed in Chapter 5) and the novels of Maximin simultaneously return to and drift away from the revolutionary Romantic ideology that perversely informs the antirevolutionary novels of Hugo and Maynard. Rather than emphasize a straightforward historical narrative, then, I have chosen to structure this book antiphonally, emphasizing a pattern of (un)likenesses—to use a word that will be central to my analysis of Coetzee's *Foe* in Chapter 2—that loosely groups together the colonial and postcolonial in the paradoxical commonplace of their modernity, a place best rendered by the slash in post/colonial.

The two main components of this book's subtitle, "creole identities" and "post/colonial literature," have now been introduced in a preliminary manner: the one component signaling the site of a tension between the creole, the "new thing" that is incessantly being produced out of the global crossing of cultures that "are in the process of changing through their exchange [*se changent en s'échangeant*]," and the old identitarian ways in which we cannot help speaking about it; and the other component pointing toward an uneasily shared common place to which the colonial and the postcolonial are both consigned, a modernity of which they must be read as cosignatories. It remains to say a few words about the main title itself, *Islands and Exiles*, which I have taken from the Barbadian poet and cultural critic Kamau Brathwaite (it is the heading of the third chapter of his influential 1967 collection, *Rights of Passage*). The complex relations that I have been outlining between a given identity and the *estrangement* from this identity that is inseparable from the experience of creolization is well conveyed by the topos of the island, of which George Lamming once remarked that there is "no geography more appropriate to the study of exile."[26] The island is a figure that can and must be read in more than one way: on the one hand, as the absolutely particular, a space complete unto itself and thus an ideal metaphor for a traditionally conceived, unified and unitary, identity; on the other, as a fragment, a part of some greater whole from which it is in exile and to which it must be related—in an act of (never completed) completion that is always also, as it were, an ex-isle, a loss of the particular. The island is thus the site of a double identity—closed and open—and this doubleness perfectly conveys the ambivalences of creole identity that I outlined above. If insular thinking is at the root of a traditional identity politics, the relational thinking that emerges out of the cross-culturalizing dynamics of the creolization process puts this insularity into question. As the main narrator of Glissant's *Mahagony* puts it, "were there not other islands, there would be no island to call home; were there not other planets, the island-earth would not exist" (p. 220). We live in a hybridized world of transcultural, transnational relations in which every island (ethnicity, nation, and the like) is but a fragment of a whole that is always-already in the process of transforming the particular into something other than its (original, essential) self. And yet because this loss of self cannot be fully recorded or even acknowledged, one returns, repeatedly and impossibly, to that which has been left behind and can never be truly recovered.

Depending upon one's perspective, the island can be viewed in either a negative or a positive light, as we see from the following quite randomly chosen passages in which this topos plays a central role. As a negative figure, the island becomes the site of a debilitating or dangerous isolation: at the very beginning of *Explosion*, Esteban's cousin Carlos is suffering from "the claustrophobia induced by living in an island, by being in a country where there were no roads leading to other lands along which to wander" (p. 14)—although, ironically enough, it will be Esteban and Carlos's sister Sofia, not he, who end up leaving Cuba behind for an encounter with the "totalité-monde." This negative vision often makes itself felt in the realm of identity politics, as when Richard Wright defines the word "Negro" as a "psychological island . . . within whose confines we live," going on to add that "its rocky boundaries have remained unyielding to the waves of our hope that dash against it."[27] As Paul Gilroy has pointed out in his *Black Atlantic* (pp. 146–86), it is within those insular racial confines that critics have consistently attempted to place Wright as a writer, concentrating on the "blackness" of his earlier books and more or less ignoring his life as an exile in Europe and the diverse intellectual interests that resulted from it. Derek Walcott also provides a dire vision of his own "isolation" as a "mixed race" poet of equally mixed intentions in his essay "The Muse of History," an angry response to the exclusionary politics of "pure black Afro-Aryanism," written at a time (the early 1970s) when Caribbean intellectuals were for the most part (at least in his eyes) still sadly in thrall to an abrasive politics of Negritude: those who, like himself, refuse to confine themselves to a single identity and its supposedly imperative themes are doomed, Walcott laments, to become "increasingly exotic hybrids, broken bridges between two ancestries, Europe and the Third World of Africa and Asia, in other words, they will become islands."[28] The dangers of a self-enclosed thinking, and the need for a relational identity, is intimated in the title of Daniel Maximin's first novel *L'isolé soleil* (1981; *Lone Sun*). In a gloss on its anagrammatic title, contained in a brief section entitled "Identity," one of the novel's two main narrators comments on these dangers, noting "I wanted to be SUN / I played with words / I found (myself) ISOLATED" (p. 105; "Je voulais être SOLEIL / J'ai joué avec les mots / J'ai trouvé L'ISOLÉ"). Bernardin de Saint-Pierre's fanciful explanation of the origins of the letter O, which "owes its shape to that of the sun," provides a further commentary on Maximin's title: as Bernardin goes on to remark about this letter, in a typical example of the "combinatory" thinking that (as I will argue in Chapter 3) surprisingly anticipates a poetics of métissage, "with Arabic numerals, when it is on its own, it is only a zero, without value, but it multiplies tenfold the number to which it is joined, a hundredfold if added on twice, and so on, resembling in this respect the sun, which needs to be combined with one of nature's powers if it is to have any effect."[29] In its isolation, the island needs to be supplemented by what it lacks, as Aimé Césaire suggests in the following lines from his poem "Dit d'errance": "every island beckons / every island is a widow" ("toute île appelle / toute île est veuve").[30] As he wanders through his "dismembered" archipelago, the poet dreams of a "lost body" for which his island is calling out in the hope of someday being reattached to it—a dream that will, to be sure, from the perspective of a later generation of writers critical of Césaire's Negritude, be attacked for its insistence on thinking his Caribbean island not in terms of the world as a whole but in terms of a particular mainland, Africa.[31]

However, the figure of the island also beckons in another more positive direction, offering the prospect of defined boundaries and a desirable self-sufficiency. It is this positive vision of the island that haunts Carpentier's Esteban in his transatlantic wanderings, causing him to long for a return to the closure of the "family circle" and "the pastoral, cloistered life of the island" (p. 152). Very soon after his shipboard meditations on the encounter of the Olive and the Maize, he takes stock of his situation and comes to the nostalgic realization that he is "surrounded by islands which resembled the one island [Cuba] he could not reach; condemned, perhaps for a lifetime, to smell the smells of his childhood, to find tokens of his adolescence in trees, houses, tricks of the light . . . , but without having what was his—what had belonged to him since childhood and adolescence—restored to him" (p. 184). To pursue a few more examples of this alternative, and inherently backward-looking, vision of the island and the self: if, in *Insularismo* (1934), his polemical account of Puerto Rico's "debased insularity and debilitating isolation," Antonio Pedreira bemoans the "tragic isolation" of the island,[32] that same situation can be read in exactly the opposite way, as Gustavo Pérez Firmat has noted with regard to a contemporary of Pedreira's, Jorge Mañach, who attributes the ills of Cuba to "excessive contact with the outside world."[33] It is this sort of excessive contact that a writer like Herman Melville laments in *Typee*, his 1846 novel about Polynesian life, where he notes the "polluting examples" Europeans offer the "poor savages" and concludes that "thrice happy are they who, inhabiting some yet undiscovered island in the midst of the ocean, have never been brought into contaminating contact with the white man" (p. 50). This exoticizing valorization of the figure of the island and of an autonomous, uncontaminated self has its match in postcolonial authors who, unlike Melville, speak about the Other from the perspective of cultural insiderism. The Jamaican writer Michelle Cliff's understanding of "the landscape of [her] island as female" is, for instance, exemplary of this desire for a self that can be defined in terms of identifiable boundaries: Cliff asserts that her own work "has been a movement back, to homeland and identity" and goes on to note how she "represents this homeland, this landscape of identity, as female, the contours of a female body."[34] One of the most important genealogical sources for these visions, or dreams, of the island as the ideal figure for a discrete identity is Jean-Jacques Rousseau's account of his stay on the Ile de Saint-Pierre: evoking, in the fifth of his *Les rêveries du promeneur solitaire* (1777/1782), this little Swiss island where pleasure was to be had from "nothing outside the self, from nothing if not one's self and one's own existence," he claims that

I would have liked it if they had turned this refuge into a permanent prison, if they had confined me there for life and if, depriving me of all means and hope of getting off it, they had forbidden me all contact with the mainland, so that—oblivious to all that was going on in the world—I might have forgotten its existence and they might also have forgotten about mine.[35]

Rousseau's desire to confine himself to "this beloved island" and forget the world exemplifies the will to identity that generates both personal and communal assertions of a stable self under the irremissibly unstable conditions of modernity. Not only does the island offer a perfect model for the would-be autonomous self (be it bourgeois, gendered, ethnic, or national), but it promotes a sense of continuity with the past. As the narrator of Victor Hugo's *Les travailleurs de la mer* (1866) notes, "to be isolated is to have a long memory, and an island is isolated"; hence, he adds, "the persistence of memory one finds in islanders, [for whom] traditions are never-ending." "It is impossible," Hugo concludes, "to break this thread that extends into the night for as far as one can see."[36]

For Rousseau, then, the island space offers a "refuge, it favors the exploration of a forgotten or buried authenticity, a return to who one really is."[37] It is notable, however, that his vision of the Île de Saint-Pierre and the self-identity that it represented to him is a nostalgic one, fraught with a feeling of loss, an awareness of the terminability of the memories and traditions of which the exiled Hugo speaks. The modern problematic of identity is, indeed, inseparable from a sense of crisis, for as Douglas Kellner has pointed out, "only in a society anxious about identity could the problems of personal identity, or self-identity, or identity crises, arise and be subject to worry and debate."[38] A preoccupation with the self is inseparable from an anxiety about the possible destruction—or, to use a favorite word of Rousseau's that will be important to our analysis of *Paul et Virginie*, "disfigurement"—of that self, as is clear in another passage from the fifth *Rêverie*. Giving a different, more ominous, twist to Césaire's "toute île appelle," Rousseau there describes how he fulfilled his dream of peopling a smaller island on the same Swiss lake with a "colony" of rabbits. More important for our purposes than the way that the isolated bourgeois subject here reveals his complicity with the colonial enterprise is the apocalyptic vision that he offers of this smaller island's eventual fate. He notes, in an elegiac tone that we will come across often in our readings of post/colonial literature, that this smaller island "will be destroyed in the end [*à la fin*] because soil is constantly being taken from it in order to repair the damage made by waves and storms to the big island." "So it is," he sighs, "that the substance of the weak is always used for the benefit of the powerful."[39]

This second vision of the island as the site of an identity under threat of dissolution inseparably complements the first, and its relevance to an increasingly interrelated world is obvious: as Françoise Péron notes, at the beginning of her detailed study of the group of small islands off the west coast of France, "one can almost go so far as to ask oneself: is not the very idea of the island today no more than an illusion, insofar as the technological advances of the end of the twentieth century appear to be cancelling out geographical particularities, shortening distances, delocalizing people, standardizing lifestyles, and thus banalizing island environments?"[40] Banalization, homogenization, assimilation: these are constant motifs in discussions of cultural identity in the postmodern and postcolonial age, and Rousseau's scenario—his preoccupation with ending ("à la fin")—clearly anticipates this turn. The little island's actual fate, though, is much more ambivalent than this simple moment of ending that Rousseau prophesies: as one twentieth-century editor points out, the island is "now linked up on one side to the big island and on the other to the south bank of Lake Biel by a narrow strip of land."[41] What has taken place, in other words, is that hitherto autonomous locations have been joined together in a series of relays that transform, as it were, "la substance du faible" without simply eradicating it or the need to talk about it. If there is, as Péron goes on to argue, a real loss of insularity in the twentieth century for the reasons cited above, this does not mean the identity that might once have attached to it is no longer available for discussion: indeed, "entering into relations with the rest of the world," she states, actually renders the feeling of being an islander more acute and "develops an insular identity" (19). Insular thinking takes on a renewed meaning in a world that is becoming ever more relational: "the longing for islands certainly expresses the quintessence of a need for the return to the local; individuals feel lost in a planetary world without bounds" (p. 159). Constantly troubled by the exigencies of a world to which the island is substantially connected, this return to the local can nonetheless play a vital role in helping us situate ourselves in the chaotic unfolding of a global(izing) modernity, but only, I would add, if the identity to which it gives us access remains just that: a role, whose essentially performative and fictional nature we have responsibly kept in sight.

As should be clear from many of the examples cited in the preceding pages, the islands of the Caribbean will provide the primary focus for my exploration of the creolization process and the identities that (do not) ensue from it. Notwithstanding the book's point of departure in the Indian Ocean and its final point of arrival in the Pacific Islands of New Zealander Keri Hulme's *the bone people* (Chapter 8), most of the discussion will bear on texts from the (francophone) Caribbean.[42] From the moment of its second, post-Columbian beginning at the end of the fifteenth century, the Caribbean has been the site par excellence of the "irruption dans la modernité" that, according to Glissant, characterizes the New World of the Americas and its literature as a whole, which "arises in a system of modernity that is sudden rather than consecutive or 'evolved'" (*DA*, p. 258). The Caribbean's abrupt and necessarily total encounter with modernity via a colonizing process that wiped away virtually the entirety of its indigenous peoples and thereby created the grounds for the proliferation of creole cultures violently forged out of the coming together of the Old Worlds of Europe, Africa, and Asia does not (as some might argue) make it an historical aberration to be contrasted with "healthier" cultures whose contact with the global(izing) forces of modernity has been more gradual and less traumatic. Rather, this foundational encounter makes it a site that has, from its very beginnings, borne witness to a relational way of life that no one, in the late-twentieth-century world of the "new global cultural economy,"[43] can now avoid confronting. For this reason, as the exiled Cuban writer Antonio Benitez-Rojo has persuasively argued, the open-closed basin of the Caribbean—a place with no "stable cultural origin"—has always contained within it the seeds of a "postmodern perspective" that puts into question, at the same time as it continues impossibly to demand, an identity that was once and for all lost with the voluntary and forced migrations out of which it was constructed. From the Caribbean perspective, identity will always be the subject of an "impossible search": "one never becomes a wholly Caribbean person; one is also something more or something less, one always falls just short of or just beyond it, one is always involved for both the near and the long term in the search for Caribbeanness, and above all, one writes page after page concerning that search or the illusion of having completed it."[44] In a no doubt overly exuberant and totalizing manner, Benitez-Rojo also notes that

> every Caribbean person, after an attempt has been made to reach his culture's origins, will find himself on a deserted beach, naked and alone, coming out of the water as though shivering and shipwrecked . . . without any identification papers other than the uncertain and turbulent memorandum inscribed in his scars, tattoos, and skin color. . . . Every person of the Caribbean is in exile from his own myth and his own history, and also from his own culture and his own Being, now and always, in the world. (p. 217)

As we have seen, this Caribbean exile consistently lends itself to at least two readings: one negative, in the manner of a V. S. Naipaul, for whom islands inevitably function as metaphors for a debilitating isolation, and for whom the shipwreck serves as "an image almost wholly of abandonment and alienation, of a marginality the only answer to which is flight, recurrent and unending";[45] and the other positive, as in Walcott, for whom "the shipwrecks of Crusoe and of the crew in *The Tempest* are the end of an Old World" and "the beginning, not the end of our history."[46] These responses to the Caribbean and its "shipwrecked" condition mark the two extremes of what I will be referring to as the creole continuum of post/colonial identity politics: neither can be taken as final, each is an aspect of the other, and directs us toward another position, somewhere between the two, in a middle space that cannot be located with any exactitude but toward which the Caribbean has been inconclusively turned since its "discovery" some five centuries ago.

In the second section of the following chapter I will be elaborating upon the importance of the Caribbean to the formation of Brathwaite's and Glissant's seminal accounts of the creolization process, as well as looking more closely at the question of cultural identity as it has been discussed in recent postcolonial theory. Before arriving at this point, however, I would first like to engage in a less direct and rather more evocative reflection upon the issues explicitly dealt with in that section by returning to one of colonial literature's most notorious shipwrecks, that of Crusoe—a shipwreck with which the modern novel can be said to begin and that was never far from Rousseau's mind as he explored the contours of his own little islands and built on them (as he puts it in his *Confessions*), "like another Robinson, an imaginary dwelling-place."[47] More precisely, I will be turning to the South African writer J. M. Coetzee's already canonical revisiting of this island in his *Foe*, a novel that self-consciously establishes a precious dialogue between the colonial and the postcolonial. What *Foe* forces its reader to come to grips with is the loss of an original, or "native," identity—a loss that is the precondition for the emergence of that "new thing" briefly and incompletely envisioned by Carpentier's protagonist "within the shady hold" of *L'ami du peuple*. Notwithstanding its foundational absence, this lost identity, Coetzee will show, remains an essential component in any thinking of the world of relations that has opened up in its wake. The coda to Esteban's "transcendental encounter" with the mixed realities of transculturation would appear to confirm this point: as we have seen, his epiphany of a creolized "totalité-monde" there proves inseparable from a sense of exile, for he finds himself "surrounded by islands which resembled the one island he could not reach; condemned, perhaps for a lifetime, to smell the smells of his childhood, to find tokens of his adolescence in trees, houses, tricks of the light . . . but without having what was his—what had belonged to him since childhood and adolescence—restored to him." In this world of resemblances, of what I will be referring to as (un)likenesses, Esteban stands in a memorial relation not only to the original identity that he has lost but to the future identity that he had, through the Revolution, once hoped to gain. It is the dimensions of this double space, neither here nor there, but always in between and in transit, that I will be exploring in the remainder of this book.

2 *"A Glow of After-Memory"*

(BEYOND) IDENTITY POLITICS IN
POSTCOLONIAL LITERATURE AND
THEORY

*"Lost in the Maze of Doubting": J. M. Coetzee's 'Foe'
and the Politics of (Un)likeness*

> The likenesses will meet and make merry, but they won't
> know you. They won't know the you that's hidden some-
> where in the castle of your skin.
> —George Lamming, *In the Castle of My Skin*

Toward the end of his revisionist treatment of Daniel Defoe's *Robin-son Crusoe*, the South African writer J. M. Coetzee has his eponymous protagonist Foe make the following comment:

In a life of writing books, I have often, believe me, been lost in the maze of doubt-ing. The trick I have learned is to plant a sign or marker in the ground where I stand, so that in my future wanderings I shall have something to return to, and not get worse lost than I am. Having planted it, I press on; the more often I come back to the mark (which is a sign to myself of my blindness and incapacity), the more cer-tainly I know I am lost, yet the more I am heartened too, to have found my way back. (pp. 135–36)

In the chronically evasive world of Coetzee's novels, isolating any one state-ment and identifying it with the author's views can only be a dangerously mistaken strategy. And yet, as any reader of these opaque allegories knows, Coetzee actively encourages such mistakes, planting row upon row of signs in his text that demand to be read as something other than what they are. A passage of the sort just cited may, nonetheless, be of particular relevance to an interpretation of *Foe* because, rather than simply laying the ground for such errant readings, it self-reflexively points to this very ground.[1] The "maze of doubting," the scene of a repeated error, would for this reason appear to be crucial to Coetzee's enterprise: this doubtful terrain where all one can effectively know is that one is lost, where all signs point only to one's blindness and incapacity, and where "future wanderings" double back upon themselves in an uncanny and yet "heartening" return of the past, bears a provocative if arguable resemblance to the world of Coetzee's novel as a whole. It is out of such problematic resemblances, out of likenesses that may be grounded in nothing at all, that the skeptically post/colonial vision of *Foe* emerges.

The self-reflexivity of this passage is not limited to the problem of error; it also points to the relationship of intertextuality that connects *Foe* with the original novel to which it has found its way back. In pressing on in his exploration of the novel as a symbolic form, Coetzee has come up against a text, *Robinson Crusoe*, that marks one of the genre's points of departure, and one of our modernity's seminal gestures; this colonial text must now be read as a sign of blindness to which his eyes are open—a blindness that may well characterize an entire literary tradition—but that cannot be simply wished away. Refusing to posit a way out of the labyrinthine modernity that *Robinson Crusoe* inaugurates, Coetzee makes a case for postcolonial literature as the site, not of a radical break with old and discredited stories, but of an incessant *reflecting back* on colonialism, in both a temporal and spatial sense: he establishes a double reflection, back *upon* colonial and pre-colonial pasts from which the novel cannot detach itself, and back *at* a still present power of which the novel, notwithstanding its trenchant critique of that power, cannot help producing mirror-images.

Foe's incessant return to the sign of its own blindness, its parasitic attachment to the already-told stories that it recites, revising without in any decisive way overturning them, is eminently deconstructionist in its epistemological concerns and its insistence on the necessity of inhabiting the very thing that it puts into question (be it, as here, the language of colonialism, or, in Derrida's case, that of metaphysics). For those with a more "activist" vision of what literature—postcolonial or otherwise—ought to accomplish, such concerns can only be of dubious value, and must lead to a politically reprehensible dead end: speaking of deconstructionism, one critic has argued, for example, that "such a position can lead only to quietism, since no action at all can be validated from its theoretical endpoint, or to a false radicalism which engages in constant but ultimately meaningless transgression of all defended viewpoints."[2] For those who still believe in the possibility of a "true radicalism," Coetzee's work must seem nugatory in its insistence on the unfoundedness, the errancy, of our future ideological wanderings. For those, by contrast, who are willing to begin to think the foundational absence of any simple resolution to the mazelike condition of a now global modernity, there may after all be something "heartening" about the situation that Foe has described. Coetzee's novel promotes a vision that is not undone by the knowledge of its blindness but founded upon it. Epistemological scruples must be the essence of any well-considered politics; this does not lead to quietism but to a more guarded view of what it means to "press on" into the uncharted future and back toward an apparently mapped out past. We cannot help supplementing our doubts with theoretically indefensible, errant and/or erroneous actions; a knowledge of the invalidity of such actions attenuates them, to be sure, weakens what might at first have been thought to possess an unquestionable strength, but it does not render them simply meaningless. With a rigorous awareness of his blindness and incapacity, Coetzee moves forward, in a gesture of ambivalence that always also takes him back to the (lack of a) ground from which he began, and upon which he has planted the sign of a post/colonial literature that takes an apparent dead end as its repeated point of departure.

Foe is divided up into four very distinct parts. The first is the narrative of and by a certain Susan Barton, which describes her being cast away on a desert island already inhabited by a taciturn man named Cruso and his mute slave Friday. They are eventually rescued, but Cruso does not survive the passage back to England; Friday, forcibly brought along on the return voyage by Barton, remains in her care while she attempts to make literary capital out of her story. Barton's narrative, it turns out, is addressed to the famous, albeit debt-ridden, author Foe, who Barton hopes will transform the bare outlines of her story into a work of art. Part Two is made up of a series of Barton's letters addressed to Foe, in which she recounts her pursuit of the elusive author, who is in hiding from his creditors, and her unsuccessful attempts at sending Friday back to Africa and thereby (in her view) freeing him. The third part, no longer in epistolary form, but in straightforward first-person, past-tense narrative, takes place in Foe's refuge, which Barton has finally succeeded in finding; it features a good deal of philosophically elevated dialogue, much of it on the subject of Friday, and ends with Foe and Barton sleeping together and Friday, at Foe's insistence, beginning to learn how to write. The very brief and enigmatic Part Four features two similar but nonetheless clearly differentiated first-person, present-tense accounts by an unnamed narrator of his (or her) entry into Foe's refuge; both accounts end with this narrator interrogating the mouth of a Friday who is either asleep, buried, or dead, with an ear to what words will emerge from his hitherto silent orifice.

Coetzee's novel displays a series of tantalizingly obvious similarities to and divergences from its original model: unlike Defoe's Crusoe, for instance, this Cruso keeps no journal, is indifferent to salvation, and instead of assiduously reproducing the Old World in the New (or like Derek Walcott's Crusoe exuberantly renaming it in Adamic fashion)[3] has contented himself with manufacturing a bed and a great number of apparently useless terraces on his island; Friday, who is clearly identified as an African rather than Defoe's "tawny" Indian, maintains a silence that contrasts starkly with the first Friday's comically expressive pidgin. This issue of Friday's voice is one to which we will return, for it constitutes the novel's (absent) kernel. However, it only emerges to the side of the most obvious difference that Coetzee's novel puts into play in the face of its original: namely, the presence of a woman, and her voice, in what had once been an entirely masculinized world. The most persistent narrative trajectory in *Foe* explores Barton's relation to Defoe's original narration, and the attempt to construct a woman's story that would differ from it. From the by now familiar perspective of feminist revisionism, Barton's disruptive presence on the primordially male island, and her desire to make a story of her own heard, would appear to lay the foundations for an authentic retrieval of woman's hitherto silenced voice. Barton's wish to transform herself into "the author of my own story" (p. 40) is one with which no sensitive reader can fail to identify.

Coetzee, however, while clearly invoking this dream of a marginal discourse asserting itself in the face of an oppressively hegemonic one, consistently undermines it: in her efforts at getting her story told, Barton is time and again depicted as pursuing essentially the same *authoritative*, and *authoritarian*, projects as the writer Foe to whom she is at once opposed and linked. Spurred on by the same "promise of fullness" that motivates a writer like Foe, Barton revealingly states that she wishes "to be father to my story" (p. 122); (this) woman's voice is clearly founded upon the same presuppositions of plenitude and "substantiality," of property and propriety ("*my* story"), as that of her male counterpart. As one critic of the novel disapprovingly puts it, "the feminist discourse seems to have been constructed simply in order to be de(con)structed."[4] In pointing out the extent to which Barton's project of giving voice to herself remains subject to the very authoritarianism it purportedly opposes, Coetzee stringently critiques a feminist identity politics that would naively overlook its own complicitous relationship with power.[5] When the white male Cruso bellows the word "*Masa* or *Massa*," in a self-accusatory fever that disturbingly echoes his original's appallingly complacent sense of identity (after saving Friday from his fellow cannibals, Defoe's Crusoe remarks that "I likewise taught him to say Master, and then let him know, that was to be my name" [p. 209]), the white female Barton notes that it is "a word with no meaning I can discover" (p. 29). Preoccupied with her own exclusion from one "massa" narrative, (this) woman cannot hear the extent to which she too is an accessory to what this word means, as is made abundantly clear not only in her quest to father her own story but in the paternalistic relationship she maintains with Friday.

Barton's desire to have "disposal" of her own story is ironically matched by her belief that she is in a position to dispose of Friday: "If Friday is not mine to set free, whose is he?" she questions, patently ignoring the possibility that people, like stories, might belong to no one. Barton asks this question after she has taken it upon herself to write a deed granting Friday his freedom (p. 99), which she signs in Cruso's name and then sews into a little bag that she hangs on a cord around his neck. Significantly enough, the anonymous narrator of Part Four, attuned to the dangers and (inescapable) violence of writing, will discover a scar around Friday's neck, "left by a rope or chain" (p. 155): Barton has left a rope or chain of "emancipatory" signifiers around the neck of the colonized subject, and thereby scarred him; she has chosen, in Kiplingesque fashion, to take on "the burden of our story" (p. 81)—not of hers alone, a woman's story already fraught with many contradictions and a problematic relation to the authority that it would contest, but of Friday's as well, a post/colonial story that uneasily overlaps with and in most respects counteracts her own. The ironies inherent in Barton's obliviousness to the fact that she is to Friday what her male foes are to her suggest, as Gayatri Spivak has pointed out in a careful discussion of *Foe*, that "feminism (within 'the same' cultural inscription) and anticolonialism (for or against racial 'others') cannot occupy a continuous (narrative) space."[6]

Such discontinuities are central to the labyrinthine terrain that Coetzee's novel maps out. In identifying these, however, it is by no means certain that Coetzee is engaging in a definitive critique of feminist revisionism, or, for that matter, of Foe's own authority, in the name of some eventual continuity that others—for instance the silent (or silenced) Friday—might embody. That both Barton's and Foe's discursive choices have been revealed as being founded upon an unjustifiable appeal to their own potential for a "fullness" they do not and cannot possess does not entirely vitiate them. In bringing the in many ways incommensurable projects of Foe and Barton together in the same textual space, in the same way that they as characters are physically brought together in Part Three of the novel, and in juxtaposing them with the as yet unannounced project of Friday, Coetzee appears to be arguing for the necessity of thinking them all together, *relationally*—as part of a collaborative, and contaminatory, dialogue that will not lead them to the fullness of truth, and thus out of the maze of doubting, but may at least draw them closer to one another. At the same time as he is undermining the authoritarian logic of both Barton's and Foe's approaches to writing, Coetzee is also partially, and carefully, valorizing the very strategies that he has incapacitated.

The skeptical position Foe outlines in the comments that provided us with our point of departure for this chapter does not represent his primary approach to writing; rather, it supplements his main discursive strategy, what we might call his *narrato-logical* perspective. Having heard the story of Barton's life on the island, he insists on situating it within the context of a larger, sequentially oriented story that begins with Barton's departure from London for the New World in search of her lost daughter and ends with a fictional reunion of mother and daughter:

We therefore have five parts in all: the loss of the daughter; the quest for the daughter in Brazil; abandonment of the quest, and the adventure of the island; assumption of the quest by the daughter; and reunion of the daughter with her mother. It is thus that we make up a book: loss, then quest, then recovery; beginning, then middle, then end. As to novelty, this is lent by the island episode—which is properly the second part of the middle—and by the reversal in which the daughter takes up the quest abandoned by her mother. (p. 117)

Foe's is the language of ratiocination ("thus," "therefore"), of totalization ("in all"), of closure ("reunion," "end"), of property and propriety ("properly"). The arrival at aesthetic fullness to which he as author aspires will be achieved through the incorporation of many parts within one master narrative—a narrative that, interestingly, contains the same sort of simple "reversal" to which a strongly revisionist feminism or anticolonialism aspires. The deficiencies of Foe's linear, narrato-logical perspective are glaring: its straightforwardness is achieved at the expense of simplifying or omitting details from Barton's account, and even of fictionalizing them in the name of a tidy ending (as with his recourse to the idea of Barton's lost daughter taking up the search for her mother).

In opposition to Foe's tactics, Barton adopts as her primary approach to writing a *hermeneutic* perspective; if Foe's quest for the "full story" leads him to flesh out Barton's account of her life on the island, to add to it in the name of a narrative completeness that he must always fall short of, then Barton's quest for the full meaning of her story takes the opposite tack of reducing its many episodes to one central enigma, "the heart of the story" (p. 141)—as she puts it in nicely Conradian fashion—upon which she comes to think everything else hinges: namely, the mystery of Friday's silence, how it came about, and what he would say were he able to tell his own story. She wants to dig up "the true story [that] is buried within Friday" and, having uncovered it, thereby discover the underlying meaning of her own. She believes that only once she has filled this gaping hole in her narrative can she hope to understand the story that she is in the process of living. This belief engenders a language of penetration, based upon an opposition between surface and depth that parallels Foe's distinction between beginning and end, and that Barton shares with a great number of protagonists in Coetzee's other novels: when the imperial magistrate who narrates *Waiting for the Barbarians* (1980), for instance, says of the barbarian woman whom he has rescued from indigence that she offers "only a surface across which I hunt back and forth seeking entry" (p. 43), he is speaking the same "predatory" language as Barton. Barton, the hermeneutic subject, who is always also an imperial subject, lives in the hope of recovering the "secret body" that she, like the magistrate, feels is lacking to her—that deeper truth hidden below the surface of things in which a long and venerable line of modernity's critics, from Marx to Baudrillard, have placed their faith.[7]

In her simultaneous attempt at digging and filling holes, Barton keeps coming up against the hermeneutic circle. "Who but Cruso," she asks, "who is no more, could truly tell you Cruso's story?" (p. 51), even though she herself has already established that what little Cruso had to say for himself was an undecidable mixture of truth, lies, and rambling (p. 12). "Yet the only tongue that can tell Friday's secret," she laments, "is the tongue he has lost!" (p. 67). This circle inevitably leads her not forward, as does Foe's simplified, ends-directed narrative, but back. In her efforts at fathoming the mystery that is Friday, or that she feels him to be, she must build a bridge back "to the time before Cruso, the time before he lost his tongue" (p. 60); she must gain access to "the time before, when he was a savage among savages" (p. 95). As her recourse to the discredited rhetoric of savagery bears witness, Barton has no real idea of what this past was like; she can only conceive of it upon the basis of unfounded hypotheses that are themselves grounded in a highly ideologized language that inadequately (re)presents it. Perhaps it was an awareness of this inadequacy that accounted for Cruso's own decision not to write—not to, as Barton once urged him, "set down what traces remain of [your] memories, so that they will outlive you" (p. 17). What Barton's words point to here, although she herself does not appear to be aware of the nuance, is that the memories that she would have Cruso recover, and that she would dig out of Friday, are themselves nothing more than *traces* of memories—and thus at a double remove from an original that is, viewed in this light, in what Barton at one point calls "a glow of after-memory" (p. 104), even more unattainable than might at first be imagined.

Neither strategy, then, is wholly satisfactory, grounded as each is in questionable, and often objectionable, assumptions. Which is not to say, however, that Coetzee is arguing they ought to be abandoned, but only that they need to be pursued carefully: we cannot simply stop constructing linear narratives of the sort envisioned by Foe; nor can we ignore the necessity of circling back upon a past that we can no longer properly envisage because of our distance from it—the distance of a modernity that Defoe's *Robinson Crusoe* inaugurates. Coetzee is implying that both are necessary; they must be thought together, not apart, despite their inadequacies and their apparent and very real differences. In Part Three of the novel, the adversarial moment becomes what it literally is: not an exclusion of one's apparent opposite, but a turning *toward* it, and a consequent (con)fusion, as in a mirror, of the one with the other. Opposition is always also apposition: Barton and Foe at once antagonize and complement one another in their desire for a return to or an arrival at a wholeness that they consistently fall short of. Such failure, Coetzee would claim, is that to which language—in its partiality, its *figurality*—is destined: that we inhabit an essentially figural world, a world of "similitudes" (p. 80), of likenesses which are always also unlikenesses, is the brunt of the poetics, and politics, that Coetzee traces out in *Foe* and that I will be pursuing throughout this book in my account of the (un)likenesses brought about by the creolization process.

The problem of (un)likeness is foregrounded from the very beginning of the novel, which describes Barton's arrival on the island. The first paragraphs put into play an emphatic series of similes pointing in two very different directions (p. 5): toward the diversity of the material ("like a flower of the sea, like an anemone, like a jellyfish of the kind you see in the waters of Brazil") and, on the other hand, the totality of the abstract ("like all the saved"). Language occupies the intermediate space between these two extremes, a space of (un)likeness that marks the absence of the very things toward which it gestures. The disruptive presence of a second "Susan Barton" in the novel, who improbably claims—possibly at the instigation of Foe—to be the original Barton's lost daughter, further draws our attention to this space. Placing her hand against that of her supposed progenitor, this second Susan, who appears to have been grafted onto the narrative from another of Defoe's novels, *Roxana* (1724), offers her the "sign by which we may know our true mother": "see," she says, "we have the same hand. The same hand and the same eyes" (p. 76). Yet her hand is short, and Barton's long; the eyes are grey, and Barton's brown. Brought face to face with this unwanted double once again in Part Three, the original Barton objects that she is "unlike me in every way," to which it is responded that this "daughter" of hers is "like you in secret ways" (p. 132)—yet another variation of the hermeneutic credo, only this time turned against its exponent Barton, that one can uncover a secret logic motivating what would otherwise be no more than an arbitrary conjunction of signs.

The novel's emphasis on (un)likeness serves to counter the idea of adequacy—of a simple one-to-one identity, or lack thereof, between figure and ground—upon which the original *Robinson Crusoe* depends and that is at the heart of a conventional identity politics (as Wilson Harris suggests, in an argument that meshes nicely with my own, when he notes that "the politics of culture assume that like to like signifies a monolithic cradle or monolithic origin" and goes on to contrast this essentially narcissistic assumption with a more complex vision attuned to "subtle likenesses *through* contrasting densities or opposite and varied appearances").[8] When Defoe's Crusoe comes across the famous footprint, one of the first signs that others—or, quite simply, the Other—might inhabit his island, he initially tries to measure it by his own, to "see if there was any similitude or fitness, that I might be assured it was my own foot" (p. 166). Crusoe's discovery of an essential *un*likeness between his own foot and this trace of another's will in turn allow him to posit an essential likeness, a perfect "similitude or fitness," between that sign and the "substantial body" of an as yet unseen savage; it will empower his categorizing and astoundingly paranoid colonial rhetoric. Simultaneously invoking and vacating this dream of returning figures to their literal ground, Coetzee creates a world that is, to use Spivak's terminology, "catachrestic"[9]—that is to say, one in which figures lack the literal referent that they inescapably evoke. Coetzee has Barton and Foe inhabit, despite themselves, the same insubstantial realm of a language that will not, and is not, fit; finally resigning herself to this, Barton will conclude at the very end of Part Three that "we are all in the same world" (p. 152). This is a world in which, as Barton puts it, "all my life grows to be a story and there is nothing of my own left to me" (p. 133). It is a world where "my own," and the self-identical property and propriety of the self, can only be conjured up through a partial likeness, within the terms of a language from which that self is fundamentally estranged and yet in which it remains hauntingly present.

Responding to Barton's comment that "we are all in the same world," Foe is quick to point out, however, that in saying this she has omitted Friday. In one respect, Foe is simply reiterating here what we already know to be the case. He is admonishing Barton for her continued, perhaps constitutive, inability to include Friday within "her own" idea of the world— the fundamental incommensurability of the feminist and anticolonial or postcolonial projects that Spivak has argued for. Foe's comment is also, though, a self-referential nod on Coetzee's part toward his own tactical omission of Friday from the authoritative, but foundationless, realm of language that the other characters inhabit. In emphasizing Friday's silence, Coetzee allows the reader to imagine him in terms of uniqueness and sheer alterity (as Derek Attridge, for one, has eloquently argued);[10] rather than inhabiting a world of figures that cannot be reduced to a body, he appears to stand as a body that cannot be reduced to the figural world of Barton and Foe.

Friday's silence serves the heuristic purpose of reminding us, impossibly, of what we have lost, and continue to lose over and over again, in our accession to, and acquiescence with, both a language that implicates us in the dubious workings of authority and a power that colonialism exemplifies. Moreover, in the purity of that silence, Friday appears to hold out the potential for a native voice that would not, like those of Barton and Foe, be founded upon the absence and loss of what it purports to convey. The figure of Friday, as one critic puts it, "anticipates the silent, transformative potency of the body of history, the body of the future."[11] While these sorts of interpretations are comforting, because they establish a fundamental difference between the colonizers and the colonized or post-colonized, between a redeemed, "potent" future and a sullied past, I am arguing, by contrast, that although Coetzee encourages this superficial reading, he also wants us to view Friday as already a part of that world of which Barton speaks: Friday too is "(a)mazed," at an insuperable remove from the silent body that has been conjured up both as a false lure for the reader in search of unsullied, extra-labyrinthine points of reference upon which to base a post-colonial politics, and as a reminder of the necessity of continuing to imagine these points of reference. We must continue to imagine them, notwithstanding our awareness of the fact that we *are* all living in the same creolized and creolizing "community-world" and our awareness of the possibility that we *are* all possessed of "the same hand and the same eyes" (however unlikely it may seem from the narcissistic standpoint of the identitarian "politics of culture" that a writer like Harris so rightly castigates).

Coetzee's rhetorical emphasis on silence is doubled by a careful insistence throughout the novel on Friday's access to the language of power in the mode not of speech but of writing. Friday's encounters with writing become particularly marked toward the end of Part Three, when Foe prods Barton into beginning to teach Friday this art, but these climactic scenes merely serve to reenact on more familiar ground an entry into language that Friday has already undergone on the island, as one particularly important episode attests. Barton spies him paddling out to sea on a log of wood, and observes him reaching into "a bag that hung about his neck" (p. 31), from which he draws forth white petals that he scatters upon the waves. Although it provides Barton with a first revelation of something stirring "beneath" Friday's "dull and unpleasing exterior," and thus lays the foundation for her hermeneutic enterprise, she cannot read what he has written: for her, it leaves no trace (p. 32). We as readers must learn how to read this (as) writing, as Foe himself implies when he later remarks that even "the waterskater, that is an insect and dumb, traces the name of God on the surfaces of ponds, or so the Arabians say" (pp. 143–44). Friday's scattering of petals is a form of writing (and as such it is intimately related to his captivity, his Lacanian "captation": it is not only Barton's deed of freedom that will leave the scar around his neck that the anonymous narrator discovers at the very end of the novel; in arming himself with the tools of writing, Friday has also contributed to his own mutilation); the ritual of the petals takes place upon a one-dimensional surface that calls forth "depths" it cannot reach. What is Friday remembering? What loss does his writing memorialize? And what does he gain through this opaque gesture that can only be read with the greatest of difficulty?

Barton is not simply incapable of reading Friday's flowery script because of its dissimilarity to her own; she has a very hard time coming to terms with the (un)likely nature of writing itself. This becomes clear when she first attempts to teach Friday how to write as part of the educative process Foe recommends. On a slate she draws a picture of a house, and below it writes "the letters h-o-u-s" (p. 145). Not only does she here pictographically attempt to establish a one-to-one correspondence between image and word—an attempt that has already proved futile (pp. 67–70)—but she ignores the difference that writing makes, the *e* that can only be heard in writing, and that makes the written word (un)like the spoken original upon which it is based. This fifth letter is the sign, as it were, of what comes after the body of the word, a sign that both signals a loss of that body and serves as a supplement to it (and is it not this supplement, the missing fifth chapter, that the four constituent parts of *Foe* call forth?). Under her coaxing, Friday eventually writes the four letters h-o-u-s, "or four shapes passably like them: whether they were truly the four letters, and stood truly for the word *house*, and the picture I had drawn, and the thing itself, only he knew" (pp. 145–46). Here, in an attempt at resolving the tension between "passably like" and "stood truly," Barton pointedly overlooks the difference, the (un)likeness, that constitutes writing: in writing down these four letters (h-o-u-s), firm in the belief that they can be made to stand truly for the word they sound like (house), she ignores the distance of the written word from its originary sound—a distance embodied in the letter *e*. Writing is (un)like speech: words can be made to stand for themselves only by inscribing them as essentially (un)like themselves, and if this proves a source of confusion on Barton's part, it may nonetheless, we are led to hope, provide the point of departure for Friday's own writing.

Barton then goes on to attempt to teach Friday how to write three other words—"ship," "Africa," and "mother"—the last two of which convey the same foundationalist assumptions as the word "house." Guided by Barton's hand, Friday performs his task passably well, but when she motions him to write the words on his own, starting with "ship"—the one word out of these four, interestingly enough, which does not fit, evoking not a scene of origins but one of *middle* passages, of transport and captivity—he chooses to write it otherwise: "h-s-h-s-h-s he wrote, on and on, or perhaps h-f; and would have filled the whole slate had I not removed the pencil from his hand" (p. 146). What Friday appears to be doing here is, on the one hand, coyly reducing language to the Manichean oppositions of colonial and anticolonial discourse,[12] in which a world of difference is reduced to the counterpoint of two extremes, and on the other, engaging in a decolonizing gesture of reversal, in which a letter takes precedence over the one that had hitherto come before it (s-h → h-s), and perhaps even transforms the latter (h-s → h-f). Barton is understandably discouraged by this reversal and transformation of her own script, but Foe, suggesting that "there are many kinds of writing," seems more optimistic about the results.

While Foe and Barton debate the matter, Friday settles down with the slate and begins to write. Barton describes the following scene:

> Glancing over his shoulder, I saw he was filling it with a design of, as it seemed, leaves and flowers. But when I came closer I saw the leaves were eyes, open eyes, each set upon a human foot: row upon row of eyes upon feet: walking eyes. (p. 147)

What one might at first glance have mistaken as a "design" of flowers, as in the episode of Friday scattering petals over the sea, turns out, upon closer examination, to be one of "walking eyes." The word "design" is carefully chosen: not only does it ironically evoke the original Crusoe, who uses the word with great frequency (as, for instance, when he revealingly speaks of his "rational design" [p. 170]), but points to the fact that every sign, when perceived as such—that is to say, as figural, signifying something other than itself—always also de-signs, gesturing toward that which the sign does not and cannot contain. The language of flowers in which Friday originally wrote—by design, one might add, in order for Coetzee to mark a difference between it and "normal" writing that cannot, ultimately, be substantiated—has become one of eyes. This marks a shift from the natural world—a world that, as in the novel's opening paragraphs, comes to us only through similitudes—to the world of the human: a world of mobility, of that transport or *translatio* evoked by the word "ship."[13] Moreover, as is suggested by the reference to eyes, always of symbolic importance in Coetzee's work, it also marks a shift (and, viewed from a certain perspective, a fall) into the world of power.

In Coetzee's novels, eyes are consistently associated with power and authority, as we can see from this particularly relevant passage in his first novel, *Dusklands* (1974), where a murderous eighteenth-century Boer colonist by the name of Jacobus Coetzee reflects upon his relation to the African wilderness that he is exploring:

> Only the eyes have power. The eyes are free, they reach out to the horizon all around. Nothing is hidden from the eyes. As the other senses grow numb or dumb my eyes flex and extend themselves. I become a spherical reflecting eye moving through the wilderness and ingesting it. Destroyer of the wilderness, I move through the land cutting a devouring path from horizon to horizon. There is nothing from which my eye turns, I am all that I see. (p. 79)

In this passage, Coetzee reveals the horrific underside of the European travel writer's apparently innocent way of looking at the world, an *"out*-look" exemplified, for instance, by Pierre Poivre (*Intendant* of the Île de France during Bernardin de Saint-Pierre's stay there in the late 1760s and author of several works about Southern Africa) when he speaks of "the intelligent traveler who travels with his eyes, sees everything, examines closely the most interesting items, does not disregard the little things, who always has notebook in hand and never tires of seeing, interrogating, studying, and learning."[14] The two visions, of imperial conquest and of what Mary Louise Pratt has termed "anti-conquest,"[15] double one another, both setting into motion that "collective moving eye" on which the sights (and sites) of alterity are registered and then translated into the writing of colonizers and mere travelers alike. What is Friday's relation to this power? That, I would venture, is the question to which he is responding in his design. First and foremost, of course, he is the object of these devouring mobile eyes, synecdoches for the cannibalizing world of colonialism that would ingest him, be it out of a despotic egotism (Cruso) or a patronizing charity (Barton). If this brutal, destructive power has to be questioned, however, can it be simply avoided? Speaking of *Foe* in a 1987 interview, Coetzee asked, "how can one question power ('success') from a position of power? One ought to question it from its antagonist position: namely, the position of weakness."[16] If Coetzee is obviously talking here, at one level, about his own necessarily ambivalent position as a white South African who wants to criticize the racial master-narrative through which so much of his country's history has been filtered, he is also raising a more general problem regarding the workings of power—a problem leading to uncomfortable conclusions that must nonetheless be addressed. In occupying the "antagonist position," that of foe, is one not already caught up in the workings of the power that one would contest; and, even more crucially, is it even possible for a writer to occupy this "position of weakness," this "point of 'authenticity'"?[17] Has not this position been vacated the minute one entered the realm of a (groundlessly) authoritative language and thereby learned to see with one's eye, and to say I?

Coetzee is arguing that the foundational "weakness" of writing, white or otherwise, is that one can never occupy a position of weakness without transforming it into one of power. Writing can never be more than this double, duplicitous game, in which the odious Jacobus Coetzee mirrors a J. M. Coetzee who would have us think otherwise than his namesake but knows himself to be incapable of speaking that nonauthoritative thought without in some way betraying it. This is the dilemma of the writer that Friday outlines in his design: if Friday's portrait of the colonizer functions as a scathing indictment of the fact that he has become an object in their eyes, it also serves as a self-portrait. The numbness or dumbness of his other senses

notwithstanding, he too has become a "reflecting eye," flexing and extending himself over the migrant terrain of the written word—with a difference,
of course, a difference that lies sheerly in his ability to see openness where
Jacobus Coetzee imposed closure. He does not portray this eye (I) of his,
and of others, as a spherical whole but as "open": an open eye signals both
surveillance and vigilance, but it is also an open *I*, an *i*—one that is no
longer fully itself, its hypothetical continuity and *I*-dentity having been broken into by a space that intervenes between its separated parts. Friday's is a
writing, like Coetzee's, that has inscribed this hole, this sign of its own
blindness, upon its surface: that is the only difference between it and the
self-oblivious reflections of a Jacobus Coetzee. The author of *Foe* is suggesting that we must learn to live with the weakness of this difference,
which does not allow for an escape from the language of power that colonialism exemplifies but merely serves to put us on our guard against it. If
Coetzee the critic has at times endorsed the possibility of "a novel that is
prepared to work itself out outside the terms of class conflict, race conflict,
gender conflict or any of the other oppositions out of which history and the
historical disciplines erect themselves,"[18] Coetzee the novelist knows better:
he stresses that rather than engage in the naively pastoral gesture of reading
the "dark figure" of Friday as being outside or upon the margins of a hegemonic language that his silence, impossibly, leads us to believe he might
overturn or redeem, we must begin to explore, from the inside, the dimensions of the simultaneously powerful and self-critical world that Friday,
(un)like Defoe's Crusoe before him, has designed and placed himself at the
center of. The foe of Foe, of patriarchy, of colonialism, of modernity itself,
is always also caught up in the logic, and the language, of what he or she
would contest.

Friday will take his place, has already taken his place, in this world of
writing. The third part of *Foe* ends with him writing the letter *o*. "It is a beginning," says Foe to Barton (p. 152)—a beginning that literally marks the
end of Cruso and his story. Tomorrow, Foe continues, "you must teach him
a." Here, in this passage from omega to alpha, Foe appears to be gesturing—predictably, given his narrato-logical perspective—toward a break between a canonical, colonial story that has come to an end and a post-colonial beginning that the end of this story cannot help invoking. As we know
from the history of Barton's name, however, which was originally Berton
but "became corrupted in the mouths of strangers" (p. 10), the new beginning that this *a* would represent always contains within it the trace of an
e.[19] Situating us squarely in the middle, at a remove from both absolute beginnings and definitive endings, this silent *e*, which brings to an end the
original "hous" that Barton was attempting to (re)construct, is a sign of the
corruption that makes writing possible and that makes of omega and alpha

not opposites but apposites, standing complicitously side by side, their apparent adversarialness notwithstanding. The post/colonial beginning will always carry with it the trace of a difference that denies its claim to a prior foundation and throws it back upon the very ending, and the very power, it would oppose but can only add on to; this ambivalent beginning has already been translated into the mouths of strangers like Barton and Foe, who find themselves at an insuperable distance from the home that their differing discursive strategies nonetheless attempt to recuperate. Friday, too, is a part of this "unhomely world" (in Homi Bhabha's words); he, too, is a "stranger," whose writing, in its efforts at inscribing a once and future self, a pre-colonial origin and a post-colonial telos, can only translate—in a series of memorial, oppositional, and transformative practices—a native voice that, as his silence attests, cannot make itself heard in any Other way.[20] Friday's writing, Coetzee augurs, will take as its point of departure the strange and estranging knowledge "that no such unity exists, that writing unveils not the truth, nor the true origins, but a series of repeated gestures and ever renewed beginnings."[21]

Friday, like the others, exists in what we might call a trance, "trance being the interval between self-identity and self-difference."[22] This is not the "trance of possession" that Barton at one point in her narrative claims for him, imagining that "his soul [is] more in Africa than in Newington" (p. 98), but what we might call the *trans- of (dis)possession* that constitutes him as post/colonial subject. Friday will not be able to supply us with the self-identical story that Barton would like to hear: if she asserts that "the true story will not be heard till by art we have found a means of giving voice to Friday" (p. 118), then Friday, and Coetzee, offer another view of art and of what it means to "give voice." This voice can only be given in a spirit not of fullness but of lack: if Foe asserts, momentarily adopting Barton's hermeneutic language, that "till we have spoken the unspoken we have not come to the heart of the story" (p. 141), then Friday, and Coetzee, register the absence of that heart from the translated world of their writing. Like Barton, the skeptical and self-critical Foe is himself partially aware of this absence: "I said the heart of the story," he quickly corrects himself, as he ponders over what drew Friday out to the depths on his log of wood, "but I should have said the eye, the eye of the story." Friday has alerted both of them to the existence of a hole in the ground upon which they would have liked, authoritatively, to stand; this solid ground has proved, in fact, a beckoning sea, carrying within it a mere reflection of one's own eye (I), rather than the stable foundation they might once have anticipated.

In his discussion of this eye, interestingly enough, Foe excludes Friday, thus providing one last teasing intimation of a radical difference that would exempt him from the "unhomely world" of the other protagonists:

Friday rows his log of wood across the dark pupil—or the dead socket—of an eye staring up at him from the floor of the sea. He rows across it and is safe. To us he leaves the task of descending into that eye. Otherwise, like him, we sail across the surface and come ashore none the wiser, and resume our old lives, and sleep without dreaming, like babes. (p. 141)

Friday is here depicted as one who, childlike, simply floats upon the skin of death, in a sleep without dreams. This exclusion, and all the others to which Friday has been repeatedly and tactically subjected in the novel, produces a double reading in which Friday marks the sign of an absence, and is himself absented from the problematic world of "relations" in which Barton and Foe find themselves. On the one hand, each of these exclusions constitutes Friday as the "sign by which we may know our true mother": he becomes the puzzling site of allegory, a gap in the text that conjures up an alternative and as yet unvoiced reading, a sign of the irrecuperable "true mother" that we might not otherwise have known was lacking to us. The silent Friday stands as a sign of Barton's and Foe's blindness, alerting them, and the reader, to the fact that they are in a maze of doubting in which their dreams of an authoritative fullness will not be substantiated, despite the fact that they cannot help pursuing these dreams; the apparent silence of his position with regard to their own makes it possible for this sign to be read. On the other hand, Foe's portrait of Friday coming ashore "none the wiser" can be read, athwart its paternalism, in a much more positive light: on this reading, Friday—as one who knows enough to remain on the surface (that eminently postmodern location)—can be thought of as somehow immune to the lure of those murky ideological depths that beckon his colonial forebears. The text encourages this double reading, in which Friday simultaneously serves as a blind spot that makes the inadequacy of old readings visible *and* as the potential site for a radically new reading that (attuned, in Iain Chambers's words, to the "ontological reality of signs, surfaces and everyday life") would return us safely ashore, passing over the powerful eye (I) that enthralls the likes of Foe and Barton, and that the anonymous narrator of Part Four will plumb.

This potential for the radically new is inevitably present in the novel, but it does not, I would argue, constitute the main trajectory of Friday's story, or the part of it that especially interests Coetzee, as we might guess from the curious turn that the novel takes in the last section. In these final pages, Coetzee appears to go against the antifoundationalist grain of the rest of *Foe* by breaking the surface upon which his characters have hitherto found themselves. In two brief episodes that partially mirror one another, an anonymous narrator undertakes the (by this point thoroughly problematized) challenge of discovering the truth of the silent Friday, as he really is—a truth to which the rest of the novel has pointedly denied us access.

The first takes place solely in Foe's chambers, while the second moves on from there to a submarine landscape where the narrator explores the dark mass of a wreck containing Friday's body: both episodes end with the opening of Friday's mouth, from which "issue the sounds of the island" (p. 154) or "a slow stream, without breath, without interruption" (p. 157), which beats across the face of the interrogating narrator. Part Four ecstatically affirms, in other words, the presence in Friday of a native voice that has been rigorously denied up until this point in the novel and considered only in the light of its absence: the anonymous diver claims that where he (or she) has arrived is "not a place of words" but "a place where bodies are their own signs" (p. 157). Given all of the cautions that have preceded this affirmative moment, the narrator's arrival at "the home of Friday" can only seem an altogether unlikely *inventio* of the nonfigural, of the "secret body" and the secret of that body as it pours forth in a seemingly natural, gushing "stream" of consciousness.

This encounter with the very thing that the rest of the novel has put into question cannot, for that reason, be fully credited; but it clearly marks Coetzee's insistence on the necessity of thinking in such (re)constructive terms. These final affirmations are, to be sure, not merely rendered hollow by all the doubts that have preceded them, but themselves contain further grounds for skepticism, if only because the identity (and hence positionality) of the first-person narrator remains an enigma. Such skepticism is further exacerbated by the fact that *two* possible affirmative endings are being juxtaposed. At the same time that the double ending invokes an emphatic form of ideological closure, recuperating the nonfigural home of Friday and finally breaking his silence, it also maintains the reader in the realm of (un)likeness that appears to have been finally left behind. In their (un)likeness, the two final episodes provide alternative endings, and any decision to privilege one over the other can only be arbitrary. Both the necessity and the arbitrariness of closure are thus emphasized in this double ending, which puts into question, with ambivalent finality, the bodily presence and the native voice that it strategically affirms. This theoretically unviable affirmation of what has already died, this (re)presentation of a voice that has already been translated into writing and thus become different from itself, marks the paradoxical double imperative of Coetzee's politics of (un)likeness—a politics in which the problem of identity, so central to the postcolonial enterprise, becomes a question of ambivalently confronting the very lack of that identity. It is only in exploring this absence that we may find—that is to say, invent—the self that is (not) hidden in the castle of the skin we are forced to inhabit, the labyrinthine surface upon which we are reduced to wandering in search of a dead body that is always also the "body of the future."

In the light of the preceding analysis, one last, admittedly speculative, point can be made here. In excluding Friday from the task of descending into the depths of the eye that the anonymous narrator of Part Four interrogates, Foe remarked that he prefigures another diver (p. 142). While this statement is most easily read as a reference to the actual author of *Foe*, I would venture an additional suggestion: that Friday, far from having gone ashore like a dreamless babe, is himself this other diver, a post/colonial author split into two selves; initiated into the realm of writing, he is now in a position to reflect back upon himself, to plumb the depths of a self to which he no longer has true access. Rather than being radically unlike the others, paddling over an authoritative eye (I) without feeling compelled to plumb it, to seek out what lies at its (false) bottom, Friday is like them, in all the ambivalence of this word. He, too, finds himself at a distance from himself, forced into speaking about his once and future self in the third person and from a perspective that cannot deny its complicity with the power that threatens to engulf it and that it endlessly interrogates. Friday is this other diver, impossibly trying to find a way back into his own mouth, to (re)inhabit a home that will now have a place only in the figural world of his writing. Friday finds himself in exile, simultaneously moving away, in his "future wanderings" as a writer, from the island of his self—"the eye / lands, my is- / lands," in the words of Brathwaite's poem "Dawn"[23]—and circling back upon that self in a strange, and estranging, encounter with the mouth of the dead man he once was. Friday, the anonymous narrator of Part Four, as yet lacking a name, a name that he can never truly speak and that he must henceforth invent, moves toward this dead self, bearing only a stub of candle that hangs on a string around his neck, yet another in the chain of signifiers that will scar him and signal his captivity: "I hold it up before me," he notes, "like a talisman, though it sheds no light" (p. 156). Guided by this light which sheds no light—the light of writing, the "glow of after-memory"—Friday returns to himself, in an impossible and necessary gesture of recuperation that marks the infinitely rehearsed beginnings of a post/colonial poetics, and politics, that will be skeptical, engaged, and strangely familiar.

Between the Banyan and the Rhizome: Kamau Brathwaite, Édouard Glissant, and the Creole Continuum of Postcolonial Theory

> Hybridity is the perplexity of the living as it interrupts the representation of the fullness of life.
> —Homi Bhabha, "DissemiNation"

In one of the founding documents of postcolonial literature, Aimé Césaire's *Cahier d'un retour au pays natal* (1939/1947), the poet notoriously augurs: "My mouth shall be the mouth of those calamities that have no mouth, my voice the freedom of those who break down in the solitary confinement of despair" (*CP*, pp. 44–45; "Ma bouche sera la bouche des malheurs qui n'ont point de bouche, ma voix, la liberté de celles qui s'affaissent au cachot du désespoir"). Strategically revising these lines in the 1950s, his compatriot Édouard Glissant, who the previous decade had attended the lycée in which Césaire taught, will speak, by contrast, of "those who have not had a voice and of whom we would not know how to be the voice, since we are only a part of their voices" (*IP*, p. 197). What should have emerged from my discussion of Coetzee's novel is not only the difficulty of this claim for the future staked out in Césaire's poem—a difficulty ably identified in Glissant's conditional rewriting of it—but its urgency. The author(ity) of the *Cahier* will give voice to the unrepresented, yes, but in thus transforming himself into a representative of his people, the poet ineluctably puts himself at a distance from both those he is supposedly representing and this voice of his to which he lays claim. On the one hand, the *je*'s emphatically singular and troublingly "demiurgic" position in the text obviously does not correspond with the voiceless plurality for which he would speak (and nor does the use of French mesh easily with the Creole spoken by the vast majority of those for whom this *je* purports to speak);[24] and on the other, this voice comes to us only in the translated form of a writing that is (un)like it, that cannot truly return to the place—the "pays natal," Brathwaite's "is-land"—from which it originated.

Césaire's ambitious dream, his belief in the possibility of eliminating this distance that separates him both from the people for whom he would speak and from his own self, is also discernible in another of the *Cahier*'s key lines, where the poet, in a statement that bears directly on the question of identity, asserts: "I am forcing the vitelline membrane that separates / me from myself" (pp. 56–57; "Je force la membrane vitelline qui me / sépare de moi-même"). An egg yolk's transparent covering, the vitelline membrane is a barrier that, precisely because of its apparent transparency, the poet believes he might succeed in breaking through. I have suggested a view of the post/colonial self, by contrast, that stresses the impenetrability of this membrane, or what Glissant would term its "opacity"—that by which, in Glissant's words, the other (and one's own self) "escapes me, ensuring that I must, with vigilance, always go toward him" (*DA*, p. 278). The word "membrane," importantly, is etymologically connected to both parchment and memory. It is with this memorial inscription that the post/colonial writer must (re)cover the "lost body" he or she claims to be in the process of uncovering. The self that in the *Cahier* Césaire attempts to "re-join," to reunite (with), amounts to nothing more (or less) than what the anonymous narrator of *Foe*'s duplicitous last chapter heard when listening at the mouth of Friday for "the call of a voice" (p. 154): a sound emptied of life, like "the roar of waves in a seashell"—an echo made possible by the foundational absence of the very thing that is supposedly being heard. The truth about Friday will go unsaid, cannot be "forced" either by himself or by others who attempt to disinter it. This is the situation that one of the many narrators of the Moroccan writer Tahar Ben Jelloun's postmodern classic *L'enfant de sable* (1985) registers, when he suggests that "truth goes into exile; I only have to speak and the truth becomes distant, forgotten, and I turn into its gravedigger and its exhumer, the master and the slave" (p. 45). It is this truth-in-exile that Glissant, choosing to follow a more circuitous route than that offered by the *Cahier*'s redemptive project of direct representation, would take as the point of departure for his own writing. Identifying himself in his first theoretical work, *Soleil de la conscience* (1956), as the "ethnologist of myself" (p. 15), Glissant would henceforth situate himself within the double space of digging and undigging of which Ben Jalloun's narrator speaks, estranged from the truth that he must nonetheless attempt to tell about himself and his people(s).

My emphasis on belatedness and estrangement exemplifies, to be sure, a postmodern perspective on the postcolonial condition, if, as the New Zealand critic Simon During once disapprovingly noted, such thought recognizes "that the Other can never speak for itself as the Other."[25] From this perspective, it is taken as a given that when it comes to identity politics we are always dealing with a script (or scrypt) that has taken the place of the authentic words we might once have spoken. From this perspective, it is equally clear that questions of identity and alterity have long since become matters of relationality and (dis)similarity, given the fact that, as Michael Taussig puts it, "First World and Other Worlds now mirror, interlock, and rupture each other's alterity to such a degree that all that is left is the excess—the self-consciousness as to the need for an Identity, sexual, racial, ethnic, and national, and the roller-coastering violence and enjoyment of this state of affairs."[26] And yet, as During also pointed out, postmodernism is "that thought which refuses to turn the Other into the Same." It recognizes the necessity of continuing to create a space for such identities, even if these are in the final analysis nothing more (or less) than fictions that are inadequate to the complex realities of global(izing) processes—notably, the "incorporation of all areas of the world and all areas of even formerly 'private' life into the money economy"[27]—that repeatedly put these identities into question. Such processes do not (simply) lead to the dissolution of difference, the Coca-Colonization of McWorld, but (also) to the obsolescence of the opposition between global homogenization and local heterogeneity that has for centuries played such a central role in structuring the exotic imaginary, be it the imaginary of the colonial or the anticolonial writer.

Without denying difference, a postmodern writer like Coetzee insightfully suggests that what counts most is that "we are all in the same world." In *Foe*, this creolized and creolizing world of "relations" is imperfectly represented by Foe's chambers, which are no longer simply occupied by the isolated bourgeois self and his man Friday, the colonized (and homoerotically charged) double fantasized by Defoe; to the great (con)fusion of those who find themselves living there, these chambers are now inhabited by a disparate group of people inextricably connected to one another and engaged in an ongoing process of (unequal) "negotiation" where, as Homi Bhabha has remarked, "no discursive authority can be established without revealing the difference of itself" and where as a result "the signs of cultural difference cannot . . . be unitary or individual forms of identity because their continual implication in other symbolic systems always leaves them 'incomplete' or open to cultural translation."[28] If our postmodernity is characterized by a growing awareness of these negotiations and the cultural translations they entail, it also remains, as I have attempted to argue in my reading of *Foe*, hauntingly subject to the discursive authority that it puts into question. Shifting the terrain from fiction to cultural criticism, I would now like to resituate this simultaneous contestation of and acquiescence with "unitary or individual forms of identity" in the specific context of postcolonial theory, first through a brief overview of the field and then through a more detailed look at how this paradoxical dynamic of identity and diversity, of the local and the global, manifests itself in the theoretical work of the two writers who have provided what are to this date probably the most vital and influential accounts of the creolization process, Kamau Brathwaite and Édouard Glissant.

Julie Dash's 1991 *Daughters of the Dust* is a groundbreaking filmic evocation of Gullah culture at the turn of this century. Living on the Sea Islands off the mainland of South Carolina and Georgia, the Gullah were, as is stated in the film's opening credits, able "as a result of their isolation" to create and maintain "a distinct, imaginative, and original African American culture."[29] Dash's portrait of this insular culture is breathtakingly effective, at both the aesthetic and political level. Working from what bell hooks identifies as a "mythic" as opposed to "documentary" perspective, Dash exposes her audience to many of the surviving Africanisms in this distinctive syncretic society; she subverts conventional (patriarchal) cinematic patterns of viewing, and—in line with her womanist agenda—attempts to represent the un(der)represented ("I always knew I wanted to make films about African American women. To tell stories that had not been told. To show images of our lives that had not been seen").[30] The end result is a superb example of cultural remembering that already stands as an historical milestone in the development of both Afro-American and postcolonial cinema.

In a perspicacious account of *Daughters*, the late Toni Cade Bambara— an important influence on Dash's own work—approvingly maintains that the film conveys "an unabashedly Afrocentric thesis in the teeth of current-day criticisms of essentialism."[31] Attempting at one point in her assessment of the film to place Dash in a more global context, Bambara sees her as one among many recent "filmmakers who argue for cultural authenticity" and who are attempting to forge a "diasporic hook-up." As one example of these like-minded filmmakers, she cites Martinique's Euzhan Palcy and specifically her first feature film: "in her [1983] screen adaptation of the [Joseph] Zobel novel *Rue Case-Nègres*," Bambara informs her readers, Palcy "invents the character Medouze (who tells [the young autobiographical protagonist] Jose about Africa) for the purpose of linking the Caribbean to the Continent"; by means of this invention, Bambara argues, Palcy demonstrates a "continuum" (p. 128) between Africa and the worlds of its diaspora. Now, what is especially interesting about these comments, which are grounded in a polemic with anti-essentialists whose position Bambara patently does not share, is that in her anticanonical haste to identify a canon of filmmakers who have the good sense to "argue for cultural authenticity" she ends up inventing a woman director who has "invented" a diasporic connection that, one can only presume from the account she gives of it, was absent from Zobel's original novel (first published in 1950). As anyone who has actually read Zobel's influential and highly popular novel knows full well, the old storyteller Médouze, and with him the connection to an ancestral Africa, in fact plays an important role in *Rue case-nègres*—a role, incidentally, bearing no small resemblance to the one played by Pa in an Anglo-Caribbean novel that is contemporary with Zobel's, George Lamming's *In the Castle of My Skin* (1952). To be sure, the character of Médouze comes across much more forcefully in Palcy's film. It is no doubt significant that in Zobel's novel, unlike in Palcy's film, José (and thus the reader) is never allowed to hear the old man's stories in their entirety, either because his grandmother calls him away before Médouze has finished or because the old man does not tell his *contes* quickly enough: "I'm never able to hear a story all the way through to the end," Zobel's José notes.[32] The invocation of Africa and the ancestor theme is but one element in a novel that is notable more for the cultural and psychological divisions and ambivalences that it assiduously registers: notably, the autobiographical (and autoethnographical) splitting of José into narrated child and narrating adult, the never final divisions between a closed time of myth and the open time of (colonial) history, and the subtle interconnections between the island's creole culture and its on the one hand partially remembered African and on the other partially assimilated

French counterparts.[33] If Zobel has linked the Caribbean to the African continent, he has done so in a way that registers the limitations of this link, and forces us to view the connection not (only) from the isolating perspective of "diasporic unity" and "cultural authenticity" that Bambara is so eager to promote, but (also) from a creolized and creolizing perspective that emphatically situates pre-colonial, colonial, and post-colonial worlds in an inseparably compromised relation with one another.

The sort of ambivalences, divisions, and mixtures that Zobel's novel registers can be traced to what Paul Gilroy has identified as "the fragmentation of self (doubling and splitting) which modernity seems to promote." In his own polemic with "the ethnic absolutism that currently dominates black political culture" (*BA*, p. 5), Gilroy is arguing that we need to take the *modernity* of diasporic cultures into account, something that Bambara's vision signally fails to do, committed as it is to what Gilroy has critiqued as the "uni-directional notion of diaspora as a form of dispersal which enjoys an identifiable and reversible originary moment" (as opposed to the "much more complex 'chaotic' model in which unstable 'strange attractors' are also visible").[34] Contrary to Bambara's sense of the current intellectual climate, Gilroy contends that furthering an awareness of this modernity, and the fragmentation it has promoted, is *less* fashionable these days and that "appeals to the notion of purity as the basis of racial solidarity are more popular."[35] Whether the appeals of a Molefi Keti Asante to Afrocentricity are more popular than those of a Homi Bhabha to cultural hybridity, or whether what Gilroy scathingly refers to as Spike Lee's "campaign against difficulty, complexity, and anything else that does not fit the historical binary codes of American racial thought to which he subscribes" is more appreciated than, say, the "black British" director Isaac Julien's cinematic transgression of those codes,[36] need not concern us for the moment. Rather, what needs to be pointed out is simply the extent to which this (ineradicable) opposition is itself at the foundations of postcolonial theory.

It is Asante-like "appeals to the notion of purity" that During seems to privilege in the article cited above (published in 1987), when he takes issue with the postmodernism that he has so precisely identified. Noting that because of its global dimensions, postmodernity is always constructed "in terms which more or less intentionally wipe out the possibility of post-colonial identity," he presents the case for a "post-colonialism" defined as "the need, in nations or groups which have been victims of imperialism, to achieve an identity uncontaminated by universalist or Eurocentric concepts and images." It is certainly this need that generates Bambara's anxiety about "current-day criticisms of essentialism" and her erroneous claims about Palcy's film and Zobel's novel. As During goes on to say, if "the post-colonial desire is the desire of decolonized communities for an identity"

(p. 43), then we can, and ought to, distinguish between those who share this desire and those who do not or cannot: between, respectively, what he calls the "post-colonized" and the "post-colonizers." Where the latter, and he cites Salman Rushdie as an example, are in many ways complicit with the legacy of colonialism ("if they do not identify with imperialism, [they] at least cannot jettison the culture and tongues of the imperialist nations" [p. 45]), the former "identify with the culture destroyed by imperialism and its tongue" and thus attempt to (re)create an uncontaminated political space and literary language, and here he cites the work of Ngugi wa Thiong'o, who—on the basis of an unrelenting distinction between "imperialist tradition" and "resistance tradition" and a firm belief in "the coming inevitable revolutionary break with neo-colonialism"—has famously argued, for instance, that one can and must distinguish between truly African literature and a "hybrid tradition, a tradition in transition, a minority tradition that can only be termed as Afro-European literature; that is, the literature written by Africans in European languages."[37] We find this desire for a decontaminated and truly post-colonial condition voiced with exceptional force, for example, in Césaire's *La tragédie du roi Christophe* (1963)—the first play in his 1960s "decolonization trilogy"—when the dying king of Haiti, Henri Christophe, laments his partial assimilation of colonial values and apostrophizes, in the name of a liberated future, the Africa of his ancestors: "Africa! Help me to return home, carry me like an aged child in your arms and then you will undress me, you will cleanse me. Rid me [*défais-moi*] of all these clothes, rid me of them as, when dawn comes, one is rid of the night and its dreams."[38] This desire for a purificatory "undressing" and redressing of colonialism, During further notes, is one that only seems realizable in certain locales: where a country like Australia "has almost no possibility of entry into the post-colonized condition," its neighbor New Zealand "retains a language, a store of proper names, memories of a pre-colonial culture, which seductively figure identity" (p. 45).

As Bambara sarcastically acknowledges, it has become a theoretical commonplace to point out the deeply problematic, if for some still very seductive, nature of the appeals to an autonomous pre- or post-colonial identity made by Henri Christophe and apparently valorized by During (who would, however, soon arrive at a much more nuanced position akin to Gilroy's in his various revisitings of these issues),[39] as well as to note the fact that such appeals have their philosophical origins in "Western" conceptions of cultural identity. Critics as diverse as France's Alain Finkielkraut and Ghana's Anthony Appiah have noted, for example, the extent to which contemporary ethnic identity politics has its source in the anti-Enlightenment proto-nationalist thought of Johann Gottfried Herder. As Finkielkraut forcefully argues, the cherished idea of "cultural identity" amounts to little more than a modern translation of Herder's *Volksgeist*;[40] Frantz Fanon's commitment to the idea of a "génie national" (which other thinkers of the decolonization period would rephrase in racial terms: Negritude, Black Power, and so on) shares a common philosophical ground with, say, the early-twentieth-century French nationalist Maurice Barrès's deeply conservative cult of "la terre et les morts" (p. 108), and it is a dangerous ground that, Finkielkraut points out, many people continue to tread in the ostensibly "plural" guise of multiculturalism. In a similar vein, Appiah has delivered an influential critique of what he calls "nativism," an ideology that is spectacularly exhibited in "that now-classic manifesto of African cultural nationalism," *Toward the Decolonization of African Literature* (1980), where its three Nigerian authors argue that "African literature is an autonomous entity separate and apart from all other literature . . . [having] its own traditions, models and norms."[41] Appiah demonstrates how this desire for "apartness" is itself substantially determined by the dictates of the West's Herderian legacy, its notion of a *Sprachgeist*, and its entanglement in what Nietzsche once called "the problem of race [*Rasse*]": namely, that "it is simply not possible that a human being should *not* have the qualities and preferences of his parents and ancestors in his body, whatever appearances may suggest to the contrary."[42] The "reverse discourse" of these Nigerian authors is generated out of the very discourse that it would contest (and that made possible the invention of "Negroes" in the first place):[43] "the pose of repudiation actually presupposes the cultural institutions of the West and the ideological matrix in which they, in turn, are imbricated." "Railing against the cultural hegemony of the West, the nativists are of its party without knowing it" (p. 59), Appiah points out in *In My Father's House*. We need, he concludes, to "transcend the banalities of nativism—its images of purgation, its declarations, in the face of international capital, of a specious 'autonomy,' its facile topologies" (pp. 71–72); this transcendence will only happen once we leave behind "the language of empire—of center and periphery, identity and difference, the sovereign subject and her colonies" (p. 72), and recognize that "we are all already contaminated by each other" (p. 155). While such recent arguments not unsurprisingly prove anathema to the more strident postcolonial critics, who argue that they deprive formerly colonized peoples of an "insurgent" agency (Benita Parry, for instance, has remarked of Appiah's critique that "in exposing the operation of a 'nativist typology'—inside/outside, indigene/alien, western/traditional—it installs a topology of its own, where the coloniser is dynamic donor and the colonised is docile recipient, where the west initiates and the native imitates"),[44] they in fact simply reinforce what a great number of postcolonial writers have been saying for decades in less theoretically charged language.

At the opposite end of the spectrum to Ngugi and the authors of *Toward the Decolonization of African Literature*, visionary writers like Derek Walcott and Wilson Harris have consistently written against the "strenuous attempts to create identity" that Appiah has so lucidly critiqued. The acerbic attacks on "pure black Afro-Aryanism" that Walcott launched at the height of the Black Power movement in the States have gained a renewed relevance in the age of Asante, Louis Farrakhan, and Leonard Jeffries. As Walcott astutely remarked of the turn the politics of decolonization was taking in his home islands at this time, "once we have lost our wish to be white we develop a longing to become black, and those two may be different, but are still careers" (a sentiment that itself echoes Fanon's well-known assessment of Negritude a little under two decades earlier: "it seems that, after the great white error, people in the Antilles are now in the process of living out the great black mirage").[45] Opposing such colonial careers, Walcott would argue for the cleansing virtues of an Adamic perspective through which the individual Caribbean man—regardless of ancestry— might greet what he poetically refers to as "the enormous, gently opening morning of his possibility, his body touched with dew, his nerves as subtilized to sensation as the mimosa, his memory, whether of grandeur or of pain, gradually erasing itself as recurrent drizzles cleanse the ancestral or tribal markings from the coral skull, the possibility of a man and his language waking to wonder here."[46] Like Walcott, Harris has been amongst the most vocal postcolonial critics when it comes to contesting the "retreat into patterns of closure or identity within (say) areas of the Third World in the twentieth century" and to criticizing a narcissistic reliance on "fields of experience geared to uniform (rather than cross-cultural) parentage of tradition."[47] Arguing for the freedom of "far-flung, regenerative, cross-cultural possibility," he points out that "concepts of invariant identity function in the modern world as a block imperative at the heart of cultural politics[:] the oppressor makes this his or her banner[;] the oppressed follow suit." "Such," he concludes, "is the tautology of power."[48] If Harris has consistently warned his readers against this tautology and the doom that "resides in the acceptance of absolute structure within partial institutions that have masqueraded for centuries as the divine parentage of the modern world," and if he has urged us to follow up on any and all traces of "unstructured vision or unconscious arbitration,"[49] his search for a "doorway into a conception of genuine breakthrough from tragedy," or what Brathwaite has called Harris's "syncretic/synthetic ideal,"[50] is nonetheless always tempered by a deconstructionist insistence on the "infinitely rehearsed" nature of the redressals of colonial structure that he is advocating: what he calls the "consumption of bias" is an unending process, in which we incessantly fall back upon the "tragic" structures and constructs that we are attempting to disarticulate. In a like manner, despite Walcott's emphasis on a "cleansing" amnesia and his quarrel with the "muse of History" and the fixed identities that (cultural, racial) memory seductively and dangerously offers us, he is a poet who, as one commentator puts it, "seems to become enmeshed in history the more he tries to escape from it."[51] Walcott's effort at forgetting and Harris's will to a breakthrough from tragedy are "doomed" consistently to turn back upon themselves, thereby forcing us to reconsider the very identities away from which these two writers have insistently and heroically directed us.

Notwithstanding Appiah's stinging critique in *In My Father's House* of "our entrancement with the polarities of identity and difference" and "the rhetoric of alterity" that it generates (p. 72), it is no coincidence that he goes on in the same book to admit that "because the value of identities is . . . relative, we must argue for and against them case by case" (p. 180). If "a self-isolating black nationalism *within* England or France or the United States" strikes him as a very bad thing, he nonetheless asserts the desirability, "however false or muddied its theoretical roots," of "another Pan-Africanism"—one that would not, this time around, be based upon "the project of a racialized Negro nationalism." Such heartfelt, if ultimately arbitrary, appeals to a "usable identity" are a far cry from his simultaneously voiced call for "transcending" the "language of empire," the language of "identity and difference"; here, we are being told not simply to go "beyond identity," but to recuperate its language carefully, "strategically," in light of the fact that "the label works despite the absence of an essence."[52] It is this same duplicitous position that, notwithstanding his withering attacks on "ethnic absolutism," Paul Gilroy maintains with regard to the diasporic connections that Bambara uncautiously championed: as he argues in his *Black Atlantic*, despite "the dangers of idealism and pastoralisation associated with this concept" (pp. 80–81), a Pan-Africanist politics should be carefully pursued while keeping in mind all that it excludes. We need, he stresses, to occupy the middle ground of an "anti-anti-essentialism" that would be capable of mediating between the two poles of radical essentialism and constructionism which, despite (or precisely because of) their prima facie opposition, "have become locked in an entirely fruitless relationship of mutual interdependency."[53] The most pressing task on the agenda of postcolonial theory, he suggests, may well be to produce a "model whereby identity can be understood neither as a fixed essence nor as a vague and utterly contingent construction to be reinvented by the will and whim of aesthetes, symbolists, and language gamers" (*BA*, p. 102).[54]

If, as some critics have rightly pointed out, this "anti-anti-essentialist" model itself degenerates at times in Gilroy's work into yet another version of "cultural insiderism,"[55] this would appear to be an inevitable, but not necessarily debilitating, result of the double game that he is urging us to play in the arena of identity politics. Appiah's and Gilroy's delicate—and by no means logically coherent—recuperation of an identitarian logic that they have so effectively demystified suggests that the only fruitful place to situate future discussions of (racial, ethnic, cultural, sexual) identity is squarely in the shifting and incoherent middle of a continuum that extends from the two unrealizable poles of its assertion and its transcendence. Even a critic as unsympathetic to the politically "contaminated" position adopted by Appiah as Benita Parry has, after her intransigent attacks on the likes of Bhabha and Spivak in the mid-1980s, come around to a rather more nuanced position in which, while continuing to argue predictably for "resistant" nativisms, nationalisms, and so on, and against critics who construe "the colonialist relationship in terms of negotiations with the structures of imperialism," she nonetheless seems more willing and able to acknowledge the constructed (discursive) nature of any and all "resistant" selves, and to reread "liberation theories" accordingly: Césaire's Negritude, for instance, thus becomes not an ontologically grounded essentialism but "a textually invented history, an identity effected through figurative operations, and a tropological construction of blackness as a sign of the colonised condition and its refusal."[56] Despite the obvious divergence of their views, then, Parry and Appiah are thus inextricably linked to one another in a mutually contaminatory dialogue— the former offering (to cite the subtitle of a recent article of Parry's) "two cheers for nativism," the latter countering, as it were, with "two cheers for hybridity."

It is this shifting middle ground of divergence and convergence that I will be calling (to adapt a term first used by linguists)[57] the "creole continuum" of post/colonial identity politics. In the preceding paragraphs I have attempted to give an admittedly schematic account of the nature of this multidimensional continuum; I will now proceed to map out some of its contours in a more specific analysis, by showing how it gets negotiated in the work of two of the most influential theorists of creolization, Brathwaite and Glissant. As we will see, both writers veer away, though in quite opposite directions, from the intermediary creolized ground that each has played such a large role in drawing to our attention: Brathwaite's trajectory takes him (back) toward a position that at times resembles the essentialist arguments of a Toni Cade Bambara; Glissant's takes him (forward) toward one that closely approximates the vision of "asymmetric infinity" promoted by a Wilson Harris. Paradoxically occupying the same middle ground and diametrically opposing poles, Brathwaite and Glissant stand in a simultaneously complementary and contradictory relation to one another that perfectly exemplifies the latter's definition of creolization—one that perhaps now reads somewhat less opaquely than it did in my first chapter—as "une dimension inédite qui permet à chacun d'être là et ailleurs, enraciné et ouvert, perdu dans la montagne et libre sous la mer, en accord et en errance" (*PR*, p. 46).

In his groundbreaking *The Development of Creole Society in Jamaica, 1770–1820* (1971), the poet, historian, and cultural critic Kamau Brathwaite examined Jamaican society at the turn of the eighteenth century and discovered there the requisite elements for a way of thinking about the Caribbean that would serve as an alternative, or at least a supplement, to two earlier models: on the one hand, the pessimistic "plantation-society" model offered by Orlando Patterson in his influential *Sociology of Slavery* (1967), which declined to read Jamaican slave society as "a total social system"; on the other, the "plural society" model put forward by M. G. Smith, which attempted to understand that society in terms of its division into "culturally distinct aggregates."[58] Of this latter model, in which, for instance, Jamaicans are seen as moralizing "incessantly about one another's actions in order to assert their cultural and social identity by expressing the appropriate sectional morality," Brathwaite commented: "the classic plural society paradigm is based on an apprehension of cultural polarity, on an 'either/or' principle, on the idea of people sharing common divisions instead of increasingly common values."[59] It is an emphasis on these "common values" that would generate his vision of creolization, which he glossed in *Development* as "a way of seeing Jamaican [and by extension Caribbean] society, not in terms of white and black, master and slave, in separate nuclear units, but as contributory parts of a whole" (p. 307), not as made up of "culturally distinct aggregates" but as "an historically affected socio-cultural continuum" (p. 310). Notwithstanding "the dehumanizing institution of slavery" and the tremendous injustices that were a commonplace of colonial rule in Jamaica, Brathwaite found a great, if virtually unexplored, potential in the confluence of the two worlds of Europe and Africa, master and slave, white and black: both groups had "to adapt themselves to a new environment and to each other." "The friction created by this confrontation was cruel," Brathwaite admits, "but it was also creative" (p. 307).

Elaborating on this creative confrontation in another book written around this time, *Contradictory Omens*, and implicitly referring his reader to the earlier work of Fernando Ortiz, Brathwaite identified the term creolization as a "specialized version of the two widely accepted terms *acculturation* and *interculturation*," the former referring to "the process of absorption of one culture by another" and the latter to "a more reciprocal activity, a process of intermixture and enrichment, each to each" (p. 11). While unsurprisingly privileging the interculturative over the acculturative (assimilatory) aspects of the creolization process, Brathwaite nonetheless acknowledged that, given the colonial dynamics of Jamaica's creole society, these two aspects were often inseparable from one another. This double-edged process at work in late-eighteenth-century and early-nineteenth-century Jamaica did not, Brathwaite went on to argue, result in a satisfactory outcome: "the movement towards cultural wholeness or homogeneity was halted" (CO, p. 22).[60] Jamaican society, he argued in the conclusion of *Development*, did not recognize the "elements of its own creativity," and this blindness to its creolized potential resulted in "the failure of Jamaican society" as a whole: the colonial power structure came to prefer a "bastard metropolitanism—handed down to the society in general after Emancipation— . . . to a complete exposure to creolization and liberation of their slaves" (p. 307). The islanders remained caught in the trap of a dualistic thinking that failed to correspond to the cross-cultural reality in which they were actually immersed—a reality with which, as Brathwaite has insisted throughout his career, in both his poetry and his theoretical works, not only the diverse worlds of the Caribbean but the world as a whole must come to terms if a significant diminishment in the sectarian violence produced and exploited by neocolonialism and rigidly identitarian ways of thinking is ever to be achieved.

As Peter Hulme has noted, "the term 'creole' seeps across any attempt at a Manichean dividing line between native and settler, black and white."[61] Brathwaite's early insistence on the value of this elusive signifier clearly ran counter to an ideological emphasis on "resistance" in the work of certain historians intent on promoting the view that "slaves tried at all costs to maintain their cultures and their original languages against a colonial society that, with an inverse determination, attempted to divest them of these [cultures and languages]";[62] more generally, it contested the simplistic rhetoric of colonialism and anticolonialism, each of which is founded upon claims of the essential apartness of colonizer and colonized. Rather than stressing the separation of cultures, Brathwaite identified their coming together as the necessary precondition of the future emergence, at the local level, of healthy Caribbean societies and, at the global level, of a functional world order, and thus helped initiate the anti-Manichean direction of so much of what has been called "post-anti-colonial critique."[63] In our fin de siècle, old certitudes about the Other—what Sara Suleri has referred to as "the simple pieties that the idiom of alterity frequently cloaks"—are rapidly giving way to an awareness of the ambivalences of cultural and racial identity. "The rhetoric of binarism that informs, either explicitly or implicitly, contemporary critiques of alterity in colonial discourse," as Suleri puts it,[64] seems ever more inadequate as a means of giving expression to our increasingly creolized—or, to put it in less culturally specific terms, hybridized—selves.[65] And yet, at the same time as Brathwaite has continued to engage this increasingly familiar way of thinking that he helped pioneer in the early 1970s, he has nonetheless also stressed, and with an increasing insistence in recent years, the continued *presence*, and I intend all the Derridean connotations of that word, of the original cultures that one would suppose the creolization process to have utterly transformed.

We can get a sense of the double direction of Brathwaite's work by looking at a passage from *Development* where he is first and foremost insisting on the "infinite possibilities" that obtain under conditions of creolization:

> From their several cultural bases people in the West Indies tend towards certain directions, positions, assumptions, and ideals. But nothing is really fixed and monolithic. Although there is white/brown/black, there are infinite possibilities within these distinctions and many ways of asserting identity. (p. 310)

While the central orientation of his claim is obvious, one cannot help noticing his appeal to the idea of cultural bases and his unproblematic use of the verb "is" in the phrase "there is white/brown/black." It is clear that the existence of "culturally discrete groups" is not really being put into question here. Similarly, in a careful discussion of Brathwaite's ideas, Nigel Bolland has remarked upon the extent to which Brathwaite's "juxtaposition of master and slave" can make it seem "as if these are individuals who have an existence independent of each other, rather than social roles that are mutually constitutive and defined by their relationship."[66] Brathwaite's theory is thus in certain respects not (in Bolland's words) "dialectical" enough; it holds back from its insights into creolization by continuing to posit the autonomous existence of his creole society's constituent parts. Moreover, Bolland adds (pp. 71–73), Brathwaite's vision of creolization is built upon untenably simple oppositions, which may be hard to avoid in practice but that are clearly too cut and dried for understanding such a complex process. Brathwaite's opposition between "colonial" and "creole," for instance, the former being "metropolitan and reactionary" and the latter "local and creative," seems altogether too pat. Positing this opposition, in turn, forces Brathwaite into constructing an historical narrative of dilution and loss in which the colonial wins out over the creole at the midpoint of the nineteenth century. For all its credibility, his claim that "the creatively 'creole' elements of the society were being rendered ineffective by the more reactionary 'colonial'" (*DCS*, p. 100) downplays the continued, indeed increasing, relevance of creolization as an *ambivalent* (rather than simply a positive) process in post-Emancipation Jamaica, and the fact that, as Glissant has pointed out, "creolization, even when it is practiced in a negative manner, nonetheless keeps on advancing" (*ID*, p. 31).

The same sort of caveats apply to Brathwaite's claim that in the Caribbean "we have a psychosomatic dilemma (Euro | Afric) which is at the same time a creole (Euro-Afric) dialectic."[67] Can the dilemma be so easily distinguished from the dialectic? In fact, it is essential to Brathwaite that this be the case because it allows him to maintain the "Euro" and the "Afric" as distinct entities—a distinction that is, notwithstanding his critique of the "plural society model," basic to his thinking, as can be discerned from his own appeal to the idea of a "prismatic" society, "where all the colours meet and become visible."[68] The prism offers him the model of what he calls a "convergence without merging," in which "ancestral heritage" continues to play a foundational role in shaping the dynamics of the creolization process; the prismatic model, he notes,

> conceives of all resident cultures as equal and contiguous, despite the accidents of political history, each developing its own life-style from the spirit of its ancestors, but modified—and increasingly so—through interaction with the environment and the other cultures of the environment, until residence within the environment—*nativization*—becomes the process (creolization) through which all begin to share a style, even though that style will retain vestiges (with occasional national/cultural revivals back towards particular ancestors) of their original/ancestral heritage.[69]

We would appear to be dangerously close here to the insidious segregationism of "rainbow coalitions" and Benetton advertisements. The important question that such a passage raises is how much weight, and of what sort, is one to give this "original/ancestral heritage"? If convergence *with* merging would clearly entail the definitive transformation and dissolution of any and all cultural bases, what is the actual status of such bases in Brathwaite's prismatic vision of converging but unmerging cultures?

That an "original/ancestral heritage" has always been important to Brathwaite is unquestionable; as he argued around the time he wrote *Development*, it is the artist's duty to explore "an ancestral relationship with the folk or aboriginal culture [that] involves the artist and participant in a journey into the past and hinterland which is at the same time a movement of possession into present and future."[70] While noting this emphasis, the authors of the influential postcolonial primer *The Empire Writes Back* (1989) strategically downplay it when they state that the views Brathwaite has expressed on "the importance of the African connection ha[ve] sometimes obscured his increasing concern with Creolization";[71] although this claim fits in with their own straightforwardly anti-essentialist agenda, it would be altogether more exact to claim the reverse and speak of a *decreasing* concern with creolization in Brathwaite's later work. In his theoretical interventions over the last decade and a half, Brathwaite has become much more insistent about the importance of this journey into the past for the artist-traveler, and much more specific about what this journey will reveal to him—not simply "vestiges" but an ancestral *essence* upon which the de-essentializing process of creolization is increasingly seen as hinging. He will refer to this originating essence as *nam*, "an indestructible culture-core, imparting to each group an identity which in normal times one is proud enough of, but which, at times of crisis, may be fiercely defended by its possessors."[72] Even if modern travel and technology have made a global cross-culturalism and "shared style" inevitable, he argues in this same article from the mid-1980s, "the essentiality of each culture must also be recognized and employed in the new transcendence." A distinct cultural identity remains substantially present and for that reason, he asserts, "interculturation ... is not the final answer." "No matter how intimate the symbiosis," he continues, "there remains the residual nam which, at moments of crisis, has the ability to re-activate itself" (p. 63). As examples of this "re-activation" he cites such events as the Indian Mutiny, Black Power in the United States, and the Soweto uprising in South Africa—a move that paradoxically serves, I would argue, to *de*historicize these eminently historical responses to the political and cultural convergences that colonialism necessarily promotes.

In seeing as complementary two things that would appear to be in contradiction with one another—an original and a creolized identity—Brathwaite gives evidence of the double bind that is central to contemporary thinking about race and ethnicity and that is exemplified by the differences, say, between Bambara's Afrocentric position and the syncretism of a "mulatto culturalist" like Harris (as Brathwaite once rather revealingly called him [*DCS*, p. 305]): in Harris's case a desire to stress the liberatory possibilities of cross-culturalism, and in Bambara's a desire to assert the substantiality of distinct cultural entities and identities (be these in pure or hyphenated form) that have somehow escaped the transformative process of creolization. Brathwaite does not shy away from but, rather, situates himself at the very heart of this bewildering double bind. As we have just seen, he insists upon the presence of a culture-core, an essential identity, and yet while advocating this position he also freely admits that this essence is itself the product of an historical transformation: nam actually contains within it the idea of loss, for it is, Brathwaite notes, "the reduction of one's name to its essentials."[73] He goes on to add that, in the Caribbean context, this reduction, the loss of an *e* that once marked a culture's self-identity, was the work of colonialism:

The name that you once had has lost its "e," that fragile part of itself, eaten by Prospero, eaten by the conquistadores, but preserving its essentialness, its alpha, its "a" protected by those two intransigent consonants, "n" and "m." It can return to name. But we are saying that this return is already present, and that one must start in the middle.

The essential—cultural identity—thus emerges as nothing more or less than a *reduction of the original*, its translation into something other than what it once was (indeed, "nam" itself, Brathwaite has remarked, is the inversion of "man"—a chiasmatic reversal which, for enslaved Africans, took place at the half-way point of the Middle Passage): nam, "the essentials," thus proves essentially incomplete, lacking a part of itself, the *e* at its end. To restore this missing letter would be to recover one's authentic identity, one's "true-true" name (or what both he and Bambara privilege as *nommo*); but this restoration can only, Brathwaite acknowledges, be the work of an impure, ever more creolized and culturally decentered or multicentric, future that "starts in the middle"—one that in simultaneously "re-membering" and adding on to the culture-core (respectively, putting *nam* and *e* back together again, and supplementing *nam* with *e*) cannot help but register the unoriginality of the very origin that it would invoke.

The double-directedness, or even duplicity, of Brathwaite's assertions here certainly encourages one to read them, as would Coetzee (to recall our discussion of the contaminated and contaminatory letter *e* in *Foe*), against their emphatically essentializing grain: if the "essentials"—the core of one's identity—are nothing more or less than a transformation of some even more original identity to which one can only return by taking the middle, rather than the beginning, as one's point of departure, then just how originary, and how essential, are they? Notwithstanding this obvious tension, there can be little doubt of Brathwaite's commitment to the reality of this original, and for him still active, identity. It is this commitment that motivates his politics of *likeness*, his straightforward quest for the "similarities" and "continuities" linking Africa and the (African) Caribbean (CO, pp. 41–42), and that, in turn, generates his call for a "literature of reconnection" that would establish in the New World links to the supposedly "organic whole" that is African culture. His comments on a passage from one work that instantiates this "literature of reconnection," Paule Marshall's *The Chosen Place, the Timeless People* (1969), are revealing:

It is rhetorical, even romantic. But Paule Marshall's *intention* is crucial, and in it she unquestionably succeeds: to transform the Afro-Bajan out of his drab, materialistic setting with meaningful correlates of custom from across the water in ancestral Africa.[74]

The essentially *rhetorical* nature of Marshall's literary act of reconnection is here conceded, and yet Brathwaite appears surprisingly oblivious to the consequences of this admission. In her transformation of the Afro-Bajan and his (from a certain highly ideologized perspective) "drab, materialistic setting" Marshall is performing the perhaps necessary yet anything but "organic" act of creating from a distance a hypothetical, and in this case patently romanticized, identity; this performance amounts to nothing more (or less) than a (re)creation of an absent original. For any writer attuned to the purely rhetorical nature of such acts of restoration, the sheltered *a* in which Brathwaite places such faith can only be an always-already corrupted letter, a false beginning inhabited—like the *a* in Susan Barton's name—by the trace of a letter that signals not the desired end of some restorative project, but a further translation of a lost original within the confines of the maze of doubting that Coetzee maps out in *Foe*. Placing us in a (dis)continuous relationship with what a "literature of reconnection" would read in terms of simple continuity, this deconstructive knowledge evacuates, without denying the urgency of, the affirmations of "untranslated" identity that Brathwaite feels compelled to posit alongside his provocative insights into "that process of mutation and adaptation we call creolization."[75]

Brathwaite's problematic *a* of beginning is, of course, the first (and last) letter of Africa itself, but it is also the letter with which the Antilles begins (but does not end), and it is an acute sense of this other beginning (and its plural ending) that has served as the point of departure for Glissant's theoretical work, which in many respects is situated at the other, anti-essentializing pole of our creole continuum. Notwithstanding his frequent emphasis on the (dis)continuities that link Caribbean societies to Africa, Glissant has been at pains throughout his career to mark his distance from the sort of Afrocentric positions that, through the massive influence of Césaire, gained such currency in his native Martinique and that continue to find ample expression in much Afrodiasporic thinking, be it in the ludicrous form of pseudoscientific appeals to the power of melanin or in the subtle and provocative claims of a writer like Brathwaite. While acknowledging, for instance, that the West African *griot* has a "part in our voice," Glissant also insists upon the obvious fact that coming to terms with "today's Africa obliges us to abandon all fantasies of projection and to try and be ourselves" (*DA*, p. 392). Trying to be one's creole, Caribbean self is, for Glissant, not a matter of identifying culture-cores but of registering one's distance from any and all points of origin and exploring the historically contingent contours (and detours) of the composite identity that has resulted from the loss of such origins. If, Glissant notes, it makes sense—at least from a certain perspective—to speak, say, of the Jews as "a people who continue themselves elsewhere, *who maintain Being*," the transported Africans who came to the Caribbean are, he contends (making tactical use of a binary opposition that is theoretically incompatible with his anti-Manichean poetics of creolization), "a population that changes itself elsewhere *into another people* . . . and that thus enters into the always renewed variance of relationality [*la Relation*] (of the relay, of the relative)" (*DA*, p. 29). The Caribbean, "dead to its essence" for the last five centuries (given the almost total extermination of its indigenous population), has since that time been the site par excellence of what he refers to as a "digenesis" (*FM*, p. 267), a second beginning that doubles and contradicts the first. It is thus an ideal location for the cross-cultural experience that Glissant sums up in the words "la Relation," by which he intends many things: not only the cultural relations and "interstanding" (Brathwaite's term) that are at the heart of the creolization process, but a relating of stories and histories, a relaying of them across time and space, as well as the relativizing of any and all ideological beliefs in an increasingly desacralized age.

In order to get a better sense of Glissant's vision of relationality, it will be useful at this point to recall two key elements of our discussion of Carpentier in the preceding chapter: namely, the limits of his account of mestizaje and of his vision of the Caribbean as a second Mediterranean. The Cuban writer's account of cultural "mixing and commixing" seemed, as we recall, greatly dependent upon the fixed identities that one might have supposed his emphasis on mestizaje to be contesting. Glissant is very aware of the trap into which Carpentier apparently falls in the passage from *Explosion* that we analyzed. His own definition of métissage, which he put forward in his monumental *Le discours antillais* (1981) and then refined in the *Poétique de la Relation* (1990), explicitly confronts this issue: "to affirm that peoples are *métissés*, that métissage is a value," he notes, "means deconstructing a [racial] category '*métis*' that would as such be an intermediary between two 'pure' extremes" (*DA*, p. 250). In the *Poétique*, moreover, he acknowledges that certain forms of métissage still serve to "concentrate," whereas what he by this point more frequently calls creolization "diffracts": if the former is "a meeting between and a synthesis of two differences, for us creolization appears as a métissage without limits, the components of which have been increased and the consequences of which are unforeseeable" (p. 46). He also makes his readers aware of the theoretical limits of a writer like Carpentier in his comments on possible analogies between the Mediterranean and Caribbean Seas, in which he again invokes the distinction between "concentrating" and "diffracting." Though sharing Carpentier's interest in the analogy, Glissant points out that the parallel is not appropriate, largely for geographical reasons: while the former is "an inland sea, surrounded by lands, a sea that concentrates," the Caribbean is "a sea that splinters lands, scattering them in an arc." This geographical splintering results in a different cultural sensibility: "the archipelagic reality, in the Caribbean or in the Pacific, naturally illustrates the thinking of relationality, without it being necessary to deduce from this any situational advantage whatsoever" (*PR*, p. 46). As with his distinction between two types of diasporic peoples, perhaps the most interesting aspect of such comments is the way that they tactically retain the *same* binary structure of thought characteristic of Carpentier's vision, for all that they arrive at quite different conclusions. My discussion of Glissant in Chapter 4 will be in large part concerned with how he "*e*-laborates"—that is to say, literally, works his way out of—these dualistic oppositions in his later highly metafictive novels through such techniques as a parodic and palinodic (re)citation of previous theoretical claims (for instance, in his most recent novel *Tout-monde* [1993], he notes that "there is no landscape that encloses you by its very nature" [p. 497], implicitly referring his reader back to earlier claims about the "concentrating" nature of the Mediterranean). For now, however, it is enough for us to take such comments at face value and to demonstrate how Glissant's vision of the Caribbean as a multirelational site connects up with his revision of traditional identity politics.

As "the estuary of the Americas," the Caribbean is inextricably connected to the mainland(s) in a way that necessitates reconceptualizing the very nature of islands: in this relational context, "insularity takes on another meaning." As Glissant points out, "one ordinarily makes insularity out to be a mode of isolation, like a spatial neurosis. Yet in the Caribbean, every island is an opening out" (*DA*, p. 249). This newly conceived island space, one of relational openness rather than of isolated closure, serves as an appropriate model for the transformed sense of identity that must emerge if one is to go beyond the colonial (and pre-colonial) vision of the world that he describes in the following passage from *Intention poétique*:

For a long time the world . . . was an idea of the world, the world-as-solitude, or as-identity, which widened its base solely on the evidence of known particulars and annexed the Whole as a simple extension of these particulars. The one who left his home far behind, the Discoverer, and the one who remained on his own land, the to-be-discovered, shared this common belief. To be born into the world is finally to conceive (to live) the world as relation: as composite necessity, consenting reaction, a poetics (and not a morality) of alterity. As the unfinished drama of this necessity. (p. 20)

By thinking the world in terms of alterity rather than (simply) in terms of identity, by emphasizing the global relations out of which we are composed rather than the particulars by which we have hitherto defined ourselves, we establish the conditions for being born into the creolized world in which, from the infinitely repeated moment of Discovery, we have always-already been living. To conceive and to live this diversified world is the poetic imperative of Glissant's work. Although the colonial "Découvreurs" created the material conditions for the realization of this imperative, they remained committed to an "unworldly" vision that distinguished sharply between self and other, identity and difference. This vision was shared, ironically enough, by the architects of decolonization in the 1950s and 1960s. Reflecting some thirty years later on the decolonizing process, in which he himself was actively engaged, Glissant notes its reliance upon an insular thinking of the closed, negative sort and its consequent failure to disengage itself from a colonial and colonizing politics of identity: "most of the nations that liberated themselves from colonization," he points out in the *Poé-tique*, "have tended to form themselves around the idea of power, the total-itarian drive of the single root, rather than in a founding relationship with the Other" (pp. 26–27). "Identity for colonized peoples," he continues, "will in the first place be an 'opposed to,' that is to say at the outset a limi-tation." "The real work of decolonization," he concludes, "will have been to go beyond this limit" (p. 29). Our entry into a truly post-colonial condi-tion depends upon learning how to reject what in *Tout-monde* he refers to as "the univocal pretension of the identitary" and the "insanity of sectarian identities and domination" that structured the colonial enterprise and gen-erated the aftershocks of decolonization, which continue, as he points out, to make themselves "atavistically" felt across the globe in such places as Eastern Europe and such events as the Gulf War (pp. 434, 465).

Glissant is careful to point out that opening oneself up to the possibility of unlearning one's colonial and/or decolonized identity does not mean (as one might have inferred from the distinction between "monde-comme-identité" and "monde comme relation") that the act of positing one's own identity no longer makes sense. Rather, one must learn how to perform that act anew, detaching it from the idea of "the identical" (*l'identique*) that has so often served as its foundation. As he puts it in one of *Tout-monde*'s many chapter epigraphs, which would eventually find its way—in slightly modified form—into his *Traité du Tout-monde* (1997):

To question the identical is not to divert [attention away from] identity. How many former masters, and master thinkers especially, revel in the words of those they once oppressed when these words 'bravely' withdraw into themselves and give off the ring of a supposedly primordial authenticity [*quand cette parole se renferme vail-lamment sur elle-même et sonne l'authenticité prétendue primordiale*]. . . . What they have in common, the former master and the formerly oppressed of this ilk, is precisely the belief that identity is a matter of one's stock [*souche*], that this stock is exclusive, and that it must prevail. Meet that [belief] head on. Go ahead! Make that rock explode. (p. 158)

Although, as we will see in the second section of Chapter 4, the metafictive dynamics of Glissant's later novels create a situation in which such appar-ently clear theoretical distinctions (identity versus identicality) and unprob-lematic imperatives ("faites exploser cette roche") cannot be fully credited, the general direction of Glissant's thinking should be clear from this pas-sage. Colonial and anticolonial thinkers, oppressors and oppressed, share an unproductively insular desire for an identity that has "closed itself off" to all other identities and that would be rooted in some "authenticité pré-tendue primordiale." Against this purportedly coherent and organic vision of one's self, Glissant goes on to advocate a "calculated" sense of being, one that will be arrived at by gathering up the pieces of the exploded rock of a traditionally conceived identity and distributing them across the increasingly chaotic "surface" (*étendue*) of the "community-world."

This critique of the role that (the fiction of) identicality plays in the construction of identities is central to the anti-essentialist, hybridizing arguments that have gained such prominence of late in postcolonial theory. Glissant's vision, elaborated over the course of the last forty years, resonates in the many recent critiques of what Trinh T. Minh-ha has termed "the identity enclosure,"[76] and it has been explicitly championed by an increasing number of postcolonial theorists for whom it serves, in the words of Françoise Lionnet, to "demystif[y] all essentialist glorifications of unitary origins, be they racial, sexual, geographic, or cultural."[77] Glissant's valorization of métissage holds forth for a critic like Lionnet the promise of a radical transformation of society, an absolute refusal of the "hegemonic" colonial legacy:

We can be united against hegemonic power only by refusing to engage that power on its own terms, since to do so would mean becoming ourselves a term within that system of power. We have to articulate new visions of ourselves, new concepts that allow us to think *otherwise*, to bypass the ancient symmetries and dichotomies that have governed the ground and the very condition of possibility of thought, of "clarity," in all of Western philosophy. (pp. 5–6)

Lionnet's call to arms is seductive, indeed. But it is precisely here, at the moment of its greatest promise, that I feel compelled to distance myself from Glissant's position, or at the very least from this critic's rather too euphoric appropriation of it. While there can be no doubt that his work often promotes a vision of this radically different future, it seems equally clear to me that Lionnet's insistence upon this vision, despite (or precisely because of) its chiliastic fervor, serves only to reinscribe her within a rigidly symmetrical way of thinking (put bluntly, in with the new, out with the old) that has been at the revolutionary heart of the West's modernity for centuries, if not millennia. Her will "to bypass the ancient symmetries and dichotomies" is subtly complicit with them, as becomes clear, I will now argue, in her mistaken equation of Glissant's views with those of his self-styled disciples, Jean Bernabé, Patrick Chamoiseau, and Raphaël Confiant, the authors of the highly influential *Éloge de la Créolité* (1989).

Lionnet approvingly remarks that their cult of "Creoleness implies the recognition and acceptance of multi-racialism as a 'new' term or syncretic category that transcends the binarisms of colonialism" (p. 102). For her, Glissant and the authors of the *Éloge* are engaged in one and the same "transcendent" project; all are prophets of what the latter refer to as "this new dimension of man, of which we are the prefigured silhouette."[78] What is obvious, however, after reading the *Éloge*—and, as we will soon see, this is a criticism that Glissant has himself made on numerous occasions since its publication—is that the authors' praise of an "identité créole" remains, as was the case with Carpentier and Gratiant, trapped within and committed to the very thing they are supposedly contesting: a foundationalist politics of identity grounded in claims of authenticity. The opening words of the document—"neither Europeans, nor Africans, nor Asiatics, we proclaim ourselves Creoles" (p. 13)—clearly affirm a New World identity that is logically equivalent to the Old World identities that are being renounced, notwithstanding their insistence on "the torrential ambiguity" of their new "mosaic identity" (p. 53).[79] A composite of geographical (Caribbean) and cultural (creole languages and practices) solidarities, the creole identity that they embrace evokes the same hermeneutic approach to the self that obsessed Coetzee's Susan Barton and that was enigmatically enacted at the end of *Foe*. The authors frequently assert, for instance, the necessity of "plunging" into the self, as when they speak of "this cultural entity into which we are today attempting a salutary plunge" (p. 16), in an unintentionally ironic echo of Fanon, who used the word critically in his comments on the Negritude movement's fascination with the African past and what he saw as the historically inevitable but dialectically inadequate "plunge into the innards of his people" to which the colonized intellectual had been "condemned."[80] In neo-Sartrian fashion, the authors of the *Éloge* speak frequently and with great passion about "our authenticity" (p. 23), about an "inner vision" that would not (as, according to them, has been the case for virtually all works of literature written in the Antilles up to this point) be "subjected to the bewitchments of alienation" (p. 24). Their critique of "our aesthetic shipwreck" (p. 51) and the consequent call for the emergence of a future literature, a literature of the future, that would be self-sufficient and original—"our literature must go into itself and not encounter, during the time of its consolidation, anything else: that is to say, no cultural displacement" (p. 42)—in fact does little more than repeat the avantgardist imperatives upon which, half a century before, the modernist enterprise of Césaire and his colleagues had itself been based.

It would not be a difficult task to deconstruct this affirmative vision of "creole identity" and its obsessive recourse to a language of authenticity and foundations (the word "fondement" is used with great frequency as a way of describing their "Creoleness" [*Créolité*]). Nor would it be hard to question the simplistic historical metanarrative through which the authors of the *Éloge* understand the Créolité that they are in the process of praising—a narrative that, in its linear progression and its commitment to progress, bears obvious allegiances to the sort of Enlightenment thinking one would have imagined them to be in the process of shaking off: "the world is heading into a state of Créolité," they proclaim, and "the old national tensions are giving way in the face of federations that will themselves perhaps not endure very long" (p. 52). Indeed, Glissant has since the *Éloge*'s publication frequently posed objections to their position: in a recent interview, for instance, he notes that Créolité, as opposed to creolization, is "a prison, like [Barrès's] *latinité* . . . or [Senghor's] Negritude." Where the one is an "essence," the other is "a universal process"—a process that, like the "chaos-world" in which we live, "is moving at such a speed that we can barely follow it."[81] As he puts it in the *Poétique*, the concept of Créolité "has designs on Being" (it involves "une visée à l'être") and thus constitutes "a step back with regard to the functionality of creolizations," a more or less innocent regression "back toward Negritudes" (as a main advocate of the similar-minded *Créolie* movement in Réunion, Gilbert Aubry, seems to admit when he states that "here, we are living on Créolie as elsewhere one lives on Negritude or on Occitania").[82] By contrast, Glissant says of his own position that

we are not offering [a vision of] being, nor models for humanity. What prompts us is not simply the definition of our identities, but also their relation to the entire realm of the possible: the mutual mutations that this play of relations generates. (p. 103)

In short, as he goes on to suggest in the passage from *Tout-monde* that I quoted earlier, where he is arguing against the idea that "l'identité est souche," Glissant sees his disciples as having in part given themselves over to the lure of the "identical": with the incessant "relaying" of identities in the closing decades of the twentieth century, "hidden hierarchies, or those surreptitiously enforced in the form of an *éloge*, are now being revealed as empty claims. Do not consent to these manoeuvres of the identical. . . . Open up your identity to the world" (p. 158).

Glissant's remarks, which gain an added piquancy if one keeps in mind the fact that, some forty years earlier (1950), the father of Negritude, Léopold Senghor, had himself written an "éloge du métissage,"[83] are very much to the point, and it is difficult not to conclude that "Créolité may itself be falling prey to the trap of universalism and essentialism so vigorously denounced in the *Éloge*."[84] Indeed, I very much doubt that a critic like Lionnet would pin her "transcendent" hopes on the authors of the *Éloge* now in the way that she did in 1989 (especially given the increasingly authoritarian tone with which they have defended their concept of Créolité in the intervening years, as we will see in the coda to Chapter 6). The important point to register, however, is not that the *Éloge* somehow falls short of a truly creolized perspective but, rather, that its authors are Glissant's followers, in all senses of the word, rather than simply "unenlightened" precursors like Carpentier and Gratiant. This apparently regressive enmeshment in the language of an exclusionary identity politics, this slippage back into what Edward Said has condemned as "fixed ideas of settled iden-

tity and culturally authorized definition,"[85] on the part of those who have
been most influenced by Glissant not only serves as a cautionary reminder
of how difficult it is to avoid the sort of hierarchical thinking that Lionnet
wants us to bypass, how hard it is to transcend those (again, in Said's
words) "exclusivist biases we so often ascribe to cultures, our own not
least," but, I would argue, puts the very project of that transcendence into
question. Coming after Glissant, these elogists are engaging in the *recon*-
structive process that I am suggesting must, for better and for worse, follow
upon every such *de*construction as Glissant is attempting and that is, moreover, itself part and parcel of this deconstruction. Instead of the radically
new, we are left with a "strangely familiar" text that marks an inevitable
return to what Glissant's emphasis on creolization is bent upon undoing,
but a return that must always and increasingly be read alongside and
athwart this emphasis.

The complexity of the creolization process resides precisely in this: that
it is impossible in an age of hybridity (not) to disengage the question of
identity from the closed strictures of the identical, or, as Bhabha might have
put it, "the perplexity of the living" from "the representation of the fullness
of life." Glissant himself seems to acknowledge this point in the previously
cited passage when he states that "ce qui nous porte *n'est pas la seule* défi-
nition de nos identités, mais *aussi* leur relation à tout le possible" (my italics): in this statement, the prison house of a defined identity and the open
field of a chaotic relationality stand side by side, simultaneously contradicting and supplementing one another. What this statement suggests is that
the connection between fixed and relational identities is not (simply) a matter of either/or but (also) of both/and. Its "not only . . . but also" logic can
be found at many other points in the *Poétique*, as when Glissant states that
"identity is no longer only permanence, it is the capacity for variation, a
variable, be it under or out of control" (pp. 155–56). To be sure, it is the
"capacity for variation" that Glissant privileges, because it serves as "evidence that ontological thinking no longer 'functions,' no longer procures a
foundational certitude, grounded [*ensouchée*] once and for all in a restricting territory" (p. 156); but it is vital to note the way in which the predictably antifoundationalist second half of this remark remains in a binary
dialogue with its first half, which emphasizes the *continued* presence of a
"permanent" identity and ensures that if, as he argues in the *Poétique*,
"contrary to the situation of exile, wandering [*l'errance*] leads to the negation of every pole or metropole" (p. 31), then our increasingly nomadic and
migrant wanderings in an ever more hybridized world will remain haunted
by an ineradicable sense of exile.

Notwithstanding his primary emphasis on creolization, Glissant's work
is itself deeply marked—though certainly not in as *overt* a fashion as is the

Éloge—by this binary dialogue and the duplicitous thinking it entails. We can see this by returning for a moment to our earlier discussion of his comments on the Caribbean and on métissage. As regards the former, Glissant's emphatic praise of "Caribbeanness" (*Antillanité*) in *Discours antillais* is obviously subject to the same sort of criticisms he will level at his followers' later concept of Créolité: both would appear to share the common ground, as it were, of their essentializing suffix.[86] Moreover, given the fact that for Glissant Antillanité is a theory that "envisions for the entire Caribbean a convergence of re-rootings in our true place [*lieu vrai*]" (p. 182), the problem of restricting identities would seem to be inevitable inasmuch as his definition of Caribbeanness presupposes the existence both of a "true place" that one must assume can be distinguished from an inauthentic one and a collective subject that would be "at home" in this place but not elsewhere. In this respect, the identity-model offered by the authors of the *Éloge* seems in some ways much more elastic than Glissant's, inasmuch as it is not merely limited to the Caribbean but establishes far-flung connections with other creolophone and insular parts of the world (notably, the Indian Ocean and the Pacific).[87]

As regards the second issue, it is important to keep in mind the fact that Glissant's use of the word "creolization" has emerged only recently in his theoretical work, as a partial substitute for a term, "métissage," that had come under fire from a certain number of critics. The Jamaican novelist and theorist Sylvia Wynter, for instance, questioned his reliance on this word, in a Foucauldian critique that stressed, à la Lionnet, the need for an epistemic break with the "Word of Man" and its universals (humanism, proletarianism, genderism, and so on). She pointed out that her one difference with Glissant lay in his choice of this word, "since the syncretism of culture can now be seen as a recombination of cultures (Native American, Judeo-Christian, African) into a new Caribbean and American synthesis, whereas the term *mestizo* (mixed) becomes simply the recombination of two variants of the human genome."[88] For Wynter, this term too obviously remembers the very thing that must be forgotten if we are truly to "bypass the ancient symmetries and dichotomies" against which both she and Lionnet are arguing. Glissant's substitution of creolization for métissage responds to this criticism, but by continuing to define the former in terms of the latter, to speak of it as a "métissage without limits" (*PR*, p. 46), or as "métissage with the added value of unpredictability" (*ID*, p. 19), Glissant would appear to have retained a significant trace of these limits, reinscribing the very thing that Wynter, in her insistence on epistemic rupture, wanted to erase; in so doing, he cannot help putting into question the theoretical lack of limits that has played an increasingly prominent role in what I will be referring to as the post/nationalist phase of his career as a writer.

As I will argue at some length in Chapter 4, Glissant's theoretical trajectory takes him from the nationalist agenda that is at the core of *Discours antillais* and its call for the decolonization of Martinique to a much less overtly political position in the *Poétique*, in which certain earlier concepts—for instance, Antillanité, métissage—are modified according to the more emphatically creolizing tendencies of his later theoretical work. Notwithstanding his increasing focus on transcultural relations in the *Poétique*, however, Glissant remains adamant in asserting the "particularity" of individual cultures, even if he stresses that these cannot be broken down into "primary components" (such as race or ethnicity) because *la Relation* is always-already acting upon them, both internally ("from each culture to its constituents") and externally ("from each culture to others in which it is interested") (p. 183). The impetus for his continued assertion of the particularity of cultures and nations in an age of global hybridity can be traced to his long-held belief that, in the words of Fanon, "it is at the heart of national consciousness that an international consciousness arises and becomes vitalized."[89] Indeed, in an early essay, "Le romancier noir" (1957), Glissant specifically identifies the words "particular" and "national" with one another when he speaks of "the various initiatives for regenerating particular (national) cultures [*les entreprises de régénérescence des cultures particulières (nationales)*]" that will be integral to the process of decolonization.[90] The emphasis on emancipation and independence in the following passages from the *Poétique* bears witness to the continued influence of this belief, despite his sensitivity to "the destructuring of a national solid(ar)ity [*la déstructure des compacités nationales*] that prevailed until very recently" and the ensuant "difficult and uncertain birth of those new forms of identity that are seeking us out" (p. 30): "relationality exists, only inasmuch as the particulars, which constitute it as an interdependency, have first emancipated themselves from all approximation of dependency." This interdependency, he continues, is profitable for everybody involved "only at the moment when it governs, not indistinct amalgamations, but defining divergences [*des écarts déterminants*]" (p. 157). How, he asks, can this cultural heterogeneity, these divergences (not only, he adds, "with regard to the prescribed, or imposed, norm, but perhaps also with regard to the norms or beliefs that we have passively inherited") be put into practice "if we have not beforehand, and fully, mastered that which is of us and belongs to us" (p. 170)?

In this call for independence, this rhetoric of emancipation and mastery, this unproblematic positing of a collective subject to which certain things "belong" and a particular "place" to which that subject properly belongs,[91] we can read the traces of Glissant's earlier commitment in *Discours antillais* both to the nation ("there is not a single people in the modern world who are not called upon to exist as a nation, if they are not to disappear as a collectivity" [p. 316]) and to what he identifies as "national literature" ("this urgency for each and everyone to name themselves to the world: that is to say, this necessity of not disappearing from the world stage but, rather, of contributing toward its enlargement" [p. 192]). Well aware of the potential dangers of Fanon's appeal to "national culture," which in its homogenizing vision of "the people" can be read as sweeping under the carpet "the disquieting, untidy presence of the other,"[92] the Glissant of *Discours antillais* is, certainly, careful to insist that "the nation is not separation; it is an unalienated mode of relation to the other [*autre*], who thus becomes others [*autrui*]" (p. 463), but his lingering commitment to the idea of the nation, and the particular type of "tribal" self-definitions that this idea entails ("each tribe that is abandoned, or denigrated, separates us from harmony" [*IP*, p. 13]), is nonetheless unquestionable. Through such memories (of the nation, of the particular), Glissant attempts to ward off the possibility that creolization might degenerate into its negative mirror-image: global homogenization and the resultant *loss* of difference such leveling entails.

One might well criticize Glissant's emphasis on this specific mode of relationality, or his recourse to the highly ideological and extremely dubious concept of "alienation," and I will indeed have occasion in this book to do so. Here, however, the point that needs to be made is simply that the Glissant of *Poétique* has not fully abandoned, although he has certainly adapted and attenuated, the sort of particularistic logic that undergirds traditional identity politics and that a superficially euphoric understanding of the creolization process would appear to put into question once and for all. As should be clear by now, I believe that this paradoxical coexistence of two differing logics is actually fundamental to that process, rather than an anachronism needing eventually to be bypassed in the sort of epistemic leap that critics like Lionnet and Wynter yearn after. Given this double identity of the creolization process, the fundamental distinction that Glissant makes in his *Poétique* between a rooted and a relational identity—between "identité-racine" and "identité-relation" (pp. 157–58)—needs to be read in at least two ways. The most obvious approach to this distinction is to view the two concepts as simply polar opposites, each denoting only one thing: thus, where the first and now historically surpassed version of identity is grounded in a roots-oriented logic of filiation and legitimacy, the latter is "linked, not to a creation of the world, but to the conscious and contradictory lived experience of the contact of cultures." In our global present, Glissant continues, identity "is no longer linked, if not at times anachronistically, and more often murderously, to the sacred mystery of the root"; rather, "it is reliant on the manner in which a society participates in the global relation, enters into its velocity, does or does not control the reins" (p. 155).

However, a less oppositional, more equivocating, reading of the phrase "identité-relation" is also possible—one that takes into account each of its three parts, all of which need to be read, with difficulty, together if we are to come to terms with what it means to be "travelling through the networks of a world bearing the tension between our particular inheritance and potentially common culturescapes."[93] The phrase "identity, hyphen, relation" does not simply direct us forward, as it were, to the creolized relations that have taken the place of the ancestral root, but also back to the two other elements that precede these relations (and that this phrase shares, in epistemic complicity, with "identité-racine"): namely, identity itself, in all the exclusionary particularism that the word implies, and the hyphen that *both* interstitially joins together the old world of a necessarily circumscribed local identity and the new world of increasingly chaotic and globalized cross-cultural relations *and* indicates the space of a neither/nor (neither identity nor relation)—a space that not only renders inevitable but puts into question the imperative of the both/and that I identified a few pages back. This space of the neither/nor defines the creole continuum of post/colonial identity politics: a continuum that is bounded at each end by what in both theory and practice are the equally unattainable and fictional poles of that fully rooted identity and that truly migrant relationality to which Brathwaite and Glissant's positions respectively tend.

This alternative, ternary rather than unitary, reading of the phrase "identité-relation" informs an important metafictive passage from Glissant's most recent novel, *Tout-monde*, where he outlines the ideological choices facing his fictional alter ego, the young writer Mathieu Béluse, in the years following the Second World War. He does so by means of a metaphorical distinction between banyans, rhizomes, and the tree known in Martinique as the *figuier-maudit* (pp. 55–56). Mathieu associates the first with the poetry of his fellow Antillean, and perhaps greatest poetic influence, Saint-John Perse: reflecting on the opening lines of Perse's "Pluies" ("banyan-like, the rain takes hold of the city . . . " ["le banyan de la pluie prend ses assises sur la ville . . . "]), he reads into them a "prodigiously descending verticality . . . that had joined together the surge and the root, the spiritual murmur and the savor, the spirit and the flesh, all the vapors of the wind above with all the pleasures of what is below." Mathieu's consideration of the banyan tree, in all its verticality and roots-orientation, and of the profoundly unifying impulse—what we might call the modernist impulse—to which the austere poet from Guadeloupe gave expression then leads him to consider a very different perspective: that of "the expanding surface [*étendue*], the multiplication of the rhizome, which the philosophers of *Mille plateaux*, Deleuze and Guattari, would establish later in the landscape of imagery, a sort of foreknowledge of the *Tout-monde*." Here the young Mathieu has (to cite the adjectives he then uses to characterize

Deleuze and Guattari's thinking) the premonition of a "jostling and joyful" world of relations—an uprooted postidentitarian world that multiplies itself horizontally and schizophrenically, upon an ever "expanding surface," in the opposite direction to that of the banyan—in the direction, let us say, of postmodernism.

However, rather than identify himself with one or the other of these positions, Mathieu will end up situating himself squarely between the two:

Between this verticality and this expanding surface, Mathieu for his part had tried to mark out the relation (even if at this moment he only frequented in his imagination and by way of premonition the spectacular upsurge of rhizomatic thinking, and even if he had mistrusted in those days what the thinking of the banyan tree covered over), and he did so through recourse to the figuier-maudit present in the Martiniquan countryside.

As yet not fully exposed to the postmodern, rhizomatic world of cross-cultural global relations that Glissant's growing insistence on the creolization process will attempt to account for in positive terms, and already distrustful of what the modernist, roots-oriented ideologies of the banyan tree covered over, the young Mathieu chooses to think that which is neither the one nor the other, but that is equally both, since the figuier-maudit is a tree, as the narrator puts it, that both "delves down" (*fouille*) and "uproots" (*déracine*), that descends into the earth and simultaneously unearths. The figuier-maudit, and the hyphen that it contains, stands paradoxically as a relay between the banyan and the rhizome but also as an interval between them—an intervening space, a space of intervention, that in separating off the one from the other, the rooted from the creolized identity, creates the possibility, and urges the necessity, of a simultaneous de- and re-construction of both. "Under identical and dissimilar forms," as the narrator puts it, the banyan, the rhizome, and the figuier-maudit that ambivalently relates the one to the other all contribute in their different and mutually implicated ways to a now global process of (dis)ordering that Paul Gilroy has nicely characterized as "the fractal patterns of cultural and political exchange and transformation that we try and specify through manifestly inadequate theoretical terms like creolisation and syncretism."[94]

The relation of (dis)similarity that joins together, and separates, the banyan, the rhizome, and the figuier-maudit is itself inseparable from their relation to the *earth* in which they are ambivalently rooted and out of which they grow; the existence of this other relation raises one last point that needs to be engaged with here, and it is a point that leads us back to the authors discussed at the beginning of this section, Césaire and Coetzee. The "prodigiously descending verticality" that the young Mathieu found in Saint-John Perse's banyan tree is equally crucial to the work of a fellow modernist like Césaire, as we can see in these lines from his poem "Pour

saluer le Tiers Monde," written in the late 1950s at the height of the decolonization movement, and dedicated, significantly enough, to the other great
exponent of Negritude, Léopold Senghor (who was himself in the habit of
thinking about trees "vertically": describing his discovery in the early 1930s
of Black Africans' "Force vitale," for instance, he praises "the casuarina,
whose roots plunge into the sands and whose branches, flowering with
stars, sing with the trade winds").[95] Looking out longingly from his as yet
undecolonized "half-sleep of an island," the poet of "Pour saluer le Tiers
Monde" sees history making "the sign that I was waiting for" and salutes
the newly emerging African nations:

> Je vois l'Afrique multiple et une
> verticale dans la tumultueuse péripétie . . .
> Et je redis: Hoo mère!
>   et je lève ma force
>   inclinant ma face.
>   Oh ma terre!
>
> I see Africa multiple and one
> vertical in the tumultuous upheaval . . .
> And I say again: Hoo mother!
>   and I raise my strength
>   lowering my head.
>   O my earth!

(CP, pp. 352–53)

In such lines we have many of the standard elements of what must, from a
certain perspective, be deemed Césaire's untenably romanticizing effort at
envisioning, on the one hand, Africa as a nurturing "mother" and, on the
other, himself as a "forceful" poet. In all its verticality, the "good earth" of
Africa and its "good voice" provide Césaire with an unproblematic access
to some perduring "truth" lying beneath false surfaces and that is just waiting to be uncovered:

> Terre, forge et silo. Terre enseignant nos routes,
> c'est ici, qu'une vérité s'avise
> taisant l'oripeau de vieil éclat cruel.
>
> Earth, forge and silo. Earth showing us our paths,
> it is here, that a truth is perceived,
> quieting the flashy rags of the old cruel parade.

In this apostrophe to the earth, Césaire inscribes himself within a venerable
political and poetic tradition that has been exploited by many Caribbean
writers. Gustavo Pérez Firmat has pointed out, for instance, with regard to
"criollist" writing, that its intent is "to achieve an ever closer link with *la
tierra*, regarded as the matrix of individual and national identity" (CC,

p. 88). For Césaire, though, this link with his own earth was an extremely problematic one, given his acute sense of the historical displacements that constituted him as a native of the Caribbean; an authentic connection to the earth, to the true mother, could be much more easily figured for Césaire—and this is a characteristic of his thinking upon which later generations of Caribbean writers intent on asserting their Antillanité or their Créolité have not looked kindly—in terms of a descent into the soil of some originary and perduringly "black" Africa.

The inadequacy of Césaire's position from a perspective that takes the facts of creolization and the consequent troubling of root-identities into account is evident. But that does not mean that his call to the earth, his appeal to what Brathwaite has termed the need for "groundation,"[96] is not an essential gesture in a post/essentialist age. It is a call that Glissant, in his own way, perpetuates, despite his ultimately critical appraisal of Césaire's poetry—with its "plunge into the black convolutions of the earth" (*IP*, p. 144)—and his acute awareness that "the earth has ceased to be an essence, it is becoming a relation" (*IP*, p. 196). This "unearthly" relation has, from its colonial beginnings, always characterized the Caribbean. The extermination of the native peoples and the immigration and/or importation of nonindigenous peoples "is precisely what founds a new connection with the earth: not the sacralized absolute of an ontological possession, but a relational complicity" (*PR*, p. 161). It is in the context of this "complicité relationelle" that Glissant has argued, with an increasing sense of urgency, for reactivating an "esthétique de la terre"—for engaging in an ecological thinking that would not, as he cautions in the *Poétique*, be "mystical," rooted in a sense of *belonging* to the earth (the equivalent, say, of Pétain's Barrès-like call for a "return to the earth" [p. 161]) but would, rather, be founded upon a sense of our distance from the very thing that we cannot salvage but upon which we must learn to survive. It is on this (lack of a) ground that one must learn how to combat the unearthly products of our global(izing) modernity, establishing a "relational solidarity" between all parts of the earth in the face of "the international standardization of consumption" (p. 160). Glissant's call for a worldwide ecopolitics, which Brathwaite echoes in his insistence on the need "to return to the notion of subsistence as opposed to accumulation[,] with rational planning and sharing of the globe's resources,"[97] is a necessary supplement to the cultural politics of identity that has dominated postcolonial theory up to this point in time and that I will be chiefly concerned with in this book; as Paul Gilroy has suggested, rightly I believe, by contrast with our own century "the central axis of conflict" of the twenty-first "will no longer be the colour line but the challenge of just, sustainable development and the frontiers which will separate the overdeveloped parts of the world (at home and abroad) from the intractable poverty that already surrounds them" (*BA*, p. 223). As with the problem of cultural identity, I believe that what is called for now is a skeptical but engaged relation to what is left of this earth—to, in Brathwaite's memorable words, "the land [that] has lost the memory of the most secret places."[98] It is only in the wake of that memory and this loss that we may, castaways, survive the now global shipwreck of our ecologically catastrophic modernity.

Perhaps no other postcolonial writer has meditated with greater care and attention on the problematic dynamics of our relation to the earth than Coetzee, and it is with a brief look at two episodes from his novels that I will draw this chapter to a close. The first is taken from *Life and Times of Michael K* (1983), where he provides a perfect gloss for Glissant's distinction in the *Poétique* between "territoire" and "terre," the former being "something one must plant on and that legitimizes one's filiation" and the latter being "without limits" (p. 166). In a South Africa torn apart by civil war, the vagrant Michael K finds himself the momentary occupant of an abandoned Afrikaaner farm where he has planted some pumpkins: in accord with, as one commentator puts it, "the minimal and ahistorical way he would like to live on the land—refusing to be a settler,"[99] he reflects that "the worst mistake . . . would be to try to found a new house, a rival line, on his small beginnings out at the dam" (p. 104). The unsettling and duplicitous dynamics of Coetzee's novel lead us as readers to a sense of both the justice of Michael K's insight and the ineluctability of this "worst mistake": Michael K's desire for the earth and the lack of limits it offers is consistently deconstructed by the historical (re)territorializations to which he is subjected and through which his subjectivity is constituted, but a thinking of this earth nonetheless emerges as the novel's utopian imperative—in a double movement that closely resembles the way that *Foe* both puts into question the positing of an identity and yet also proffers it as a once and future (im)possibility.

Despite *Foe*'s emphasis on issues of cultural identity, a meditation on the problem of the land, while certainly peripheral to the novel, is not altogether absent from it, as the second episode that I wish to cite in closing bears witness. This episode returns us to the figure of Cruso, so different from and yet so similar to his industrious colonial predecessor. One of the few activities in which Coetzee's otherwise slothful castaway engages is the building of terraces and walls, for which Susan Barton can see no obvious purpose, although when she suggests to him that he "set down what traces remain of [your] memories, so that they will outlive you," he counters that "I will leave behind my terraces and walls" and that they will be "more than enough" to memorialize his presence on the island (p. 18). Barton later describes Cruso's landscaping in the following terms:

There were twelve levels of terracing at the time I arrived, each some twenty paces deep and banked with stone walls a yard thick and at their highest as high as a man's head. Within each terrace the ground was levelled and cleared; the stones that made up the walls had been dug out of the earth or borne from elsewhere one by one. (p. 33)

For Barton, the purpose of all this leveling and clearing remains uncertain: "what will you be planting, when you plant?," she asks him, to which he responds, in words that remain "dark" to her: "the planting is not for us. . . . We have nothing to plant—that is our misfortune. . . . The planting is reserved for those who come after us and have the foresight to bring seed." "I only clear the ground for them," Cruso adds, noting that "clearing ground and piling stones is little enough, but it is better than sitting in idleness." While Cruso's motives must remain forever in doubt, as doubtful, indeed, as those of the silent Friday, the effect of his actions can nonetheless be read: Cruso's terraces render the absence of the earth visible, forcing us to confront the critical transformations that have been effected by the colonial world that his literary predecessor helped inaugurate. In the word "terrace" (which, in Defoe's original, is revealingly spelled *terras*),[100] we find not (simply) the original root word, *terra*, but (also) something quite different, if curiously (un)like it: the root has been added on to, and as a consequence we are now compelled to read it also in terms of the *trace* with which it has become intermingled. The earth is no longer present to us in and of itself; it appears to us in a different form, scarred with traces that mark the absence of the original *terra* toward which they point. What Cruso has done is little, but it is, indeed, "more than enough." The colonial appropriation of the earth that his labors exemplify is something that will never be forgotten, and in its doubling back to one of the sources of our now worldwide ecological crisis, Coetzee's novel pointedly reminds us of all that we have lost through the unremitting development of the planet. And yet, as Cruso himself ventures, and as I will venture with him, it may well be that this apparently sterile terrain, the violently cleared ground of a global colonialism, is a place especially reserved for "those who come after us," for those who will have had the foresight to bring seed and the will to begin planting, in the shadow of walls that have not fallen, on the unsettling common ground—the post/colonial (lack of a) ground—that these terraces provide. That, at least, is the relatively heartening perspective that will be generating my inquiry in the remaining chapters of *Islands and Exiles*.

Part **11**

IRRUPTIONS: BERNARDIN DE
SAINT-PIERRE, ÉDOUARD GLISSANT,
AND THE DOUBLE TIME OF
MODERNITY

But what we have in common is *the irruption into modernity.*

—Édouard Glissant, *Le discours antillais*

3 "The Shadow of What One Will Be"

BERNARDIN DE SAINT-PIERRE'S
INSULAR RELATIONS

Displacing Modernity, Restoring Diversity: Bernardin de Saint-Pierre and (the Death of) Enlightenment Exoticism

> Risorge chiara dal passato fosco
> la patria perduta
> che non conobbi mai, che riconosco....
> —Guido Gozzano, "Paolo e Virginia: I figli dell'infortunio"

Rousseau, as we have seen, had a certain fascination for islands. Indeed, at one point in his *Discours sur l'origine et les fondemens de l'inégalité* (1755) he puts forward the hypothesis that "it is at the very least plausible that society and languages originated on islands, and that they were perfected there before becoming known on the continent."[1] Islands, which were detached from an original continental mass through a series of cataclysms (great floods and earthquakes, "revolutions of the globe"), appear to Rousseau as the most likely site for the emergence of human language: "it is understandable that a common idiom would form among men brought close in this way and forced to live together, rather than among those who were freely roaming about in the forests of the mainland," he notes, adding that it is thus "very possible that after their first attempts at navigation it was islanders who brought us the use of speech." Because of its circumscribed territory, the island offers the ideal space for the creation of "a distinctive nation [*une Nation particulière*], bound together in customs and characteristics not by regulations and laws but by the same style of life and type of food, as well as by a shared climate" (p. 169). The confines of the island put an end to wandering and allow for the possibility of a fixed language (and, as Defoe's *Robinson Crusoe* attests, a fixed self ostensibly impermeable to external influences) that can in turn be brought to, or imposed upon, others.

As I emphasized in the opening chapter, the figure of the island can be read in at least two ways, both of which are apparent in Rousseau's story about the origins of language. On the one hand, the closed space of the island, and the fixing of language and identity it enables, supplies the perfect model for a nonrelational outlook on life. Hence the island's importance in the literature of imperialism, from Defoe on: as Diana Loxley argues in her study of the deployment of the island topos in nineteenth-century British and French colonial fiction, it is an imperial space par excellence because it "draws a line around a set of relationships which do not possess the normal political, social and cultural interference," and thereby enables "a simplifi- cation of existing colonial problems and thus an ideological process of wish-fulfilment."[2] The attenuation or occlusion of such interference is ba- sic to the project of a novel like *Robinson Crusoe*, in which the island func- tions as a "crucible of manageable proportions in which to act out the fan- tasies of colonial power,"[3] and it is equally instrumental in the attempts of much anticolonial counterdiscourse to break away from the oppressive in- fluence of that power, to cease being—in John Donne's famous phrase—"a piece of the Continent, a part of the main."

However, the example from Rousseau also points in another direction. The place of origins that it posits is also patently a *secondary* space, depen- dent for its existence upon the loss of the primary (continental) identities that have there been brought together and (con)fused with one another. The emergence of the insular "common language" that Rousseau is here hy- pothesizing can be seen, from this second(ary) perspective, as nothing less than a prefigurative account of the creolization process itself. Explaining the emergence of creole languages and cultures in the Caribbean and the Indian Ocean, and more specifically among peoples "brought together [*réunis*] in the cradle of the plantation economy," the authors of the *Éloge* point out that "these peoples were called upon to invent new cultural schemata that would allow for the establishment of a relative cohabitation among them" (p. 31). These new island populations are not at the origins of "l'usage de la parole" but, as the etymology of this word itself suggests (*parole* → *para*-bole), *to the side of* the continental cultures and languages that they rework and reinvent in the post/colonial "contact zone" (to cite a term used by linguists with reference to the creolization process and popu- larized by Mary Louise Pratt).[4] Committed to an account of the prehistoric origins of language, Rousseau's description also, no doubt despite itself, evokes an ongoing history in which insular locations have become the site of a global *réunion* that puts all natural and cultural fixtures into question, opening them up to the "political, social and cultural interference" of chaotically cohabiting worlds.

This double space of the original and the secondary, which will prove constitutive of the textual universe of Bernardin de Saint-Pierre's *Paul et Virginie*,[5] has been a commonplace of (the discourse of) modernity. This commonplace, a tactical (re)citing, and (re)siting, of the millennia-old myth of lost origins so predominant in Judeo-Christian thought, emerges in response to the political and industrial revolutions of the last decades of the eighteenth century, which were responsible for a specifically modern sense of cultural fragmentation and dispersal that had first been anticipated, centuries before, in the violence of the colonial rupture (Discovery, genocide, slavery) that gave birth to the creole societies of the New World. An awareness of this state of fragmentation produces a double-directed longing, backwards and forwards: a longing for the past, in which a now lost totality was thought to have been possible; and for the future, in which that cultural wholeness might be reconstructed. Nowhere is this awareness more visible than in a Rousseauesque work like Schiller's *On the Aesthetic Education of Man* (1795), with its elegiac argument that "civilization" (*die Kultur*) has inflicted a wound upon modern man, severing "the inner unity of human nature," breaking up the social "totality" to such an extent that "one has to go the rounds from one individual to another in order to be able to piece together a complete image of the species."[6] As a result of the "corruption of the age," there has arisen a pressing need for "the split within man" to be "healed" (*aufgehoben*, the same word that Hegel would use to describe the process of dialectical sublation) and his nature "restored [*entwickeln*] to wholeness" (p. 45). This future-oriented healing and restoration, Schiller argues, must be effected by a "higher Art"—an "art of semblance" that will allow us to restore (*herstellen*) "the totality of our nature" (p. 43).[7] "Humanity," Schiller affirms, "has lost its dignity; but Art has rescued it and preserved it in significant stone"; "truth lives on in the illusion of Art, and it is from this copy, or afterimage [*Nachbild*]," he concludes, "that the original image [*Urbild*] will once again be restored [*herstellen*]" (p. 57). This claim for the restorative powers of art is one that would be loudly echoed in much postcolonial literature, as when in 1959, at the height of the decolonization movement, Aimé Césaire noted that it is the task of black writers and artists "to reestablish the double continuity broken by colonialism: the continuity with the world, and the continuity with ourselves,"[8] or when, thirty years later, the anti-Negritude authors of the *Éloge* voice, ironically enough, this very same sentiment, speaking of the need for Caribbean writers to "return" to their creole loam "in order to reestablish that cultural continuity (associated with the restored historical continuity) without which collective identity is difficult to affirm" (p. 37).

Schiller's image of "significant stone" (*bedeutenden Steinen*), in which the Truth "lives on" even in the face of "the noisy market-place of our century" (p. 7), resonates in a pair of related episodes from Goethe's *Elective*

Affinities (1809) that will lead into my discussion of Bernardin de Saint-Pierre. Put on display throughout the novel, the displacing energies of modernity are nowhere more evident than in the decision of one of the central protagonists to "beautify" the burial ground of her large estate and thus provide for "the demands of sensibility." As we learn very early on in the novel, Charlotte—who along with her husband Eduard is a German aristocrat in the process of self-consciously downgrading herself into an exemplary bourgeois subject—has decided to move all the gravestones from their original location, set them up against the wall and at the base of the church that stands on their property, and then level the ground and sow it with "various kinds of clover, which provided a fine green and flowery expanse," "a gaily coloured carpet instead of a field of rough and rugged gravestones" (p. 156):

With every consideration for the ancient monuments she had managed to level and arrange everything in such a way as to create a pleasant place which was nice to look at and which set the imagination working.

The oldest memorial [*Stein*] of all had been put in a place of suitable honour. In the order of their antiquity the gravestones were erected against the wall, inserted into it, or lodged in some other way. The base of the church itself was ornamented and augmented by this arrangement. (p. 32)

Charlotte's leveling intentions are clearly at one with a new historical and aesthetic vision that insists upon mechanical as opposed to organic temporalities ("in the order of their antiquity") and that deprives objects of their original use-value by transforming them into pleasurable ornaments.

Goethe strategically returns to this site of displacement in the second half of his two-part novel, as if to acknowledge the repetitive, serial nature of the leveling that modernity effects and the conditions of secondariness it promotes. There were, Goethe's narrator notes, some parishioners "who had already expressed disapproval that the place where their ancestors reposed was no longer marked, and that their memory [*Andenken*] had thus been so to speak obliterated. There were many," he adds, "who said that, although the gravestones which were preserved showed who was buried there, they did not show where they were buried, and it was where they were buried that really mattered." As one especially upset parishioner remarks, "it is not the stone itself which draws us to the spot, but that which is preserved beneath it, that which is entrusted to the earth beside it"; he then distinguishes on these grounds between a grave and a monument, which has "in itself little real meaning" (p. 157). All monuments, by this definition, are thus examples of "insignificant stone," their meaning contingent upon the retention of an organic connection with the past and the earth. Countering that one ought to renounce particular places but not "memorials" (*Andenken*), Charlotte's architect argues, by contrast, for "well-conceived, well-executed monuments, not scattered about all over the place but erected on a spot where they can expect to remain" (p. 159).[9] Not coincidentally, the architect wants "to restore [*herstellen*] both exterior and interior [of the newly ornamented church] to their original condition and to harmonize them with the churchyard" (p. 161); this dream of restoration in no small measure resembles Schiller's, motivated as it is by the hope that the original can be preserved through the semblance of Art and its afterimages. That this semblance is itself a product of the conditions it would remedy, an "obliteration" of that which it would remember, is what Goethe suggests in *Elective Affinities*, with an ambivalent mixture of desire and repugnance that makes this novel one of the most recognizably liminal texts of what Goethe himself refers to as "modern times" (p. 162).

In the light of these episodes from Goethe's novel, an apparently insignificant detail from Bernardin de Saint-Pierre's biography gains a symbolic resonance: one of the few tasks that he was officially assigned as a King's engineer during his mostly unproductive stay from 1768 to 1770 on the Indian Ocean island of Mauritius (or as it was called at the time, the Île de France) was to turn the old cemetery of the capital Port-Louis into a timber yard; this cemetery and its "insalubrious" contents would subsequently be relocated outside of the town.[10] This episode can be read as a relatively innocuous instance of a modernizing and sanitizing process that is basic to the violence of imperial conquest and colonization—a disruptive and global violence that antedates and anticipates those revolutionary disruptions that swept across the European continent around the turn of the century and with which *Elective Affinities* genially attempts to negotiate.

The ambivalent acceptance of modernity and its displacements in Goethe's novel, so different from the ethos of dissatisfaction that one finds in Schiller's writings of the previous decade, is certainly not a mood that predominates in the vast oeuvre of his contemporary Bernardin (whom Goethe surely had in mind when writing *Elective Affinities*, a novel that uncannily doubles and displaces the idyllic sentimentality of *Paul et Virginie*). As his role in the relocation of the Port-Louis cemetery suggests, Bernardin was acutely aware of the unearthly leveling process to which Goethe's novel bears witness; indeed, he frequently draws his readers' attention to burial grounds that are undergoing a process of obliteration similar to the one in *Elective Affinities*. His repeated meditations on urban cemeteries in the never-completed *Harmonies de la nature* are exemplary in this regard: as he points out, what results from the modern reliance on a "common grave," necessitated by too many dead bodies and not enough land, is an effacing of differences that were once central to the order and meaning of society. The son looks in vain for "the one who gave him life":

How could he even recognize [his father] among the crowd of intermingled corpses, covered over with only a little earth. To tell the truth, there is not even enough time for them to be eaten away. In such a populous city, the old graves are soon dug up in order to make new ones. . . . A Paris cemetery is nothing more than a human refuse dump. (8.178–79; see also 9.366–67)

The interminglings of the Parisian cemetery that Bernardin here describes are certainly a far cry from Charlotte's tranquil beautifications, but the affinities that link these two visions should nonetheless be obvious, since both register the loss of a sacred ground, the confusion that stems from a lack of monuments, and a distorted (in this case, accelerated) temporality. Such changes are, for Bernardin, at least partially attributable to the onset of a modernity that is indissociable from the French Revolution. In his *Suite des voeux d'un solitaire* (1792), for instance, he notes that one result of "this new order of things" inaugurated in 1789 has been the reopening of a cemetery that encroaches on his property and that has been "invaded by the town authorities, who have turned it into a mephitis-ridden place through daily burials" (11.206). Reflecting the often deadly and confusing energies unleashed by the Revolution, this malodorous invasion can, however, also be ascribed to human passions that are in no way contingent upon social and political revolutions: Bernardin prefaces this particular account of the city's rapidly changing landscape with the claim that, "like water flowing in a river, one man is succeeded by the next, who is himself replaced in turn, but their passions remain the same, just as a river remains in its bed." "It was always a matter of the same ambitions," he continues, "with the only difference being that the ambitions of the lowly had now mastered those of the powerful, in a struggle where neither showed any respect for laws ancient or modern" (11.206). Bernardin's writings as a whole, and *Paul et Virginie* in particular, are founded upon this sort of oscillation between, on the one hand, an acute sensitivity to the historical changes wrought by revolution and, on the other, philosophical appeals to an unchanging human nature that owe much to his Enlightenment predecessors.

Complicating this unresolved tension yet further is a plethora of intermediate claims that problematically fall somewhere between historical specificity and philosophical abstraction: namely, proto-ethnographical generalizations about specific cultures and nations, which to some degree acknowledge history but which nonetheless also tend to categorize peoples and places as if their identities were once and for all fixed, as in the following example from his *Études de la nature* (1784): "all natural peoples, and even the majority of civilized peoples," he notes, "have made the tombs of their ancestors the center of their devotions and an essential part of their religion, with the exception of the peoples of western and southern Europe, where a sad and cruel education has made fathers hateful to their children"

(5.82). The sort of invasive and obliterating dislocations that Goethe's Charlotte effects would by this account be attributable to a condition that is neither entirely divorced from historical time (since it is the product of an "educative" process) nor separable from ahistorical generalizations having to do with "European" peoples.

It is precisely in this middle space, where historical (secondary) and essentialist (originary) claims uneasily exist side by side, that the colonial dimension of Bernardin's work is most visible; it is here that he must attempt to articulate the differences between the West, the expanding influence of which he more often than not condemned on ecological and moral grounds, and a multiplicity of other worlds with which he was often in profound sympathy but that he feared were becoming ever more subject to a process of colonial "disfigurement." This grievous process involved the effacement of supposedly natural differences and their replacement by a plethora of unnatural colonial relations—such as slavery, which according to Bernardin was responsible for the "denatured character" of many Africans (5.396)—brought about by the mixing together of hitherto separate cultures and the consequent emergence of a globalized economy based on "artificial needs" (8.274). With Bernardin, the abstract philosophical vision that characterized Enlightenment thinking about the exotic begins to give way to an historical insight, traceable in great part to Bernardin's own lived encounter with the colonies, that destabilizes such generalizations without fully abolishing them. Among the first European writers to grapple with the global dissemination of a colonizing modernity, his work assiduously registers the various disfigurements that ensue from it; if, for the most part, Bernardin laments these disfigurements, upon occasion he attempts, as we will see, to reconfigure them in more positive terms as a potentially redemptive grafting of diverse peoples and cultures onto one another.

In line with his mentor and close friend Rousseau, whose own use of the word "disfiguration" often (as in his late *Rêveries*) serves to acknowledge a slippage between fact and fiction that his rhetoric of truth-telling incessantly attempts to contain,[11] Bernardin consistently deploys the word in order to convey an unhappy falling away from the original, a displacement and translation of it, that he sees as basic to the leveling energies of modernity. In the first of his *Études*, notably, Bernardin indirectly addresses the issue of colonialism when he critiques contemporary geographers and their artificial representations of the globe: rather than mapping the earth in terms of its "natural subdivisions, they present it to us with an array of gaudy colored lines, which divide and subdivide it into empires, dioceses, seneschalcies, *élections*, bailiwicks, *greniers à sel*" (3.25). "They have disfigured or replaced with meaningless names," he adds, "those that the first inhabitants of each region had bestowed and that expressed the nature [of the places] so well," and they have thereby "deprived nature's work of its characteristics and nations of their monuments."[12] This act of replacement, and the dangerously amnesiac and fictional order that ensues from it, is but one example of a far-ranging process of disfiguration that for Bernardin embraces both the realm of the social and of the aesthetic, as when he speaks, for instance, of those who have been "more or less disfigured by our institutions," and "those who have been disfigured by the vice-inducing effects of our upbringings and our habits" (4.177, 178), or when in the foreword to the 1789 edition of *Paul et Virginie*, while praising writers like Homer and Virgil "who lived so near to nature," he critiques "the courtier poets, such as Ariosto," for "strangely disfiguring" nature and succeeding only in painting caricatures of it (p. 91).

Offering innumerable critiques of this sort, founded upon the belief that "the more man grows remote from his origin, the more he deviates from nature" (12.148), Bernardin nonetheless consistently holds out the possibility of putting this process of disfigurement and estrangement to an end and returning the figure, as it were, to its original state. Those disfigured people referred to above can, he asserts, "reform their traits" (4.178); the stated purpose of the old man who narrates most of *Paul et Virginie*, and who at one point remarks that the majority of illustrious names from the past, such as those of Homer and Socrates, "have come to us disfigured by a number of satirical barbs used to characterize them" (p. 229), is to counter this process and to restore the original figure by leading his interlocutors back to nature (p. 217; "les ramener à la nature"). Jean Starobinski has shown a similar doublespeak at work in Rousseau, for whom disfiguration (and other such related processes: deformation, degeneration, and so on) is not only a definitive event but also, and contradictorily, simply a matter of occultation: "primitive nature persists, but *hidden*, shrouded by the veils cast over it, the artifices under which it has been buried, and yet always intact."[13] "Rousseau tells us," Starobinski continues, "that man has irretrievably destroyed his natural identity, but he also asserts that the original spirit, being indestructible, remains forever identical to itself underneath the masks that have been superimposed upon it" (p. 27). These disfiguring masks must thus be torn away if the essence of the lost original is to be made manifest. Bernardin assiduously attempts to duplicate this pattern of thought, to erase the realm of the obstacle and to substantiate his own "essentialist conception of language" in which, as Coetzee puts it in a discussion of the strategies of white South African pastoral, "there is no split between signifier and signified, and things are their name,"[14] or in which, as Bernardin himself puts it in his 1789 foreword, "words correspond to things [*les mots suivent les choses*]: Rem verba sequuntur" (p. 90).

Where he differs from his Swiss mentor, however, is precisely in the greater worldliness of his argument, which attempts to literalize Rousseau's largely conceptual primitivism (with its appeal to a state of nature "that no longer exists, that perhaps did not exist, that probably never will exist")[15] by providing it with a precise geographical and cultural location, most notably, the Île de France in *Paul et Virginie*; he thereby necessarily draws the reader's attention to a colonial dimension that Rousseau's work is better able to marginalize. Citing the example of "those peoples who still live close to nature" (4.445), Bernardin will hold out the hope that there is a positive response to the question he poses in his *Études*: "will a new Arcadia never reappear in some corner of the globe?" (3.358). Notwithstanding his awareness of the fact that "our harvests and our forests sail over the seas bringing sorrow to both hemispheres" (3.17), and that "although we Europeans boast that in many respects we have been particularly favored by God, it is certain that we cause the unhappiness of three-quarters of the world" (*VF*, p. 251), he clings to the exoticizing belief that "there are still places in the New World where one can change the nature of our institutions" (5.165). In *Paul et Virginie*, his self-styled "espèce de pastorale" (p. 78), Bernardin attempts to envision one such space; however, as we will see, in departing from the pastoral genre's well-established convention of situating its protagonists in a timeless Arcadia by locating his "true story" on a recently colonized island in the Indian Ocean, he opens it up to the "historicity" that, as Starobinski points out with regard to the writings of Rousseau, is always visible in the gap that intervenes between "the initial and the restored transparency" (p. 115), between the original spirit and its unmasked double.

The pastoral impulse to transparency that generates Bernardin's *Paul et Virginie* and its oppositional relationship to modernity is fundamental both to the Romantic vision of nature that his novel anticipates and to early postcolonial ideologies such as Negritude, which ostensibly critique the Romantic vision but also spectacularly reinscribe it, as we can see by briefly turning to one of the central topoi of postcolonial revisionist literature, Shakespeare's Caliban. For the Romantics, a figure like Caliban exemplifies the sort of organic connection to nature that writers like Césaire and Senghor would over a century later come to associate with pre-colonial societies: Hazlitt, for instance, noted that Shakespeare "has described the brutal mind of Caliban in contact with the pure and original forms of nature; the character grows out of the soil where it is rooted uncontrouled, uncouth and wild"; Coleridge, for his part, asserted of Caliban that "all the images he utters are drawn from nature, & are all highly poetical."[16] While neither of these examples are entirely positive (indeed, they would appear to demand the imposition of some form of "prosaic control" over the "wild" forces of nature by a Prospero figure capable of organizing "all knowledges into a coherent imperial whole"),[17] they certainly lay the foundations for the sort of postcolonial rehabilitation of Caliban that a writer like Césaire would attempt in his parodic adaptation of Shakespeare's play, *Une tempête* (1968–69).

The artist figure Prospero, so appealing to the Romantic imagination, becomes for Césaire the arch-colonist, while Caliban is recast as "the man who is close to nature, whose contact with it has not yet been interrupted." Indulging in not only Senghor's rhetoric of "participatory" cultures but that of Carpentier's "marvelous" reality, Césaire goes on to assert that this unbroken connection allows Caliban to "participate in a marvelous world."[18] Césaire's interest in the figure of Caliban is matched by a linguistic primitivism that is at the heart of the modernist aesthetics he had been championing from the outset of his career: some twenty years earlier, for instance, after defining the "true poet" as the one who makes use of "the primitive word," "the primitive phrase," he would go on, in language that significantly echoes Bernardin's, to assert of this poet that he "leads language back to its pure state" ("sa langue *ramène* le langage à l'état pur" [my italics]).[19] Such modernist, and primitivist, gestures are equally ubiquitous in the work of the other founder of Negritude, Senghor, who once argued that the merit of Romanticism, and especially of Surrealism, was to have "transcended the antinomy reason-imagination, by restoring the latter to its rightful place at the fore"; such acts of restoration were not necessary for his own people, since "it happens that Black Africa did not make this error: it did not forsake the Kingdom of Childhood [*le Royaume d'Enfance*], which is that of the art of poetry."[20] Senghor's identification of Africa as the unadulterated site of imagination and childhood, which not only consorts with Bernardin's pastoral vision but, more alarmingly, with Hegel's notorious definition of the continent as a "Gold-Land compressed within itself— the land of childhood, which lying beyond the days of self-conscious history, is enveloped in the dark mantle of Night,"[21] is one that later generations of postcolonial writers would, of course, amply rebut—as when, for instance, Derek Walcott in the early 1970s lashed out against "a fake exoticism of poverty and the pastoral," satirizing the fascination of certain Afrocentric or revolutionary writers with the figure of Caliban, and putting into question their desperately mythologizing attachment to "the songs of triumph, the defiance of the captured warrior . . . the nostalgic battle chants and the seasonal songs of harvest, the seeding of the great African pastoral."[22] Walcott's own vision of the New World as the potential site of an Adamic rebirth—a "green world, one without metaphors"—is itself, to be sure, by no means immune to his own powerful critique of the pastoral impulse. His insistent appeals in "The Muse of History" to the "maturity" of his poetic work, his claims about being condemned to "middle age" (p.

20), his rejection of the "adolescent" aesthetic of those who remain in Clio's servitude, belie an obvious anxiety of influence—one that situates him squarely within rather than beyond the post/colonial continuum that links such apparently diverse writers as Bernardin, Césaire, and Senghor in their contestation of the "self-conscious history" of colonialism.

Bernardin's recourse to the genre of pastoral, like that of many postcolonial authors writing during the early years of decolonization, is impelled by a sense of historical crisis and the imminent prospect of radical social change. Pastoral briefly flourished in France in the years immediately preceding the Revolution as an apotropaic response to the possibility of this crisis. In one of his many astute analyses of Bernardin's work, Jean-Michel Racault has demonstrated the problematic nature of the version of pastoral put forward in *Paul et Virginie*: notwithstanding Bernardin's insistence in his brief 1788 preface that "it was not necessary for me to write a novel in order to portray happy families" (p. 78), Racault shows some of the many ways in which this supposedly true story opens out onto "the degraded novelistic universe" that it was intended to occlude.[23] My own argument about *Paul et Virginie* pursues Racault's general approach (one that is itself greatly dependent upon Georg Lukács's well-known theory of the novel) with the specific goal of showing how Bernardin's text negotiates one particular issue that is of central concern to my analysis of post/colonial literature: namely, the integral connections between *novelization* and *creolization*. For Bernardin, (colonial) history proves synonymous with the complexities of a novelistic condition that necessarily marks the attenuation or eclipse of a simple genre like pastoral and of the primary connection to nature that it would assert. If, as Bernardin once put it in his *Études*, "it is only the history of men that fiction renders more beautiful [*embellit*], while it degrades that of nature" (3.32), then it is precisely the presence of such secondary "embellishments" that constitutes *Paul et Virginie* as a novel and ensures the degrading contamination—or, viewed from another perspective, the invigorating creolization—of his text.

The twin revolutions, political and industrial, at the turn of the eighteenth century mark the definitive onset in Europe of a modernity that will, according to Franco Moretti, find its most appropriate expression in the nineteenth-century *Bildungsroman*, which—because of its emphasis on development and its predisposition to compromise, its capacity for coming to terms with the "intrinsically boundless dynamism" of modernity—emerges victorious in a quasi-Darwinian struggle of symbolic forms at this time. "Industrial and political convulsions," Moretti notes,

acted simultaneously over European culture, forcing it to redraw the territory of individual expectations, to define anew its "sense of history" and its attitude toward the values of modernity. For all sorts of reasons, the *Bildungsroman* was the symbolic form most apt to solve these problems—the fittest for surviving in the new, selective context. And the *Bildungsroman* did indeed survive, while the *Erziehungsroman* and the *Entwicklungsroman* and the *Künstlerroman*, the allegorical, the lyric, the epistolary [and . . .] the satirical novel, all perished in that veritable struggle for literary life.[24]

The details of Moretti's no doubt overly schematic argument need not concern us here. What I am privileging, rather, is simply his emphasis on the Bildungsroman, which he for all intents and purposes identifies with the "classic" nineteenth-century novel *tout court*, as a site of compromise in which the transformative (social, political, scientific, and so on) energies that were gathering steam at this point in world history can most effectively be negotiated. Rather than simply expunging these energies in a nostalgic gesture of longing for lost traditions or sublating them in a vision of some radically post-modern future, the Bildungsroman contains them, in both senses of the word, *including* them but also, inasmuch as the invocation of *Bildung* presupposes an eventual end to their growth, fictionally *controlling* them. Schiller's degraded present will be the preferred terrain for the nineteenth-century novel, a secondary space, contaminated and contaminatory, from which both the primacy of the fixed origin and the finality of a telos are absent, if not forgotten. "The fate of these [extinct] forms hung on their respective 'purity,'" Moretti argues in his *The Way of the World*; "that is to say, the more they remained bound to a rigid, original structure, the more difficult their survival[,] and vice versa: the more a form was capable of flexibility and compromise, the better it could prosper in the maelstrom without synthesis of modern history."[25]

Moretti's definition of the novel as the "most bastard" of symbolic forms, an "impure" genre not bound to any one original structure but weakly linked to many, has obvious relevance to a consideration of the creolization process, and fits in well with the appeal to mongrelization and migrancy in recent postcolonial and postmodern thinking. While it would be illegitimate simply to conflate the terms novelization and creolization, much of my argument in this book does indeed rest on a loose identification of these two ongoing processes of development that have been generated out of "the maelstrom without synthesis of modern history" and that, for this very reason, must repeatedly fall short or overshoot the mark of the very thing they insistently look forward to or back upon: namely, that "conclusive synthesis of maturity," in Moretti's words (p. 19), that the double vision of modernity has either relegated to the past, as with Schiller's Greeks who "combined the first youth of imagination with the manhood of reason in a glorious manifestation of humanity," or reserved for a radically different future in which "Truth's triumphant rays," again in Schiller's words, shall have "penetrated the recesses of the human heart" and brought a definitive end to "the corruption of the age which besets [us] on all sides."[26]

Bernardin's recourse to pastoral is, then, a reactive strategy that attempts to defer the confrontation with a convulsive modernity that would soon find its (im)proper expression in the nineteenth-century novel. This literary strategy works in tandem with the proto-ethnographical vision of fixed identities that, as we have already remarked, finds its way at many points into Bernardin's theoretical and fictional writings in the wake of systematizing "natural historians" such as Buffon and Linnaeus, whose "global classificatory project," as Mary Louise Pratt puts it, was based upon an act of naming that "brings the reality of order into being," extracting "all the things of the world and redeploy[ing] them into a new knowledge formation whose value lies precisely in its difference from the chaotic original" (*IE*, p. 33). If, after its brief flowering in the latter part of the century, pastoral as an identifiable prose genre was on the verge of literary extinction (to be recuperated under a myriad of other antimodern literary guises), the same cannot be said of this categorizing and categorical vision that, as Nicholas Thomas has recently argued, was by the end of the eighteenth century emerging as the dominant representational mode of a specifically *modern* colonial discourse. In contrast to the constructions of cultural alterity that dominated European writing until the early eighteenth century (which were grounded in a Christian—or, better, post/Christian—world view and thus tended to conceive of non-European peoples "not in any anthropologically specific terms, but as a lack or poorer form of the values of the center," envisioning them primarily as pagans, "incomplete or imperfect forms, rather than as 'peoples' of a comprehensibly distinct kind"), the Enlightenment and, a fortiori, the nineteenth century witnessed the emergence of "a worldview that imagines a plurality of different races or peoples,"[27] or of what Francis Affergan, in a similar argument, has referred to as a "classifying mode of thought wherein others [*autrui*] are *integrated* only in their calculable form: as a difference in a descriptive logic."[28] We find this new world view at work, to take but one notable example from the decade in which Bernardin wrote his *Études* and *Paul et Virginie*, in the cultural pluralism of a Johann Gottfried Herder, for whom "the European has no idea of the boiling passions and imagination which glow in the negro's breast; and the Hindu has no conception of the restless desires that chase the European from one end of the world to the other."[29] Such generalizations are basic to eighteenth-century natural histories and nineteenth-century ethnographies, which—in Thomas's words—are generated out of a "discourse [that] proceeds through confident assertion about the natures of whole populations, and is marked consistently by the slippage . . . whereby the behaviour of particular peoples towards Europeans, or the responses of the latter to the former, are taken as emanations of the natives' essential characters, rather than facts arising from the circumstances of contact."[30] As Thomas concludes, "modernity has been an epoch of anthropological typification" (p. 90), and this modernity, grounded in an avoidance of the "facts arising from the circumstances of contact," finds ample expression in Bernardin's predominantly antimodern oeuvre.

Buffon's classificatory logic pervades Bernardin's oeuvre, perhaps most notably in his frequent reliance on the former's division of humanity into four main groups on the basis of skin color, which are in turn equated with the "four ages in the life of a man" (a childlike America, an adolescent Africa, a "virile" Europe, and a senescent Asia; see 8.95–140). As stated, Bernardin's repeated appeals to a people's essential "character" are basic to this rhetoric (as when he notes in *Voyage à l'Île de France* that "the character of blacks is naturally cheerful" [1.142–43]), but they prove almost invariably subject to a process of historical development, or disfigurement, that necessarily undoes—at the same time as it furthers—that rhetoric (as when he feels compelled to add of the blacks whose cheery nature he has just characterized that "after being enslaved for a while, they become melancholic"). A few more examples of this "anthropological typification" are worth citing here inasmuch as they specifically bear upon Bernardin's attempts at containing the complex effects of a cross-cultural contact that, as I will argue in a moment, he was also capable of viewing in a more positive light that refreshingly anticipates a poetics and politics of creolization. At certain points in the *Études*, for instance, he speaks of "la figure européenne," which is supposedly characterized by simplicity, and contrasts it favorably with others that are "disfigured by African or Asiatic characteristics" (5.97). In a similar vein, describing the lives of European colonists who live in the tropics, he speaks of "the European type [*caractère*], which in a hot climate is always fearful of seeing its own blood become denatured like that of its slaves, and that yearns after new alliances with its compatriots, in order to get the vivid, fresh colors of the European blood, and the even more vital affection for the homeland, circulating in the veins of its offspring" (5.165). This closed circulation is in stark contrast to a "denaturing" cultural opening of the sort that he describes in his *Voyage*, where the deficiencies in the character of the island-born whites are partially attributed to their practice of using black women as wet nurses for their children: Bernardin there speaks disapprovingly of "the vices of the black women, which they suck in with their milk, along with the whims that they will tyrannically exercise upon their poor slaves" (1.137).

What this last example suggests, however, is a point for which Bernardin frequently argued: namely, the importance of an *educational* process in shaping, and reshaping, supposedly essential characteristics (a point also stressed by Buffon, whose classification of the human race into four main groups was, as Béatrice Didier has argued, intended less as a means of keeping them separate than as the grounds for thinking their underlying unity and the ubiquitous métissages through which that unity reveals itself).[31] As he puts it in his precipitous response to the outbreak of the French Revolution, Voeux d'un solitaire (1789), "not only our acquired knowledge but our feelings, which it seems as if we were born with, depend almost entirely upon our education" (11.158–59). "Change a man's education," he asserts, "and you change the way he eats and dresses, his philosophy, his moral code, his religion, his patriotism, etc." Depending upon the milieu in which they are raised, he continues, "the African will think like the European, and the European like the African: the republican will have despotic sentiments and the despot republican ones" (11.158). Thus, while examples of Bernardin's reliance upon a systematic thinking could be multiplied almost ad infinitum, they would by no means tell the whole story. There is also an ample resistance to closed systems in Bernardin's work that runs against the grain of his insular thinking, opening it up to "the perplexity of the living" and to the creative process of education that may, after all, be at the etymological heart of the word "creole," with its probable connections to the Spanish verb "criar" (to grow [plants], to breed [animals], to raise and educate [children]), itself derived from the Latin "creare" (to create).[32]

As one instance of this creole openness, Bernardin's sensitivity to the contingencies of place can be cited for the way in which it attenuates and diverts the categorical imperatives of natural history and its typologizing systems: "how greatly naturalists have mutilated the most noble portion of natural history," he notes, "by providing, as most of them are wont to do, isolated descriptions of animals and plants, but without saying anything about the season and the place in which they were found" (4.150).[33] The will to realism that finds repeated expression in both his scientific and fictional work—of Paul et Virginie he states, for instance, "I have described real sites, customs of which one might still find examples in various solitary parts of the Île de France, or the neighboring island of Bourbon [present-day Réunion]" (p. 95), and notes that it has been "corroborated by several settlers [habitants] whom I came to know on the Île de France"—ensures that this work will be fraught with the ambivalence that marks any attempt at negotiating between the strictures of an abstracting representational language and what Edward Said has so nicely termed "the disorientations of direct encounters with the human."[34] Realism, to be sure, is a double-edged sword: as Homi Bhabha once pointed out, colonial discourse "employs a system of representation, a regime of truth, that is structurally similar to realism."[35] One effect of so assiduously reinscribing the "real" in a work of travel literature such as the Voyage, or of locating a fictional work like Paul *et Virginie* in that same colony, is to turn the act of writing into a proprietorial gesture: as Lennard Davis has argued, "the seemingly neutral idea that novels must take place in locations was actually part of a collective structure of defenses that gave eighteenth-century society a way to justify the ownership of certain kinds of property."[36] This novel emphasis on location, which for Davis distinguishes, say, Crusoe's island from the one in Shakespeare's *Tempest*, where the point is simply "that the action takes place on an island—any island—and the lack of specificity is not important,"[37] assuredly motivates Bernardin's prose (and in this light it is certainly no coincidence that the primary site in *Paul et Virginie*, the isolated basin where his protagonists live, had earlier been identified by Bernardin, in his role as King's engineer concerned with the military problem of defending the island, as a place where "all the inhabitants of the island and their blacks" could be safely gathered should the Île de France come under attack).

And yet the realistic dimension of his work also productively opens it up to the beginnings of an encounter with "creole life" and the "contact zones" in which that life flourishes.[38] This encounter puts into question, without dissolving, not only the proprietorial impulse at work in the techniques of realism that were taking shape in the eighteenth century, but also the characterological biases and pastoral impulses that, as we have seen, were so much a part of Bernardin's enterprise. If *Paul et Virginie* is, in the words of the nineteenth-century poet Leconte de Lisle (himself a native of the Île Bourbon), an "immortal pastoral," it is also, as he recognizes, a work "in which the precision with which the landscape and creole customs are rendered is second only to the indescribable charm that it exudes."[39] Bernardin was himself profoundly attuned to this creole dimension of his pastoral. Noting, in an unfinished article on colonies focused on the Indian Ocean islands, that "nothing is rarer on the islands than a moral feeling that would attach Creoles to their country," Bernardin states, with an emphasis on the need for rootedness that anticipates, say, the rhetoric of nineteenth-century Latin American intellectuals intent upon transforming the Americas from a space of exile into a (literary) homeland, that "it is with the specific intention of attaching the habitants to their country that I wrote the story of Paul and Virginie, where I drew a picture of the happiest life possible" (*VF*, p. 435). To be sure, in referring to Creoles and to the habitants Bernardin is here thinking primarily of the island-born "white" population but they are for him, as his writings on the Indian Ocean islands invariably bear witness, inextricably joined together with all the other islanders in a complex cultural and biological mix that provided Bernardin with a positive foretaste of what a truly "diverse" society might look like, as in the following description from the *Suite des voeux* in which he describes for his readers the results of the interracial marriages that took place during the early days of the colonization of the Île Bourbon. "It is very common there," he points out in an argument for extending the rights of French citizenship to the *gens de couleur libres* (free mulattoes and blacks), "to see nephews and nieces, male and female cousins, brothers and sisters, fathers and mothers, of all different colors." "Nothing interested me more than this diversity," he notes, adding that "these families, at one and the same time white, mulatto, and black, united by blood ties, represented to me the union of Europe and Africa, much more so than those fortunate lands themselves, where the shade of the pine and the palm tree are commingled" (11.227–28).

This creolizing will toward diversity *and* (re)union that is present throughout Bernardin's work did not escape at least one nineteenth-century reader of *Paul et Virginie*, the influential Orientalist Edgar Quinet, author of *Du génie des religions* (1842), "a work that," as Said repeatedly stresses in *Orientalism*, "announced the Oriental Renaissance and placed the Orient and the West in a functional relationship with each other."[40] In this book, Quinet astutely remarks that with Bernardin "a new spirit filters into the eighteenth century."[41] Speaking of the *Études*, Quinet asks, "what reader is not aware of the fact that they were produced in the vicinity of the Indies, and does one not find there the gentleness of a Creole in that love for flowers, bodies of water, and the smallest of insects?" (pp. 71–72). Portraying Bernardin as a sort of "Christian Brahmin" (p. 72), he contends that "one could compare Virginie with certain figures from the sacred poetry of the Hindus, such as Sakuntala, Damayanti, and one would be astonished to see how the same soil, the same harmonies have produced the same poetic creatures in the mind of Orientals and in that of a man from the West" (p. 71). For Quinet, *Paul et Virginie* is a hybrid text, its identity shaped by and rooted in its creole surroundings (a view that can be usefully contrasted with Chateaubriand's "monotheistic" interpretation of Bernardin's eclogue, in which "the two *exiled* Christian families" [my italics] are read purely in terms of European origins, with no regard to the post/European insular formation that Quinet stresses).[42] No more than Bernardin's own pronouncements about "l'union de l'Europe et de l'Afrique," to be sure, can Quinet's comments about Bernardin's work be separated from a colonial framework that to a great extent erodes his apparently synthesizing message. Significantly enough, Quinet's paean to Bernardin is immediately followed by an equally positive assessment of "one of the most ingenuous admirers of Bernardin de Saint-Pierre," Napoléon Bonaparte, whose Egyptian campaign in its own way marks for Quinet "l'alliance de l'Occident et de l'Orient" (p. 72)—an unholy alliance, indeed, inasmuch as, in Said's words, the Napoleonic occupation of Egypt set in motion specifically modern Orientalist processes "that still dominate our contemporary cultural and political perspectives."[43] The links between Quinet's positive appraisals of Bernardin and of French imperial expansion need to be asserted, certainly, no less than those between Bernardin's laudably prescient interest in *diversité* and his (hetero)sexist tendency to conceive of it predominantly in terms of physical intercourse. What one must also keep in mind, though, is the extent to which such mixed messages are basic to *any* attempt at thinking cross-culturally: the very inconsistency of pioneering visions like those of Bernardin and Quinet, so visibly caught in a translational space between insular biases and universal claims, is perhaps in the end more consistent with the (unrepresentable) truth of "that process of mutation and adaptation we call creolization" than any amount of more programmatically "correct," multicultural "happy talk" that vaingloriously attempts simply to banish such tensions and contradictions.

Notwithstanding the obviously mixed message that they convey, however, the visions of cultural change and exchange that frequently surface in Bernardin's writings are in many ways remarkably "advanced" for their time (to invoke an obviously questionable linear view of intellectual history): many, though by no means all, of his incipiently hybridizing visions have at their core the scenario of interracial coupling, which is also central to the "sexually liberated, miscegenated world" that Diderot, in his less pessimistic moments, occasionally proposed as a way of combining colonizers and colonized, in Anthony Pagden's words, into "a new society for which we might all have greater hopes than we can at present have of any existing community 'civilized' or 'savage.'"[44] Doubtless the simplest and among the most problematic models for conceiving of cross-cultural relations,[45] this scenario is nonetheless a vital one given that, as Brathwaite has maintained, "it was in the intimate area of sexual relationships that the greatest damage was done to white creole apartheid policy and where the most significant—and lasting—inter-cultural creolization took place" (*DCS*, p. 303). If this scenario finds perhaps its most extended narrative expression in the posthumously published play *Empsaël et Zoraïde*, which would have been more easily produced "in Morocco than in Paris," as Bernardin noted at the height of the Revolution (11.231),[46] it crops up all over his published and unpublished work in the decades surrounding the publication of *Paul et Virginie* as part of what we might term a *neopastoral* fantasy of global harmony that is grounded in the belief, as he put it in his article on colonies, that "if the chorus of voices offered by the different birds in the forest is so charming, than how much more so the voices of men of diverse nations in the same landscape" (*VF*, p. 436), and that should such a place exist where this "concert d'hommes de diverses nations" could be assembled, "even were it in the glacial regions, it would be the most pleasant, abundant, and happiest place on earth" (*VF*, pp. 446–47).

One particularly dramatic version of this fantasy is the philanthropic experiment urged in the last of his *Voeux*, the "Voeux pour les nations," in which Bernardin imagines a veritable Noah's Ark of peoples translated into the heart of France, "men once divided by languages, governments and religions brought together [*réunis*] in the midst of abundance and freedom by French hospitality" (11.188). This reunion would, ideally, be duplicated by all other nations: "Oh! how worthy of an enlightened, rich, and generous nation to naturalize foreigners, and to see in its midst Asiatic, African, and American families multiply, surrounded by the very plants for which we are indebted to them!" (11.172). Bernardin's literal-minded conception of this experimental transplantation leads him here to imagine these "hommes étrangers" as being "surrounded by the plants and animals of their own countries": a Senegalese in the valley, cultivating "in a greenhouse prickly pears full of cochineals"; a Laplander on the highest mountain, "putting his reindeer out to graze in the summer next to a glacière," and so on (11.181). Here, to be sure, in the revealing slippage between the political usage of the word "naturalize" (the admitting of "an alien to the position and rights of citizenship" [*OED*]) and its nonanthropocentric meaning (that introduction of animals or plants "to places where they are not indigenous, but in which they may flourish under the same conditions as those which are native," which is itself, as Confiant reminds us, an important aspect of the creolization process),[47] Bernardin attempts to contain the estrangement that is inseparable from all acts of human translation, to bracket out the anything but harmonic dynamics of displacement and adaptation that they entail and that he himself registers, in a different context, with his use of the word in the *Voyage* when he notes that "by dint of familiarizing ourselves with the arts, we have become estranged from nature" (2.86; "à force de nous naturaliser avec les arts, la nature nous devient étrangère").

Notwithstanding this slippage, though, to say nothing of the (absurdly) experimental nature of Bernardin's naturalization scenario and its potential affinities with an essentializing multiculturalist vision that Jean-Loup Amselle has dubbed "racisme du métissage,"[48] the estranging space of crosscultural exchange makes itself visible in the Carpentieresque vision of fusion that concludes this passage from the *Voeux*. The eventual result of Bernardin's experiment in transplantation would be the breakdown of "natural" boundaries between these displaced peoples through a sexual rapprochement. Bernardin envisions the marriage of the children of the Ganges and the Thames, of Amerindians and Spaniards; "the Negress from Guinea, with her coral necklace and ivory teeth, would smile at the son of the European who once placed her forefathers in irons, and would desire no other vengeance this time around than shackling the son in her ebony arms." For Bernardin, such marriages lead us into a multiracialized future where it becomes possible again to conceive of the eventual reunion of "the members of mankind's vast family" (3.94), as is even clearer in a slightly earlier version of this same experimental scenario that he included in his *Études*:

What joy for us to delight in their joy, to see their dances in public and to hear the sound of the blacks' ivory horns echoing round the statues of our kings! Ah, if we were good, I imagine them [*je me les figure*] being touched by the excessive and unhappy population of our cities and inviting us to spread out on their lonely expanses, to enter into marriages with them, and through these new alliances to draw closer the various branches of mankind, which are becoming more and more distant from one another, and which national passions divide even more than centuries and climes. (3.95)

What we are presented with in passages like this is an emphasis not on the categorical logic of disfiguration that generates much of Bernardin's work and that enables the vision of "closed circulation" we looked at a few pages back but, rather, the privileging of a very different sort of "figuration," a productive reconfiguration of the "nouvelles alliances" to which he also referred in that passage ("le caractère européen . . . soupire toujours après de nouvelles alliances avec ses compatriotes").

Contesting the divisive and increasingly deadly "passions" that have been such a consistent feature of the modern nation-state, Bernardin's neopastoral scenario of cross-cultural fertilization—notwithstanding its lingering biases and its evident utopianism—is of obvious genealogical relevance to recent evaluations and valorizations of the creolization process, as the following passage from the *Éloge de la Créolité* clearly attests:

Cultures are merging, and are full of subcultures that are themselves generating other cultural aggregates. To think about today's world, about a man's identity, about a people or a culture's first principles, in the terms of the eighteenth or the nineteenth century would be an impoverishment. More and more, a new humanity will be emerging, one that will have the characteristics of our creole humanity: all the complexity of Créolité. Born and living in Peking, the son of a German married to a Haitian woman will be torn between several languages, several histories; he will be caught up in the torrential ambiguity of a mosaic identity. (pp. 52–53)

The (un)likeness of Bernardin's scenario to this one from the *Éloge* should be obvious, and it both confirms and puts into question the progressivist rhetoric that the latter invoke in their critique of "impoverished" eighteenth- and nineteenth-century conceptions of identity (while also, of course, drawing our attention to the male "gendering" of Créolité).[49] The "claire harmonie du monde" envisioned by Bernardin has certainly been replaced by a more dissonant and ambiguous model for thinking about the world, one that can better conceive of opaque and centrifugal ("diversal") relations in which fragmentation has become the point of departure for a new humanity rather than the obstacle that must be overcome if it is to be achieved. And yet the postcolonial vision of métissage doubles back upon its colonial predecessor in its continued reliance on, for example, national identities and heterosexual coupling as the means through which the complexity of an "identité mosaïque" can be figured. If, as it has been argued, postcolonialism "is perhaps the sign of an increasing awareness that it is not feasible to subtract a culture, a history, a language, an identity, from the wider, transforming currents of the increasingly metropolitan world,"[50] then the cosmopolitan scenarios of both Bernardin and the authors of the *Éloge* inscribe that same sign, although each does so with a more or less lingering investment in "subtractive" conceptions of culture, language, and identity that testifies to the never-finalized status of this "increasing awareness."

Writing during the years immediately preceding and following upon the outbreak of the French Revolution, Bernardin was peculiarly well situated to bear witness to the "increasingly metropolitan world" that was taking shape at this time. As his immediate successor in the realm of exotic fiction, Chateaubriand, put it in 1814, "today, when news travels from St. Petersburg to Paris in a fortnight; when it takes only a few minutes for a dispatch from Strasbourg and even Milan to reach the Tuileries; when all the nations are acquainted with one another, have mixed together, and know each other's languages and history; when the printing press has become an always open rostrum that anyone can use to make themselves heard, there is simply no way of isolating oneself and of escaping from the march of Europe."[51] Chateaubriand's comments about such things as the mixed nature of national identity, the impossibility of cultural and political isolation, and the ubiquity of print culture, could already be extended to include the entire world, as Homi Bhabha has suggested in his discussion of Goethe's "profoundly Eurocentric" but nonetheless groundbreaking formulation of a "world literature" in the opening decades of the nineteenth century: as Bhabha points out, this idea can and should be read as an "emergent, prefigurative category" that extends beyond the parochial boundaries within which Goethe situates it, establishing the grounds for "a comparative method that would speak to the 'unhomely' condition of the modern world," interrogating the "border and frontier conditions" that a transnational modernity promotes (*LC*, pp. 11–12). It is an open confrontation with this unhomeliness that the recourse to pastoral in *Paul et Virginie* attempts to defer, exemplifying the horrified reaction to "cultural fragmentation and mobility" that characterizes the antimodern critical tradition inaugurated by writers like Rousseau and Schiller—a tradition that, in Iain Chambers's words, has fought "an endless rearguard action against modernity," disavowing "the discontinuous tempos and cultures of the city, commerce and modernity" and persistently seeking "radical alternatives in the assumed continuities of folk cultures, 'authentic' habits and 'genuine' communities."[52]

But, as I have tried to show in this "global" survey of Bernardin's oeuvre, the author of *Paul et Virginie* is acutely aware of the transnational implications of even the most local of actions and this awareness generates a contrary critical position—simultaneously neopastoral and creolizing—that works with(in) the "increasingly metropolitan" world that a part of him would like to reject but that he often also draws to his reader's attention, as when he notes in the *Études* that "today, a savage is oppressed in the American desert, and the flight of his arrows leads from family to family, from nation to nation, and war flares up in the four corners of the world," and concludes from this that "we are all of us interdependent" (3.63; "Nous sommes tous solidaires les uns pour les autres"). It is this same global solidarity that he points to in his 1789 account of the transnational origins of the French Revolution, where he refers to "the last war, which mobilized England, France, Spain, Portugal, Holland, the Cape of Good Hope, the East Indies, North and South America, and which brought the government's deficits to such a state that the Estates-General have now had to be convened," and notes that this war, in turn, "owed its origin to the East India Company, which wanted to force the inhabitants of Boston to pay a tax on tea" (11.78). To face up to the relational complexities of the cosmopolitan world that Bernardin here describes is to put into question, without denying the urgency of, the search for radical alternatives that begins to dominate political and cultural discourse in the closing decades of the eighteenth century, and that takes the double form of a quest for assumed continuities with the past or calls for breaking with the present in the name of a revolutionary future. Appearances to the contrary, such appeals to the future are yet another sort of rearguard action bent on erasing the unhomely conditions that elicit them; under these conditions, any revolution—from the natural revolutions that Rousseau posited as being at the insular origins of human language to the political apocalypses that have so obsessed our modernity and its countercultures—will result not in an entirely new language or a "new humanity" but in an ever more perplexing and contradictory mixing together of old ones.

The question of (the nostalgia for, and of) revolutionary futures will occupy us at length in later chapters of this book. What I will be looking at in my reading of *Paul et Virginie* is the other side of modernity's double-directed longing, Bernardin's pastoral attempts at invoking the simplicity of a past time from which the creolizing-colonizing-novelizing energies of the present would be absent; the conflictual presence of these two times makes for the liminality of his text, which is at once the culminating example of the Enlightenment's ahistorical exoticism and the opening salvo of a post/colonial literature that is inextricably implicated in the chaotic unfolding of global history. If, as one critic puts it in a description of literary exoticism during the age of Enlightenment, "before the French Revolution, colonial life such as men of letters represented it seemed to unfold outside time and on the margins of history . . . frozen in its exotic changelessness,"[53] then Bernardin's pastoral, despite its best (or worst) Rousseauesque intentions, enacts the death of this exoticism and the consequent birth of a new double vision of the world, simultaneously colonial and creole. It is this same death that Édouard Glissant described at the very outset of a career that has taken the dissolution of the essentializing and pastoralizing absolutes of the Negritude movement as its point of departure:

Exoticism is well and truly dead from the moment geography ceases to be absolute (that is to say, limited to itself) and begins joining up with its history, which is that of mankind. The apposition of landscapes confirms that of cultures and sensibilities: not as an exaltation of the Unknown, but as a way of finally shedding one's skin in order to see oneself projected in another light, as the shadowy outline of what one will be [*comme manière enfin de se débarrasser de son écorce pour connaître sa projection dans une autre lumière, l'ombre de ce que l'on sera*]. (SC, p. 69)

Often (mis)understood as the very model of the conventional exoticism whose death Glissant is here celebrating, *Paul et Virginie* must also be read as initiating us into the loss of an "absolute" geography. It confronts us with a land- and culture-scape that certainly recalls to us, to play off the lines from the early-twentieth-century Italian poet Guido Gozzano that serve as epigraph to this section,[54] "the lost homeland" that we never knew (Glissant's "Unknown") but that equally compels us to "re-cognize" that country, to know it again, translating the exotic into the relativizing and relational terms that signal its death, projecting it anew, rereading it in the problematic light of our ever present modernity, as both the shadow of what it once (never) was and "l'ombre de ce que l'on sera."

Colonial Endings, Creole Beginnings: The Mimetic Affinities of 'Paul et Virginie'

> In the labyrinth where I had lost my way, I stubbornly set
> about looking for the thread that would lead me back to
> the old world of childhood.
> —Marie-Thérèse Humbert, *À l'autre bout de moi*

In 1904, Victor Segalen wrote the first of a series of notes toward a never-finished *Essai sur l'Exotisme* that has come to be viewed by many postcolonial writers (notably, Glissant and the authors of the *Éloge*) as one of the founding documents in a truly post-exoticist approach to cultural diversity. In this note, Segalen sets out his project: "To write a book on Exoticism: Bernardin de Saint-Pierre—Chateaubriand—Marco Polo the initiator—Loti."[55] It is only toward the very end of the decade, however, that he will begin to elaborate upon this project, and by this time a radical change in his thinking has occurred that leads him to abandon the sort of conventionally linear history he had previously envisioned. This palinodic shift can be read in the gloss of his earlier reference to Bernardin in a 1911 entry from the *Essai* written in China: "Read only here at Tientsin seven years later. Doubtless cited [an illegible word] contempt for his insipidity" (p. 766). Whatever the illegible word may have been, the negative tone of Segalen's reaction to his "insipid" predecessor is unmistakable, and reflects the canonical modernist (mis)understanding of Bernardin's work through which any rereading of it must be filtered.

We find this same gesture of distancing at work in Alejo Carpentier's response to the question of whether or not his *Explosion in a Cathedral* had been at all influenced by Bernardin de Saint-Pierre. Carpentier is adamant about the lack of any such influence. The attraction that a writer like Bernardin could exercise on him, he notes,

is virtually nil. Given that the novel takes place in an age when Europeans were, in practice, discovering exotic nature, there could be some coincidence as far as descriptions and so on are concerned. However, if you look carefully, you will see that, in effect, my descriptions of landscape are very timeless; that the same thing could have been written down in the eighteenth century as in the present age. On the other hand, I must confess to you that I have always greatly admired a book like Albert Camus's *Noces*.[56]

Carpentier's account of his own novel here privileges what in the opening pages of this book I have characterized as the natural (as opposed to cultural) manifestation of "lo real maravilloso," which reveals itself through the senses to any individual who, like Esteban, is capable of momentarily escaping the absurd confines of his bureaucratized, historical identity. The appeal of Camus's *Noces* (1938) is not, in this context, hard to understand: programmatically avoiding any confrontation with the colonial context out of which they emerged, the young Camus's essayistic portraits of his native Algeria oscillate between, on the one hand, self-absorbed poetic meditations on such things as solitude, silence, and death and, on the other, the occasionally voiced "foolish hope that perhaps, unwittingly, [the French Algerians]—a people without a past, without traditions, and yet not without poetry—are in the process of shaping a culture in which the greatness of man will finally find its true expression."[57] For the Camus of *Noces*, ultimately, "the world always ends up defeating history" (p. 65), and Carpentier's admiration for its "timeless" qualities testifies to the close connections between his vision of a marvelous reality and the existentialism that

Walcott once decried as "simply the myth of the noble savage gone baroque."[58] While Carpentier's remarks about the temporality of Bernardin's exoticism appear simply to be insinuating its dated quality, they also alert us (in a perhaps unintentionally perceptive manner) to the inseparability of this exoticism, its pastoral intentions notwithstanding, from an intimate engagement with history that makes *Paul et Virginie*, from the modernist perspective Carpentier here adopts, the very model of an unreadable text—in Camus's (anxiously?) dismissive characterization of it, a "truly pathetic piece of work."[59] Needless to say, it is precisely the temporality of Bernardin's text that ensures its rereadability in a post/modern age that is especially critical, though by no means free, of "modernism's purist break with history."[60]

When he arrived on the Île de France in 1768, the thirty-year-old Bernardin was already an experienced traveler, having spent the past decade wandering from one European country to another, hawking his talents as a military engineer and seeking the patronage of the likes of Catherine the Great, to whom he once proposed the idea of founding a "colony of adventurers" who would pursue the realization of his "Projet d'une compagnie pour la découverte d'un passage aux Indes par la Russie" (2.310). Reflecting on these repeated displacements from his native Normandy, Bernardin speaks regretfully of having "forgotten his own language,"[61] and his later work as an author can be viewed as one long attempt at rediscovering that lost tongue. His sojourn on the Île de France represents the last episode in this youthful phase of migrancy. Attracted to this colony by the same instincts that motivated a prominent Enlightenment writer such as Rousseau to look to an island (Corsica) as the most likely site for his envisioned social reforms, he set out from France as part of an expedition that was to establish a colonial settlement on Madagascar, but quickly fell out with the leaders of that expedition (who, far from being motivated by his utopian ideals, were simply intent on developing the trade in slaves on the island). He disembarked at Port-Louis, after an arduous four-and-a-half-month journey out, where he took up his appointment as King's engineer. The rapidly growing colony was at that time in flux,[62] the group of islands known as the Mascarenes having been only a few years before (1765) placed under the direct administration of France after four decades of being controlled by the Compagnie des Indes (the previously uninhabited Île de France had been initially colonized by the Dutch in the seventeenth century, abandoned by them in 1710, claimed by France five years later, and subsequently recolonized starting in 1721).

Bernardin's first account of his over two-year stay on the island was the epistolary travelogue, *Voyage à l'Île de France* (1773), "a heterogeneous mixture of discursive practices" that anticipates the fragmentary and idiosyncratic nature of much of his later work.[63] A financially unsuccessful effort, it nonetheless made him some prominent friends in France (most notably, Rousseau, whose disciple Bernardin would become during the last years of the Genevan philosopher's life), but also greatly offended the island's (white) creole population, who succeeded in having sale of the work banned there. This reaction was due mostly to Bernardin's negative portrayal of master-slave relations on the island—a place where, as he said of the "Fortunate Isles" in his autobiographical allegory "Voyage de Codrus," there was "neither liberty, nor society, nor honest emulation," and of which he concluded that "of all the countries I have seen, I have not found another where it is more disagreeable to live" (6.326). The predominantly negative tone of the Voyage bears witness to a typically Enlightenment critique of the worldwide excesses of European militarism and imperialism (describing his many travels abroad in the later Études, he asserts that "I have only seen countries frequented by Europeans and desolated by war and slavery" [3.223]), but this critique has itself become inseparable from a more personal dissatisfaction with the world of "second contact" that colonialism creates—a dissatisfaction that anticipates the peculiarly modern sense of belatedness that would be at the heart of so many nineteenth-century encounters with the exotic. Bernardin's first published work records the absence of those "virginal beauties" that he imagines were seen by "the first sailors to discover uninhabited islands" (3.223). The world he describes in the Voyage is one in which there can be no positive response to the ubi sunt question that he poses at the very end of this book: "where are the games of childhood [du premier âge], those days that were so full, without cares and without bitterness?" (2.92). It is only in the wake of such insights into the island's unnatural, secondary condition that his own "second contact" with it in Paul et Virginie can be read and a response to those questions given, as Bernardin takes up the imaginary thread that he hopes, like the protagonist of the Mauritian novelist Marie-Thérèse Humbert's À l'autre bout de moi (1979), will lead him back to the "vieux pays de l'enfance." Reversing the disenchanted trajectory of the Voyage, which ends with Bernardin back in France and "restored to a natural life" (2.82), Paul et Virginie effects a knowingly fictional return to a renaturalized island that is situated at a memorial distance from the original upon which it is based.[64] If, as Racault has pointed out, "for Bernardin islands are the topographical figure of immanence, of coinciding with oneself,"[65] then this figure, and the remedies it offers ("it was to offer men a refuge from the evils of the continent that nature formed islands" [VF, p. 425]), will be repeatedly disfigured and refigured in the face of this distance and the exilic knowledge that, as Sainte-Beuve so nicely put it in his sensitive 1836 portrait of Bernardin, "those Arcadias, those Fortunate Isles, exist only in the mists of hope or of memory."[66]

It was no doubt to augment the impression of an immanent, self-enclosed world that, when writing the definitive version of *Paul et Virginie*, Bernardin changed the birthplace of its eponymous male protagonist from France to the Île de France, thus making it match that of his "Dioscuric" counterpart Virginie.[67] By virtue of their purely insular origins, these "two Creoles" (to cite the title of an 1806 pantomime based on Bernardin's book)[68] appear more completely at home in the genesial world that Bernardin is attempting to construct for them in order to prove his thesis that, as he puts it in the 1788 preface, "our happiness consists in living according to nature and virtue" (p. 78). The irony, of course, will be that in thus insulating his characters from the outside world he has also more fully creolized them, attaching them to a cross-culturalized home that will always also be for its inhabitants an unhomely place, at a remove from any and all ancestral sites of origin. Given the recent establishment of the French colony (Paul and Virginie would appear to have been born in 1725 and 1726, respectively), their parents are of necessity not island-born; as a result, the problematic of exile from France, "la patrie" (p. 105), is largely mediated through them. Paul's mother is a peasant woman from Brittany who was impregnated out of wedlock by a nobleman and who subsequently decided to "go hide her misdeed in the colonies" (p. 106); the mother of Virginie, Mme de La Tour, was born into an aristocratic Norman family but married beneath her rank and emigrated to the island with her husband, who himself died very soon thereafter. Brought together by that Providence in which Bernardin so firmly believed (p. 105), the two women live side by side on their settlements (*habitations*), in an isolated basin on the mountain overlooking Port-Louis, attended only by an adult male neighbor and two older and zealously devoted slaves, the Wolof Domingue and Marie from Madagascar, whom the women managed to secure after their arrival on the island and who have since married one another.[69] Paul and Virginie spend the idyllic childhood described in the first third of the text within the pastoral confines of this little community, which (re)creates the matriarchal conditions that for Bernardin first enabled the founding of human society ("the first founder of human society was a mother" [p. 357]) and that ensure a harmonious relation to nature (since women, as he puts it in the *Études*, "are always closer to nature [than men]" [5.10]). The rest of the text chronicles the melancholic aftermath of this childhood: rather than let nature take its course and permit the two children to marry young, the still class-conscious Mme de La Tour allows the fifteen-year-old Virginie to be sent to France to be "educated" by her rich aunt, a traumatic exile from which neither of the two adolescents will ever recover. Almost three years later, returning to the island, Virginie will die in a shipwreck within sight of her native land (refusing, in an egregious display of virtue, to take off her garments so that a

sailor can help her swim ashore), a watery end that is then reinforced by the
deaths in rapid succession of the remaining members of the two families.

The story is told by the neighbor who had helped the two women establish themselves on the island. His is a belated narrative, taking place well
after the events chronicled. Now an old man, he relates the story of the two
families to an unnamed individual who has found his way to the isolated
locale and who in fact narrates the opening pages of *Paul et Virginie*.[70] It is
this old man, double of the author himself, who lays the foundations for a
pastoral interpretation of the story that he is telling, both within the tale
and in the telling of it: he describes himself, for instance, as having engraved
a line from Virgil's *Georgics* in praise of the rural life onto the bark of a
tree under which Paul sometimes sat (p. 145); his narrative is, moreover, interwoven with a set of post facto theoretical interventions that attempt to
fix the meaning of his characters by connecting them back to earlier literary
and cultural models—in much the same *allegorical* manner, say, as Columbus attempted to make the New World comprehensible by renaming it
(with)in the terms of the Old. The most notable of such models used to further the organic thesis that he so insistently voices (e.g., "their life seemed
linked to that of the trees, like that of fauns and dryads" [p. 162]) is, predictably, the story of Genesis:

Their youth had all the freshness of dawn. They were like our first forebears in the
garden of Eden when, emerging from the hands of God, they saw one another and,
drawing near, began to talk with one another like brother and sister: Virginie, gentle, modest, trustful like Eve; and Paul, similar to Adam, having the height of a man
and the simplicity of a child. (p. 163)

The *identification* of Paul and Virginie with Adam and Eve is, of course,
also an act of *translation*, as with any recourse to an allegorical mode of
representation, which establishes a temporal relation between texts, between past and present, that necessarily undermines the narrator's claims
for the timelessness of characters who "had neither clocks, nor almanacs,
nor books of chronology, history, or philosophy" (p. 161). The translational condition that allegory enacts is, moreover, a basic feature of all intertextual relations. As several critics have pointed out, the narrator's rejection of "you Europeans" (p. 161) and his appeals to an insular nature are,
given the ubiquity of "citational utterances" in *Paul et Virginie*, on extremely unstable ground since "from the outset the supposedly sheltered
world is, in a more or less direct fashion, striated with the values of the antagonistic universe."[71]

To make such broad-ranging deconstructive claims about the destabilizing role of allegory and intertextuality in *Paul et Virginie* is a necessary first
step in any interpretation that attempts to read it as a text that has something interesting to tell us about post/colonial literature and the creolization

process. In order to take the next step, we must more exactly situate the narrator's allusion to Eden in the context of his narrative: it occurs at a point about a third of the way through the text when the narrator is making his most forceful interpretive claims about "these two children of nature." Within a very few pages, the temporal problematic that is at the core of allegorical representation will be explicitly confronted in the form of Virginie's "mysterious illness"—the first stirrings of puberty and of an unacknowledged sexual desire for Paul that will eventually lead to the dissolution of their "première enfance" (p. 118) and her exile from him and the island. As Renata Wasserman points out, the myth of paradise "breaks up at the irruption of sexuality, at the introduction, with the notion of successive generations, of historical time." For Bernardin, "nature beckons with a promise of abolishing alienating social rules, but the biological fact of puberty carries along with it all the rules governing the exchange of sexual partners and, implicitly, the transmission of culture."[72] The narrator's claims at this particular juncture in the text are thus part of a peroration, marking the end of the primary part of his argument, and clearing the way for the onset of the second(ary), more (im)properly novelistic, part of the text.[73] The beginning of this second(ary) part has, however, itself been repeatedly preenacted in the first third of *Paul et Virginie*, and nowhere more crucially than in the episode that immediately precedes the narrator's climactic claims—an episode that features what is perhaps the text's most telling insight into the creolized culture upon which he has been constructing his (theories of an) Edenic nature.

Describing the outdoor meals that he was in the habit of sharing with the two families on Sundays, the narrator notes that Virginie would afterwards sing, and

quelquefois, à la manière des Noirs, elle exécutait avec Paul une pantomime. La pantomime est le premier langage de l'homme: elle est connue de toutes les nations: elle est si naturelle et si expressive, que les enfants des Blancs ne tardent pas à l'apprendre, dès qu'ils ont vu ceux des Noirs s'y exercer. Virginie se rappelant, dans les lectures que lui faisait sa mère, les histoires qui l'avaient le plus touchée, en rendait les principaux événements avec beaucoup de naïveté. (p. 157)

sometimes, in the manner of the blacks, she would perform a pantomime show with Paul. Mime is the first language of man: it is known to all nations; it is so natural and so expressive that once they have seen the children of the blacks doing it, the white children learn it quickly. Recalling the stories that her mother used to read to her, Virginie would act out with great ingenuousness the principal episodes of those that had most touched her.

Here, the primary and the natural ("premier," "naturelle") are affirmed and yet at the same time rendered as the secondary effects of a mimesis made possible by cross-cultural relations, since the "first language of man" and its gestural vocabulary has to be learned from others ("à la manière des Noirs"). The loss of nature that reveals itself in this crossing of cultures is, moreover, even more emphatically evident in Virginie's reliance on written texts, previous readings that connect their supposedly "naive" pantomime to the "sentimental," in Schiller's sense of the word, problematic of history ("les histoires") and exile. The two stories that Bernardin cites are biblical, the first—the story of Moses at the well of Midian—being taken from the beginning of Exodus (significantly enough, the *second* book of the Bible), and the other being the story of Ruth. Both readings are themselves caught up in the intertextual dynamic of translation and *mis*reading, most obviously in their elision of the cultural mobility that underlies each biblical narrative. The episode from Exodus (2.15–22), of course, occurs during Israel's bondage and rather than simply ending, as does Virginie's pantomime, with the marriage of Moses and Zipporah (2.21), its final verse records the birth of a son whom Moses calls Gershom because, as he puts it, "I have been an alien [*ger*] residing in a foreign land" (2.22). The other reading is at an even further remove from its original model, inasmuch as the story's protagonist is erroneously identified as "the unfortunate Ruth, who returns widowed and poor to her own country, where after a long absence she finds herself a foreigner [*étrangère*]" (pp. 157–58). Here, the "strangeness" of Ruth has been domesticated, her linear (im)migration to a foreign country transformed into a circular return to the place of her birth; the act of translation that is at the very heart of Ruth's story, and that has made it such a touchstone for recent critics interested in the textual and political connections between Self and Other,[74] has been erased and replaced by the strangest of "absences"—an absence grounded in a presence that never was. In this glaring distortion of a well-known biblical story, Bernardin forces the reader to think in terms of the very displacements that have dropped out of sight in Paul and Virginie's translated version.

Ultimately, the pantomime episode leads into a general consideration of issues of theatricality, and of representation itself, that would take us too far afield from the specific concerns of our analysis: by explicitly situating his characters in the context of a theatrical "spectacle" (p. 158), Bernardin subverts his own intentions, exiling his characters to a world in which, to cite Rousseau's 1755 *Discours*, "being and appearing" have become "two entirely different things" (a distinction that, according to Rousseau, has promoted "gaudy pomp, deceitful ruse, and all their attendant vices").[75] Moreover, in forcing the reader to confront this gap between appearance and being, between the (secular) figures who act and the (sacred) originals that they (re)enact, this episode functions as a veritable *mise en abyme* showing up the extent to which the pastoral life that the two families are living is itself, like their own pantomimic "representing" of the "patriarchal" life (pp. 157, 158), nothing more than an appearance, a representative fiction. For our purposes, however, it is the cross-cultural dimension of this episode that is of most interest because it points toward the mimetic education, and the education in mimesis, that is at the heart of the creolization process. As Bhabha has pointed out, mimicry is a mode of colonial discourse that is constructed around an ambivalent, unsettling *resemblance* between colonizer and colonized: in "problematiz[ing] the signs of racial and cultural priority" and "destroy[ing] narcissistic authority through the repetitious slippage of difference and desire" (*LC*, pp. 87, 90), such mimetic relations displace the Manichean divisions that are essential to the imposition of colonial authority and identities. Always present as a potential menace to colonial discourse (and to the equally narcissistic authority of anticolonial discourse), such relations of (un)likeness are *also* the ambivalent ground upon which creole societies are created, and become creative.

Such relations are both impeded and facilitated by the fact that the protagonists live on a remote island. On the one hand, their isolation can be seen as promoting a cultural stasis, and Bernardin's narrator certainly engages at times in a not entirely positive portrayal of creole life that is complicitous with the sort of classificatory outlook we examined in the first section of this chapter: from this typological perspective, it is possible to speak, for instance, of "idle Creoles and their customs" (p. 245), of Paul being "indifferent as a Creole when it came to what was happening in the world" (p. 200), or of the young children not knowing how to read or write and thus being "ignorants comme des Créoles" (p. 117). Such relatively neutral characterizations obviously lay the foundations for a more negative assessment of (white) creole life, of the sort that one finds, for instance, in Leconte de Lisle's dismissive account of his fellow islanders in the short story "Sacatove" (1846). "The Creole is a prematurely solemn man," he informs us, "who only interests himself in what can show a clear profit, in irrefutable sums, in the harmonious sounds of minted metal; after that, everything else is pointless—love, friendship, desire of the unknown, intelligence and knowledge: all that is not worth a single coffee bean."[76] But, viewed from another perspective, this "ignorance" of and "indifference" to the world create the conditions for the emergence of a creolized society, one that does not defer to ancestral models but shapes itself according to the intercultural demands of the location itself. As Bernardin once put it, "an island is a little world in miniature" (4.415), meaning not only that islands are worlds unto themselves but also that the world itself can be found within them. Precisely because Paul and Virginie "believed that the world ended where their island ended, and could imagine nothing pleasant that was not right where they were" (pp. 117–18), their lives are in many respects supremely open to the world and to the sort of mimetic cultural interactions conveyed in a phrase like "à la manière des Noirs" (one that is also used to describe Paul's technique of lighting a fire [p. 128]).

This sort of mutual understanding, this cultural "interstanding" (in Brathwaite's words), potentially differentiates the two creole children from their parents, who maintain a lingering commitment to the values of the metropole in which they were brought up (an attachment that will lead to Virginie's exile from "the place where I was born" [p. 206], and to her eventual death). We are told, for instance, that the two women rarely went to Port-Louis, "for fear of being looked down on because they were dressed in the same coarse blue Bengali cloth as the slaves used" (p. 112). They continue to read this cross-cultural dressing, as it were, within the negative terms that their European education demands—hierarchical terms that the (white) inhabitants of Port-Louis themselves clearly (attempt to) retain, their supposed indifference to and ignorance of the outside world notwithstanding. The colonial society remains in great part attached to metropolitan values that it cannot fully replicate but that remain decisive for the containment of the "more reciprocal activity, a process of intermixture and enrichment, each to each" that is ideally constitutive of creole societies.[77] What results from this mimetic attachment to Europe is, in Bhabha's phrase, a world that is "almost the same but not quite," as the very name of the Île de France, in the (im)perfect doubling of its distant eponymn, bears witness.[78] The two mothers remain attached to the world that they have left behind, as is evident from the fact that they "gave the names Brittany and Normandy to the little plots of land where they had sowed corn, strawberries, and peas" (p. 146). Ironically enough, this allegorical practice of connecting the unfamiliar new world to, and thereby disconnecting it from, the familiar old one can itself be learnt through the very same process of cross-cultural mimesis that enables the emergence of creole society, as when we find Domingue and Marie duplicating Mme de La Tour and Marguerite's acts of naming: "desiring, in imitation of their mistresses, to recall the places in Africa where they were born, [they] gave the names Angola and Foulpointe [in Madagascar] to the two spots where the grass with which they wove baskets grew and where they had planted a calabash tree" (p. 146). Subject to the complexities of cultural translation, such allegorical practices are necessarily imperfect, as both the Wolof Domingue's obvious misnaming of his place of birth and the inextricably mixed Caribbean and African referents of the name of the tree they (trans)plant suggest.[79] By virtue of their second generation status, Paul and Virginie are more open than their elders to the possibilities of "indigenization," that creative grounding in one's native land out of which an "authentically" creole society might emerge from the shadow of its Old World antecedents—a never complete emergence, to be sure, and an always problematic authenticity since it cannot be fully disentangled from the sort of mimetic complications that we have been looking at (as Brathwaite cautions, when he notes of Caribbean societies that "our real/apparent imitation involves at the same time a significant element of creativity, while our creativity in turn involves a significant element of imitation" [CO, p. 16]). In thus opening out onto the possibilities of a creole narrative, however, *Paul et Virginie* ineluctably moves away from the site of pastoral origins that Bernardin is trying to locate in his text but that, as the pantomime episode suggests, can only be mimetically (re)presented there.

The very phrase "creole narrative" needs to be read as a tautology, inasmuch as the cultural transactions upon which creole identities and practices depend are part of an additive (and also subtractive) process that is indissociable from narrative itself. To take an extremely banal example, it is this supplementary process that the narrator of *Paul et Virginie* identifies when (with a Carpentieresque attention to the fruits of the vine) he notes how, for his outdoor meals with the two families, he would bring along "some bottles of old wine, in order to add to [*augmenter*] the gaiety of our Indian meals with these sweet and invigorating products of Europe" (pp. 155–56). It is this narrative process of augmentation that Bernardin identifies in a curious passage from his *Harmonies* that serves as a deconstructive gloss on the "première enfance" he is trying to depict in his pastoral. As Bernardin had pointed out in the *Études*, "the very word *enfant* comes from the Latin *infans*, that is to say, one who does not speak" (5.14). In the *Harmonies*, he reflects at greater length on the original components of this word and their "weak" relation to it: "in general, compound words [*les mots composés*] are much stronger than their roots; but they often have quite another meaning. . . . *Infans*, child, conveys more than *non fans*, one who does not speak" (10.32). An act of composition has resulted in the loss of the word *enfant*'s original meaning (its "signification primitive") and the emergence of a secondary, "stronger" meaning. At times, Bernardin goes on to warn, it will be necessary for him to draw both meanings to his reader's attention, and for that reason "I will be careful to separate by a hyphen compounded words from their prepositions [e.g., *in-fans*], whenever I find it necessary to reduce them to their original meaning [*les ramener à leur signification primitive*], which will be more expedient than a periphrasis and less unfamiliar than a new word" (10.33). As he also notes, "merely by separating compound words with a hyphen one sometimes gives them a different meaning from what they had when they were compounded. Often, this new meaning is weaker: *Vis unita major*, in unity there is strength [*les forces augmentent par leur union*]" (10.32–33).

What this example points to, of course, is the secondary nature of the "enfance" that in *Paul et Virginie* Bernardin is attempting to portray in terms of primacy: in order for this "enfance" to be spoken, it must first be composed, drawn from an original silence into the realm of a speech in which it has only the appearance of strength—an appearance that any awareness of its mixed origins necessarily attenuates. The irony of this situation is itself doubled by the fact that the return to these original roots and to the word's "signification primitive"—a return that so emphatically echoes the narrator's stated enterprise in *Paul et Virginie*: namely, to lead back (*ramener*) his listeners "à la nature"—is here seen as resulting not in the resurfacing of old meanings but in the production of a *new* one in the form of a tripartite word ("in-fans") that is visibly marked by the same hybrid condition we identified in our reading of Glissant's phrase "identité-relation" (at the end of Chapter 2). Bernardin's deconstructive analyses of *enfance* and of *in-fans* thus both, in their different ways, break down the sense of primacy and unity that these words at first sight evoke and that is central to the anti-narrative intentions of *Paul et Virginie*; in so doing, they draw our attention to a more complex state of affairs, a state of com-position and dis-unity symbolized by the *trait d'union* that divides even as it unifies.

As I argued in the first half of this chapter, Bernardin's writings are often refreshingly open to the supplementary possibilities of creole narrative, and *Paul et Virginie* bears traces of this openness, despite its deep resistance to narrative. This resistance stems from the fact that Bernardin associates narrative primarily with colonial expansion and the dissemination to all parts of the globe of "our history, which has been nothing more than one long series of conflicts, supplying more wars, atrocities, lawsuits, feuds, duels, and robberies than all the rest of the world put together" (*VF*, p. 251). "Colonial narrative" is, after all, just as much of a tautology as "creole narrative," which raises the question of exactly how to separate the "augmentations" of the one from those of the other. The *pre*-narrative pastoral world that dominates the opening third of *Paul et Virginie* is constructed as a way of avoiding this (ultimately unanswerable) question altogether. That this world self-de(con)structs is what I have suggested in my analysis of the novel up to this point. In the remainder of this chapter, I will demonstrate some of the ways in which Bernardin actively inscribes, rather than occludes, the destructiveness of colonial narrative in his text, and then attempts to put an end to it in an apocalyptic gesture of closure that actually replicates the violence of the very narrative that he is contesting.

For Bernardin, the narrative of colonialism has as its central protagonist an authoritative father figure who stands in opposition to the primitive matriarchy upon which the pastoral fiction of *Paul et Virginie* is founded, and who also functions as a negative double of the benignly paternal authority (ostensibly) embodied by its narrator—and by the author himself.[80] This figure was, in fact, present at the very beginning of the old man's narration in the person of M. de La Tour, who had come to the island in 1726 to "seek his fortune," and having left his new wife at Port-Louis, "embarked for Madagascar, in the hope of buying some blacks and quickly returning to set up a plantation [*former une habitation*]" (p. 104). M. de La Tour thus exemplifies that "ambitious spirit" Bernardin identified as the peculiar vice of Europeans, one that had introduced slavery to the island "and thereby turned every habitant into a tyrant . . . and that divvied up the land [there] into what are called habitations, of which the smallest are 200 arpents and of which I have seen 80 habitations, 16,000 arpents, granted to the same owner" (*VF*, p. 431). The ambitious M. de La Tour quickly dies of the "pestilential fevers that prevail [in Madagascar] for half the year, and that will always prevent European nations from settling there on a permanent basis" (pp. 104–5). Notwithstanding this sacrificial gesture through which the pastoral world is cleansed of its colonial preconditions, the repressed figure of the father repeatedly comes back to haunt the text; most obviously embodied by the slave-owning habitant who lives on the banks of the Black River and around whom the text's first extended narrative sequence is centered (pp. 124–38),[81] this malignant authority is that which eventually, through the dictates of the colony's governor, M. de La Bourdonnais, puts an end once and for all to Paul and Virginie's isolation, drawing them into a world of colonial relations that for Bernardin can only be synonymous with exile and death.

In the lengthy 1806 "Preamble" to *Paul et Virginie*, Bernardin speaks very favorably of Mahé de La Bourdonnais, "that illustrious founder of the French colony of Île de France" ("all the most useful and most effectively carried out things that I saw on this island were his work" [pp. 340, 342]), but within the terms of his exotic fiction this male *fondateur*, who governed the island from 1735 to 1746, serves as the embodiment of an unnatural colonial power that works against the best interests of creole society and for those of decadent *métropolitains* for whom the island can only be a "country of savages" (p. 206). La Bourdonnais's role in the novel is primarily to serve as a mediator between the two families and Mme de La Tour's rich French aunt. It is in this context that we are first briefly introduced to him near the beginning of the story: his entry into the text is prefaced by the second of its three explicit references to historical chronology ("finally in 1738, three years after the arrival of M. de La Bourdonnais on this island, Mme de La Tour learned that the governor had a letter from her aunt to deliver to her" [p. 121]), thus linking him back to M. de La Tour's 1726 arrival on the island and subsequent slaving expedition to Madagascar and forward to the shipwreck of December 24, 1744, in which Virginie dies. The aunt having self-servingly maligned her niece in her attached note to the governor, La Bourdonnais treats Mme de La Tour with an extreme coldness when handing over the hypocritically judgmental letter, thus marking his suscep-tibility to the rhetorical distortions of (the aunt's) writing, his undue regard for what Bernardin would term, in the 1789 foreword, a deceptive elo-quence that "paints nothing as it is [*au naturel*]," that makes "small things big and big ones small, as it was once defined by an interested party, a rhetorician," and to which he opposes a "natural eloquence" that is "the very body of human thought" rather than simply its clothes (p. 93).

This brief exposure to the forces of history and rhetoric anticipates La Bourdonnais's second, and this time fatal, appearance in the novel, which occurs very soon after the revelation of Virginie's "illness" and in the midst of Mme de La Tour's anxieties about Marguerite's suggestion that they sim-ply let the two adolescents marry (such early marriages being, incidentally, entirely in accordance with creole practices on the island at that time). Protesting that Paul and Virginie are still too young, Mme de La Tour ar-gues for imposing a waiting period that would allow for the family for-tunes to be augmented: "by sending Paul to India for a short period of time, trade would provide him with enough [money] to buy a slave or two" (p. 174), she suggests, revealing her continued allegiance to the colonial out-look of her dead husband. The narrator charges himself with the task of asking "M. de La Bourdonnais for authorization to make this trip" (p. 175), but Paul refuses to engage in such fortune-hunting activities, citing the advantages of simply staying on the island and cultivating what land they possess. In maintaining this insular position, he shows himself to be as yet untouched by the *novelistic* condition that afflicts a character like De-foe's Robinson Crusoe and that generates all of his adventures: namely, the "general plague of mankind" that consists in "not being satisfy'd with the station wherein God and nature had placed them" (p. 198).

It is at this point that Mme de La Tour receives a second letter from her aunt: much more conciliatory than before, the old lady enjoins her niece to send Virginie to France, where she will see to her education and material comfort. That this is more than a simple suggestion becomes clear the very next day when La Bourdonnais, accompanied by two slaves, pays an unex-pected visit to the isolated habitants as they are eating breakfast. As Wasserman notes, one effect of this episode is to show that "the continua-tion of the idyllic life of the valley depends on the tolerance—or protec-tion—of an external power aligned with the authority of history, not na-ture."[82] It is, moreover, a *colonial* intrusion into a *creole* world, as is sug-gested by the fact that when he enters the house, Virginie has just served "coffee and boiled rice, *in line with the customs of the country*" (p. 178; my italics). The message he brings Mme de La Tour regarding her daughter could not be blunter: "I won't hide from you the fact that your aunt has en-listed the help of officials [*l'autorité*] in order to ensure that she goes there."

"The administration [*les bureaux*]," he continues, "has written advising me to use my power in this matter, if necessary" (p. 178). Directly emanating from a colonial "bureaucracy" (a word that originates precisely in the last decades of the eighteenth century), La Bourdonnais's "power" and "authority" is itself inseparable from that of the writing that authorizes him to seize Virginie should the family prove recalcitrant to the aunt's wishes. The governor does not immediately exercise this power, trying first to persuade Mme de La Tour with the thought of the riches that she will gain through her compliance. After all, he asks, "why does one come to the islands if not to make one's fortune?"; "isn't it nicer," he suggests, "to go and find it in one's own homeland [*patrie*]?" (p. 179). La Bourdonnais then reinforces this appeal to the commercial imagination and his insistence on a European as opposed to a creole homeland by depositing on their table "a big sack of piastres that one of his blacks was carrying," which serves to draw a subtle metonymic connection between the financial wealth of the metropole and the institution of slavery. Having clinched his point with Mme de La Tour, the governor then accepts their offer to sit down and dine with them, eating "in the manner of Creoles, with coffee mixed in with boiled rice" (pp. 179–80). The governor's highly problematic relation to the creole population over which he rules is captured in the ambivalence of this phrase "à la manière," which here conveys a sense, not of a coherent set of cultural practices based upon imitation (as in the examples we looked at earlier), but of a casual, quasi-touristic act of sampling such practices. After this meal, the episode ends with Mme de La Tour agreeing to put Virginie at the governor's "disposition"—a decision that will be strengthened by the subsequent intervention of "a sacred authority" in the person of her confessor, a missionary sent by the governor to convince Virginie that her going to France is "ordered by God" (p. 183). In the end, however, notwithstanding all these acts of rhetorical and financial persuasion, the colonial authorities will virtually have to abduct an unwilling Virginie in order to get her on board a ship bound for the fatherland. As Mme de La Tour explains to an angry Paul, who was absent on the morning of Virginie's abduction from her island home: "it being time for the ship to cast off, the governor, followed by some of his officers and the missionary, had come to take Virginie away in a palanquin and . . . in spite of her remonstrances, her tears and those of Marguerite, and with everbody shouting that it was in all their best interests, they had taken the half-dying girl away" (pp. 197–98).

In large part responsible for Virginie's departure, M. de La Bourdonnais also oversees the death of this young woman, as the ship bearing her back home (after she has been disinherited by her villainous aunt) sinks during a hurricane within sight of the island. Arriving to witness the wreck of the *Saint-Géran*, the governor is followed by "a detachment of soldiers, armed with rifles, and a great number of habitants and blacks" (p. 246), a description that serves to confirm the connections between colonial government and military force as well as to foreground a distinction between "habitants" and "Noirs" that has been downplayed throughout *Paul et Virginie* but that is basic to the Manichean workings of the colonial power La Bourdonnais embodies. What the governor will bear witness to is a power greater than his own, that of a tropical nature put into play by Bernardin as a way of bringing (his) narrative to an end in a violent act of closure that contests, but also inevitably repeats, the violence of colonial power. Killing off Virginie provides the author with a possible way out of the labyrinth of that colonial narrative into which his characters have fallen. This closural gesture is greatly facilitated by Bernardin's recourse to a religious framework that can make sense of this violent death through appeals to an afterlife, a definitively post-narrative condition: as Virginie is swallowed up by the sea—refusing a naked sailor's offer to divest her of some of her clothes and help her swim ashore[83]—she raises her eyes to the sky and "seemed an angel taking flight to the heavens" (p. 252). This angelic *appearance* is but one instance among many of the shift from a secular to a sacred register that marks the final part of *Paul et Virginie*, what Racault has termed its attempted "surpassing of the novelistic condition" ("dépassement du romanesque").[84] Bernardin's distortion of history in his account of the wreck, changing its date from August 17, 1744, to December 24 of that year, is another such instance: Virginie's apocalyptic end, situated one day before the new beginning that is the birth of the Christ whom she in so many ways resembles,[85] returns us to the "essentially medieval, Christian (or Judeo-Christian) vision of Time" with which, as Johannes Fabian has argued, "Enlightenment thought marks a break"—a break "from a conception of time/space in terms of a history of salvation to one that ultimately resulted in the secularization of Time as natural history."[86]

The nineteenth-century novel will be fully inscribed within this secularized time: Bernardin's belated reversion to a sacred temporality and the comforting idea of an afterlife as a way of resolving the anxieties raised by his (colonial) narrative will be at best only a parodic option for later writers, who nonetheless face the same peculiarly modern dilemma with regard to closure as does Bernardin. As D. A. Miller has suggested, the nineteenth-century novel, which he refers to simply as the "traditional novel," is generated out of a structural contradiction between what he calls the "narratable" ("the instances of disequilibrium, suspense, and general insufficiency from which a given narrative appears to arise") and the "nonnarratable" (that "state of quiescence assumed by a novel before the beginning and supposedly recovered by it at the end").[87] While perhaps basic to any narrated text, this tension between a quiescent state of beginning and/or ending and the intermediary movement of narrative is especially critical to the production of the nineteenth-century novel, a reactive genre (to recall Moretti's argument from the first section of this chapter) in which the "intrinsically boundless dynamism" of modernity is symbolically put on display in a story of Bildung that can serve, in the end, either to contain that dynamic growth or to celebrate it (the former case being exemplified, for Miller, by Jane Austen's "closural world of proper names, categories, feelings, and relationships" [p. 24], and the latter by Stendhal's "notorious resistance to closure" [p. 268] and his consequent openness to erotic and semiotic drift). Inasmuch as an attempt is made by the author of *Paul et Virginie* to inscribe a pastoral state of quiescence *within* the text (*after* its beginning), and to conceive of the end of narrative in sacred rather than secular terms, it must be thought of as a pre-traditional novel (that is to say, from Miller's perspective, not really a novel at all). But it is also what we might call a pre/modern novel, not only because, as we have seen, that quiescent state is, from the beginning, subject to "the logic of insufficiency, disequilibrium, and deferral" that is indissociable from narrative, but also because the appearance of the sacred in Bernardin's text can be read as just that—an appearance, one that is of only momentary consolation and that is itself immediately supplemented by a series of events that situates the problem of ending more squarely within the secular framework that dominates in, say, the novels of Austen. Like Bernardin, Austen needs to locate her texts (in Miller's words) "within a controlling perspective of narrative closure, which would restore the world (and with it, the word) to a state of transparency, once [and] for all released from errancy and equivocation" (p. 265); again like Bernardin, she envisions closure as a means of recovering "a time before narrative, before the failure or *fêlure* from which a narrative has untowardly bulged" (p. 101). But what Bernardin, like Austen, will in the end come up against is the "self-betraying inadequacy," as Miller puts it, of the traditional novel's attempts at closure (p. 267): because "the narratable is stronger than the closure to which it is opposed in an apparent binarity" (p. 266), narrative never really comes to an end, at least within its own terms.[88] The ending that it calls forth, like that of modernity itself, remains an absence that unendingly haunts the text.

Virginie's death leads not beyond but back into the world of a secular story (and history) that it contests. Her dead body washes back into the narrative, and becomes the object of two potentially competing narratives: colonial and creole. The body is discovered on the shore by Domingue and the narrator, who carry it to a fisherman's cabin, "where we gave it over to the keeping of some poor Malabar women, who took charge of washing it" (p. 256). Only the unspeaking subaltern, one might suggest, can have access to the unclothed body of Virginie, a body that must otherwise be conceived of at a mediated distance, in terms not of presence but of representation (terms that Virginie has herself clearly accepted, as is suggested by the fact that when her body is found one hand is clinging to her clothes and the other is closed over a little box containing a portrait of Saint Paul the Hermit given to her by his namesake).[89] Virginie is quickly commandeered, though, by the political and religious authorities: the narrator notes that "M. de la Bourdonnais sent secretly to inform me that on his orders Virginie's body had been brought into town, and that from there it was going to be moved to the church at Pamplemousses" (p. 257). The administration orders an elaborate funeral ceremony in honor of the virtuous Virginie, which draws the inhabitants of the entire island together: the orderly procession is led by grenadiers, who are followed by "eight of the most prominent young ladies of the island, dressed in white" and acting as pallbearers, a chorus of hymn-chanting children, and then "all the island's most distinguished habitants and officers, behind which walked the governor, followed by the people in a crowd" (p. 258). This is colonial spectacle with a vengeance, but what is undoubtedly most interesting about the episode of the funeral is that at a certain point in the procession all this "pompe funèbre" is interrupted by a spontaneous outburst of the entire people: "the hymns and the songs ceased, and on the plain only sighs and lamentations were heard" (pp. 258–59). An unofficial clamor rises up in place of the official ceremony, and not coincidentally this disruption of the colonial script leads directly into a more diversified description of the crowd when the corpse arrives at its burial place:

Negresses from Madagascar and Caffres from Mozambique laid baskets of fruit down around her, and hung bits of cloth on nearby trees, following the custom of their countries. Indians from Bengal and the Malabar coast brought cages full of birds, which they set free over her body. So greatly does the loss of a lovable object affect all nations, and so great is the power of unhappy virtue, which draws together [*réunit*] all religions around its tomb! (p. 259)

This sort of cross-cultural reunion is the necessary precondition of a truly creole society: as Racault has rightly argued, through Virginie's death the islanders attain a new sense of collective identity, and for this reason her death can be read as "the founding act of a future creole nation,"[90] the inaugural vision of what Glissant once called "la nation future," which "is not only a State . . . but a Poetics of being-in-emergence [*Poétique de l'être qui se trouve*]" (*IP*, p. 51). As Bernardin himself once pointed out, "one of the great disadvantages when it comes to the colonies is that the habitants are constantly seduced by Europe, by military distinctions [*les croix de Saint Louis*], by alliances with the rich and powerful, by pamphlets, the opera, pretty women; all of that attracts them away from their country and toward Europe, where they think their happiness lies" (*VF*, p. 434). Virginie's death has the effect of at least momentarily making the islanders of

European descent forget the seductions of the fatherland and settling them more firmly on the native ground they share with peoples of African and Asian descent. And it is perhaps this vision of a new collective identity that Virginie glimpsed in the end, if we are to believe the otherwise curiously bifurcated explanation the narrator later gives Paul as to why she was happy at the moment of her death: "either because she had a glimpse of an entire colony plunged into universal grief on her account, or of you running fearlessly to her rescue, she saw how dear she was to all of us" (pp. 272–73). The sentimental romance of Paul and Virginie here proves inextricable from a protonational unification that provides an alternative narrative and ending to that of colonialism.[91]

Although *Paul et Virginie* briefly looks forward to this post-colonial moment of unification, a positive secular conclusion that might adequately take the place of the sacred transcendence after which it longs, the text does not, as Racault goes on to point out, end on this uplifting note: "far from concluding with the advent of a regenerated community that has Virginie's funeral as its founding act, the novel ends with a poignant vision of abandonment, death, and separation."[92] Its concluding pages serve as a melancholy supplement to this collective ending, one that cannot move forward but only back: back into the degraded world of colonial narrative, on the one hand, and back into a desirable past that is now nothing more than an irrecuperable memory. Like certain Caribbean writers whom Walcott once described as being able to "contemplate only the shipwreck," the surviving characters will succumb to the fatal malaise of "an oceanic nostalgia for the older culture and a melancholy at the new."[93]

Our last sight of La Bourdonnais comes right after the funeral: after trying to console the two families and belatedly speaking out against the aunt's cruelty (the always belated regrets of colonial power), he advises Paul to go to France, where a place in the King's service will be reserved for him; the governor then offers his hand to the young man, who refuses it, "withdraw[ing] his own hand, and turn[ing] his head away so that he would not have to look at him" (p. 260). The creole subject here definitively rejects what might once have tempted him—an identification with *la patrie* and with the authority that derives from it—but he has nowhere else to go. He will spend the last two months of his life in a "sombre and melancholy" state (p. 263), despondently wandering around the island, revisiting "all the places [*lieux*] that he had visited with his childhood companion" (p. 265) and that "recalled to him the memory of her loss" (p. 266). In an effort at drawing Paul out of this state, the narrator tries to distance him from such *lieux de mémoire* by taking him to another part of the island, and "to that end, I led him to the inhabited heights of the Williams district, where he had never been" (p. 266). What they see there is the bustling world of the

colonial present, in which "agriculture and commerce were generating . . .
a great deal of lively and varied activity [*beaucoup de mouvement et de
variété*]" (p. 266). This world in movement bears an ironic resemblance to
the timeless pastoral world that it has displaced: "there were groups of carpenters who were squaring timber [*qui équarrissaient des bois*] and others
who were sawing it into planks; carts were coming and going along the
roadways; large herds of cattle and horses were grazing there in vast pas-
tures, and the countryside was scattered with habitations" (a description
that significantly leaves out one element that had been present in an earlier
version of this quasi-pastoral vision of plantation life: "there was in this
area a considerable amount of movement[,] *one could see blacks harvesting
the corn*, carts loaded up with planks and beams, groups of carpenters who
were squaring off timber[,] large man-made meadows where horses were
grazing" [my italics]).[94] Within the terms of a colonial narrative, this would
be an appealing vision indeed: a colonized and colonizable space (as the
narrator points out, because of the freshness of the air in this part of the island, it is a locale that "even favors the health of whites"); a formerly wild
place that has been thoroughly domesticated, and in which "les bois"—
earlier identified as the labyrinthine abode of the maroons (p. 138)—are in
the process of being "squared off" (*équarris*), after having been "cleared
away" (*éclaircis*; the narrator notes that "here and there one saw harvested
corn on the plain, carpets of strawberry plants in the clearings [*dans les
éclaircis des bois*], and rosebush hedges along the roadways" [p. 266]). But
Paul, for whom this colonial vision has nothing to offer, quickly suggests
that they return home—a now unhomely home that proves quite simply
uninhabitable: Paul and the two mothers die off one after the other in the
months that follow upon Virginie's death, and the aging Domingue and
Marie are then taken into the "care" of the government. All that remains in
this colonial aftermath is for the narrator himself, like Paul, endlessly to revisit the "lieux qui lui rappelaient le souvenir de sa perte." Anticipating the
"pastoral allegories of cultural loss and textual rescue" that, as James Clifford has pointed out, so pervasively structure the salvage operation that is
twentieth-century ethnography,[95] the narrator will translate the pastoral
story of the two families into a story about the loss of pastoral, a story that
could only have occurred in a past that bears little or no relation to the
degradations of the colonial present (hence the narrator's occasional reminders to his narratee that the story of Paul and Virginie took place during the very early years of the island's colonization,[96] when, for instance,
"this island did very little trade with the Indies" [p. 107]).

The colonial present founds itself upon the gap that opens up between a
lost original and its translation. As Racault has pointed out, this gap can be
read in the very name of the "plaines de Williams," which defies the sort of

obvious allegorical reading to which most of the other geographical names in the book (e.g., "la baie du Tombeau" [Tomb Bay]) appear to lend themselves, being "transparent names that 'speak' for themselves, fulfilling the old dream of [Plato's] *Cratylus* that there exists a necessary relation between the word and the thing, a perfect 'affinity' between the name and the site it designates."[97] The name "Williams," itself an anglicization of a Dutch or German name,[98] offers no such transparency. Rather, it points toward the obstacle of a colonial history that is difficult to read; it locates us in a secondary realm where the word does not, in (Bernardin's distortion of) Horace's phrase, "follow the thing," but follows upon it (just as the French have followed upon the departed Dutch in their colonization of the island). A version of this unreadability extends, in fact, to many of the ostensibly more transparent names in *Paul et Virginie*, notably the three that are referred to in italics at the very end of the text. Noting that "the voice of the people, which is silent when it comes to monuments that have been erected to the glory of kings, has bestowed upon several parts of the island names that will perpetuate [the memory of] Virginie's loss," the narrator cites as evidence of this "a place called *la passe du Saint-Géran* [the Saint-Géran channel]," "*le cap Malheureux* [the Cape of Misfortune]," and "*la baie du Tombeau*, where Virginie was found buried in the sand" (p. 283). This claim, which also has the cyclical effect of linking the very end of the text to its beginning since the latter two of these names were first mentioned in the opening paragraph (p. 101), is a provocatively misleading one on Bernardin's part: it supplants the real historical referents of these names (Tomb Bay, for instance, in actuality most probably owed its name to the much earlier drowning of a Dutch captain), falsely ascribing their origin to the factual episode—the sinking of the *Saint-Géran*—that provided the climax of his fictional story.[99] Here, fact and fiction, cause and effect, origin and supplement, voice and writing, confusingly combine to mirror one another in "a specular movement in which," to borrow Roberto González Echevarría's description of chiasmus (*retruécano*) in Carpentier's *Explosion*, "it is impossible to tell what takes precedence over what, what is the reflection of what."[100] The effect of the narrator's claim, coming as it does at the very end of the text, is to leave the reader with the uneasy sense that it may be impossible to separate what *Paul et Virginie* commemorates (nature, virtue, childhood, origins) from an act of falsification, an uncanny construction that, like Cruso's terraces in Coetzee's *Foe*, is only possible in, and because of, the absence of the very thing toward which it points.

As Bernardin himself once said, "when it comes to nature, our books on the subject are nothing more than novels, and our exhibition rooms nothing more than tombs" (3.30): the reflection on names that draws *Paul et Virginie* to a close openly confronts us with this novelized condition that

Bernardin so obviously wants to resist. This supplemental state of affairs is the starting point of post/colonial literature, one that cannot be entirely divorced from the sepulchral condition with which a pastorally minded writer like Bernardin often identifies it, but that always also, and increasingly so in our postcolonial age, can be read more productively as the (lack of a) ground upon which cross-cultural relations alone are possible. By way of concluding this chapter, I would like to return to the pantomime episode and examine one last aspect of its spec(tac)ular mimesis that especially anticipates this world of productively creolized relations.

As the reenactment of the Midian story begins, with Virginie in the role of Zipporah timidly advancing toward the well where she will first meet her protector and eventual husband Moses, she is accompanied by the "sound of Domingue's *tam-tam*" (p. 157). Exactly what is Domingue playing? The answer, on a first reading, is simple: as the cliché-obsessed protagonist of the Guadeloupean novelist Maryse Condé's first novel, *Heremakhonon* (1976)—a trenchant anti-Negritude critique of its Caribbean protagonist's attempts at getting back in touch with her African "ancestors"—puts it in a rhetorical question, "who hasn't heard about the African tam-tam?"[101] The Wolof Domingue would appear to be playing that same "black tom-tom" that one finds, many generations later, still beating in the poetry of his countryman Léopold Senghor,[102] for whom it served as a perfect metonym for the naturally "rhythmic" character of African culture as a whole. This "tam-tam noir" has been instrumental in accounts of African and Afro-diasporic literature penned by both cultural "outsiders" and "insiders." Picking up on Sartre's statement in "Orphée noir" that "Negritude is," among other things, "that far-away tam-tam beating at night in the streets of Dakar,"[103] for instance, the critic Jack Corzani suggests that "the black poet aims at the heart more than the ear: his text, like a tam-tam, is intent on raising, slowing down, unsettling the rhythm of the heart, bringing it to the point of suffocation, unbearable asphyxiation, or the mystical trance, the momentary source of complete happiness."[104] The ending of Aimé Césaire's poem "Le verbe marronner" (1955), addressed to the Haitian writer René Depestre, perfectly complements this account. Chiding the poet, "courageous tom-tom rider" ("vaillant cavalier du tam-tam"), for agreeing to follow the Eurocentric stylistic dictates of Aragon and the French Communist Party rather than developing a poetics of his own that would accord more naturally with "the bad manners of our blood" ("les mauvaises manières de notre sang"), Césaire concludes by exhorting Depestre to join him once again, like renegade slaves, in an act of stylistic *marronnage* (one that is, and perhaps this says something about the sexual politics of the Negritude movement, inseparable from a cosmic "rutting"): "believe me as in the old days beat the good tom-tom for us / splashing their rancid night / with a succinct rutting of moudang stars" (*CP*, pp. 370–71; "crois-m'en comme jadis bats-nous le bon tam-tam / éclaboussant leur nuit rance / d'un rut sommaire d'astres moudangs").

Such appeals, as Condé's narrator well knew, run the risk of becoming nothing more than clichés, and it is not surprising that in his trenchant critique of Afrocentric Caribbean writers Walcott referred with distaste to those "epic poets [who] create an artificial past, a defunct cosmology without the tribal faith," as "the glorifiers of the tom-tom."[105] We find a version of this same critique in Confiant's recent book-length portrait of Césaire, who is guilty, from the former's rather dogmatically creolizing perspective, of neglecting the realities of his native Caribbean in favor of the idealities of an imaginary Africa. At one point, indeed, Confiant specifically addresses the question of the "black tam-tam" in Césaire's work (*AC*, pp. 96–97), citing a 1962 interview in which Césaire (of whom Senghor had once said, in an early poem dedicated to his "beloved Brother," that "the tam-tams give rhythm to your song")[106] proudly notes the fact that Africans have told him his poems are "among the rare ones that can be easily beaten out on a tam-tam." Remarking sarcastically that certain poems of Césaire's can also be very well recited to Wagner or Debussy, "without having to conclude that because of this he is a classical European author," Confiant stresses that "it would be helpful to know exactly what Césaire understands by 'tam-tam,' which is a word that is totally unknown in the Antilles, where one says, exclusively, 'tambour.'" "The *tambour antillais*," he continues, "has two origins: one African, the other European," the *tambour bèl-air* (*tanbou bèlè* in Creole) and the *tambour basque* (*tanbou-dibas*), respectively. These drums, he points out, "are both perfectly creole or creolized, even if each is played to its own rhythm," which leads him to pose the following question: "exactly which tam-tam is it that Césaire so proudly claims can accompany his poems: the *basque* or the *bèl-air*?"

The question is perhaps a little illogical, inasmuch as it precludes the obvious answer (namely, that Césaire, immersed in Afrocentric clichés, is talking about neither), but Confiant's excursus on the creolized—non-European, non-African—identities of "le tambour antillais" does point the way toward a more historically sensitive reading of Domingue's tam-tam, one that detaches it from its apparently obvious African referent and resituates it in the cross-cultural context out of which it originated. The onomatopoeic creole word "tam-tam" has its etymological origins in the Indian subcontinent (the *OED* entry for the related English word "tom-tom" cites Hindustani, Sinhalese, and Malay variants as sources) and refers to a type of East Indian percussion instrument. Bernardin's uses of the word here and in the earlier *Voyage* are, in fact, among the very first in a French-language text.[107] The association of (West) Africans and tam-tams that Bernardin establishes in *Paul et Virginie* thus marks the beginning of a translational process that would over the course of the next century turn the word itself into a virtual metonym for African culture, one that writers like Senghor and Césaire would in turn invoke in the service of the Negritude movement. That the simplicity of essentialist arguments always emerges out of the complexity of creolized conditions is the main lesson that one can take away from this example—a lesson that is even further complicated by the possibility that what Domingue is playing is not a tam-tam at all but rather the stringed instrument that in the *Voyage* Bernardin himself *mis*identifies as a tam-tam and associates with Africans: "a type of bow fitted to a calabash shell" from which "the blacks extract a sort of gentle harmony, with which they accompany the songs they compose" (1.140). As Robert Chaudenson has pointed out, this instrument would have been more "properly" designated in Indian Ocean Creoles as "'bobre,' 'bob' or 'bombe' (from the Portuguese 'bobra' or 'abobora')."[108]

The African tam-tam so cherished by Senghor and Césaire is a (colonial/creole) production, an "entangled object" (in Nicholas Thomas's phrase) that both filters, and thus distorts, our vision of the past and determines our relations to the future. Notwithstanding the falsified *image* of reality that they (re)present, such objects have real effects in the determination of our identities. Bernardin's otherwise improbable account of the origins of Paul's name becomes, from this perspective, uncannily perceptive in its claims for the generative power of images: the narrator informs us that Paul's mother, while pregnant with him, carried around with her a portrait of Saint Paul the Hermit to which she was much devoted; "it even happened," he continues, with a nod to the theory of "maternal impression,"[109] "that . . . by dint of contemplating the image of this blessed hermit, the fruit of her womb had acquired some resemblance to it, which made her decide to give [the baby] that name" (p. 173). We live in a world of images, of afterimages, that resemble, in an (un)likely manner, the originals upon which they are (not) based and that in turn produce other images, other resemblances inextricably woven together to form what Michael Taussig has called the "interzone of mimetic space,"[110] a world of endlessly proliferating copies that can either be viewed with a nostalgic despair for lost origin(al)s, or, as Taussig suggests, with "an appreciation of mimesis as an end in itself that takes one into the magical power of the signifier to act as if it were indeed the real, to live in a different way with the understanding that artifice is natural, no less than that nature is historicized" (p. 255). This naturally artificial, or artificially natural, world is one in which the cross-cultural, mimetic relations initiated by the "first contact" of colonialism have become the global norm, forcing us, on the one hand, to abandon what Taussig calls the "border logistics" that would treat identity as a "thing-in-itself" rather than a "relationship [created in the] colonial mirror of production" (pp. 133, 66) and, on the other, to "enter into the 'second contact' era of the borderland where 'us' and 'them' lose their polarity and swim in and out of focus" (p. 246).

It is the ripening of this second contact, which "disassembles the very possibility of defining the border as anything more than a shadowy possibility of the once-was" (p. 249), that I will be examining in the following chapter on Édouard Glissant, whose poetics of relationality so nicely complements Taussig's portrait of a mimetically reconstellated world in which our actions and reactions "are 'relative' to each other more than they are 'relative' to what we used to call their 'own cultural context,'" and in which "the border has dissolved and expanded to cover the lands it once separated such that all the land is borderland" (p. 249). Such a world, where we can do no more or less than, in Taussig's words, "live reality as really made-up" (p. 255), necessarily appears to us in the wake of a disenchantment that Rousseau was among the first to voice in his many accounts of how, as he puts it in the 1755 *Discours*, "with primitive man [*l'homme originel*] gradually fading from sight, the only spectacle Society now offers the wise man is that of collections of artificial men and false passions, which are the handiwork of all these new relations, and which have no real foundation in Nature."[111] The primary impulse of a writer like Bernardin was to follow Rousseau and reject these "nouvelles relations," to insist upon insular solutions to the problems of a global modernity, or else to mourn their absence; as Bernardin once remarked, "a tomb is a monument located at the place where two worlds meet [*sur les limites des deux mondes*]" (5.83), and his oeuvre as a whole and *Paul et Virginie* in particular often serves this sepulchral function, conjoining worlds only in order to commemorate their loss. That Bernardin's "limits" can and must be read otherwise, that his tomb is also, as it were, a womb, its colonial endings inseparable from the (re)productive potential of creole beginnings, is what I have attempted to suggest in my reading of his preliminary but insightful mapping of the ever-expanding borderland of "second contact" that has put a (never final) end to any and all dreams of separating the real from the really made-up, the islands of our once and future dreams from the mainland of the post/colonial present.

4 Resisting Memories

> Everyone was following a trail.
> All of these trails did not amount to a path.
> —Édouard Glissant, *Malemort* (1975)

> The desperate irony of an old militant, who renounces
> a part of himself in order to secure, or so he believes,
> something of what still remains.
> —Édouard Glissant, *Faulkner, Mississippi* (1996)

"Changing Color With Position": Lafcadio Hearn's 'Youma' and "the Phenomena of Creolization"

Most famous for his writings on Japan, where he spent the last fifteen years of his life, marrying into a Samurai family and eventually becoming a Japanese citizen, the itinerant Irish-Greek-American Lafcadio Hearn would spend the years immediately preceding his departure for Asia in the Caribbean, after a decade-long sojourn in Louisiana. His stay on Martinique, from October 1887 to May 1889, resulted in the substantial travelogue *Two Years in the French West Indies* (1890) and a novel entitled *Youma* published that same year. Most importantly, while in Martinique Hearn transcribed a good many of the island's creole folktales (six of which were translated into French and published posthumously in 1932 under the title *Trois fois bel conte*), which have played an influential role in the development of Franco-Caribbean literature, in both its modernist and postmodern phases.[1] Writing from the town of St. Pierre, often referred to as the Paris of the Caribbean before its complete destruction in the 1902 eruption of the Mt. Pelée volcano, Hearn remarked in a letter to Henry Alden, then editor of *Harper's Magazine*, that "the romance of Bernardin de Saint-Pierre never could have taken place in Martinique; I doubt if it ever did in Mauritius. There are Virginias, but no Pauls."[2] Providing a rather cryptic reason as to why Martinique could never serve as the backdrop for the sort of exotic romance with which he associates his literary predecessor, Hearn goes on to explain that "tropic life" is too "material." It may well have been an overbearing sense of this materiality that the twelve-year-old Bernardin came away with from his own brief and disillusioning visit to the island as a passenger aboard his merchant uncle's trading ship; already an active hub of international commerce, Martinique must have offered to Bernardin's adolescent eyes no outlet for the heroic dreams with which his repeated readings of *Robinson Crusoe* had filled him, and barely a trace of this encounter with the Caribbean has remained in his writings. As we saw in the preceding chapter, Bernardin's initial reactions to the material conditions on the Île de France were equally negative: his positive vision of "the patriarchal simplicity of olden times, and of ways of life worthy of the golden age," which the very first reviewer of *Paul et Virginie* found painted there,[3] would only emerge retrospectively, an insular fiction embellishing and supplementing his real disillusionment with the island and its modern, all-too-modern condition. Signs of this colonial condition, I argued, repeatedly rise to the surface of *Paul et Virginie*, drawing Bernardin's text into the space of a relational culture that the creolophone peoples of the Mascarenes and of the Antilles had and continue to have in common.

Hearn's coy and somewhat puzzling assertion that there are Virginies in Martinique but no Pauls would lead us to believe, however, that he still partially subscribes to the "romance" that he is certain cannot take place there. Who, we might ask, are these surviving Virginies to whom he refers, and why are there no Pauls to match them? And how, moreover, does the issue of race fit into his commentary about an island where "there are at least five men of color to one white."[4] We get the beginnings of an answer to these questions in *Youma*, a novel first published in *Harper's* and that is of interest to us here not only because of the way it implicitly rewrites Bernardin's sentimental pastoral from a late-nineteenth-century fin de siècle perspective, but in its explicit and historically prophetic engagement with the problem of creole identity—an engagement that amply justifies Chamoiseau and Confiant's identification of this "man of multiple identities" as a writer who had "the intuition of Diversality."[5]

Hearn's novel takes place in nineteenth-century Martinique in the years leading up to the abolition of slavery in 1848. His Virginie is Youma, a *capresse* (light-skinned woman of color), who has grown up in a béké household and whom the Peyronettes purport to treat as one of the "family."[6] When the mistress's daughter unexpectedly dies young, Youma becomes the logical candidate to care for Mayotte, the surviving child of her "foster-sister," and she is prematurely pressed into service as nurse, or *da*—a social role that the narrator, in the novel's quasi-anthropological prefatory chapter, refers to as "the one creation of slavery perhaps not unworthy of regret—one strange flowering amid all the rank dark growths of that bitter soil" (4.263).[7] Because Madame Peyronette looks upon her beloved

Youma's enslavement as "a moral protection" (p. 270), she does not allow her "pet slave" to marry Gabriel, the robust, independent-minded, and very black *commandeur* (foreman) of her son-in-law's plantation, to whom Youma is instinctively drawn despite the inhibitions of her "civilized" education. Hearn's descriptions of the attraction that Youma and Gabriel feel for one another are typical of the age in which he wrote, reminding one especially of Joseph Conrad's early Malay romances such as *Almayer's Folly* (1895) and *Outcast of the Islands* (1896) in the way that they desperately attempt to preserve the category of "nature" that was so central to Bernardin's post/Enlightenment enterprise: namely, by identifying nature with an exotic "savagery" that can then be pointedly contrasted with a modern "civilization" in which writers like Conrad and Hearn have lost faith.[8] The narrator asserts of Youma and Gabriel, for instance, that "the two strange natures comprehended each other without speech—drew and dominated each other in a dumb, primitive, half-savage way" (p. 302). Under the influence of Gabriel, we are told, "the nature of the savage race whose blood dominated in [Youma's] veins" bursts its bonds (p. 309)—exactly the sort of blood memories that would serve as the stable ground of Lawrentian primitivism only a few decades later but of which a Hearn or a Conrad could not wholly approve, despite the ambivalent fascination such memories exercised over them. However, despite her passion for Gabriel, the virtuous Youma refuses to flee with him to the neighboring island of Dominica (where the English had already abolished slavery), feeling that it is her moral duty to remain with the family and take care of her young white charge. Soon thereafter, during the riots that broke out in May 1848 between the time that abolition was officially proclaimed in France by the architects of the Second Republic and the actual arrival of that proclamation in the colonies, a house full of whites, including Youma's family, is set on fire by what Hearn calls the "negro mob" (p. 363)—significantly over-determining his exotic narrative with the sort of apprehensive invocations of mass society that were such a common feature of fin de siècle culture.[9] Given the chance to escape from the burning house, Youma refuses, since the mob will not allow her to take Mayotte along with her. Pointing out that their retribution is just an "imitation" of white violence (p. 366), Youma sacrifices her life, à la Virginie, in order to preserve her virtue and sense of propriety.

The story of Youma, as we have already mentioned, is itself prefaced by an "objective" account of the role of the da during "old colonial days" for which the narrator seems altogether nostalgic: plantation life, he notes, echoing the terms in which Bernardin's novel was first reviewed, was "patriarchal and picturesque to a degree scarcely conceivable by one who knows the colony only since the period inaugurated by emancipation"

(p. 277). Invoking "this colonial country life, so full of exotic oddities and unconscious poetry" (p. 278), the narrator adds that "even to-day the stranger may find in the gentler traits of this exotic humanity an indescribable charm—despite all those changes of character wrought by the vastly increased difficulties of life under the new conditions" (p. 341). That Hearn shares his narrator's nostalgic perspective can be verified by flipping through the pages of his autobiographical *Two Years in the French West Indies*, which also promotes both a fin de siècle longing for exotic horizons that are rapidly disappearing from sight and a bittersweet critique of "the present era of colonial decadence" (p. 22). (One can also find traces of this longing and this critique, ironically enough, in contemporary writers from the Antilles such as Chamoiseau and Confiant when they look back with approval on the relative cultural and economic autonomy that obtained in Martinique and Guadeloupe prior to the islands' formal incorporation into France in 1946 and subsequent, in Glissant's words, "Hawaii-ification.")

Ironically, it is within the framework of these exotic memories that creolization—the hybridizing wave of our own fin de siècle's future, according to many postcolonial theorists—comes into play, for the narrator's discussion of creolization and things creole is inseparable from his nostalgia for a less culturally homogenized time than the colonial present. What we need to address first, though, is simply the ambivalent way that the word "creole" functions in Hearn's text, serving partially to erase and displace the issue of race while at the same time compelling the reader to remember and make continued use of it. In *Youma*, the word "creole" ambivalently supplements, but by no means supplants, a wide array of racial and cultural taxonomies. Some of these taxonomies serve to establish predictable bipolar oppositions: for instance, "civilized" versus "savage," or "white" versus "black" (and other variants of the word: "Negro," "colored," or the quintessentially colonial label "of color" [p. 269], which has gained such a renewed if problematic popularity in recent years).[10] Other taxonomies, while grounded in these oppositions, serve more to enhance the exotic quality of the novel, identifying a carefully gradated middle ground between white and black, as in the case of such lovingly cited and by the time of writing already anachronistic mulattoisms as "capresse," "griffe," and "mestive." All such labels, in any case, bear ample witness to Hearn's quasi-scientific chromatic obsession with "race types" (one that is on especially glaring display in *Two Years in the French West Indies*).

As opposed to these definitive categorizations, the word "creole" points toward an altogether more ambivalent situation, which is especially apparent in the following description of Youma:

[She] represented the highest development of natural goodness possible in a race mentally undeveloped, kept half savage by subservience, but physically refined in a remarkable manner by climate, environment, and all those mysterious influences which form the characteristics of Creole peoples. (p. 263)

In this passage, the deterministic discourse of race retains a certain validity, but appears to apply only to the realm of *mental* development. It unfolds alongside an equally deterministic but altogether more "mysterious" appeal (one apparently limited in this instance to the realm of the *physical*) to the formation of "Creole peoples," whose identity in this passage is clearly not dependent upon race but upon location. It is a similar situation that Hearn directs us toward—in what, if we are to believe the *Oxford English Dictionary*, is the first occurrence of the word "creolization" in an English-language text[11]—when he notes that "the subject race had . . . been physically refined by those extraordinary influences of climate and environment which produce the phenomena of creolization" (p. 341). Stressing the importance of such influences was, to be sure, a commonplace of nineteenth-century literature about (white) Creoles; we find it at work, for instance, in the degenerative scenario that propels Charlotte Bronte's *Jane Eyre* (1847), where Bertha Mason's lunacy and lasciviousness is clearly a result of her identity as a Creole; as Jenny Sharpe has argued, Bronte uses the figure of the Creole to demonstrate "that 'whiteness' alone is not the sign of racial purity," but, rather, that such purity can only be ensured by means of an identification with "English national culture."[12] Hearn's account recalls such negative scenarios at the same time as it reverses them, by identifying the process as refining rather than degenerative, and expands them, by identifying it as common to all of the island's "races." In this respect, Hearn marks a new and potentially more positive stage in the apprehension of the phenomena of creolization, laying the foundation for a communitarian thinking that would put into question the racial categorizations and cultural sectionalism that the Limbaughs and Farrakhans of our own day and age have inherited from the Victorians.

However, the inclusionist, communitarian sense of the word "creole" by no means exhausts the possible meanings of this shifting signifier in Hearn's novel. Its slipperiness in *Youma* is not surprising, given the historically diverse uses of this word in the Americas and Africa.[13] In the Indian Ocean island of Mauritius, for instance, the word has for centuries primarily designated those of African or mixed descent (although Bernardin's use of the word to describe the island's white habitants testifies to a more comprehensive application of it in the colony's early days),[14] while in neighboring Réunion the word has consistently included all native-born islanders (those of Chinese and Indian descent at times constituting an exception to this rule). This all-inclusive usage had also characterized the Antilles during the early years of their colonization, although the word soon became limited to peo-

ple of "pure" European descent born on the islands (a fact that recent advocates of creole identity like Confiant have untiringly pointed out in their
attempts at undoing this "monopolization of the designation 'Creole' by
the béké caste").[15] In the Louisiana that Hearn knew so well, the word's
meaning was similarly contested, and an exclusionary sense of the word
had been gaining ground over the course of the century, as Virginia
Domínguez has pointed out in her thorough study of the gradual transformations in racial coding that followed upon the colony's purchase by the
United States.[16] Consistent with discursive practice in New Orleans and the
Antilles, the exclusionary sense of the word predominates in Hearn's novel
(see pp. 261, 266, 268, 272, 277, 299, 309, 341, 364), severely curtailing
the racial ambivalence—and the cross-cultural and communitarian potential—that was so readable in the above-cited passages.

Notwithstanding the potential to which Hearn's text alerts us, then, his
use of the word "creole" more often than not reinscribes all sorts of social
and ethnic cleavages that have historically attached to the label.[17] But this
reinscription is itself problematized by the resolutely unstable nature of the
word, and the racial limits and divisions that the exclusionary usage would
enforce often get lost sight of in the novel. Thus, as an adjective meaning island-born, the word "creole" also attaches to words like "Negro,"
"Negress" (pp. 261, 357); moreover, its use as a noun in a phrase like the
"white Creoles" (pp. 346, 363) stands in obvious contradiction to the more
frequent, racially particularistic usage of the word since it implies that
"white" and "Creole" are not necessarily synonymous. Such contaminated
usages, in which race partially gives way to place, themselves at points slide
into an even more inclusionary sense of the word that, while not predominant, is nonetheless emphatically present in the novel, surfacing in references to the Creole spoken by virtually all the islanders (pp. 271, 280, 325,
355), cultural practices involving the "Creole story-teller" (p. 288) and his
"contes créoles" (p. 282), or more broadly to "Creole tradition" (p. 301),
"fancy" (p. 303), and "legend" (p. 320). The word's conflicting appearances in the novel prevent us as readers from settling upon a final meaning
for the word, be it inclusivist or exclusivist, forcing us to make interpretive
choices about what the word is actually designating that are based on an always shifting context (choices that are even harder to make when it is attached to actual Creole vocabulary such as "bitaco" [peasant, p. 330]).
This undecidability (which, indeed, ultimately makes a mockery of the
clear-cut partitioning of meanings in which I have just been engaging) is especially apparent in what is doubtless the most historically poignant and
difficult to read use of the word in the entire novel (and I will have listed
them all here): namely, the phrase "Creole slave" (p. 304), in which the adjective simultaneously attaches to the body of the slave (referring, that is, to

an island-born black slave) and to the proprietor of that body (referring to the slave of an island-born white).

While undoubtedly not in control of the shifting signification of this word (and it is precisely this lack of control that makes his account exemplary of the indeterminacy that characterizes the creolization process), Hearn is nonetheless emphatically committed to what he thinks it stands for—or, rather, stood for. It is precisely "Creole peoples" who, the narrator argues, are most threatened by the "colonial decadence" that he so abhors: with the increasingly difficult conditions that followed upon Emancipation, he notes, "Creole life shrank into narrower channels; and the character of all classes visibly hardened under pressure previously unknown" (p. 264). "The races," he continues, "drew forever apart when they needed each other most." This nostalgic scenario about the waning of "Creole life" and the ensuant isolation of "the races," which revealingly anticipates the argument of Brathwaite's *Development of Creole Society*,[18] is patently, and dangerously, rooted in exactly the sort of racial categorizations that one might expect a sensitivity to the cross-cultural dynamics of creole societies to have transcended: Hearn's admiration for "a people of half-breeds—the finest mixed race of the West Indies" (*Two Years*, 3.36) clearly borders on the fetishistic, and it is just as obviously linked to his pathological fear of a black planet. For Hearn, the decadence and dissolution of creole society can only lead to the victorious assertion of blackness in a not-so-distant future that he figures in predictably devolutionist terms: as he argues in his Caribbean travelogue, "all these mixed races, all these beautiful fruit-colored populations, seem doomed to extinction: the future tendency must be to universal blackness, if existing conditions continue—perhaps to universal savagery." "The true black element," he continues, "more numerically powerful, more fertile, more cunning, better adapted to pyrogenic climate and tropical environment, would surely win" (3.110–11). In this apocalyptic winner-take-all scenario (which itself prefigures the nightmarish visions of cultural homogenization that mechanically underwrite so many critiques of postmodernity), the island's "white population" and its economic viability end up being completely obliterated by the "true black element." Here, as with Bronte, such claims recall a familiar nineteenth-century position, perhaps most memorably voiced in the dystopian narrative of Thomas Carlyle's "Occasional Discourse on the Nigger Question" (1848/1853), where he speculates that England has "'emancipated' the West Indies into a *Black Ireland*."[19] The difference, of course, lies in the fact that Hearn's scenario not only predicts the blackening of the island but also registers the loss of a racial and cultural middle ground to which his work prophetically, if problematically, alerts us (a hybrid ground, incidentally, that struck Carlyle as equally or even more frightening than a purely "Negro" emancipation).[20]

Steeped in nostalgia, Hearn's vision of creoleness is indisputably racist, in both an objective and subjective sense: it is, to use Appiah's terms, both "racialist" in its commitment to the objective reality of "race" as a valid cultural and scientific category and "racist" in its subjective evaluation of the hierarchies that obtain between the "white," the "black," and "those beautiful fruit-colored populations" that for him mediate between these two extremes.[21] We have, doubtless, "progressed" in our apprehension of the phenomena of creolization. If I have chosen to linger over Hearn's *manifestly* inadequate position, however, it is in order to suggest that his inadequacies are, less openly but in no less determining a fashion, still our own. Hearn's vision, in its receptivity to "those strange Creole words which, like tropic lizards, change color with position" (p. 325), not only provides a prescient glimpse of the interstitial terrain that current theorists of creolization are charting, but also an idea of its contradictory limits. The tensions in Hearn's fin de siècle novel—its oscillation between, on the one hand, an appeal to (white, black, and mixed) race and, on the other, to that ambiguous something else toward which the word "creole" also directs us—are not resolved in *Youma*, and nor, I would argue, are they—or need they be—resoluble in our own fin de siècle, notwithstanding our enhanced awareness of the problems with Hearn's rac(ial)ist account and our increased sensitivity to the ambivalences that his text unrelentingly, if quite unwittingly, opens up. The shuttling back and forth in *Youma* between a particular type of settled identity (in this case, racial) and another (creole) identity that both does and does not correspond to the former—an identity that is (un)like it—anticipates the necessarily duplicitous way in which we cannot help talking about our own increasingly creolized selves. It is this duplicity that I am gesturing toward in the title of this chapter with the phrase "resisting memories," where (racial, national, cultural) memory is both that which we must resist—because it hinders the (*inter*racial, *trans*national, *cross*-cultural) process of creolization—and that which persists, for better and for worse, as a force of resistance. If Hearn's work obviously falls short of the fluid, diversal practices of the poetics and politics of creolization argued for by Glissant, it nonetheless provides a vital glimpse of what these practices might be and where they might lead. If the Guadeloupean critic Roger Toumson somewhat exaggerates the case when he identifies Hearn as the "first [writer] who knew how to show the Lesser Antilles as they really are,"[22] it is assuredly the case that this "strange questioner"—as Césaire would refer to him in his tribute-poem "Statue de Lafcadio Hearn"[23]—stands as an important genealogical precursor to a writer like Édouard Glissant,[24] whose own reflections upon the strange and estranging question of creole identity will occupy us in the remainder of this chapter.

Maroon(ed) Narratives: National Disenchantment and the Novels of Édouard Glissant

> I think that in the context of globalization the modalities
> of resistance will change. And they will have to be changed
> because all of those with which we have become familiar
> over the past fifty years—heroic and sensational as they
> most certainly were—have resulted in the unspeakable, be
> it in Algeria, black Africa, Asia, or elsewhere. And new
> ways of resisting will have to be invented, because it is
> obvious that the old ones no longer work.
> —Édouard Glissant, *Introduction à une Poétique du Divers*

In one of the opening chapters of his most recent novel, *Tout-monde*, Édouard Glissant recounts the youthful adventures of his partially autobiographical protagonist Mathieu Béluse in Italy during the early 1950s. Mathieu, a central character in Glissant's five previous novels, is staying in the town of Vernazza on the Ligurian coast, at both a significant proximity to and remove from the city of Genoa—the birthplace of the European who first "discovered" his native island of Martinique. While sojourning in Vernazza, Mathieu becomes fast friends with a group of Italian youths who share his enthusiasm for cycling and swimming in the bay. What must be especially avoided during these otherwise pleasant dips in the Mediterranean are the stings of the *méduses*, those multicolored jellyfish about whose geographical origins his friend Pino is extremely curious: "Tell me, Mathieu," Pino repeatedly asks, "do they come from your neck of the woods, these medusas?" (p. 37). As the omniscient narrator of this chapter then goes on to explain, Pino's apparently innocent question actually has its basis in an all-too-familiar logic, and poetics, of exoticism; it exemplifies an "ends-of-the-earth type of thinking" ("pensée de bout du monde") that would figure the space of the Other as a mysterious and more often than not Edenic site of origins, an "over there" ("là-bas") detached from the "here and now" of Europe and its modernity. Mathieu, "who was already beginning to sense that another logic—perhaps that of all those countries roused by hunger, oppression, and extermination—would soon take over from this one [*cette logique-là serait bientôt relayée par une autre*]," is quick to counter Pino's exoticizing vision, responding that "medusas can be found all over the world" and that they "do not have a country of origin." He does so because he "wants to make it understood, perhaps as much to himself as to this dry, gnarled, almost black-skinned child, that there was no longer such a thing as the ends of the earth and that there would soon be no more center from which one might set forth in the direction of strange and phantom-like peripheries" (p. 38). Exclaiming "*non è vero*," young Pino simply rejects this prophetic vision of the death of the exotic, but there can be no doubt that one of the major thrusts of Glissant's novel is to underwrite its truth—to confront the reader with a decentered world in which, as the narrator puts it toward the very end of *Tout-monde*, "the procession of 'Over theres' has risen up into a tempest of 'Heres.' The *Tout-monde* is radiating with 'Heres' that are relaying one another" (p. 490). Glissant's most recent novel is a concerted attempt at rendering in narrative form this increasingly relationalized late-twentieth-century world, at mapping out a global poetics of creolization that would not only take up the relay of an exhausted European exoticism but also that of the decolonizing politics of which the young Mathieu has a premonition—the Third Worldist politics of resistance produced by "tous ces pays soulevés par la faim et l'oppression et l'extermination" that flowered in the late 1950s and early 1960s and to which Glissant himself once subscribed, but that he will in his later novels find it necessary to *recant*, in both senses of the word (to renounce, and as the etymology suggests, to sing again).

Although the primary role of the medusa in this passage is thus to serve as a floating signifier, referring us back toward an untenably exotic differentiation and forward to emergent global relations, one could pursue this image along somewhat different interpretive lines, stressing its vertical as opposed to horizontal dimensions as well as drawing out the etymological connection with Greek myth. Glissant has himself metonymically invoked the image of the medusa—floating upon the surface and yet reaching down toward submarine depths—as a way of describing the abyssal experience that Africans must have undergone during their forced migration to the New World. In an account of this experience in the *Poétique*, Glissant identifies three stages in this exilic process of defamiliarization, the first two being "the wrenching away from the home country" and the subsequent encounter with "the marine abyss" that opens up when the slaves are thrown into the belly of the ship (pp. 17–18). The third and final stage in this series of paralyzing experiences that constitute the pre-text for the creolization of these enslaved Africans (their "irruption dans la modernité") is the crossing of the Middle Passage itself, "the most petrifying aspect of the chasm" (p. 18; "la face la plus médusante du gouffre"). Mathieu's simultaneous fear of and fascination with the figure of the medusa thus also exemplifies his response to the challenge of facing up to history, that "angel with whom all we Caribbean Jacobs have to wrestle, sooner or later, if we hope for a blessing."[25] It is this encounter and its ambivalences that Glissant gestures toward in his choice of matching epigraphs for the *Poétique*: Walcott's "Sea is History" and Brathwaite's "The unity is sub-marine," which point toward one and the same experience and yet from very different perspectives. Walcott's claim—made in the name of an Adamic amnesia—has consistently been that the "confrontation of history" is a petrifying one for the artist: indeed, he calls it "that Medusa of the New World."[26] Brathwaite, by contrast, has consistently stressed the need to explore those historical depths that the medusa, in its alluring transparency, points down toward. Glissant's yoking of the two (dis)similar claims of Walcott and Brathwaite situates us, from the outset of the *Poétique*, in a double space where it is not only possible but necessary to think them together rather than apart, to gaze upon the Medusa's face of history and simultaneously to turn away from it.

If the image of the medusa here thus draws us into the space of Glissant's own most recent theoretical reflections, it also ironically throws us back to a much earlier intertext—one with which the young Mathieu would doubtless have been familiar: Aimé Césaire's poem "Ode à la Guinée" (from the 1948 *Soleil cou coupé*). This surrealist text, written in the spirit of Césaire's Afrocentric poetics of Negritude, ends with the poet's cosmic appeal to the "Guinea / silenced in myself with the astral depth of medusas" (*CP*, pp. 206–7; "Guinée / muette en moi-même d'une profondeur astrale de méduses").[27] Césaire's project is to (re)sound the silent ancestral land that supposedly lies within him, to explore the astral depths of a cultural unconscious more or less identical with what Brathwaite terms a people's nam. The emphasis in Césaire is not on horizontal processes of displacement but (as we argued toward the end of Chapter 2) on a vertical descent—the hermeneutic process that was so central to Coetzee's *Foe*—in search of a lost home for which the poet nostalgically longs (a search that could very well be construed as an unwitting repetition of that fascination with *là-bas* that was the cornerstone of European exoticism). In his own use of the image of the medusa as a trope for global relationality, Glissant can thus be read as ironically signifying upon Césaire's own exoticizing use of it in his quest for cultural origins. The implicit polemic with Negritude and its Afrocentric avatars that partially determines Glissant's choice of this medusal image will, indeed, become perfectly explicit toward the end of *Tout-monde* when he criticizes "our" temptation to return to Africa "as if it were a territory that was owed us," to treat it as a place frozen in time since "the days when our ascendants were forcibly taken from there, and to believe that we in turn will find there a vital essence [*une force essentielle*]"—to act, in a word, as if the inhabitants of the continent had not changed, "and we would like, impertinently, to share this essence with them, to claim their kinship as if they were paralyzed referents, to freeze-frame them [*les tenir pétrifiés*] in the eternity of some [illusory] age in which we and our grandparents are one" (p. 429).

This petrifying, essentialist vision of Africa is one that Glissant has, from the beginnings of his career as a writer, vocally contested—most notably, perhaps, by substituting (Caribbean) Negritude's romanticizing cult of a mythic là-bas with a localized politics of Antillanité, "the awareness of a Caribbean reality that has Africa as one of its components, the predominant component, but not the only one."[28] In this critique he has not been, of course, alone in the Antilles; as the young Mathieu, like his alter ego Glissant, would have been well aware, the ideology of Negritude had already been severely criticized by Fanon in *Peau noire, masques blancs* (1952), and was, as Michel Leiris put it in a 1955 overview of France's new Caribbean *départements*, well on its way to becoming a cliché that "seems little by little to be veering toward inauthenticity, manifesting itself as an aesthetic or sentimental theme, one that is all the more arbitrary given the considerable cultural, to say the least, distance that in fact separates even the darkest person from the Antilles and a black African."[29] It is this attention to cultural distance and geographical difference that generates Glissant's call for Antillanité—a call to which later generations of Franco-Caribbean writers have proven especially sensitive in their at times revealingly Oedipal responses to Césaire who, in their opinion, has been supremely guilty (in Confiant's words) of "forgetting that whatever little bit of Africanness that has been retained in the Antilles has necessarily been filtered through creole culture (and thus been deconstructed in it)" (*AC*, p. 37). For these writers, the creole culture with which Lafcadio Hearn was so awkwardly beginning to grapple in *Youma* from the limited perspective of his own nostalgic exoticism has become one of the exemplary models for reading a globalized, and in important respects postmodern, condition. As Confiant puts it, in a passage that we have already had occasion to quote in part, "the term 'Creole' is . . . eminently modern, not backward-looking and colonial as some might think; indeed, it is even postmodern insofar as it signals the emergence of a new model of identity that one might call 'multiple' or 'mosaic,' which is in the process of developing and making itself visible everywhere in the world, notably in the West's megalopoli" (*AC*, p. 266).

Glissant's long-standing and clearly articulated commitment to what Confiant has called "this irreversible phenomenon," of which "creolization has been, over the course of the last three centuries, in a way the foreshadowing" (p. 266), explains the central role that his theoretical works play in my own explorations of the postmodern condition. But it is not simply his prescient vision of creolization that will be of interest to us in this particular chapter; rather, I will be concerning myself with the way that this vision is inextricably tangled up with other ideological commitments that appear to push him in quite different, post/modern directions. Notwithstanding the critique of Césaire and the ideology of Negritude that his invocation of the medusa implies, it is undoubtedly also significant that despite his best efforts at avoiding contact with them, Mathieu nonetheless eventually gets bitten by the very thing that he is attempting to avoid, at which point he comically shouts out in his questionable Italian, "*sono battuto delle meduse!*" (p. 38). This apparently innocuous phrase will be repeated at the very end of the novel in a list of many such phrases taken from the novel— a list prefaced by the author's claim that his book is "filled with sayings and citations to which you have perhaps paid no attention, secure in the conviction that you have grasped their meaning [*persuadé que vous êtes de les avoir pénétrées*]" (p. 516). In the light of the attention that we have paid to this particular image, it is possible to venture at least two possible interpretations of this uneasily penetrable sentence. First of all, this contact with the medusa marks the impossibility of swimming safely away from the historical depths that, as we saw in the passage from the *Poétique*, it conjures up: rather than simply moving forward into the creolized future, the Glissantian oeuvre—touched, as it were, by the *m(éd)use* of history—will remain inseparable from an ambivalent encounter with and attachment to the past. Second, given the intertextual connections that bind this medusa to those in Césaire's "Ode à la Guinée," might not the recollection of Mathieu's "beating" at the hands of these Césaire-surrogates be an admission on Glissant's part of the extent to which he has himself, notwithstanding his stated opposition to Negritude and his personal ambivalence (at best) toward Césaire, failed to negotiate entirely the minefield of these and other such petrifying essentialist ideologies and ideologists? Might Glissant not be admitting to the presence in his own work of traces of the very thing that he has consistently put into question and yet with which, in a sly gesture of self-portraiture and self-critique, he here reveals himself as having been on intimate terms? To what extent is Negritude, say, still contained within the apparently quite different politics of Antillanité? Or, to pose another such question, one that will be absolutely vital to our discussion of Glissant's novels in this chapter, how does a Fanonesque politics of national identity and anticolonial resistance—an ideological position to which (as was certainly never the case with that of Negritude) Glissant once seemed wholeheartedly committed—fit in with the anti-ideological poetics of *inter*national creolization that he has so productively pursued over the entirety of his career as a writer and especially over the course of the last decade?

These are the sort of *genealogical* questions with which Glissant, especially in his novels, has become increasingly concerned, and it is the importance of such questions, and of their being posed, that I want to argue for in this chapter. In his latest novels, *Mahagony* and *Tout-monde*, Glissant adopts an explicitly metafictive position in which he puts many of the authoritative ideological claims and posturings of his earlier novels and works of theory into question—ironizing them, and yet also preserving them in the form of memorial traces that continue to have their ambivalent place in a present to which they are no longer adequate. It is this inadequacy to the present that, despite the younger Glissant's differing responses to them, joins together such apparently diverse positions as Césaire's Negritude and Fanon's nationalism. As my reading of the episode of the medusas suggests, these positions may well be inadequate to the present, yet they are still inevitably, if problematically, present in it. Given this situation, the task of the writer becomes one of carefully registering the dimensions of this "phantom-like" presence rather than, to put it in metaphorical terms, simply taking upon him or herself the heroic role of Perseus and, in a straightforward act of decapitation, putting an end to these petrifying ideologies, or even to the Medusa of ideology itself. As I will be arguing in the following broad overview of Glissant's work as a novelist, it is the dream of such definitive acts that his novels have been gradually declining away from since the publication of his first, *La Lézarde*, in 1958. As I will then go on to show in the last section of this chapter, it is only with the appearance of *Mahagony* in 1987 that Glissant finds a textual mechanism for coming to grips with the inadequacy of the ideologies to which he once subscribed but that he finds himself in the uncomfortable position of having survived. In *Mahagony*, Glissant metafictively reflects upon his own survival as a writer: upon what has indubitably been lost and what may well have been gained in what I will be arguing is his transition from the *engagement* (in Sartre's sense of the word) of modernist ideologies to the "(dis)engagement of the postmodern." If, as Glissant once put it early on in his career, "the writer is always the ghost of the writer he wants to be" (*IP*, p. 36; "l'écrivain est toujours le fantôme de l'écrivain qu'il veut être"), then *Mahagony* can be best understood as a dialogue between these two writers, between the writer Glissant once hoped to be and the other—the *fantôme*, the *revenant*—that he has become. It is the events leading up to this recanting dialogue that we must now begin to address.

In order to discuss the gradual shift in Glissant's novels from a modernist to post/modernist perspective, one that he has himself begun to thematize in autobiographical asides in his most recent theoretical works (as the second of this chapter's epigraphs testifies),[30] a brief overview of his life and works is in order. Born in 1928, Glissant attended the Lycée Schœlcher in Fort-de-France during the years of the Vichy occupation in Martinique, at the same time that Césaire was teaching there and editing the journal *Tropiques*. Often misrepresented as having been one of Césaire's students, Glissant from the beginning of his career as a writer struck out in a rather different aesthetic and political direction from the author of the *Cahier* (and I will be returning at the beginning of Chapter 7 to the problem of gauging the relations between the work of these two literary giants). After the liberation of the island and its formal incorporation into France as a département, Glissant left for the *mère-patrie* in 1946 and began to establish a reputation for himself, first as a poet and soon after as a literary critic, novelist, and playwright, with such works as *Les Indes* (1956), *Soleil de la conscience* (1956), *La Lézarde* (1958), and *Monsieur Toussaint* (1961), respectively. During this time, he was also becoming personally involved in the decolonization movement that was then reaching its apex in Africa and the Caribbean: close friends with his fellow-islander Frantz Fanon, Glissant would help found with the Guadeloupean poet Albert Béville (better known as Paul Niger) the Front Antillo-Guyanais, an independence-minded movement that was disbanded by De Gaulle in 1961. Because of his new status as a political dissident, Glissant would be prevented from returning to his native island until 1965, a year after the publication of what remains perhaps his most substantial novel, *Le quatrième siècle*. Having finally been allowed to return to Martinique, Glissant would, over the course of the next decade and a half, not only publish several more novels (*Malemort* [1975], *La case du commandeur* [1981]), but continue—albeit in a less directly politicized manner—to combat what, with an increasing pessimism, he was coming to see as the "successful colonization" of Martinique by the French: notably, by founding L'Institut Martiniquais d'Études in 1967, the stated goal of which was to "connect teaching to a non-parodic culture developed by the Martiniquan community,"[31] and starting up the journal *Acoma* (published sporadically between 1971 and 1973). Some of the articles from *Acoma* would find their way into his magisterial *Discours antillais* (1981), a wide-ranging work of theory for which he is perhaps best known in the English-speaking world and where many of his ideas on métissage and the creolization process were first formulated. Since the beginning of the 1980s, his career has taken on a more global dimension: he served for several years in Europe as the director of the *Courrier de l'Unesco*, moving on in 1988, a year after *Mahagony*'s publication, to act as chair of Louisiana State University's Center for French and Francophone Studies, a post he recently left for a teaching appointment at City University of New York.

The most comprehensive biographical account of Glissant can be gleaned from the more than seven hundred pages of Alain Baudot's bibliographical reference guide to both his writings and their critical reception over the past four decades.[32] Given the many genres in which Glissant has worked, generalizations about this reception are difficult to make, but in the case of his novels it is fair to say that, at least until quite recently, an admiration for his "poetic" style has more often than not been balanced by a cautionary appraisal of that style. From the outset, with the very mixed reviews of *La Lézarde*, Glissant would be tagged with the reputation of being a difficult writer whose emphasis on style (the frequent rupturing of traditional syntax, the insistent creolizing of standard French, the baroque convolution of personal and historical narratives, and so on) at times seemed intrusively to conflict with the readability—and hence for some readers, political efficacy—of his novels, which were often viewed as being "so hermetic that one has to question the social value of what he has produced."[33] As the Martiniquan critic René Ménil put it, with Glissant "the way of telling tends to win out over what is being told"; this is not necessarily a bad thing, Ménil added, but "the criticism that can be made of Glissant is that his style is too showy and his various [stylistic] devices are as a result too much in evidence."[34] Maryse Condé once complained, in a similar vein, that "Glissant's work is so obscure that it is often necessary to turn to commentaries on it in order to try and elucidate it," going on to wonder "whether his work—precisely on account of its extreme abstruseness—can have the therapeutic power he is striving after. Can one envisage a therapist who cannot communicate with his patients?"[35] Glissant has always been at pains to counter such criticisms (which, given his rapidly increasing stature, have become much less frequent of late) by adopting the Stendhalian position that he is the "prefacer" of a literature that has yet to come into existence,[36] arguing that the colonial condition of the Antilles, and the subaltern condition of the Caribbean as a whole, gravitates against the very act of an *in*formed reading of his work in the present ("les lecteurs d'ici sont futurs," as he puts it in *Malemort* [p. 231]). Moreover, he supplements this essentially historical argument with an ethical, and indeed ontological, appeal to what he calls "opacity." If, however, the later novels of this "préfacier d'une littérature future" continue to pursue, by means of this opaque style, a future that remains to be read *otherwise*, we will see that in *Mahagony*, and a fortiori in *Tout-monde*, this "unreadable" style is one that now markedly differs from itself, because it has been self-consciously reinscribed alongside a plethora of other more accessible voices whose presence in the text puts into question the prophetic, and some might even say pompous, claims about the present and for the future to which the earlier novels, and the earlier novelist, unironically subscribed.

The authors of the *Éloge de la Créolité* provide a very revealing account of their own mixed reactions to Glissant's work. Describing their attempts as young writers who, refusing "to shut themselves away in the ideology of Negritude," were trying to come to an understanding of their own Caribbeanness, they note that Glissant was in the beginning of little use to them: "Glissant himself was not much help to us, taken up as he was with his own work, distanced by his rhythm, persuaded that he was writing for readers of the future." "Faced with his texts," they continue, "it was as if we found ourselves faced with hieroglyphs, vaguely detecting there the rustling of a path [*voie*], the oxygen of a perspective" (p. 23). This relative indifference (and even, at least in the case of Confiant, hostility)[37] to Glissant and his work, motivated by the sort of concerns mentioned in the previous paragraph, eventually gave way to a belated conversion on the part of the authors of the *Éloge*. Glissant's consistent critique of Negritude, and his increasing emphasis on creolization—as both a cultural and textual practice—began to strike them as a viable foundation for their own literary projects. Since the mid-1980s, Chamoiseau and Confiant have become enthusiastic disciples (and some would argue vulgarizers) of Glissant, whom they praise for having managed to distance himself from the sort of ideological errors to which earlier writers—intent on assimilating themselves to an *elsewhere*, be it Europe or Africa—were subject, and perhaps even from ideology itself. With typical gusto, Chamoiseau and Confiant claim that "he does not fall into any illusion, be it that of Europe or that of Africa," because "he understands that these two terms of the equation must be supplemented with all the others, in their boundless internal interactions, out of which arose another cultural reality that can no longer be divided into its main elements, even if these elements can be located."[38] And it is certainly this absence of illusions toward which Glissant's work tends, in its attempts at thinking about cultures in terms of relationality, and relativity, as opposed to aboriginality, and absolutes. Glissant urges us to think in terms of a contradictory whole (or what he like Schiller calls "totality") as opposed to isolated parts of that whole: as he puts it in the *Poétique*, describing the merits of a global perspective, "if the imagination of totality helps no one organize resistance, one can at least believe that it might enable all of us to protect ourselves from so many of the mistakes that resulted from the old ideological ways of thinking [*se garantir contre tant d'errements qui sont provenus des anciennes pensées de l'idéologie*]" (p. 217).

As with the sort of double-edged claims from the *Poétique* that we analyzed toward the end of Chapter 2, however, the limitations of this global imaginary are patent: if "structuring resistance" remains part of the postcolonial writer's agenda, as in a world full of inequalities and injustice it undoubtedly must, then this relational thinking has its limits. Once these limits are crossed, however, any guarantees against the "errements qui sont provenus des anciennes pensées de l'idéologie" (or what Lyotard famously referred to as "metanarratives") would appear to be ruled out. The above sentence thus situates us *between* an open totality that, in its complexity, cannot be read in any univocal way and the simple act of structuring resistance that still depends upon the very *errements* away from which Glissant is apparently directing us. As I will be demonstrating both in this chapter and at strategic points in my later discussion of Maximin (who functions in my argument, for better and worse, as the very model of a postmodern writer), Glissant's work is, from start to finish, committed to any number of ideological errors made in the name of structuring resistance; these errors stem, for instance, from a *questionable* (which is certainly not to say wrongheaded) belief in the reality of such things as national identity and cultural alienation, as well as, in his portrayal of Martinique and the average Martiniquan, a reliance upon such dubious tropes as "the dying island" and the "happy zombie"—to say nothing of his enthusiastic allegiance to the ethnographically and ethnocentrically problematic ideas of French theorists like Deleuze and Guattari. The most obvious repository for these errors is his most politically grounded and committed theoretical work, *Discours antillais*,[39] which as Jack Corzani once pointed out often seems to have been written from the intolerably authoritative perspective of the "Martiniquan-who-knows-everything-about-Martinique-and-the-Martiniquans."[40] Maryse Condé has also noted this penchant for order(ing) in her acerbic analysis of "the various commands decreed about West Indian literature" by generations of male authors: in his many attempts at providing models for a national literature, Glissant—like Césaire before him—has put forward a series of stylistic and political imperatives that may actually contribute more to the consolidation of the problem of literary creation in French Caribbean literature than to the realization of its envisioned solution. If malaise there is, it can, according to Condé, be attributed "to the very commands enumerated throughout the history of West Indian literature by the various generations of [male] writers"—commands that even more emphatically structure the aggressive rhetoric of a manifesto like the *Éloge* as well as Chamoiseau and Confiant's hyperbolic claims on behalf of Glissant.[41]

That these claims are erroneous would hardly be worth arguing (although given the ongoing canonization of Glissant in French and North American literary circles, and the effusive commentaries his work has generated, one certainly needs to keep his limitations in mind). It is, however, a necessary pre-text for the argument that I *am* in the process of making here: namely, that Glissant's novels have always worked against, at the same time as they invariably embodied, the sort of authoritative, ideological imperatives to which a writer like Condé rightly objects and that abound in *Discours antillais*. In this respect, the novels have always contained within them an element of postmodern self-critique, while at the same time actively pursuing the sort of questionable ideological agendas adumbrated in the previous paragraph. The metafictive dynamics of *Mahagony* and its magnificent sequel *Tout-monde* formalize this postmodern dimension, displacing the political concerns of earlier and more visibly committed novels without simply erasing them; these novels "e-laborate" such concerns, working their way *out of* what they are nonetheless simultaneously expanding upon. At times this elaboration appears to take the form of a simple reversal: for instance, if the Fanonesque idea of alienation had in the past been central to his analyses of what was wrong with his native Martinique, Glissant has increasingly shown the capacity to turn against this rhetoric, as when in *Tout-monde* he discusses the apparently problematic identity of the so-called *Négropolitains* (people of Antillean descent living or born in France) and rejects the very categories upon which Fanon's anticolonial vision of the world was based. There is no point, Glissant argues, tearing oneself apart "between those impossibles (the alienated being, the liberated being, this-that-and-the-other being)" (p. 274), for to do so is to ignore the manifest possibilities offered by the complex and novel state of *be(com)ing* that is creolization, which "permits each and every one of us to be both here and elsewhere, . . . harmoniously at rest and restlessly wandering," simultaneously (in Trinh T. Minh-ha's words) "rooted and rootless."[42] As stated, however, this "e-laboration" of previous positions is never a simple matter of palinodically overturning the past: if the conception of an "être aliéné" (and of its counterpart, the "être libéré," which in Glissant's earlier writings—as we will see—was most often figured in the guise of the heroic maroon) no longer plays a central role in Glissant, it remains present on the margins as a (re)sounding echo that gets ambivalently translated into his increasingly postmodern novelistic universe—a universe from which the ideological resolutions he once might have hoped for are emphatically absent.

As the critical literature on Glissant's novels overwhelmingly attests (and part of what I am attempting to do in this section of the chapter is simply introduce the reader to some of the more important contributions to this literature), an initial reading of Glissant's first four novels lends itself to viewing them in (the no doubt theoretically inadequate) terms of a linear trajectory from the relative optimism of *La Lézarde* to the pessimism of *Malemort* and *La case du commandeur*. The pessimism of these latter novels results from a sense of cultural fragmentation and directionlessness: the novelistic protagonists, and history itself, are increasingly portrayed as following a bewildering array of trails that do not amount to a viable path for the Antilles and its peoples—to allude to one of this chapter's epigraphs ("Chacun suivait une trace. Toutes ces traces ne faisaient pas un chemin" [p. 219]). In 1955, Michel Leiris pointed to the difficulty of finding this path, given the culturally dislocated position of France's *départements d'outre-mer*: "to find one's path [*voie*] in a situation where one can neither adhere absolutely to the culture disseminated by a distant and very different (in its population as in its living conditions) metropole, nor turn for support to a culture of long-standing tradition that to a certain degree would be a

national culture, obviously constitutes a difficult problem."[43] Notwithstanding the difficulty of resolving this "problem" in the Antilles, as opposed to what at the time appeared (at least in the mind of someone like
Aimé Césaire) the relative simplicity of doing so in the context of an Africa
in the process of decolonization,[44] it was precisely such a resolute path, in
the form of a synthetically unified culture, that the young Glissant gestured
toward at this same moment in history in his *Soleil de la conscience*:

Now, in the Antilles, where I come from, one can say that a people is positively
building itself. Born in a hotbed of cultures [*un bouillon de cultures* (a culture
medium for bacteria)], in this laboratory where each table is an island, here is a synthesis of races, of customs, of knowledge, but that is aiming toward a unity of its
own. The question is, in effect, can this synthesis achieve that unity? (p. 15)

As with Carpentier's formulations of Caribbean identity in the coetaneous
Explosion, Glissant's account here seems tempted by the vision of a finished *unité* in the future as opposed to that of the unfinished *synthèse* that
confronts him in the present. To put it in terms made famous by Fernando
Ortiz (and nicely glossed by Gustavo Pérez Firmat), Glissant seems here to
be raising the possibility of an eventual "neoculturation," of a "new cultural synthesis created by the merging of elements from the old and new
cultures."[45] As Pérez Firmat notes, Ortiz conceived of this "synthesis"
(Glissant's "unity") as the end product of the formative process of cultural
interaction that he labeled "transculturation"—a word that Ortiz occasionally used to refer to this future synthesis of cultures but that, as Pérez
Firmat points out, more "properly designates the fermentation and turmoil
that *precedes* synthesis" (*CC*, p. 23). For Pérez Firmat, it is precisely this
state of "transition, passage, process" that is "the best name for the Cuban
[and by extension Caribbean] condition"—a condition of "indefinite deferral" (p. 25) in which the finality of "neoculturation" is neither likely nor
desirable. Although an appreciation of this indefinite deferral will eventually become a cornerstone of Glissant's poetics, the author of *La Lézarde*—
published two years after *Soleil de la conscience*—is still very much intent
upon finding a definitive response to the question of cultural unity.

Glissant's first novel, and in many ways his most accessible (it is as yet
the only one to have been translated into English and upon its publication
in France it received the illustrious Prix Renaudot), *La Lézarde* tells the
story of a revolutionary band of young men and women—modeled on a
group called *Franc-Jeu* to which the young Glissant had belonged—who
have taken it upon themselves to assassinate a local government official assigned the task of quelling political unrest on the island in the days leading
up to the 1945 electoral campaigns that would result in Césaire being voted
mayor of Fort-de-France and a representative of Martinique in the French

Chamber of Deputies. As one critic especially invested in the aesthetics of social realism has put it, this first novel is "refreshingly optimistic": Glissant "appears to be insisting on the perfectibility of the human being and the possibilities of a deepening ideological consciousness, given the appropriate circumstances."[46] *La Lézarde* moves forward in a relatively straight line toward an assertion of what in a 1958 interview Glissant identified as "the moral autonomy that our particularity as islanders demands."[47] There is an unfolding sense that, as the narrator puts it, "a people is slowly returning home to its kingdom" and that they "know the road to take" (p. 51). This *route* leads both through and beyond, enacting and transcending, what Glissant would broadly (re)define in *L'intention poétique* as the fleeting moment of "negritude" (which I will translate here with a small *n* to mark its difference from Senghor's essentialist concept): "negritude is always a moment in time, a total combat and, as a consequence, fleeting and fiery. Everywhere that Negroes are oppressed, there is negritude. Each time that they take up a knife or a gun (their) negritude ceases." It is this "deed through which [negritude] transcends itself" ("l'acte par quoi elle se dépasse"), and by means of which "a person achieves possession of himself" (*IP*, p. 148), that *La Lézarde* attempts to write into existence. As Glissant had argued a year before in the pages of *Présence africaine*, only such self-possession—the logical end-product of decolonization—can ensure the flowering of the novel in black nations: on the day when, by virtue of his being "free to express himself within the parameters of his own country and addressing it directly, the novelist will have thus overcome the difficulties related to his art, on that day the black novel [*le roman nègre*] will reach its full maturity, its very own classicism."[48] In the same way that the nineteenth-century Bildungsroman projected a state of maturity as the culminating point of its protagonist's narrative trajectory, *La Lézarde* looks forward to this day of liberation and the waning of a "pre-classical" adolescence within the bounds of which it nonetheless remains—as one of its main protagonists, Mathieu Béluse, notes when, some thirty years later in the pages of *Mahagony*, he comes to reflect upon this first novel in a metafictive conversation with the author of *La Lézarde* and characterizes it as being primarily a report on the "adolescent unrest that had for us figured the foaming crest of a burgeoning wave, the first stammerings of the word [belonging to] those peoples who were beginning to rise up on the world's horizon" (p. 156).

If there are ample traces of *La Lézarde*'s political optimism in Glissant's second (and, at least until *Tout-monde*, most ambitious and substantial) novel, *Le quatrième siècle*, it is nevertheless obvious that the forward impulse of the first has in large part given way to a tragically Faulknerian reconstruction of the past (a point I will be developing at the beginning of the next chapter). The passage toward a classical maturity appears to have been blocked off, entailing an aesthetically felicitous but politically indeterminate detour through several centuries of Martiniquan history. This history is revealed over the course of a decade-long dialogue between the young schoolboy Mathieu and an old *quimboiseur* (sorceror, healer) Papa Longoué, who each in their differing but increasingly compatible ways—the way of the archivist and of the storyteller, of writing and orality, respectively—attempt to clarify the dark "night" of the past, to unravel the events that brought their respective ancestors to the island in 1788 and that followed upon this arrival in the New World (the "ante-Béluse" having taken the path of apparent compromise, accepting his slavery, and the "ante-Longoué" that of overt resistance, becoming a maroon immediately upon disembarking from the slave ship). The vertiginous detour into the past that Glissant effects in this novel marks a moment of divergence from the revolutionary ideology of Fanon. Glissant here remains only partially loyal to the moving, and still very relevant, critique of a mythologizing and narcissistic obsession with history that concludes Fanon's *Peau noire, masques blancs*: "the discovery of the existence of some black civilization from the 15th century does not testify to my humanity. Whether one likes it or not, the past is of no help in guiding me in the present."[49] In line with this sentiment, a veil is cast over Africa in *Quatrième siècle*: the continent functions as an absent origin to which the reader is given no access. Glissant thereby stresses that what is important is the passage of the ancestors from one world to the next, their negotiation of a middle space of constantly renewed beginnings that is situated between an entirely African past and a wholly Caribbean present.

But even this negotiated past has no place in the liberated future that Fanon envisioned: both whites and blacks, he continues, "need to distance themselves from the inhuman voices that were those of their respective ancestors, in order for authentic communication to begin. Before taking up this affirmative voice, freedom requires that we try and put an end to our alienation" (p. 187). In stressing the need to understand what in *Quatrième siècle* is called "the mechanism inherited from the past" (p. 280) and the extent to which the present is inextricably related to that mechanism, Glissant disrupts the affirmative voice (*voix*) and the straightforward path (*voie*) into the future that Fanon would have the decolonized subject take up after the necessary "effort de désaliénation." If, as Glissant would argue several decades later in an article entitled "D'un baroque mondialisé," "all human cultures have gone through a period of classicism, an era of dogmatic certitude" (*PR*, p. 93), then it is fair to say that *Quatrième siècle*, in its indeterminate interrogation of the past, supplements the progressive cultural model of decolonization, just as the baroque does the classical, and thereby prepares the ground for the eventual disappearance of what had once been dogmatically held ideological certitudes about the future. And yet this baroque reconstruction of the past by no means entirely covers over the classical intentions that were so prominent in *La Lézarde* and that Glissant continues to point toward in his second novel, most notably in the figure of Marie Celat (Mycéa), the future wife of Mathieu. Primarily concerned with issues of praxis, she acknowledges the importance of digging into the past, but also knows that the memorial concerns of Mathieu and Papa Longoué will be fruitless if not oriented toward the future and made in the name of that *acte* which motivated the revolutionary group in *La Lézarde*: Mycéa embodies a faith, which the novel ultimately appears to share, that she and Mathieu "will together go beyond [*dépasseraient*] knowledge in order finally to enter into the deed—not the evanescent gesture, not the short-lived passion of before, but the fundamental deed itself, which would establish its own permanence, confirm its own existence" (p. 273).

It is no doubt significant, as we learn from later novels, that the programmatic marriage of Mathieu and Marie Celat does not last for long: Mathieu leaves the island, Mycéa remains, and in this separation one gets a premonition of the growing pessimism that characterizes Glissant's next two novels as they attempt to articulate the relation between writing and action in a Martinique that he was increasingly coming to view and lament as having been "successfully colonized," as having been (to cite a particularly relevant phrase uttered some thirty years earlier by Césaire) "robbed of its revolution."[50] After a ten-year hiatus in which he reestablished himself as a political and cultural presence on the island, Glissant published *Malemort* in 1975, stylistically his most experimental novel and one that, like *La case du commandeur*, was intimately linked to the scathing indictments of Martinique's "morbid society" that he published throughout the 1970s and that would eventually be collected in *Discours antillais*. In these novels, as Richard D. E. Burton puts it, "the future-directed chronological progression" of the first two novels is gone and their "carefully contrived plenum" has become a vacuum.[51]

Glissant had once remarked that "the suffering of peoples cannot be expressed; only their hope, their presence" (*IP*, p. 13). In *Malemort* he puts this dictum to the test, confronting the unspeakable situation of a world from which hope—conceived in terms of national liberation and cultural autonomy—is largely absent. Although the novel ranges across the centuries—and indeed takes the reader back to a time on the island well before *Quatrième siècle*'s 1788 point of departure—it is primarily concerned with the degradations of the present, being an abrasive account of "the turbulences of deracination in the Antilles" (as he described the novel in the in-

troduction to an excerpt from it published separately in the pages of
Acoma),[52] of the suffering and absurdities to which the island's inhabitants
are subject, but also subject themselves. Notwithstanding, or precisely because of, the island's relative material prosperity (vis-à-vis the rest of the
Caribbean), Glissant's Martinique is in a sorry state: parasitically dependent upon French capital and social assistance, it is a society of pure consumption where little or nothing is produced, a client economy with a hy-
pertrophied tertiary sector, a political dependency inhabited by peoples
whose minds have been zombified by the mass media of France and the
United States.[53] This novel shifts the focus away from highly individuated
characters like Mathieu and Marie Celat or the discrete ancestral lineages
of *Quatrième siècle* to a disparate cast of characters of whom a trio of odd-
job's men, collectively referred to as Dlan Medellus Silacier, emerge as the
most prominent. Like most everyone else in the novel, these *djobeurs* are
following "traces déracinées" that lead no place in particular (p. 61); "the
avatism of the characters, their lack of revolutionary or ideological initiative, distinguishes them from the characters of the first two novels."[54] Indeed, the aimlessness of this deracinated present is enough to generate a
nostalgic perspective in which the narrator of *Malemort* almost ends up fa-
voring such "full caricatures" from the past as the assimilationist professors
of the Third Republic over "the sort of elongated shadows that we have become" (p. 151). In this mournful situation (not surprisingly, the novel begins with a lengthy account of a funeral procession, seeming to mark the
fact that, as Césaire had recently put it, "traditional Martinique is well and
truly dead"),[55] even the act of asserting one's cultural identity has been
cleverly preempted by the "paracolonial" authorities. In a section revealingly entitled "Télés," the "Minister in charge of the *Territoires d'Outre-
mer*" notes that "obviously, it's up to us to facilitate the emergence of this
country's cultural identity. People don't give enough thought to cultural
identity" (p. 194). Appropriating the rhetoric of cultural identity, this tele-
vised bureaucrat stands as a monstrous double of the author himself, whose
work is intent upon a similar task of salvaging, and producing, that very
identity.

   The "root metaphor" of blocking and/or blockage has always been, as
Sylvia Wynter argues, central to Glissant's oeuvre,[56] but with *Malemort* this
metaphor finds no outlet beyond itself. Where obstacles impeding the
movement forward toward political and cultural autonomy appeared eminently removable in *La Lézarde*, they have by this point taken on an air of
permanence. Viewed historically, Glissant's growing sense of frustration in
the early 1970s is clearly a special variant of that "national disenchantment"—in the Tunisian novelist Hélé Béji's phrase—that was setting in
over much of the recently decolonized world at the time and finding ex-

pression in its literature. Following upon the euphoria of independence and the "celebratory novels of the first stage," what Anthony Appiah identifies as the second and properly "postcolonial stage" of the African novel is "postoptimist": this stage is typified by the production of "novels of delegitimation" that are "no longer committed to the nation" (*IMFH*, p. 152). Béji's *Désenchantement national* (1982) is an exemplary meditation on this loss of commitment and the dilemmas it provokes: for her, nationalism—and its ideological corollaries such as "national culture" and "cultural identity"—"has kept none of its promises."[57] "The national breakthrough and its revolutionary transparency has lost this transparency," she notes; "the bedazzlement is over" (p. 14). Independence has failed to arrest "the collapse of social life and communal culture that began with colonialism" (p. 125). This pessimistic global vision informs Glissant's novels, overdetermining his own local anguish in the face of the Antilles's ongoing integration into France. Glissant's persistent attempts at writing "our novel" ("le roman de nous")—to cite a phrase of his that J. Michael Dash has rightly taken as emblematic of his novelistic enterprise as a whole[58]—are thus compromised by the double knowledge that what Césaire once advocated but never delivered upon has not come to pass in the Antilles ("if freedom is always mediated through the nation, then the scantiest of nationalities will always be infinitely more substantial than the richest of imperial abstractions")[59] *and* that the dream of the nation-state and the transparent community it was to have embodied has already proved, to say the least, a highly problematic reality in other parts of the decolonized world. If, as Alain Finkielkraut has put it, the *nous* was once "the pronoun of a recovered authenticity" in societies undergoing decolonization, it has now become that of "an obligatory homogeneity": formerly the "warm space of a combatant fraternity," the *nous* has turned into "the glacis where public life withers and congeals," a convenient way of papering over (ethnic, religious, sexual) diversity in the name of an artificially integral community,[60] of protecting oneself from what Bhabha has referred to as "the anxiety of [the nation's] irredeemably plural modern space" (*LC*, p. 149). Under these changed conditions, what (sort of) sense does it still make to speak of "us"? This is the question that haunts Glissant in *Malemort*, and if a positive vision of this collective subject seems more and more unlikely, he nonetheless continues to assert the reality and necessity of this subject by conserving it in such typically *negative* pronouncements as "we now use up what little strength we have in efforts at erasing ourselves by resembling others" (p. 156).

His fourth novel, *La case du commandeur*, poses this same question, attempting to elucidate "our difficult obscurity" ("cette obscurité difficile de nous"), to reassemble "these disconnected selves" ("ces mois disjoints") into a coherent whole (p. 239), but the situation proves as or even more dire than in *Malemort*: as Frederick Ivor Case rightly pointed out at the time, "of the four novels this is the one in which the least hope for 'redemption' of Martiniquans is expressed."[61] As was by this point de rigueur for a Glissant novel, *La case du commandeur* is made up of a series of tangentially related episodes (many of them intertextually generated from stories told in his previous novels) that leap back and forth across the centuries. The final section takes up the story of Marie Celat from where *La Lézarde* and *Quatrième siècle* had left it, chronicling her separation from Mathieu, the loss of her revolutionary faith in both the *acte* and the future that it was to have inaugurated, the premature death of her two sons, and her gradual descent into what would "officially" be termed madness. The novel is prefaced by an extract from the *Quotidien des Antilles* that describes Marie Celat's madness in a parodically assimilationist journalese and it ends with another, equally inane, extract in praise of Martinique's psychiatric hospital, the supposed envy of the entire Caribbean. These newspaper clippings provide the ironic parentheses within which the "unofficial" account evolves—an account that attempts to unravel "these knots of commingled silence and night" (p. 28), to give voice to the collective subject toward which the novel obsessively drives but that, from the very first sentences, it seems virtually resigned to falling short of.

"*We* who were perhaps bound never ever to form, in the final accounting, that one body by means of which we would begin to enter into our span of earth or into the surrounding violet sea (its birds now defunct, itself shot through with a volley of tar) or into those prolongations of it that weave for us the world at large [*l'au-loin du monde*] . . . " (p. 15): thus begins the novel's lengthy second sentence and in it we find clustered many of the central concerns of the *Discours*—a sense of ongoing ecological disaster, of the Martiniquan's failure to take true possession of the land, to become aware of fundamental connections with "la mer violette" that surrounds the island (the imperative of Antillanité), or to enter into meaningful relations with the tout-monde. The absence of this "corps unique" creates a situation in which "each self, becoming 'I' or 'he'" imprisons itself "in a faltering opacity, like that of an island disappearing into some elusive blue yonder" (p. 16). This is the insular condition that the novel analyzes, corroborating Glissant's vision of the "Hawaii-ification" of the Antilles and looking forward with horror to the day when, as he put it in an interview around this time, "Martinique will disappear as a community."[62] A single paragraph constitutes each of the novel's twelve chapters: the resulting absence of paragraph breaks has the effect of making virtually every page look alike, rectangular blocks of print that visually figure the blocked nature of what he is describing. If the very end of *Case* leaves the reader with some dim glimmer of hope in the resurfacing of Marie Celat from the depths of her madness, the overall vision of the novel is relentlessly down-beat, as Burton—writing in 1984—makes perfectly clear: "the vision of *La Case du commandeur* (as of *Le Discours antillais* and, before it, *Malemort*) is so extraordinarily pessimistic that one wonders quite how—if at all—Glissant's writing will develop in the future."[63] It is precisely this question that I will eventually be addressing in my reading of *Mahagony*.

Before doing so, however, I would like to flesh out this general portrait of Glissant and of the itinerary traced in his novels by briefly elaborating upon one of the most prominent features of the "national disenchantment" with which his third and fourth novels are infused: namely, the breakdown or attenuation of the binary structures upon which both colonial and anti-colonial discourse depended—structures that our modernity both demands of us and in its complexity incessantly dissolves (as we saw, for instance, in the case of Bernardin's nature/culture, here/there dichotomies). Béji stresses the importance of this breakdown to an understanding of the postcolonial scene: "there are no longer two realities, colonial and national, confronting one another, but two realities overlapping with one another," she argues.[64] It is no longer possible to see these realities as simply antithetical—a mat-ter of *nous et les autres*—or in terms of a simple linear succession from colonial dependency to independent nation. It was precisely such binary op-positions, by contrast, that were at the heart of Fanon's analysis of colo-nialism and revolutionary struggle during the last years of his life. At the very beginning of *Les damnés de la terre* (1961), he asserts, for instance, that "le monde colonisé est un monde coupé en deux," and then goes on to show—in a way that anticipates Glissant's own "exploration of landscape as a key to consciousness"[65]—how that division is inscribed in the physical disposition of colonial territory: "the dividing line, the boundary, is marked by the military barracks and the police stations," he notes, adding that these two zones are "inhabited by different species."[66] Such stark divisions are central to Glissant's work, the classical frame upon which his increas-ingly baroque figurations are hung: as he put it in a 1964 interview, "in every person from the Antilles there is a being who accepts and one who re-fuses."[67] In his early novels "this deeply rooted duality in the Antillean character" finds expression, most notably, in his symbolic treatment of the island's physical and cultural geography: as Burton points out, "the essen-tial binary opposition of Glissant's vision of Martinican history" is supplied by "the polarity of lowland/plainsfolk/bondage and highland/hill-folk/free-dom."[68] The hills serve as the site par excellence of authentic resistance and *grand marronnage*, while the plains symbolize submission and the compro-mised (or from another perspective creolized) identity that was to emerge on the plantations and then later be refined in the degraded urban setting that the narrator of *Quatrième siècle*—in a typically modernist attack on cities—revealingly identifies as "the unspeakable thing that raises its voice in order to muffle the call of the heights . . . the vacuum into which the history of the land and the knowledge of the past is sucked, and in which it gets lost" (p. 221).[69] For Glissant, such historically determined partitions of nature must, to be sure, eventually be dissolved—that is, dialectically resolved—in order for a truly integral Martiniquan identity to constitute itself. As Jacques André notes, an "elemental reunification of the morne and the plain, of the land and the sea" is the necessary precondition in Glissant for the emergence of that "new man" prefigured by the *actes* of the revolutionary group in *La Lézarde* or by the resistance of the "splendid and isolated maroon, who avoids the detour of the Plantation and the acts of submission it repeatedly involves."[70]

As the young narrator of *La Lézarde* comes to realize, anticipating Glissant's later claim that it is the Caribbean writer's task "to lay bare [*dévoiler*] the life-giving dynamism of a rekindled dialectic between Caribbean nature and culture" (*DA*, p. 133), the purpose of the story (and the history) that he is recounting is to rejoin (in both senses of the word) a nature from which its protagonists have been severed. The heroic tale of his companions "had been but one long ferocious rush to escape from the pettiness that was being forced upon this country, and with which it was being bombarded at the same time that shame and poverty were being distilled from it"; it was "an absolute attempt at rejoining the flamboyant, the great silk-cotton tree, the gleaming sandbar" (p. 216). The figure who most consistently embodies in Glissant's work this rejoining of man and nature is the maroon, an ancestral model for the sort of revolutionary activity with which the first novel is engaged. As Sylvia Wynter approvingly notes in her reading of *La Lézarde*, Glissant opposes a "Maroon identity" to an "imposed and nihilated identity" and valorizes the former's "defense of a still-autocentric tribal-lineage model of being secured by a retreat to the mountains and to the ancestral past."[71] Burton fleshes out this portrait in his description of the Glissantian maroon:

[He is] the unconditional refuser of the system, usually African-born, who succeeds in creating an authentic culture and community outside the plantation with which he retains only the most tenuous of links; he is the absolute outsider, and he and his progeny embody a continuing tradition of wholeness and dignity that contrasts sharply with the accommodations and compromises with the system made by those who remained on the plantations and those who today inhabit the lowlands and, above all, the towns.[72]

Fresh off the boat from Africa, the ante-Longoué of *Quatrième siècle* immediately escapes and instinctively heads for the hills and the only place "where the dogs would never be able to track him down" (p. 45). His pursuers, who cannot follow his trail ("la trace du marron" [p. 47]), are forced to acknowledge his victory and in this way he succeeds in effecting a "rejection without the slightest compromise of a servile nature."[73]

This act of resistance, through which the maroon "opts out of the System,"[74] allows for the establishment of two major binary oppositions in the novel. The first is that between "un être qui accepte et un être qui refuse," between the "marron du premier jour" and his arch-enemy, Béluse, who by contrast does not flee upon embarkation. This opposition remains a foundational point of reference for the politically militant novels of, say, the Jamaican novelist Michelle Cliff, as when she didactically reminds the reader of her autobiographical novel *Abeng* (1984) of the myth that "in the beginning [in Jamaica] there had been two sisters—Nanny and Sekesu. Nanny fled slavery. Sekesu remained a slave. Some said this was the difference between the sisters" (p. 18). The second opposition is that between the maroon and the man who would have been his master, La Roche. In one of the most memorable scenes from *Quatrième siècle*, Longoué and La Roche meet head-to-head ten years after the former's initial act of marooning, and engage in a "conversation" that, as André notes, significantly bypasses "the false harmony and the illusory community of Creole" (p. 118): the one speaking proper French, the other an African language "that he was doubtless making use of for the first time in ten years," they are situated in sovereign opposition to one another, two mutually inaccessible selves engaged in a strange "dialogue that was not one" (p. 106). This is the sort of polar division that characterizes Fanon's (de)colonized world and that is forcefully invoked in the ending of Césaire's *Une tempête*, where the arch-colonial Prospero, having decided to stay on "his" island rather than return home to Milan, nostalgically calls out to a Caliban who has long since fled his former master and taken up residence in nature: "Well then, my old Caliban, it's only us two on the island, only you and me. You and me! You-Me! Me-You!"[75]

In the above examples, the presence of a binary opposition allows for the composition of a particular identity: the "maroon" and the "slave," or "Caliban" and "Prospero," are the *effects* of this doubling process rather than its cause. The very act of positing a fixed identity, indeed, may well be inseparable from this process. Let us return for a moment to a key passage from Rousseau that we discussed in Chapter 1: as Louis Marin has pointed out, given Rousseau's autobiographical project of self-representation and his symbolic equation of this self with the circumscribed topos of the island, the appearance of a second island on Lake Biel should come as little surprise to the reader. The smaller island that Rousseau would like to "colonize" is, as Marin puts it, an essential element for conceiving of the first: "identical double, simulacrum, phantasm, the image itself or its negative, archaic or anticipatory, the 'other' island will play its part in the economy of insularity and its 'sameness,' serving as its external point of reference [*repère*], but one that is as near as possible, in order to constitute and institute, properly, the [self's] refuge [*repaire*]." The appearance of the *other* island allows for the refuge of the *same* to produce and think itself, "to found itself in its own truth [*dans sa propre vérité*]."[76] What are we to make of this "proper truth" and the identity that it enables? My claim has been that Glissant takes them, and the oppositional logic that they enable, very seriously in his earlier novels; however, one must immediately supplement this claim with a contrary one that acknowledges the potential *absence* of this "proper truth" in these same novels. A double reading of Glissant is always possible, one in which he is read as not only inscribing and consolidating binary oppositions, but as showing up the extent to which such oppositions mark not (only) distance but (also) complicity. Thus, in *La Lézarde*, Garin and Thaël, the collaborator and the revolutionary activist assigned to kill him, are said to be "complicitous in their distance from one another" (p. 122), and this same remote complicity characterizes Longoué and La Roche's "dialogue qui n'en était pas un," which unfolds athwart "that mutual lack of understanding in which they find themselves bound to one another" (p. 111; "cette incompréhension mutuelle dans laquelle ils se retrouvaient solidaires"). Not only, then, do such oppositions provide the potential ground for the revolutionary praxis of decolonization, but they are also, first, examples of what Wilson Harris has referred to as the "diseased, cultural and psychical twinships" that play such a central role in colonial systems and that ought to be absent from a truly post-colonial literature,[77] and second, premonitions of the (un)likely solidarity upon which a poetics and politics of creolization is (to be) built.

It is a performance of this sort of double reading, I have argued, that post/colonial literature demands: this demand can be explicitly acknowledged by an author (as it will be in Glissant's later metafictive writings) or it can be more or less ignored (as I believe it is, to the detriment of a more complex rendering of Caribbean reality, in the examples from Cliff and Césaire referred to a few paragraphs back).[78] Between these two poles stretches a continuum within which Glissant's first four novels "e-laborate" the binary oppositions and dialectical strategies that were central to his initial project (in the Sartrean sense) as a writer and yet that he knows he must decline (away from) once their viability in the newly decolonized nation-states begins to appear ever more doubtful (an unviability that is all the more apparent in a still ambivalently colonial society like that of his own Martinique, where dominant and dominated "do not form a pair of contradictory opposites [but are], rather, each in the other," and where "no binary logic could account for their relations").[79] In André's words, "a dialectic that begins with what can only be at the end is a flawed one, to say the least,"[80] but it may be precisely this type of "bien mauvaise dialectique" that is the most appropriate for coming to grips with the compromised realities of the post/colonial world.

Several years after writing *La case du commandeur*, Glissant would refer to the period from 1960–1980 as "our tempest years" ("notre passé de tempête").[81] What form will politics take after the passing of this tempest? This is the question that Glissant's writings have confronted over the past two decades. Any response to this question must come to grips with the realization that the project of nation-building can no longer be convincingly formulated in Fanon's radically oppositional terms, and it must take into account the fact that in the Antilles everything, including the post-1981 France-wide policy of "decentralization," seems to be pointing toward the islands' "renewed integration into the core of the nation as a whole."[82] Under these conditions the figure of the maroon can no longer play the role of ancestral model in the same way that it once did for Glissant, as was already becoming clear in his novels from the 1970s. As Burton points out, "it is precisely in th[e] no-man's-land between hauteurs and habitation, especially in towns, that the vast majority of Martinicans today live, move, and have whatever being is vouchsafed them and from that same in-between world that the characters of *Malemort* and *La Case du commandeur* will principally be drawn."[83] In these novels from the (end of the) tempest years, Glissant is increasingly forced to acknowledge the primacy of this intermediate space, this indeterminate milieu in which the paths of resistance and submission meet and become virtually indistinguishable one from the other; as a result, "the maroon figure loses its actuality and recedes toward the realm of timeless myth."[84] In these novels there is, as Bernadette Cailler has pointed out, "a constant and perhaps growing tension between the exaltation of a primordial, quasi-allegorical Maroon and the attention paid to the daily life and sufferings of the common people" (and of women in particular); tellingly, the maroons in *Case*, who "constitute the anecdotal framework" of the novel, "remain for the most part silent presences."[85]

Despite their disciplelike relationship to Glissant, it is significant that Chamoiseau and Confiant (who has argued recently against Martiniquan independence and for a "commonwealth" relation to France along the lines of that obtaining between the United States and Puerto Rico [*AC*, p. 298]) do not take the figure of the maroon as the central touchstone for their post/Glissantian poetics. Where the maroon functioned for the Glissant of *Discours antillais* as "the only true popular hero in the Antilles" (p. 104), the historical figure of most significance for these exemplars of the generation of writers who have followed in Glissant's wake is the creole storyteller, who does not exist on the peripheries of colonial society but in close proximity to its center. The storyteller is someone who has an "official" function in the world of the habitation, which Confiant defines as "the primary mould in which the Martiniquan personality was formed" (*AC*, p. 59). As Chamoiseau puts it, the storyteller is "a man who has been 'civilized' [*un homme policé*], who in his daily life in no way resembles a maroon."[86] Capable of living "in the very heart of negation,"[87] he serves as the model for an attenuated and complicitous resistance that does not attack from without but erodes from within. Glissant himself, writing in the aftermath of the tempest years, will come to a similar (re)evaluation of the cultural importance of the plantation and its policed subjects. In the *Poétique*, for instance, Glissant defines the plantation as one of the testing grounds for that "always multilingual and often multiracial entanglement" that he sees as characteristic of a globally creolized world (p. 86). Far from being, in the words of Frederick Douglass, "a little nation of its own," characterized—as in the exoticizing vision of Hearn's *Youma*—by "isolation, seclusion, and self-reliant independence,"[88] the plantation is

one of the principal sites where some of our present modes of relationality [first] developed. This world of domination and oppression, of muted or openly declared dehumanization, saw the decisive and obstinate elaboration of [new] forms of humanity. The tendencies of our modernity make their appearance in this outmoded place on the margins of all [historical] dynamics. (p. 79)

It is no doubt this belated sensitivity to both the oppositional and relational aspects of plantation life—to the dissimulated resistance and the ambivalent accommodation that were both equally a part of the "shared process of creolization" it promoted, albeit largely unbeknownst to master and slave alike—that explains why Papa Longoué, lying on his death-bed in *Toutmonde*, comes to the realization that, unlike his earlier incarnation in *Quatrième siècle*," he was more deeply moved by the first Béluse than by the first Longoué" (p. 93). Longoué's shift in perspective with regard to the two ancestors who arrived in Martinique in 1788 doubles that of Glissant himself as he begins to renegotiate the blocked passageway in which the receding tempest had, as it were, left him marooned.

The trajectory I have been sketching in this chapter does not, however, simply end with a shift from one poetics and politics to another, from the maroon and the heights to, say, the storyteller and the plantation. To give precedence to a cultural paradigm that is apparently more in tune with the historical realities of our own fin de siècle may well be inevitable, but it is also once again to fall into the errors and exclusions of ideology, as Glissant well knows. Thus, he is quick to caution that if "the Plantation is one of the wombs of the world" in which some of the formative laws of "the cultural métissage that engages all of us" can be discerned, it is most assuredly "not the only one, but simply one among so many others" (*PR*, p. 89). To have perceived—indeed, to have lived through—the inadequacy of one cultural paradigm is, one might hope, to have learnt to approach all such paradigms with the greatest caution and sense of both their relativity and their relatedness. It is not (merely) the various points of departure or end products of Glissant's trajectory as a novelist that are of value to the reader but the *transitions* from one error to another: these transitions open up a space of what Bhabha would call "interstitial intimacy" (*LC*, p. 13), one in which the new errors can be read not only as contradicting but as supplementing the old, translating them into the present in the form of inadequate memories that nonetheless disturb what might otherwise appear to us in the here and now as ideological certitudes. Such transitions and translations, which become visible in the sort of linear readings (from optimism to pessimism, and so on) that I have been performing in this section but which ultimately put into question the usefulness of such readings by situating us between the two ends of the line, are—as Benitez-Rojo has argued—typical of "Caribbean discourse" (and, I would add, of post/colonial literature as a whole). Writing in the aftermath of his own break with Castro and the Cuban Revolution that he once served so enthusiastically, Benitez-Rojo asserts that "Caribbean discourse" is "never a matter of *subtracting*, but always of *adding*," for it carries

a myth or desire for social, cultural, and psychic integration to compensate for the fragmentation and provisionality of the collective Being. The literature of the Caribbean seeks to differentiate itself from the European not by excluding cultural components that influenced its formation, but rather, on the contrary, by moving toward the creation of an ethnologically promiscuous text that might allow a reading of the varied and dense polyphony of Caribbean society's characteristic codes. (*RI*, p. 189)

The desire for integration is generated out of a lack of foundations, and this desire, in turn, attempts to generate those foundations (in such forms as "Africa," "the maroon," "the creole storyteller"): this is the ongoing and incomplete(able) transitional process that I have been describing. Viewed from a certain perspective, to be sure, it *can* be understood in terms of subtraction, if one focuses solely on either the original lack or the collapsing of a particular foundation that was generated in order to answer this lack (the loss of Africa, the disappearance of the heroic maroon, the death of the authentic storyteller, and so on); equally, this transitional process can be seen as subtractive if one fixates only upon the glaring absence of those final solutions toward which our ideological errors inevitably tend, but that this process endlessly defers. But what Benitez-Rojo is saying—and what Glissant's transition from a modernist *engagement* to the "(dis)engagement of the postmodern" confirms—is that this ongoing process of supplementation can *also*, and more fruitfully, be seen as paving the way for the creation of a common cultural ground in which apparently contradictory positions are conjoined in an unlikely manner without ever being resolved into the sort of synthetic unity that the continued absence of a "collective Being" monogamously (to keep in the spirit of Benitez-Rojo's admittedly suspicious sexual metaphor) demands of us.

In an early essay on Mallarmé, Glissant once spoke of "a poet's heroic perseverance in preparing the coming of what he knows will not take place (*IP*, p. 65; "l'héroïque obstination d'un poète à préparer un avènement dont il sait qu'il n'aura pas lieu"). We should by now be in a position to see that this problematic advent has, in the case of Glissant, turned out to be a double one that is generated, on the one hand, by a continued if increasingly frustrated allegiance to certain ideological metanarratives that he can no longer support with the conviction of former times and, on the other, by a growing awareness of and sensitivity to a common cultural ground that can never—by virtue of its transitional nature—be realized in and of itself, but that must always be approached via one or more of the erroneous positions that "promiscuously" constitute it. It is the non-place, the not-having-a-place, of this double advent that is the site, and the condition, explored in Glissant's later novels—an exploration that is both in marked contrast to and profoundly continuous with his earlier work.

Both this contrast and this continuity are on display in a brief episode from *Tout-monde* with which I will close here. Just after his encounter with the medusas, the young Mathieu meets a rather mysterious Italian woman called Amina who tells his fortune: she predicts that he will be wounded in a combat but, despite Mathieu's repeated questioning ("will it be in a war, the Third World War? . . . a revolution, a riot, fighting in the streets?" [pp. 41–42]), she is unable to supply him with any more details. A few pages and some thirty years later, the two meet again and converse, comparing the old and the new Vernazza and sharing their ideas about the rapidly changing world. In response to one of Mathieu's comments, Amina remarks: "You no longer talk about things in the same way, no. You've changed. And then, isn't this all a little pompous?" (p. 46). Through her deceptively simple remark, Glissant makes two essential points about his trajectory as a writer. First, he has indeed changed over the years—a change that can be understood not only in terms of the shift from optimism to pessimism that I have outlined in my account of the first four novels, but, to extend the story beyond *La case du commandeur*, in terms of the gradual emergence of a post/pessimism capable of modifying the dire perspective voiced in the novels that he wrote in the 1970s. From this post/pessimistic perspective, the "disenchantment" of the world is a given, and it is no longer a question of simply trying to prevent or circumvent such things as what Mathieu angrily, yet also resignedly, refers to in *Tout-monde* as "the slow trivialization [*banalisation*] of the Martiniquan landscape, buried under concrete, and the polluting mediocrity of progress" (p. 52), but of acknowledging that in many important respects the damage has already been done and that the challenge of this banalized world resides in learning how best to circulate within it rather than posit—in a nostalgia for the past or a projection onto and into the future—a definitive way outside it. It is this disappearance of horizons that the eventual fulfillment of Amina's prophecy at the very end of the novel confirms. When she predicted that Mathieu would be wounded in combat, his immediate reaction was to think of this struggle in the potentially world-historic form of a revolution or a riot, and as the novel progresses he repeatedly muses over her prediction and its possible referents. The wound that Mathieu eventually suffers, though, is anything but heroic: he will receive it at the hands of a couple of wandering vagabonds who, in the banal episode with which the novel ends, break into the island residence of the now successful Martiniquan author and attack him with a cutlass, possibly killing him.

What the ending of the novel thus effects is a critique of the prophetic vision that once generated both Glissant's revolutionary claims and his jeremiadic diatribes. In the place of these claims and diatribes emerges the very different vision of, as he puts it toward the beginning of *Tout-monde*, "un voyage sans voyage organisé, une rupture d'horizons" (p. 48): an "unpackaged" tour of a world that can no longer be organized with an eye to ideological horizons that have been once and for all breached, that have undergone a rupture that consists precisely in the absence of the sort of ruptures that were basic, say, to the rhetoric of decolonization (a rupture of ruptures, as it were, similar to what Derrida—as we will see in Chapter 7—refers to as "apocalypse without apocalypse"). All of this, then, points toward the different "way of speaking" that, as Amina notes, characterizes the older Mathieu. And yet the two Mathieus do have something in common, and it is what Amina refers to as "pompousness" (a word, one should remember, that also means "magnificence"). To speak of the "rupture of ruptures" is no doubt as pompous, and erroneous, as to speak simply (in terms) of ruptures. Mathieu has not stopped producing theories about the world, for all these theories are very different from the ones that previously engaged him. All that has changed is the newly ironical perspective on these theories—an irony that Glissant forces us to acknowledge by including Amina's commentary on them. It is such commentaries with which *Mahagony* and *Tout-monde* abound, and that significantly differentiate them from his earlier novels. If all his novels have been attuned, à la Faulkner, to the problematic and subjective status of narration, *Mahagony* is the first, as we will now see, where Glissant explicitly puts into question his own "pompously" authoritative claims, ironizing them, reframing them, whilst at the same time cautiously preserving and persevering in them. In so doing, he takes readers beyond the ideological endings, and the mournful end of ideology, that marked his earlier novels—thereby offering, if not a way out of, then at least other ways of looking at, and living through, the badly (and banally) ended story of a "successful colonization" that was chronicled in those novels. In a lexicon at the end of *La case du commandeur*, Glissant provides the following definition of the "malfini" (chicken-hawk), a bird that makes frequent appearances in his work: "Large shore bird. Disappearing" (p. 247). Without denying the importance of this disappearance and the badly ended (*mal fini*) story it entails, we can nonetheless supplement the preceding definition with a second and differing vision of the end that this word evokes: the "*mal*fini" is, after all, always also the *incompletely* finished. It is precisely in the ambivalent space between these two endings that the post/pessimistic fiction of *Mahagony* and *Tout-monde* will locate itself.

(Un)ending Colonialism: The Place of Memory in Édouard Glissant's 'Mahagony'

> A tree is often all that one requires in order to characterize the needs of a country's people and the care Providence bestows upon them. Trees are the real monuments of nations.
> —Bernardin de Saint-Pierre, *Études de la nature*

From the perspective of conventional literary history, Bernardin de Saint-Pierre and Édouard Glissant could not be further apart, and yet to peruse the former's dauntingly vast oeuvre is to become aware of the fact that he is not (merely) the caricature that our own century has made him out to be, the sentimentalizing author of an "ouvrage proprement affligeant," to recall Camus's description of *Paul et Virginie*, but a prescient thinker remarkably sensitive not only (as I argued in the preceding chapter) to the complex dynamics of cross-cultural mixing but to the urgent need for thinking the poetics of place (*lieu*)—a need that in our own transnational age has become all the more pressing as we attempt to understand the interface between the global and the local with which we are confronted on a daily basis. As Bernardin puts it at one point in his *Études de la nature*, "every place has its very own harmonies and . . . displays them in turn" ("chaque lieu a ses harmonies qui lui sont propres, et chaque lieu les présente tour-à-tour").[89] It is a preoccupation with reading such places, with defining the contours of the local, that draws him closer than one might initially think to a writer like Glissant, whose insistent emphasis on place is one of the most defining features of his own oeuvre. In an epigram from *Tout-monde* entitled "Le lieu" (attributed to Mathieu Béluse and taken from his *Traité du Tout-monde*, a title that playfully doubles a work of the same name that Glissant would publish in 1997), he notes that a sense of place is "uncircumventable" (*incontournable*), a central fact of one's existence. However, he (or, if you will, Mathieu) goes on to caution, "if you want to prosper in this place [*profiter dans ce lieu*] that has been given to you, take into consideration the fact that henceforth all the places of the world, and even the stars, converge [*se rencontrent*]": "the lieu," he adds, "widens out from its irreducible center just as much as from its incalculable outer edges" (p. 29). If Bernardin and Glissant thus share a sensitivity to place—a will to identifying (with) the local—they are nonetheless separated by two centuries in which Bernardin's quest for harmony, for the "proper" dimensions of a place, has become an increasingly complex one. Bernardin's own chaotic and diffuse theoretical work, indeed, suggests this complexity, given its inability to maintain the orderly ("tour-à-tour") succession it desires in the face of the historical dissonances and "improprieties" that we examined in the previous chapter; his writing consistently exposes its own inability to separate the *lieu* from the world that (in the form of colonialism) molests the local and that thereby renders its borders incalculable. Eminently aware of his island's chaotic relations to the tout-monde that he knows is always-already present in it, Glissant's Mathieu is, of course, much better equipped to deal with this incalculability; and yet, no less than his Enlightenment predecessor, he continues to figure his own place as possessed of a "centre irréductible" from which alone one can profitably explore that which overlaps and interferes with it (and that which, in Glissant's most pessimistic scenarios, threatens to inundate it).

At one point in *Quatrième siècle*, the narrator notes—in accordance with the Manichean outlook that I commented on in the previous section— that there is a "natural division" between the plains and the mornes of the island, but that it did not have "the time to harden, to set": as a result, the division has been "sown everywhere" in an untimely manner (p. 147). The island is thus striated with histories that in their dissemination deny us any unmediated access to the place as it "naturally" is; this loss of nature, and the consequent predominance of what Edward Said has termed the "hybridizing intrusions of human history,"[90] is something that Bernardin repeatedly comes up against in his work, and two passages from his nonfictional accounts of the Île de France are worth citing here because they nicely introduce the issue of memory that will be central to my discussion of *Mahagony* in this section. Both passages revolve around the presence of maroons (a presence that proves indissociable from their absence), who wind up embodying the impossibility of the sort of orderly exposition that

Bernardin's poetics of place would like to achieve. The first passage comes during the central narrative moment of the *Voyage*, Bernardin's journey on foot around the island: having just left a particularly idyllic scene ("ces beaux lieux"), he encounters a government troop of blacks armed with rifles and in the company of a woman captured after a successful raid on a maroon camp. She is carrying on her back "a sack made of screw pine leaves. I opened it. Alas! inside was a man's head. The beautiful landscape disappeared, and I could see before me only a place of abomination" (1.204). This is the abominable place of history from which the "landscape" (*paysage*), a key term in Glissant's poetics, has disappeared: it is now to be read only retrospectively, a palimpsest shrouded over by the historicized body of the decapitated maroon. In similar fashion, in a passage from the *Études* where he again recalls his circumambulation of the island, Bernardin enthusiastically describes his encounter with an uninhabited part of the Île de France "which seemed to me the loveliest part of it, even if," he adds, "the runaway slaves [*les noirs marrons*] who take refuge there had, on the beach, cut down latanias [fan palms] (with which they make their ajoupas [huts]) and, on the hillsides, palm-kernels (of which they eat the edible tips) and lianas (which they use for their fishing nets)" (3.224). As in the first episode, the image of cutting is central, although here it is the maroons who exercise agency, an agency that (as their absence suggests) cannot be brought within the sentimentalizing and prototouristic terms of Bernardin's prose. This prose, as in the first passage, can only figure the maroon in terms of either (female) captivity or a (male) decapitation that is synonymous with the (re)appearance of history in his text—terms that anticolonial counterhistories would themselves inevitably appropriate and turn to their own uses.[91] What is most important for our purposes, however, is that in both cases this disruption of his story, and the irruption of history into his orderly world, creates a space for memory, a space of conservation: in spite of "these disorders," Bernardin notes in his account of the maroon refuge, "this stretch of the island had preserved the traits of its age-old beauty." This site has become a *living* monument to the original that once stood in its place: it is this paradoxical conjunction of the organic and the monumental, ultimately, that the whole of Bernardin's work attempts to valorize.

It is significant that the maroons have disrupted this site by cutting away at various types of trees, because trees serve as Bernardin's primary metonym for the identity of a place and as his preferred metaphor for the organic memory by which he hopes to trace his way back to the harmonies of an "antique beauté." As he says of trees in the *Études*, "more than one might think they help attach us to the places in which we have lived. Our memory fastens onto them, like points of convergence [*points de réunion*] that share secret harmonies with our soul" (5.227). The old man in *Paul et Virginie* confirms the importance of such memorial "points de réunion" when he speaks of the two Indian coconuts planted at Paul and Virginie's birth, out of which arose "two coconut trees that were these families' only archives" (p. 147), or when he apostrophizes the papaya tree planted by Virginie: "O tree whose posterity still lives on in our forests, I looked upon you with more interest and reverence than the triumphal arches of the Romans!" (p. 222). This praise of the living archive or monument inevitably provokes a negative commentary on real monuments such as the Roman triumphal arches, which are less effective in conserving the past precisely because they are *intended* to conserve it. This opposition, basic to Pierre Nora's influential distinction between memory and history (as we will see in a moment), crops up everywhere in Bernardin's work: as he says at the end of his eleventh *Étude*, the villager "does not need architectural monuments to ennoble his landscape. A tree in the shade of which a virtuous man has rested leaves one with sublime memories; the poplar tree in the forest recalls the combats of Hercules, and the leaves of the oak tree the triumphal wreaths of the Capitol" (4.433–34). This example is revealing, of course, because of the way nature gets routed back into the very realm of culture that it supposedly precedes: the harmonies of place, and the living monuments in which we can read this place, lead us back to the combats of Hercules or the wars of the Romans in the same manner that the pastoral of *Paul et Virginie* leads us back to the ravages of a colonialism that was the real source of those disorders he identified in his account of the maroon refuge. (It should be added that the ecologically minded Bernardin was very well aware of these colonial disorders: speaking, for instance, in his *Études* of the *acajou* [mahogany tree] and how the islanders use it to build canoes because "sea worms" never attack them, he notes that "this lovely tree has found more formidable enemies than worms—namely, the European inhabitants of these islands, who have almost totally destroyed the species" [4.391].)

If I have once again rehearsed the double bind that is at the very foundations of Bernardin's writerly enterprise, it is because his emphasis on trees and his association of them with memory is so central to Glissant's *Mahagony*. As the Martiniquan Serge Denis remarked in the notes to his 1932 French translation of the creole folktales that Lafcadio Hearn had transcribed some forty years earlier, "in the North, a tree is simply a tree," whereas in the Antilles "it is a personality, one that imposes itself; it possesses a vague physiognomy, an undefinable *moi*. It is an individual, a Being."[92] The opening sentences of each of *Mahagony*'s first two paragraphs reflect the same kind of logic as Denis's (a logic that would be entirely familiar to Bernardin): "trees that live a long time," we are told, "secrete mystery and magic"; we are then informed that "a tree is a whole country, and if we inquire what this country is, then right away we find ourselves plunging into the thicket of time, the ineradicable darkness we struggle to clear away, injuring ourselves on its branches, which leave our legs and arms indelibly scarred" (p. 13). After these opening claims, we are then introduced to the individual subject who is in the process of producing such apparently authoritative statements about trees and the way that they "are" a country: this *je* notes that for a long time he had confused the *mahogani* and the ebony tree, "on account of having first encountered them only in the form of a piece of furniture or a block of wood, both reduced to the same indefinable state by human hand or by the wear and tear of time [*par l'équarrissage ou par les usures du temps*]," and "even now I still wasn't sure whether one of them might not go under the name of *acajou*" (pp. 13–14). This first-person narrator thus situates himself on a trajectory leading from nomenclatural confusion to greater clarity—a trajectory that takes him away from unnatural reductions of the tree (such as the "équarrissage" that we also remarked upon in Bernardin's portrait of the Williams Plain) to a more organic but still incomplete idea of it that bears a family resemblance to the earlier arboreal visions of a Bernardin and that will empower our narrator to see this tree as a symbol, a living monument, of the island's history.

We soon discover that this narrator is Mathieu Béluse, main protagonist of several of Glissant's earlier novels, who is itching to get out from under the pen of the man he refers to as his "chroniqueur," an author who shares many of his obsessions—both are, for instance, "obsessed with places, every one of which is a potential character" (p. 24)—but from whose supervision Mathieu now longs to break free. It is this metafictive dimension of the novel that I will be chiefly concentrating upon in my discussion of *Mahagony*, showing the way in which it allows Glissant to expose, in both senses of the word, the sort of authoritative statements that Mathieu makes in these opening paragraphs: to continue putting them on display (pursuing, that is, a rhetoric with obvious affinities to the organic vision of Bernardin and Hearn's translator, and that also engages the sort of "secret depths" we saw at work in Coetzee's *Foe*), but also to put these statements into question by *con*-textualizing them, that is, placing them side by side *with* other texts, within the framework of a multiply authored story that cannot help but relativize Mathieu's claims.

For the moment, though, I would like to pursue a little further the metaphor of the tree and its relation to place and memory by turning to the French historian Pierre Nora's distinction between (deep, organic, lived) *memory* and (superficial, inorganic, written) *history*. History, Nora contends, "is the always problematic and incomplete reconstruction of what no longer exists"; it is a "representation of the past." By contrast, memory "is an always current phenomenon, a connection lived out in the eternal present." This lived as opposed to reconstructed link with the past can accommodate the sacred and its poetry, whereas "history, always prosaic, chases it away."[93] Such binary oppositions proliferate in Nora's account, and consistently reveal his animus against the dead time of a history that, unlike its "absolute" counterpoint, "knows only the relative." "Memory is life," he asserts, "and living groups its bearers; for this reason it is permanently evolving, open to the dialectic of recollection and amnesia, unconscious of its successive distortions, vulnerable to all sorts of utilizations and manipulations, given to long periods of latency and sudden revitalizations" (p. xix). But the immediacy of this "mémoire vraie," Nora contends, is becoming increasingly rare, our access to it mediated by a history that is necessarily at a distance from its object and that can only recuperate the past in the form of "traces" (p. xix)—traces that negate the very thing toward which they point (for instance, "the sacred has become entangled with the trace, which is its negation" [p. xxvii]). Nora's binarisms inevitably produce (since they are themselves produced by) a nostalgic scenario in which this collective memory, "toujours portée par des groupes vivants," is threatened or completely dispersed by the forces of history. Thus, the nation (to take an example that is of particular relevance to Glissant's political and aesthetic trajectory), which was one of the primary means by which "our memory kept touch with the sacred" (p. xxii), "is no longer the unified framework for a closely-knit collective consciousness" (p. xxiii). The disappearance of this "cadre unitaire," and the resulting privatization of memory,[94] is for Nora simply the last moment ("the memory-nation will have been the last incarnation of memory's history") in a dialectic of "enlightenment" that has cut us off from "real memory, social and untouched, for which the so-called primitive or archaic societies provided the model and of which they carried away the secret" (p. xviii).

Nora's distinction between "the tree of memory and the bark of history" (p. xxi; "l'arbre de la mémoire et l'écorce de l'histoire") is, of course, only one of the latest in a series of highly influential binary oppositions that have arisen since the age of Rousseau as a way of understanding our modernity: from Schiller's opposition of the naive and the sentimental, to Ferdinand Tönnies's 1887 distinction between *Gemeinschaft* and *Gesellschaft* societies, in which he "transformed his account of traditional memory into a systematic *nostalgia for memory*,"[95] to Walter Benjamin's auraticizing distinction between authentic and inauthentic experience (*Erfahrung* and *Erlebnis*),[96] and ending up with Baudrillard's apocalyptic and implicitly nostalgic critiques of "a prolonged symbolic order . . . an order of history, science, and museums" that is characterized by an "irreparable violence toward all secrets, the violence of a civilization without secrets."[97] It is this line of thought that Mathieu perpetuates in his organicizing account of trees and the "secretion" of mystery and magic that they still offer to those capable of properly reading them; it is the *end* of this line that Glissant will explore in *Mahagony* through his ironic and yet also sympathetic "contextualization" of Mathieu's vision—a vision that continually makes claims for, and in the name of, a living and organic memory that it can only monumentalize in the form of a nostalgic and artificial history. The distance that opens up between Mathieu's vision and the text's is, as I will now briefly suggest, the tenuous distance separating Glissant's modernism and his post/modernism.

As Glissant once pointed out, a novel like Faulkner's *Absalom, Absalom!* puts into play "first the affirmation of a secret, of something hidden, of a fundamental trace," and then "the process by which one tries to reveal them (to oneself), not so much in the clarity of their truth as in the sheer vertigo of this process" (*IP*, p. 178). Modernist literature of the Americas— or at least of the "other America" that, according to Glissant, is founded upon a traumatic encounter with a suddenly imposed (rather than evolved) modernity[98]—has as one of its defining features an anxiety about cultural origins and traditions that are in the process of becoming ever more occulted under conditions of modernity. What we might call first-level works of modernism like Jean Toomer's *Cane* (1923) or Carpentier's *Écue-Yamba-Ó!* (1933) are attempts at bringing this secret to light, at making the Black Southern or Afro-Cuban tradition speak its originary truth, without excessively foregrounding the conditions of narration that make this speech possible. Faulkner's *Absalom, Absalom!* and Glissant's resolutely Faulknerian *Quatrième siècle*, while continuing to pursue the "fundamental trace" of the past, most often situate themselves at a second, more self-reflexive level that insistently draws our attention to the vertiginous narrative operation by means of which this past is revealed or reveals itself to the reader. The "true" nature of this past becomes a secondary, although by no means inessential ("*moins* dans leur vérité nette") consideration in such novels; the past proves obscure, a "night" to be endlessly and perhaps erroneously traced by characters who are as much narrators as actors. And yet, for all that the self-reflexivity of these second-level modernist texts complicates the project of revealing the place of the past in the present, that project is not itself put into question: indeed, there is a sense in which such texts are even *more* committed to the existence of a past that, in Faulkner's famous words, "is never dead, it's not even past," than those of Toomer's or Carpentier's, where the narrative voice often feels compelled to (re)present the realm of tradition through the filter of a quasi-ethnographic discourse and thereby effectively deaden it.[99] The past lives on in *Absalom, Absalom!* and

Quatrième siècle (hence the importance of family genealogies to both novels): this ensures the possibility of memory, in Nora's sense—a memory that does not move forward in a straight line like the deadly forces of the history to which it is opposed but that follows the circuitous lay of the land, taking the natural route, the "tracée," rather than the artificially imposed direction of the "route coloniale."[100]

Indeed, in *Quatrième siècle*, the opposition between memory and history is explicitly thematized in the persons of the two main narrator-protagonists, the old quimboiseur Papa Longoué and the young student Mathieu Béluse, who join together in an attempt at fathoming the closely related stories of their two families, from the moment the two male ancestors (were) disembarked on Martinique in 1788 to the present in which, over a space of years (1935–45), they are narrating, and thus reliving, those stories. Mathieu, as a result of his colonial education, is estranged from the past as a living entity: for him memory has been translated into the terms of history. It has become, in Nora's words, "intentional and deliberate, lived as a duty and no longer spontaneous; psychological, individual and subjective, and no longer social, collective, encompassing" (p. xxv). Already beginning to dig around in the colonial archives (the *registre*), the young Mathieu's goal is to "establish the chronology of this history" (p. 31), to seek out the "logical coherence" of the series of episodes that he and Papa Longoué are attempting to recuperate. Papa Longoué, by contrast, rejects as artificial and sterile this sort of logically ordered history, affirming that all one can find in the archives, in the "old papers" that stand as a metonym for writing itself, is a bare-bones narrative—"arrival, sugar cane, death" (p. 213)—that reveals nothing of the past and its magic, a magic that he himself practices and embodies. A reader of nature, of "the wide open sky and the night that lies within it," Papa Longoué nonetheless seems at least partially resigned to the fact that Mathieu's history is going to supplement his own memory, acknowledging that "order and reasoning are the thing these days." His death in the novel, rather like the death of Médouze in Zobel's *Rue case-nègres*, anticipates the eventual loss of memory that will ensue if he and everything he stands for are forgotten—and it is this loss of memory that Glissant's subsequent two novels in large part lament. But in *Quatrième siècle*, Longoué remains everywhere present, figuring forth the possibility of a living, oral memory that doubles, and to some extent trivializes, the sort of archival history that the young Mathieu is learning how to write.

It is this memory that, ironically enough, the much older Mathieu in *Mahagony* has come to valorize, as his comments in the opening paragraphs about trees and the magic they secrete bear witness. Mathieu has, as it were, learned the lesson of *Quatrième siècle*: that, without the supplement of lived memory, (written) history is a lifeless product—a piece of furniture or a block of wood "ramenés au même indéfinissable par l'équarrissage ou par les usures du temps." Mathieu has, then, come to see that his archival project of elucidating the past requires this supplement, but it is precisely that insight, basic to the modernist poetics and politics of *Quatrième siècle*, that Glissant in turn *relativizes* via the later novel's metafiction, forcing the reader of *Mahagony* to put into question the authoritativeness of any statement that is grounded in this sort of binary distinction. Rather than speaking the truth at the beginning of *Mahagony*, Mathieu is quite clearly constructing it, and this construction itself retroactively reflects back upon a character like the Papa Longoué of *Quatrième siècle*, forcing us now, in the aftermath of the "tempest years," to read him differently than we might have at first: no longer to read him as the living embodiment of a people's memory, but as the modernist author's (rhetorical) attempt at positing him as such. The seeds of this postmodern insight into the fictional nature of what Nora referred to as memory are, in fact, sown in several brief but key passages in *Quatrième siècle* itself, as when Longoué—after delivering a long speech made up of what he himself refers to as words that are "too reasoned"—pauses to consider the conditions that made his speech possible, and in so doing implicitly draws our attention to the person who is narrating him and thereby translating his words into the stuff of (historical) novels: "the old man meditated over this flood of words, assessing whether he was really the one who had churned them out, or if it was another person, an inappropriate stranger [*un étranger inconvenant*] who had taken his place next to the fire, tapping his clay pipe on the nearest stone just like him" (p. 33). This other who is speaking in Longoué's place, this inappropriate stranger, can be none other than the narrator, briefly revealing himself here as the author of this stream of "mots trop raisonnés"—words that have been placed in the mouth of a quimboiseur who is not so much the embodiment of living memory as a textual site that calls this absent memory to mind.

Nora's well-known account of the binary opposition between memory and history is not, of course, as simple as I have thus far made it out to be: although his argument hinges upon the existence of these two extremes, it also leads away from and implicitly undoes them by mapping out an intermediary space, neither memory nor history, that he calls the "lieu de mémoire." Referring with this term to any number of things (museums, archives, holidays, "invented traditions," and so on), he notes that these *lieux de mémoire* are only possible in the absence of more organic *milieux de mémoire* (p. xvii): "the time of these lieux is that precise moment when a vast store [of cultural capital] disappears, no longer to be lived in the intimacy of memory, but living on only in the form of a history where it is reconstituted" (p. xxiii). These lieux are virtually *posthumous* (re)creations, "vestiges," "no longer entirely alive, but not entirely dead": they are, he notes, in an image that calls to mind the ending of *Foe*, "like shells on the shore when the sea of living memory recedes" (p. xxiv)—that is to say, like objects that produce (fictional) echoes of something that is no longer (and was never) present. Although they appear to sound, and to resound with, the living voice of memory, these *lieux* are ultimately empty of the past they evoke: as Nora admits (rather reluctantly, given his unabashed nostalgia for memory), they "have no referents in reality. Or rather, they are themselves their own referent, signs that refer only to themselves, signs in a pure state" (p. xli). The Papa Longoué of *Quatrième siècle* is one such sign, although this is by no means obvious on a first (modernist) reading in which he might have served the reader as both a guide to and an embodiment of the Martiniquan past; in the light of a work like *Mahagony*, this Longoué is himself revealed as one of the first in a series of "lieux de mémoire," posthumously signed by an author who can no longer lay claim to reviving the past that might once have acted as the unifying framework for the collective identity he wishes to postulate.

The postmodern turn of Glissant's work consists in his growing awareness of the sheer textuality of both the past and of the collective identity that the asserted presence of this past had once allowed him to posit. To address this past, he will find, is to situate oneself in a place from which it is absent, to strike out in a direction that leads away from it; after *Quatrième siècle*, this form of address that marks a turn away from the very thing being addressed (and that I will be identifying in Chapter 7 as the rhetorical figure of *apostrophe*) increasingly characterizes the intertextual world of his novels. As one critic rightly points out, the third novel, *Malemort*, has in certain respects become more of a meditation on the previous novels than "a reflection on the past, proposals for action in the present, and the outline of a plan [for the future]."[101] As another critic puts it, "the novelistic text is no longer the reflection of a reality but the diffraction of several meanings that might go toward making it up."[102] It is this textual turn, already incipiently present in *Quatrième siècle* and increasingly evident in the two subsequent novels, that is explicitly brought to the fore in the "after-the-tempest" metafictions. One critic has argued that in Glissant "the lieu is never a plane surface on which actions are performed; rather, it is a depth in the memory and in the passions of the characters."[103] In *Mahagony*, however, these depths of memory and passion are replaced by "lieux de mémoire" that only *superficially* recall the past after which Glissant's modernist works aspired, and it is in this respect that one can make sense of Bernadette Cailler's astute remark that "*Mahagony* stands out as the logical outcome of a lifelong narrative scheme which was to reach its apex in *La case du commandeur*; but it also represents its subversion."[104] Whereas a great deal of *Mahagony* continues to deal with the usual Glissantian concerns—the figure of the maroon, the critique of neocolonialism and consumerism, the passage from the oral to the written,[105] and so on—what is radically different in this novel is the way that it continually relativizes, and thereby partially undoes, these concerns by having parts of the novel self-consciously narrated by an author-figure, Mathieu Béluse, who serves as a parodic mirror of the politically engaged and modernist *chroniqueur* who authored *La Lézarde* and *Quatrième siècle*. What both Mathieu and the reader will eventually find out in the course of the novel is that in the shift from character to author Mathieu has himself entered the very domain of ideological (mis)representations—of both his own identity and that of the others whose history he shares and would relate—that he was trying to leave behind by divorcing himself from an author whose viewpoint was so clearly flawed and yet whose writing his own uncannily resembles. Neither Mathieu nor his chronicler nor the various other minor narrators of *Mahagony* will get the story, or history, right, and this admission of error into the novel opens up a space of skeptical reflection that puts any and all truths that it might credit permanently into question.

This skeptical relativization and undoing of what might once have passed as authoritative stories about cultural traditions and identities, this transformation of lived milieux into textual "lieux de mémoire," is a move that is basic to the postmodern sensibility. We find it at work, for instance, in Patrick Chamoiseau's Prix Goncourt-winning novel *Texaco* (1992); parodically (re)engaging the genre of the historical novel that has had such currency in the Caribbean, Chamoiseau frequently disrupts the linear progression of his novel and the homogeneity of the popular-culture milieu chronicled therein with metafictive passages that introduce an authorial double, an erudite town planner (*urbaniste*), who comments in pointedly theoretical and ethnographic terms both on the characters he has met in the shantytown of Texaco and on the very meaning of Texaco itself. Chamoiseau's insertion of such heterogeneous elements into the text serves to distance the reader from the (predominantly oral) community that is being evoked in the main body of the text, transforming that community and its place into the object of (a necessary) memory, a (necessary) theoretical construct. The town planner, like Glissant's Mathieu, is himself not entirely aware of the irony of his position, as can be seen from the following passage:

To wipe Texaco off the map, as I was being asked to do, would amount to amputating the city of a part of its future and, above all, of its irreplaceable treasure, memory. The creole town, which possesses so few monuments, itself becomes a monument through the care bestowed on its "lieux de mémoire." Here, as throughout the Americas, the monument is not a monumental erection; it sprawls. (p. 369)

The town planner believes that his refusal to tear down the shantytown will have led to its preservation as a living monument, something that is not an "architectural monument," to recall Bernardin's words, but that sprawls in quasi-organic fashion. For him, the creole town's "lieux de mémoire" are real, living reminders and remainders of a past that he hopes can still infuse the future. The irony of his situation, however, is that his disruptive presence in the text actually alerts readers to the "historical" (in Nora's sense of the word) identity of this quarter of the "ville créole." The town planner's presence in this site of resistance to cultural oblivion is the sign of its contamination by history; moreover, his authoritative claims about Texaco cannot be taken as such by the reader, who has access to other, (un)equally nonauthoritative and relativized-relativizing, stories about the world that he is attempting to (re)construct. His apparently living monuments are textual sites, at a double remove from the object they would memorialize—a double remove that the narrator of *Mahagony* evokes in the word "ressouvenir" (p. 140) and that is synonymous with writing itself.

This double remove, readable from the very outset in the modernist literature of an (other) America that was anxiously intent upon locating itself with regard both to its ancestry and to a modernity that threatened to obliterate any and all links with the past, rises to the surface in self-reflexive novels like *Mahagony* and *Texaco*. The postmodernism of such works consists in the distance that they force us to take from both the cultural traditions and practices in which one might once have hoped to ground one's identity and the ideological imperatives (e.g., nationalism) that might once have attached to this identity. This distance does not simply result in a forgetting of the past but, rather, in its being reinscribed, as it were, in the place of memory (and in place of what Nora referred to as memory). Rather than (only) producing a disengagement from the past and its ideologies (as the familiar postcolonial critique of a "politically ambivalent" postmodernism would have it),[106] this distance (also) allows us to engage again with that past and the sort of political *engagements* that might once have gone, but can no longer go, unproblematized. This ambivalent process of loss and recovery can be referred to as the (dis)engagement of the postmodern. At the same time as the postmodern collapse of metanarratives imposes upon us a global responsibility to disengage ourselves from the ideologies in which we might once have believed wholeheartedly, this disengagement can never be final; indeed, it necessarily turns back upon itself, resulting in provisional disengagements from that very disengagement, the continued pursuit of an *engagement* that will nonetheless never again be founded in the sort of comfortable certitudes to which we once (thought we) had access. This (dis)engaged postmodern vision does not simply renounce the dreams of earlier generations: it parodically and always also nostalgically doubles back upon these dreams, (re)citing them in such a way that both their impossibility and their (questionable) necessity are simultaneously maintained. Evoking both this impossibility and this necessity, Glissant's *Mahagony* will engage with, by skeptically (re)engaging, the sort of emancipatory narratives through which alone the end of an unending colonialism and its modernity might begin to be thought.

> My political activity . . . proves to me that I embody the
> archetypal image of the pharmacist, for I dream of provok-
> ing reactions in a sick country: I dream of infiltrating it, as a
> sulphate or a soluble, in order to influence (by acting on the
> diencephalic centers) the course of its death throes, and to
> transform this agony into regenerescence.
> —Hubert Aquin, *Trou de mémoire*

The very structure of *Quatrième siècle*, with its four sprawling chapters that indistinctly flow into one another, mirrors at the level of form the spontaneous and permanently evolving mode of collective consciousness that Nora identifies with memory. By contrast with this typically modernist appeal to organic form, the structural framework of Glissant's subsequent novels becomes decisively more pronounced and rigid, as if to emphasize the artificial, constructed nature of the story, or (hi)story, or better yet, (hi)stories that are being relayed to the reader. Glissant has carefully divided *Mahagony* into three parts, each with six chapters; the historical focus of each part is established by the tripartite "Chronology" that (as with all but the first of his four preceding novels) he attaches to the end of the novel, a linear set of dates that serves as ironic clarification of the historical events that are being circuitously presented in the body of the text. As this chronology makes clear, the first part of the novel circulates around the *marronnage* of a youth called Gani in the early decades of the nineteenth century; the second invokes the story of Maho (first chronicled in *Malemort*), who, some hundred years later, finds himself on the run for having murdered a white "colonist"; while the last part, which serves to supplement the story of Marie Celat as it was recounted in *La case du commandeur*, tells of the flight from "justice" of a not entirely admirable youth by the name of Mani in the late 1970s. The novel's three parts (which are entitled Le Trou-à-Roches, Malendure, and Le Tout-Monde)[107] can clearly be read as separate episodes in an ongoing history of resistance, of marronnage. Rather, though, than simply being distinct episodes in a linear history—a history that in many respects lends itself to a pessimistic reading, given the decreasing heroism of the maroon figures both from one Glissant novel to the next and within this novel from Gani to Mani[108]—the three episodes, despite their formal separation, are also clearly meant to be read synchronously, as the title itself suggests in the mixing together of their three names and the consequent (con)fusing of their stories, and of history itself. What these three parts most obviously have in common is the fact that each features, alongside the historical material, at least one metafictive chapter entitled "Mathieu," in which Mathieu Béluse reflects upon both his relation to his chronicler and to the three stories of Gani, Maho, and Mani that they (both Mathieu and Glissant) are attempting to reconstruct and, perhaps illegitimately, relate to one another. It is these metafictive "Mathieu" chapters, and especially the two with which the first part of the novel begins and ends, on which I will be primarily concentrating in the remainder of this chapter.

From its very first pages, *Mahagony* registers a shift away from the collective identity that was on such prominent display in the opening pages of his previous novel, *La case du commandeur*—an identity demanded by the modernist politics of decolonization and embodied in that famous line from Césaire's *Cahier*, "we are standing now, my country and I" ("nous sommes debout maintenant, mon pays et moi"). A first-person narrator (whom we soon realize is Mathieu Béluse) introduces himself on the very first page, which in itself immediately sets *Mahagony* apart from Glissant's previous novels.[109] After a few pages it becomes clear that the resolutely subjective nature of this *je* differentiates it from earlier manifestations of the first-person singular pronoun in Glissant's novels, where for the most part, as Jack Corzani points out in reference to *Quatrième siècle*, "the 'I' ['*Je*'] is a collective 'I' ['*je*'], a crowd of 'narrators' composing an almost legendary narrative in the course of which the word, which for a long time had been only a cry, in turn enchants, 'dazzles,' orders the world of the past, prepares the future, makes the need for action felt, becomes 'deed' [*acte*]."[110] This singular-yet-plural subject that Corzani describes coincides nicely with Glissant's own early claim regarding his "true" self: "I throw my lot in with the 'I' who is the 'we' of a people [*je me groupe au je qui est le nous d'un peuple*] . . . and even if I should live a truncated or unnatural existence, it would still be in the wake of a history of this 'we'; I would be an avatar of the 'we,' who with me 'here' says 'I'" (*IP*, p. 38). But it is precisely this always-already collective subject that has been displaced from the beginning of *Mahagony*, replaced by (or supplemented with) a *je* who, as Mathieu later notes of himself, is capable of maintaining a cautious distance from "that *nous* which I sometimes wanted to express or to live" (p. 86). He thus resists, at least *up to a point*, a temptation to which the man who authored him—a chronicler resembling no one so much as Édouard Glissant himself—has in Mathieu's view all too frequently given in: namely, the temptation of "merging into a beneficent 'we' that would just as easily have allowed me to vanish within it." He goes on to note that

the example of my biographer kept me from yielding to such a natural and logical propensity, remembering how abundantly and with what conviction he had preceded me along this path. I was not going to start up that racket again, pile on more of that old baggage [*Je n'allais pas recommencer la sarabande, ajouter au bataclan*]. (p. 85)

Here, Mathieu takes his necessarily ambivalent distance from the ideological presuppositions that underpinned earlier Glissant novels and in so doing opens up a space from which these presuppositions can be interrogated. Drawing attention to the author(ity) who makes truth claims about such things as an a priori collective (national, cultural) identity, the metafictive agon between Mathieu and his chronicler necessarily weakens and defers these claims: if, as we will see, Mathieu himself eventually ends up recommencing this same *sarabande* and adding on to the *bataclan*, he will do so only in the wake of an initial deferral and the skeptical understanding that this deferral makes possible.

Mathieu's commentary on his author's proclivity to speak in the first-person plural is exemplary of the metafictive dialogues that are scattered throughout the five chapters of the novel that he openly narrates. Of these chapters—all of which (with one final exception to which we will return) are simply entitled "Mathieu"—it is the first, which Mathieu himself styles as a "preface" to the narrative as a whole (p. 33), that most fully draws out the dynamics of these dialogues. As the novel opens, it is 1979, and Mathieu has returned to his native island after an absence of many years; as is only "natural," he finds parts of the island greatly changed, as for instance "this town that was not so long ago [*naguère*] flush with the stench of its sugar cane factories, which a chronicler named [in *La Lézarde*] Lambrianne, but which I know is called Le Lamentin, a town that is today caught up in the pincers of its roads, its residential developments, the bustle of its airport and the nostalgic miasma of its dying sugar refineries" (p. 14). These are the sort of modernizing degradations, from bad to worse, that generated the pessimistic vision of novels like *Malemort* and *La case du commandeur*, but if Mathieu registers them with distaste he is nonetheless more preoccupied for the moment with the uncanny effect of returning to a place where he had once, "as a creature of fiction," wandered "by the decree of a power that still imposed itself on me and barred me access to my own self" (p. 31); this uncanny sensation itself doubles what he had felt upon reading his author's previous novels and finding "in the pages of a book the channeled echo of what one has lived, and of which one only felt the tremor without having had to do more by way of naming it" (p. 18). Not only do these comments on his return to the island point to a troubling confusion of reality and fiction, and of past and present, but they explicitly raise the problem of *representation* that is at the heart of so much postcolonial literature, making itself heard, for instance, in Césaire's "ma bouche sera la bouche des malheurs qui n'ont point de bouche, ma voix, la liberté de celles qui s'affaissent au cachot du désespoir" (as we discussed in Chapter 2). What is the nature of the decree that has empowered the chronicler to represent this individual, to take him—or rather, Mathieu notes, "this image he had of me"—"for a character in his narratives, conferring an exemplarity on me that, in its mechanical simplicity, hardly did justice to me" (p. 18)?

Questions such as this motivate Mathieu's attempts to escape from under the mechanically simplifying pen of the man who had turned him into the "type and model of his own explorations in the maelstrom of our past" (p. 21). Like the maroon or renegade characters whose own stories Mathieu is trying to research and write (and that will be told alongside the metafiction of *Mahagony*), he too, Mathieu remarks of himself, is an escapee, "but from a chronicle in which I had not requested to appear, and where the author had represented me without informing me or asking for authorization" (p. 25). It is thus partially in order to redress this "ambiguous portrait" that, in "a corrective counterpoint" (p. 29), Mathieu aspires to take up the "relay" (p. 25) from his author and supplement the latter's chronicle, which "had taken up the first thread of the story but had not been sufficient for the weaving of it" ("avait enroulé le premier fil de l'histoire sans pour autant suffire à la trame"): "other words," he continues, "had to compete with it [*devaient y concourir*]" (p. 16). Developing this idea of competing-converging words,[111] he then goes on to remark that "since I was the thread, I could just as well become the unraveler [*le révélateur*], and no need for a chronicler in order to get that job done" (p. 22). This supplement, he hopes, will amend some of the errors that had found their way into the chronicler's own works, as well as incorporate important details that had been omitted from these earlier versions and avoid the infamous opacity of his author's previous work. Ultimately, Mathieu believes that in liberating himself from his author's quest and hurling himself into "the ardent confusion of this land in order to seek out there, to imagine there, light and transparency" (p. 22) he will perhaps finally render obsolete his own function in Glissant's novels as the writer-archivist who vertiginously plunges into the maelstrom of his island's "non-histoire." Thus, armed with his "reserve of dates (1831, 1936, 1978)" (p. 31), which direct him toward what he feels are the interrelated lives of three shadowy maroons or renegades (Gani, Maho, and Mani, respectively) from various periods in the Martiniquan past, he takes upon himself the authorial burden of enlightenment ("I had good reason to believe that once these dates were specified and these connections established they would serve to shed light over [*éclairer*] the whole mass of events" [p. 25]). He does so with the conviction that he can find a "rule," "some sort of law that would have imposed a hidden, or at least a yet to be discovered, order" and that would allow him to show that—their different historical identities notwithstanding—the stories of Gani, Maho, and Mani "represented the same figure of an identical force diverted from its normal flows" (p. 22).

As the preceding passage makes clear, Mathieu is himself implicated in the exemplary project of representation that has in the case of his own "ambiguous portrait" proved so *mis*representative. Aware of his author's deficiencies in this regard, Mathieu is nonetheless following along the same well-trodden path in his attempts both at self-portraiture and at historical reconstruction and it is precisely this conjunction of insight and blindness that comprises the double bind in which he is situated and out of which Glissant is writing him(self). Simultaneously the antagonist of his author— that "hagiographer of sites, who was given to spending much of his time blending together the inhabitants, their lineages, their faces, into one and the same indistinct and over powerful identity" (p. 33)—and his double, Mathieu too, like that "chronicler loaded down with his fragile datings" (p. 20), is committed to an orderly representation of the self and of the past, which would provide him with an access to that "Being" Hearn's translator saw embodied in the trees of Martinique. Thus, Mathieu remarks at the very outset of his prefatory chapter, in terms that explicitly echo Nora's distinction between "l'arbre de la mémoire et l'écorce de l'histoire," that "the being of an old tree is evasive, as long as one has not tried approaching it from all angles, taking up a scrap of bark and [from that] piecing together the entire masting" (p. 14; "l'être du vieil arbre se dérobe, tant qu'on n'a pas tenté de faire le tour, de reprendre par quelque bout d'écorce et de reconstituer l'entière mâture").[112] Writing in the belief that the hidden can be revealed, and with the intention of "replying to the old obscurities of my chronicler with a burst of light [*une poussée de lumières*]" (p. 34), Mathieu nonetheless keeps bumping up against, without ever fully admitting to, the problematic nature of his representational enterprise (a problem, one might add, that is subtly enforced in this passage by the substitution of "mâture" for "arbre"—a metonymic displacement that historicizes what ought to be natural, drawing it into the circuit of human production and, more specifically, calling to mind the means of transport that made possible both Europe's colonization of the Americas and the transatlantic slave trade). His reply keeps folding back into the very thing to which he is attempting a response, as he himself notes at several points in the novel where he finds himself in the compromising position of imitating the author whom he wanted to correct (pp. 31, 92). Such intermittent admissions of complicity register Mathieu's never more than partial insight into the fact that he remains squarely within the logic of authoritative (mis)representations from which he is trying to escape: his own "prescriptions"—the rules according to which he hopes to order his material—are written in a language that mirrors and re(as)sembles his predecessor's. The prospect of a cure that these prescriptions offer, to flesh out the etymological ironies implicit in the Québécois novelist Hubert Aquin's proto-Derridean use of the *pharmakon* metaphor in *Trou de mémoire* (1968), proves inseparable from the poison that they are meant to combat. Contaminated by the same arbitrariness and opacity, Mathieu's "corrective counterpoint" is as *subject* to error as was his former chronicler's.

If the example of Mathieu's supplementing and/or doubling of his au-thor's (mis)representations forces the reader to confront the potential erro-neousness of the laws that would impose "une ordonnance cachée ou tout au moins à découvrir," it is nonetheless also true that the reader cannot simply dispose of these laws and of this order: indeed, the text of *Ma-hagony* is incomprehensible without some recourse to the rule of historical equivalence that Mathieu has established. As a result, we as readers are forced to confront the possibility that the stories of Gani, Maho, and Mani *do* represent "la même figure d'une même force dérivée de son allant nor-mal" since, for what may ultimately be entirely arbitrary reasons, they have been juxtaposed within the pages of the same novel, and we are now forced to read them in tandem. In this respect, Mathieu's dubious rules of order accomplish the same performative work as he argues the *image* does when he notes that although his own "bookish image" has been imposed upon him by another person it "nevertheless ended up defining that which I re-ally was" (p. 29). Notwithstanding the unfoundedness of this image, it has a reality of its own—a reality that may, indeed, be the only one to which we have any access, as Homi Bhabha suggests when, in arguing against the idea of recuperating identity as an a priori or finished product, he privileges by contrast the "image of identity," which "is only ever possible in the *negation* of any sense of originality or plenitude," and goes on to define that image as "at once a metaphoric substitution, an illusion of presence, and by that same token a metonym, a sign of its absence and loss" (*LC*, p. 51). Glissant's metafiction confronts us with a world of images, alerting us to the *produced* and *producing* status of the ideas and identities it presents, and thus situating us at a point from which their authority can be put into question, but also, and inevitably, reproducing that authority and its effects. Our awareness of this ongoing production of reality, which is a necessary consequence of the novel's metafictive encounter between author and char-acter, thus creates a double perspective in which we as readers can neither fully credit nor discredit what we are told by Mathieu or any of the other secondary narrators in "this narration of mingled voices" (p. 251), this "in-finite relay of singular voices" (p. 252) that makes up the novelistic text of *Mahagony*. (That this also holds true of seemingly more authoritative and monological texts, such as his theoretical interventions, is a point that Glissant stresses at the very beginning of his *Poétique* by paraphrasing without comment an extended passage from one of Mathieu's later monologues in *Mahagony*, in which Mathieu finally gives in to the temptation of speaking in the person of the collective *nous* that he had earlier renounced and to whose authority we as readers can as a consequence no longer mechanically defer [cf. pp. 215–16 and *PR*, pp. 18–19].)

The importance of Glissant's shift away from the *nous* and toward the first person singular at the beginning of *Mahagony*, as well as his insistence on the way that authority repeats itself in spite of—or perhaps even because of—our efforts at critiquing it, can be gauged by briefly comparing Glissant's position with that of Deleuze and Guattari, whose work has so greatly influenced Glissant. In the preface to their voluminous *Mille plateaux* (1980), the French philosophers make two points that are extremely relevant for such a comparison. First, explaining the collective nature of their enterprise, they begin their work with the assertion that one should arrive at the point "not where one no longer says 'I,' but at the point where it is no longer of any importance whether one says 'I' or not," and then go on to urge their readers not to "attribute this book to a subject."[113] Second, arguing for a rhizomatic and nomadic way of thinking, they critique "arborescent" systems of thought: noting that the figure of the tree is inseparable from the verb "to be" (p. 36), and that it has "dominated occidental reality and all of occidental thought" (p. 27), they claim that they "are tired of trees" and that "we should no longer believe in trees, in roots and radicles" (p. 24); rather, we should embrace the multiplicity of the rhizome which, "by contrast with the tree . . . is not an object of reproduction—neither external reproduction like the tree-image nor internal reproduction like the structure-tree" (p. 32). As Christopher Miller has pointed out in his brilliant deconstruction of their ultimately specious postidentitarian argument, Deleuze and Guattari, notwithstanding their own claims about having broken free from the world of subjective authority and arborescent reproduction, consistently end up replicating the very patterns of thought that they are supposedly contesting (as their insistent and moralizing recourse to the verb "should" amply bears witness). Miller proves this most specifically through a close reading of those footnotes in *Mille plateaux* that direct the reader toward reference material concerning the nomads whose praises Deleuze and Guattari sing in the face of rooted, sedentary societies and selves: as Miller shows, their dependence on these sources (some of them quite dated and written from an openly colonial perspective) implicates Deleuze and Guattari in the "science of identity" par excellence—anthropology.[114] Their frequent and unexamined borrowings from anthropological sources consistently draw them back into "the mortal and dangerous world of representation" (p. 17) that they are supposedly rejecting.

In short, what recent revisionist anthropologists have critiqued as "ethnographic authority"—an authority that a metafictive text like Chamoiseau's *Texaco* both acknowledges and interrogates—proves "intrinsic to the discourse of *A Thousand Plateaus*" (p. 24), which is not, as Miller goes on to argue, in and of itself a bad thing:

the problem is not the presence of authority within *A Thousand Plateaus*; the problem is the *denial* of authority, the claim to be nonauthoritarian, and the consequent failure to come to terms with the consequence of the authority that the authors put into practice. (p. 20)

This denied authority is ubiquitous in their work, with its incessant recourse to, in Miller's words, "heavy-handed cultural representation through dualisms" from which they attempt to absolve themselves but that are clearly essential to their work (p. 32), with its all-too-familiar nostalgic appeals (in Europe, they claim, "we have lost the rhizome" [p. 28]) and its consequent exoticizing privileging of the Other ("is there not in the East," they ask, "notably in Oceania, something like a rhizomatic model that is opposed in every respect to the occidental model of the tree?" [p. 28]). As Miller sums it up, *Mille plateaux* "sets out to 'strangle' but winds up at least partially reproducing all of the following: representation, anthropology, evolution, primitivism, universalism, dualism, Orientalism, and of course negation itself" (p. 30). This inevitable reproduction, and the subjective biases that generate it, surely must be taken into account if one is to arrive at "a more convincing ethic of flow": "the delusion of 'nonauthority,'" Miller concludes, "must be abandoned" if we are effectively to work toward a "cosmopolitanism of knowledge [that] would have to face up to the consequences of the representational authority it assumes, [rather than] pretending to have no authority at all" (p. 33).

I have been arguing that it is precisely this confrontation with the consequences of "representational authority" that the metafiction of *Mahagony*, which at once conscientiously displaces and (re)places that authority, triggers. As Miller notes, "when faced with a forest, we should not simply declare that we don't 'believe in trees'" (p. 33). If Deleuze and Guattari, in their provocative but also disturbingly shallow attempts at challenging all models, are incapable of owning up to their own beliefs, or of situating them—relationally—in the context of other such erroneous ideologies (the global forest, as it were), the Glissant of *Mahagony* is committed both to relativizing and affirming those beliefs of his that have been put into question by the historical trajectory of "national disenchantment," the collapse of that radically different and truly post-colonial future to which the modernist literature of decolonization looked forward. In the wake of modernism and its failed *engagement*, he responds, as I have said, with the (dis)engagement of the postmodern, a purposefully ambivalent term by which I mean to convey Glissant's nuanced response to the postmodern condition. This response is to be distinguished from both a lack of *engagement*—a straightforward renunciation of political commitment—and from the surreptitious prolongation of modernist *engagement* that we find at work in Deleuze and Guattari, whose anti-authoritarian appeal to "imperceptible ruptures," "nomadic flows," and "rhizomatic adventitiousness" is itself clearly a last, desperate attempt at establishing an authoritative discourse with which to understand and remedy what they see as an all-too-arborescent modernity, and at preserving (to cite Spivak's critique of them) "an essentialist agenda" under the cover of a "postrepresentationalist vocabulary."[115] Neither an unexamined continuation of modernist *engagement* (Deleuze and Guattari) nor the sort of simple disengagement from it that, as we will see toward the beginning of Chapter 7, characterizes the world-weary pronouncements of a disenchanted modernist and former Marxist like the Haitian writer René Depestre, Glissant's (dis)engagement of the postmodern negotiates between these two responses, as he ironically disengages himself from his once-cherished beliefs and yet at the same time skeptically (re)engages those beliefs and in so doing prolongs a discredited but (perhaps) still vital manner of thinking that would disengage us from the postmodern and clear a space for other worlds.

Everything, in the final analysis, still depends upon what sort of stories one chooses to tell, and if Glissant's decision to put his beliefs and his stories into question is not subject, or not entirely subject, to the standard critique that a self-reflexive postmodern literature is politically regressive or insufficiently attentive to questions of "agency," it is because of his continued allegiance to the dreams of an exhausted modernism, to the "erroneous" narratives of opposition and to a logic of (re)solutions in which he can no longer entirely believe (and which, indeed, stands in an uneasily contradictory relation with his creolizing poetics) but through which alone we can think the end of an unending colonialism. Although the political ramifications of this (dis)engagement must ultimately remain *doubtful*, since those who choose to follow the pathways of a committed skepticism are always in a position of weakness with regard to the "true believers" (in Salman Rushdie's words) whose commitment knows no such bounds, there can at the very least be little question of the invigorating effect that Glissant's adoption of such tactics in *Mahagony* has had on his work as a novelist: a minor masterwork in and of itself, *Mahagony* serves as prodromus to the even more emphatically metafictive *Tout-monde*, his most recent and, in my view, most aesthetically satisfying work of fiction.

A more detailed study of Glissant's fifth novel would take us well beyond Mathieu's lucid and programmatic preface and explore the ways in which

he pursues his representational project in subsequent "Mathieu" chapters
and the ways in which that project intersects with those of the novel's other
narrators and their written or oral narrations, such as (to limit ourselves to
Le Trou-à-Roches): the journal of Hégésippe, the old hoer who has pain-
stakingly and at great risk learned how to write and whose secret journal
makes up several chapters of this first part of the novel; the monologue of
his "wife" Eudoxie who looks upon Hégésippe's writing as simply an "imitation" of the colonial *registre* (p. 58); or the brief conte of the errant storyteller Lanoué. Viewed hierarchically, these historical narrations (which
are all obviously meant to provide evidence of "the constant subversive desire originally clearly evident in the autopoesis of the slave autobiography
to blend and transcend key Western categories: narrative and documentary;
history and literature; ethics and politics; word and sound")[116] occupy a
level—or plateau, as Deleuze and Guattari would say—beneath the historian Mathieu's. Yet at the same time that Mathieu exploits this primary material as the substratum for his own orderly reconstruction of the events
surrounding Gani's curious marronnage in 1831—an account that takes up
most of the second "Mathieu" chapter, which draws the first part of *Mahagony* to a close—he is also careful to point out the extent to which the
different levels of narration cannot be truly separated because the original
"documents" are themselves of doubtful historical origin, filtered through
a variety of mediatory sources. We do not know, for instance, whether the
original of Hégésippe's journal was written in Creole—"in which case one
would have to ascribe to my informants the adapted version of which I was
made aware and of which, like an ethnologist out in the field, I had tried to
respect the letter, at times imagining it" (p. 75)—or in a rough paraphrase
of the French spoken by his self-styled masters. This same uncertainty that
comes from the blurring of distinctions between different levels of narration
will eventually extend to the historian's own words, for (as we learn toward
the middle of the novel's third and final part) Mathieu eventually renounces
his own project, handing back the role of narrator to his author, "the one
who comments." This commentator, identifying himself as "the signatory
of this narration," affirms that "he has built it around what was confided
to him by the one who declaimed it [i.e., Mathieu]," adding that "the permission to ratify such a document, which was most certainly accorded,
does not mean that the author may not have added onto the words of the
said declaimer or perverted it in places, having moreover been invited to do
just that, or mixed in with it his own feelings about things" (p. 228). With
this shift, Mathieu's first-person declamations are themselves reduced to the
same level as those of the historical characters whose stories he wanted to
relate: perverted, (re)constructed, and thus situated in an undecidable relation to the truths that they would contain. And yet even this reduction is

not the novel's last word, for the author's commentary in this chapter (and his "allusive and incomplete" glossary of Creole words [pp. 230–33], mirroring those with which *Malemort* and *La case du commandeur* concluded) are themselves supplemented, first, by a brief chapter written in the third-person and devoted to Mycéa and, then, by one last chapter, entitled "Passion, selon Mathieu" ("The Passion According to Matthew"), that Mathieu narrates some four years after he has supposedly renounced the project of (self-)representation and handed that responsibility over to his author.

Who, then, is responsible for these supplementary words with which this potentially unending relay of voices ends (a relaying of voices, it should be noted, that extends into *Tout-monde* in the form of a dialogue between Mathieu and two of his characters in which they comment on the plot and structure of *Mahagony* [pp. 180–83])? And what are we to make of the undecidable situation that has resulted from this dynamic (con)fusion of narratorial levels where, as "the commentator" puts it, "in the end neither the informant nor the author could have recognized themselves apart from one other; and not even an attentive reader could, at least without perplexity [*sans vertige*], distinguish between them" (pp. 228–29)—a doubling of narrators that in *Tout-monde* will become an even more complex proliferation of authorial alter egos, all of whom stand in a *relation* of (un)likeness to one another ("Mathieu, the chronicler, the poet, the novelist, to say nothing of he who, or that which, is writing at this moment and who is not to be confused with either Mathieu, that chronicler, that novelist, or that poet" [p. 271]). Finally, is there actually a place for "passion" in the vertiginously self-referential world of this novel, which is so resolutely situated to the side of the real agony of endangered lives that, like Mathieu's eponym at Gethsemane, it can only record in the secondhand form of textual echoes, *ressouvenirs*? These are some of the pressing questions that a more detailed study of the novel would have to address, but at this point it is time for me to draw my own argument in this chapter to a close.

In order to do so, I will cite one last metafictive episode from the novel, which occurs toward the end of the second part, Malendure. Mathieu is recalling a recent conversation between himself and his "author and biographer" in which he questioned the latter's methods of telling the story of the renegade overseer Beautemps (Maho) in *Malemort* and suggested to this man, "who had not so long ago [*naguère*] enveloped the story of Maho with a veil of mystery and poetic confusion, how natural and profitable it would be to revisit it, keeping to a summary of the facts, an exact posting of the story [*au strict report des relations*]" (p. 154). It is not the ironies implicit in Mathieu's revisionist appeal to a "strict report des relations" (the word *report*, after all, designates not just a copy, the transference of reality onto the page that Mathieu desires, but a postponement, the deferral of that same reality—a deferral that Derrida has shown to be synonymous with writing but with which Mathieu has not yet come to terms), nor the author's rather pompous response to this assertion that is crucial to us here ("no study, howsoever detailed, would give an idea of the whole, which we have got to live totally," he asserts, counseling Mathieu against immersing himself in petty little investigations that only do a disservice to the past by commodifying and monumentalizing it in the form of reported tales that amount to nothing more than "pale replications" (pp. 154–55; "pâles réc-its conformes"). Rather, what interests me in this passage is Mathieu's use of the word *naguère*, which in this instance clearly reflects his (temporal) distance from the chronicler's earlier novel and its stylistic and ideological approach. Discontinuities of this sort are repeatedly invoked in *Mahagony* (we saw them at work, for instance, in Mathieu's reflections on the differences between present-day Lamentin and the Lambrianne of *La Lézarde* [p. 14]), and with such invocations the novel pursues an historicist vision that was central to Glissant's earlier work, as we can see from the following passage in *Intention poétique*, where he is describing the drying up of the Lézarde:

Not so long ago [*naguère*], the river was like a delta of very small irrigation channels, teeming with leeches, where the swarming of mosquitoes assumed the proportions of some altogether natural disaster. I derived from it (even before memory imposed an idealized image of it upon me) the dream of childhood, the desire for being. But today it is a gutter, its delta filled in. The Lézarde of my childhood is no more. (p. 220)

Such uses of the word "naguère" establish a fissure between the present and the past, inducing a nostalgia that cannot be satisfied: a negative double of the rupture between degraded present and redeemed future that was to have been effected by the revolutionary act, this discontinuity of past and present is the central element of the narrative of decline that generated Glissant's increasingly pessimistic vision of Martiniquan history in the years following upon the publication of *Quatrième siècle*. And yet, as we have seen in the case of Mathieu's relations with his author, this fissure (or as Glissant himself might have put it, this *lézarde*) is by no means as simple as it might appear. Mathieu himself, for instance, invokes and then complicates the idea of temporal discontinuity inherent in the above usages of "naguère" when, upon returning to Martinique, he reflects upon his relation to his former self: "the same speaker, changed by what he says, revisits the same spot in the same country, only to find that this spot also has changed, as have the perceptions of it that he once had [*comme a changé la perception qu'il en eut naguère*], or the chronology of what took place." "Trees that live a long time," he concludes, "are always changing, while remaining" (p. 16). If the first sentence simply marks an inalterable distance between the past and the present, the second—in its affirmation of that which "changent toujours, en demeurant"—points toward the possibility of a (dis)continuous relationship between the two; this is a relationship that does not erase but supplements and complicates the belief in historical ruptures that generates the pastoral nostalgia and the revolutionary utopianism that are as basic to Glissant's vision of modernity as they were to Schiller's.

To be sure, Mathieu alerts us to this (dis)continuity by means of a metaphor that itself testifies to a questionable investment in an "organic" vision that he shares with the likes of Bernardin de Saint-Pierre (and with those postcolonial theorists who have been enthusiastically latching onto the idea of the "changing same" as a way of resolving the problem of our relationship with the past and its traditions [see Chapter 8]). That there are other, equally (un)satisfactory, ways of gesturing toward the complexities of the ambivalent temporality that Glissant explores in *Mahagony* is the insight toward which, I would suggest, the novel's second epigraph directs us, and which is itself prepared for in the first epigraph, an "example of grammatical whimsy in the French language" (namely, "ces bonnes gens sont fous," a seemingly whimsical if historically explicable clustering of feminine and masculine adjectives around one and the same noun, cited as having been often invoked by the punctilious grammarian Monsieur Lannec, an old-style assimilationist earlier parodied in the pages of *Malemort*). This second epigraph is taken from the Franco-Mahgrebian literary critic and novelist Salim Jay and reads as follows: "Naguère qui prend la relève / c'est Agoni faisant des livres" (p. 9; "Of late the one who has been taking up the relay / is Agoni writing books"). Here, beginning the sentence with "naguère" establishes the expectation of a straightforward distinction between past and present, as in the conventional uses of the word that we looked at in the previous paragraph. However, instead of the imperfect tense that a pedagogue like Monsieur Lannec might well have anticipated (*prenait, c'était*), these lines confront us with an uneasy—but also possibly jubilant—mixture of the past and the present that puts into question such conventional readerly expectations. This idiomatic conjunction of "naguère" and the present tense, which could be read as reactivating—as re*presenting*—the *a* in "naguère" (the word itself being a contraction of "il n'y a guère"), is of the same potentially invigorating nature as the "error" that Glissant has inscribed in the novel's tactically misspelled title (mahogany → mahagony).[117]

In one of the many apocryphal epigraphs sprinkled across the pages of *Tout-monde*, we are told that some of the names from Glissant's "strange poem" *Pays rêvé, pays réel* (1985) such as "Mycéa" or "Mahogany" have "a symbolic meaning in dialectal Arab (Moroccan or Egyptian) or in classical Arab." Thus, "*Mahogany* means: 'He [or it] has not come,' with the sense of a desperate waiting, and the sighs that result from it" (p. 423). If this is true (and I doubt very much that it is!), then can we not read the misspelling of *Mahagony* as a rewriting of this "desperate waiting," one that explicitly acknowledges and accepts the *agony* that Aquin's revolutionary-cum-pharmacist—ideologue of the radical cure—once dreamt of turning into "régénérescence," and yet that also subtly works within and against it, situating the end (of modernism and its dreams) at the beginning and making of this end a beginning (that is to say, putting the omega in the place of the alpha and the alpha where the omega once was), and conducting all such contaminatory and ungrammatical transformations *in a middle space* that has its (im)proper place at neither the beginning nor the end? If the question is an illegitimate one (given the dubious foundations of the translational claims upon which it is based), it is not, I would venture, a question without a response. *Mahagony* is Glissant's positive response to this question. Exploring the ambivalent double time to which the unconventional use of the word "naguère" alerts us, Glissant's response—and the responsibility that attaches to it—is one that locates us squarely "between our stormy past and our dolorous future" (p. 23), in a place of memory where we can forget neither: the post/colonial present.

Part **III**

ERUPTIONS: (REWRITING)
CARIBBEAN ROMANTICISM

It will no doubt be inquired of us whether we need to worry about any new and even more substantial explosions than the one that concerns us today. It is impossible to make pronouncements about the future, without the possibility of their being proved wrong; but several centuries' worth of observation has proved that, in most cases, a great number of years separates one violent eruption from the next. . . . For this reason, it is fair to assume that we are no longer in danger . . .

—*Rapport fait aux citoyens Victor Hugues et Lebas, agens particuliers du Directoire exécutif aux isles du vent par la commission établie en vertu de leur arrêté du 12 vendémi-aire, an 6 de la république, pour examiner la situation du* VOLCAN DE LA GUADELOUPE, *et les effets de l'éruption qui a eu lieu dans la nuit du 7 au 8 du même mois*

5 The Memory of Hayti

WILLIAM FAULKNER, VICTOR HUGO,
AND THE SAINT-DOMINGUE
REVOLUTION

"Nothing Fault Nor False": Writing Over Revolution in William Faulkner's 'Absalom, Absalom!'

> Masters and slaves alike were haunted by a dream of blood
> and fire—the memory of Hayti.
> —Lafcadio Hearn, *Youma*

As the recent publication of his lengthy *Faulkner, Mississippi* (1996) demonstrates, Édouard Glissant is among the most prominent of the many Latin American, Afro-American, and Caribbean novelists who have looked to the work of William Faulkner for inspiration in their attempts at coming to terms with the hybrid complexities of their New World heritage. Over the course of the last thirty years Glissant has returned again and again in his theoretical writings to Faulkner, and especially to *Absalom, Absalom!*, a novel that his own early masterpiece *Quatrième siècle* emphatically doubles, in its antilinear approach to (hi)storytelling, and critically supplements, in its revisionist emphasis on the centrality of a black experience that remains for the most part on the silent or inarticulate margins of the Southern writer's oeuvre. The following description from *Intention poétique* of Faulkner's technique of (hi)storytelling epitomizes the approach that Glissant himself adopts in *Quatrième siècle*: "There is only this: the veiled, the unveiling. First the affirmation of a secret, of something hidden, of a *fundamental trace*, and then the process by which one tries to reveal them (to oneself), not so much in the clarity of their truth as in the sheer vertigo of this process" (p. 178). Both novelists establish an agonistic dialogue between something veiled (essence, truth, identity) and the potentially limitless task of its unveiling. In *Absalom, Absalom!*, Quentin Compson and his father, among others, insistently speculate upon the (racial, biographical) origins of the Sutpen dynasty, affirming as truths what the reader soon discovers are no more than provisional and often contradictory or erroneous hypotheses. In *Quatrième siècle*, Mathieu Béluse and the man who serves as his spiritual father, Papa Longoué, relentlessly interrogate the Béluse-Longoué family tree, with such enthusiasm that they at times forget what the reader cannot: namely, the existence of an "enormous distance between them and the events [of the past], that ocean to the bottom of which they dived (without even thinking that things could have happened in some other way, that there could have been other nuances to the gestures and the words of those bygone days)" (p. 75). The secret (of) identity persists in Faulkner and Glissant, but can only be revealed indirectly, in the very process of its revelation—a vertiginous operation through which the past is (re)constructed, thus becoming other than what it was; the "trace fondamentale" that might, if unearthed, have provided the stable ground for an American identity (be it that of a "white" Southerner or a "black" Martiniquan), proves nothing more or less than a vestige of doubtful value, a *trace* in the Derridean sense of the word, alerting us to the fundamental lack of any "pure unveiled" and of any "certain 'reason'" (*IP*, p. 178).

Absalom, Absalom! and *Quatrième siècle* are thoroughly modernist in their insistence upon the problematic revelation of a past that, having become "veiled," seems in danger of getting lost. Modernism, broadly speaking, can be thought of as a rearguard project of cultural recuperation (or, the flip side of the same coin, as cultural iconoclasm [e.g., the avant-garde] in the name of an unalienated future). Self-consciously aware of the difficulties involved in this project, the modernist writer inaugurates a shift in focus that postmodernism exacerbates—from telling, as it were, the story of *origins* to the *story* of origins. Faulkner's and Glissant's novels are as much (if not more) about the dialogic process through which Quentin and his father, Mathieu and Papa Longoué, vertiginously narrate their respective pasts and affirm their places of origin as they are about that which is being sought after through these acts of narration. It is this modernist sensibility that generates Glissant's critique in the *Poétique* of a too readable novel like Alex Haley's *Roots* (1976), with "its overconfident filiation" and its "calendar-like" approach to memory, which are not suitable for conveying the "entangled" reality of the Americas (p. 86). Haley's linear and literalist approach—grounded in what the authors of *Toward the Decolonization of African Literature* have valorized as the need "to reclaim and rehabilitate our genuine past, to repossess our true and entire history"[1]—contrasts, unfavorably, with that of a novelist like Faulkner, who engages with "the obscurity of this impossible memory, which speaks louder and carries farther than the chronicle or the census" (p. 86). In a novel like *Absalom, Absalom!*, rather than providing the reader with ready-made genealogical solutions to the problem of cultural identity, Faulkner confronts us with an "entwinement" (*enroulé*) that "involves a quest and its impossibility" (*DA*, p. 146).

As Glissant elsewhere argues in the *Poétique*, it is this double insistence on memory and its impossibility, on a necessary but unending quest, which makes possible the relational thinking characteristic of Faulkner's "in some ways theological" body of work:

It starts off being a question of digging about for the roots of a self-evident place, the South of the United States. But the root takes on the appearance of a rhizome, certitude proves unfounded, the relation is tragic. The tangle over the source [*le démêlé de la source*], the sacred but henceforth inexpressible enigma of rootedness, makes this world of Faulkner's one of the points where the modern poetics of relationality can be found simmering. (p. 34)

Glissant then immediately goes on to note, in a rather cagey autobiographical statement, the influence that this tragic universe once exercised on his own imagination, admitting that "in the past I had regretted that such a world had not spilled over more into surrounding regions: the Caribbean, Latin America." "But this reaction," he continues, "perhaps only stemmed from the unconscious pique of one who had felt himself excluded from it" (p. 34). The Glissant of the *Poétique* thus appears to be distancing himself from the tragic modernism of his literary predecessor, whilst acknowledging its "reactive" influence on his own earlier representations of Martiniquan history in a novel like *Quatrième siècle*, which so clearly partakes of Faulkner's grandiosely tragic sensibility. This is only half the (modernist) story of *Quatrième siècle*, though, because, the novel also patently offers us the hope of a solution that, as Glissant points out, is apparently absent from Faulkner's novels (*IP*, p. 178); it aspires to providing "a prophetic vision of the past" (*DA*, p. 132), in which the past becomes the redemptive ground out of which a different set of relations—and a revolutionized future—might be thought to emerge (and in which, for instance, the painfully oedipal filiations and rivalries that both join and separate Faulkner's narrators as well as their characters will have been transformed into more livable bonds of affiliation and solidarity). The "désir historique" that causes Glissant, and his narrator-characters, to plunge into the night of the past produces both a tragic insight into the irrecuperability of that past and a comic belief that new possibilities can nonetheless result from this ground-less encounter. Viewed in the light of my analysis of *Mahagony* as a post/modern novel, the later Glissant's palinodic appraisal of Faulkner would thus stem from an ambivalent out-living of his own modernist point of departure as a novelist—a further but never final distancing of himself from tragically veiled origins and a prophetically envisioned telos.

The specifically American dimension of Faulkner's and Glissant's modernism and their "impossible quest" is rooted, as it were, in the dynamics of racial and cultural entanglement. Any attempt at clarifying the past, at "disentangling the source," sooner or later leads them to a confrontation with the ineluctably mixed origins of the "other America" they inhabit, that America which is "neither the One nor the Other but something else besides," as Bhabha so often puts it in his *Location of Culture*.[2] One critic has noted that "the question of inter-racial contact is the crucial point of contact between Glissant and Faulkner,"[3] and it is the ubiquity of this contact that prevents the various narrators of *Absalom, Absalom!* and *Quatrième siècle* from tracing their way back to a single origin, an undisputed truth. The foundational lack of such certainties, their (im)purely translational existence as a confused and confusing mixture of truth and falsity, of "black" and "white," is what Thomas Sutpen will spend an entire lifetime trying to deny, struggling to disentangle himself from the rhizomatic dissemination of his past relations—a futile enterprise, for as Glissant has noted, "foundations and filiations are not something one can start up again, and Sutpen's (hi)story catches up with him" (*PR*, p. 70). Whereas Glissant stresses this entrapment by refusing to trace—à la Haley—the (hi)story of the Longoués and the Béluses back to Africa, thus emphasizing that it only begins—and can only begin to be told—aboard the slave ship that took them to the Americas, Faulkner dramatizes it in a different manner, by providing Sutpen, and the narrators of *Absalom, Absalom!*, with (the illusion of) a "pre-history," rendering the mixed realities of (Sutpen's) American identity all the more visible by positing a time of lost innocence. This is a time before the "monkey nigger" tells the youthful Sutpen to go around to the back door of the Virginia plantation house, a time before Sutpen ventures as an adolescent to the West Indies and—attempting to forward the elusive "design" that he identifies as his life-project and that both echoes and, in its inarticulateness, differs from that of a predecessor like Crusoe (to recall our discussion of that castaway's "rational design" in the first section of Chapter 2)—unsuspectingly enters into marital relations with a woman whom he eventually realizes, or at least believes, is "part negro." Where Glissant's emphasis works to defuse an Afrocentric nostalgia, Faulkner's questions the status of "whiteness" by treating it as the object of, at best, an ironized nostalgia; both approaches lead away from the site of (African and/or European) origins and toward a place where "the traditional grounds of racial identity are dispersed," and where it has become possible to think that "the Negro is not. Any more than the white man" (to quote Bhabha quoting Fanon).[4] Surprisingly enough, in Faulkner's novel, this place of racial dispersion goes by the name of Haiti.

Sutpen's design begins, and effectively ends, on the "little lost island" of Haiti. As narrated by Quentin to his Harvard roommate Shreve (a narration itself constructed out of memories of the past tellings of his father, grandfather, and of Sutpen himself), the island emerges as a doubled space, its split identity ensuring, ultimately, that it cannot be remembered properly, in and of itself, but only as in some way other than it is. Haiti is not (simply), as one might expect, the home of an insurgent blackness, a predictably Conradian darkness, but (also) the site of an overwhelmingly pervasive métissage, which unsettles any recourse to unitary terms such as "black" and "white," rendering them profoundly unreadable and thus highlighting, in Bhabha's words, "the impossibility of naming the difference of colonial culture" (LC, p. 129). Notwithstanding the aggressively nostalgic dimensions of Faulkner's novel and its encounter with the past, the acknowledgment of this "impossibility of naming" in Absalom, Absalom! clears a space for a way of thinking that, while never transcending the rac(ial)ist identities upon which both it and American (in the largest sense of the word) society are grounded, is nonetheless capable of provisionally questioning those identities and the names by which we (falsely) know ourselves and (violently) subject others.

Like Faulkner's Haiti, his novel is itself split into two: the narrative proper, in all the vertiginousness of its (re)telling, and the straightforward chronology-genealogy that supplements it, ironically clarifying details of historical sequence and personal biography that remained opaque or were resolutely withheld in what came before (like the name of Sutpen's first wife, Eulalia, which is never given in the narrative itself). Within the terms of this supplement, the place of Haiti could not be more defined: "1827: Sutpen married first wife in Haiti"; "1831: Charles Bon born, Haiti. Sutpen learns his wife has negro blood, repudiates her and child" (the certainty of this last truth-claim, of course, being itself undermined by the fact that in the original edition of the novel, Faulkner identifies Charles Bon as being born in 1829, two years before Sutpen "learns his wife has negro blood"— an "error" that has been corrected by editors sensitive to an historical timeline from which they believe their author to have carelessly strayed). Such determinate sitings of the island, Faulkner implicitly maintains, while by no means inessential to an understanding of the events chronicled by the novel's several narrators, must remain secondary to the more indeterminate mapping of history and character provided by those narrators. Haiti supplies this alternative map with its meridian: "named" as such only a half dozen or so times in the narrative proper, the words "Haiti" and "Haitian" prove ones to which no historical, ethnic, or even geographical referent can be definitively attached; they thus visibly signal a zero-point of semantic invisibility that casts its long shadow over the entirety of the narrative—an elusive point of origin that provokes the various narrators into situating their characters, and themselves, in relation to it and yet that equally dooms any such attempts at stabilizing meaning through recourse to its instability, at localizing identity in the face of its unlocatability.

The place that is (not) Haiti makes its first appearance in the seventh of the novel's nine chapters—the chapter in which the story of Thomas Sutpen's early years is belatedly, if only partially, revealed to the reader, who by this time has a fairly clear idea of the details of Sutpen's life in Mississippi, from his arrival there as a young man of twenty-five in 1833 to his murder a few years after the end of the Civil War. Haiti emerges as part of a story initially told by Sutpen himself to Quentin's grandfather in 1835, during their pursuit of the runaway "French architect" from Martinique, creator of Sutpen's mansion and his virtual slave during the two-year period of its construction. Having told Grandfather Compson the story of his early days as a "poor white" in the mountains of what would become West Virginia and of his family's migration back east to work on a Tidewater plantation, and having analyzed in some depth the traumatic encounter at the front door of the master's house that led to his decision to leave the Virginia plantation and go to the "West Indies," Sutpen pauses for a while. As darkness falls and the pursuit of the architect continues on into the night, he confusingly launches back into the narrative of his youth, abruptly getting himself and Grandfather Compson "both into that besieged Haitian room as simply as he got himself to the West Indies by saying that he decided to go to the West Indies and so he went there; this anecdote no deliberate continuation of the other one but merely called to his mind by the picture of the niggers and torches in front of them" (p. 199). At Grandfather Compson's prompting, Sutpen eventually begins to shape this disorderly rush of details about the time he served as "overseer or foreman or something to a French sugar planter" (p. 199) into a more coherent narrative, starting over again "with at least some regard for cause and effect even if none for logical sequence and continuity"—a (re)telling that itself does not make "absolutely clear—the how and the why he was there and what he was" (p. 199). We find out that having learned to speak a "new language" (presumably Creole), and still possessed of the "innocence" that (he feels) is his single most defining characteristic, Sutpen has become the overseer of a sugar plantation on an island the soil of which has been "manured with black blood from two hundred years of oppression and exploitation" (p. 202). Sutpen peacefully goes about his business of overseeing, "not knowing that what he rode upon was a volcano" (p. 202). A common metaphor for revolution in Caribbean literature, which we will be examining at some length in Chapter 7 (C. L. R. James speaks in *Black Jacobins*, for instance, of revolution as that moment "when the ceaseless slow accumulation of centuries bursts into volcanic eruption" [p. viii]), the volcano eventually erupts in the form of what, in the manuscript version of the novel, are referred to as "insurrecting niggers"[5]—a distinct identity and revolutionary motivation that are significantly less apparent in the published version. Sutpen eventually succeeds in lifting the siege, walking out "into the darkness and subdu[ing] them" in an act of masterful assertiveness that he appears not to have described to General Compson, who is himself forced into hypothesizing as to the exact nature of this improbable act. In any case, Sutpen's valiant actions earn him the hand of his employer's daughter, a fittingly romantic reward for having saved, as he puts it, "the lives of all the white people" on the place (p. 211)—a phrase that, as it turns out, may well refer only to Sutpen himself, or perhaps even to no one at all if, as James Snead has suggested, Sutpen is "the carrier of an originless blackness that clandestinely inserts its way into the presumably pure genealogies of Southern whiteness."[6]

In his representation of this episode, Faulkner ostentatiously "regresses" back into the sort of language and mood that dominate Marlow's encounter with a "black and incomprehensible frenzy" in Conrad's *Heart of Darkness* (p. 100).[7] Sutpen's bewildered encounter with Haiti is a self-conscious echo on Faulkner's part of Marlow's journey into the heart of an Africa that he can never bring himself to name as such: unbeknownst to himself, Sutpen finds himself on well-trodden Conradian ground, "hearing the air tremble and throb at night with the drums and the chanting and not knowing that it was the *heart* of the earth itself he heard," believing "that earth was kind and gentle and that *darkness* was merely something you saw, or could not see in" (p. 202; my italics). Defending the plantation house, the owner and his future son-in-law "fired at no enemy but at the Haitian night itself, lancing their little vain and puny flashes into the brooding and blood-weary and throbbing darkness" (p. 204). This passage thoroughly Africanizes the Haitian night in its overt recollection of the French man-of-war's apparently purposeless shelling of the bush, witnessed by Marlow on the initial stage of his journey while traveling down the coast to the Outer Station: "in the empty immensity of earth, sky, and water," Marlow remarks, "there she was, incomprehensible, firing into a continent" (p. 29). Faulkner's emphasis on "little vain and puny flashes" recalls Marlow's own insistence on the "tiny," "feeble" quality of the man-of-war's offensive ("a small flame would dart and vanish, a little white smoke would disappear, a tiny projectile would give a feeble screech"). Moreover, the statement that Sutpen was firing at "no enemy" but at the "Haitian night itself" reinscribes the moment of linguistic skepticism with which Marlow's brief account of the coastal shelling concludes (someone on board informs him that the shelling does indeed have a purpose, since "there was a camp of natives—he called them enemies!—hidden out of sight somewhere"). Perhaps the most notable effect of this particular intertextual conjunction, which links the shelling of Africa to the defense of the plantation house, is

to reverse the spatial opposition of inside and outside that apparently structures Sutpen's colonial encounter: those who are *inside* the French plantation owner's house are, in the light of this conjunction, repositioned *outside*; these defenders of the hearth can now be read, like the French man-of-
war, as being on the periphery of what they are aggressively attempting to
conquer and penetrate. *Heart of Darkness* is, of course, highly critical of
this colonial violence and, as the ironization of the term "enemy" testifies,
very attuned to the lack of (moral and epistemological) foundations upon
which such acts are based. And yet, ironically, such penetrating violence is
itself at the heart of (Conrad's) modernist narrative, which unnervingly
doubles the "hermeneutic" movement of the colonial enterprise that it critiques, in its repeated attempts at going beyond "surface-truths" to the
heart of the matter, its never-completed gesture of unveiling, its concerted
shedding of inadequate light on a darkness that remains alluringly inscrutable and that (Conrad's) modernism cannot do without, because—like
the primitive—this darkness signals a stable if inscrutable point of origin
from which one has been displaced and to which one must return if the
"truth of things" is ever to be arrived at.

To be sure, Conrad's primitivism in *Heart of Darkness* is not that of a
D. H. Lawrence (a point I will be returning to at the beginning of Chapter
8): to recall a distinction made in the previous chapter, his is a second-level
work of modernism, one that self-consciously registers the impossibility of
those "journeys to the source" that were so central to the modernist imaginary. For this reason, Conrad's Africa, like Faulkner's Haitian night, is presented in terms of its unreadability, as that which can never be properly figured or, rather, that which must always remain a figure, one that shrouds its
literal referent in a self-consciously "blank darkness" (to allude to Christopher Miller's memorable account of Africanist discourse, which Conrad's
novella strategically [re]cites and thus estranges). In both Conrad and
Faulkner, attempts at naming the origin give way to an emphasis on its sheer
unnameability as such: they recognize that it can only be gestured toward in
the form of its absence, through tropes such as metonymy ("the drums and
the chanting"), irony (Marlow's "enemy," an irony that is itself turned
upon, [re]troped, in Faulkner's "no enemy"), or metaphor (as when Sutpen
finds himself facing "a blank wall of black secret faces, a wall behind which
almost anything could be preparing to happen" [p. 203]). Willfully "tropical" gestures of this sort tentatively distance us from the often intolerable
readability of nineteenth-century colonial discourse—Carlyle's "The Nigger
Question," for example, where, lamenting the turn for the worse that he
sees the British Caribbean as having taken after Emancipation, he cites the
condition of independent Haiti as the logical result of ending slavery, identifying it as an island "with little or no sugar growing, black Peter extermi-

nating black Paul, and where a garden of the Hesperides might be, nothing but a tropical dog-kennel and pestiferous jungle."[8] Carlyle here shows himself woefully oblivious to the problem his names pose, ignoring (or, what amounts to the same thing, reveling in) the figurality of his account of Haiti, the biblical allegory and bestial metaphors out of which it is constructed. Conrad rigorously empties out this colonial language, directing us toward the (impossible) responsibility of naming its referent properly by emphasizing the impropriety of his own representations of it. This deconstructive methodology, while clearly not offering a final solution to the problem of a colonial discourse that Conrad's novella at once mimics and contests,[9] supplies us with a compelling model for how best to live in a post/colonial world that consistently falls short of the post-colonial fantasies it generates.

The typically modernist interrogation of language and the (putting into question of the) search for origins that I have just described is as central to *Absalom, Absalom!* as it is to *Heart of Darkness*, but these are supplemented in Faulkner's novel by a sensitivity to mixed (up) identities that Conrad's has difficulty envisioning. Faulkner's Haiti is Conrad's Africa, but it is also "something else besides," not (simply) the place of the absent origin but (also) the post-originary space of métissage, of cross-cultural transactions that have rendered the modernist quest for origins not merely tragically impossible but, ultimately, beside the point. Viewed in this light, the uncanny resemblance of Faulkner's Haiti and Conrad's Africa is not so much the coincidental result of a shared modernist mentality, but the product of a self-conscious pastiche on the Southern writer's part, one that ultimately serves to direct the reader's attention beyond the familiar Conradian terrain that it maps out. Faulkner's pastiche, in other words, renders inevitable a modernist reading of the Haitian episode, generating certain readerly expectations concerning primitive origins, only to deflate those expectations by overdetermining the Conradian story with a second narrative—one that highlights the thoroughly secondary nature of the American (in the largest sense of the word) world he is chronicling. Through his echoes of Conrad, Faulkner both promotes, and critically reflects upon, the modernist need for primitive origins that generates the work of his literary predecessor.

It is doubtless significant that Marlow's account of Africa is least responsible (in the sense of the word outlined above), most forthcoming in details, and thus at odds with the unreadable enterprise I have just described, when accounting for those Africans who have in one way or another visibly entered into the transcultural realm of the contact zone, the existence of which poses a threat to Marlow's hermeneutic enterprise of penetration and unveiling. Marlow has little difficulty naming the difference of the hybrid: he conjures it up in a series of apotropaic descriptions that are grounded in either an ironic or a romantic language that he elsewhere treats as groundless, as tropic(al) representation. Marlow's description of the steamer's "fire-man," "a thrall to [the] strange magic" of its "vertical boiler," marks him out as a troublingly impure mixture of "steam-gauges" and "ornamental scars," a mimic man who has proven sadly adequate to the inadequate rep-resentations of a colonial discourse that would identify him as an "improved specimen"; "a few months of training had done for that really fine chap," Marlow concludes, noting that the sight of him was "as edifying as seeing a dog in a parody of breeches and a feather hat, walking on his hind legs" (p. 52). The ironic (and metonymic) portrayal of the fireman is matched by the romantic individuation of Kurtz's mistress, a "wild and gorgeous apparition of a woman" (p. 77) who has become "readable" as a result of her role in an interracial romance and the specter of métissage that such an alliance raises; rather than signaling the "substitution of the female for the primi-tive,"[10] her presence in *Heart of Darkness* serves not to consolidate but to threaten the primitive and its pre-historic blankness/blackness, directing the reader toward (as Marlow's uncharacteristically libidinized prose testifies at this point) an erotic history in which the boundary lines separating suppos-edly "different" worlds have become troublingly permeable.

The critique of imitation (the fireman) and the temptation of romance (Kurtz's mistress) are the two most familiar ways in which colonial dis-course filters and contains the disruptive presence of cultural hybridity (and the consequent absence of cultural originality), and these containment strat-egies take on additional importance in the light of modernism's stress on artistic innovation and its resistance to conventional plots. Such acts of con-tainment, of course, themselves testify to the continued presence of that which they would exclude and in so doing cannot help, as if by contagion, replicating themselves. Once repressed, the figure of the fireman inevitably returns in an uncannily similar form as the strutting helmsman (so similar, indeed, that certain critics appear unable to distinguish the one from the other);[11] "educated by my poor predecessor," he provides a casebook study of colonial dependency, steering "with no end of a swagger while you were by[,] but if he lost sight of you, he became instantly the prey of an abject funk" (p. 60). More importantly, though, this quickly suppressed figure—who, fittingly enough, is killed off by the primitive itself, pierced by the "shaft of a spear" that contrasts tellingly with the empty Martini-Henry ri-fle he has been waving about (p. 62)—offers a brief glimpse of what is at stake for Faulkner in his encounter with Haiti, when he casts the ship's cap-tain a dying look that, Marlow asserts, "remains to this day in my mem-ory—like a claim of distant kinship affirmed in a supreme moment" (p. 67). This is (the memory of) a claim that Conrad's *Heart of Darkness*, in-tent upon primitive origins and cultural difference, is regrettably uninter-ested in exploring, but it is one that is fundamental to Faulkner. The acknowledgment of this claim (what Marlow calls the "subtle bond" created between himself and the helmsman [p. 67]), and the world of entangled relations that it entails, puts into question the modernist enterprise of Conrad that Faulkner pastiches in his "Africanized" vision of Haiti; the "American" Haiti, Faulkner insists, is a place where such entanglements and transfusions are the rule, not (as in Conrad) the lamentable exception.

For Faulkner, neither Carlyle's racist certainties about blackness nor their Conradian critique and redeployment are adequate for coming to terms with the hybrid ground out of which American identity has emerged. He polemically forces his reader to confront the pervasiveness of this mixed identity by associating it first and foremost with "black Haiti," "the Negro republic," officially "liberated" from the oppressive yoke of the two-decades-long United States occupation in the very year (1934) that Faulkner began serious work on *Absalom, Absalom!* The originary "darkness" of the Haitian night turns out to be not, as in Conrad, the primary source of identity but the (after)effect of an event that has, from its post-Columbian beginnings, brought the island into the partial "light" of a (violent) conjunction of worlds. Sutpen's island is not "One or the Other" but a meeting ground in which neither can be what they once might have been. It is, Quentin tells us, in a description that is itself made up of the repercussing traces of words passed down to him by earlier narrators,

a little island set in a smiling and fury-lurked and incredible indigo sea, which was the halfway point between what we call the jungle and what we call civilization, halfway between the dark inscrutable continent from which the black blood, the black bones and flesh and thinking and remembering and hopes and desires, was ravished by violence, and the cold known land to which it was doomed, the civilised land and people which had expelled some of its own blood and thinking and desires that had become too crass to be faced and borne longer, and set it homeless and desperate on the lonely ocean. (p. 202)

A familiar irony scrapes away here at words like "jungle" and "civilization," but to an altogether different end than Conrad's: namely, that of rendering visible the space of relation, the relativizing space, that has opened up between these two poles. Ironized, a binary opposition such as this nonetheless remains necessary in order to begin to position the intermediary zone in which the "inscrutable" and the "known," the "black" and the "white," have lost their original meaning and become unrecognizable as such.

Faulkner's Haiti is a place of "homelessness," where what Wilson Harris would refer to as the biases of ancestral or national cultures are consumed in attempts at making sense of the "nonsensical" (Bhabha) place that has risen up between, and thereby estranged, two mainlands—an estrangement that no mathematical formula ("the halfway point," "the third space") can adequately account for, and no race-based taxonomy (mulatto, octoroon, etc.) truly name, without betraying its essential incalculability, its sheer unreadability. Such betrayals are inevitable, to be sure. No more than anyone else can Faulkner avoid the language of race to which history has doomed him and his (black-white, white-black) people; but by explicitly allegorizing Haiti, of all places, not (just) as a site of insulated blackness but (also) as one of relational métissage, he pointedly directs us away from the binary segregations of "us" and "them" through which his people have so consistently attempted to (re)construct their ancestral and national home(s). Insisting that the search for origins is above all else the discovery of their absence, Faulkner posits this absence as being at the foundations of an American identity that is constitutively impure, chronically adrift, untranscendentally homeless. If Faulkner cannot explicitly embrace the impure and the migrant, as will Glissant (an embrace that, as I attempted to show in Chapter 2, can in any case never be more than *inconsistently partial*), he nonetheless prepares the (lack of a) ground for a way of thinking in which the recourse to the transcendental and the pure that we find, to take but one random example, in Miss Rosa's description of the "mulatto" Clytie's *"brooding awareness and acceptance of the inexplicable unseen inherited from an older and a purer race than mine"* (p. 110), will have been, if not thankfully abolished, then productively attenuated.

Faulkner draws our attention to this (absent) identity not only by his relative restraint in actually naming Haiti as the site of métissage, and his willingness (as we will see in a moment) to cast doubt on the propriety of this name, but by refusing to give any straightforward historical account of the island's history, even though the above passage about the island's mixed origins clearly implies and calls forth some such account. Faulkner rigorously denies his reader access to this implied "real" history of Haiti, most notably through a skillful use of anachronisms that destabilizes without erasing a referent that must remain as elusive as possible if the sort of betrayals discussed in the previous paragraph are not to overwhelm the narrative; Haiti as the site of métissage, as the site of that which puts into question the stable language of identity, cannot be properly remembered within the (chronological-genealogical) terms of this language: thus the crucial importance of Faulkner's anachronisms as signs reminding the reader of this unavoidable forgetting. The following brief account of the Haitian episode in a recent New Historicist interpretation of *Absalom, Absalom!*, which usefully explores the role of New Orleans and its creole society in the novel, is exemplary in the way that it delicately handles the impossible problem of situating that episode within the terms of a history that cannot adequately respond to the questions Faulkner poses it:

Thomas Sutpen lives in French Haiti from the early 1820s to 1833. He serves for a time as overseer on a sugar plantation owned by a French planter; he "subdues" an uprising of Haitian slaves who threaten the planter with their Vodou in what is probably one of the many skirmishes that made up the long and bloody Haitian revolution of the late eighteenth and nineteenth centuries; he marries Eulalia, the planter's daughter by a Spanish creole; his son, Charles Bon, is born in 1829; and Sutpen makes the "discovery" that causes him to repudiate Eulalia in 1831, two years before he arrives in Yoknapatawpha County and not long before his spurned wife arrives, with their son, in New Orleans—still a logical destination for a West Indian creole at this time.[12]

As we will see, any such conscientious attempt at (new) historicizing these events necessarily betrays Faulkner's self-consciously faulty memory of Haiti, by smoothing over the fissures, inconsistencies, and displacements through which he directs us toward an alternative (to) history, a place where the lived reality of cross-cultural contact could be satisfactorily named.

We are a long way in this account, to be sure, from Myra Jehlen's infamous assertion that "Faulkner pointedly describes [Sutpen] landing in Haiti ('a soil manured with black blood') just before the slave rebellions of 1791–93 which haunted American slavers forever after,"[13] but the references to "French Haiti" and "Haitian slaves" are puzzling, given the fact that—as the author of the historical summary is clearly aware—Haiti won its independence from France in late 1803 (an independence that France officially acknowledged in 1825, although it would not be recognized by the United States until 1862) and slavery had been once and for all abolished at that time, confirming its initial abolition in 1793. Might the reference to "French Haiti" be a way of distinguishing it from "Spanish Haiti," the republic of Santo Domingo on the eastern part of the island of Hispaniola, which was annexed by Haiti in 1822, a state of affairs that would last until 1844?[14] More likely, the reference to "French Haiti" simply attempts to make sense of the sugar-plantation-owning "French planter"; such a planter, though, would have been an impossibility in postrevolutionary Haiti, given the fact that whites and foreigners were prohibited from owning property under Dessalines's 1805 constitution (hence Sutpen's design could never have been realized in Haiti and any document, such as his marriage settlement, that purported to deed him property would indeed have been "misrepresentation" of a crass nature [p. 211]). And what of the uprising of Haitian "slaves" (a word that Faulkner significantly does not use in his description of the Vodou-related siege)? Why would "slaves" be rising up against their "French" master if they have already won their freedom? The New Historicist author tries to finesse this question by evasively identifying this "uprising" as "probably one of the many skirmishes that made up the long and bloody Haitian revolution of the late eighteenth and nineteenth centuries," leaving open the question of when this "revolution" ended, but strongly intimating that 1803 is not the date she has in mind when asserting that "the" Haitian revolution extended into the nineteenth century. Presumably the slave-owning French are not the only objects of this problematically ended revolution, for a little later she speaks in passing of "the formation of Haiti as the first mulatto government in the New World" (p. 538), and one is left to assume that this event occurred before Sutpen's arrival on the island (as, in a sense, it did—the "black" kingdom in the North and the "mulatto" republic in the South having been united in 1820 under the "mulatto" President Jean-Pierre Boyer), although one is less sure of what its possible relevance to the events on the "French" planter's estate might be. The sort of historical evasions and slippage that can be thus identified in what might at first glance appear to have been a straightforward summary of Sutpen's years in Haiti climax in the use of the word "creole" to describe the never-named "Eulalia" ("West Indian creole") and her mother ("a Spanish creole"): the historical and racial ambiguity that Faulkner's vision of Haiti has opened up generates a recourse—a perhaps unjustified one in the case of the mother, identified simply as a "Spaniard" in the actual text—to a word that seems capable of containing such ambiguities, leaving open-ended the question of racial identity. To read *Absalom, Absalom!* is, ideally, to discover the necessity of this word, and the open-ended creole identity to which Faulkner has covertly, and with great difficulty, directed us.

Doubtless, it would be possible to (re)construct a more historically coherent account of Haiti in the 1820s and to argue for its relevance to Sutpen's youthful West Indian experiences. The "French planter," for instance, would thus be a light-skinned mulatto plantation owner, in which case Sutpen's story, or Grandfather Compson's understanding of it, would be based upon an act of racial and national *mis*identification as "ignorant" as the redneck Wash Jones's conception of Charles Bon as "that durn French feller" (p. 106): the phrase "French planter" would be yet another sign of the inability to read race and/or nation that enables Sutpen's great "mistake" (and Faulkner himself alerts us to the possibility of this reading in the genealogy when he refers to Eulalia's father as a "Haitian sugar planter of French descent" [p. 307], a description that allows for the possibility that he, too, like his wife, could be labeled a "West Indian creole"). The "revolutionary" uprising faced by this light-skinned planter would, further, be nothing more (or less) than one of countless examples of the random social unrest that accompanied the break-up of the old colonial plantation system in the decades immediately following upon the independence of Haiti; despite government attempts at perpetuating this system, and preserving the old (mostly mulatto-owned) plantations, the period from 1820 to 1842 saw a drastic decline in sugar exports, from two and a half million pounds to six thousand pounds,[15] and the consolidation of a neopeasant economy increasingly based on small holdings. Even more specifically, we might read

the uprising quelled by Sutpen as part of a reaction against the notorious
1826 *Code Rural*, enacted in the twenty-third year of Haitian independence by Boyer "in order to maintain the supply of cheap labour, by attaching rural workers to specific plantations and by punishing vagrancy."
This harsh piece of legislation, which David Nicholls characterizes as "an
attempt to order the lives of the majority of rural workers for the prosperity of the few large landowners" (*FDD*, p. 68), launched a concerted attack
on idleness (*vagabondage*), decreeing that "all persons who are not proprietors, or renters of the land on which they are residing, or who shall not
have made a contract to work with some proprietor or renter" be arrested
by a newly empowered rural police and then forced to employ themselves
in agricultural labor (article 174); contractually binding themselves to their
maître for periods of three to nine years, they would be compelled to labor
five, and when necessary six, full days a week (article 183), with the added
benefit, given their status as "free" citizens, of paying taxes to a cash-
strapped government that had recently (1825) promised massive indemnities to France as compensation for land expropriated during the Revolution
and in return for a formal acknowledgment of independence.[16]

Sutpen's Haitian beginnings thus coincide with the historical moment
(the late 1820s) that Carpentier chooses as the depressing end-point of his
own novel about the Haitian Revolution, *The Kingdom of this World*,
when the former slave, Ti-Noël, squatting on the dilapidated estate of his
former master Lenormand de Mézy, is forcibly displaced by the new masters of the Plaine du Nord, "this spurious aristocracy [*esa aristocracia entre
dos aguas*], this caste of quadroons, which was now taking over the old
plantations, with their privileges and rank" (p. 177). This new aristocracy
works hand in glove with the surveyors (*Agrimensores*), whom Carpentier
allegorizes as the agents of a process of Weberian rationalization that is incompatible with Haiti's marvelous reality but inseparable from the degraded world of Europe, its realist novels and their bourgeois individualist
protagonists like Robinson Crusoe with his "innate reverence for bookkeeping and the law of contract."[17] Armed with telescopes that mediate
and falsify their vision of reality, bristling "with measuring rods and
squares," "measuring everything and writing things in their gray books
with thick carpenter's pencils" (p. 175), these surveyors are committed to
the totalizing imperatives of the *Code Rural*, which proclaims that all lands
not yet surveyed (*arpentés*) shall be so within a year from the publication of
the Code (article 15). There is no room for the likes of Ti-Noël in this (vision of the) world: "to remove him from the field of vision of his tele-
scope," one of the surveyors gave the old man "a sound whack across the
belly with his measuring stick" (p. 176). In a final moment of clarity, the se-
nile Ti-Noël realizes that, appearances to the contrary, the Haitian Revolu-

tion is not over, and he launches one last defiant cry of revolt, hurling a "declaration of war against the new masters," before dying—a cry of revolt that, like the uprising on the plantation overseen by Sutpen, shows little respect for the letter of the law and its demand that "labourers shall be submissive and respectful to the proprietors and farmers with whom they have contracted, as well as to the overseers" (article 69; "les agriculteurs seront soumis et respectueux envers les propriétaires et fermiers avec lesquelles, ils auront contractés, ainsi qu'envers les gérans").

This is perhaps as close as one can get to a "proper" historical and sociological contextualization of Faulkner's Haiti and, of course, in the final analysis, as Mr. Compson would say, "it just does not explain." Given the relative silence or misinformation that has surrounded this episode and its problematic evocation of Haitian history such contextualization is certainly necessary, but what is one to make of the confusions and contradictions that surface once a closer familiarity with this history is gained? One of the first critics to linger, howsoever briefly, over Faulkner's anachronistic foray into the West Indies argued that since "all this has little to do with the historical Haiti" Sutpen's island is "not Haiti then so much as a projection of American anxieties."[18] While this is certainly a plausible critical response, it pointedly begs the question of exactly what those anxieties might be,[19] and too easily renounces the decentering of American identity that results from Sutpen's sojourn in the Caribbean. In a recent article entitled "Looking for a Master Plan: Faulkner, Paredes, and the Colonial and Postcolonial Subject," Ramón Saldívar, reading the novel from an Hispanic perspective that emphasizes the fluidity of national boundaries and the indeterminacy of racial identities, has recently made a relevant case for the importance of its "colonial" referent: privileging "a class of racialized identity that is neither black nor white but distinct, even if determined in the last instance by its racial pedigree," Haiti's three-tiered colonial society (white, mulatto, black) offered "a more intricate expression of difference and the understanding of difference" than was possible in the nineteenth-century United States.[20] Saldívar argues that Haiti provided Sutpen with "a missed possible colonial alternative to his later American tragedy"—a tragedy that would stem from refusing to live the "experiential blur" between master and slave that had been possible in Haiti because of the "ideology of mutually imbricated racial and social identities underpinning aspects of colonial Haitian life" (pp. 105, 106). In short, in line with my own argument, Saldívar sees Faulkner as having portrayed Haiti, correctly, as a place where identity has been thought differently, in terms not only of separation but of mixture, and thus as a place that puts into question the miserably segregationist history of the United States. This Haiti offers not (just) the specter of black independence, "the San Domingo hour" (to cite a phrase from *Uncle*

Tom's Cabin) that Carlyle and his United States counterparts feared or held in contempt, but the even more threatening one of a black-white interdependence that would lead, that *has already led*, to the erasure of black and white as discrete identities.

Notwithstanding his productive emphasis on this "colonial" blurring of color lines, however, Saldívar strangely fails to theorize the relation between the "colonial and the postcolonial subject" that the title of his article posits, but that he refers to only once, in passing, in his actual article when he identifies *Absalom, Absalom!* as being "the narrative of Faulkner's most enthralling encounter with the colonial and the emerging postcolonial subject." The word "postcolonial" is otherwise curiously absent from this article, which refers time and again to the "Haitian colonial world" or "Haitian colonial society" as if Haiti had undergone no substantive change since (before) the time of the Revolution, as if the collapse of Saint-Domingue's ternary social structure and its replacement, in theory, by universal blackness (Haiti's first constitution having proclaimed "that all Haitians no matter what their shade of skin were to be called 'black'")[21] and, in practice, by a new two-tiered variant of the old colonial arrangement (mulatto, black), had not taken place. This "colonial world" occupies in Saldívar's argument the time of a seemingly eternal present tense: arguing, for instance, that the opposition between colonizers and colonized invariably leads to the emergence of "subcultures" in colonial society, Saldívar notes that "in Haiti, these subcultures form a mediating middle ground between the overwhelming polarities of the racially and economically supremacist white people and the dominated blacks" (p. 104). In other words, Saldívar (unintentionally, it would appear) reinscribes the same confusions and contradictions that are to be found in Faulkner's novel, repeatedly situating us *before* a revolution that he knows has already happened and that ought to have marked a definitive break between "colonial" society—with its "supremacist white people," its "dominated blacks" and its intermediate subcultures—and a radically different state of affairs of the sort C. L. R. James gestured toward when, in 1963, he noted that "whatever its ultimate fate, the Cuban Revolution marks the ultimate stage of a Caribbean quest for national identity."[22]

How can one exist in this paradoxical time that is simultaneously pre- and post-revolutionary? How can one live in a world where the "defining moment" that should have separated the colonial from the post-colonial is nowhere to be found, where the ultimate stage of a quest for national identity has already given way to a decidedly more penultimate sense of that identity, and where, as a result, one finds oneself living in what, from the standpoint of conventional history, can only appear as an intolerable contradiction, a troubling absence, an impossible mixture? These are the sort of questions that Faulkner's account of Haiti brilliantly insinuates and that are as relevant to us today as they were in 1843, when the French abolitionist Victor Schœlcher, reflecting upon his recent visit to the birthplace of Toussaint Louverture, noted that "Saint-Domingue has disappeared, but Haiti does not yet exist" ("St-Domingue a disparu, mais Haïti n'est pas encore").[23] This troubling non-place between Saint-Domingue and Haiti, the oxymoronic conjunction of these two places,[24] goes under many names: to cite just one such name, Jean Baudrillard has referred to it as "the aporia of modern revolutions," which is created out of the sad knowledge that "controlling and clampdown mechanisms proliferate at the same pace as (and doubtless even more quickly than) the liberating virtualities [of these revolutions]."[25] As I have been suggesting, another name for this uncanny place that Faulkner has so ably, and with the greatest ambivalence, identified is "the post/colonial condition."

Quentin's (re)telling of the Haitian episode ends abruptly, with Sutpen— having recovered from the wounds he incurred when putting down the siege—becoming engaged to the planter's daughter. "Then he stopped," Quentin concludes, with unusual brevity (p. 205). Shreve urges him to "go on," but Quentin merely repeats his previous statement: "I said he stopped." Shreve's response to this repetition, as "flat and final" as Sutpen's own abdication of narrative (p. 206), shows the extent to which he has not understood, or is willing to misrepresent, what Quentin has been telling him:

I heard you. Stopped what? How got engaged and then stopped yet still had a wife to repudiate later? You said he didn't remember how he got to Haiti, and then he didn't remember how he got into the house with the niggers surrounding it. Now are you going to tell me he didn't even remember getting married? (p. 205)

Whereas Quentin has shifted back to the level of discourse (Sutpen's stopping of the story), Shreve remains within this story, wondering what Sutpen stopped in Haiti. Further, in his own summary of what Quentin has said about Haiti—here identified for the first time by name (as opposed to being metonymically evoked, in the form of the adjective "Haitian")—Shreve distorts what he has "heard," transforming what Quentin (and, presumably, Sutpen) have simply not narrated into something that they have forgotten. This is but one instance of the productive confusions that characterize the Quentin-Shreve dialogue and that by the end of the novel's seventh chapter will have resulted in Shreve assuming a greater role, and responsibility, as narrator of a story that he has been up to this point merely hearing; his gradual transformation from listener to storyteller in the second half of the novel culminates in the eighth chapter's ecstatic communion with Quentin, in which "it did not matter (and possibly neither of them conscious of the distinction) which one had been doing the talking" (p.

267). From his privileged site on the margins of United States culture, the Canadian Shreve confusingly adds his own voice to that of his Southern double (a doubling to which Glissant unintentionally drew his reader's attention in *Intention poétique* when he identified Quentin as Shreve! [pp. 179–80]). Shreve jump-starts a narrative in danger of "stopping," adding an element of playfulness to it—"let me play a while now," he says, before briefly taking over the narrative of Sutpen's murder (p. 224)—and thereby attenuating its tragic aspects, which threaten to overwhelm a Quentin who (in the earlier *Sound and the Fury* [1929]) has already shown himself all too willing to put a "stop" to his own story.

One of the potential casualties of Shreve's error-prone, playfully skeptical interventions as narrator is "Haiti" itself, the referential status of which he will put into question at the beginning of the eighth chapter. Describing Sutpen's first wife in the years following upon her move to New Orleans and the "implacable will for revenge" that (may have) motivated her, and her young son's possible reactions to the "hate and the fury and the unsleeping and the unforgetting" that (might have) characterized her, Shreve pictures Charles Bon creating for himself "his own notion of that Porto Rico or Haiti or wherever it was he understood vaguely that he had come from" (p. 239). Here, Shreve inserts an element of doubt (Bon's or his own?) into the Haitian story, floating the possibility that Sutpen himself may have mistaken another island—say, Martinique, where slavery had not yet been abolished—for Haiti. Whatever the exact location of this island, it is a place to which (in Shreve's account) Bon's mother has no intention of returning and that she has transformed for her son into something "that you were to thank God you didn't remember anything about . . . yet at the same time [that] you were not to, maybe dared not to, ever forget" (p. 239). The young Bon's relation to this indeterminate yet unforgettable place quickly assumes a more personal importance to Shreve, as he adopts and extends Bon's (hypothetical) relation to his native island in two further variations of the phrase "Porto Rico or Haiti." First, the young Bon is said to have imagined that the "incomprehensible fury and fierce yearning and vindictiveness and jealous rage" of his mother is simply "a part of childhood which all mothers of children had received in turn from their mothers and from their mothers in turn from that Porto Rico or Haiti or wherever it was we all came from but none of us ever lived in" (p. 239). From this supposition, he (Bon) immediately draws the conclusion that he too will some day have to pass on this inheritance and that "hence no man had a father, no one personal Porto Rico or Haiti," but only affronted and ever-breeding "mother faces" swooping down on their progeny, on "all boy flesh that walked and breathed," on that "perennial and ubiquitous" brotherhood that has stemmed from the "one ambiguous eluded dark fatherhead" against which the mother(s) rage (pp. 239–40). To paraphrase these intriguing comments is already to have ventured into metaphysical and psychoanalytic terrain that substantially voids the historical referentality of Haiti, which has here become some far more general and abstract place, an Origin to which—like Heidegger's Being—we cannot return, condemned as we are to *living* in time (Shreve's first variation), or (his second variation) the realm of the Father, of the Symbolic, which lawfully determines a "personal" (male) identity that remains threateningly subject to the "abject" (in Kristeva's terms) assaults of the maternal. Pursuing Shreve's audacious and productive suggestions would lead us rather too far from the place to which my own argument must return: namely, the historical Haiti temporarily put into question by Shreve's remarks. For our purposes, his treatment of the Haitian referent here can be looked upon as simply a provocative moment of doubt, a flagrant suspension of belief, that is typical of what we might call the nascently postmodern outlook of *Absalom, Absalom!*, in which the materiality of history repeatedly seems on the verge of being transformed into nothing more than the material of a story, the true facts into "faulty" fictions.

It is no doubt only a coincidence that the word immediately preceding "fault" in the *Oxford English Dictionary* (2nd ed.) is "Faulknerian." Be that as it may, variations of the word play a highly significant role in *Absalom, Absalom!* Sutpen's narrative about his time in Haiti itself originates from a "fault": his telling of this part of his life story to Grandfather Compson begins during a lull in their pursuit of the escaped architect. "He and Grandfather," Quentin notes, "were sitting on a log now because the dogs had faulted" (p. 193)—a "fault" being, in hunting terminology, a "break in the line of scent; loss of scent; a check caused by failure of scent" (*OED*). To be "at fault" is thus to have lost the scent, but also to be "puzzled, at a loss," and even "not equal to the occasion, in the position of having failed." It is precisely this puzzlement and this failure—this "amazement" (as Faulkner repeatedly terms it)—out of which (Sutpen's) narrative is generated. He and his men have failed, at least for the moment, in their ruthless pursuit of the "French" architect from Martinique (and given the extremely dubious referentiality of that adjective in *Absalom, Absalom!*, one might well hazard a guess that this shadowy figure with "coon-like hands" [p. 207], the one "artist" in the novel [p. 29], so gifted in the techniques of marooning, may well—like Charles Bon—"be" someone altogether other than he appears). The architect has escaped by climbing a tree, leaving behind a sapling pole with his suspenders still knotted about one end of it— suspenders that have somehow permitted him to cross "a gap to the next nearest tree that a flying squirrel could not have crossed" and then to travel from tree to tree for over a half mile before once again touching ground. While the physics of this escape—the architect's calculation of "stress and distance and trajectory"—remain somewhat obscure (at least to this reader), the presence of the suspenders pointedly signals the suspension of the pursuit, which becomes the occasion for the West Indian narrative—a narrative that unfolds in this time of suspension made possible by a "fault."

Sutpen, to be sure, remains blind to the possibilities of this fault out of which his story emerges; the ultimate failure of his narrative, its dangerous naiveté, lies in his belief that this fault can be once and for all done away with. For him, Haiti is the location of an "old mistake in fact which a man of courage and shrewdness . . . could still combat if he could only find out what the mistake had been" (p. 215). Sutpen believes that "mistakes" can be remedied, just as the "misrepresentation" through which (he believes) his Haitian in-laws tricked him appears to dissolve once the "fact" that they withheld from him is revealed and he realizes that, "through no fault of her own," his first wife could not be "adjunctive or incremental to the design which I had in mind" (p. 194). And yet, as he obscurely knows, an understanding of where he went astray can only be gained by admitting the fault, by telling the story and thus falling back into the realm of (mis)representation from which he seeks a reprieve. He will, of course, temporarily escape from this intolerable situation, stop his telling, take up again his hunt for the marooning architect so that he (the architect) can complete the stable structure in which Sutpen would house himself. The alternative home that the architect has, through his flight, constructed for him, with its faulty foundations, is one that Sutpen cannot bear to inhabit, just as he could not acknowledge the "fault" in his first wife, in a failure of seeing, and reading, cross-cultural difference that seals his doom. Like the "doomed ships" fleeing indeterminately to and from the island of Haiti (p. 202), Sutpen will have escaped "in vain" from the second chance that the telling of his story offered him. The repercussions of what Mr. Compson refers to as "that mistake which if he had acquiesced to it would not even have been an error and which, since he refused to accept it or be stopped by it, became his doom" (p. 41), will pursue him to the grave, shipwrecking him repeatedly in the vast and "lonely ocean" that lies between the lost mainland of a single identity he so violently mourns and desires, and the paradoxical fertility of the double island that his story of métissage promises us.

In the company of Shreve, Quentin is able, tentatively, posthumously, to "go on" beyond his suicidal ending in Sound and the Fury, acceding to the post/apocalyptic realm of a narrative in which his ultimate fate can yet remain uncertain. In a gesture of reversal that we will also observe at work in the ending(s) of Daniel Maximin's Soufrières, and that is the underlying conceit of Wilson Harris's 1960 Palace of the Peacock (with its antirealist insistence that one can live, and die, a second time; that one can, in the unlikely space that opens up between one's first and "second death," learn from the "ghost of a chance" that this afterlife offers), Faulkner relativizes what might otherwise have seemed an absolute conclusion, allowing Quentin partially to "redress" (in Harris's words) his existence, to begin the process of growing up by learning (how) to live with his "faults" rather than being vanquished by them. In the novel's penultimate chapter, with Shreve's support, Quentin manages to evade at least one aspect of the psychological impasse that led to his earlier doom: finally walking "out of his father's talking" (p. 142), he overcomes provisionally the Oedipal anxieties that haunt him and begins telling his own (version of the) story. In thus disengaging himself from paternal authority (a disengagement that is the necessary precondition of novelistic Bildung),[26] he achieves what Bon apparently could not, if we are to judge from (what Quentin and Shreve imagine to be?) his obsession with his father's face, "*the shadow of whose absence my spirit's posthumeity has never escaped*" (p. 254), as well as from the overall texture of his life story as it gets told in the eighth chapter.

Significantly, Bon's italicized remarks about the inescapability of his father's absence and the shadow it casts are preceded by what is perhaps the novel's most euphoric moment, which consecrates the faulty vision that I have been sketching in the last few paragraphs. Quentin and Shreve are on the verge of talking about love and we are told that

> it did not matter to either of them which one did the talking, since it was not the talking alone which did it, performed and accomplished the overpassing, but some happy marriage of speaking and hearing wherein each before the demand, the requirement, forgave, condoned and forgot the faulting of the other—faultings both in the creating of this shade [Charles Bon] whom they discussed (rather, existed in) and in the hearing and sifting and discarding the false and conserving what seemed true, or fit the preconceived—in order to overpass to love, where there might be paradox and inconsistency but nothing fault nor false. (p. 253)

The many differing senses of the words "fault" all run together here to make possible the participatory ethos of (hi)storytelling that Faulkner is valorizing. The Faulknerian fault involves a transgression, something wrongly done, perhaps even to the point of blasphemy;[27] a confrontation with the defective, the incomplete, the failed; an expression of censure (as in "finding fault with"); an act of dislocation (as in its geological meaning, "a dislocation or break in continuity of the strata or vein," with a consequent displacement of one side of the fracture with respect to the other). The word "faulting" itself refers solely to this geological dimension, describing "the process of producing faults, dislocation of strata" (*OED*), and thence the creation of "fault lines," interstitial zones that paradoxically divide and unite and in which, figuratively speaking, Quentin and Shreve have learned to exist. This confusing admixture of transgression, error, bias, and dislocation occasions the "overpassing" to a place where love can, paradoxically and inconsistently, happen and where, for this very reason, it is possible to "go on," without "stopping," or, ideally, even "faltering." (After Shreve has "played a while" with Quentin's story at the beginning of the eighth chapter, we are told that "there was no harm intended by Shreve and no harm taken, since Quentin did not even stop. He did not even falter, taking Shreve up in stride without comma or colon or paragraph" [p. 225].)

What this defective and dislocating process ultimately enables is a successful relocation, at the level of *discours*, of a love that the *histoire* itself cannot adequately supply. Tragically played out in the Henry-Judith-Bon triangle, the paradigms of heterosexual and homosocial romance, which (as we will see in the following sections of this chapter) dominate the Romantic exoticism of a novel like Hugo's *Bug-Jargal* and which, in turn, prove central to the articulation of the novel as a genre in the nineteenth-century Americas (be it in the form of the utopian, cross-cultural reconciliation that Doris Sommer has identified as the "foundational fiction" of the Latin American novel,[28] or in the guise of the dystopian racial divides that striate a plantation novel like Maynard's *Outre-mer*), gain a renewed vigor from being translated out of the realm of the story and into that of its telling. This translation from *histoire* to *discours*, which effectively relativizes Émile Benveniste's famous distinction between the two, allows for the possibility that Quentin and Shreve's lovers' discourse can itself become the foundation for a new history, conceived—as Celia Britton has argued of Mathieu and Papa Longoué's dialogues in *Quatrième siècle*—no longer as "'histoire' . . . but [as] a quasi-performative 'discours,'"[29] a lived performance in the present that might, through faultily (re)constructing the past, bring about a brighter future, one that is altogether more visible in Glissant's novel than in Faulkner's, but that is nonetheless also apparent in Quentin's and Shreve's (to be sure, resolutely privatized) collaboration as narrators.

Despite its allure and its potential, though, we must approach cautiously this sort of faulty performance, for does it not (and here is the bone of contention picked by countless critics with regard to a supposedly ahistorical postmodernism, a politically inert deconstructionism, and a radically constructivist postculturalism) mark a renunciation of the "truth," a forgetting of the "material."[30] Does it not irresponsibly glamorize "play" as a solution to real problems—and to the problem of the real—that merit a less skeptical approach, a more deeply rooted commitment? And, a logically related but quite opposite question, does not the belief that there is "nothing fault nor false" about this particular performance, or the paradigms of (heterosexual-homosocial) romance upon which it appears based, signal the further danger of eventually taking *too* seriously what were originally nothing more than fictions, "playful" or otherwise, and thus losing sight of their contingent nature? These are all questions that Faulkner's novel, with its insistent emphasis on the *narrativized reality* of history, necessarily opens up for consideration, but this fact—to state the obvious—hardly makes it the sort of radically postmodern document that would invite (from some quarters, at least) a series of disapprovingly affirmative responses to such questions. It is important to note that Faulkner is not claiming Quentin and Shreve have actually arrived at a place where there is "nothing fault nor false" (although, as lovers are prone, they may themselves indeed feel that they have achieved this state): such a position would be utterly incompatible with the novel's emphasis on the productive inescapability of the "fault." Shreve's and Quentin's "faulting of the other," which leads them to a provisionally felt love for and identification with Bon and Henry, and produces a *certain* story about them, has its all-too-evident faults, which other aspects of Faulkner's multilayered novel at least partially address, and redress: their romantic vision, for instance, tends to marginalize (Judith) or even demonize (Bon's mother) women; their empathetic fascination with the "white" Bon implicitly highlights their relative lack of interest in, or sympathy for, those "blacks" of a darker hue; the privileged location (Harvard) from which they narrate their story renders it politically suspect in no small degree. Gender, race, class: the holy trinity of contemporary North American literary criticism can be ranged against Quentin and Shreve's story, and not without justice. Faulkner's own love of his characters, however, permits him to "forgive," even to "condone," the faults and faulting that have made their story possible, while at the same time rigorously preventing us from forgetting the uncertain ground out of which their eventual certainties have emerged: the ground of a material history that their discourse, like any discourse, necessarily loses sight of in order to constitute itself, but that Faulkner consistently draws to our attention through his emphasis on the forgetfulness of his narrators and the faultiness of their narratives.

The last two of the eight explicit references to Haiti in the novel proper mark a limited return to a *certain* story that Shreve's skepticism had put momentarily into question. Not long after his doubt-inducing comments about "Porto Rico or Haiti" (p. 239), Shreve permits the geographical referent to restabilize, imagining Bon "in search of the meaning of his whole life, past—the Haiti, the childhood, . . . the woman who was his mother" (p. 250), and this (im)possible stability of the referent carries over into the final and most dramatic occurrence of the word. Shreve's playful intervention having relieved Quentin of his anxieties about the oppressively authoritative story that has been passed down to him by his father (the authority of patriarchal tradition), Quentin is now able to return to that story and appropriate elements of it for his and Shreve's retelling of it. Reliving the episode of Henry and Bon's Christmas departure from Sutpen's Hundred in 1860 and their arrival in New Orleans, the two narrators find themselves, along with their protagonists, at Bon's mother's house, sitting "in that drawing room of baroque and fusty magnificence which Shreve had invented and which was probably true enough," and in the presence of "the Haiti-born daughter of the French sugar planter and the woman who Sutpen's first father-in-law had told him was a Spaniard (the slight dowdy woman with untidy gray-streaked raven hair coarse as a horse's tail, with parchment-colored skin and implacable pouched black eyes which alone showed no age because they showed no forgetting, whom Shreve and Quentin had likewise invented and which was likewise probably true enough)" (p. 268). Here, a *certain* story is restored, in which Quentin and Shreve have become immersed and to which the third-person narrator accedes, while nonetheless supplementing it with a cautionary reminder of the extent to which this story must remain an indeterminate admixture of invention and truth; located in the chiasmatic space of the "likewise," this admixture puts into question without finally undoing the language of absolute certainty that Sutpen "had doomed all his blood to, black and white both" (p. 216). Sutpen's doomed and dooming language is one that can account neither for this confusing blend of truth and invention nor for the cross-cultural mixing that is the inescapably faulty ground of a diasporic American identity; it is a language that remains subject to arbitrary laws and determinations (for instance, "the laws which declare that one eighth of a specified kind of blood shall outweigh seven eighths of another kind," as Mr. Compson's Bon puts it [p. 91]) and that thus can never respond "truly" to the question posed Charles Bon's passably "white" son: "'*What are you? Who and where did you come from?*'" (p. 165).

Attempts to provide a definitive answer to this question have bedeviled the United States from its inception. A long series of sadly mistaken and genealogically connected political strategies have vied to represent, and thereby contain, the imbricated (lack of an) identity and the unsettling truth—the unsettling of truth—that the posing of this question reveals: they range from the "peculiar institution" of slavery and Jim Crow segregationism to the "well-intentioned" fallacies of multiculturalism and the highly problematic efforts at institutionalizing "biracialism" that are now, some seventy-five years after the category of "mulatto" was removed from the United States census, being tentatively introduced as a way of preserving the cherished logic of race while trying to do lip-service to the more *visibly* hybrid environment of our late-twentieth-century world(s). What all such divisive rhetorics and institutional practices anxiously respond to and attempt to foreclose upon is the reality of that which has always-already emerged and has yet to emerge: namely, the positive reality of what Jean Toomer referred to as "the American type," whose identity has been, and will be, fashioned out of "a spiritual fusion analagous [*sic*] to the fact of racial intermingling."[31] Toomer's faulty spelling is (unintentionally, no doubt) exemplary of what is needed in order to begin, impossibly, to (re)envision this "type": his productive error troubles the *logos*, transforming the letter of ending, *o*, into one of beginning, *a*; this is a new beginning that nonetheless remains inextricably tangled up in a nominal structure that points toward the same old ending, that continues to inscribe that which it at the same time inflects and contests (its "correct" analogue), in much the same way as every variant of Creole simultaneously marks an initiatory divergence from and a distorted repetition of the original languages out of which it is composed.

Sutpen's tragic "mistake" can be traced to his inadequate grasp of this new-old language of Creole, as Mr. Compson makes clear in a passage that I have already had occasion to quote but that I would like to (re)cite and slightly augment here: once in Haiti, we are told, Sutpen found himself "in a country and among a people *whose very language he had to learn* and where *because of this* he was to make that mistake which if he had acquiesced to it would not even have been an error and which, since he refused to accept it or be stopped by it, became his doom" (p. 41; my italics). Sutpen's mistake is primarily linguistic, in Mr. Compson's ambivalent formulation, which not only suggests that this mistake was caused by a failure to learn enough of that people's language to understand what was going on around him but *also* that it stemmed from having learned *too much* Creole, from having become sufficiently creolized as to have entered into that disorienting translational space in which another self can begin to speak in another language that strangely resembles and differs from one's own. Speaking this other language, this other self can begin to live differently, to live (with) difference by inaugurating new relations that can only appear mistaken from the perspective of one's original language and the grammatical restrictions that it imposes. Language, Grandfather Compson remarks at one point in his ur-telling of Sutpen's Haitian interlude, is a "meagre and fragile thread . . . by which the little surface corners and edges of men's secret and solitary lives may be joined for an instant now and then before sinking back into the darkness where the spirit cried for the first time and was not heard and will cry for the last time and will not be heard then either" (p. 202). Sutpen's failure to weave with this thread or, alternately, to recognize what he has already woven with it, mirrors the profound failure and misrecognition of Faulkner's thoroughly hybridized society as a whole, which is unable to rise out of the darkness of absolute beginnings and final endings and to make itself heard, *as it is*, in the intermediary and mediating space of communication and community that this "meagre and fragile thread" makes briefly, but repeatedly, possible.

It is on this note of failure and misrecognition, of course, that Faulkner, with a crushing realism, ends his novel, after the euphoric possibilities entertained in the second-to-last chapter. In the final section of my own penultimate chapter I will examine in some depth the problematic of ending, the sad inevitability of "stopping," as it gets rehearsed in the final pages of Maximin's *Soufrières*. Here, we need only note that in the character of Jim Bond Faulkner emphasizes, one last time, the unlikeliness of the language of hybridity ever being heard in a society that seems constitutively incapable of unlearning the language of race. The black-white, white-black Bond bellows "in human speech" (p. 300), but such speech can have no meaning for those who, inhumanly, have failed to (learn how to) listen to him, or live with him, and for whom (as Shreve puts it, mimicking with appalling accuracy the language of the story that he has just heard and attempted partially to redress) Bond is nothing more than the last remaining "nigger Sutpen." As Shreve reminds Quentin in his final tirade, however, Bond is also "something else besides": playing off of and adapting the sort of dystopian vision that we saw at work in Hearn's negative vision of "universal blackness" (Chapter 4), Shreve puts forward an alternative account of Bond that sees him not as the site of an apocalyptic ending but as the eventual progenitor of a thoroughly hybridized world (so fully hybridized, indeed, that it can include not only the future but the past—as Shreve's curious recourse to the future anterior suggests: "in a few thousand years, I who regard you will also have sprung from the loins of African kings" [p. 302]). In this parodic harangue, self-consciously saturated with the language of racial paranoia to which he knows Quentin is all too susceptible and from which he (Shreve) is attempting to wean him (Quentin), what can be read—between the lines, along the fault line, beyond the color line—is a positive invocation of radical métissage, a salutary vision of human *relations* in which race will have been finally forgotten, its "last word" spoken.

This is the ultimate tendency of Faulkner's novel, albeit one that it can only faulteringly enunciate. As Frederick Karl has argued, and I find myself in complete agreement with his assessment, *Absalom, Absalom!* is the novel in which Faulkner moves toward "his most radical statement on race, the furthest he would ever go"; it is, Karl continues, a statement that is "possible only in fiction, and it clashes directly with nearly everything he said in his public statements. Here he appears on the edge of suggesting that the resolution of the South's (and the nation's) racial dilemma was in a single race, one that would transcend black and white by becoming black-and-white."[32] Faulkner's provocative portrait of "black Haiti" as the site par excellence of a *mixed* identity anticipates this daring, if faultily rendered, prophecy of a monoracial South (and nation) in which Jim Bond might finally have his proper place. In the final analysis, to be sure, even in this most visionary novel of Faulkner's, we remain still and always "on the edge" of (voicing) any such transcendence, not only for obvious historical reasons, but because this very transcendence—conceived of in terms of a definitive "overpassing"—is itself incompatible both with the elusive mobility of human interactions and the rigidifying stasis of an (in)human language out of which one can never fully translate oneself and that thus directs us not only forward into a progressively creolized future but also repeatedly back toward what Derek Walcott has so nicely referred to as "the primal fault / of the first map of the world, its boundaries and powers."[33] If this "primal fault," and the "boundaries and powers" that it makes possible, is one that (Faulkner's) writing can never truly right, or put a definitive "stop" to, his own secondary (re)mapping of the world, for all its faults, and because of them, reminds us that this primal inheritance can and must be, in all the ambiguity of the phrase, *written over*.

It is with two instances of "writing over" (which entails, among other things, repetition, revision, palimpsest, and defacement) that I would like to conclude this account of Faulkner's novel. The first derives from Quentin and Shreve's description of Sutpen's first wife, specifically the (true and/or invented) claim that she has "parchment-colored skin." What this description so beautifully suggests is that a determination of (her) skin color is first and foremost contingent upon an act of writing that inscribes itself upon, and thereby defaces, what is—literally—neither black, brown, yellow, or white, but simply parchment. To write any such color on this parchment would be to write over it, to mask it with a metaphor that can itself—once it has been revealed as metaphor—be unmasked and revised. At the same time, the word "parchment" is itself obviously a metaphor, which blocks—in palimpsest fashion—a literal reading of the skin, encouraging one to read beneath it, and thus return the figure to its ground (cream, beige, ochre, beige-ochre . . . ?). But this ground of color to which one might return is, as we have seen, itself figural. How, then, to make the materiality of her skin visible if it must always be written over, in one way or another? Perhaps only by not naming, by not writing at all, and if Faulkner has chosen to leave this woman unnamed in the novel proper, it is because he wants to remind us of the violence with which she has been written over, her human reality reduced by Sutpen to the inhuman and ultimately figural considerations of race. And yet without a name of some sort her story, and history itself, would go forgotten. Under these circumstances, in the face of the familiar double bind in which (Faulkner's) writing situates us, the only "solution" must be to betray her presence with as little violence, and to preserve her traces with as much vigilance, as possible. To attenuate the violence of a language that names, Faulkner suggests, one must draw the figurality, the groundlessness, of those names to the fore; to be vigilant in the recuperation of the material, in all its lived complexity, he equally suggests, one must register the extent to which it comes to us in the form of memorial traces that can only faultily (re)present it. To "write over" is to engage with (the categoricality of) language and (the necessity of) memory in the spirit of these uncategorical and uncategorizing imperatives.

If my first instance of "writing over" had primarily to do with the problem of language, the second one concerns memory, and can be read in the falterings of a passage from the manuscript version of *Absalom, Absalom!*, at the point where Sutpen has just launched confusingly into the telling of his Haitian story. Sutpen, it will be remembered, got himself and Grandfather Compson "both into that besieged Haitian room as simply as he got himself to the West Indies by saying that he decided to go to the West Indies and so he went there; this anecdote no deliberate continuation of the other one but merely called to his mind by the picture of the niggers and torches in front of them" (p. 199). In the manuscript version of the novel, the hinge binding these two phrases to one another reads with just the slightest difference: "so he went there—this memory [?], no this anecdote. . . ."[34] What this earlier version reveals, archaeologically, is a (questionable) "memory" that precedes and underlies the "anecdote" of the published version, and that stands in a double relation to it: one of complementarity, in which the memory and the anecdote seem compatible, and one of contrast, in which the negation—a negation that has itself been struck through—asserts their incompatibility. Here, then, is a perfect allegory for the sort of tenuous remembering that I have been attempting to identify, and argue for, in my account of Faulkner's Haiti (all the more tenuous, indeed, given the fact that, as published, this manuscript version of *Absalom, Absalom!* is apparently "flawed by mistranscriptions and errors of fact").[35] Made possible by a faulty comparison, called to mind by a picture of "niggers" that does not correspond to the reality of cultural mixing that it will convey, this is a memory that can and must be read, if only with the greatest of difficulty. Recalling, and writing over, Marlow's famous description of himself traveling "in the night of first ages, of those ages that are gone, leaving hardly a sign—and no memories" (p. 51), this is a memory that has learned how to read the paucity of signs and the abundance of light that they shed.

From Revolution to Representation: Romancing
the Creole in Alejo Carpentier, Jules Levilloux,
and Heinrich von Kleist

Alejo Carpentier's attitude toward Bernardin de Saint-Pierre was, as we saw in Chapter 3, largely dismissive, to say the least. Bernardin, along with his famous novel, makes several telling appearances in Carpentier's *Kingdom of this World*, where his name functions as a metonym for the (naiveté of the) Enlightenment and for representational strategies that are patently inadequate to the task of conveying either the alternately marvelous and horrific reality of life in the colonies or the libidinal energies underlying colonial encounters and revolutionary history. The plantation owner Lenormand de Mézy, Ti-Noël's original master, is the first character in the novel through whom Carpentier's critique of Bernardin's exoticizing vision is filtered. Reflecting with irritation upon recent events in revolutionary France (the year is 1791) and "those Utopian imbeciles in Paris whose hearts bled for the black slaves," Ti-Noël's master notes that the dangerous notions about human equality held by those supporting the Revolution could only have been exacerbated by the misleadingly benign representations of the exotic available to them there. From "pictures of indolent mulatto girls and naked washerwomen, of siestas under banana trees engraved by Abraham Brunias and exhibited in France along with verses of [the Île Bourbon poet] De Parny and [Rousseau's] the 'Profession of Faith of the Savoyard Vicar,'" how easy it must be, the plantation owner surmises, for these liberalists, "full of theories from the *Encyclopédie*," "to envisage Santo Domingo as the leafy paradise of *Paul and Virginia*, where the melons did not hang from the branches of the trees only because they would have killed the passers-by if they had fallen from such heights" (pp. 71–72). By this account, reformist or revolutionary politics turns out to be little more than the logical end-product of faulty representations emanating from the metropole—a belief that, as we will see in our examination of the nineteenth-century Martiniquan plantation novel *Outre-mer* in Chapter 6, is at the foundations of what can be termed "creolist discourse."

Ironically, Lenormand de Mézy's caustic reflections come only hours before his plantation is sacked, as part of the mass uprising in the Northern Province that saw the slave population finally enter the fray of an ongoing civil war that had hitherto been limited to *grands blancs*, *petits blancs*, and *hommes de couleur* (free men of color). The slave uprising (in Carpentier's account) marks a carnivalesque overturning of the rationalized and theatricalized régime of a colonizing modernity: significantly, it is the plantation's bookkeeper (*contador*) who is the first to fall in the attack on the plantation, and the chapter devoted to this attack ends with Ti-Noël raping de Mézy's wife, Mlle Floridor, a mediocre actress given to declaiming "bravura passages" from Racine in front of her bemused slaves. In the same way that Carpentier filters his critique of Bernardin's exoticism through the reactionary musings of a plantation owner, his account of the slave revolt, with its emphasis on drinking, looting, and raping, seems curiously compatible with the sort of simultaneously apocalyptic and trivializing representations of black insurgency that one finds at work in any number of nineteenth-century novels such as *Outre-mer*. Lemuel A. Johnson, indeed, has gone so far as to argue that "at bottom, its magical realism notwith-standing," Carpentier's novel "is driven by an exotic but clichéd and fool-ish sexuality that, here and there, threatens to reduce the slave uprising to a penis erection."[36] Whether one agrees with this view or not, it is clear that the critique of Bernardin's Enlightenment exoticism in *Kingdom* is not as straightforward as it might at first appear: filtered through the reac-tionary lens of creolist *ressentiment*, this critique is inseparable from a libi-dinized counterrepresentation of historical reality that in certain respects actually seems to reinforce, rather than negate, the sort of falsified vision that a writer like Bernardin supposedly perpetuated.

We find a similar tension at work in the novel's second reference to Bernardin—actually, a cluster of references attaching to the figure of Pauline Bonaparte, wife of the general (Leclerc) whom her brother had charged in 1802 with the mission of reinstituting slavery in Saint-Domingue and restor-ing control over a nominally French territory that, under Toussaint Louver-ture, had won full internal self-government. As the frigate loaded with troops nears the island, the sight of the Cap and the Plaine du Nord "de-lighted Pauline, who had read *Paul and Virginia*, and had heard *L'Insulaire*, a charming Creole *contredanse* of exotic rhythm published in Paris on the rue du Saumon" (p. 93). Her experience of the island will be, in Bovarystic fashion, shaped by the exotic novels she has read: once settled on the island, she feels herself "part Virginia, part Atala" (p. 95), thus exhibiting an overdetermined sense of self common to many nineteenth-century novelistic protagonists, whose mimetic engagement with the world is often compli-cated by an excess of potentially contradictory texts from which to choose when modeling their identities. Pauline's unlikely presence on the island, which had already attracted the attention of W. E. B. Du Bois in his 1938 play *Haiti*,[37] supplies Carpentier with an opportunity once again to insist upon the inadequacies of Bernardin's Enlightenment exoticism, which not only fails to represent the colony as it really is (de Mézy's critique), but also remains blind to the libidinal underside of human psychology and revolu-tionary history. During the early days of her stay on the island, before the war takes a turn for the worse and her husband dies of yellow fever, Pauline takes to cavorting with her black masseur Soliman, engaging in erotic games (whipping him, for instance, "with a green switch without hurting him, for the fun of seeing the face of feigned suffering he made"), and, from time to time, rewarding him for the loving care he lavishes on her beauty by "per-mitt[ing] the Negro . . . to kneel before her and kiss her feet in a gesture that Bernardin de Saint-Pierre would have interpreted as a symbol of the noble gratitude of a simple soul brought into contact with the generous teachings of the Enlightenment [*ilustración*]" (p. 95). Soliman's fetishism, to say noth-ing of his and Pauline's soft-core bondage routine, pushes the reader aggres-

sively beyond the pale of Bernardin's interpretive framework, toward an altogether "darker" and more "realistic" view of human existence. Part of
what is at stake in establishing this alternative framework can, in turn, be
gauged from the way in which, only a few pages later, Carpentier's narrative
briefly grants Pauline a more "authentic," less Bovarystic, engagement with
life: as the war turns from bad to worse and Leclerc lies dying, Pauline
comes increasingly under Soliman's sway, and finds herself trying out his
various magic spells and conjures, which stir up in her "the lees of old Corsican blood, which was more akin to the living cosmogony of the Negro
than to the lies of the Directory, in whose disbelief she had grown up [*en
cuyo descreimiento había cobrado conciencia de existir*]" (p. 99). In the
same way that the implied sexual interpretation of Pauline's relations with
Soliman renders hopelessly naive the "enlightened" reading of (Carpentier's)
Bernardin, the appeal to a blood logic here serves as a counter to the
mimetic world of "romantic lies" (to recall the terms of René Girard's *Mensonge romantique et vérité romanesque* [1961]) that Pauline formerly inhabited—and to which she will quickly revert, once Leclerc dies and she returns to Europe.

   The novel's unexpected shift in focus away from Ti-Noël, who has accompanied his exiled master to Cuba, and onto Pauline occurs at a crucial
moment in the text: not only does the Pauline episode occupy the actual
midpoint of the novel (pp. 90–101), but it also overlaps with the climactic
events of the Haitian Revolution—the imprisonment of Toussaint and the
final push to independence led by Dessalines, Christophe, and Pétion. The
Pauline episode situates the reader at a significant distance from and yet
proximity to these world-historical events, which serve, for example, as the
triumphant climax of C. L. R. James's history of the Revolution, *The Black
Jacobins*, but which in *Kingdom* are passed over in virtual silence (Toussaint Louverture, indeed, is not mentioned once in the novel). In the place of
revolutionary history, in excess of it, we are given a figure who, while herself historical, seems to come from an entirely different universe, a novelized
world of romance. This displacement from the center to the periphery, from
history to romance, forcibly draws the reader's attention to the *absence of
revolution* that Carpentier has placed at the very center of his four-part
novel, the first half of which deals with French-ruled Haiti (Part I being focused around Macandal's 1757 slave revolt; Part II chronicling the outbreak
of the 1791 slave revolt and concluding with the Pauline episode and the
briefest of postscripts concerning the final defeat of the French), and the second half of which examines Haiti after it gained its independence (Part III
dealing with the end of Henri Christophe's harsh rule in the North and his
suicide in 1820; Part IV evoking, as we saw in the discussion of Faulkner,
the consolidation of Boyer's mulattocracy in the mid- to late-1820s). It is

this displacement, this excessive connection between romance and revolution, upon which nineteenth-century Romantic novels like Hugo's *Bug-Jargal* and Maynard's *Outre-mer* depend: to talk revolution, for them, is equivalent to talking (interracial) romance. Carpentier self-consciously addresses this connection in *Kingdom*, treating it not as one of equivalency but of incompatibility: the presence of romance in his text marks the absence of revolution, the impossibility of the latter being satisfactorily represented within the terms of the former. But, to rephrase a point made in the preceding paragraphs about Carpentier's disturbing complicity with the discursive practices and literary traditions he is ostensibly critiquing, this attempt at reading romance and revolution apart from one another has its obvious limits, since in self-consciously drawing the reader's attention to the excess of romance rather than simply excising it from the novel he runs the risk (as Johnson's critique suggests) of reinscribing the very connection that he is in the process of undoing.

Whether the excess of romance can be as easily expunged as the preceding sentence suggests must remain an open question here. What is certain is that in *Explosion in a Cathedral*, his subsequent novel about the French Revolution and its ramifications in the Caribbean, Carpentier insists more openly on the essential unrepresentability of revolution: rather than implicitly suggest this through a disruption of narrative continuity (of the sort effected by the Pauline episode), he does so through an explicit meditation on the necessarily allegorical nature of all representation. When Esteban first arrives in revolutionary France with Victor Hugues, it seems to him as if he is "in the midst of a gigantic allegory of a revolution rather than a revolution itself, a metaphorical revolution, a revolution which had been made elsewhere, which revolved on a hidden axis, which had been elaborated in subterranean councils, invisible to those who wanted to know all about it" (p. 95). By this account, revolution can only appear as other than it literally is, in allegorized form, if it is to be known and rendered visible. This problem of (mis)representation is signaled in the novel most notably through the recurring appearances of the "apocalyptic painting" entitled "Explosion in a Cathedral," which metafictively points toward Carpentier's own self-consciously inadequate efforts at giving artistic representation to the historical process of revolution.

This painting, which is capable of generating a "multiplicity of interpretations" (p. 253), records "the apocalyptic immobilisation of a catastrophe": to view it is to be struck by "the terrible suspense of this static earthquake, this silent cataclysm, this illustration of the End of Time" (pp. 18–19). For Esteban, and for the reader, this painting cannot help evoking the ongoing revolution, albeit uncannily and even illogically (given the fact that it was painted long before the outbreak of the events to which it tantalizingly seems to refer), and yet it can do so only by stopping the movement of history, freezing it in a static representation that betrays the dynamic presence of revolution and the new time (as opposed to the End of Time) that revolution supposedly initiates. Moreover, not only does this painting immobilize history, and thus misrepresent it, but—given its excessive interpretability—it renders the meaning of history all too mobile, subjecting the singular reality of material change to the multiple vagaries of human interpretation. Both terrifyingly fixed and dizzyingly multivalent, the painting serves to remind Esteban of the inescapability of representation and the consequent impossibility of gaining certain knowledge about the revolution in which he finds himself bewilderingly entangled, and it is thus not surprising that at one point in the narrative he attempts to destroy it and the frustrating (lack of) knowledge it conveys. At the end of the novel, however, the painting—now hanging in Esteban and Sofia's Madrid apartment, its "gaping wound" having been "inexpertly healed over with patches" by an unknown hand (p. 340)—makes one final appearance: this return of the repressed signals that what "Explosion in a Cathedral" duplicitously represents—both the problem of revolution and the problem of (mis)representation—cannot be simply done away with in a counterrepresentational gesture of denial, or, rather, that such gestures must be conceived of in an altogether different manner, which acknowledges the fundamental inadequacy of representation while pointing—impossibly, allegorically—to a revolutionary elsewhere, an aporetic present, that no representation can ever contain. It is precisely into this unspeakable, unrepresentable space and time of the revolutionary present that Esteban and Sofia dissolve at the end of the novel, vanishing without a trace into the crowd of Spaniards who, on May 2, 1808, rose up against the French occupation in an uprising that, so history tells us, "set off the wars of liberation in the Spanish colonies."[38]

Esteban and Sofia's sudden and unexplained disappearance from the novel is the price they pay for entering history and thereby escaping the problematic realm of representation. Perhaps this opposition between a lived presence and its textual (mis)representation, between (revolutionary) history and a (fictional) story in which that history can only appear as a foundational absence, is itself nothing more or less than a subtle reinscription of an ultimately questionable opposition between authenticity and inauthenticity. Be that as it may, at the very least the later Carpentier no longer conceives of this opposition in terms of a simple conflict between authentic and inauthentic *representations*, as so often happens in an earlier work like *Kingdom*, where the catastrophic immobilization that "Explosion in a Cathedral" puts on display is treated not as the necessary precondition of all art but as the characteristic feature of a certain type of (degraded, European) art, as we can see by returning one last time to the figure of Pauline

Bonaparte. Pauline's departure from the island does not mark the end of her role in the novel; rather, she reappears in Parts III and IV as a monumental reminder of the continuing, pernicious influence of Europe on a now independent Haiti: first, in the form of a bust that once adorned her house at the Cap and that has found its way to Sans Souci, Henri Christophe's ostentatious palatial residence, and then in the form of Canova's statue of her, which a transplanted Soliman discovers to his horror in the rooms of the Borghese Palace in Rome. Under the shadow of Pauline's bust at Sans Souci, Henri Christophe's daughters—the little Princesses Athenaïs and Améthyste—play at battledore and shuttlecock (p. 116), one minor sign among many of the mimetic excesses that Carpentier associates with Christophe's Europeanized court. Soliman's drunken nocturnal encounter with Canova's *Venus*, in turn, leads him to the brink of madness and death, as he massages the familiar form, at first believing it to be Pauline herself, only to realize from the "chill of the marble"—in a mistaken interpretation that reveals a deeper truth—that this statue "was the corpse of Pauline Bonaparte" (p. 166). His hallucinatory encounter with her reproduced "dead" body causes Soliman, who contracts a fatal malarial fever that very night, both to long for the island that he left behind in order to follow Christophe's widow to Europe, and to remember penitently his African ancestry and his neglected Vodou beliefs. We last encounter him on the point of death, seeking "a god who had his abode in far-off Dahomey, at some dark crossroad, his red phallus on a crutch he carried for that purpose" (p. 168): this invocation of Papa Legba and his phallic authenticity contrasts sharply with the theatrical inauthenticity of Soliman's life in Rome prior to his nightmarish encounter with Pauline's "corpse" (we are, for instance, informed that his Italian acquaintances, as a joke, once took him to one of "the narrow, foul-smelling theaters where *opere buffe* were sung" and pushed him onto the stage; "his unexpected appearance was such a hit with the spectators that the manager of the company invited him to repeat the performance whenever he liked" [pp. 161–62]). *Kingdom of this World*, in short, establishes a central counterpoint between two different types of representation, whereas *Explosion in a Cathedral* engages in an argument about the conditions of representation per se, thus putting into question the straightforward antitheses (such as authentic and inauthentic, virile and effeminate, marvelous and theatrical, African and European, original and mimetic, epic and novelistic, oral and written) upon which the earlier novel relied.

Notwithstanding this crucial difference, what these two novels of Carpentier's obviously share is the will to interrogate and revise the well-established conventions of the historical novel, a subgenre that emerged in the first decades of the nineteenth century as a response—be it progressive or, as in the case of a novel like *Bug-Jargal*, reactionary—to "the French

Revolution, the revolutionary wars and the rise and fall of Napoleon, which for the first time made history a *mass experience*, and moreover on a European scale."[39] One might well adapt Lukács's sentence to read "on a global scale," since the well-chronicled rise of the historical novel coincides with and is indissociable from a fundamental transformation in colonial literature. Henceforth, the problem of history (and along with it, that of race) would come to dominate this literature. Léon-François Hoffmann points out in his seminal study of "le nègre romantique" that it is only after 1800 that historical characters start showing up in novels with exotic locales; he notes, moreover, that after the revolution in Saint-Domingue, "it became impossible to pass over in silence the racial tensions that characterized life in the colonies."[40] As evidence of this, he goes on to cite the preface to Maynard's *Outre-mer* where, justifying the pervasive "bloodiness" of his novel, Maynard affirms that "colonists in all the colonies know very well that it is no longer possible today to turn an account of their society into the stuff of rosewater- or orange-flower-scented volumes" (1.vii). For postrevolutionary writers, the exotic can no longer be disentangled from the colonial; the loss of pastoral, which—notwithstanding Carpentier's and Pauline Bonaparte's (mis)reading of *Paul et Virginie*—Bernardin repeatedly inscribes in his famous novel (most notably, through his use of the historical character La Bourdonnais), becomes a foregone conclusion, their (more often than not lamented) point of departure.

Alexandre Dumas makes this point with a nice irony in his novel *Georges* (1843), when he has his eponymous hero, a superlatively gifted and "satanically" proud mulatto who has returned from France to his native island of Mauritius with the intention of singlehandedly killing "the prejudice that no homme de couleur had yet dared to combat" (p. 121), and who has been jailed and sentenced to death for having led a failed slave revolt, read the "calm and poetic story" of *Paul et Virginie* on the eve of his execution (p. 408).[41] Only a decade after Bernardin published *Paul et Virginie*, his protégé Jean-Baptiste Picquenard had similarly, if with none of Dumas's irony, juxtaposed that "calm and poetic" pastoral with revolutionary history in his *Zoflora, ou La bonne négresse* (1800): set in Saint-Domingue, the scene shifts at one point to the tranquil Spanish colony of Santo Domingo on the eastern half of the island, and it is at precisely this point in the novel that Picquenard pays tribute to his mentor in a lengthy apostrophe to the "happy bard of *Paul et Virginie*, true painter of nature" (2.159–62). Picquenard's double island—revolutionized Saint-Domingue, pastoral Santo Domingo—is an apt metaphor for the transitional nature of his novel, awkwardly positioned as it is between an ahistorical Enlightenment exoticism and the history-bound narratives of a postrevolutionary writer like Victor Hugo. For this generation of writers, Picquenard's double island could no longer be conceived of spatially, but only temporally, in terms of a lost past and a problematic present. Confirming Maynard's opposition between a bloodily historicized and a sweet-smellingly timeless narrative, his compatriot Jules Levilloux stated, in the preface to *Les créoles* (also published in 1835), that he purposefully situated the beginning of his novel during "the last days of the old colonial régime" for the purpose of dramatic contrast: "I chose the time in which nothing had changed, when everything was still untouched in the Antilles [*où tout était encore vierge aux Antilles*], a time contemporaneous with the revolution that was beginning to cast some disquieting glimmers of light as far as the New World" (p. 14).

This "virginal" point of departure is soon left behind in Levilloux's novel, which allegorizes the coming of revolutionary change to the Antilles by ambivalently entertaining the possibility of a marriage between a light-skinned métis, Estève, and a (white) Creole, his friend Briolan's sister Léa. As we saw at the beginning of this chapter, Levilloux raises this possibility only to negate repeatedly the "conciliatory gesture of romance" (in Sommer's words): Estève and Briolan have deceived the prejudiced Léa, allowing her to think that she is marrying a (white) Creole, but the marriage ceremony is broken off, in *Jane Eyre*-like fashion, after a last-minute revelation of Estève's "true" identity; the lovers are both killed off very soon after the interrupted wedding, to be united only in death when Briolan, to his mother's horror, has them buried in a common grave. The only character left standing by the end of *Les créoles* is Briolan, still committed to the egalitarian ideals of the French Revolution, despite the disasters that have resulted from his attempts at transplanting them to the barren soil of the Antilles. Finding he "cannot exist in his own country," disgusted with and beaten down by its seemingly ineradicable prejudices, Briolan will depart for France in 1792 on the same boat as Jean-François Coquille Dugommier, accompanying this soon-to-be hero of the revolutionary wars on "his providential march toward the immortality of history" (p. 254), in a move that bears some resemblance to Esteban's departure from Saint-Domingue with Victor Hugues near the beginning of *Explosion in a Cathedral*.[42] In the novel's brief epilogue, the prematurely aged Briolan dies in the battle of Sierra-Negra (November 17, 1794) alongside General Dugommier, the man who (as Levilloux put it in an article published around the same time as his novel) "drove the English out of Toulon, singled out Bonaparte while he was still a lieutenant, expelled the Spanish from the South of France, and died—victorious and pure—in the battlefields of Catalonia."[43]

This double death, the eradication of both the fictional protagonist Briolan and the historical figure Dugommier, confirms one last time Levilloux's inability to approach the subject of revolution in any but apocalyptic terms that negate the possibility of historical change and put into question the superiority of "political principles" (revolutionary egalitarianism) over "colonial customs" (racial prejudice) that he seems to be arguing for in the preface to his novel (p. 14). In this respect, Levilloux ends up promoting the same antirevolutionary perspective as his compatriot Maynard whose novel, as we will see in the following chapter, ends in an orgy of destruction that might be thought of as the necessary prelude for restoring the old order of things, erasing historical change, and—in the words of the 1814 Charter (the constitutional document under which the Bourbon dynasty returned to power after the fall of Napoléon)—"linking back up the chain of days that harmful deviations had undone."[44] "The ideal of Legitimism," as Lukács puts it, "is to return to pre-Revolutionary conditions, that is, to eradicate from history the greatest historical events of the epoch."[45] Such an ideal was, of course, quite simply unrealizable, and even an adamant royalist like Chateaubriand, in his *Réflexions politiques* of 1814, took as his point of departure the disappearance of the old way of life and the consequent need to compromise with the postrevolutionary world: "in life, one must take as one's point of departure the place at which one has arrived," he maintained, adding that one must take men "as they are, rather than always seeing them as they are not and as they no longer can be; a child is not a mature adult, and he in turn is not an old man."[46] In this passage, Chateaubriand acknowledges the reality of change and attempts to control it through an organic metaphor, equating radical transformations in social structure with the gradual development of the human organism: this (limited) acceptance of change is, as Franco Moretti has argued, the ideological imperative that generates the Bildungsroman tradition in the early decades of the nineteenth century. Charting the passage from childhood to maturity through an unstable transitional space of adolescence, the Bildungsroman makes it possible to imagine a happy ending to the transformative process initiated by the French Revolution. However, for writers committed to Restorationist values—like Maynard, and the young Victor Hugo—the possibility of Bildung can only be a monstrous one: their main protagonists are for this reason doomed to an eternal adolescence that can never reach fruition. And yet, just as Levilloux's novel incessantly reinscribes the values of a prejudiced world to which it is ostensibly opposed, so too do novels like *Outre-mer* and *Bug-Jargal*, in opening themselves up to the restless energies unleashed by a revolution that they bitterly contest, unintentionally dissolve the ideological certainties that their repeated acts of narrative closure would enforce.

Before turning to Hugo's novel about the Haitian Revolution, though, I would like to pause very briefly over another well-known Romantic account of those events, which also insists on tragic closure as opposed to the carefully orchestrated openness of Bildung: namely, Heinrich von Kleist's "The

Betrothal in San Domingo" (1811; *Die Verlobung in St. Domingo*). Kleist's brief tale is of special relevance here because of the way that it reroutes his familiar post-Kantian preoccupation with semantic instability and epistemological doubt through the territory of racial discourse and, specifically, that ambiguous zone of it occupied by the word "creole." The story takes place in 1803, as Dessalines is leading his troops toward their final victory. In its very first sentence the events in Saint-Domingue are characterized as a simple struggle between whites (*Weissen*) and blacks (*Schwarzen*), the latter of whom seem fittingly embodied by the "ferocious" African-born Congo Hoango whose violent revenge against his kindly former master, Guillaume de Villeneuve, is indicative of "the general frenzy of vindictive rage that flared up in all those plantations as a result of the reckless [*unbesonnen*] actions of the National Convention" (p. 231).[47] This black-white struggle is somewhat complicated by the presence on the former Villeneuve plantation of Congo Hoango's mulatto wife Babekan and her European-born "mestiza" daughter, the fifteen-year-old Toni. Both the *Mulattin* and the *Mestize* are, however, clearly on the black side as the story begins, eagerly participating in the "hideous deception" to which Congo Hoango subjects fleeing wayfarers who come to the old plantation house seeking shelter. This deception consists in lulling "white or creole refugees" (p. 232; "weisse oder kreolische Flüchtlinge") into a false sense of security, lowering their defences, and thereby preparing the way for Congo Hoango to murder them: we are told that Toni's "yellowish complexion [*ins Gelbliche gehenden Gesichtsfarbe*] made her very useful for the purpose of this hideous deception"; all that glitters, clearly, is not gold—a point the story will make even more emphatically by transforming Toni and her fool's gold complexion into the true heroine of an interracial romance. For now, we simply need to remark that the narrator's initial use of the word "creole" establishes a semantic indeterminacy that will never be dissipated, and will only be deepened by its subsequent occurrences: "creole" obviously marks a difference from "white" but of what sort? Does it mean island-born white as opposed to European white? Mulatto? It would appear, in any case, that whites and Creoles are on one and the same side. And yet when the story's male lead, the Swiss officer Gustav von der Ried, tells Babekan and Toni about the violent rebellion in Fort Dauphin from which he and his uncle's family are fleeing, he states, apparently contradicting the narrator, that "the mad lust for freedom which has seized all these plantations has driven the [N]egroes and [C]reoles to break the chains that oppressed them, and to take their revenge on the whites for much reprehensible ill-treatment they have had to suffer at the hands of some of us who do our race no credit" (p. 241; "der Wahnsinn der Freiheit, der alle diese Pflanzungen ergriffen hat, trieb die Negern und Kreolen, die Ketten, die sie drückten, zu brechen, und an den

Weissen wegen vielfacher und tadelnswürdiger Misshandlungen, die sie von einigen schlechten Mitgliedern derselben erlitten, Rache zu nehmen"). Immediately after, Gustav differentiates between a "white planter" ("einem Pflanzer vom Geschlecht der Weissen") and a "creole planter" (the peculiarly capitalized "Creolischen Pflanzer"),[48] neither of whom would appear to be on the "black" side (p. 242). How can Gustav use the word "creole" in these two apparently differing senses? And between himself and the narrator, whose is the more authoritative use of the word? Are they referring to one and the same thing, and do either of them really *know* what they are talking about? And where, if at all, does the question of race fit into all this? (Interestingly, in the above passages, the story's translator oscillates between reading race into the text—Kleist speaks not of "some of us who do our race no credit" but of "some bad members [*Mitglieder*] of the whites"— and partially ruling it out—the planter is not merely "white" but "from the stock [*Geschlect*] of the whites," and thus ancestrally grounded in a way that the creole planter is not.)

Such questions, versions of which we have already encountered in our examination of Hearn's *Youma*, seem irresoluble—and it is precisely the linguistic, and thence political, ramifications of this indeterminacy that Kleist's postrevolutionary oeuvre so rigorously identifies and explores. The characters in "Betrothal" provide a dizzying and often contradictory series of responses to such questions—at times with a cynical deceptiveness, at times with a sincere pathos, but in the final analysis, always with a fatal result. Despite his initial fears that the Villeneuve plantation house may not be a safe refuge for him, the fleeing Swiss officer is assured by Babekan that she is not a Negress but a "mulatto woman," that her daughter is a "mestiza" (p. 233), and that they are both subject to the persecutory whims of the "black" Congo Hoango. This act of naming serves to calm Gustav and confirm his visual perceptions: he believes he can trust the old woman because "in your face, like a gleam of light, there is a tinge of my own complexion" (p. 236; "aus der Farbe eures Gesichts schimmert mir ein Strahl von der meinigen entgegen"). And yet her naming of herself as "mulatto" also confirms the anxiety that seeing her provokes, since she is a woman, as Gustav puts it, who "as the whole cast of your features shows are a mulatto and therefore of African origin" (p. 236; "die ihr nach eurer ganzen Gesichtsbildung eine Mulattinn, und mithin afrikanischen Ursprungs seid"). Explaining why she is an enemy of Congo's, despite her appearance, Babekan resolves this tension between the "gleam of light" in her complexion and her visibly African origins through recourse to the word "creole" and its ambiguous referentiality: it is, she states, Congo Hoango's dearest wish "to inflame the vengeance of the blacks against us white and creole half-dogs, as he calls us [*über uns weisse und kreolische Halbhunde, wie er uns nennt*]"

(p. 237). In this particular instance, the adjective "creole" seems quite clearly to serve as a synonym for "mulatto" and yet its appearance here is ironized by the fact that it is a name given by Congo Hoango, or rather by Babekan in Congo Hoango's name, and thus is part of a lie meant to expedite Gustav's misunderstanding of the situation, to complicate his attempts at determining to "what race [*Volksstamm*] the people living here belonged" (p. 239). These attempts were from the very outset grounded in an illusion, as Toni suggests in a playful account (addressed to her mother but performed for Gustav's benefit) of his initial meeting with her: his imagination (*Einbildung*), she notes, "was obsessed with blackamoors and negroes, and if a lady from Paris or Marseilles had opened the door to him, he would have taken her for a negress" (p. 239).

Toni herself proves equally adept at imaginatively (mis)taking one thing for another by quickly falling in love with the man whom she is supposed to treat as an enemy and who is, likewise, taken by her. Initially repelled by her "complexion" (p. 243; "Farbe"), he nonetheless finds her strangely moving, not only on account of her beauty but because of a "remote resemblance [*Ähnlichkeit*], he did not himself yet rightly know to whom, which he had noticed as soon as he entered the house and which drew his whole heart towards her" (p. 243). It turns out that (he thinks that) she resembles his old fiancée, a certain Marianne Congreve who was put to death in Europe by agents of the Revolutionary Tribunal while bravely protecting her lover from a similar fate. Here, Kleist emphasizes the extent to which human identity, and desire, is an uncanny combination of repetition and difference—a relation of (un)likeness, of *Ähnlichkeit*, that estranges the familiar and draws what is remote close to us, situating us in a place that is neither here nor there, locating our selves as neither Same nor Other. The "strange mixture of desire and fear" (p. 247; "eine Mischung von Begierde und Angst") that Toni generates in Gustav is a sign of this uncanny combination and leads to the physical consummation of their relationship (an act of love that itself troublingly mirrors the unrepresented act of rape in a story like "The Marquise von O—"). After their night together Toni, as was the case with Marianne Congreve, will have to protect her "betrothed" by acting out a lie, playing the part of his enemy in order to convince Congo Hoango, who has unexpectedly returned to the plantation house, that she is still loyal to the black cause. She manages, however, to contact Gustav's uncle and the rest of his family and lead them to the plantation where they succeed in overcoming Congo Hoango and the rest of his band; apparently on the verge of triumph, Toni declares to her outraged mother, "I am a white girl [*ich bin eine Weisse*] and betrothed to this young man whom you are holding prisoner; I belong to the race [*ich gehöre zu dem Geschlect*] of those with whom you are openly at war and I will be answerable before

God for having taken their side" (p. 264)—her use of the word "white" here thus marking a quasi-performative redefinition of the term, opening it up to the diversity of all those who belong, even if only partially, to that stock, rather than limiting it to the singularity of a purely defined race.

However, before Toni's new identity can take hold her story is brought to a tragic close when the freed Gustav, still under the illusion that she has betrayed him, shoots her. As she lies dying, Toni utters her famous last words—"you should not have mistrusted me" (p. 267)—and Gustav, by now aware of his monstrous mistake, confirms them, noting that "you were betrothed to me by a vow, although we had not put it into words" (p. 267; "denn du warst mir durch einen Eidschwur verlobt, obschon wir keine Worte darüber gewechselt hatten!"). Here, Gustav portrays language as a vow that, even if unspoken, might be capable of determining reality, but the naive pathos of his belief in language is by this point in the story all too evident: to believe in the exchange of words, to trust them blindly, is to have failed to register their problematic referentiality, to have overlooked the fact that they can be made to stand only uneasily for the reality that they would represent in a world that is neither "black" nor "white" but fully (in Kleist's ambivalent sense of the word) "creole." Overcome with regret, and shamed by the emptiness of his vow and the language with which he has made it, Gustav blows out his own brains, while the rest of his family manages to escape the island. The story ends with a brief and highly ironic description of his uncle's house near Rigi in 1807, which situates us in much the same "monumental" territory as did the passages from Goethe's *Elective Affinities* that we examined in Chapter 3: "among the bushes of his garden," we are told, "one could still see the monument he had erected to the memory of his cousin Gustav, and to the faithful [*treuen*] Toni, Gustav's bride" (p. 269). Toni's faithfulness, her "truth," can only be known and inscribed posthumously, in a memorial writing that tries impossibly to fill in the void she has left, to restore the absence that it fatally marks. The unquestionable truth and the certain knowledge produced by this writing constitute the ultimate betrayal of Toni's life, relegating this life to a state of eternal changelessness with words that, in their disarming ability to switch sides and change colors, must (as Kleist has repeatedly insisted) always fall short of the monumental certainties they are meant to enshrine. To know this, of course, is to know both everything and nothing: to confront this conclusive and yet trivial knowledge is to be faced with a choice between the inhuman silence of eternity or the human sounds of a language that cannot mean what it says. Kleist, of course, eventually chose eternal silence, following in Gustav's footsteps by committing suicide only months after the publication of "Betrothal"; to choose human language, in all its referential mobility and uncertainty, would be to embrace the difficult (one might even

say revolutionary) possibilities of growth and development that are tragically absent from the world of Kleist's "Betrothal," or present only in
a sadly distorted form that betrays the processual reality of Bildung—
whether that betrayal takes the form of a dehumanizing insistence on physical appearance (*Gesichtsbildung*) or that of the self-deceptive certainties of
an imagination (*Einbildung*) that mistakes race for reality. As we will now
see, it is this same refusal of Bildung, and these same betrayals of it, that
Hugo offers his postrevolutionary audience, in a novel whose melodramatic
excess sharply contrasts with the tragic concision of Kleist's tale, signaling
Hugo's even greater complicity with the new worlds he cannot abide, and
his ever greater distance from the old world he cannot restore.

Double Portraits: Scapegoating the Mulatto in Victor Hugo's 'Bug-Jargal'

> I have often said to myself that one cannot really know a
> man from an earlier era unless one has at least two portraits
> of him. That of his youth, although it fades more quickly
> and loses its resemblance after a few years, is nonetheless of
> the greatest importance. Let us then see for ourselves how
> this applies to our contemporaries and how, before our very
> eyes, they are more or less completely transformed. When
> one only knows people, and especially sensitive and imagi-
> native people, after they have reached a certain age, and
> during the second half of their life, one is far from knowing
> them at all in the way nature made them: the sweet turn
> sour, the tender become rough; one would understand noth-
> ing about all this if one did not possess the first memory.
> The portrait fills in that gap.
>
> —Sainte-Beuve, *Portraits contemporains*

At one point in a brief article entitled "National Identity and 'Mestizaje,'" the poet Nicolás Guillén, arguing for a "mestizo Negritude," recalls reading about an epistolary exchange that took place between the
Columbian-born author Félix Tanco and Domingo del Monte, leader of a
prominent literary circle in Cuba during the 1830s. In his 1830 letter, Tanco
questions del Monte regarding his opinion of Victor Hugo's recent novel on
the Haitian Revolution, *Bug-Jargal* (1826; originally published as a short
story in 1820). Tanco then goes on to note his own favorable impressions
of it, or at the very least of its mixed style: "I'd like for us to write in the
style of this little novel. Think about it. Blacks in the Island of Cuba are
our Poetry, and that's that; but not the blacks alone, rather blacks with
whites, all mixed together [and then forming the picture, the scenery] . . .

May our Victor Hugo be born, and may we know at long last what we are."[49] These nineteenth-century creole writers, in their search for a (cultural, national) identity, turn to Hugo as a literary model, who has himself already turned to the Caribbean for the ingredients of what—in his 1832 preface to *Bug-Jargal*—he would refer to as his "premier ouvrage," his point of departure as a novelist (p. 25). This, then, is a perfect example of what Mary Louise Pratt has identified as "the transcultural dimensions of what is canonically called European Romanticism" (*IE*, p. 138)—a Romanticism that is unthinkable without the sort of global criss-crossing of influence and imitation we find at work here, and that continues to make itself felt, long after the official death knell of Romanticism, in the quest for a national literature and identity upon which a poet like Guillén was himself engaged. This quest, as Tanco's letter suggests, is inseparable from an encounter with a "mixed" reality that translates the finality of pure poetry ("blacks in the Island of Cuba are our Poetry, *and that's that*") into something far more indeterminate ("not the blacks alone, rather blacks with whites, all mixed together").

Implictly present in Tanco's letter as a positive value and explicitly valorized in Guillén's advocacy of mestizaje (an "éloge du métissage" that nonetheless also remains attached, in a productive oxymoron, to the "Poetry" of Negritude), this indeterminate identity is, by contrast, viewed as a distinct threat in Hugo's *Bug-Jargal*. What Hugo attempts to do in this novel (which is a point of reference for Glissant also, incidentally)[50] is, as it were, to determine the identity of this threateningly indeterminate identity, to give it a name in order the more effectively to suppress it. The figure whom Hugo thus identifies and violently suppresses, in an act of narrative containment that, ironically, only serves to render more visible the "unpoetic" condition that the young French Romantic would like to contest, is that of the mulatto. Dramatically visible in the 1826 version of *Bug-Jargal*, this figure is virtually absent from the original 1820 conte, and it is an account of this fundamental difference between the original and its novelized sequel that I will be providing here. The attention paid to the mulatto in Hugo's act of rewriting marks a decisive moment in the development of his own emerging poetics of mélange, his energetic celebration of that "fertile union of the grotesque and the sublime types" from which, as he put it in the preface to *Cromwell* (1827), "modern genius" is born.[51] Reenvisioning as a "féconde union" the métissage that he looked upon with horror and scapegoated in *Bug-Jargal*, Hugo will lay the foundations in France for an identifiably modern aesthetics, a Romanticism that aggressively recuperates the realm of pure poetry but that, in the process, displaces and forgets (ever so more effectively than did the narrative violence of *Bug-Jargal*), the confusingly mixed and prosaic realities of a colonial history and of a postrevolutionary identity too indeterminate and too compromised for (his) genius to contemplate.

Bug-Jargal was first published anonymously in the 1820 May-June issue of the journal *Conservateur littéraire*, which the seventeen-year-old Hugo and his brothers had started up in December 1819, its title a homage to Chateaubriand's highly successful *Conservateur* (founded in October of the preceding year). This ambitious adolescent, spurred on by the mimetic desire "to be Chateaubriand or nothing," was at the time a thoroughgoing royalist, and in the same year as the publication of the first *Bug-Jargal* this enthusiastic supporter of the Bourbon Restoration would, indeed, receive a stipend from Louis XVIII for his "Ode sur la mort du duc de Berry." A late example of the "literature about the horrors of Saint-Domingue [that flourished] under the Consulate and the Empire [1799–1815],"[52] Hugo's conte features an extremely simple plot: a good many years after the fact, Captain Delmar is recounting an episode from his youth to a group of his fellow soldiers. At an early age, the orphaned Delmar had been sent from France to his uncle's plantation on the north coast of Saint-Domingue; distressed by the "absolute despotism" of his rich uncle, the seventeen-year-old Delmar befriends a highly respected slave by the name of Pierrot who has fallen into his uncle's bad graces and been imprisoned. Having succeeded in obtaining the uncle's pardon, Delmar arrives at the prison only to find that Pierrot has escaped, three days before "the famous night of August 21–22, 1791" (p. 232), the beginning of the slave insurrection that would lead, two years later, to the de facto abolition of slavery on the island. During those first days of the insurrection, Delmar witnesses massacres aplenty, and the burning down of the Northern Province's capital and a good many plantations; he also looks on helplessly as Pierrot abducts his uncle and the uncle's youngest son—a "perfidious" act that Delmar supposes is generated by the slave's desire for vengeance. The insurrection continues under the leadership of Biassou, Jean-François, and Boukman, real-life historical figures whose "ferocity" contrasts strongly with the generous conduct of the fourth leader of the revolt, a certain Bug-Jargal. In a skirmish between the colonial army and the rebels, who have retreated to the mountains, Pierrot inexplicably allows himself to be captured by the French, and Delmar is himself taken prisoner and led to Biassou's camp. Pierrot makes a sudden appearance in the camp and explains himself to the enraged Delmar, who still believes him to be a brigand and an assassin: it turns out that Pierrot and Bug-Jargal are one and the same person, the son of an African king, and that far from abducting Delmar's uncle with the intention of killing him Bug was rescuing him from certain death at the hands of angry black slaves. Once again friends, the two must part company because Delmar has promised Biassou, who has allowed him to roam freely about the camp, that he will under no circumstances attempt to escape. Taken by Biassou's soldiers to an abyss, into which he is to be hurled, Delmar is saved by Bug, who then hurries back to the French camp where he has promised to return with Delmar. Believing Delmar to be dead, the French are on the point of executing ten black prisoners when Bug arrives back at the camp; maintaining an inexplicable silence regarding the success of his venture, the noble African takes the place of the prisoners and allows himself to be shot dead before Delmar has had time to return to the camp. Albeit in a far less masterful and provocative way, the young Hugo's conte reflects upon the same confusion of appearance and reality, of sign and referent, that haunts Kleist's "Betrothal," although its insights into the (mis)interpretability of human acts and the groundlessness of language remain undeveloped since, in the final analysis, the two protagonists are still portrayed as living in a world where words mean what they say and a promise is a promise.

The romance scenario through which Kleist filtered his account of the Haitian Revolution is decidedly absent from Hugo's tale of male friendship, present only subterraneously in the homoerotic intensity that binds the two men to one another ("I embraced him, I beseeched him to live with me from that moment on," Delmar states, for instance, after Bug has rescued him [p. 251]) and that, interestingly, gives rise to the single use of the word "revolution" in the conte (upon learning from Bug that his uncle is still alive, Delmar notes that "this extraordinary man had just, through his latest words, turned my whole world around [*venait . . . d'opérer en moi une révolution*]: I was afraid that I had judged him too quickly" [p. 244]). By contrast, both revolution and romance are brought to the fore in the greatly expanded—*novelized*—second version of *Bug-Jargal*, which in its opening pages explicitly situates the now twenty-year-old French protagonist, renamed Léopold d'Auverney, in the context of the massacres that "had marked the invasion of the revolution in this magnificent colony" (p. 33), and, fleshing out a passing reference in the first version to a cousin that Delmar was meant to marry (p. 226), introduces a new character, Marie—daughter of d'Auverney's uncle, betrothed to d'Auverney, and desired by an unknown rival who, it eventually turns out, is none other than Pierrot. With this triangulation, Hugo self-consciously moves beyond the idyllic coupling immortalized in *Paul et Virginie* and naively envisioned by d'Auverney (who in Paul-like fashion claims that he had been "accustomed from a very young age to consider as my future wife one who was already in a way my sister" [p. 39], and who speaks of "a love felt and shared since childhood by the woman who was destined to be mine" [p. 40]). Instead, he invites us to read, in René Girard's terms, the desire of these two men, and colonial desire *tout court*, as inseparable from a mimetic rivalry in which ostensibly

distinct individuals reveal themselves to be little more than monstrously indistinct doubles of one another (a point I will be developing in Chapter 6).
It might be ventured that such interracial mimetic rivalries, and the specter
of racial indifferentiation they entail, supply the ur-script of the nineteenth-
century (French) colonial novel, the "novelistic truth" (in Girard's phrase)
that works like *Bug-Jargal*, Dumas's *Georges*, or Maynard's *Outre-mer* tentatively expose, only to cover it up again in a series of "romantic lies" that
serve (like the racial taxonomies and taboos structuring colonial society) to
police the boundaries between Self and Other that get momentarily destabilized in these novels. Hugo wards off the threat of contamination, for instance, by having Pierrot for all intents and purposes renounce his desire,
transforming him into the noble savage Bug-Jargal, exoticizing (and, as we
will see, "negrifying") him; the obstacle that he poses at the beginning of
the novel gradually disappears, replaced by—or dissolved into—the altogether larger but somehow more comforting obstacle of history itself, in the
form of the slave revolt that breaks out on the night of d'Auverney and
Marie's wedding, preventing its consummation and, like the storm in *Paul
et Virginie*, eventually causing her death. And while history does its dirty
work, the threat of indifferentiation posed at the beginning of the novel by
the rivalry of d'Auverney and Pierrot is further alleviated through Hugo's
scapegoating recourse to the figure of the mulatto as the singular embodiment of that threat: incarnated, given a name, the threat becomes containable, at least in theory; however, the underlying if unintentional irony of
this "antimulatto novel,"[53] and other such works of colonial fiction is, of
course, that such acts of containment necessarily draw the reader's attention to and thereby promote the "racial indefiniteness, th[e] new shade of
social meaning" that they would like to violently suppress.[54]

A rereading of *Paul et Virginie* was only one of several external stimuli
that contributed to the twenty-three-year-old Hugo's decision to rewrite a
short story that he had published over five years before and written even
earlier (1818).[55] Most notably, France's official recognition of Haitian independence in 1825 lent, as Hugo himself points out in his 1826 preface, the
conte's subject matter "a new degree of interest,"[56] although he quickly
goes on to claim that this was merely a happy coincidence, his actual mo-
tive having been to preempt a Paris bookseller from republishing the original story and, by "revising and in certain respects redoing . . . [his] anonymous sketch," to "spare the author's pride a bit of vexation" (p. 23). In the
years between 1820 and 1826, and in the passage from adolescence to
adulthood, much had changed in Hugo's life: the death of his mother in
1821 opened the way for his marriage to Adèle Foucher the following year,
and a rapprochement had been effected with his father, Léopold, the Bona-
partist general (and author in the previous decade, as Roger Toumson re-

minds us, of a *Mémoire sur les moyens de suppléer à la traite des nègres par des individus libres, et d'une manière qui garantisse pour l'avenir la sûreté des colons et la dépendance des colonies* that certainly influenced his son's thinking on colonial issues).[57] That Hugo's novel is in some sense a commentary on his relationship to parental authority is unquestionable, given the new name of his French protagonist, which yokes together that of his father (Léopold) and one associated with his mother (the Trébuchet family possessing property in Auverney), and the fact that Hugo had occasionally signed his articles for the *Conservateur littéraire* with the name d'Auverney. If the individualizing project of novelistic Bildung depends, as I have argued in connection with Faulkner, on a break with previous generations—one that symbolically repeats the revolutionary passage from ancien régime and traditional status-society to the world of modernity and the more mobile identities it makes possible—then the recuperation of these parental names is one obvious sign of Hugo's continued allegiance to an antimodern ideology of Restoration, albeit one that is itself now divided (Bonapartist | royalist, father | mother) in a way that reflects the gradual evolution of, and eventual disenchantment with, conservatism that would mark his thinking from the mid-1820s on.[58] If at this point, Hugo is still "drifting around in total ideological conformism," the second *Bug-Jargal* is nonetheless, in Toumson's words, "a transitional text" in which the uncomfortable contradiction between a traditionalist politics and the antitraditionalist (Romantic) aesthetics that he would fully enunciate in the preface to *Cromwell* is already beginning to make itself felt. As Toumson puts it, "after *Bug-Jargal*, nothing will be as it was before": "things begin to give way," he points out, "as if Hugo, stunned, was discovering that, in narrating Saint-Domingue, he had inadvertently adopted, out of sheer complacency, some grossly erroneous points of view; as if he felt the need, in order not to lose his way, of equipping himself with different structures for accommodating [his ideas]."[59] Transcending (or evading?) the unsettling contradictions contained in the rewritten *Bug-Jargal*, Hugo will self-consciously distance himself from his early royalism in the years immediately preceding the fall of the Bourbon dynasty, embracing a mildly republican liberalism more compatible with what Baudelaire once referred to as Hugo's "revolutionary, or rather reformist, literary doctrine."[60]

In the novelized version of *Bug-Jargal*, Hugo is at pains to display the deeper familiarity with the culture and history of Saint-Domingue that has resulted from his perusal of various written sources.[61] As he points out in his 1826 preface, several distinguished individuals who, either as colonists or as government officials, were "mixed up in the Saint-Domingue troubles" supplied him with material, much of it unpublished, which allowed him to "rectify what in captain d'Auverney's account was incomplete as regards local color and uncertain in relation to historical truth" (pp. 23–24). The single most important instance of this "rectification" with regard to local "color," I will be arguing, is Hugo's new and obsessive insistence on the existence and importance of diverse racial gradations in colonial Saint-Domingue, where before he spoke only of "noirs" and "mulâtres" (and in a manner that, as we will see a little later on, treated the two as practically indistinguishable). As the lengthiest of the many authorial footnotes that supplement the 1826 version of *Bug-Jargal* makes clear, this new emphasis on métissage derives largely from the notorious taxonomy of color put forward in the Martiniquan Moreau de Saint-Méry's *Description . . . de la partie française de l'Isle Saint-Domingue* (1797–98): occurring very early on in the novel (in the fourth of its fifty-eight brief chapters), this long footnote—most of it taken verbatim from the "Note relative à la population de couleur" with which Baron Pamphile de Lacroix begins his 1819 *Mémoires* on the Haitian Revolution—is provoked by the appearance in the novel of an entirely new character, a "Spanish dwarf" by the name of Habibrah, the only one of his slaves that d'Auverney's uncle looks upon with favor and, we are told, a "griffe de couleur" (p. 38). Noting of this word *griffe* that "a precise explanation may be necessary for understanding it," the (plagiarized) authorial voice of the footnote then launches into an extended paraphrase of Moreau de Saint-Méry's "system," which "classified into generic types the different shades offered by the colored population's mélanges," basing itself on the notion that "mankind has one hundred and twenty eight shades in all, ranging all the way from the white to the black" (p. 38). After listing the nine major intermediate "espèces génériques" between the noirs and the blancs—namely, *sacatra, griffe, marabout, mulâtre, quarteron, métis, mameluco, quarteronné, sang-mêlé*—the authorial voice then focuses on the sang-mêlé and the griffe, noting of the latter that he "can have between twenty four and thirty two parts white [blood] and ninety six or one hundred and four parts black," and of the former that "if he keeps on combining with the white, he ends up in a way merging with this color. However, it is claimed that he always retains on a certain part of the body the indelible trace of his origin" (p. 38; "le *sang-mêlé*, en continuant son union avec le blanc, finit en quelque sorte par se confondre avec cette couleur. On assure pourtant qu'il conserve toujours sur une certaine partie du corps la trace ineffaçable de son origine").

This confusion "en quelque sorte," of course, marks the extreme point of anxiety for any such racial taxonomy and Moreau himself notes that "arbitrariness enters into the entire classification,"[62] and that in the case of some sang-mêlé "one needs very well trained eyes in order to distinguish such mixtures from pure whites, and it can be said that in general there is hardly anything but oral or written tradition that can serve as a guide in this respect" (1.79).[63] With virtual disregard for this arbitrariness, Hugo will seize upon these racial categories, repeatedly personifying the excesses of revolutionary violence in a figure such as the griffe Habibrah; where even the reactionary Moreau could permit himself the occasional positive comment regarding these intermediary "species" (for instance, "of all the combinations of the white and the Negro," he affirms, "it is the mulatto in whom the greatest number of physical advantages are to found; he is the one who has come away from all these crossings of races with the strongest constitution and the one most suited to Saint-Domingue's climate. To the sobriety and strength of the Negro, he joins the graceful figure and the intelligence of the white"),[64] Hugo rigorously identifies all mixed-race characters in negative terms, preserving thereby, as we will see, the noble purity, the pure nobility, of his white and black protagonists, d'Auverney and Bug-Jargal, and distancing himself from the "striking confusion" that besets the captive French soldier when Biassou reviews his troops, that strange and disorderly procession of Negroes, Negresses, mulattoes, and griots, "from time to time laced with heterogeneous detachments of *griffes, marabouts, sacatras, mamelucos, quarterons,* free *sang-mêlés,* or with nomadic hordes of maroons bearing themselves proudly" (p. 152).

Since Moreau's taxonomies now appear patently ludicrous (if perhaps only a little more so than those that continue to dominate discussions about "race" in the United States), it is impossible for the modern reader to credit the authority of the authorial voice in this footnote, and that of the impersonal third-person pronoun ("on assure") upon which it depends. This is a banal point, to be sure, but one that becomes more interesting if we take into account the fact that this lack of authority has already been (unwittingly?) inscribed in the novel's very first footnote: preceding the explanation of griffe, this footnote authorizes what would, for much of Hugo's audience at the time, have immediately been seen as a glaring error, and that for this reason has the effect of ironizing the purportedly certain knowledge conveyed in all the footnotes that follow upon it. This note provides a gloss on a reference to the *club Massiac* made by one of the soldiers listening to d'Auverney's tale, lieutenant Henri, who interrupts the captain's description of the effects of his uncle's "absolute despotism" on the slaves with the cynical suggestion that his account of "the misfortunes of the ci-devant 'blacks'" ought to be supplemented with "a bit of speechifying on the duties of humanity, *et caetera.*" "We wouldn't have gotten away with anything less at the Massiac Club," he concludes (p. 37). "Our readers have no doubt forgotten," the authorial voice helpfully explains, that the Massiac Club was "an association of *négrophiles*" formed at the outset of the Revolution and that it "had provoked most of the insurrections that broke out in the colonies at that time." In an acerbic antirevolutionary outburst, the au-

thorial voice then goes on to identify it as the meeting place of those dangerous "philanthropists" who "still reigned at this time by grace of the executioner" (pp. 37–38). In reality, of course, the Massiac Club was a reactionary syndicate of mostly absentee colonial landlords and noblemen who
were doggedly intent on defending their financial interests, on preserving
slavery and denying the hommes de couleur full civic and civil rights; as described in 1837 in the pages of the *Revue des Colonies*, the "colored" peri-
odical run by Cyrille Bissette that we will be examining in the next chapter,
the Massiac Club was "the meeting place of all that was most hostile to giving the hommes de couleur their rights and the slaves their freedom" (III.x:
394). Repeated later on in the novel when the sympathetically portrayed
General de Rouvray, a royalist and the one voice of reason in a room full of
bickering *grands* and *petits blancs*, states that "all the horrors that you are
now witnessing in Saint-Domingue were conceived in the Massiac Club" (p.
78), this error establishes, from the outset, the authorial voice's lack of authority, the questionability of the information with which this voice corrects
the reader's supposedly faulty memories. What are we to make of this error,
which, as Toumson notes, "is at all events an egregious one,"[65] and who
(Henri? the authorial voice? Hugo himself?) is ultimately responsible for it?

While there is a slim chance that this mistake is not intentional (although
a proven source like Pamphile de Lacroix's *Mémoires* is very clear on the
ideology of the Massiac Club),[66] by virtue of its very egregiousness it cannot be simply written off as meaningless: this error testifies to an at the very
least latent awareness on Hugo's part of the extent to which mistranslation
and misunderstanding is built into every act of telling history and of the extent to which bias inflects every ideological pronouncement (in this case,
Hugo's Restorationist ideology, which is rendered questionable by its complicity with such obvious errors of fact). The very decision to render history
in the form of a romance necessarily draws to the fore this troubling of discursive authority, although Hugo would appear to be as yet not fully prepared to confront the relativizing consequences of his choice. *Bug-Jargal* is
a novel that only verges upon an exploration of the postmodern dimension
that, as Diane Elam has argued, potentially characterizes all historical romances, from Walter Scott's to Umberto Eco's. In her account of the "infla-
tionary footnotes and marginalia" in Scott's novels, for instance, Elam argues that they promote a postmodern troubling of what she calls "the certainty of modernist history," with its authoritative chronologies that, their
precision and accuracy notwithstanding, contribute to the effective erasure
of the past in the name of the present's ideological imperatives.[67] Because,
Elam notes, "in romance there is an inevitable misprision of history," it
"must always lead to a confusion of fact with fiction, a confusion of history
with romance" (p. 60), and this inevitable confusion can be usefully de-

ployed as a tool for "challenging the way we 'know' history" (p. 12)—a
way of "knowing" that is inseparable from the legitimation of certain ideological perspectives and the disempowering of others. Romance, when self-
consciously rather than naively deployed (Scott's *Waverley* as opposed to
Bug-Jargal, say), responsibly reminds us of the extent to which we lack a
privileged access to the past; evoking "the absolutely irrepresentable" (p.
76), "romance remembers the past as that with which it cannot come to
terms, as that which is always never fully present or recuperable" (pp.
62–63). For this reason romance memorializes the past—in all the past's
excessive and productive difference from the present—more effectively than
the authoritative narratives of "modernist history," with which we cannot
simply do away but that we must nonetheless rigorously interrogate. Of
course, as Peter Hulme has pointed out, the romance form can also be
"useful to the colonial enterprise precisely because it *reduces* . . . a potentially embarrassing cultural complexity to the simplicity of the essential romance terminology: heroes and villains" (*CE*, p. 211), and it is this sort of
Manichean reductionism that dominates in an early production of Hugo's
like *Bug-Jargal*, which cannot openly acknowledge the awareness of epistemological and cultural complexity that is nonetheless at work in the novel
generating its anxiously authoritative footnotes and its assertively negative
portrayals of mulattoes.

Toumson is the critic who has been the most explicit in identifying the
connection between the young Hugo's Manichean (as opposed to dialectical) logic, which is "impervious to the union of opposites," and his portrayal of mulattoes: given this imperviousness, "it is understandable that
the monstrous as such should derive from the compenetration of extremes,
that mixture, miscegenation, should for him be 'antiphysis,'" and that
"Habibrah is thus monstrous because a mulatto."[68] What I want to add to
this general assessment is an account of how this monstrosity *emerges* in the
translation of conte into novel: if this emergence is most obvious in the addition of a completely new character like Habibrah, it is also readable in the
subtle reformulation of the historical figure Biassou's creole identity, as well
as in his greatly expanded role in the second version. Georges Biassou, "a
fire-eater, always drunk, always ready for the fiercest and most dangerous
exploits," as C. L. R. James described him (*BJ*, p. 73), was one of the early
leaders of the slave insurrections of 1791–93 and the man under whom
Toussaint Louverture would first serve and whose leadership he would eventually supplant.[69] His presence in the original conte may perhaps have been
determined by a reading of Jean-Baptiste Picquenard's *Adonis, ou Le bon
nègre* (1798),[70] where Biassou plays a central role, the main white protagonist finding himself, like Delmar, imprisoned in the rebel leader's camp in the
early days of the insurrection. In Picquenard's novel, Biassou is described as

an "ignorant and superstitious Negro, who had succeeded in winning the trust of his brothers-in-arms through a cruelty of character so pronounced that it inspired terror even in the most bloodthirsty among them" (p. 12). He is treated as the unwitting tool of French royalists and thence the British, eager to stir up trouble in the prized colony. Picquenard's Biassou is also the source of memorable atrocities, sanctioning a mass torture of whites in which, for instance, one sees the rebels flailing away at pregnant women, "tearing out of their quivering wombs the tender fruit of their marital union, which they chopped up into bits, forcing the wretched victims of their cruelty to eat this revolting flesh, which they violently rammed down into the pit of their stomach," while "the young girls were tortured in another but no less cruel fashion, since these brigands did not let go of them until the moment when they realized that all they were now holding in their arms was an insensate corpse" (p. 79).

Biassou's cruelty, referred to in passing in Hugo's conte, will be all too colorfully amplified upon in the novel, the middle third of which he dominates. More importantly, for our purposes, in the conte Picquenard's "nègre" is referred to simply as a bizarrely-dressed "noir" when Delmar is first led into the cave where he holds court: "between two lines of mulatto soldiers, I caught sight of a black man seated on a baobab trunk, covered with a carpet made out of parrot feathers" (p. 241). In the 1826 version, this gets rewritten as, "between two lines of mulatto soldiers, I caught sight of a colored man [homme de couleur], seated on an enormous acajou trunk, half covered by a carpet made out of parrot feathers," and is immediately supplemented by the following information: "this man was a sacatra, a species distinguishable from Negroes only by an often imperceptible nuance" (p. 107). D'Auverney's emphasis on the difficulty of perceiving this "species" echoes Moreau's statement that "this class can barely be said to exist, and although it is looked upon as superior to the Negro, it differs from them only in an almost imperceptible manner, since it is only one part white as against seven parts black" (1.79). However, notwithstanding—or precisely because of—the virtual imperceptibility of this difference Hugo insists upon it and the separations it makes possible, the veritable abyss that it opens up between a mixed and a pure racial identity, between this "sacatra chief" (p. 108), an island-born créole, and the truly black Bug-Jargal, an African-born congo. Biassou's new status as an homme de couleur, moreover, provides a racial ground for the physiognomic and psychological description of him in the first version: "his ignoble features offered a singular mixture of shrewdness and cruelty" (p. 241), a description retained in the second version (with the substitution of "rare" for "singular" [p. 108]). In all his monstrous "rarity," the sacatra Biassou becomes the scapegoat figure in whom the confusions of revolutionary politics and the ambivalences of cultural hybridity can be contained. He also becomes the figure onto whom negative Africanist stereotypes (such as his large appetite, which "had something terrifying about it" [p. 148]),[71] are most forcefully displaced, permitting the fuller delineation in Bug of positive racial characteristics that hark back to the Enlightenment's noble savage and look forward to the enchanting primitives of modernism. Moreover, Biassou is a figure who can be further contained through an overdetermining recourse to orientalist references (he is first revealed, for instance, behind a curtain of "Tibetan cloth" [p. 107]) that will be even more in evidence in the descriptions of the griffe Habibrah and that nicely serve to familiarize and thereby deflect attention away from the "new shade of social meaning," the creole identity, he so threateningly embodies.

As soon becomes clear, what is primarily at stake in the representation of Biassou is the fate of representation itself. Biassou becomes the figure through whom Hugo can explore, and yet at the same time (attempt to) dispel, one of the commonplace anxieties of postrevolutionary writers: namely, that arising from the evaporation of an authentic connection between signs and their referents, the melting of all that is solid into air. Having described his initial impression of Biassou, d'Auverney takes note of the many flags and banners in the cave, among which those representing French royalism, French republicanism, and Spanish royalism ("le drapeau blanc fleurdelysé, le drapeau tricolore et le drapeau d'Espagne") hang impossibly side by side, along with other "extravagant battle ensigns" ("enseignes de fantaisie"); from this senseless conjunction of signs—in which, divorced from their "true" referent and metonymically identified with one another, the flags have become equivalent to mere fantasies—his gaze then shifts immediately to a portrait hanging over Biassou. It is "the portrait of that mulatto Ogé" who, d'Auverney informs his audience, had been brutally tortured to death the year before along with his lieutenant Jean-Baptiste Chavannes and "twenty other blacks or sang-mêlés." In this portrait, "Ogé, son of a butcher from Cap français, was represented in the manner in which he customarily had himself painted: in the uniform of a lieutenant-colonel, with a 'croix de Saint-Louis' and 'l'ordre du mérite du Lion,' which he had bought in Europe from the prince of Limburg" (p. 108). We will have more to say about the historical figure of Vincent Ogé in the following chapter;[72] at this point, we need merely note the way that the "representation" of this historical figure here consecrates a false order of things made possible by the slippage from a "real" identity determined through paternal filiation ("son of a butcher") to an illegitimately assumed one created out of the deceptive manipulation of signs (military uniform, medals) and a liberal dispensing of money. Viewed from a different perspective, of course, Ogé's ascent from the realm of the father to that of the self-made man resembles the story of, say, a Julien Sorel, but this Stendhalian story of Bildung is one that the young Hugo is ideologically disinclined to tell or, rather, that he will only tell obliquely and disparagingly, through the racially mixed, culturally hybrid figure of a mulatto like Biassou, for whom Ogé's portrait functions as a dangerous model to imitate, in much the same way as Napoléon's did for Sorel.

The initial description of Biassou in the conte includes mention of a "croix de Saint-Louis" hanging from his belt (p. 241). Within the terms of analysis established in this first version, Biassou's inappropriate appropriation of this French badge of honor (one with which, we recall, Bernardin suggested the Creoles of the Île de France were all too fascinated) can be explained as the result of an innate characteristic that he shares with others of his race and/or color: Delmar speaks a page later of "the foolish vanity of the blacks, who were almost all loaded down with military ornaments and religious vestments [that they had] stripped from their victims" (p. 242). The inappropriate presence of the "croix de Saint-Louis" as part of Biassou's patchwork uniform thus demands to be read here as a sign of his "blackness" pure and simple. In the novelized version, Ogé's portrait provides a supplementary and more unsettling explanation for the cross's presence, which can now also be interpreted as the result of a mimesis made possible by the contaminatory powers of (bad) representation. Biassou's mimetic relationship to the portrait of Ogé establishes a significant distance between these two mulattoes and the naturally vain "blacks," although, to be sure, the original reading of Biassou's appropriative nature maintains a certain credibility since Delmar's appeal to black vanity is repeated virtually verbatim by d'Auverney in the second version (p. 105). Without entirely replacing the argument from nature, the new "mulatto reading" of Biassou displaces and stands in potential contradiction with it, directing the reader's gaze toward an "unnatural" second nature in which reality and image have become inextricably entangled with one another and in which identities can be re-created, and signs redeployed, accordingly. Biassou's vanity does not (only) stem from some essential, racialized self, and for precisely that reason it can be passed on to any and all with whom he comes in contact, as it was passed on to him by means of the portrait. How to limit the spread of this infectious vanity? How to control the influence of (bad) representation? Hugo's scapegoating insistence on the figure of the mulatto in the second Bug-Jargal is his far from satisfactory response to these questions. This attempt to cordon off the mimicry that representation promotes through a negative representation of this mimicry can, however, only lead Hugo further into the world of unbridled vanity from which he is attempting to distance himself—a world in which, to cite René Girard, it is no longer possible to distinguish "the spontaneous being who desires intensely from the lesser being who desires weakly, who copies [the desires of] Others."[73]

Notwithstanding its skirting of the paradox that "in tarring mimesis one risks getting tarred oneself with the same brush,"[74] Hugo pursues this response at length in the novel's greatly expanded portrait of Biassou, obsessively exploring and warning against the distressingly "unnatural" condition that the sacatra embodies, the contaminated and contaminatory "second nature" that this "lesser being" prefigures. The unnaturalness of Biassou's mimetic condition is repeatedly emphasized by Hugo in the process of rewriting, making itself oppressively felt in even the smallest details, such as (to cite but one example) the subtle transformation of the two mismatched epaulettes, one gold and the other of blue wool, that formed part of the original Biassou's patchwork costume (p. 241). In the second version, not only do his epaulettes not match but, "not being bound *in their natural place* by cross braids, they hung down both sides of the chief's chest" (p. 107; my italics). Moreover, these unnaturally positioned epaulettes have themselves been further adorned in Hugo's novelistic translation of the conte: "two silver brigadier's stars" have (as is only natural) been added to the gold epaulette, but onto the wool epaulette have been affixed, "doubtless in order to make it worthy of appearing next to its shiny companion" (p. 107; "sans doute pour la rendre digne de figurer auprès de sa brillante compagne"), "two copper stars, which would appear to have once been spurs' rowels." The critique of Biassou's mulatto figurations resonates, finally, even at the (perhaps unconscious) level of word choice: the two "copper stars" ("étoiles de cuivre") necessarily recall the "copper complexion" ("le teint cuivré") of Biassou's mulatto troops (p. 92), while the color of the wool epaulette has itself been changed from blue to yellow, making it not only a pale imitation of the other truly gold epaulette but yet another reminder of the inauthentic nature of "the yellow caste" ("la caste jaune"), to cite a label that Victor Schœlcher would later popularize as a way of referring to Haiti's mulattoes (as we will see in the following chapter). As I have been stressing, this inauthentic nature, this "order of mimesis" (in Christopher Prendergast's phrase), is something that Hugo's *Bug-Jargal* has in common with classic nineteenth-century French novels such as *Le rouge et le noir* and *Madame Bovary*. The novelty of Hugo's youthful novel is that, in the process of rewriting his earlier conte, he first discovers this condition abroad, in the colonies, and it is this colonial (re)location, or even (pre)location, of the "second nature" that will be chronicled in such detail in the domestic French novel (on the margins of which Hugo's later novels are so uneasily situated) that constitutes the primary interest of *Bug-Jargal*. In precociously drawing together two ostensibly separate spheres in which the problem of cultural mimesis has been conceptualized—namely, the already well-established critique of colonial populations or primitive peoples as prone to imitation, which would itself feed into Europe's understanding of the Haitian Revolution,[75] and the emerging novelistic insight into the mimetic underpinnings of modern French society that we find in the likes of Stendhal and Flaubert—Hugo globalizes a condition that one might otherwise have been tempted to read as either purely domestic or purely colonial.

This postrevolutionary awareness of a contaminatory mimesis that cuts across supposedly fixed (e.g., racial) boundaries is the monstrous double of the Enlightenment belief in a commonly shared human nature into which we can all be educated and thus be (in Bernardin's phrase) "reunited" despite our differences. We still find remnants of this belief in Picquenard's treatment of the "exécrable Biassou" for, while he repeatedly emphasizes the black leader's singular barbarism, this disciple of Bernardin also includes one scene that openly harks back to the *mentalité* of Enlightenment exoticism. Notwithstanding his cruelty, Biassou is at one point represented as being still capable of hearing the voice of "childhood" when two black youngsters, Zozo and Zéphyr, beg him not to execute two young whites, Joseph and Paulin, who were wet-nursed by their own mother. Faced with the pleas of these children on behalf of their "frères de lait," Biassou finds himself unable to "resist this first cry of nature, of innocence, and of humanity: his heart was moved, perhaps for the first time in his life; he was choked with sobs, and plentiful tears streamed down his face. The more difficult it was for sensibility to make itself felt in his heart," the narrator concludes, "the stronger and more expansive its explosion," and Biassou readily spares the white children, allowing them to circulate freely amongst the black population (pp. 81–82). Indeed, Picquenard rationalizes his decision to include the horrific account of black-on-white violence that we examined a few paragraphs back by prefacing it with the comfortingly universalist claim that "men must be taught, through the most dreadful lessons, what crimes our species is capable of when education has not developed the precious seed of sensibility that nature has placed in all hearts" (p. 77). Such appeals to nature and a single human species can have no place in a postrevolutionary text like *Bug-Jargal*, which alternately promotes a belief in absolute racial difference—be that difference positive, as with Bug, or negative, as with Biassou—and translates the positive Enlightenment vision of a common education into the nightmare of an endemic mimesis.

This mimesis is indissociable from the rampant theatricality that will be so frequently critiqued in nineteenth-century novels, and Hugo's Biassou has been rightly described as a "consummate actor."[76] His first dialogue with d'Auverney at an end, Biassou retains the French prisoner in his cave, allowing him to serve as captive witness to a series of "dramas" and "ludicrous scenes" (p. 129) that are enacted by, or for the benefit of, what amounts to a holy trinity of mulattoes—Biassou seated on his throne of acajou, the leader of the Southern mulattoes, André Rigaud, seated to his left, and the camp *obi* or sorceror to his right (who turns out to be the griffe Habibrah, wearing a disguise that d'Auverney, despite many painfully obvious clues, cannot penetrate). Their theatrical "simulations" (to cite a word that gets repeated several times in the novel: for instance, Biassou is at one point described as "mixing in with his simulated anger several phrases in bad Latin, à la [Molière's] Sganarelle" [p. 146]) are many and it must suffice here to comment on only one of them in detail. Immediately after his initial dialogue with d'Auverney, Biassou asks his obi to cover himself with his "priestly vestments, and celebrate for us and our soldiers the Holy Sacrifice of the Mass." When the obi replies that they have no altar, Biassou brusquely replies,

Mais qu'importe! depuis quand le *bon Giu* a-t-il besoin pour son culte d'un temple magnifique, d'un autel orné d'or et de dentelles? Gédéon et Josué l'ont adoré devant des monceaux de pierres; faisons comme eux, *bon per*; il suffit au *bon Giu* que les coeurs soient fervents. Vous n'avez point d'autel! Eh bien, ne pouvez-vous pas vous en faire un de cette grande caisse du sucre, prise avant-hier par les gens du roi dans l'habitation Dubuisson? (p. 110)

What does it matter! Since when does the good Lord require a magnificent temple to hear our prayers, or an altar decorated in gold and covered with lace? Gideon and Joshua worshipped him in front of a pile of stones. Let's do as they did, my good padre; all the good Lord wants is that our hearts be fervent. You don't have an altar! Well then, couldn't you make one out of this big sugar crate, seized by the "king's men" from the Dubuisson plantation the day before yesterday?

This "parody of the divine mystery" (p. 110) transforms a sacred ceremony into theatrical representation and understandably disturbs the French captive, all the more so given the fact that the tabernacle and the ciborium that are used in this ceremony have been taken from the same parish church where d'Auverney and Marie had been wed. Forced to his knees by two "vigorous mulattoes," d'Auverney is nonetheless made to offer up "a simulacrum of respect for this simulacrum of worship" (p. 111), and it can be said that, quite despite himself, Hugo too, in his parodic rendering of this parody, his mimesis of a mimesis, his simulating of these *simulacres*, cannot help falling captive to the power of the groundless images by which he is at once repulsed and yet obviously fascinated.

  Biassou's ceremony thus lends itself to a double reading, at once colonial and postcolonial, with and against the grain of Hugo's text. Despite all attempts to control, to write over, the disturbing power of Biassou's performance—for instance, the authoritative footnotes that identify phrases like *bon Giu* and *bon per* as "creole patois" and translate them back into proper French—this power remains visible and easily recuperable for a modern-day reader. The brief passage cited above, for instance, is a veritable treasure trove of familiar postcolonial strategies: linguistic subversion of the colonizer's language and its authority (Biassou's Creole disrupting the integrity of the French language, chipping away at the rule of the colonial father [*père* → *per*]); strategic (re)citation and appropriation of the Western literary canon (the Bible) and modes of interpretation (allegory); contestation and revision of colonial values (turning a container in which colonial merchandise is *exchanged* to an entirely different *use*); representing one's people and one's self as opposed to being represented by others and as an Other (for instance, renaming the former slaves—or what d'Auverney frequently calls "hordes"—as "gens du roi" and himself as "*généralissime*" [p. 111]).[77] It is these sorts of transformations, these turnings (tropes), that postcolonial literature and theory so often enact. Lacking a cross, the obi will use a dagger in its place—thus displaying his ability to live with metaphor, to work with signs that have been detached from their original referent, to channel the powers of mimesis. This ability—to trope, to simulate—creates a situation of extreme undecidability that forestalls any and all decisive judgments regarding the authenticity of human actions: after the ceremony has ended, Biassou turns to d'Auverney and cites it as proof that "we are good Catholics," and d'Auverney has to admit that "I don't know if he was speaking ironically or in good faith" (p. 112). In this world of imitated actions and dislodged signs, one can be both ironic and in good faith, and at the same time neither, and this is precisely what is so devastating about Biassou's "extraordinary pantomime" (p. 115), which he at once controls (a euphoric postcolonial reading) and is controlled by (a dismissive colonial reading). Neither fully in control nor out of it, inhabiting a world where image and reality can no longer be separated from one another (and yet, of course, still must be), the tensions that Biassou's theatrical performance opens up are exemplary of a post/colonial condition that can only be spoken in a mixed language, with a forked tongue, through "parables" (p. 113) that must appear diabolical when viewed from any perspective that valorizes what it (mis)takes as substantial truth over performative fiction.

Biassou's "eloquent" performances (p. 115), in which he succeeds in voicing an astonishing number of postcolonial concerns (e.g., Antillanité),[78] are themselves complemented by the performances he requires of others, perhaps the most notable of which involves a bloodily comic deconstruction of racial categories and a counterbalancing revelation of the performative nature of race. As our discussion of the phrase "gens du roi" showed, Biassou is eminently aware of the necessary, and necessarily rhetorical, nature of self-representation: in a lengthy dialogue in which he toys with one of his captives, a self-styled "négrophile" who earlier on in the novel had shown his true colors when he called for the brutal extermination of hundreds of his own slaves even though they were not among those who had rebelled (p. 79), Biassou puts this same awareness to work on racial categories. Reacting, with a "simulated anger," to this colonist's assertion that he is "on close terms with all the most famous defenders of Negroes and mulattoes," Biassou interrupts him: "*Nègres* and *mulâtres*! What do you mean by that? Are you here to insult us with those odious names, invented by the contempt of the whites? Here, there are only 'hommes de couleur' and 'noirs,' do you understand that, Mister colonist?" (p. 132). Having made this point about the right to self-entitlement, Biassou eventually sentences the negrophile to death at the hands of another prisoner we have already encountered in the novel, "a rich planter whom the whites would only grudgingly admit into their company and whose equivocal color raised doubts about his origins [*faisait suspecter l'origine*]" (p. 43). This "planteur équivoque," with whom d'Auverney once had a duel because he had dared to dance with Marie, now finds himself desperately attempting to claim as "brothers" those from whom he has spent a lifetime dissociating himself, citing as proof that he is a sang-mêlé "this black circle that you can see around my finger nails" (p. 140).[79] While an authorial footnote confirms the existence of such signs of identity ("several sang-mêlés do indeed have this sign at the base of their fingernails [*à l'origine des ongles*], which disappears as they grow older but reappears in their children" [p. 140]) and d'Auverney's narration leaves no doubt that the planter is indeed a sang-mêlé (p. 141), Biassou demands that the planter supply him with a very different type of sign if he wishes to prove that he is not white and has been on their side all along: he must kill both the negrophile and d'Auverney (who reflects that he is in "an odd situation with regard to this man; he had already almost killed me in order to prove that he was white; he was now going to assassinate me to show he was mulatto" [p. 143]). After some hesitation, the planter does indeed kill the negrophile; satisfied, Biassou then spares d'Auverney, declaring the planter a "true brother" and naming him "army executioner" for good measure. The planter's pusillanimity, to say nothing of the signs on his fingernails, serves as sufficient proof that he is not a white, putting an end to the "equivocation" that he incarnates: such is clearly the main point that Hugo wants to make by means of this "horrible spectacle" (p. 143); what also comes through, however, is a quite different vision of race as, at the limits, a performance, a limited performance that has no permanent meaning.

D'Auverney refuses to perform for Biassou or, rather, this refusal becomes itself a performance (a manifestation, Hugo would say) of Frenchness, which differentiates him from both the black and mulatto "natives" (p. 114; "indigènes") and the creole whites. At several points in the second version, Biassou offers to spare d'Auverney's life if the Frenchman will help rewrite a letter that the rebel leaders, who find themselves in a difficult situation militarily, have addressed to governor Blanchelande and the Colonial Assembly and in which they state their conditions for making peace: desiring that there be nothing in the letter "that could provoke the arrogant *burlerias* of our former masters," Biassou asks d'Auverney to "correct any mistakes in our dispatch that might invite the laughter of the whites" (p. 156). Too proud to take on "the role of Biassou's diplomatic proofreader," d'Auverney refuses not once but twice to help him "redo" the letter "in the *white style*" (p. 190). Ludicrous as it might appear, Biassou's obsession with "spelling faults" is yet one more sign of his exploitation of and dependence upon the power of representation, and d'Auverney's refusal to perform in the role of (re)writer signals his supposed freedom from this power (and if he seems to retain this freedom in the act of [re]telling his story, it is precisely because, as in *Heart of Darkness*, orality is here conceived of as a more "authentic" means of representation than writing). But can Hugo himself as decisively decline to enter into the realm of (bad) representation? In choosing to (re)write history, and his own conte, has he not committed himself to the same sort of degraded rhetorical performance that d'Auverney heroically resists?

If d'Auverney proudly refuses to redo Biassou and Jean-François's letter, Hugo is unable to resist the opportunity of transcribing and imitating their prose, once again entering the contaminatory zone of mimesis, exposing himself to the very thing against which he would immunize himself and his readers. Biassou reads this letter to d'Auverney, and the Frenchman in turn recites it in its (fictional) entirety to his audience (noting that, improbably, the memory of it had "stuck in my head word for word" [p. 156]). The letter that his fellow soldiers hear, and that we read (pp. 154–56), is a truncated and distorted version of a real letter sent by the leaders of the slave revolt in early December 1791, where they establish the terms under which they would be willing to end the insurrection and help restore the "broken equilibrium" (these conditions included a general amnesty as per a recent decree of Louis XVI's, freedom for the leaders, and some willingness on the part of the colonists to declare "through a decree ratified by the General, that your intention is to deal with the future status of the slaves"). Hugo, who copied parts of the letter from Lacroix's *Mémoires* (1.148–52), obviously intends this letter to be used as evidence of the ignorance of the rebel leaders and yet the real letter poses a problem in this regard since, as the reactions of both contemporary commentators and later historians confirm, it is a document that has already been (re)written "en *style blanc*" and that is thus grammatically, if not politically, quite unassailable,

Describing their self-styled "profession of faith concerning the present troubles" to the French National Assembly in early 1793, Charles Tarbé noted that this particular letter lacks "the character of coarseness and deepest ignorance" that was to be found in the rebels' earlier communications.[80] C. L. R. James comments, in turn, that "in its skilful use of both the moral and political connection between the mother-country and the colony, its dangling before the colonists the chance to restore the former prosperity 'of this great and important colony,' its firm but delicate insistence on political rights, duly certified by law, for the freed men, its luxuriance whenever it dealt with things that cost nothing such as peace, good-will, etc., the letter could have come from the pen of a man who had spent all his life in diplomacy" (*BJ*, p. 83), which is by no means a compliment since for James this letter, with its stress on reconciliation and restoration, and its deferral of the slaves' freedom to a vaguely defined future, represented an egregious betrayal of the revolutionary cause.[81] Hugo's perspective is not James's, but the letter suits his purposes no better than it did those of the author of *The Black Jacobins*. For this reason, he quotes only a few passages from it, filling out his pastiche of a letter with bits and pieces from communiqués written several years later, under very different circumstances, and also culled from Lacroix. The penultimate paragraph of Hugo's letter, for instance, contains a problematically sincere appeal to royalist principles, taken more or less verbatim from comments made in 1793 by the rebel leader Macaya: "we are the subjects of three kings, the king of Congo, master-born of all the blacks; the king of France, who represents our fathers; and the king of Spain, who represents our mothers," and because of this triple affiliation, Hugo's Biassou concludes (or, rather, is made to conclude), he and the other leaders will not serve under the revolutionary assemblies (p. 155). The (fictional) letter ends, moreover, with a distorted echo of another (real) letter from July 1793, this one indeed signed by Biassou and Jean-François, which claims that in helping the French and Spanish kings they are promoting the "cause of humanity" and that even if "these majesties should fail us, we would soon have '*throned*' a king" (p. 156).[82] Through this anachronistic pastiche, Hugo indeed succeeds in creating an absurd document and, at least in the case of the 1793 contributions, a primitively written one (as the ungrammatical use of the verb "trôner" attests). However, he can only do so through a manipulation of historical evidence that undermines, in an even more flagrant way than did his earlier account of the Massiac Club, the authority of the footnote that he appends to this letter, in which he notes that "it would appear this ridiculously characteristic letter was actually sent to the assembly" (p. 156). Moreover, one of the unintended results of creating this "ridiculously characteristic" document by grafting together dispatches from late 1791 and mid-1793, by which time Biassou and Jean-François's allegiances were clearly with the Spanish (counterrevolutionary) camp, is that Hugo's own Restorationist ideology itself gets implicated in the "ridiculousness" of their royalism.

Into such distortions of history and complications of his own ideological position do his efforts at representing Biassou and the problematic figurations of this "mulatto" lead Hugo. From the mixed realities that Biassou represents, and the carnivalized language(s) in which he represents them, it is with understandable relief that Hugo turns to Bug, the noble African, characterized by "the purity of his language" (p. 65).[83] Glissant once described Faulkner's *Light in August* (1932) as succumbing "to the unconscious impulse of prejudice against mulattoes or métis: the 'pure' Negro is always for him more noble, in any case more 'healthy,' than the mulatto" (*IP*, p. 176), and these prejudices and preferences (which will be "e-laborated" in the later *Absalom, Absalom!*, expanded upon and worked out of) are also what generates Hugo's rewriting of *Bug-Jargal*. The seed of prejudice out of which the 1826 version is generated was, indeed, already present in one apparently offhand remark in the 1820 conte that will be unfolded spectacularly in the novel: it is Bug himself who makes this comment, telling Delmar at one point that Biassou is "treacherous" because "he's not a black, he's a mulatto" (p. 247), a definitive indictment that is understandably retained in the second version (p. 184). While it pointedly registers the historical tensions between (enslaved) blacks and (free) mulattoes on the island—tensions that were themselves duplicated within the black (slave) camp, since "Creole goals and those of their African fellow combatants were not always the same"[84]—Bug's comment is an interesting anomaly in the first version because it bluntly registers a distinction that the conte cannot otherwise systematically make. Everywhere else in the conte, the terms "noirs" and "mulâtres" circulate indifferently, as we can see from examining a passage that would become the novel's brief twenty-second chapter.

The word "mulâtre" first occurs in the conte during the buildup to the battle in which both Pierrot and Delmar are taken captive. The colonial army has pursued the rebels toward the mountains; night is falling, when they hear a "fearsome chanting" and see a fire breaking out on the rocks above them. "The fire's livid light," Delmar notes, "disclosed to us numerous bands of mulattoes on the neighboring summits, whose copper complexion seemed red in the flames' light. These were Biassou's men" (p. 236). Only a few lines later, though, these same *mulâtres* have reverted into *noirs* ("the blacks, instead of taking advantage of the disorder in which we found ourselves frozen, watched us, while chanting the *Oua-Nassé*"). Thus, a distinction between the two groups is present in the first version (Delmar speaks a little later on of "les noirs et les mulâtres" [p. 240], for instance), but the adolescent Hugo is not yet in a position to pin down the exact relation of these confederated forces.[85] In the second version, Hugo addresses the problem of their earlier interchangeability with a series of minor but revealing corrections: d'Auverney now sees "de nombreuses bandes *de nègres* et de mulâtres dont le teint cuivré paraissait rouge à la lueur des flammes" (p. 92; my italics), and the word "noirs" a few lines down has been translated into the more generic "les révoltés." A distinction between blacks and Biassou's mulattoes having been established, this sets the scene much more effectively for Pierrot/Bug's entry into the battle: the phrase from the first version—"a gigantic black man appeared, alone, on the highest peak over-looking Grande-Rivière" (p. 236)—is more or less retained (p. 92), but the *difference* of this "noir gigantesque" has been more effectively rendered vis-ible, since he now emerges from out of a group of "révoltés" instead of, as in the first version, from a group of other "noirs" who are themselves con-fusingly identical with Biassou's mulattoes. After Bug's emergence, the bat-tle—which in this second version is now identified as unfolding in a place called *Dompte-Mulâtre* (literally, "the Mulatto-Tamer," so named because of "the rough edges of its steep slopes" [p. 91])—will henceforth be a black-white affair: the one further reference to "mulâtres" in the first ver-sion's description of the battle (p. 237) is accordingly changed to the more indeterminate "rebelles" (p. 92) in the second, and a new centrality is given to Bug's hard-fighting "Morne-Rouge band," which is later identified as a "horde made up only of blacks" (p. 120), and one that Biassou wishes the colonial army would get rid of for him ("I hate them; they are almost all *congos!*" [p. 149]). Only after the heroic battle has been fought, only after Bug has let himself be captured and d'Auverney in turn has fallen into the hands of the retreating rebels, is there any further mention of the mulattoes around whom the extended, anything but heroic, account of life in Biassou's camp will revolve (p. 97). This camp, significantly, is situated in a valley "in the very heart of the mornes, in what are called in Saint-Domingue *the double mountains*" (p. 98): as we have seen, Hugo's microrevisions enforce this doubleness, accentuating the Manichean contrasts (heroic whites I heroic blacks, heroic blacks I perfidious mulattoes) that were so much less clearly defined in the earlier version.

In Hugo's revision, the mulatto—embodied most spectacularly by Bias-sou and Habibrah—emerges as the place, the topos, where an anxiety about racial (in)differentiation can play itself out; sheer (African) blackness can, as a result, be treated more positively than before. In the conte, Bug is explicitly distinguished from his fellow blacks (who are themselves, as we have seen, not entirely distinguishable from mulattoes): "his face [*figure*], on which the characteristic signs of the black race were less apparent than on those of the other Negroes, presented a mixture of ruggedness and majesty that would be difficult to imagine" (p. 227), Delmar states, when introducing Pierrot into his narrative. This phrase undergoes a significant change in the second version, where Pierrot's entry into the novel does not occur in a single moment but in a series of deferred revelations, since we first encounter him indirectly through his words (the romance he sings to Marie, in which he identifies himself as a former king and a black) and his actions (the repeated substitution of bouquets of wildflowers in place of the roses with which d'Auverney adorns the pavilion where Marie, in Virginie-like fashion, is wont to repose).[86] D'Auverney's first direct vision of the man whom he does not yet realize is his mysterious rival comes when he runs down to the pavilion to rescue Marie, after hearing her cry out: what d'Auverney sees there is "a young black of colossal stature" protecting his betrothed from a monstrous crocodile, which d'Auverney then shoots. Marie's unknown protector having disappeared into the bushes, d'Auverney runs over in his mind the "similitudes" between this "Negro, of an almost gigantic size," and his unknown rival, and it is at this point that Hugo inserts the earlier description of Bug: noting that his rival had, in the romance sung to Marie, declared himself to be a king whereas her rescuer "was only a slave," d'Auverney can nonetheless not help being struck, "and not without astonishment, by the air of ruggedness and majesty stamped on his face in the midst of the characteristic signs of the African race" (p. 56). The change is subtle but important: Bug's noble features no longer simply differentiate him from "la race noire"; rather, they majestically supplement the "signes caractéristiques de la race *africaine*" (my italics) without necessarily contradicting them. The stage is thus set for the valorization of an (African) blackness that is best embodied by Bug, in all his virile glory,[87] and that can be set against the dangerous mimicry of the mulattoes. At a distance from their theatrical world (his change of name from Pierrot to Bug-Jargal thus takes on its full significance only in the second version),[88] this exemplary African stands, like his white European double, d'Auverney, as a force capable of resisting (bad) representation, an ideal figurehead for the sort of elemental struggle Hugo describes in his 1832 preface to *Bug-Jargal*, where he notes that the novel's subject is "the revolt of the blacks of Saint-Domingue in 1791, a struggle of giants, three worlds having a stake in the matter, Europe and Africa as combatants and America as battleground" (p. 25). His valorization of (African) blackness in the second version thus allows him to displace attention away from the mixed realities of a creolized "America" (which in Hugo's formulation appears here only as a place, a battleground on which peoples from *elsewhere* engage in mortal combat) toward a Manichean conflict more amenable to the primal inclinations of this "Maître du tam-tam," as Léopold Senghor once referred to Hugo.[89]

Even in the case of Bug, to be sure, this displacement is never more than partially successful. Toumson speaks of him as "a hybrid being" created by Hugo out of, on the one hand, a negrophilia that turns blacks into faithful servants or noble savages and, on the other, a negrophobia that envisions them as dangerous rivals and sadistic rebels.[90] If Hugo effectively manages to control this hybrid identity in the course of the novel by offloading this negrophobia onto the figure of the mulatto, the threat it offers nonetheless

makes itself uncomfortably felt in the opening sections of the novel: as suggested at the outset of our discussion, Pierrot poses a problem to d'Auverney, and to Hugo, inasmuch as he occupies the third point of a romantic
triangle that positions the two men as rivals and mimetic doubles of one
another, thereby disturbing the supposed autonomy of their antithetical but
complementary black or white identities. From his first appearance the
stage is set for Pierrot to embody the "pure" black that he will become, yet
in the early chapters of the novel he remains subject to desires and impulses
that conjure up the possibility—indeed, already testify to the existence—of
a mixed identity that would conflict with this ideal role. Nowhere is this
more apparent than in the "Spanish romance" that he sings to Marie (pp.
49–50), which ends with the lines: "You are white, and I am black; but the
day needs to join with the night in order to bring forth the dawn and the
sunset, which are more beautiful than it!" (p. 50). It is precisely this colonial desire that, in both versions (pp. 244, 179), is cited as the original fault
that led to Bug's enforced exile from Africa, since his family's enslavement
was the result of his father naively following a Spanish captain who had
promised him both power ("countries vaster than his own") and interracial
sex ("white women"). The narrative burden of the second Bug-Jargal will
be to reverse this trajectory, to extricate Bug from the fallen world of colonial desire and the metaphorical language of romance, restoring to him the
transparency of his original African identity and conjuring away the problematic opacity of the translated, or "smuggled," self inscribed in the title
of his "signature" tune (p. 69), the Spanish air Yo que soy contrabandista.

    If the contradictions in Bug's character are never fully resolved, if the pu-
rity of the African origin does not entirely cover over the impurity of (its)
American translation, they are nonetheless massively offloaded, as I have
demonstrated, onto the character of Biassou and, in an especially obvious
fashion, that of Habibrah. Hugo's treatment of Biassou as a mulatto has
gone virtually unremarked by critics and for that reason I have concentrated
on it in my account of Bug-Jargal, but a few words about the griffe Habibrah
need to be said here in closing, specifically about the way he is made to enter
and exit the text. Given to d'Auverney's uncle by the governor of Jamaica,
Lord Effingham, Habibrah is a dwarf whom the uncle has made "his fool, in
imitation of the feudal princes of yesteryear, who kept jesters in their courts"
(p. 39). First described and, as we have seen, footnoted in the novel's fourth
chapter, Habibrah enters the narrative a few chapters later, at the very moment after d'Auverney's unseen rival has finished singing his romance to
Marie. "This deformed wandering minstrel, this idle slave, with his ridiculous outfits, [which are] gaudily strewn with braids and scattered with bells"
and which contrast so emphatically with Pierrot's "nakedness" (pp. 40, 56),
is placed in the role of interpreter for a bewildered d'Auverney who franti-

cally asks the griffe if he has seen anyone in the woods or heard a "voice." Habibrah coyly replies, "*Que quiere decir usted* by a voice, master? There are voices all over and voices for all; there is the voice of the birds, there is the voice of the water, there is the voice of the wind in the leaves" (p. 51). This bilingual response effectively contests d'Auverney's faith in language, his unreflecting belief in the simple referentiality of words and his obliviousness to their metaphorical and changing nature—as changing, indeed, as Habibrah's own face and the "bizarre mobility of its features" (p. 39).

Undeterred, d'Auverney offers the dwarf the entire contents of his purse if he will reveal the identity of the singer. Noting that this purse is filled with enough coins "to sow the field of the Grenadin magician Altornino, who knew the art of growing *buenos doblones* there" (p. 52), Habibrah then pays the impatient Frenchman back with double-talk, providing a duplicitous account of the singer's identity, which he derives from a parodically literal interpretation of the last lines of Pierrot's romance:

Or, si cette chanson dit vrai, le griffe Habibrah, votre humble esclave, né d'une négresse et d'un blanc, est plus beau que vous, *señorito de amor*. Je suis le produit de l'union du jour et de la nuit, je suis l'aurore ou le couchant dont parle la chanson espagnole, et vous n'êtes que le jour. Donc je suis plus beau que vous, *si usted quiere*, plus beau qu'un blanc. (p. 53)

Now, if this song is right, the griffe Habibrah, your humble slave, born of a black woman and a white man, is more beautiful than you are, my little lord of love. I am the issue of the marriage of day and night, I am the dawn or the sunset referred to in the Spanish song, and you are only the day. I am thus the more beautiful one, if thou willst, more beautiful than a white man.

As Habibrah well knows, the only way to make this song speak the "truth" that d'Auverney wants to hear is to misread the metaphors out of which it has been constructed: if the nature of metaphor is to reveal its referent only by casting a veil over it, (re)presenting it as different from itself, then the act of unveiling, in erasing this difference, betrays the truth of metaphor. From this perspective, nothing could be falser than a definitive reduction of metaphor to its literal referent, and Habibrah reminds d'Auverney of this by engaging in a patently unsatisfactory and yet logically coherent interpretation of the song's "true" meaning, from which he concludes that the identity of "*el hombre* who could have sung such *extravagances*" must be that of a "fool just like me." Habibrah's strategic (mis)reading of his own métissage as the literal ground of the song's metaphors, which voids them of their ostensible romance and draws out the sexual threat that Bug's desire for Marie poses, makes a mockery of d'Auverney's belief that the irreducible doubleness of (metaphorical) language can be abolished by uncovering its definitive referent. Moreover, read against the grain, in the spirit of the "double reading" (colonial *and* postcolonial) that *Bug-Jargal* promotes despite itself, Habibrah's reductionist interpretation parodically doubles and thereby slyly comments upon the foolishness of Hugo's own extravagantly "literal" attempts at locating the malaise of an impure postrevolutionary condition in the hybrid figure of the mulatto.

The dangerous play of Habibrah's language is matched by the unsettling deformity of his body: "this hideous dwarf was fat, short, paunchy, and moved about with an unusual speed on two spindly, frail legs, which, when he sat down, folded up under him like those of a spider" (p. 39). No less than his evasively figurative language, Habibrah's monstrous appearance, significantly diverging from the positive physical portrait of the griffe in Moreau de Saint-Méry,[91] serves as a transparently readable sign of his inner self and of his absolute difference from the colossal Bug, whose own dangerous complicity with the metaphorical language of romance can begin to be unthought once this contrast has been established (not uncoincidentally, d'Auverney's first direct vision of Bug, protecting Marie from the crocodile, comes immediately after Habibrah concludes his unlikely interpretation of the song). Such stark contrasts are grist for Hugo's Manichean mill—as Toumson puts it, "Bug-Jargal is good, Habibrah is evil. The heights are reserved for the former, the abysses for the latter. One has the strength of the giant, the other the weakness of the dwarf"[92]—and it would be superfluous at this point in our analysis to detail the many ways in which Hugo reinforces these contrasts throughout the novel in his representations of Habibrah's transparently monstrous body. Patently, Hugo's reading of this body is as spurious as the "metoposcopic" readings of facial traits in which Habibrah, in the guise of camp obi, engages for the amusement of Biassou and his troops (as when he notes, for instance, that "the figure of the three close-set S's, on whatever part of the forehead they are found, is a very ill-fated sign, and the one who bears this sign will drown without fail, unless he is extremely careful to stay away from water" [p. 120])—readings that, from a postcolonial perspective, can be productively (re)read as parodically reflecting upon, in their patent ridiculousness, the even more ludicrously arbitrary reading of bodily signs upon which racial science and Hugo's own interpretation of the "figure" of the mulatto are based.

If a full portrait of Habibrah is not necessary here, a few words about the manner of his death will add one last element to our discussion of the almost pathological pattern of Hugo's revision of his adolescent conte. In the original, Biassou has assigned to his guards, referred to simply as "les noirs" or "les nègres," the task of throwing Delmar into the abyss; in the novel, d'Auverney and the guards are accompanied by the obi, his face still covered by the "white veil" (p. 103) that has kept his true identity hidden from the Frenchman, who has been under the illusion that Habibrah died along with his uncle during the first days of the slave revolt. Eager to get as much pleasure as possible out of the death of the nephew of his former master, Habibrah takes this occasion to reveal his identity, first exposing his chest so that the Frenchman can read the signs that are quite literally "printed" there "in whitish letters"—the names of his two masters, Effingham and d'Auverney (p. 194)—and then unveiling his "deformed face," its usual air of "mad gaiety" replaced by "a threatening and sinister expression" (p. 195), a change that renders him practically unrecognizable to d'Auverney. Habibrah acknowledges that his antagonist must "find it hard to recognize me in this new light," since "you only ever saw me looking happy and cheerful; now that nothing prevents my soul from appearing in my eyes, I must no longer look like myself [je ne dois plus me ressembler]. You only knew my mask; here is my face!" (p. 197). This gesture of unmasking yet again confirms the monstrosity of Habibrah, rendering the answer to the rhetorical question he poses at one point in his lengthy monologue—"do you think that just because I am a mulatto, dwarfish and deformed, that I am not a man?" (p. 196)—distressingly obvious. From a postcolonial perspective, of course, this gesture can also be (re)interpreted as an empowering act of self-representation, in which alienating "white masks" are once and for all dropped and the authentic, decolonized "soul" makes itself visible, with the help of a little "necessary violence."

These two readings, colonial and postcolonial, of Habibrah's unveiling are in fact variations of the same reading, and it is precisely the inadequacy of such definitive "solutions" to the problem of identity that Habibrah's play with language and "sly mimicry" has exposed throughout the novel, and with it the consequent necessity for the self always, in Habibrah's words, to resemble itself, to be (un)like itself. It is a relief to believe that signs can be traced back to a single referent and the need to interpret thereby eliminated, or that human actions and desires can be attributed to an original source and the anxiety of influence thus curtailed, and it is precisely this relief that Habibrah seeks in his confrontation with d'Auverney and his attempted abandonment (to cite a Platonic distinction) of "the dissimulations of mimesis (speaking in the name of another)" for the "virtues of simple diegesis (speaking in one's own name)."[93] This confrontation, of course, ends badly for Habibrah, who eventually finds himself trapped on the root of a tree that sticks out over the abyss, and pleading with d'Auverney for mercy. Lured back to the edge of the abyss by the dwarf's words—in saving a criminal, Habibrah suggests, "will you not be giving proof that whites are more worthy than mulattoes, and masters better than their slaves?" (pp. 203–4)—and impressed by the "pleading and distressed" expression that he sees on the endangered man's face, d'Auverney extends his hand to Habibrah and falls into the trap that the dissimulating mulatto has set. Despite appearances, the "demonic" Habibrah does not want to "as-cend" back to safety and instead grabs hold of d'Auverney with "his two bronzed and calloused hands" (p. 205), vigorously attempting to drag the Frenchman down with him to their mutual death. This physical trap is itself doubled by the moral one into which d'Auverney has fallen, for in responding to Habibrah's suggestion, he has unwittingly revealed the actual basis of (his) philanthropy, which here allows itself to be read as stemming not from natural inclinations but from an extremely unnatural, vain desire to prove the "worth" of the white as opposed to the mulatto and the superiority of the master to the slave. Armed with this last insight made possible by Habibrah's dissimulating language, one might well argue that the novelization of *Bug-Jargal* was created out of this same colonial vanity—a vanity different from, but intimately related to, that "amour-propre d'auteur" playfully but revealingly spoken of by Hugo in the 1826 preface as having provided him with the impetus to rewrite his youthful conte.

D'Auverney is, of course, rescued at the last moment from his enemy's mulatto grasp, the root under Habibrah's feet gives way and he plunges "into the abyss." After Habibrah's fall into the rootless void and the retreat of Biassou with his army into the hills, the mulatto threat has been defused for the moment, leaving the field clear for d'Auverney and Bug to retake center stage. And yet, this aim achieved, it proves synonymous with the death of everything that Hugo has been valorizing. The story cannot continue without Biassou and Habibrah: they *are* the story, and (as Hugo's novel bitterly if indirectly testifies) history itself, exemplary figures of a confusingly modern world that is anything but black and white. As in the conte, Bug is executed by the French, this time dying immediately rather than living on "until the day after" (p. 255); as was not the case in the conte, however, his death will now be matched by d'Auverney's. We learn about this death in a "Note" appended to the novel proper and dripping in venom, where the authorial voice provides his readers with "definitive clarifications as to the fate of each of the characters in whom he has tried to interest them" (p. 215). D'Auverney will die only a couple of years after the events chronicled in his tale, at the height of the Terror, while leading the charge to take an important enemy redoubt in a "great battle won by the troops of the French republic over Europe's army" (p. 215); lacking both a wife (Marie having died in Saint-Domingue soon after being reunited with him) and the son mentioned in the first version (p. 222) but replaced by a nephew in the novel (p. 28), d'Auverney stands at the end of a noble line, his death signaling the definitive break between a valorized past and a reviled, revolutionary present that the Restoration has not succeeded in abolishing.

In its account of the circumstances of d'Auverney's death, the authorial voice of the "Note" heaps scorn on "the immolators of the Place de la Révolution" who, eager to "chop off heads and knock down crowns, were they only of thorns, like that of Louis XVI, of flowers, like those of the young ladies of Verdun, or of laurels, like those of Custine and André Chenier" (p. 216), would have arrested and put to death d'Auverney for counterrevolutionary "crimes" had he not died in battle. On the day after the battle, the General under whom d'Auverney served is visited by a "representative" of the people, who wants him to deliver up this "aristocrat"—"a counterrevolutionry, a royalist, a Feuillant [constitutional monarchist], a Girondist"—to "public justice" (p. 217), which has convicted him on four counts: having told to "a secret assembly of conspirators an alleged counterrevolutionary story aimed at ridiculing the principles of equality and liberty, and at glorifying the old superstitions known under the names of *royalty* and *religion*"; having used "expressions condemned by all good sansculottes to characterize various memorable events, notably the emancipation of the 'former blacks' of Saint-Domingue"; having used the word "monsieur" instead of "citoyen" in his story; and, finally, having openly conspired in this tale toward "the overthrow of the republic in favor of the Girondin faction or the followers of Brissot" (p. 217). From Hugo's perspective this is as flagrant (and petty) a misinterpretation of d'Auverney's story as one could imagine, and yet as a critique of the Restorationist ideology informing Hugo's novel it would appear to be more or less on the mark and his insistence on this Jacobin (mis)interpretation doubtless testifies to a growing if still latent anxiety about his own relation to his conservative ideology and the limits of the particular interpretations it makes possible. As the General points out to the *représentant* at the end of the "Note," each of them will be sending a list to the National Convention and "the same name will be found on the two lists. You denounce it as the name of a traitor, I as that of a hero; you doom him to ignominy, I to glory; you put up a guillotine for him, and I a trophy: to each his role" (p. 218). Although it is obvious which position and which vocabulary the young Hugo would have his readers adopt, the very fact that he felt compelled to juxtapose these two radically incompatible interpretations registers the frightening possibility that both revolutionary "representation" and its counterrevolutionary double are nothing more or less than roles to be played in a world where the "truth" to which each lays claim actually lies somewhere in between, in an indeterminate middle space that Hugo's apotropaic figurations of the mulatto have failed to conjure away.

An account of how Hugo (re)negotiated this middle space in the years immediately following upon the publication of the novelized *Bug-Jargal* and responded to the interpretive dilemma with which it ends is well beyond the scope of my book: it can and should be argued that any account of his aesthetic and political "progression" in those years—the substitution or "supplementing" (to recall Sainte-Beuve's terms) of one portrait for another[94]—

needs to take into consideration the extent to which the adolescent certainties that Hugo mourns and yet also buries in the rewriting of his conte are not simply transcended in his "mature" work but evasively translated into the extremism of Romantic poetics and the temporizing of a mildly republican politics. Rather than do so here, however, I would simply like to close with a few reflections on another passage from Hubert Aquin's *Trou de mémoire*, which resonates nicely with my discussion of the role of métissage in *Bug-Jargal*. In this highly metafictive novel, one of several editors commenting on a manuscript supposedly written by the revolutionary Québécois writer, Pierre X. Magnant, notes that it has been "altered [*retouché*] as regards everything pertaining to its description of Africa." Elaborating on these alterations of the original manuscript, the editor notes that "without wanting to make a bad pun, it all smacks of the 'griffe' as they say in the Antilles about certain forms of interbreeding [*cela sent la 'griffe' comme on dit aux Antilles de certains métissages*]." Although he stresses (in geological language that resonates with our discussion of Faulkner) that it is impossible to know exactly "how far this fault of inauthenticity extends," the editor urges the reader "not to confer too much truth on the Africa narrated there" since it is not "a real Africa" but one that has been "grafted on by someone other than Pierre X. Magnant" (pp. 119–20; "greffée par un autre que Pierre X. Magnant"). In his retouching of *Bug-Jargal*, Hugo grafts himself onto the text of his former self and thereby opens up a "faille d'inauthenticité" that he will try to contain in the figure of the mulatto but that his every act of revision further exposes and deepens, betraying the conservative "reality" of the original in the very act of attempting to conserve it.

This same ambivalent traffic between the original and its translation, reality and its imitation, can also be read in two other, closely related definitions of the word "griffe" that undoubtedly feed into the "bad pun" that Aquin's editor wants to avoid. In Larousse's *Grande dictionnaire universel du XIXe siècle* (1872) we are told that the word "griffe" is used to refer to the "characteristic signs through which one recognizes that a work is by a particular writer or a particular artist," as well as to a "stamp imitating a person's signature" (8.1525): the word thus has a double meaning, one that sign(al)s both the authentic and the inauthentic, the original and the copy. In the case of Pierre X. Magnant, then, the very inauthenticity of his account of Africa, the evident presence of another hand at work in the writing of it, could—given this inextricably double meaning—be read as the very sign(ing) of his own authorship: an apparent paradox that must, to say the least, unsettle anyone who, like Aquin's editor, might want to keep the original and its imitation(s) distinct from one another. The author of the entry on "griffe" in Larousse's *Grand dictionnaire* would appear to be one such person, for he goes on to note, reflecting upon the uses to which a "stamp imitating a person's signature" can be put, that "the griffe does, in effect, present serious dangers: it can be easily imitated or affixed by subordinate employees not authorized to use it [*par des employés subalternes non autorisés à s'en servir*]."[95] What I would ultimately like to suggest with regard to Hugo's mature rewriting of his adolescent *conte* is that it inscribes a crisis in his sense of literary authority, a frightened recognition of the extent to which (his) writing is imitation—or even an imitation of an imitation—and an anxiety about the extent to which he is master of his craft or merely a "subaltern" who has illegitimately grafted himelf onto an illustrious tradition that has no place for him. Hugo's portraits of the mulattoes Biassou and Habibrah take on, in this light, a strangely autobiographical dimension: the attempt to ensure the legitimacy of his own signature by identifying and containing the illegitimacy of theirs is never, as we have seen, fully successful and his every gesture of parodically distancing himself from these subaltern mimic men only ends up binding him further to them in a complicitous relationship that, as I have tried to show, his text repeatedly remembers and exposes to view.

It is one last memory in *Bug-Jargal* of what Hugo must, but cannot, forget that I would like to recall here in closing, taking us back for a moment to Biassou's cave, where Habibrah has just finished his metoposcopic examination of the sacatra's forehead: faced with a strange combination of lines on Biassou's forehead, Habibrah notes that "your brow offers the most striking of all signs of prosperity, a combination of lines forming the letter *M*, the first letter of the Virgin's name. On whatever part of the forehead, on no matter what wrinkle, this figure appears, it heralds genius, glory and power" (p. 126). Habibrah's "authoritative" reading comes, significantly, only a few pages after we have already been exposed to another quite different interpretation of the letter *M*: describing a missive from *généralissime* Jean-François delivered to Biassou, d'Auverney notes that it was "a piece of unrolled parchment bearing a seal whose imprint represented [*figurait*] a heart in flames. In the middle was a monogram formed out of the characteristic letters *M* and *N*, doubtless intertwined to designate the union of free mulattoes and enslaved Negroes" (p. 122). Between these two occurrences of the same letter, as between the two identical names on the very different lists of the General and the *représentant*, we are left with an impossible choice; we are faced, in fact, with the possibility that this choice—between the sanctity of the Virgin Mary and the illegitimacy of the dissimulating mulatto—is no choice at all and that the singular identity this sign apparently conveys is irreducibly plural, indeterminately mixed. It is this possibility that Hugo has violently contested and yet unwittingly inscribed in the rewriting of his youthful *conte*—a work first published in the *Conservateur littéraire* under the signature . . . "M."

6 *1835, or 'Le troisième siècle'*

THE CREOLE AFTERLIVES OF
CYRILLE-CHARLES-AUGUSTE BISSETTE,
LOUIS DE MAYNARD DE QUEILHE,
AND VICTOR SCHŒLCHER

> To tell the truth, prejudice is more than simply a matter of
> prejudice these days: it is a matter of anger, of hate. The law
> of April 24, 1833, in abolishing the distinctions established
> by the old colonial legislation and in bestowing political
> rights on free men of all colors (whether they were born
> so or became that way as the result of being individually
> emancipated), has brought into relief the instinctive antago-
> nism toward one another that was still felt by the [white
> and free colored] classes. The law is a good one, since it
> obviously prepares the way for fusion: the benefits that will
> accrue in the future are assured; but as yet it has only aggra-
> vated the existing seeds of rivalry. Things had to be this
> way. Before the recognition of their political rights, the free
> men of color were the clients of white-skinned patricians;
> they have now become their rivals, and like all rivals who
> find themselves placed on a lower rung, they want—because
> they share in the passions that are peculiar to mankind—
> more than equality: they would like to dominate. Today,
> patrons and clients hate and despise one another: the former,
> because they see their old servants aspiring to rise up the
> ladder; the latter, because this feeling of equality that they
> have been allowed to express and the possibility of gaining
> any and all forms of employment render even more intolera-
> ble the education, wealth, positions, and predominance that
> is amassed in the hands of their former patrons.
> —Victor Schœlcher, *Des colonies françaises*

In the very brief thirty-ninth chapter of *Bug-Jargal* (pp. 157–58),
which stands out from the rest of the novel by virtue of its lyrico-philo-
sophical content, d'Auverney pauses to reflect on the change in fortune that
has led to his becoming a prisoner in Biassou's camp. After having been
given twenty-four hours to reconsider his refusal to proofread the rebel
leader's letter to the Colonial Assembly, the Frenchman's arms are bound

behind his back by the "mulatto Candy," the captain of Biassou's guard (and in real life, Garran de Coulon informs us, a cruel man with the reputation of "tearing his prisoners' eyes out with a corkscrew"),[1] and he is led away from the cave. The memory of this episode provokes d'Auverney into generalizing about the condition of those who have had a hitherto uniformly happy life broken into by "extraordinary events, anguish, and catastrophes." The unhappiness produced by such brusque interruptions of "the soul's slumbering," he notes, does not at first "seem an awakening, but only a dream":

Everything about our life's horizon has changed, its atmosphere and prospects; but a long time goes by before our eyes lose the sort of radiant image of past happiness that pursues them and that, continually intervening between them and the melancholy present, changes its color and lends an indefinable falseness to reality. At that point, everything seems impossible and absurd; we scarcely believe in our own existence because, finding nothing around us of what once composed our being, we do not understand how all of that could have disappeared without sweeping us away along with it, and why we are all that remains of our life. (p. 158)

The temporal dislocation that d'Auverney describes—and the impossible, absurd world of afterimages, the space of ambivalent survival, that it engenders—is as apt a description of the postrevolutionary condition as one could wish for. In the context of this chapter, it can be read more specifically as exemplifying not only the embittered outlook of the dispossessed colonists of Saint-Domingue (or, by extension, the sentiment of dispossession that generated Hugo's Restorationist ideology) but that of the white creole elite on the Anglo-Caribbean islands in the years immediately following upon Emancipation (1833). The half-sleeping, half-waking vision described by d'Auverney certainly brings to mind the bewildered apprehension of historical change that, in the case of Jamaica and Dominica in the late 1830s, Jean Rhys's *Wide Sargasso Sea* (1966) both analyzes and, well over a century later, still exemplifies.[2] As power "changes color," passing from the hands of the old planter family (the Cosways) into those of a more efficient metropolitan-born elite (the Masons), of the newly emancipated black masses and, perhaps most threateningly of all, of an educated colored population (embodied by the sinister Daniel Cosway), a discomposing vision of former happiness comes to haunt and confuse both the novel's protagonist Antoinette and its author herself, situating them in a lonely place between dream and waking, between an impossible past and an absurdly real present without horizons.

    The British Parliament's Emancipation Act of 1833 (which provided for the official abolition of slavery as of August 1, 1834, while imposing a four-to-six-year period of forced labor, or "apprenticeship," on many of the former slaves) was matched on a much less dramatic scale that same year by the French government's decision finally to grant full civil and civic rights to the free colored population in their Caribbean and Indian Ocean colonies. The "Charte des Îles" of April 24, 1833, last in a series of reforms ending discrimination against the *gens de couleur* that had been enacted in the years following the collapse of the Bourbon dynasty and the inauguration of a constitutional monarchy under Louis-Philippe in 1830, enshrined their right to vote and run for office (although in practice, the elevated property and tax qualifications [*cens*] required to vote and be elected to the newly inaugurated *Conseil colonial* made a mockery of this right).[3] For fifteen years, until the end of the July Monarchy and the abolition of slavery under the Second Republic in 1848, the French Caribbean was the site of a curious interregnum, in which the old order was slowly dying and a new one had yet to be born (to paraphrase a comment of Gramsci's to which Nadine Gordimer gave postcolonial currency in the 1980s).[4] On the one hand, the granting of full rights to the free colored population marked a definitive rupture with the past: writing in 1835, a year after the foundation in Paris of the *Société pour l'abolition de l'esclavage* led by the Duc de Broglie, even one of the most reactionary French writers of the period, the confirmed *esclavagiste* Granier de Cassagnac, had no reservations in stating that "the colonies are on the eve of a complete and radical reorganization; the hommes de couleur demand it, the colonists grant it, the metropole will iron it all out. The principle has triumphed; it is now only a matter of time."[5] On the other hand, notwithstanding the triumph of principle and the inevitability of further changes, the old traditions remained quite firmly in place, both legally (in the continued distinction between citizen and slave, and the undemocratic requirements of the cens) and psychologically: as the very different-minded Abbé Dugoujon pointed out in his abolitionist tract *Lettres sur l'esclavage dans les colonies françaises* (1842), the "shameful prohibitions of old have been taken off the books but they still live on in the colonial customs that they created."[6] Focusing on Martiniquan literary and political culture during this confusingly double time of the 1833–48 interregnum, a time of attenuated change and problematic survival, I will be attempting in the following pages to sketch out a number of responses to the "impossible and absurd" situation, the curious afterlife, identified by Hugo's d'Auverney.

This interregnum was a time of economic decline: "between 1830 and 1848, the planters of Martinique found themselves in the grip of a prolonged crisis that reduced the once flourishing colony to poverty."[7] Perhaps not coincidentally, the mid-1830s also witnessed the emergence of the first sustained literary activity in Martinique and Guadeloupe (as well as in the former Saint-Domingue): corresponding to the "series of political readjustments" was a "literary ferment (poems, novels, pamphlets, newspaper articles, scholarly papers) stimulated by the blossoming of Romanticism in

France,"[8] and associated with (white) creole writers like Louis Maynard, Jules Levilloux, Poirié Saint-Aurèle, as well as writers of color like Cyrille Bissette, Eugène Chapus (and in Haiti, the Nau brothers and the *cénacle de 1836*). Part of my focus in this chapter will be on the criticism and fictional work of Louis Maynard, or Louis de Maynard de Queilhe as he sometimes signed himself: known (in the context of studies of Franco-Caribbean literature) only for his 1835 novel *Outre-mer*, he also authored in these years many articles on literature and art, as well as a number of short stories, published in key journals of the day like the *Revue de Paris* and *L'Europe littéraire*. I will be reading the entirety of his oeuvre for what it has to tell us about what we might call "creolist discourse," as well as about the eclipse of that discourse—and the discomposition of the (white) creole identity it made possible—in the years immediately following upon the 1833 Charter. As my epigraph from the abolitionist Victor Schœlcher suggests, one of the effects of the Charter was to exacerbate a long-standing rivalry between (white) Creoles and mulattoes, and Maynard's conception of his own identity will prove inseparable from a (dis)identification with this newly legitimized class and its own emergent discourse. For this reason, I have prefaced, or doubled, my account of Maynard with an extensive introduction to the work of Cyrille Bissette, the influential but little-studied editor of "the first French journal written in part by men of color,"[9] the *Revue des Colonies* (founded in 1834). In radically diverse but intimately related ways, the writings of both Maynard and Bissette respond to the question that, in a self-consciously cross-cultural dialogue, the Jewish ethnologist Gustave d'Eichthal posed his fellow Saint-Simonian Ismayl Urbain near the end of the decade regarding "this mulatto race" to which the Cayenne-born Urbain belonged:

A form of humanity that is still in the cradle, what future is in store for it? What are going to be its relations with the old form of humanity, with its father and its mother? Is it going to assimilate them and appropriate their life in the same way that the child quickly absorbs the life of its parents, reproducing them in himself, until he too brings forth a child and it is his turn to waste away? Or what limits should be placed on the proliferation of this race, on its own development, and on the cross-breeding [*croisement*] of the black race with the white race?[10]

In examining their respective responses to these questions, we will not only discover the limits of Maynard's and Bissette's discursive positions, and of the (white and mulatto) subjects who speak, or are spoken, through these positions. What I will ultimately be suggesting is that these limits are in certain important respects those of the creolization process itself, and thus ultimately as relevant to an understanding of our present condition as they are to that of the "ancienne humanité," and its eclipsed horizons, that ambivalently lives on in the work of these two long-forgotten rivals.

"C'est du papier ou de l'Histoire en marche?":
The Revolutionary Compromises of Cyrille
Bissette's *'Revue des Colonies'*

Exactly two years before the launching on July 1, 1836, of Émile de Girardin's daily *La presse* (the "journal à quarante francs" that, selling for half the price of other newspapers, would revolutionize media culture in France and provide an ideal forum for the *roman-feuilleton*), a new monthly publication appeared in Paris entitled *Revue des Colonies, recueil mensuel de la politique, de l'administration, de la justice, de l'instruction et des moeurs coloniales, par une société d'hommes de couleur* under the direction of Cyrille-Charles-Auguste Bissette (1795–1858).[11] Son of the illegitimate daughter of Joseph Tascher de la Pagerie (and thus related to Napoléon's creole wife, Joséphine), Bissette was by 1834 already a prominent figure on the French political scene, his notoriety stemming from events that had occurred some ten years before in his native Martinique. What would become known as the "affaire Bissette" evolved out of the distribution in 1823 of an anonymous pamphlet entitled *De la situation des gens de couleur libres aux Antilles françaises* (most probably authored by the Marquis Renouard de Sainte-Croix after a visit to the Antilles). Bissette and his fellow hommes de couleur Jean-Baptiste Volny and Louis Fabien were arrested for having reportedly read to their friends this "brochure . . . that called for several improvements in colonial regulations and practices" (as Bissette later laconically described it in the pages of the *Revue* [see I.viii: 16–20]). The anonymous author of *De la situation des gens de couleur libres* began by demanding, "in the name of justice and of humanity," that the government of Louis XVIII destroy the special laws that govern the gens de couleur libres, "and that they be granted legislation that accords with the present state of civilization."[12] "Tearing away the veil that masked so many iniquities" (p. 29), "finally breaking an overlong silence" (p. 32), the author then went on to enumerate the various indignities to which these supposedly free people were subject in the French colonies.

The following passage is typical of the pamphlet's exposé of conditions in the colonies and worth citing as a reminder of the milieu in which Bissette was raised. Pursuing his account of the "odious 'honours' awarded the gens de couleur libres," the author reminds his readers that they are

excluded from certain public squares and walks; [follow them] to a theater auditorium and you will see them forced to sit in the midst of their servants, with whom, however, it is forbidden for them to be seen in public, under pain of a large fine, or to eat or drink (if they are slaves), under pain of being expelled from the colony. If, leaving the auditorium, we then go into the church, we will see there the *humble* and *devout* members of the privileged class arrogantly sauntering up to the foot of the altar, which the gens de couleur libres are not allowed to approach until after [the whites] have themselves withdrawn. But let us leave this holy place and move on to the colonial battlefield; there, we will see the gens libres, who form the greater part of the militia, rushing to wherever danger calls them, bravely giving battle, being badly wounded, crawling to the door of the hospital, only to be mercilessly expelled by the privileged class, who are the only ones admitted there, and whose properties [the militia] has been defending. (pp. 26–27)

The dissemination of such reformist ideas and of this all-too-realistic portrait of Martiniquan life was deemed seditious, and the three men were branded in 1824 by the Cour royale de la Martinique "and condemned to hard labor for life." After being branded on the shoulders, they were banished from the island (their original sentences having been overturned by the Cour royale de la Guadeloupe), along with hundreds of other supposed associates, and transported to France where further legal battles ensued over the next several years, while the three men remained imprisoned in Brest.[13] When the final verdict was reached on March 28, 1827, it confirmed the banishment of Bissette from the French colonies, but otherwise exculpated everyone who had been implicated in the *affaire*.[14] Neither in Martinique, where colonial censorship merely whetted people's appetite for texts like *De la situation des gens de couleur libres*,[15] nor in France did the brutal and ill-considered reprisals have their desired effect. In the mère-patrie, Bissette and his companions were looked upon with great sympathy, and the path was cleared for Bissette to become a prominent advocate in Paris of the cause of the hommes de couleur. Serving as one of their accredited representatives with the colonial ministry (Ministre de la Marine) in the years immediately following upon his release from prison, Bissette led "a spirited campaign against the colonial system and helped trigger a far-reaching movement of sympathy for the 'colored' class."[16] He published a series of polemical pamphlets in the late 1820s and early 1830s, recognizing the opportunity for equality that print culture made available to him; throughout his career, he used the media as a way of forcing people to respond to his attacks (or his praise), of drawing them into the same discursive arena and thereby establishing a *relation* between his words and theirs.[17] His role as a political agitator having been facilitated by the proclamation of April 24, 1833, in the following year he launched the *Revue*, which was published on a monthly basis for the first three years of its existence, and then intermittently until 1842. Once the *Revue* ceased publication, Bissette went on to play a critical role in Martiniquan politics after the fall of the July Monarchy, but I will defer my discussion of his later years to the last section of this chapter, limiting my account here to his work for the *Revue* in the years 1834–42 and (for reasons that will become clear as this chapter progresses) his early relations with the abolitionist Victor Schœlcher.

As we will see, despite the fact that the *Revue* was directed by a "société d'hommes de couleur," its exploration of cultural and political issues and its calls for social justice were broad-ranging and in no way limited to the intermediary free colored caste; indeed, the abolition of slavery quickly emerged as its main objective and Bissette has been rightly described as "the first important advocate of complete and immediate emancipation in July Monarchy France."[18] However, even without taking into consideration the highly problematic—"reactionary," "right-wing," "populist"—politics of Bissette's later years, his identity (and self-identification) as a (mulatto) homme de couleur, and his allegiances to the French mère-patrie that legitimated this category in 1833, necessarily involved what we might call a certain (dis)identification with blackness, so it is worth prefacing my positive assessment of his work in the *Revue* with a passage from Patrick Chamoiseau's *Texaco* that recalls the "affaire Bissette" and reflects critically on the limits of the mulattoes' political vision at this point in history. Discussing the early decades of the nineteenth century, the narrator Marie-Sophie Laborieux lingers for a while over the "extraordinary" mulattoes who were always lamenting the "cruelty of the békés," and contrasting it with "the generous eternity of France, that kindly mother" (p. 83). She comically evokes "a politicized mulatto, bon viveur but a reader of newspapers, an admirer of another mulatto named Bissette, exiled by the békés after the publication of a little red book" (p. 85). This innkeeper "carried that booklet around with him from table to table as if it were the sacred host. It was an unsigned brochure, of around thirty-two pages, printed in Paris. The politicized mulatto would just stammer out the title, over and over again: 'De la situation des gens de couleur libres aux Antilles françaises.'" Enthusiastically waving this "newly penned Genesis" ("texte de Genèse") in the face of his clients, he repeatedly asks them, "What's this, then, . . . just some paper or History on the march? What he wanted you to do was answer back *It's History on the march,* which is what everybody did"— everybody, the narrator continues, except for a certain Théodorus, given to fevers and "rotting" of syphilis: in a last delirious outburst, he responds *"What History, what's this History? Where are the niggers in it?"* before breaking out into a "frenzied song and dance" and "collapsing onto the ground . . . , dead and already fetid, the little book, which he had succeeded in grabbing hold of, crumpled in one hand" (p. 85). Critiquing the mulatto vision of History, its faith in France and in print culture, Chamoiseau alerts us to the possible limits of Bissette's position and the deleterious effects of buying into the colonial distinction between "homme de couleur" and "nègre" (a distinction that still haunts the Antilles and Haiti and that, ironically enough, continues to make itself felt in the antimulatto rhetoric of the likes of Chamoiseau and Confiant—be it humorously, as in *Texaco*, or offensively, as in Confiant's recent book on Césaire).[19] If it is necessary to keep such cautions in mind when surveying the career of this prolific pamphleteer (who fills up four pages of the Bibliothèque nationale's 1903 *Catalogue général des livres imprimés* [vol. 13, columns 649–55]), it is equally important to register his impressive achievements and to assess undogmatically the difficult mixture of resistance and complicity that made these achievements possible. Ultimately, in his "Atlantic peregrinations" from Martinique to Paris (and, as we will see at the end of this chapter, back to Martinique again) Bissette is someone who fits very well Paul Gilroy's description of those black writers whose "itinerant lives and the dissident political observations which they facilitate can only disappoint and frustrate absolutist understanding of racialised cultural forms and the overintegrated conceptions of self, kinship and community to which they remain invariably bound." The intermediary space "officially" occupied by a mulatto writer like Bissette is not simply a colonial creation but also anticipates a postcolonial world of "unofficial," creolized identities that defy, in Gilroy's words, the "ruthless simplicity of undifferentiated racial essences as a solution to growing divisions inside black communities."[20] Between conformism and dissidence, Bissette's writings evoke a doubled, post/colonial identity—homme de couleur and "something else besides"—that demands to be read not in either primarily positive or negative terms but only with the greatest of ambivalence.

While welcoming as a first step the 1833 colonial charter and its "recognition" of the hommes de couleur and their rights as French citizens, "installing them, without distinction of race, in the very midst of the great family" (I.ii: 8), the *Revue* stressed from its very first issue in July 1834 (e.g., in "Coup d'oeil sur le régime colonial et ses effets" [I.i: 8–13]) that the new voting laws were "a work of treacherous deception" (p. 10), given the elevated cens; indeed, the chicanery had been made even more blatantly obvious by the fact that the cens in Martinique and Guadeloupe, islands "where the 'colored' population was very large and not too badly off," had as a precaution been fixed at a substantially higher level than in the other two colonies to which these laws applied (Bourbon and Cayenne) (p. 11). In short, egalitarian theory had in no way displaced inegalitarian practice. As Bissette put it the year before in his initial assessment of these laws, they "are the old régime, only legalized, with all its odious caste prejudice": the elevated tax and/or property requirements, "far from being a right for the hommes de couleur, become a privilege for the white colonists" on account of their wealth.[21] This "odiously ironic" tergiversation on the part of the mère-patrie, which had only served to consolidate the power of the colony's "racial aristocracy" ("aristocratie de peau") at the expense of "the mass of black, mulatto, and even white workers" (I.ii: 12), was but one instance among many of the new government not living up to its initial promise, at home or in the colonies. If in the years before 1830, "the hommes de couleur especially, more advanced than the unfortunate slaves, turned their eyes toward France with love and trust, . . . feeling that each link in the chain of the old Europe that came undone was for them a further assurance of their eventual freedom" (p. 9), and if the Revolution itself "made one believe for a moment in France's awakening" (p. 10), that love and trust had been severely tested in the four years since the "trois Glorieuses," rendering necessary a journalistic enterprise like the *Revue*, as the "Prospectus" with which the first issue begins makes clear:

The suffering and oppressed classes continually protest and struggle, always without success. To stimulate the listless efforts at doing what is right with which the government contents itself, it is necessary to bundle together the legitimate claims that are being raised from all quarters. To be successful, these claims, these grievances, must receive as much publicity as possible: that is the purpose of our *Revue*. (I.i: 3)

Stressing the need to narrow the gap between theory and practice ("in general, the colonies have as yet only encountered the grand principles of philanthropy as a theory; as for the actual practice of freedom, forget it"), the *Revue* would insistently remind its readers of the government's unfulfilled obligations toward a colony such as Martinique that had, since its establishment in 1635, been the site of untold and unpunished horrors ("It has been almost three centuries now that the most appalling things have been happening in our colonies without their being punished. When will the Ministre de la Marine decide that it is time to say 'enough'?" [I.v: 13]), and where "the art of being illegal even under the rule of equality" (I.viii: 20; "l'art d'être illégal dans l'égalité même") was becoming ever more refined in the face of ostensibly more humane but largely inoperative legislation.

Over the course of its nine-year existence, the *Revue* would pursue a literary and cultural agenda that has much in common with the project of postcolonial revisionism. Its many articles on the Haitian Revolution, for instance, contest Eurocentric representations of colonial history and put the spotlight, à la C. L. R. James, on those who successfully ousted the French (although to point this out is equally to acknowledge the extent to which a work like *Black Jacobins* does not merely revise but perpetuates nineteenth-century historiography). Its inclusion of biographies of African rulers or African-descended writers such as Ignatius Sancho and Phillis Wheatley points toward an alternative canon bearing no small resemblance to those advocated over the last several decades in North American universities (although, again, this resemblance alerts us to the deeply *conven-*

tional nature of canon expansion and revision, its unconsidered affiliation with a nineteenth-century mentality). In turn, the many poems and short stories by "colored" writers from such places as Haiti, the Mascarenes, and Louisiana,[22] as well as the trenchant critiques of (white) creole writers like Poirié Saint-Aurèle (III.vi: 262–65), testify—as would, more emphatically, a journal like Césaire's *Tropiques* a century later—to the *Revue's* attempts at rendering visible an indigenous literature that, while bearing an undoubted resemblance to that of the metropolitan center, was nonetheless identifiably on its margins exploring a different geographical and psychological terrain. The ubiquitous presence of such strategies, which supplement the *Revue's* primary emphasis on colonial politics and jurisprudence (lengthy reports on debates in the French Chamber of Deputies or in the Colonial Councils, assessment of verdicts reached by various metropolitan and colonial courts, and so on), not only makes the *Revue* a recognizably modern document worthy of something more than "mere" historical consideration but also alerts us to the underlying complicity—the post/colonial affinity—of our own prized revisionism with that of an earlier, less "enlightened" time.

Such literary and cultural revisionism is only one of the many strategies operative in the *Revue* that anticipate a postcolonial outlook. The emphasis on Haitian history and literature, for instance, is part of a larger Pan-Caribbean perspective that anticipates Glissant's vision of Antillanité: predominantly concerned with Martinique and Guadeloupe, the *Revue* nonetheless assembled in each issue commentary on and correspondence from other areas of the Caribbean, closely following, to be sure, the ongoing process of Emancipation in the British islands but also reporting on a wide range of events and issues in the English- and Spanish-speaking islands. To this more expansive *local* focus was added the further dimension of a resolutely *global* vision that insisted on reading these islands in the light of black-white relations in other parts of the world (e.g., race riots in the United States), and of the spread of (mostly French) colonialism to such places as West Africa, Asia, and Algeria (the ongoing colonization of which was greeted with a very cautious approval [e.g., I.ix: 12–16]). Given special attention is the Indian Ocean colony of Bourbon; indeed, during the 1836 trial of the mulatto Thimagène Houat, future author of the novel *Les marrons* (1844) and supposed ringleader of an uprising against the island's ruling elite (the "complot de Saint-André"), the *Revue* would be cited by Bourbon's public prosecutor Ogé-Barbaroux (whose speech would in turn be quoted at length in the *Revue*) as having helped fuel a spirit of revolt on the island. "When the *Revue des Colonies* circulated among the inhabitants," he affirmed, "all classes of society were agitated; a deep sense of worry seized hold of them, and passions that were cooling down heated up

again, only stronger" (III.x: 400). Emphasizing its strongly abolitionist
agenda, starting with the "image of the shackled black man that adorns its
cover" and under which was written the phrase "Am I not a man and your
brother?," the prosecutor continued: "to hear them tell it, it seemed that
what was required—without delay, without precautions, without prelimi-
naries, without compensation—was putting an end to colonial property
and bringing about a sudden and complete restructuring [*déclassement*] of
our social order" (p. 399). Although Ogé-Barbaroux's assessement that the
Revue's doctrines were "subversive of the established order" was not (as
we will see in a moment) necessarily shared by its editor, it may well have
had the effect he claims on certain of its readers; in any case, the episode
testifies to the *Revue*'s dissemination and reception in the colonies, even if
most of its impact was in Paris, where it would provoke a number of
polemics and lawsuits notwithstanding "its very limited readership."[23] Be it
the colonial center, its colonized peripheries, or the Caribbean archipelago,
Bissette and his collaborators realized that an adequate understanding of
the situation in the Antilles was not possible without taking into account
these diverse zones of what Glissant would call the tout-monde. As Bissette
noted in the article "Coup d'oeil sur le régime colonial et ses effets," "in
the destiny of peoples, as in that of men, nothing is isolated, and today's effects are often produced by causes that are lost in the mists of time [*qui se
perdent dans la nuit des temps*]" (p. 9). In a statement such as this we can
begin to read the Glissantian imperative of thinking beyond the clarity that
seems possible in isolation (the isolation of the Cartesian subject and of
Robinson Crusoe) and in terms of complex relations that are to be found
(and lost) in a "night" that renders them always in some way opaque.[24]

Introducing his transcript of Ogé-Barbaroux's speech, Bissette denies
the accusations that he and his collaborators had "preached rebellion" and
"endeavored to turn the colonies completely upside down": such accusations "have little to do with us really, and the three volumes of our *Revue*,
from the first line to the last, bear that out" (III.x: 396). As Bissette's comments suggest, the *Revue*'s calls for a "social revolution" in the colonies
were consistently put forward in a spirit of negotiation and grounded in an
unshakeable belief as to the efficacy of legal reform and moral (re)educa-
tion. Its vision of revolution, "a word that is simultaneously terrible and
sublime when it expresses political and social change" (II.v: 196), was thus
double: the violence of past revolutions was valorized for having laid the
foundations for a society in which peaceable ones were now possible. The
French Revolution is, quite literally, the *Revue*'s point of departure, since
the *Déclaration des droits de l'homme en société* is transcribed at the beginning of the first issue, right after the Prospectus (I.i: 5–7). Commenting
on this *Déclaration*, Bissette notes that "no matter what happens, in these

principles—sown throughout Europe by the French Revolution, by its republican and imperial armies, and throughout the entire world by its books—is a virtuality that no one will ever succeed in quashing" (p. 8). The French Revolution created a "virtual" reality of truly global dimensions—a reality that, across the Atlantic, the Haitian Revolution confirmed, as Bissette points out in his 1836 retrospective of the *Revue*'s achievements over its first two years of publication: "the Haitian Revolution, despite the massacres of the Cap, just like the French Revolution, despite the September massacres, created a new people and rendered hallow the principles of justice and humanity" (III.i: 4). Noting of Haiti that "we owe it to France to initiate it into the history of this country about which it has only false notions," Bissette cites that Caribbean republic as being a revolutionary model to learn from in a postrevolutionary age: "to see the huge steps forward taken by a slave society abandoned to its own devices and in the grip of civil and foreign wars for 25 years, is to realize that, under the enlightened protection of France, the colonies can arrive peacefully at a social revolution, that they possess all the strongest and most intelligent elements of society, if these elements are combined with justice and moderation" (III.i: 6).

This last passage, of course, exemplifies that seemingly naive faith in the mère-patrie mocked in Chamoiseau's *Texaco*. Firmly rejecting "the ridiculous system of colonial independence" (III.x: 397), which it associated with the interests of the white "oligarchy," the "petits seigneurs des îles," Bissette forcefully proclaimed his preference for "a peaceful fusion over any and all insurrectionary movements" (I.iv: 33), maintaining a vision of France as "the necessary arbitrator of all colonial problems" (III.x: 397), while repeatedly giving voice to his disappointment with the lack of social progress in the colonies ("sincerely as we may desire the unity and fraternity of the two races in the colonies, and however great our confidence in the coming universal triumph of philosophy and of reason might be, it is distressing, and quite rightly cause for lamentation, to see the government of the metropole do so little toward hastening this triumph in countries where its influence might be actively brought to bear in such a direct and peremptory manner" [I.vi: 7]). Stressing the need for education in the colonies, and noting that it was in Paris that the likes of Bolívar, Pétion, and Boyer had for several years been able "to imbibe the noble and generous ideas for which they would fight with such bravery and success," he goes on to add that

we, children of France, do not have to wish for a Bolívar who would come and deliver us from the foreign yoke. France is too dear to us, its beneficial effects too precious and its protection too necessary for us to indulge in ideas that are hostile toward her. In the domination of those who govern over us and who falsely interpret the wishes of France we see only isolated undertakings, and not the faithful expression of the intentions of the mère-patrie. (I.ii: 6)

Such professions of faith abound in the pages of the *Revue*: revolution is necessary, but violence can and must be averted; this is best—indeed, should only be—effected through the good offices of the colonial "parent" (e.g., "we are demanding that the blacks be in turn summoned to take their place among us, and in order for this revolution to occur without violence, it is up to the mère-patrie to determine the phases [of the emancipation process]" [II.iv: 164]). Bissette's (post- and anti)revolutionary vision of assimilation, his belief in the "all-powerful and maternal impulse of the metropole" (I.vi: 3), is a familiar (some would say all-too-familiar) one in the context of twentieth-century Franco-Caribbean politics, and can be read more or less verbatim into the enthusiasm with which, say, an Aimé Césaire promoted the island's *départementalisation* in 1946. Offering the first systematic articulation by a Martiniquan of this *revolutionary compromise* (in all the ambivalence of the phrase), the "mulatto" *Revue* is thus an essential genealogical point of reference for understanding not only the "black" Césaire's equivocal attitude toward revolution but also how to negotiate (in) a postmodern world where the very idea of revolution no longer seems to make the radical sense it once did.

The word that best sums up the (post- and anti)revolutionary project of the *Revue* is "fusion": as stated in its Prospectus, the *Revue* was founded with the purpose of engaging public opinion through "an always sensible and straightforward, but vigorous and never timid, discussion of the causes, whatever they might be, that are hindering the desirable fusion of the colonies' various peoples" (I.i: 3). Time and again this word is cited in order to point toward an alternative reality in which the racial divisions organizing colonial society will have been transcended: for instance, turning to the English colonies for a model in his article "De l'émancipation des esclaves, considérée comme premier élément du progrès social aux colonies" (I.vii: 3–14), Bissette notes that "production and material prosperity are moving ahead there and, in a very limited number of years, the fusion of the black and white races will turn these lands that have been wretched for so long into a country enjoying civil and political liberty and equality, having its own customs and civilization, and guarding not a trace of the hideous servitude with which it was so cruelly afflicted for centuries" (pp. 3–4). Although implicated in the project of assimilation with the mère-patrie, the ideal of fusion is clearly not identical with it: the stress is, in fact, predominantly on the formation of a creole society "ayant ses moeurs et sa civilisation propres," of the sort analyzed in Brathwaite's *Development of Creole Society in Jamaica*. In the exemplary article "De la fusion des deux races aux colonies et des causes qui la retardent" (I.vi: 3–7), there is a similar stress on the creation of a postracialized "shared homeland" ("com-mune patrie"), which would be both part of France and distinct from it:

> in effect, it is impossible that, once legitimate grievances have been satisfied, resent-ments assuaged, the playing-field leveled out, the oppressors disarmed and pun-ished, in a word, equal rights proclaimed and adequately protected by the public au-thorities, it is impossible, we say, that the white and black populations in the colonies will not fraternize and join together, in everybody's best interests, to work the land in common, their shared homeland of today, in which a better organization of labor and the development of an eminently social feeling for the fraternity of man will turn it into a homeland that is for all of them as beloved as it is free, industri-ous, and prosperous. (p. 3)

As historical prognosis, of course, a claim such as this can only strike us as painfully naive, and yet as hortatory *rhetoric* it opens up a path to a differ-ent sort of future, performing thereby a function similar to that filled by the many appeals to creolization in our own day and age. To be sure, as with Bernardin's emphasis on harmony, the concept of "fusion" now appears untenably simplifying (or synthesizing), and we are likely to rewrite it as *(con)fusion*, a more chaotic manner of being-with, a more complex and dis-concerting mode of relationality; as with Glissant's transformation of métis-sage into creolization, however, such rewriting does not result simply in the erasure of this visibly inadequate colonial precedent but, rather, in its con-tinued presence as a trace that, once read, draws our attention to the post/colonial limits of those contemporary visions of cross-cultural mixing with which it is genealogically aligned.

To promote a vision of fusion necessarily raises questions concerning identity: (how) will the old identities be different once they have been fused together? In the case of Bissette, it is helpful to recall Brathwaite's idea of a "convergence without merging," and his portrait of the West Indies as a place where "there *is* white/brown/black," but also "infinite possibilities within these distinctions and many ways of asserting identity" (*DCS*, p. 310). In a similar way, Bissette envisions an ideally fused creole identity as characterized not by the disappearance of the old racial identities ("white/brown/black") but by a productive restructuring of relations between the three classes. The mulatto is thus taken as a given, one of the colony's "di-verse populations" rather than (as was implied in Glissant's original choice of the word "métissage" to describe creolization) the very embodiment of old identities being translated into new ones. The "brown," however, is de-cidedly privileged as a middle category through which "la fusion désirable des populations diverses des colonies" can be facilitated; in thus redefining this category as a conduit between the "white" and the "black," rather than as a barrier separating them, Bissette contests the "divide and con-quer" stratagems of colonial politics and discourse, which in a myriad of ways assert the difference of the mulatto in order more effectively to exercise and maintain power (for a lengthy denunciation of such "Machiavellian" tactics see, for instance, the article "Diviser pour régner" [II.ix: 385–401]).[25] If the mulatto as a (racial, social) category goes unquestioned, Bissette nonetheless shows his keen awareness of the contingent nature of colonial identities and of the language with which the discourse of colonialism attempts to "naturalize" those historically created identities when he speaks, for instance, of "this magic word, 'hommes de couleur,' a word by means of which they had been banished to the fringes of civilization" (I.iii: 10). Such identities are fictions, a fact rendered all the more obvious in the case of this "magic word" because, as he points out, the 1833 legislation had effectively "abolished" it as a legal category. And yet to acknowledge the essentially rhetorical status of such identities is not to escape from them: they continue to exercise their power (notwithstanding the legislation, people would still speak of hommes de couleur as if they existed, thereby continuing to relegate them to "the antichambers of civilization") and their fascination (notwithstanding the legislation, people would keep on referring to themselves as hommes de couleur: the title-page of the Revue des Colonies, after all, identifies it as the work of "une société d'hommes de couleur"). The Revue is thus, inasmuch as it is produced by self-styled hommes de couleur, a posthumous enterprise, inscribed within a language of identity that has been demystified and yet that continues to have its (negative and positive) uses; nothing exemplifies better the general problematic of post/colonial identity that I have been elaborating upon in this book than the paradox of an homme de couleur writing in 1834.

Bissette cannot be summed up by this one posthumous identity, of course; the *nous* through which he speaks in the Revue does not simply designate an homme de couleur but also, depending on context, a Frenchman, a Martiniquan, a mulatto, a person of African descent, and so on. If I have lingered over this particular example, it is because Bissette's discussion of the "magic word" exemplifies a sensitivity to the groundlessness of colonial discourse in particular (if not language in general) that generates what is perhaps the single most visible critical strategy of his work in the Revue, and one that is equally central to postcolonial revisionism: a demystificatory—and one might even say deconstructionist—critique of (mis)representation, in which colonial discourse (as inscribed in government documents, legal rulings, literary texts, newspaper articles, and so on) is identified as a systematic mode of what is frequently referred to in the Revue as the "denaturing" of reality. This critique includes a salutory if predictable attention to the problem of stereotypes,[26] and the way that the conventions of fiction feed into the representation of facts (as when, to cite an example relevant to our discussion of Bernardin, the genre of pastoral is seen as informing media discussions of plantation society: "if one were to believe the official newspaper, slaves find themselves in a veritable *el dorado*, enjoying the tranquil and pure happiness that one no longer encounters anywhere except in the pastorals of d'Urfé or Florian" [I.i: 32]); but the critique is most interestingly manifested, as with his discussion of the phrase "homme de couleur," in a suspicious inquiry into the relation of individual words to their supposed referents. In repeatedly exposing the gap between colonial discourse and the reality it would represent, Bissette engages in and recontextualizes a rhetorical practice common to many of his generation: namely, Romantic irony, which "reminds us of the double nature of language (life), which cannot mean or be what it says."[27]

This problematization of (colonial) language, to consider briefly an historical episode with which the first issues of the *Revue* were much occupied, is at the center of Bissette's account of what he ironically refers to as the "*great revolution* of Grand'anse" (I.i: 37), a supposed insurrection led by mulattoes that took place in Martinique in December 1833 and that resulted in dozens of people being sentenced to death (although this verdict would eventually be commuted several years after the event). As Bissette repeatedly argues, in order to fabricate a sense of outrage and moral panic the creole elite transformed a simple "démonstration" into an aborted mulatto plot to massacre the island's white population and appropriate their belongings. Suggesting some of the ways in which "the public prosecutor's office in Martinique is laboriously giving birth to what it calls the *insurrection* of Grand'anse" (I.i: 13), Bissette also provides detailed reports on the violent repression (vigilante assassinations and such like) that followed upon this "insurrection," lambasting the government's unwillingness "to pursue the authors or perpetrators [*les auteurs ou fauteurs*] of these bloody and arbitrary saturnalia" (p. 14), and its willingness to ignore "incontestable facts" that "give proof for the hundredth time to the metropole of the systematic oppression of the 'colored' classes, the daily provocations directed against them, the persistent denial of all their rights in defiance of the laws that grant these rights to them—all those facts, in short, that show the events of Grand'anse in a true light [*qui donnent aux événemens de la Grand'anse une véritable couleur*]" (p. 15). Such facts will be "omitted, dissimulated, if necessary denied, and in all cases excused" by the government media:

Ce qu'on montrera aux colonies, à la France, dans les relations officielles et authentiques, comme on sait, du *Moniteur*, ce sera *cent dix-sept conspirateurs* comparaissant sous le poids d'une accusation de 300 pages, accusés tous de complot, car il en faut bien un au gouvernement de la Martinique; puis prévenus chacun en particulier d'avoir *pillé* deux pots de taffia et deux pots de rhum chez *Seguinot*; ou chez *Desmadrelles*, du savon, de la chandelle, une étrille de cheval; ou chez *Lereynerie*, une bouteille de genièvre (pages 85 et 86 d'arrêt de renvoi). Et tout cela imprimé par le

gouvernement de la colonie à 200 pages, intitulé pompeusement, par le plus ignorant des magistrats, *Insurrection de la Grand'anse.* (pp. 15–16)

What will be shown to the colonies, to France, in the accounts—official and authentic, as everyone knows—of the *Moniteur* will be *one hundred and seventeen
conspirators* appearing in court under the weight of a 300-page indictment, all accused of a plot, for that is exactly what the government of Martinique needs, and
each then charged in particular with having *plundered* two jugs of tafia and two
jugs of rum from *Seguinot*'s; or some soap, candles, and a currycomb from *Desmadrelles*'s; or a bottle of genever from *Lereynerie*'s (pages 85 to 86 of the court decision). And all that printed up by the government of the colony in 200 pages,
pompously entitled, by the most ignorant of magistrates, *Insurrection de la
Grand'anse.*

In this exemplary passage, Bissette shows how colonial history is, as it
were, "faultily authored" (*auteur* → *fauteur*) and achieves its illusory appearance of "weightiness." The supposedly authentic and official knowledge purveyed in a government organ like the *Moniteur* becomes the object of an ironic knowledge ("comme on sait") that is attuned to the doubtful existence of the one hundred and seventeen "conspirators" and their
acts of "pillage." That such words are merely the empty signs of power,
lacking a real referent but nonetheless brutally constructing reality, is emphasized by their being underlined. This underlining, which voids a word
like "conspirator" of its meaning, performs (through metonymical association) a similar function with regard to the colonial names (Seguinot, Desmadrelles, Lereynerie) whose establishments have been "robbed": might
not these underlined patronyms, and the authority they betoken, be as
groundless as the other underlined words in the text; might not their enti-
tlement be as empty of substance as the pompous and erroneous title *Insurrection de la Grand'anse*? Such are the questions that Bissette's ironic
interrogation of individual words raises. Repeatedly undermining the authority of colonial discourse, showing it in its true (that is, false) "colors,"
he further supplements this ironic critique with a reverse discourse that
breathes new life into the old, hollowed out words, as when he refers a few
lines later on to "the permanent conspiracy against the rights and personal
security of the 'colored' population, the permanent insurrection of the
whites against the laws of the metropole!" (p. 16).

Examples of this deconstructive irony abound in the pages of the *Revue*,
and Bissette's far-reaching unmasking of the "omissions, dissimulations, de-
nials, and apologias" of (a particular variant of) colonial discourse certainly deserves a much larger place in accounts of Franco-Caribbean literary history and cultural critique than it has hitherto received. Part of the
reason that Bissette's work has not been looked at more closely, despite its
obvious achievements (achievements that would certainly, for example,

have earned it a place in any Afro-American canon), no doubt has to do with what I have referred to as his (dis)identification with blackness, as well as with his adoption of an increasingly religious and conservative rhetoric in the post-*Revue* years. Most important, though, is the fact that over the course of the 1840s he would fashion himself into the most vocal enemy of Victor Schœlcher (1804–93), signer of the 1848 decree ending slavery in the French colonies and a figure who would take on legendary dimensions in the Antilles over the course of the next century. No discussion of Bissette can avoid his tendentious relations with his fellow abolitionist Schœlcher— relations, as we will see, that were grounded in the same "prejudice, anger, and hate," the same bitter rivalry between patron and client, that Schœlcher so ably identified (albeit with an unwarranted sense of his own detachment from the situation he was describing) in the passage that serves as epigraph to this chapter.[28] It is to this mimetic rivalry of white and mulatto abolitionists that we must now turn.

The hostile relations between Bissette and Schœlcher can be thought of in two phases; the second phase (1848–51), involving the two men's virulent electoral campaigns during the short-lived Second Republic, will be looked at in some detail toward the end of this chapter, but the first (1842–44), revolving around Bissette's two book-length *Réfutations* of works written by Schœlcher in the early 1840s, can be treated here, since the polemic with the affluent white philanthropist began to take shape in the last issues of the *Revue* and we can find much the same contestation of official colonial discourse and the histories that it authorizes in these *Réfutations* as in the passages from the *Revue* we have just analyzed. Much the same—and yet with the important difference that in the figure of Schœlcher Bissette is attempting to unmask an authority figure with whom it is hard not to sympathize, given his strong abolitionist and revolutionary credentials. Indeed, an excerpt from the first of Schœlcher's two books that Bissette "refutes" was initially published in the *Revue des Colonies* (VIII.iv: 131–48), and favorably commented on, albeit with a number of critical remarks that hint at the attitude Bissette would soon adopt with regard to the author of *De l'esclavage des noirs et de la législation coloniale* (1833) and *Abolition de l'esclavage* (1840).

Based on Schœlcher's second trip to the Caribbean, in 1840–41, the two books attacked by Bissette were the influential *Des colonies françaises: Abolition immédiate de l'esclavage* (1842, henceforth *DCF*),[29] and a two-volume sequel entitled *Colonies étrangères et Haïti: Résultats de l'Émancipation anglaise* (1842–43, henceforth *CEH*) in which Schœlcher supplemented his earlier account of the Antilles with an examination of the recently emancipated British islands and independent Haiti. The general direction of Bissette's critique is summed up early on in his response to the first book, *Réfutation du livre de M. Victor Schœlcher, intitulé 'Des colonies françaises'* (1843): "what I am refuting are the errors into which the author has all too readily fallen, treating as friends of the blacks the very people who have shown themselves to be their greatest enemies [i.e., Schœlcher's (white) creole hosts in Martinique and Guadeloupe]; the unfair criticism that he has made regarding the conduct of the mulattoes toward the blacks;[30] his malicious assessment of their principles and their morals; finally, the unfortunate tenor of a book that risks dividing blacks and mulattoes" (p. 6). These main points also inform the book that Bissette would next publish, *Réfutation du livre de M. V. Schœlcher sur Haïti* (1844), and it is this book in particular, which resituates some of the issues discussed in Chapter 5 concerning Hugo's problematic representation of mulattoes, that I would like to concentrate on in the following brief overview of the first phase of the Bissette-Schœlcher debates.

Throughout the 1844 *Réfutation*, Bissette appropriates and redirects Schœlcher's claim that his account of Haiti is intended to counter "a falsified history of the country that is being propagated here in the interests of a caste" (*CEH*, 2.225). Bissette repeatedly emphasizes Schœlcher's own "falsifications," showing how "history is disfigured at his hands" (p. 100). In this "pamphlet" (p. 3) by the would-be "*historiographer*" of Haiti" (p. 112) are to be found countless "inexact and fabricated facts" (p. 2), which can be primarily attributed to three causes. First, Bissette accuses the self-styled "écrivain négrophile" (p. 32) of having ignored Bissette's repeated warnings in the *Revue* that "one should not count on the goodwill of [the white Creoles] when it comes to effecting the social and political reform toward which the abolitionist society is working" (II.x: 460), and of having allowed himself as a result to be won over by "that fascination, that creole charm . . . , which befogged his mind in the tropics and caused him to see the facts through the eyes of the colonists" (p. 6). In his 1833 *De l'esclavage des noirs*, Schœlcher had already expressed his great admiration for aspects of (white) creole life (for example, he there asserted that "the noble and pure hospitality of olden times, which has been so completely lost sight of in our cold, vain Europe, as miserly as an old woman, has taken refuge with them" [p. 100]), and he continues to speak of the creole elite with great sympathy in the early 1840s, notwithstanding their commitment to slavery. As Bissette puts it, "Monsieur Schœlcher seems to have sacrificed historical truth; his book is dangerous, his framework is generally defective; his language—malicious and offensive when it comes to those whose cause he believes himself to be defending—reveals only too well that he was under the influence of a fascination that followed him from Martinique to Guadeloupe, and from Guadeloupe to Haiti" (p. 3)—a fascination that encourages him, among other things, to contradict himself by arguing that slaveowners in Martinique and Guadeloupe should be indemnified for the loss of property that will result from abolition, while scoffing at the indemnities the Haitians agreed to pay out to the French in 1825.[31] In short, the white philanthropist had become "creolized," to cite a neologism that the Abbé Dugoujon was among the very first to make use of in 1842 when he criticized those Europeans who, influenced by their contact with planters, represented blacks "as types of monsters or ferocious beasts that [the whites] must keep muzzled and chained up if they are not to be devoured by them."[32] Immune to propaganda against blacks, Schœlcher had proven himself all too willing, in Bissette's view, to regurgitate his creole hosts' disparaging views on the mulatto presence in the Antilles and to let those views affect his (mis)understanding of the situation in Haiti.

This antimulatto prejudice, in turn, affects the choice and interpretation of the textual sources through which Schœlcher filters Haitian history and supplements the account of his own experiences there. Throughout his *Réfutation*, Bissette does a convincing job of showing the massive extent to which Schœlcher has borrowed, quite often in plagiaristic fashion, from the same colonial pamphlets and memoirs that, as we saw, fed into the rewriting of Hugo's novel; stressing "the similitude, the identity of these phrases copied by Monsieur Schœlcher" with the original texts (p. 37), Bissette claims that "the history he is teaching us has been copied from the pamphlets and memoirs of Page, Brulley, Thomas Millet, Daugy and other Saint-Domingue colonists who were among the most ardent opponents of the blacks and of the hommes de couleur, and who were their torturers back in those days in the same way that certain of Monsieur Schœlcher's hosts still are when it comes to mulattoes and blacks in the French colonies" (p. 28). If Schœlcher disregarded or downplayed more progressive and less ideologically dubious sources that might have complicated his representation of the Haitian Revolution—such as the four-volume *Rapport sur les troubles de Saint-Domingue* (1797–99) of Jean-Philippe Garran de Coulon, "true friend of the blacks, worthy and esteemed colleague of Grégoire in the National Convention" (p. 57)—this is due not simply to his own "creolized" biases but (and here is the third main cause of Schœlcher's errors) to his overwhelming ego, his need to arrogate for himself the role of crusading hero, to establish his identity and credentials as *the* abolitionist, owing nothing to predecessors like the Abbé Grégoire or contemporaries like . . . Bissette himself. While this last, ad hominem argument regarding Schœlcher may strike us as nothing more than sour grapes, it nonetheless has the merit of putting into question the transparency of the philanthropic posture adopted by Schœlcher (*and* by Bissette)—a transparency that (to recall my analysis in the previous chapter of Habibrah luring d'Auverney back to the edge of the abyss) may well be rather more opaque than it initially appears.

While convincingly pointing out many errors in Schœlcher's synopsis of Haitian history, Bissette's main bone of contention with his rival's assessment of postrevolutionary Haiti centers around a particular chapter: "Monsieur Schœlcher's book boils down to the chapter entitled *the Yellow Faction*" (p. 69). In this chapter (*CEH*, 2.219–45), the Frenchman pursues his thesis that "the color distinction is the key to all the misfortunes of Haiti" (2.342). "This country's population," Schœlcher notes, "is unfortunately composed of two very distinct classes: the gens de couleur, who number some 60 or 100,000, and the Negroes, who number some 500 or 600,000. Now, it is the gens de couleur who head the government; hence their glorification to the detriment of others" (2.235). While acknowledging that this division is not officially formalized ("It is in vain that the two classes mingle at official gatherings; a de facto separation exists between them. I am not saying that the distance between them is something that is admitted to, I am merely saying that it exists. Outwardly, relations between the blacks and the yellows are on a perfectly equal footing; outside the *forum* they keep to themselves" [2.236–37]), and stressing that his criticisms are addressed only to a ruling faction rather than the entire mulatto class, Schœlcher nonetheless insists that the only solution to this "abnormal domination" (2.235) is for the elite to ally themselves with the "real people" and relinquish some of their power—for instance, by "reserving the top post for a Negro" (2.342), as he puts it in the book's concluding sentence. (The letter, if not the spirit, of this sentiment would be intermittently accommodated, from the mid-1840s on, by a new system of governance "whereby a black president was controlled by mulatto politicians [and that] became known as *la politique de doublure*, the politics of the understudy.")[33] Nothing, it would appear, could be more straightforward than Schœlcher's division of Haiti into a *parti noir* and a *faction jaune*, although the fact that this division is also phrased in terms of an opposition between the "vrai peuple" and other presumably less "authentic" people belies an ideological slant that, as Bissette no doubt sensed, is complicit with the sort of oppositions that structured a work like *Bug-Jargal*.

Uncontestable as it might appear, Bissette attacks as both false and dangerous Schœlcher's "idée fixe that the *yellow faction* is everywhere oppressing the blacks" (p. 7). False, because matters are not so simple in Haiti, and dangerous, because to emphasize these divisions is to risk inflaming and institutionalizing them. Schœlcher's vision of Haiti as the site of a "caste war" is, Bissette remarks, simply "a reminiscence of what he saw in Martinique and Guadeloupe" (p. 114): "since the time Africans and their descendants made themselves masters of this country and drove out the whites, there has been no more black party or mulatto party; since the time, that is," Bissette adds, implicitly critiquing the will to discursive mastery that Schœlcher exhibits in the writing of his "authoritative" account of Haiti, "that they wrote in their fundamental pact, 'No white, of whatever nation, can ever set foot on this territory as a master or an owner'" (p. 4). The recent overthrow of the Boyer régime in 1843 might, he admits, demonstrate that postrevolutionary Haiti remains the site of revolutionary ferment but it does not testify to the sort of simplistic distinctions that Schœlcher wants to make since the mulatto president was "overthrown by a revolution authored by *blacks* and *mulattoes*" (p. 95). It would be wrong, Bissette argues, to read such events in terms of distinctions of color, which "have no political meaning in Haiti, where one sees (as the revolutionary and insurrectional movements that have [recently] taken place in that re-public bear witness), blacks and mulattoes on one side, fighting mulattoes and blacks on the other side" (p. 4). Further, portraying the unified nation of Haiti as thus divided and thereby perpetuating such colonial reminis-cences in a post-colonial location can only destabilize the political situation by *creating*—or re-creating—the reality it purports to describe. (In 1845, Haiti's new black president, Louis Pierrot, would attempt to defuse this danger by decreeing in his "race relations" act that "any person whatever who indulges in idle talk about colour likely to spread dissension among Haitians and to provoke citizens one against another, will be arrested, put in prison and delivered to the courts.")[34] While thus denying that distinc-tions of color have any "political sense" in post-colonial Haiti, and stating that they are "absurd, since one is faced with nuances that simply cannot be specified precisely" (p. 113), Bissette nonetheless tactically appeals to them in order to unmask the "denigratory attitude toward mulattoes" (p. 10) that informs Schœlcher's systematic distortion of Haitian history: in de-veloping his thesis about a homogeneous "faction jaune," Bissette points out, the Frenchman has in certain instances identified blacks as mulattoes— "in order not to disturb the book's agenda and to assure the consistency of its falsely grounded ideas, Monsieur Schœlcher has turned . . . three black men (Geffrard, Magny, and Riché) into three men of the *yellow faction*, mulattoes" (p. 13)—and in other cases has turned "*blacks* into *yellow men*" (p. 14).

To be sure, in pursuing the argument that Schœlcher "does not know how to distinguish what is *yellow* from what is *black*" (p. 112), Bissette cannot help reinscribing the absurd colonial distinctions that ought to have no place in post-colonial Haiti. Schœlcher certainly invites this sort of counterargument, but it could nonetheless be said to backfire against Bis-sette; or, to put the matter another way, the contradictions it entails visibly signal the post/colonial complexities that both he and Schœlcher are in

their different ways attempting to suppress in their discussions of, as Stendhal might have put it, "le jaune et le noir." This aspect of their exchange,
which in great part replicated ongoing debates in Haiti (one finds
Schœlcher's insistence on the continued presence in Haiti of two castes in
the writings of the mulatto historian Thomas Madiou, while Bissette's objections are shared by exponents of the "mulatto legend" such as Beaubrun
Ardouin and Joseph Saint-Rémy, the latter of whom also attacked Schœlcher's book),[35] situates us squarely within the terms of a double bind, in a
place where nothing and everything has changed. Colonial distinctions and
identities continue to exercise their oppressive power, as the revolutionary
Schœlcher reminiscently argues, but, as the conservative Bissette revolu-
tionarily argues, in a country "where all citizens are free and have equal
rights" (p. 129) they have also lost that power: such are the contradictions
of a post/colonial condition that neither man can adequately account for
but that nonetheless becomes visible in a juxtaposition of their respective
positions and an interrogation of the various contradictions and errors with
which their arguments are riddled.

Much of the 1844 *Réfutation* is taken up with a discussion of the ways
in which Schœlcher depreciates and misrepresents mulatto contributions to
the Haitian Revolution: commenting on Schœlcher's devastating portraits
of people like Pétion and Ogé, Bissette deprecates the way in which this
"negrophile" seizes hold, "in one fell swoop, of men whose memory is dear
to us and, correcting history in his manner, turns them into base and con-
temptible beings, unworthy of serving as our models and rivals in excellence" (p. 68). Since it nicely supplements our discussion of Hugo's portrait
of Ogé in *Bug-Jargal*, Bissette's "memory" of this mulatto leader and his
extensive refutation of Schœlcher's (pp. 26–69) is worth pausing over here.
The latter's discussion of Ogé is inseparable from a critique of the way in
which he was being glorified in Boyer's Haiti as a representative revolutionary hero: a work like Pierre Faubert's play *Ogé, ou Le préjugé de couleur*, in representing the first colored leader of the Haitian Revolution as
having advocated "liberty for all" rather than simply his own caste's interests, sacrifices historical probity in the name of political passions, giving undue importance to a flawed and minor revolutionary figure in a fashion
analogous to that in which the "bad patriot" Pétion (*CEH*, 2.230) has been
crowned with glory at the expense of a Toussaint or a Dessalines ("of all
the countries in the world, it is in Haiti that the least tribute is paid to
Toussaint Louverture!!" [*CEH*, 2.226]). In thus drawing attention to the
distortions involved in the production of what David Nicholls has referred
to as the "mulatto legend" that, along with its *noiriste* mirror-image, dominated nineteenth-century Haitian politics and culture, Schœlcher is on extremely solid ground; Bissette repeatedly glosses over what is at stake in the

dissemination of this legend, to which he is clearly attached, and in this respect his account of the "culpable indifference" shown by the self-styled "*abolitionist historian*" to Ogé, that "martyr of freedom" (pp. 26–27), is markedly unconvincing. By contrast, when it comes to such things as Ogé's purchase of a "croix du Lion de Limbourg" Bissette's mulatto sympathies give him a clear insight into the colonial assumptions generating Schœlcher's dismissive comments thereon (assumptions that were equally on display in *Bug-Jargal*).[36] Moreover, Schœlcher's characterization of Ogé's speech to the Massiac Club as "timid and dubitative," notwithstanding the fact that it unequivocally called for an end to slavery,[37] provides Bissette with the opportunity to invoke Schœlcher's own timorous relationship to the abolitionist cause in the previous decade: "Monsieur Schœlcher would have liked Ogé to speak, in 1789, about liberty for the slaves in the way that it is spoken about today; that is to say, in the way that Monsieur Schœlcher himself did not speak about it, in 1830, since he wrote [at that time] in the *Revue de Paris* that 'those who want the abolition of slavery to happen now, spontaneously, are wasting their breath'" (p. 31). In reminding readers of Schœlcher's former belief that the final abolition of slavery could only occur toward the end of the century, and in recalling further damning statements from that article (e.g., "no more than anybody else do I see the need to infect the present society, already bad enough as things stand, with several million brutes decorated with the title of 'citizen,' who in the final analysis would be only a vast breeding-ground of beggars and proletarians"),[38] Bissette ably exposes the inadequacy of Schœlcher's anachronistic judgment of the Haitian past—a judgment that also informs the Frenchman's over simple reading of the "chef noir" Biassou as a "traitor" to the revolutionary cause (see pp. 72–75). Just one of many such "contradictions and palinodes" (p. 19) in Schœlcher's book, such judgments are enough in Bissette's estimation to expose him as a newcomer in the arena, "whose abolitionist credentials still need to be verified by us Negroes and mulattoes, the *only* ones competent to judge in this matter" (p. 68; "dont les titres abolitionistes sont encore à vérifier par nous autres nègres et mulâtres, *seuls* compétents dans la question").

In *Des colonies françaises*, Schœlcher remarked that "even today, mulattoes take it as a sort of an insult when they are called mulattoes; they ought to make it into a title of honor, glory in it until the time when differences between them and the whites have ceased being an issue." "Monsieur Bissette," he elaborated, "has constantly preached this excellent doctrine in his *Revue des Colonies*, and it is regrettable that people have not been listening to him" (p. 204). Ironically, it is only a very short step from (and perhaps even a logical extension of) this "excellent doctrine" to the argument from racial authority that generates Bissette's exclusionary comment about "nous autres nègres et mulâtres." We see a variation of this argument, which will take on greater prominence as Bissette's career progresses and his polemic with Schœlcher intensifies, at work in the autobiographical commentary through which he critiques Schœlcher's statement that "Ogé was even weak-kneed enough to ask for a reprieve on the morning of the execution" (*CEH*, 2.223). Bissette's response to this gratuitous and cavalier remark is worth quoting at length:

Well! I too, Monsieur Schœlcher, I was sentenced by your friends, by your Martiniquan hosts, and among the judges ... what am I saying! ... among the TORTURERS were to be found THE MISTERS PERRINELLE, FATHER AND SON [the former being one of the few judges who voted in 1824 that Bissette be put to death]! I too, like the unfortunate Ogé, demanded in the name of the law a reprieve, a legal reprieve, because the court charged with making a ruling on my case had not yet pronounced on it, no more than had the erstwhile King's council [pronounced] on the "legal" assassination of that unfortunate man! "They also *disdainfully refused to listen to me*" but, less unlucky than Ogé, that martyr for freedom, I was not broken on the wheel; I was only dragged to the scaffold, while your generous hosts applauded, and there, THE TORTURER MARKED ME WITH HIS BRAND!!! ... Two years after this "execution," prematurely carried out in spite of a pending appeal, the Court of Cassation NULLIFIED this despicable ruling!

But this branding, this branding will remain indelibly marked on the brow of your friends as the sign of their infamy! And it will have its part to play in the abolition of the enslavement of my black brothers. (p. 48)

This self-identification with Ogé is rhetorically powerful, and succeeds (but at what cost?) in fully differentiating Bissette from Schœlcher—as do even blunter claims stressing his "status as a descendant of Africans" (p. 24), such as when he identifies himself as "a mulatto, who is as good an abolitionist as Monsieur Schœlcher, and who is more of a negrophile than he, because his great-grandmothers were Negresses from Martinique" (p. 46). The experience of color prejudice is something that has to be lived to be understood, and a short stay in the tropics is not a sufficient base from which to make the sort of claims that are repeatedly, and *patronizingly*,[39] put forward in Schœlcher's volumes about the Antilles and Haiti; as Bissette would argue a few years later with regard to his white rival, "it is a phenomenal error on his part to assume that a few months of traveling in the Caribbean is enough to turn oneself into a fount of knowledge" and "to believe oneself capable of writing about colonial customs and all the other related issues in big fat volumes *destined to become a standard point of reference [à faire autorité]* on the issue of emancipation."[40] These are claims about authority with which we are all familiar, and if Bissette's blatantly rhetorical (re)presentation of his "signed" body strikes us—living as we do in an age that is wary of rhetoric or, rather, is easily persuaded by the rhetoric of anti-rhetoric, "the allegedly simple speech straightforwardly translating the movements of the heart"[41]—as a little bit "off color," they are nonetheless voiced here in an exemplary manner that rehearses what is perhaps the central topos of postcolonial literature and theory: "Who can speak for and/or as the Other?"

As this brief account of the first phase of their exchange should have demonstrated, Bissette's response to Schœlcher in many respects anticipates the ways in which postcolonial authors would write back against the distortions of colonial discourse. Certainly, as both Bissette's entanglement in a mulatto ideology that clearly did not serve progressive ends and Schœlcher's credentials as the eventual architect of emancipation bear witness, Bissette's response is not one that can be "purely" endorsed. In this respect, I would ultimately argue, his post/colonial confrontation with Schœlcher actually provides a more realistic model for understanding the authorization of identities and the revision of histories at work in postcolonial writing than other, more superficially attractive ones that seem to require no caveats. Be that as it may, I would now like to turn back to an earlier polemic of Bissette's that must appear altogether less problematic, since it was directed at a far "worthier" target. The account of Schœlcher in great part relied upon the technique of parodic (re)citation that he had reserved in the pages of the *Revue* for reactionary French writers like Granier de Cassagnac—or "Granier (de) Cassagnac" as Bissette liked to call him, casting ridicule on the journalist's adoption of the aristocratic particle—and (white) creole writers like Poirié Saint-Aurèle, and it is Bissette's treatment of Granier de Cassagnac's college friend, the Martiniquan Louis (de) Maynard (de Queilhe), and his 1835 novel *Outre-mer*, that I would now like to summarize, by way of introducing my own discussion of this almost completely, and no doubt justly, forgotten creole author.

Creolist Discourse, Mulatto Bildung: Louis Maynard's 'Outre-mer' and (the Failure of) the Melodramatic Imagination

Maynard was a repeated target of the *Revue* in its early years, most notably in a lengthy review of *Outre-mer* in the December 1835 issue (II.vi: 279–88). Unsigned, but certainly authored by Bissette, the article stressed the novel's objectionable ideological project ("directed against the 'colored' class" [p. 279], it attempts to establish, first, "that mulattoes are an inferior and base race," and second, "that those among them who would like to rise above their conditions will, by the very way in which the colonies are constituted, sink down to a level below their own race" [p. 282]) and its aesthetic shortcomings (it is, "speaking in literary terms, a really bad book" [pp. 279–80]). In so doing, Bissette's review entirely accorded with the handful of others that this novel received, as he gleefully notes: "the cream of the Paris press has treated Monsieur Louis de Maynard de Queilhe as he deserved; that is to say, as a truant schoolboy who has taken pen to paper as a way of ruling over the universe" (p. 280). Maynard's attempt at becoming an author(ity) having wretchedly failed, he is portrayed in the review as skulking back to the islands in shame and disgust:

The noble writer has left this fine country of France where aristocracies are not held in respect, and . . . embarked at Le Havre, carrying with him the first edition of *Outre-mer*, which served as ballast for the *Pauline*. God help this excellent young man and those who are traveling on the same boat! Theirs is indeed a perilous journey. (p. 280)

The sheer size of Maynard's book excites Bissette's sarcastic impulses, providing weighty evidence "that one can write entire volumes without having even the ghost of an idea" (p. 288). Along with the expected ideological critique ("instead of speaking out against a country where such deplorable prejudices hold sway, the author wants to justify the prejudice" [p. 283]), Bissette parodically (re)cites the entire plot of the novel and points out the extent to which it is plagiaristically indebted to works like Hugo's *Marion de Lorme* (p. 282) or, even more embarrassingly, to a novel published earlier that year by one of Maynard's fellow Creoles: "what is most unfortunate for the literary reputation of the author is that he has taken a whole mass of situations, thoughts, and details from Monsieur Levilloux's *Les créoles*, published five months before *Outre-mer*, and a book written in an altogether different spirit" (p. 288). After thus demolishing the originality of Maynard's project, the review ends with an ad hominem postscriptum in which the novel's evident distaste for mulattoes is ironically contrasted with its author's supposed proclivity for women of color: "we have been assured that the author of *Outre-mer*, during his sojourn in Paris, rendered the homage of his most tender feelings to a young woman of color, the daughter of a former colonist in Martinique, now a mercantile banker, very well known in Paris and in the colonial world. It has even been floated about," Bissette continues, "that the purpose of Monsieur Louis de Maynard de Queilhe's trip back to Martinique was simply to obtain his father's blessing for the marriage with this young lady of color" (p. 288; see also VIII.xi: 449).

Bissette pursues his parodic critique of Maynard in further issues of the review. In a discussion of "Monsieur Poirié dit de Saint-Aurèle" a year later, he remarks in passing, after having spoken of "the poetry of overseas" ("la poésie d'outre-mer"): "Ah, good Lord! *Outre-mer*! what words have I just let slip? *Outre-mer*, the first and last masterpiece of Martinique's greatest prosifier, Monsieur the viscount of Quercy, Louis de Maynard de Queilhe," adding, "Ah! Monsieur Louis de Maynard, we owe you a second article, since the *Courrier de la Guadeloupe* has been calling us names for having denounced, tactfully to be sure, all the stupid infamies, all the rubbish with which you laced your insipid novel; take my word for it, we will pay you back in short order" (III.vi: 263). And return he does, in a bitingly parodic account (III.vii: 298–304) of an article published in the *Courrier de la Guadeloupe* (and republished in *La France maritime* under the title "Voyage à la Martinique"). Ridiculing the aristocratic pretensions of the creole elite by referring to it as "les impressions de voyage de Monsieur Louis de Maynard, vicomte de Queilhe et du Quercy," Bissette once again emphasizes the monstrous proportions of the prose of this "démi-poète": "he has twice stuffed the *Courrier de la Guadeloupe* with this piece, nine immense columns of prose in the style of *Outre-mer*, and he has had the inhumanity to expedite this fabulous masterpiece to the mère-patrie, where all the regulars of that seedy café in which the *Courrier de la Guadeloupe* is read are likely to pass out from reading it" (p. 299). Further harping on the "syncopal" properties of this prose, Bissette notes that "the success of *Outre-mer* was such that, twenty-four hours after its first appearance, fifteen people were already dead as a result of a horrible heaviness of the head, followed by such violent yawns that the lower jaw being no longer capable of reaching the upper jaw, the poor wretches had expired in the midst of some remarkable convulsions" (p. 298). Elaborating on this scenario leads him to revise his explanation as to why Maynard left the country: he now playfully suggests that the police, having identified the responsible party, had been forced to expel him for having brought about too many deaths-by-yawning! (His expulsion will, however, only result in the exporting of this sleeping sickness back to the colonies, as an earlier-published "dramatic proverb" [III.iii: 135–44] that amusingly describes "a session of Martinique's Colonial Council" suggests when it begins by noting that the members of the Council are "sound asleep" and "one sees by looking at several of these notable individuals that this sleep is of such a prodigious and concentrated nature that one would be tempted to believe each of the esteemed sleepers carried in his pocket a copy of *Outre-mer*, by that nobleman from Quercy, Monsieur Louis de Maynard de Queilhe" [p. 137].)[42] More seriously, Bissette once again addresses the question of Maynard's style, pointing out its mimetic relation to the work of other Romantic writers: "Monsieur Maynard's style is neither prose nor verse; it is usually a kind of jargon [*baragouin*] falling somewhere between Breton and Toulouse patois, a series of little centos, chopped up fine, in the midst of which glitter, like pearls on manure, a few morsels stolen from Victor Hugo, Alexandre Dumas, Sainte-Beuve, and even from that joker, that

'sprightly' prosifier, Granier de Cassagnac" (p. 299; see also II.v: 204). As
we will see later on in this chapter, such an assessment of creole writing as
primarily imitative was a common one in nineteenth-century literary criticism, voiced most famously by Baudelaire; Bissette's strategy of parodic
(re)citation proves both an ideal one for registering the presence of such imitation in a writer like Maynard and is itself an example of that imitation—
one that is self-consciously adopted, and that empowers his discourse but
that *also* debilitates it inasmuch as the imitation of an imitation necessarily
becomes inextricable from the object it (re)presents.

Having given an account of Bissette's scathingly parodic portrait of his
fellow Martiniquan, I would now like to turn to the man himself, providing
a few details about his life, and surveying his various articles, short stories,
and novel with an eye for what they have to tell us about "creolist discourse." His date of birth has hitherto escaped notice: he was born on
March 29, 1811, in the parish of Vauclin on the southeast part of the island
to a French father, Louis Charles François Maynard (born in 1769 in Tulle,
in the Limousin region of central France, and deceased in 1839) and a creole mother, Adelaide Olympe la Place (born 1778).[43] Arriving in France
around 1831, he spent several years at a college in Toulouse, where—if we
are to believe the *Revue des Colonies*—"he made his literary debut with a
light comedy, which was hissed and booed by the good people of Toulouse
(to the accompaniment of stewed apples, used by the public with such
profligacy that the entirety of the year's harvest was lost)" (III.vii: 298).
Notwithstanding Bissette's dismissive assessment, and the almost complete
oblivion into which he has fallen, Maynard would actually play a role of
some significance in Romantic circles during his years in Paris (c. 1833–35).
Having become a close friend of Victor Hugo's, Maynard would author a
great many articles and short stories over the course of those three years,
including a polemical overview of political journals for *L'Europe littéraire*
in 1833 ("De la littérature des journaux politiques": July 10, 15, 26, August 15) that contributed greatly to the final rupture between the husband
of Adèle Hugo and her lover Sainte-Beuve, who assumed that a critical
comment of Maynard's directed toward him could only have originated
with Hugo. As Sainte-Beuve put it in a letter to his former friend, "everything pointed toward those articles being the more or less direct result of
some conversation of yours, at which the writer was present"; disdainfully
referring to the aesthetic preferences Maynard had voiced in his series of articles on the 1833 Salon, Sainte-Beuve asserted that "a man who so warmly
praised [the painter] Horace Vernet seemed to me hardly capable of getting
spontaneously impassioned about such a lofty artistic cause."[44] Some three
months after the publication in late June 1835 of *Outre-mer* Maynard
would depart for Martinique, where a little under two years later he would

meet his death in one of those duels for which Creoles were notorious. Interestingly enough, the exact circumstances of his death would themselves become a minor bone of contention in the Bissette-Schœlcher exchange: in *Des colonies françaises* Schœlcher, who had been a friend of Maynard's, speaks of "the unfortunate Louis Maynard, that young son of Martinique, who made himself loved in France, and who died too young, butchered [*abattu*] in a duel by the gun of a mulatto" (p. 255). With evident malice, and with his usual emphasis on the importance of attending to individual word choices, Bissette corrects the record in his 1843 *Réfutation*: "and yet it is a matter of public knowledge in Martinique that Monsieur Louis Maynard was *butchered*, to use Monsieur Schœlcher's elegant turn of phrase, by a young white Creole from Saint-Pierre, Monsieur Thounens, who thus avenged the honor of a white family into which Maynard had wanted to bring discord and dishonor" (p. 26).

Whatever the truth behind the twenty-six-year-old's death (and it would appear that Bissette's version is closer to it than Schœlcher's), it is clear that he was a young man for whom the French abolitionist had strong feelings, which would eventually generate, as we will see, a rather unexpected reading of parts of *Outre-mer*. Even more intense were Hugo's feelings toward Maynard, and it is worth lingering over the author of *Bug-Jargal*'s reactions to his death, since the brief accounts of *Outre-mer* that one finds in comprehensive histories of Franco-Caribbean literature such as those of Jack Corzani or Régis Antoine strangely fail to mention the connection between these two men, despite the fact that Maynard himself indirectly refers to it in the preface to *Outre-mer* (where, after asserting that among his ancestors was "the illustrious member of the Academy" François de Maynard de Saint-Céray [1582–1646], he adds that "I do not hope for, certainly, the same good fortune from the critics of our own day, but if Maynard was the friend of [Mathurin] Régnier, a greater poet than Régnier honors me with his friendship" [1.ii]). This connection not only assures Maynard a certain "importance" as an historical figure but also opens up interesting if unanswerable questions about the criteria according to which Hugo (and Schœlcher) judged a person's character, given the aesthetically and ideologically problematic contents of *Outre-mer*. Poignantly enough, the fullest expression of Hugo's sentiments toward his young friend would come in a letter of his dated May 21, 1837, one day before his friend's death. Noting in this letter that "distance ennobles men such as yourself, for one compares you to those who stayed and it is not you who lose out in this comparison," Hugo urges his young friend either to return to Paris or at the very least to send them some new book of his, and comments derisively on the contemporary scene in France ("As far as politics goes, things are all still second-rate and shabby . . . they have not gotten any better since you left us. Small-minded men working on small ideas; next to nothing bustling about over nothing"). These last comments lead him to conclude that, "all things considered, there are times when I envy you, poet exiled under the sun—an exile that Ovid would have enjoyed—in that Martinique you have so wonderfully depicted."[45] Hugo's exoticizing portrait of sunny Martinique in this never-to-be-answered letter begs a number of questions to which we will return; the letter provides ample evidence, in any case, of an attachment to Maynard that is even more visible in Hugo's melancholy reflections on the death of this "exiled poet" in a letter to his wife Adèle some months later. There he recalls looking out to sea while in Boulogne and pondering the loss of several of his friends that year, including his brother Eugène and "Maynard so radiant and so noble," "all dead having scarcely begun to live": "Where are they now? Do their thoughts turn to us as ours turn to them? Do they miss us, do they long after us? They now know how much I really loved them, Maynard especially, who was unfair enough to have sometimes doubted it, the only fault with which I can reproach him."[46]

Only four years before Hugo wrote his last letter to Maynard, both men had contributed statements of purpose to the editors of a new journal entitled *L'Europe littéraire* in which they—along with the likes of Dumas, Michelet, Nodier, Scribe, Sue, and Vigny—confirmed their intention of contributing to the "noble and useful" project of strengthening the bond of art uniting Europe to France, that "essentially civilizing nation" (in the words of Hugo's statement, published in the journal's Prospectus). In his own letter to the editors, Maynard notes the revisionist nature of the work that he intends to contribute to the journal:

It seemed to me that *L'Europe littéraire* had as its goal bringing the entire range of European ideas into dialogue with one another. Each country ought, then, to bring its allotted share to this enterprise. Although cast away in the New World, the colonies are intimately linked to Europe through their political and social relations. They offer the writer, moreover, a rich and unexplored mine of material to exploit. I intend then, not to provide its physical statistics, details that are of little importance to art, but to devote myself to what I would like to call its moral statistics; to make known the French Caribbean especially, which has been for such a long time the object of either unjust disdain or of emotional attacks; to identify, finally, by means of various literary forms and particularly those of the novel or the short story, the relationships, customs, habits, and prejudices of the different classes of these variegated peoples [*ces populations bigarrées*]. Such is the project that I will be undertaking.

Unexceptional as such a programmatic statement might appear to us today, it is important to register both its novelty in the context of the Antilles and its affinities with the first flowering of a specifically Caribbean literary self-consciousness in Cuba and Haiti during this same decade. Maynard's aesthetic project does not simply entail an exoticizing "exploitation" of opulent and unknown locales but also their *de*-exoticization, a (re)vision of them in the face of European misrepresentations and a (re)placing of them in "relation" to the Old World with which they are "intimately linked." This threefold project can be read in his self-identification (in the preface to *Outre-mer*) as a "Français d'Amérique" (I.v): one who speaks, that is, as a Frenchman mining the exotic, an American revising the stories Europe imposes upon its colonized Others, and a Franco-American who himself embodies the colonial relation between these two worlds, and these two identities.

Maynard's revisionist project overlaps with the strategy of "writing back" that typifies postcolonial literature and theory: the same logic underwrites both enterprises, for all that their content diverges radically. Maynard writes in order to counter the stereotypes about (white) Creoles that one finds in European writers who (as the Creole narrating his short story "Scènes nocturnes aux Antilles" puts it) "usually, when it comes to portraying an American planter, present you with the first bearish individual who happened to pop into their head, replete with straw hat, armed with a bamboo cane, and kitted out with a little roast nigger."[47] These stereotypes and the prejudices they generate form part of a discursive system identified as "philanthropy,"[48] a wolf in sheep's clothing that Maynard associated with the name of Schœlcher as early as 1833.[49] The distortions of reality that this discourse ensures have succeeded in bringing about the collapse of creole society: "their task is finished," the narrator of "Scènes" continues, "our fortunes are collapsing, the cutlass is at our throats, glimmering, and it is now our turn to pay for the crime of our color" (p. 269). What is interesting about Maynard's otherwise banal (if, in our own day, still very familiar) invocations of the power of a newly hegemonic discourse to penalize and criminalize whiteness is that they are so blatantly, even self-consciously, *imitations* of a rhetoric of victimage that is itself essential to philanthropic discourse. At one point in *Outre-mer*, the narrator notes disparagingly that "in France, where it is so easy to make oneself out to be a victim, . . . where one readily sides with the person who yells over the person who keeps quiet, the name 'Creole' had become synonymous with anthropophagite, with ferocious beast" (2.167). To speak out is potentially to redress this situation, and yet it is also to put oneself in the place of the victim, mimetically to adopt the very tactics of those one opposes. The master's voice has become reactive; in making itself heard, it has entered into a troubling relation of resemblance with that of his slaves; in *Outre-mer*, as we will see, this relation finds expression in Maynard's identification of mulattoes as the embodiment of a reactive, imitative logic that (as he is dimly aware) is in fact as essential to his own identity as a Creole and a novelist as it is to the colonial victims he is imitating and the postcolonial revisionists whose tactics he anticipates.

In pursuing this revisionist project Maynard necessarily contests representations of the islands that would detach them from postrevolutionary history; philanthropy is only one symptom of a "cosmopolitanism" that has found its way to the New World from a Europe "where the iron blade of equality has no more heads to chop off, where the death throes of liberty—that chaste goddess raped by her assassins—have come to an end," as the narrator of "Mademoiselle Lafayolle" puts it. This brief story, which recounts an episode from the very first years of the colony, begins with an ironic invocation of the Caribbean as the site of a timeless, exoticized (and eroticized) present: "Today, Guadeloupe is a raft carried out to sea by the waves. Its sky is large and serene; each palm leaf resonates like a harp. Its orange trees coat the air with perfumes. Clusters of colibris hang from the flowers, a living bouquet that vanishes at the approach of beating hooves. There, it is all grace and harmony; the women are of ivory, gold, and ebony. . . . " Such proto-Baudelairean sentiments are characteristic of an external representation of the islands that also pervades Hugo's last letter to Maynard, as when, after asking his young friend to make up for his absence by at least sending them a further example of his creative work, the author of *Bug-Jargal* remarks that "in place of the great spectacle of mankind that you had here, you have the great spectacle of nature; in place of the struggle of ideas, you have the calm harmony of things; if you have less of our century, you have more of the sun. Over there, art is bound to open up for you still more beautiful prospects." Sensitized to the realities of historical change, Maynard refuses to let such visions of a graceful and harmonious *là-bas* stand, evoking them (as at the outset of "Mademoiselle Lafayolle") only to deflate them immediately with the sort of comments about Europe cited above. These comments superimpose a very different present onto the supposedly exotic locale: a negative double of the tranquil "aujourd'hui" with which "Mademoiselle Lafayolle" begins, a conflictual and valueless present that Maynard everywhere deprecates in his work (e.g., "today when all the centers of moral action have disappeared; today when the impiety of our fathers is bearing its fruits, when cafés have replaced churches; today when the family is destroyed and along with it the paternal lesson that was once so powerful! . . . ").[50] The breakdown of cultural traditions and the contagion of a revolutionary cosmopolitanism that characterize this globally Europeanized present have for Maynard rendered hollow the "belles perspectives" of exoticism, and the pastoral vision that he dismissively associates with writers like Bernardin de Saint-Pierre.[51]

Hugo's dehistoricized vision of the islands as the site of an unsullied nature (one that actively forgets the "grand spectacle des hommes" that he had already registered in *Bug-Jargal*) has its equivalent in what we might call the "native variant" of creolist discourse: it dominates, for instance, a poem like Poirié Saint-Aurèle's "Les Antilles" (from the 1833 collection *Cyprès et Palmistes*), where he speaks placidly of "our carefree Negroes, our cheerful Negresses / And their songs and dances" ("Nos nègres sans soucis, nos négresses rieuses / Et les chants de leur calenda") and of "our fine colonists with their patriarchal customs / Reciting the peaceful annals of their forefathers" ("Nos bons colons aux moeurs patriarcales / Racontant des aïeux les paisibles annales"). Poirié's is a pastoral vision from which revolutionary tumult has been occluded (complying, in this respect, with exoticizing European representations of the islands) and yet in which the erotic possibilities gestured toward in Maynard's "les femmes sont d'ivoire, d'or et d'ébène" play only a limited role. Significantly, the poem's focus on contented blacks and patriarchal colonists leaves no room for the intermediary mulatto class; as we will see, for Maynard, it is precisely this class that embodies the problem of revolutionary change *and* of a (sexual, mimetic) desire that is inextricably linked to this problem. In "Les Antilles" only the slightest trace of such desire can be found, surfacing in the poem's final verse:

> J'aime, oh! j'aime avant tout, la sensible Créole
> À la paupière noire, à la taille espagnole,
> Doux trésor de pudeur, d'amour et de beauté,
> Le front ceint d'un madras plein de coquetterie,
> Berçant dans un hamac sa molle rêverie
>   Et la dolce farniente.[52]

> I love, oh! above all I love the tender Creole
> Her black eyelids, her Spanish waist,
> Sweet trove of modesty, of love and beauty,
> The brow encircled by a madras full of coquetry
> Who in a hammock rocks her languid thoughts
>   And her dolce far niente.

Unlike the straightforward descriptions of the slaves and the colonists, the appearance of "la sensible Créole" generates a moment of semantic trembling in the poem: while quite obviously referring to white women, the stanza nonetheless does so with a certain ambivalence, evoking images of blackness ("paupière noire") and foreignness ("taille espagnole"); these seemingly banal lines, moreover, contain (in both senses of the word) one of the dominant semes of creolist discourse, the *madras*, which in European (as opposed to native) inflections of this discourse not only conveyed a sensuality that Poirié in a limited way allows into his poem ("plein de coquetterie") but was especially associated with women of mixed race.

Eugène Sue's treatment in *Les mystères de Paris* (1842–43) of the "dangerously seductive" *métisse* Cecily is exemplary of this European deployment of the madras and the contaminated usage of the word "creole" that results from it (a usage that Poirié's poem resists). Cecily has just put on her "charming nocturnal headdress" and, after remarking upon the "titillating contrast between this fabric, brightly splashed with purple, azure, and orange, and her black hair, which, slipping out of the tight folds of the madras, frames her pale but round and firm cheeks with its thousand silky curls," Sue's narrator launches into a description of her that is both fearful and desirous:

This tall creole woman, at once slender and fleshy, sturdy and supple like a panther, was the very incarnation of that raw sensuality [*sensualité brutale*] that flares up only in the tropics. Everybody has heard about those young women of color who are, so to speak, fatal to Europeans: those bewitching vampires who, intoxicating the chosen victim with their dreadful charms, suck him dry of his gold and of his blood, leaving him with only—to use the forceful expression of the islands—his tears to drink, his heart to gnaw. (p. 663)

As Sue had earlier pointed out with regard to métisses, "only a few imperceptible signs differentiate them from white women" (p. 119); the lurid transformation of Cecily into a "vampire" certainly serves the purpose of distinguishing her from a white woman, and yet at the same time—as the juxtaposition with Poirié's poem shows—the possibility of their indifferentiation can also be read metonymically into Sue's description of this "grande créole." The madras is one sign of their potential interchangeability; in restricting his reader's access to this sign, a writer like Poirié is able to maintain distinctions that Maynard's short stories and novel also assert but cannot help troubling.[53] Resisting both Europe's negative (philanthropic) portrayals of white-black relations and its positive (exoticized) representations of the Caribbean's spectacularly ahistorical nature, Maynard nonetheless shares Sue's eroticized vision of the islands. If, however, the French writer's flirtation with the "dangerous seductions" of interracial desire simply provides additional fuel for the fire of his Romantic melodrama, a great deal more is at stake in the Franco-American writer's representations of it, which in an almost consciously suicidal fashion put into question the very foundations of Maynard's (white) creole identity, as I would now like to suggest in my reading of *Outre-mer*.

In the *Revue de Paris*, where one of its chapters had already been published in advance of the novel,[54] the young Saint-Simonian Adolphe Guéroult sums up the general theme of *Outre-mer* in the following terms: "Monsieur de Maynard's book is a mulatto drama that takes place in Martinique; he has attempted to put into play the rivalry of the mulattoes and the whites in the colonies, the pretensions (too often unjustified) of the hommes de couleur, and the crimes into which they can be led by the inferiority that, despite the law, prejudice imposes upon them."[55] This is a very exact description of (the bias of) Maynard's almost eight-hundred-page novel, which tells the story of an exceptionally gifted mulatto by the name of Marius (a name that, interestingly enough, Maynard had already used in a short story to designate a *white* pirate captain).[56] Having been educated from a young age in England by the philanthropist Sir William Blackchester, the twenty-two-year-old Marius returns to Martinique in 1829, a year before the July Revolution, and finds himself in surroundings that are entirely unconducive to his "genius." Having angrily renounced his love for the passionate mulatress Flora once he finds out that she has prostituted herself to a series of men (at her white father-owner's behest), notably the incredibly dissolute young count, Charles de Longuefort, Marius instead marries one of the black slaves owned by the vicomte's kindly father, the marquis de Longuefort, who lives near Vauclin on the eastern side of the island, far from the cosmopolitan temptations of a city like Saint-Pierre. Marius's attempt at "rehabilitating" Jeannette fails miserably: she allows herself to be sexually corrupted by the count, whom Marius then kills in a moment of rage. Despite the suspicions cast on him, Marius gets away with his crime of passion and, having gained the trust and respect of the noble marquis, ends up securing the job of overseer on the Longuefort plantation, *la Estrella.* The return of the marquis's daughter Julie from France, where she has spent most of her life, brings about new complications: this highly educated young woman becomes the object of Marius's increasingly obsessive desire, and she herself haltingly returns his love, relatively immunized by a French education against the color prejudice that holds sway in the islands. His repentant wife has taken her own life; the vindictive Flora, still desperately enamored of him, has been momentarily sidelined: the way seems clear for Marius and Julie to flee to France where their love for one another could be legitimately consummated. However, her father has other plans for his daughter: unaware of her sentiments toward Marius, he tries to marry her off to a series of young men, all of whom the mulatto succeeds in poisoning, aided by a band of maroons with whom he has entered into a "satanic pact" (2.18). Julie begins to have her suspicions about Marius's role in these deaths, and falls more and more under the sway of creole prejudices, especially once she realizes—under the tutelage of Arthur de Brétigny, a mouthpiece for the more "liberal" (2.174) position that Maynard (self-)identifies with the younger generation of Creoles, who emerges as Marius's main "rival" (2.349) for Julie's affections—that the man she loves is nothing more than the "exception" who proves the rule about the "pariah" class to which he seems not to belong (2.163). Gaining in freneticism (and ludicrousness!) as it draws to a close, the novel ends with a fictional re-creation of the insurrection that broke out in Martinique in February 1831, a direct result (in Maynard's account) of the July Revolution in France, which had brought down the Bourbons the previous year. Marius helps organize the 1831 revolt in the hopes that it will allow him finally to gain possession of Julie, similar in this respect to many a protagonist in counterrevolutionary nineteenth- and twentieth-century novels whose "private dissatisfactions lead them to their vocations as political and revolutionary militants."[57] In an apocalyptic concluding chapter, the marquis's plantation is burned to the ground, Marius kills Julie when she refuses to be his, and then, after an old black woman recognizes him as the child she was forced to abandon and identifies the marquis as his father, puts an end to his own life.

In the novels of the colonists of Saint-Domingue and Martinique, as Glissant has noted, one often finds "an involuntary Parnassian element," "the same propensity to obliterate life in all its trembling agitation—that is to say, here, the turbulent realities of the Plantation—by emphasizing the scenery and its conventional splendor" (PR, p. 84). Despite the fact that Maynard does erase many of the signs of a turbulently creolized reality, most notably perhaps the language of Creole (as he alerts the reader in the novel's preface, "you will be grateful to me . . . for not having clouded the limpid waters of the French language with all those barbaric words, which would have dropped into it like so many rocks" [1.iv–v]),[58] the central focus in Outre-mer on interracial desire and a political rivalry between whites and mulattoes that proves inseparable from this desire ensures that Glissant's statement is of only partial help in understanding this novel. Before turning to Maynard's own anxiously dismissive treatment of Martiniquan mulattoes, "that despicable class, which dreams only of destroying the whites" (as the planter Pierre Dessalles described them in 1832 after hearing that Bissette "had asked the Chamber of Deputies to free the slaves"),[59] it will be useful to contextualize his portrait by reminding ourselves of Schœlcher's disturbingly similar account of the gens de couleur and mulattoes (he often treats the terms as synonymous) that only a few years later would find its way into his Des colonies françaises.

Schœlcher, clearly, found the existence of this intermediary class scandalous, inasmuch as it complicated the straightforward dichotomies (white master | black slave) upon which his abolitionist discourse depended. The gens de couleur are, he there notes, "almost all without family, the fruits of concubinage or of debauchery." The "mediocrity" of this class, he adds, "its still problematic manner of existence, its uselessness, its reprehensible morals, its lack of dignity and the small esteem merited by the majority of those who compose it, would up to a certain point explain the pride of the whites, if they had enough philosophic intelligence to separate the wheat from the chaff, if they were not as indulgent toward the degenerates of their own caste as they are merciless toward others" (p. 190). In its separation of the exception Marius from the mulatto rule (and its scathing portrait of the depraved count), Maynard's novel partially puts into practice this "philosophic intelligence," and it should not come as a surprise (as we will see a little later on) that Schœlcher had nothing but good things to say about the novel. To be sure, the abolitionist supplements his negative evaluation of the gens de couleur with more conciliatory statements in which he claims that the "evils" of their condition are in great part "imposed": "society is always half responsible for the crimes of individuals," he points out (p. 191), and his criticisms of "the idleness that devours and debases this race" are more often than not made with the understanding that this race is "the victim of a badly organized society" (p. 190). Noting that prejudice creates contempt, contempt demoralization, demoralization prostitution, which in turn legitimates the contempt through which the original prejudice is maintained, and armed with a belief in "the gradual improvement of the races through culture [le perfectionnement progressif des races par la culture], and in the transmission from one generation to the next of the degree of intelligence thus acquired" (p. 147), Schœlcher looks forward to the eventual amelioration of this "lazy and degraded" race under different social conditions. Such "progressive" caveats are perhaps understandably left out of Bissette's enraged account of this and similar passages in his Réfutation, which he (re)cites and defamiliarizes through a recourse to such typographical strategies as capitalization and italicization: for instance, "'Women of color, he says, who ALL live IN CONCUBINAGE or in A STATE OF DISSOLUTENESS, and to whom white men come seeking mistresses as if they were in a bazaar, contribute [certainly] by their libertinism to fostering the abasement of the races that they dishonor ... The tributes paid them by the privileged class flatter them, and they would rather give themselves to an old white man, without merit or quality, than to marry a man of mixed blood. Examples of the deplorable effects of this corruption are not hard to come by.'"[60] The abolitionist's descriptions of this intermediary class, Bissette concludes, "aim at nothing less than to blacken [flétrir] and discredit our progenitors, by referring to all of us as the fruit of debauchery and of libertinism, and to our mothers as base prostitutes."[61]

Here is not the place to choose between Schœlcher and Bissette—to uphold an outsider's right to tell the harsh "truth" about a "race" of people other than his own (or about his own, for that matter) or to reject such generalizing statements and the scientifically "progressive" or sociologically "understanding" arguments through which they are deviously rendered palatable—but simply to note the close affinities between Schœlcher

and Maynard's visions of this "infamous class." In a letter to his English
mentor that takes up an early chapter of *Outre-mer*, Marius confirms that
the women of his caste "are all prostitutes" (1.66), adding with irony that
they "have turned adultery and debauchery into such a universal trade that
such vices have in this country taken on the extraordinary appearance of
good conduct" (1.67). If virtually everything in the novel confirms the fact
that, as the novel's narrator notes, explicitly recalling the words of Marius's
letter, "the privilege of libertinism is something that all women of color
have in common" (1.142), such "vice" is also at points traced back (as in
Schœlcher) to a source that explains and partially justifies it, as when Marius states in his letter that it is the whites' "purses that keep these weeds
alive and that feed them; it is their hands that pluck them in order to add
spice to their nightly orgies" (1.68)—a claim that is corroborated by the
novel's disapproving portrayal of Charles de Longuefort and the "seraglio"
that he keeps at his luxurious house in Saint-Pierre. Notwithstanding such
caveats, the appeals to endemic prostitution in Schœlcher and Maynard obviously signal a fetishistic engagement with (black) female sexuality that is
all the more apparent in Maynard's novel given that the dynamics of narrative allow him more openly to express (while ostensibly condemning) this
sexuality. The apparently solid truths of Schœlcher's account give way to
the ambivalence of a fiction in which the possibility of contagion that the
femme de couleur poses, and the moral sanction she demands, is itself inseparably (con)fused with the sexual promise she alluringly renders visible.
This scandalous (con)fusion, the ambivalent sensation of repulsion *and* attraction provoked by these women and their "overfree way of dressing"
(e.g., "the madras that lavishes upon the spectator the bounties of their
neck, the billowing lace that is pierced by their bosom . . . " [1.66]), is central to *Outre-mer*, but it does not pose the most overt threat to the creole
identity that Maynard is attempting to consolidate in his novel, even if the
generalized anxieties about eviration and feminization that typify a fin de
siècle work like Huysman's *À rebours* (1884) are already embodied in the
figure of the debauched count (who, "with the coquetry and the puerile
vanity of a young girl, adorns himself with lace, . . . with earrings that he
was not ashamed of wearing, . . . with gold chains that hung loosely over
his shoulders and that put the finishing touches on his resemblance to a
frail creature at her lying-in [*une femmelette en couches*]" [1.161–62]).
Rather, it is the *man* of color and the mimetic rivalry linking him to the
"pure" Creole that produces the most violent textual reactions on the part
of Maynard, whose every attempt at differentiating these rivals from himself testifies to their growing indifferentiation. Unlike Maynard, it should
be added, whose claiming of a creole identity in the face of his mulatto rivals testifies to an almost conscious awareness of the relatedness of these

two identities, the Schœlcher of *Des colonies françaises* is an author who believes himself to be without rivals, who feels no doubts concerning his own identity or that of those about whom he speaks with such knowing authority. However, by the late 1840s, as we shall see toward the end of this chapter, Bissette will have forced the white abolitionist into a (re)active dialogue in which the fiction of this autonomous identity can no longer be maintained.

Maynard's vitriolic portraits of the hommes de couleur (a term that he is careful to remind his readers comprises all free people who are not white, be they black or mulatto [2.300], but that nonetheless most often simply functions in his text as a synonym for mulattoes) up to a certain point correspond with the "facts" of Martiniquan history, just as Schœlcher's analysis of the role of "la caste jaune" in postrevolutionary Haiti does not strike us today as particularly unreasonable. Speaking of the situation in 1829, for instance, Maynard's narrator notes that a good many hommes de couleur were themselves slaveholders and that even though they had taken to allying themselves with the truly oppressed class this was only in order to further their own agenda of achieving "the abolition of certain of the whites' privileges and the creation of certain advantages for themselves, civil and political rights among others." "But of slavery, which was the real issue for the Negroes," the narrator adds, "they did not breathe a word" (2.173). We find a version of this same criticism at work, say, in Glissant's *Quatrième siècle*, when the narrator, describing a slave revolt, notes that "the mulattoes, half freed from the terrifying yoke of this society, were going to take part in the affair, but only with their own prospects in mind, not hesitating when necessary to bay alongside the [colonists'] dogs" (p. 101). As is not the case with Glissant's novel, however, the particular psychological complex that is responsible for generating these "historical" descriptions is readily identifiable. In its analysis of the hommes de couleur as self-interested mimic men, envious doubles of their white compatriots ("The gens de couleur are the biggest copycats [*singes*] in the world. Whatever the whites do, they are sure to imitate it" [2.157]), *Outre-mer* embarrassingly displays the origins of its own production: a fear of social and racial indifferentiation, and the consequent resentment felt toward those who provoke this fear (or desire, in the case of the woman of color). Every theory of ressentiment, as Fredric Jameson once remarked in his analysis of the late-Victorian novelist George Gissing's anxious portrayals of the lower classes, is always also "the expression and the production of *ressentiment*";[62] given this "unavoidably autoreferential structure," everything Maynard has to say about the resentful, envious, mimetic (and so on) identity of the gens de couleur and, especially, the mulattoes in *Outre-mer* ultimately needs to be read in terms of displaced autobiography, as a projection onto the rival

class of his own fears (and desires) in a gesture of expulsion that must ultimately be understood in terms of René Girard's analysis of the scapegoat.

As Girard has pointed out, "it is never their actual difference for which
religious, ethnic, national minorities are blamed, it is for not differing in the
right way, ultimately even, for not differing at all." "Contrary to what people keep on saying," he argues, "it is never difference that obsesses the per-
secutors, but always the unspeakable opposite of difference, its absence."[63]
In colonial societies, the mulatto has always embodied this threatening erosion of difference, this unspeakable "indifférenciation."[64] The proper characteristic of the class to which the mulatto belongs, as the narrator points
out in the first chapter of *Outre-mer* when describing the historical emergence of this class, is that it lacks one: "Soon a third class emerged between
the masters and the slaves, between those two classes that were two extremely clear and distinct principles; but the new element did not have a
character of its own [*n'avait pas de caractère propre*], for if it stemmed
from the master, it also stemmed from the slave. It was white and black at
one and the same time—in short, it was *mulatto*" (1.25). The mulatto's
newly legitimized political status in the early 1830s aggravated this threat
of a "character-less" indifferentiation and caused a heightening of the
scapegoat mechanisms necessary for disposing of the mulatto's (lack of)
difference; Maynard's textual violence is provoked by the postrevolutionary
world in which, epidermal distinctions apart (and even then, as the possibility of "passing" testifies, these could not always be taken for granted),
the difference "of one who is truly a Creole" (1.26; "du créole proprement
dit") from the free person of color had been substantially put into question.

This specifically colonial inflection of the problem of postrevolutionary
(lack of) difference is itself overdetermined in Maynard's novel by his acute
awareness of the political leveling that was going on at this same time on
the other side of the Atlantic and of the social identities through which this
indifferentiation was making itself felt there. One such identity was that of
the dandy, a figure that Maynard transposes from Europe to the Caribbean.
As the narrator tells us, "usually each mulatto has his own dandy for a
model, after whom he fashions himself so exactly and so conscientiously
that it is a rare thing if he does not become the dandy's double [*Sosie*]"
(2.157); the upstart mulatto lacks presence, he is nothing more than a (bad)
representation, the "living portrait, color excepted" (2.158), of his white
"dandy modèle," who is, as Maynard is well aware, nothing more than a
mimic man who himself follows European models (as his critical portrait of
one of Julie's suitors, "that flower of creole dandyism grafted onto Parisian
fashions" [2.22], makes clear). The dandy is a contaminated and contaminating figure, product of a mimesis that in turn generates further imitations: as Christopher Prendergast has argued, the dandy is "the focus of an

uncertainty of perception, of recognition and classification that, as the century unfolds, will become a veritable 'perceptual panic,' in which the basic categories of social distinction go into a kind of vertiginous spin."[65] Such perceptual panic can be resolved only through an arbitrary reimposition of difference (hence, say, the antisemitic emphasis of much nineteenth-century literature).[66] Maynard's willingness to acknowledge that the mimetic contagion is not merely limited to the mulattoes with whom both his creole compatriots and European commentators traditionally associated it but has already spilled over into his own class is one sign among many of the *limited honesty* of a novel that often borders on the self-recognition it must repeatedly reject in its attempts at asserting a less vertiginous vision of the world. This simpler vision would be one in which, to cite Peter Brooks's description of the "hyberbolic" genre of melodrama (which he defines as the "mode of the excluded middle"), "there is no place for moral indifference or nuance; there are only pure, unadulterated moral positions."[67] If the melodramatic imagination triumphs in a novel like *Outre-mer*, this victory (that is to say, this defeat) is by no means an unadulterated one: in emphasizing the mimetic relations that obtain between supposedly different (moral, social, racial) positions, Maynard cannot help drawing our attention to the "middle" that he would exclude (himself from), an "impure" place where the differences upon which racism (and a certain antiracism) would ground themselves can no longer be secured because the self has been always-already defined in relation to its other(s).

This relational definition of the self is (in Girard's words) the "novelistic truth" about identity that gets explored in the work of major nineteenth-century writers like Stendhal and Flaubert; rejecting this truth, many of Stendhal's and Flaubert's contemporaries embrace the "Romantic lie" of the exceptional (heroic or villainous) individual, (re)actively opposing to the relational (mimetic) self one finds in *Le rouge et le noir* and *Madame Bovary* an autonomous individual forcefully differentiated from all those lesser selves who remain susceptible to the inauthentic representations of postrevolutionary mass society.[68] Hugo was deeply committed to this Romantic exceptionalism (which is itself linked to what Girard calls "the Hugolian, righter-of-wrongs conception of the novel" [*MR*, p. 102]—a melodramatic conception, in Brooks's sense of the word, that feels empowered to differentiate between "pure, unadulterated moral positions"), and in centering his novel around an exceptional character like Marius Maynard was clearly imitating his literary master, as critics were quick to point out, although not always to the same end. If the *Revue des Colonies* noted that "it is evident . . . that Monsieur Louis de Maynard de Queilhe is an intimate friend of Monsieur Victor Hugo; he treats his friend in an offhanded manner, borrowing his best ideas only to spoil them" (II.vi: 282), it was simply in order to ridicule Maynard as someone who "has borrowed like a plagiarist and a schoolboy." For Guéroult in the *Revue de Paris*, by contrast, Maynard's deference to Hugo provided an excuse to attack the Romantic, melodramatic exceptionalism that the older writer had "systematized" (p. 187). "One finds in him the same poetics as in Monsieur Hugo," the reviewer notes, explaining the underlying reasons for the novel's lack of verisimilitude: "Marius definitely comes from that notorious family of heroes composed of a half part vice and a half part virtue, and who embody the inexplicable union of all the extremes, of pride, strength, noble ambition, and of cowardice, cruelty, and ingratitude." Guéroult finds this understanding of human nature "utterly false and monstrous," an attempt at "coupling together faculties that are mutually exclusive, and seeking out, through the jangling of artificial oppositions, effects that are not to be found in nature; in following this process one ends up with personified antitheses rather than human beings, for whom nature, rich as she is in contrasts, has provided gradations of feeling, nuances and transitions, which alone testify to and preserve identity" (p. 188).[69] Compromised and unoriginal, too open to the sort of mimetic contagion that he had stumbled upon in *Bug-Jargal* and then quickly suppressed in the process of fashioning his own authoritative authorial identity as French Romanticism's chef d'école, the nuanced transitional identity for which this reviewer argues could not satisfy a writer like Hugo. Following in his master's footsteps, however, leads Maynard into the paradoxical situation of having to present his mulatto protagonist as a "man of genius," immune to the contagion of mimetic desire that afflicts his fellow mulattoes: Marius can be a hero and a villain but he cannot be a mimic man. He escapes the stereotypical condition to which his identity as a mulatto ought to have doomed him; as with the eroticized madras, Maynard's openness to European literary models thus troubles the hierarchies and boundaries that would be maintained in a more properly native creolist discourse, in which the words "genius" and "mulatto" simply could not be yoked together. At the same time, however, as a Creole whose sense of identity is endangered by the rival class, Maynard is incapable of just expunging the problem of mimesis from his novel; indeed, its pervasive presence in the text threatens to undermine the Romantic lie that makes a "superior" being like Marius possible in the first place.

Given Maynard's mimetic commitment to Hugo's exceptionalist poetics, there is nothing particularly surprising about the way in which he describes his twenty-two-year-old protagonist, who is possessed of "the intelligence of a rebellious Satan" (1.350) and of a "furious passion" (2.53) that has its origin in himself rather than in the desire of others. "Extreme in all things, in good as in evil, after the crime as before the remorse," Marius is "a beast and a god at one and the same time" (2.42; "une bête et un dieu à la fois").

"This mulatto, it must not be forgotten, was not a man like any other," the narrator reminds his readers; "he was the very image of those intense sites that nature offers, full of precipices, poisonous plants, and deadly animals, but a place where one must nonetheless go to search out the most esteemed marvels of this world" (2.16). Produced by a nineteenth-century (white) creole writer, however, such descriptions *do* surprise, and Maynard clearly felt compelled to supplement his portrait of Marius as naturally superior with a more realistic explanation of the mulatto's talents, which places the emphasis not on an innate nature (as when Marius's relation to his fellow mulattoes is described in terms of a crime that "every man of genius commits by the very act of being born and for which the rest of humanity makes a point of punishing him throughout the course of his life. This crime was that of being superior to them" [2.288]), but on the anomalous education he received in England, the country "where I was happy and free, where my mind was enriched and enlarged" (1.43). Supplementing the Hugolian novel of extremes is a Bildungsroman in which natural genius is reenvisioned as part of a socially *constructed* identity that, in theory at least, can be arrived at by anyone.

The Bildungsroman attempts to grapple with, to accommodate, what would have been unthinkable under the ancien régime: the potentially upward mobility of even the most marginal of individuals. As Jean-Michel Racault points out in a discussion of Dumas's *Georges*, "the mulatto's racial bastardy is equivalent to the social bastardy from which the characters in Stendhal or Balzac often suffer,"[70] and Marius's search for recognition in many respects resembles that of a Julien Sorel or a Lucien de Rubempré, although for obvious reasons a writer like Dumas can more sympathetically explore the possibilities of mulatto Bildung (while remaining, like Maynard, contradictorily committed to a Romantic, essentially static vision of his "satanically proud" [pp. 318, 404] protagonist). As Jack Corzani has remarked, Maynard's is a "perspective loaded with flagrant contradictions."[71] Nowhere is this more apparent than in his intermittent recourse to the concept of Bildung as a supplementary explanation for Marius's natural genius: these appeals to Bildung reattach Marius's Romantic identity to the problem of mimeticism, in the form of a European education that, while it might alienate individual gens de couleur from their native surroundings (as Maynard argues with a certain satisfaction in *Outre-mer* and as Schœlcher also argued, while deploring the fact),[72] could only strengthen their position on the island were it to be applied in a comprehensive rather than occasional fashion. Acknowledging the empowering effects of (a necessarily mimetic) education in the case of Marius, Maynard must nonetheless resist this power not only because it puts into question his Hugolian poetics but because it renders new social relations possible: new dispositions of political power and, as the case of Julie and her "French education" (1.330) makes clear, of sexual desire.

One contemporary commentator noted of the creole protagonist of George Sand's *Indiana* (1832), "in our day education is making itself felt everywhere; nobody escapes from it. Indiana could thus only be imagined as a Creole, that is to say, someone born and raised in the heart of a society that in terms of its moral development is almost nonexistent."[73] The exotic difference of Indiana's name contrasts sharply with the unoriginality of Julie's, which pointedly directs us back to Rousseau's *Nouvelle Héloïse* (1761), insinuating that she is a creature of fiction, one whose identity is indissociable from the books that she has read and that have initiated her into the possibility of interracial desire. If, according to the marquis, his debauched son was someone who had "some Werther in his veins" (1.332), Julie, with her "excessive love for Shakespeare and Byron," is someone who has been well prepared for the role of Desdemona, as the fact that she has read *Othello* suggests (1.332–33). Maynard is acutely aware of the way in which works of literature provide their readers with a mimetic stimulus, leading them to acquire, in Girard's words, "an irresistible tendency to desire what *Others* desire, that is to say, to imitate their desires" (*MR*, p. 21). *Outre-mer* is scattered with insights into the workings of mimetic desire, as the following explanation of why the nearly total nakedness of many of the young black men on the island has no effect on creole women:

Education, which has been rightly termed a second nature, would be highly dangerous for a European woman, but protects their creole counterparts. They are not told: do not fall in love with a man of color. They are told nothing: they grow up in the midst of these slaves, and alongside these freed men; their hearts are in bloom, and [yet] they do not fall in love with them. Does prejudice blind these women, or disfigure the men? Be that as it may, this is the way things are. (1.349)

Maynard's narrator here—in line with Sand's *Indiana*—identifies creole women with an education that consists in a complete lack of education, a second nature that could almost be conflated with nature itself. No doubt inadequate as a description of colonial realities, this passage nonetheless amply suggests the mimetic origins of (in this case, interracial) desire, and even raises the possibility at the end, with surprising candor, that the *lack* of this desire on the part of creole women might itself be the result of an unnatural "prejudice," a colonial form of vanity that "disfigures" what is neither desirable nor undesirable in and of itself, and that renders it undesirable simply because it is not desired by others. Having lived in France most of her life, Julie does not share these prejudices (or this natural lack of inclination toward men of color, as the case may be): her French education has prepared her to desire Marius, and from the moment she sees him engaged in the heroic task of saving sailors from a hurricane-wrecked ship (a heroism that he later confirms when he sucks deadly venom from her snake-bitten foot), she is overcome by a passion for him from which only the most hideous of his actions can dissuade her, and perhaps not even those (her dying words, after all, are "Mon Marius. . . . Je t'aimais!" [2.376]).

Unlike the case of her literary predecessor and Saint-Preux, if Maynard's Julie allows Marius to gain hold of her heart ("I felt you taking possession of my heart as if it were a house that belonged to you" [2.104]) full access to it is predictably denied him. Marius's desire to enter into this house, which would accomplish at the personal level what he desires at the political level ("we must be treated as full-fledged citizens" [2.282; "il faut que nous soyons reçus dans la cité"], he proclaims in a letter to the "committee of the Saint-Pierre mulattoes" in which he agrees to participate in their revolt after it becomes clear that the July Revolution has aborted and will not result in substantial social change for the colonies), is in great part thwarted because Julie's "second nature" never fully wins out over her creole origins: "they had never been able entirely to shape this creole woman according to French fashions" (1.289), the narrator observes. No less than Sand's Indiana, Julie retains a visceral link to Caribbean nature, her first nature, which is reanimated upon her return to the islands after her brother's death: "between this nature and this girl," the narrator notes, "it was evident that there existed an insoluble bond, relations as necessary as those between mother and daughter and such that, ultimately, she had either to live in the Antilles or not live at all" (1.290–91). This renewal of her affinities with Caribbean nature is part of a process of (re)creolization in which she slowly absorbs social prejudices that, unlike those of her compatriots, Maynard cannot simply finesse as natural, given her previous education into other ways of life. As Flora explains to a disbelieving Marius, "little by little, I can tell, she is turning into a Creole [*elle se fait créole*]. That should say it all to you. The Frenchwoman loves you; the Creole will hate you, because you will have made her blush" (2.150). This process is at one with what we might call her de-Bovaryization as, under the tutelage of Marius's rival Arthur, Julie's illusions about mulattoes in general, if not Marius in particular, fall "like a veil from her eyes." Those whom she sees in Saint-Pierre "hardly corresponded with the poetic images that she had formed of their feelings and their manners; they played their part of victim so badly, they overturned so completely the ideas that had been suggested to her in France and the fantasies that she had been entertaining since her arrival in Martinique" (2.162). She has begun to realize the anomalous situation in which her (mimetically induced) desire has placed her ("you now know enough about the colonies," the narrator reminds us after Marius's declaration of love, "to understand just how strange, how unprecedented, how monstrous a mulatto declaring his love to a white woman was! Many colonists, on hearing of such a thing, would have refused to believe it," despite the manner in which they themselves "pour out their hearts and lavish their money on mulatresses" [1.348]). As a consequence, the man for whom she has "alienated" her heart begins to seem undesirable to her, notwithstanding his apparent likeness to the love-objects about whom she has read. Julie falls prey to that desire-according-to-the-other known as vanity, as Marius himself points out when the tide begins to turn against him: "it is out of vanity that you will not marry me, because you are in love with your titles, with being called lady and viscountess" [2.221]. Maynard cannot fully abandon Julie to this vanity, of course, because to do so would be to put into question the autonomy of her passion for Marius, a necessary prerequisite for the Romantic heroine that Maynard ultimately, insights into mimetic desire notwithstanding, wants to portray her as: she will, in her own way, love him until the end—an end that Maynard can only render in apocalyptic terms that directly contrast with the utopian conclusion of Sand's *Indiana*, with its evocation of an Île Bourbon that seems indistinguishable from the Île de France of Paul and Virginie's pastoral childhood.[74]

The novel's violent dénouement is only the last in a series of plot developments that conspire against Marius and his passion for Julie. That Maynard repeatedly thwarts the transgressive narrative he has set in motion is to be expected, but one of the more surprising aspects of *Outre-mer* is that its author has no definitive argument to make against the interracial relationship around which his novel revolves. Ultimately, he can only argue against it by invoking the relativistic concept of local customs that are not natural but, as he repeatedly acknowledges, something that one is educated into and can thus be educated out of: unobjectionable, or at the very least acceptable, in France, Marius and Julie's love is "wrong" only in the racially charged context of a society like that of Martinique. After Julie confesses to Arthur that she loves, and is loved by, a mulatto, he reacts in a predictably negative manner, while assuring her that the fault is not hers but that of "the education you were given, which left you defenseless against a seduction that was, certainly, unexpected but not entirely inconceivable" (2.248). And yet Arthur, one of the young Creoles who "were not hostile to any ideas involving improvement and progress" (2.168) and who are agreed that the "old colonial system" can and must be transformed (2.169), has no objections in theory to such a relationship: "as should be clear to you by now," he tells her, "I don't have any deep-rooted prejudices." "Your great-granddaughter," he concedes, "could perhaps marry his great-grandson, such things could well happen. But at present nothing of the sort is possible" (2.246–47). Here we have an argument that is very much in accord with Schœlcher's gradualist position at this time regarding the abolition of slavery: the ideal of *fusion* that is so dear to Marius's heart ("Let everything be held in common by the three classes! Let us unite them through marriages," he self-servingly enthuses at one point [2.206]) is not ruled out but simply deferred and thereby effectively legitimized.

To be sure, as Schœlcher's abandonment of his original argument in the 1840s testifies, such gradualism may well do no more than strengthen the status quo, and it is uncertain—and perhaps even doubtful—whether Maynard's thinking would have evolved any further had he lived beyond the age of twenty-six, but (as his acknowledgment of the purely customary nature of the island's sexual taboos bears witness) it had already evolved far enough to have identified the contradictory (lack of a) ground upon which his (white) creole identity was founded. Schœlcher himself would nostalgically suggest this in *Des colonies françaises* when he cited *Outre-mer* as corroborating his own argument that in the struggle "of the weak man against the strong man who is oppressing him any weapon is fair game," and that assassination is a "défense légitime" (p. 122). For Schœlcher, slavery creates a situation in which the weak are able to "represent" themselves only through "open violence or covert poisonings" (p. 123), and it is precisely because its existence "justifies any and all crimes that it must be abolished" (p. 122). Among the white ruling class, he goes on to note, there are those "who are courageous enough to admit this terrible truth": "scarcely four or five years ago, one of their most distinguished offspring admitted 'rebellion as the slave's right,' in a book where one finds both heart and talent" (p. 123).[75] Maynard's recognition in *Outre-mer* that slavery was the "real plague of the colonies" (2.173), his inability to ground the argument against "amalgamation," or "miscegenation" (as it would eventually [1864] come to be called in the United States), in anything more than relativizing appeals to custom, are but two of the most visible faultlines in a novel that can no longer effectively uphold or fully accredit the patriarchal and segregationist way of life to which it nonetheless remains in large part committed.

Soon after his nostalgic invocation of Maynard, Schœlcher launches into an attack against the religious and scientific arguments in favor of slavery— arguments that approach the problem in an absolute rather than a relativistic manner. We will have occasion at the end of this chapter to mention one of the religious shibboleths that Schœlcher takes on (the damnation of Noah's son Ham and all his [black] descendants); Schœlcher's main "scientific" target in *Des colonies françaises* is the doctor Jules-Joseph Virey, who—"driven by a sort of anatomical hatred of the Negro" (p. 139)—insisted that blacks were an intermediate species between man and monkey.[76] Such arguments, which gave a dangerous new legitimacy to the ressentiment that undergirds colonial relations, had become increasingly prominent over the first three decades of the nineteenth century and would culminate in the full-fledged emergence of racial theory in the 1840s and 1850s. The first half of the nineteenth century, a time of political amelioration that saw the abolition of the slave trade and then of slavery itself in much of the New World, also witnessed a reciprocal diminishment of positive discussions of race and métissage. As Nicholas Thomas has pointed out, a shift "is apparent from the late Enlightenment onwards . . . that saw an ambivalent array of attitudes, including humanitarian and appreciative assessments as well as more negative judgements, displaced by a more uniform, intolerant, and less subtle denigration of those whose physical inferiority and moral faults were unmistakable."[77] In a similar vein, Maurice Mauviel has noted that the relatively positive assessments of cultural contact and borrowings that one finds in late-eighteenth-century French thought (he cites *idéologues* such as the Comte de Volney and Jean-François Thurot but he could just as easily have pointed to Bernardin), and which find expression, for instance, in Thurot's claim (made in 1800) that "racial mixing [*le mélange des races*] is perhaps the most effective method of changing and ameliorating human nature," gradually give way to ideas based on "opposition, differentiation, antagonism."[78]

There are certainly traces of a properly racist vision in Maynard's novel—notably, the occasional appeal to the mulatto's African "instincts": at one point, for instance, an action of Marius's is attributed to "the ferocious nature of the African, [which] burst the barriers built up by education" (1.210), and Flora's passion is said to "reveal in all its violence the African blood that smouldered under her skin" (1.35). Furthermore, early on in the novel, in Marius's letter to his English mentor, Blackchester is chastized for his philanthropy because "scientists, phrenologists, and doctors had assured you that the facial angle of the mulatto is less open than the facial angle of the white man, and had concluded, and I must say rightly, that our intelligence is lesser than that of those who dominate us" (1.56–57). Damning as such appeals to an instinctively racial nature and to phrenology may be, however, they are more notable for their virtual absence from the novel (and this single appeal to scientific arguments is itself inherently problematic inasmuch as it is attributed to the self-alienated Marius and is not, unlike several of the other comments in his letter, given narratorial sanction elsewhere). The absolutes of racial science, which helped both in Europe and in the colonies to perpetuate a social order that political transformations had revealed as purely arbitrary, cannot yet fully assert themselves in Maynard's novel. *Outre-mer* is situated, as it were, between what Julie refers to as the "sacred customs of her country" (2.225), which were evidently undergoing a process of desacralization whereby their arbitrary nature was becoming increasingly apparent, and whatever might be thought to come after those customs, be it an admission of their inadequacy and a consequent insistence on change (as with Schœlcher), or their resacralization in the form of a racialized science that, among other things, attempted to suppress the "colonial desire" (in Robert Young's phrase) that is so openly and disturbingly on display in a novel like *Outre-mer*.[79]

As Glissant has noted in the *Poétique*, contrasting oral and popular literature in the Caribbean with its "elitist and written" (white) counterpart, "the colonists and Planters, as well as the travelers who visited them, were obsessed with the need to justify the system" (p. 84). Maynard's novel gives expression to a moment of historical transition in which this need is felt but cannot be effectively realized. Haunted by what Glissant calls the colonist's "fantasy of legitimacy," Maynard—who dedicates *Outre-mer* "to my father"—attempts through the act of writing to establish a continuity with the past and to replicate the father's supposedly legitimate authority (the "message" of his novel, he notes in his preface, "is not hostile to any of the camps, it is entirely paternal. If you will pardon the conceit, the youngest priests are called *fathers*" [1.vi]). And yet Maynard can only aspire *after* this absolute authority; the lack of legitimacy upon which his own identity is founded makes itself felt time and time again in *Outre-mer*—at the most decisive level, perhaps, in his original choice of that "most bastard" of symbolic forms (to recall our discussion of Moretti in Chapter 3), the relativized and relativizing genre of the novel, as the medium for conveying his paternal vision. Incapable of openly acknowledging his own illegitimacy, Maynard displaces it onto a figure like Marius, who ultimately must be read as an autobiographical projection of his author; nowhere is this illegitimacy more visible in the novel, however, than in the figure of the Marquis's son, the "Comte de la Négraille," whose transgressive conduct testifies to the anxieties that went into the production of *Outre-mer* and that make it such a psychologically revealing document. Even the scathing review of the novel in the *Revue des Colonies* felt compelled to point out that, in the character of Charles de Longuefort, Maynard "has not only slandered the hommes de couleur, he has done the same to the whites" (II.vi: 283–84). The count's nocturnal banquet, in which—as the Marquis exclaims before disowning his son—he goes so far as "to mix in even the Lord's texts with the filthy ravings of your wine-drenched couplings" (1.181), and that culminates in the mock-circumcision of a terrified black servant, strikes Bissette as a dangerously excessive portrait of the white ruling classes on the island:

We have (God be thankful!) enough reproaches to level at the white colonists, without needing to have them accused of such disgusting acts. No class, in the colonies, is capable of serving as the model for this portrait, which the author has borrowed from the appalling novels of the Marquis de Sade. Never would a Negress, a mulatress, or a white woman consent to the scenes of debauchery that Monsieur Louis de Maynard has painted. (p. 284)

Whether one wishes to agree with Bissette or not in his estimation of how disgustingly the white colonists might be capable of acting, Maynard's inclusion of this entire scene is an exemplary instance of what I have called his limited honesty, which gives indirect expression to what he cannot simply suppress: the illegitimacy of his own creole identity and its transgressive desires.

The sumptuous *hôtel* in which the count's orgiastic banquet takes place is located in the city of Saint-Pierre, which is portrayed in the novel as the preferred site of the island's mulatto population (with the exception of Marius, to be sure, who shuns it in favor of the countryside). At as far a remove as possible from the paternal estate of Vauclin, the bustling port of Saint-Pierre is—as is so often the case with Maynard—represented in an overdetermined fashion: the Caribbean town takes on many of the features of a *modern* European city, and this partial translation of the modern metropolis to the modernizing colonies has the effect of further highlighting the problem of indifferentiation that is at the core of the novel's anxieties. The nineteenth-century city was a place in which both social and geographical distances between the various classes were visibly closing. As one critic puts it, for the nineteenth-century bourgeoisie "the problem of contamination was bound up with the 'movement' of people through the city"; "the city was a site and sight of promiscuity: people 'mixed' in public spaces."[80] Maynard conveys a sense of this unsettling mixture in, for instance, his description of the city's courtyards (*cours*), "inundated" with billeted slaves, free people of color, and young white men who have housed "their pleasures and their debauchery" there. "Veritable thieves' dens, places that will lead to Saint-Pierre's ruin" (1.143), these yards—the sort of location that would be transformed into a carnivalesque zone of equality in a postmodern novel like Chamoiseau's *Texaco*[81]—provoke the narrator's disapproving rhetoric, but such indictments must nonetheless be read alongside several impassioned descriptions of the city in which a fascination with it, one that is also filtered through the perverse figure of the count, is more openly expressed (as when, for instance, contrasting Saint-Pierre with Fort-Royal [present-day Fort-de-France], "an old soldier that has settled under our sunny skies and who would be a thousand times happier watching the grey sky of his homeland" [1.18], the narrator identifies it—or rather "her"—as "populous, elegant, rich, joyful, and wild: a true Creole [*C'est une véritable créole*]" [1.17]). Provoking mixed emotions of fear and desire that cannot be disentangled from one another, the nineteenth-century city is a "highly mobile, ceaselessly 'turning' landscape . . . in which the perception of ranks and occupations, origins and identities, can no longer reliably orientate itself within a fixed structure of differentiation."[82]

This mixed site, symptomatic of "a universe in which, little by little, the differences between men are being obliterated," is a place where what René Girard has called "internal mediation" triumphs, a place in which fixed structures of differentiation (father | son; model | imitator; bourgeois | proletariat; black | white) have become increasingly fragile, and where formerly separate spheres "interpenetrate one another" (*MR*, pp. 23, 18). In the absence of these structures emerges a world inundated with increasingly undifferentiated rivals who mirror one another in their desires, a mimetic world of envy and vengeance ("which is always only the inverted copy of the first persecutory representation, its mimetic repetition"),[83] a world of *doubles* that Maynard's novel dimly envisions in its evocation of the "rival brothers" theme, which links Marius and Charles at the level of biology, and Marius and Arthur at the level of politics. This, as Girard puts it in a revealing metaphor, is the world of the melting pot (*creuset*):

Double mediation is a melting pot in which differences between classes and individuals slowly melt away. It works all the better in that it does not, to all appearances, interfere with diversity. Indeed, it lends to [diversity] a new but deceptive sheen: the opposition of the Same to the Same, which is everywhere triumphant, for a long time conceals itself behind traditional oppositions, which thus experience a violent revival and keep up a belief in the past's integral survival. (*MR*, pp. 127–28)

The relevance of these comments to the current obsession with multiculturalism, or the genocides in Bosnia, Rwanda, or Algeria, should be obvious, but Girard is here specifically describing Stendhal's vision of the French Restoration, in which "the old families, in a fiercer manner than ever before, set about marking the barriers separating them from the common people" (p. 128), and in which a fetishistic attention was paid to the outward, mechanical signs of difference. The obsession with such signs, however, itself confirms "the modern trend toward the identical" that these "impassioned divisions" exemplify: the very act of comparison, through which the superiority or simply the difference of one class of men is "proved" at the expense of another, attests to the fact that the superiority or difference that is being asserted is already in the process of being lost. To put oneself in a position of comparison, as Girard points out, is to assert the very equality, the very likeness, that one is attempting to refute: "in order to see oneself as superior to other men, a comparison is necessary; but to compare things is to draw the things being compared closer, to put them on the same level and, to a certain extent, to treat them identically." "One cannot deny men's equality with one another," he concludes, in a statement that nicely sums up the underlying irony of a novel like *Outre-mer*, "without first assuming it, howsoever fleetingly" (p. 122).

If I have chosen to end my account of Maynard's long-forgotten novel with a rehearsal of ideas that Girard put forward almost forty years ago it is not only because they are of obvious relevance to the Romantic era in which Maynard wrote but because these ideas have a seldomly acknowledged (in postcolonial theory, at least) relevance to an understanding of our own globally hybridized age. The negative flip side of the *chaos-monde* of relationality that a writer like Glissant privileges is the undifferentiated world that Girard describes, in which ever more violent attempts at recuperating past "differences" lead to catastrophic impasses similar to those explored, from a particularly unsympathetic perspective, in a novel like *Outre-mer*. Perhaps one cannot simply distinguish between (good) relationality and (bad) indifferentiation; perhaps our survival (if not our salvation) depends upon maintaining the volatile balance between them and self-consciously negotiating the contradictions of a post/colonial condition that provokes inextricable mixtures of desire and fear. Perhaps this negotiation is impossible without an understanding that the violence and ressentiment we are only too happy to identify with others is nothing more than a mirror-image of our own; and perhaps this understanding alone might be that which allows us to move, if not beyond, then to the side of that "almost apocalyptical vision," in Corzani's words,[84] that dominates a novel like *Outre-mer* from beginning to end—an end in which nothing and no one survives, with the exception of Arthur (and here, to be sure, is a perfect instance of Maynard's narcissistic bad faith as a novelist), who leaves for Brazil a month after the aborted insurrection, resuming "his life of adventures and travels" (2.393). In this recourse to exoticism, one that would become increasingly popular as the century drew to a close and the modernity that Maynard already identifies with France *and* Martinique came to seem ever more widely diffused, the author of *Outre-mer* preserves the (illusory) possibility of an heroic and nonmimetic individuality, but only at the cost of abandoning his native island and transforming the condition of exile into his flattering alter ego's sole remaining home.

How to end differently? That is the primary question that I will be addressing in the following chapter, which puts into question without attempting to disperse the apocalyptic imagination that one finds in a writer like Maynard. Reactionary as it might appear, this imagination is nonetheless, I would suggest, a revolutionary one. Peter Brooks has identified melodrama as "the genre—and the rhetoric—of revolutionary moralism because it states, enacts, and imposes its moral messages in clear, unambiguous words and signs"; the writer of melodrama shares the Jacobin vision of a world that is "defined by a vast Manichaean struggle of light and darkness."[85] Maynard's counterrevolutionary novel manifests this same logic, and yet, as I have tried to point out in a variety of ways, also marks the failure of melodrama in its inability to impose a clear message, in the difficulty it has distinguishing properly between "light and darkness," notwithstanding its eagerness to do so. The final struggle leads not to the victory of one over the other, but to the annihilation of both—and only in this act of total destruction can the novel restore the order after which it longs. An unacceptably high price to pay, no doubt, and one that does little to satisfy the aesthetic demands of our modern sensibilities. That Maynard was capable of writing other, more satisfying endings—endings that remain committed, but less visibly so, to the same apocalyptic vision with which *Outre-mer* comes to a stop—is evident, however, if we turn to the conclusion of his short story "Scènes nocturnes aux Antilles."

In this story, the mulatto Jupiter, who has led an unsuccessful slave revolt and been the cause of an innocent young creole woman's death, is forgiven his many crimes by the colonial authorities who are only too happy to legitimize him, as the final lines of the story emphasize by drawing us into a degraded and politicized present tense:

C'est aujourd'hui un *monsieur*, à qui le gouverneur a décerné les épaulettes d'officier de milice. Sa vénérable *épouse* est morte à l'hôpital, et, pour opérer la *fusion*, l'autorité locale serait bien aise de le marier à une jeune héritière, riche, jolie et de couleur blanche. En attendant, il est chevalier de plusieurs ordres. (p. 272)

Today, people address him as *sir*, and the governor has awarded him the rank of officer in the militia. His venerable [black] *wife* died in the hospital and, to help bring about *fusion*, the local authorities would be delighted to marry him off to a young, rich, pretty, and white heiress. In the meantime, he has been made a chevalier in several orders.

Notwithstanding his recourse to one of modern literature's favorite tropes, irony, the corrosive ressentiment of Maynard's ending is all too apparent. Surely there is nothing to be learned from it, and history has done well to relegate this story and the reactionary Creole who wrote *Outre-mer* to the dustbin of history? If the responses to questions such as these seem obvious, I would like to suggest, by way of defending my own decision to resurrect the memory of a man whom Bissette perhaps rightly dismissed as a truant schoolboy "qui prend la plume pour régenter l'univers," that the hate-full emotions so apparent in the last lines of this short story still speak to us and through us, and that the triumphant mulatto Jupiter is one and the same figure—a figure made possible by a hatred that we have not ceased imitating, for all that we continue to deny our mimicry by projecting it onto others—as the reviled bourgeois exemplar who dominates the ending of another, much more justly famous work of literature, written some twenty years later, Flaubert's *Madame Bovary*. After everything I have said about (the failure of) the melodramatic imagination in the preceding pages, the significance of this last ending and of its uncanny similarity to that of Maynard's "Scènes nocturnes" requires, I believe, no further comment on my part:

Depuis la mort de Bovary, trois médecins se sont succédé à Yonville sans pouvoir y
réussir, tant Monsieur Homais les a tout de suite battus en brèche. Il fait une clien-
tèle d'enfer; l'autorité le ménage et l'opinion publique le protège.

Il vient de recevoir la croix d'honneur. (p. 357)

Since Bovary's death, there have been three doctors at Yonville, but none of them
have made a go of it, so successful has Monsieur Homais been in running them
down from the moment of their arrival. He has acquired a hellishly large clientele;
the authorities go easy on him and public opinion protects him.

He has just been awarded the Cross of the Legion of Honor.

Masterful Originals, Slavish Imitations: Romantic Monstrosities, Metaphysical Rivalries, and the Post/Colonial Conjuncture

> Every departure is a source of aggrievement, even from
> a disagreeable land. There is something in a man that
> becomes attached to places independently of their qualities,
> like the creole lianas that just as readily wrap themselves
> around poisonous trees as around beneficial ones. And I
> was leaving behind me in France such dear and noble
> friendships!
> —Louis (de) Maynard, "Voyage à la Martinique"

> Cet homme qui naquit pour souffrir et combattre,
> Qui méprisa le nombre assemblé pour l'abattre,
> Illustre Bissette, c'est toi!
> Et quand la calomnie attachée à la gloire,
> Cherche à te diffamer, à salir ton histoire,
> Etonné, tu lui dis: Pourquoi?
> —Martialis *fils*, "À M[onsieur] Bissette"[86]

As René Girard has noted in a discussion of Stendhal's novels,
"everywhere, in the nineteenth century, spontaneity becomes a matter of
dogma, dethroning imitation" (*MR*, p. 23). This dogma, the "terrorism of
innovation," is still with us today: it is our Romantic legacy, and it is, Girard would argue, nothing more or less than a manifestation of our *vanity*,
a desire to differentiate ourselves from those whose influence we anxiously
disclaim. "Romantic disdain, hatred of society, nostalgia for the desert,"
Girard continues, "just like the herd mentality, most often only cover up a
morbid preoccupation with the *Other*." In Hugo's *Bug-Jargal*, this "souci
morbide de *l'Autre*" was simultaneously expressed and suppressed: the
mimetic condition of postrevolutionary society repeatedly rises to the fore
only to be explained away through Hugo's scapegoating of the figure of the
mulatto, who is made to assume the entire burden of a repellent unorigi-

nality. Anxiously aware of the contagiousness of mimesis, Hugo would leave its further exploration to the likes of a realist novelist like Stendhal, resolving—or, rather, camouflaging—the confusions to which the (re)writing of *Bug-Jargal* had exposed him by comprehensively denying them: this denial would take the form of the antimimetic Romantic aesthetics elaborated upon at length in the 1827 preface to *Cromwell*. In this preface, Hugo draws a clear line between the original and the copy, the model and the imitation: "To imitate?" he rhetorically asks. "Is the reflection worth the same as the light? Is the satellite that continually drags itself around the same old circle worth the same as what is central and generative, the star? For all his poetry, Virgil is only Homer's moon" (3.67). Aesthetic theory allows him to conceive of what novelistic practice cannot: namely, the existence of a "strong" poet, whose originality derives from his unimpeded access to a primal energy ("one must draw [one's inspiration] from the deepest wellsprings" [3.69; "il faut puiser aux sources primitives"], he notes, anticipating the primitivist imperatives of so much modernist literature). The strong poet has been freed once and for all from the specter of ever being mimetically influenced, and thereby enslaved, by the Other: "What is the good of attaching oneself to a master? Of grafting oneself onto a model? It is still better to be a bramble bush or a thistle, nourished by the same earth as the cedar and the palm, than to be the fungus or the lichen on those great trees. The bramble bush lives, the fungus vegetates" (3.69). Between the living and the simply vegetating, there is an abyss that cannot be crossed: this, at least, is the claim that Hugo—and all of those who have absorbed the Romantic dogma of originality—would like to enforce.

As an impassioned advocate of "our literary revolution,"[87] Maynard too promoted this aesthetic, most programmatically in his articles for *L'Europe littéraire* on the 1833 salon. As Sainte-Beuve disparagingly pointed out, Maynard devoted several of these articles to a comparison of the work of Horace Vernet with that of a neoclassicist like Ingres. Ours, Maynard notes, is an "age of inquiry and originality" and for this reason alone a painter like Vernet must have our preference: "The artist who invents and continues to progress will thus be more our type of painter than the one who copies and remains in the same place, whether as a matter of principle or powerlessness it matters little. Horace is a poet, Monsieur Ingres is a draughtsman" (April 1, 1833: 58). The true poet is inventive, progressive, and powerful. Above all, as the following passage revealingly clarifies, he is of pure descent:

In a word, the school that we are defending, the new school, does not resemble that noble animal born of the horse and the donkey. It is fertile. The horizons that it opens up to ambition are infinite as thought itself. Lofty and deep, it walks in step with human life in all its variety and rapid unfolding, reproving no aspect of that life. It declares that imitation is a step back, that the complete genius is the only one who will enjoy a glorious immortality; and in thus restoring true originality and perfection, it strives—be it in solitude or in the world, victorious or persecuted—to reach its goal: the moment when the artist, who went in search of it as a man, has arrived at his final resting-place, a god. (April 17, 1833: 85)

Far from demonstrating a profound misunderstanding of Hugo's position, a statement like this recovers its suppressed genealogy. The sterile mule, the ignoble mulatto, imitates: such is the thesis of *Bug-Jargal* and it is one that Maynard, especially attuned to the racial concerns of this novel, here writes back into the Romantic ideology through his choice of metaphor. To be sure, other less revealing and more ostensibly palatable metaphors are possible, and Maynard would come up with a number of them—as when in his critique of the *Journal de Paris*'s systematic championing in literature of the "happy medium" ("juste milieu") he notes that "two liqueurs, each of them excellent on their own, when mixed together usually produce a dreadful brew, [and] the literary 'happy medium' is that brew."[88] However, it is the same preference for purity that generates them all. As Maynard said in a critical account of classical French theater written for the *Revue de Paris* in August 1834, "to compare Racine with Sophocles is to liken [*assimiler*] the dove to the eagle; even worse, it is to elevate an unfaithful copy to the rank of a sublime and true original" (p. 32): it is precisely this *assimilation* of two unlike things, this intertwining of the copy and the original, that must be avoided at all costs—as the example of seventeenth-century neoclassicism monstrously bears witness ("The Greek of the seventeenth century was French; or rather, in that monstrous coupling of Athens and Versailles, of Louis XIV and Hercules, we were no longer French and we were not yet Greek. It was some bastard creation, estranged from all countries, all customs, all traditions: something that had never been seen before and that has not been seen since; something, in short, that would not even have made its way down to us were it not that Corneille and Racine had taken the trouble to weld it to their timeless style" [p. 32]).[89]

Maynard's (white) creole origins thus make him in many respects the perfect reader and disseminator of Hugo's Romantic poetics. His cultural identity dependent upon the sort of absolute differentiations that had been put into question with the political legitimization of the gens de couleur, and more specifically, the mulatto section of this class (or caste, or race), it is hardly surprising that Maynard should have become such an ardent disciple of Hugo, whom he repeatedly praises for renewing the French language ("this is a language that sheds [*dépouille*] its limp decrepitude in order to clad itself in the confident splendor of a renewed youthfulness").[90] The obvious irony in all this, of course, is that to be a disciple of Hugo's amounts to copying the master (just as the young Hugo copied Chateaubriand) and thus to find oneself in an anything but "revolutionary" situation. After noting in an 1835 review of *Angelo Malipieri* that when it came to Hugo's relations with literary critics "the master does not accept a partial admiration—he wants an unqualified faith, an unlimited obedience," the critic Gustave Planche poured scorn on the master-disciple relationships that Hugo's cult of originality apparently encouraged: "that young and enthusiastic minds should mistake will for power and devote themselves to the fortunes of an adventurer, that their parasitic pride should graft itself onto the master's pride and glory in his hopes, all that is straightforward enough and could have been foreseen."[91] Maynard is one such "parasite," and his dim awareness of this no doubt contributed to the sense of dissatisfaction that he felt as he departed Paris for Martinique in 1835: "I had done nothing for my literary fame," he states in that "Voyage à la Martinique" so scathingly parodied by Bissette, "and it was devastating me" (p. 361). This awareness of his failure to attain the "gloire littéraire" of the European model upon whom he had grafted himself, and his return to a homeland from which—no less than his mulatto protagonist Marius—his education had estranged him ("Despite everything I knew about the way people are, I must confess that I was still surprised by the universally cool reception accorded me. From everything that was said to me, it was obvious that I would have been a thousand times better received had I not known how to read" [p. 365]), provokes the moment of filtered autobiography that serves as the first epigraph to this section. Maynard is this "creole liana" that parasitically and indiscriminately attaches itself to the good and the bad, to the salutary tree and the manchineel, its poisonous double: neither one nor the other, but a plant that draws the two into relation and, in so doing, undoes the absolute distinction that Hugo wished to draw between the living tree and the vegetating fungus, pointing toward another life that, like the seventeenth century's exiled and bastard Franco-Greeks, uncomfortably resembles that of its models without being reducible to them.

Compared with Glissant's figuier-maudit, majestically relating the banyan and the rhizome, Maynard's creole liana is a lowly plant indeed, and he would most probably not, in any case, have recognized my no doubt over eloquent description of it. Nevertheless, to reread (as I have just done) Maynard's unoriginality as one (not particularly attractive or "successful") manifestation of Glissant's relationality is a useful gesture because it exposes the extent to which our own critical judgments are committed to a revolutionary Romantic aesthetic—the "terrorism of innovation"—that is at odds with the gradualist, mimetic process of creolization to which both men, in their very different ways, are responding. It is a cliché of literary history that the single most defining characteristic of literature written by

Creoles in the nineteenth century is its unoriginality. Such a view was consecrated by Baudelaire, who began his 1861 portrait of Leconte de Lisle (in *Réflexions sur quelques-uns de mes contemporains*) by addressing this supposed lack of innovation:

I have often asked myself, without being able to answer my own question, why Creoles, generally speaking, have not brought any originality, any power of conception or expression, to their literary work. They impress one as being womanly [*on dirait des âmes de femmes*], fit only for contemplating and enjoying. The frailness and slenderness of their corporeal forms, their velvet eyes that look without examining, the strange narrowness of their exaggeratedly high foreheads, everything that is so often charming about them indicates that they are the enemies of work and of thought. Languidness, graciousness, a natural faculty for imitation, which they share for that matter with Negroes, and that almost always lends a certain provincial air to a creole poet no matter how distinguished he is: this is what we have generally been able to observe in the best among them.[92]

This is a precious statement for what it reveals about the prejudices and anxieties underwriting Baudelaire's idea of the true artist—an idea that came down to him from the Romantics and that he will pass on to the modernists. The creole writer lacks *force*; he is feminine, provincial, as prone to imitation as the Negroes among whom he lives, and as easily summed up by a physiognomic portrait as they. Leconte de Lisle is the only exception to this general rule that Baudelaire can think of (and the exception proves the rule—just as in *Outre-mer* the extraordinariness of Marius confirms the abjection of the rest of the colored population): he is someone who has succeeded in passing as French, for there are few signs of "the poet's origin" in his work; if not for these, Baudelaire contends, it would otherwise be "impossible to detect the fact that he was born on one of those volcanic and perfumed islands, where the human soul, gently rocked by all the pleasures that one meets with there, each day unlearns the act of exercising itself in thought." Ironically enough, Leconte de Lisle has learned how to imitate a French poet so well that he has escaped the charge of mimeticism that Baudelaire has laid against other creole writers: this "genuine poet, serious and contemplative, who holds the confusion of genres in horror, and who knows that art obtains its most powerful effects only though sacrifices that are commensurate with the rarity of its goal" (p. 748), does not provoke the uncomfortable sensation of similarity-difference that the "faculté naturelle d'imitation" of all these other Creoles engenders.

Baudelaire's views have been influential—so influential, in fact, that we cannot simply reject them, our own critical attitudes being far too indebted to the Romantic fetishization of originality and purity for us simply to transcend such thinking. We can readily accede to the notion that nineteenth-century Haitian writing, for example, is simply "a literature of pure imi-

tation, a flight from difference";[93] we must nod approvingly when Chamoiseau and Confiant (following in the footsteps of Jean Price-Mars's seminal *Ainsi parla l'oncle* [1928]) refer to this same writing as exemplifying
"Haiti's collective Bovarysm."[94] Imitation is bad; good writers are not under the same illusions as a Flaubertian heroine. To be sure, Baudelaire's criteria for true poetry were Eurocentric, and we are now happy to critique
those same creole poets (and especially someone as successful at de-
"provincializing" himself as Leconte de Lisle) from a different perspective,
albeit with the same animus toward imitation: nineteenth-century Antillean
writing is, as the authors of the *Éloge* put it, "a writing for the Other, a
borrowed writing, anchored in French (or in any case external) values" (p.
14). From such writing, trapped in a complicitous dialogue with values that
are external ("hors de cette terre"), only inauthentic "falsifications" can result: discussing J. W. Orderson's fictionalized account of Barbados plantation life, *Creoleana* (1842), for instance, Brathwaite notes that it is characterized by a "tropical English" as opposed to a truly "West Indian" outlook, although as we have seen (in Chapter 2) he elsewhere reminds his
readers of the impossibility of simply distinguishing between West Indian
"imitation" and "indigenization" (as a critic like Sylvia Wynter attempts to
do).[95] Faced with, say, "the virtual identity between the [early- to mid-
twentieth-century] regionalist writers from the Antilles (be they black or
'colored') and writers from the metropole,"[96] we can only chastize these
passéiste, doudouiste authors and argue for an "authentic" Caribbean literary identity that is more often than not conveniently deferred to a future in
which that "excellent liqueur" might once and for all be tasted in an
unadulterated form. In other words, we can only imitate the arguments
about authenticity and originality that have been passed down to us by our
Romantic models; as René Girard says, "modern society is no longer anything more than a *negative imitation*, and the attempt at getting off the
beaten track irresistibly causes everybody to fall back down into its ruts"
(*MR*, p. 105).

   It is precisely this negative imitation that inspires the "revolutionary"
break of Franco-Caribbean modernism, conceived in 1932 with the single
issue of *Légitime Défense* and "triggered off" in 1940 by the "chief architect of this revolution," Aimé Césaire, with the journal *Tropiques*.[97] As
René Ménil stated in the first issue of *Tropiques*, in an article significantly
entitled "Naissance de notre art":

All our cultural manifestations, in the domain of art, have been up to this point
mere pastiches. In this domain, as in all others, imitation leads to nothing of value,
for "in imitation virtue takes leave of a substance." Thus, all this necessarily sterile
imitation has brought us only worthless "oeuvres." Worthless, because they are not
viable, being unnatural productions. . . . Useless reflections. (1.60)

In the face of these sterile and unnatural (mule-like?) imitations, Ménil and his colleagues lay claim to a virile originality, and literary historians have been more than willing to sanction this claim: Lilyan Kesteloot's notorious assertion that "before *Légitime Défense*, there was in effect no original literature in the Antilles" sums up this long-standing critical consensus.[98] To be sure, it is a consensus that is beginning to waver: J. Michael Dash points out, for instance, in a discussion of nineteenth-century Haitian literature and its supposedly imitative nature that "the pieties and received ideas of the militant thirties have become the point of departure for a whole school of literary criticism that has fixed the label of *mimétisme culturel* on the nineteenth century." "This has tended," he continues, "to obscure important and relevant issues raised in the nineteenth century particularly in Haiti where . . . a century of independence had already begun to create greater assurance and sophistication among Haitian writers."[99] The literary "revolution" that Césaire and company supposedly initiated had in certain respects already begun—one finds, for instance, in the "generation of 1836" the "stirrings of a *littérature indigène*"[100]—and, indeed, Ménil unintentionally reminds us of this nineteenth-century genealogy when he refers approvingly in *Tropiques* to the "new conception of creole beauty" that was unleashed in 1940 as exemplifying a "Caribbean romanticism" ("romantisme antillais").[101] In certain respects, to be sure, an argument such as Dash's does not so much contest the distinction between (bad) imitation and (good) originality as it does historically resituate it, simply pushing the birth of a truly Caribbean art back a century (nineteenth-century Haitian writers were more original than we give them credit for being!), but it has the signal merit of at least raising the question of what was at stake for the founding fathers of Caribbean modernism (and for so many of their enthusiastic exegetes) in their mimetic appropriation of the rhetoric of originality and its "militant pieties."

In his comprehensive account of Franco-Caribbean literature, Roger Toumson has argued that both assimilationist regionalism and the revolutionary modernism that claimed to supplant it need to be read as subdiscourses of one and the same discursive ensemble ("one mimics the dominant discourse, the other contradicts it").[102] Complicitous subdiscourses such as these, the boundaries of which are themselves extremely permeable, are not only the foundational components of a more broadly conceived (Franco-)Caribbean discourse but of that globalized discursive ensemble I have been referring to as post/colonial literature. This is a *creole* literature, in Baudelaire's sense of the word: imitative, impure, bastardized, grafted, (uselessly) reflective—to cite a number of the unflattering adjectives that we have come across in the preceding paragraphs. These adjectives can, of course, be translated into compliments: the postcolonial interest in "mongrelization" attests to this possibility, and such reversals are no doubt both necessary and beneficial. It is important, however, to register the limits of this euphoric translation, and in emphasizing the extent to which an unsuccessful and rather unattractive writer like Louis Maynard is exemplary of this creole literature I have attempted to suggest that such translations must be undertaken cautiously. It is in the same cautious spirit that I would like to cite another problematic case of post/colonial grafting by way of closing off my discussion of Maynard and reopening the case of Cyrille Bissette. The following passage is taken from an article entitled "Éloge du métissage," penned in 1950 by the father of Negritude, Léopold Senghor:

Our vocation as colonized subjects is to overcome the contradictions of the present situation [*conjoncture*], the artificially established antinomy between Africa and Europe, our heredity and our education. It is from the grafting of the one onto the other that our freedom must be born! The sweet taste of the grafted fruit, which is not the sum of its component elements. Superiority, because freedom, of the Métis, who chooses what he wants, from wherever he wants, to make from the reconciled elements an exquisite and powerful body of work. . . .

Too assimilated and yet not assimilated enough? Such is exactly our destiny as cultural métis. It is an unattractive role, and difficult to take hold of; it is a necessary role if the present situation and the "Union française" is to have any meaning. In the face of nationalisms, racisms, academicisms, it is the struggle for the *freedom of the Soul*—the freedom of Man.[103]

Here is as euphoric a translation of the condition of métissage as one could hope for: the impure, partially assimilated and yet entirely grafted identity, has become the precondition of liberty, a veritable destiny. And yet Senghor's praise of métissage, an essential if seldom-cited genealogical precedent for those *éloges* that are proliferating in our own postcolonial age, is inseparable both from the colonial context in which it is given, and from Senghor's complicity with the federalist ideal of the "Union française," which in the years following World War II seemed to offer French Africa a possible compromise between colonial status and full independence, a satisfactory way of being "different and together." In the afterlife of this failed Union what further sense can one make of Senghor's praise of métissage? As I have been arguing, whatever sense it does make is one that renders problematic the production of "exquisite and powerful" works; it is a *sens* (a meaning and a direction) that is to be found through inhabiting, rather than surmounting, the contradictions of the post/colonial "conjuncture."

The compromised position in which this representative to the French National Assembly here situates himself—and for which, to the displeasure of some, he would continue to argue in a diversity of ways as president of Senegal, a country whose independence had come, in his words, "thirty or forty years too soon"[104]—is one that Bissette too can be read as having oc-

cupied, and the Martiniquan's accommodating emphasis on the virtues of
the mère-patrie, cultural fusion, and nonviolent social "revolution" would
only become more glaring as his career progressed and his polemics with
the "radical" Schœlcher intensified. If these polemics to a great extent marginalized him in the years immediately preceding abolition—as Schœlcher's
most recent biographer puts it, "the misunderstandings that built up between the two men starting from 1842 led to Bissette's exclusion from an
abolitionist process and a political life in which he obviously ought to have
participated"[105]—he nonetheless kept up his attacks, despite their unpopu-
larity in some quarters. Bissette himself speaks of certain of Schœlcher's
abolitionist friends initially wanting to "tear out my eyes" after his *Réfutations* of books that they had not read but about which they "spoke very
learnedly, on the strength of the strong reviews that it had received in certain newpapers." "And I," he continues, "who had read and reread them
from beginning to end, who had even had the patience to learn several passages by heart, was expected to say the same thing as the *advertisements* of
those papers. I was accused of having committed a *Schœlchéricide*, a new
crime invented by a little sect of atheists, a horrible and dreadful crime according to the disciples."[106] In an exemplary letter of 1846 addressed to the
playwright Étienne Arago, Bissette aggravates this crime, putting into question Schœlcher's presumed "right and privilege to discuss our interests":
contrasting his rival's posturings with the deeds of an heroic predecessor
like the Abbé Grégoire, or the current efforts of the politically moderate *Société pour l'abolition de l'esclavage* (associated with the likes of de Broglie
and Lamartine), he notes that "these true friends of our cause, whom we
acknowledge and to whom we are grateful, never had the pretension of offering themselves to us as if they were saviors, nor of exerting the sort of
tyranny that comes from compelling, in a relentless and obsessive way, our
gratitude—for it is a genuine tyranny, Monsieur, and tyranny, in whatever
form it takes, is always odious, always revolting for those on whom it is to
be inflicted."[107] Observing that "whether or not he works toward the successful abolition of slavery, the abolition of slavery will come to pass without him," Bissette cites the disastrous effects of Schœlcher's book on Haiti
(hyperbolically blaming him for the chaos into which that country had
been plunged after the overthrow of Boyer), and ends his letter with an
open declaration of war: "whatever he does or does not do, he will never
obtain our gratitude, for it is not in his power to undo the harm that he has
caused our race through his incitements and his provocations, which have
resulted in the revival of caste rivalries, that deplorable legacy of slavery, in
a country where unity and peace are so very necessary for the resolution of
this great question that is so contested by our enemies—namely, the civilizing of Negroes under a government founded by themselves" (p. 124).

Notwithstanding his relatively marginalized position during these years, Bissette (Fig. 1) continued to devote his energies to the abolitionist cause, rigorously critiquing government legislation intended to ameliorate but not end the institution of slavery (such as the 1845 reforms associated with the Ministre de la Marine, Baron de Mackau, which he labels nothing more than a "corrected edition" of Louis XIV's Code Noir),[108] promoting the antislavery petition campaigns that were gaining force in the years before the fall of the July Monarchy, and briefly relaunching the *Revue* in 1847 under the name *Revue abolitionniste*. As his comment about a "little sect of atheists" suggests, one of the ways in which Bissette would most strongly differentiate himself from Schœlcher over the course of the decade would be to begin stressing the virtues of a Christian education, and this new religious emphasis (or rhetorical pose?) is on ample display in the revived *Revue* (as is obvious from a glance at the cover, where the old image of an enchained black has been retained with one important addition: his skyward gaze is now directed at a cross from which light is emanating toward him). The Revolution of 1848, the provisory government's decree of April 27 abolishing slavery, and the establishment of universal male suffrage opened up new political opportunities for Bissette, who would that same year be elected one of Martinique's three representatives to the Constituent Assembly, along with Schœlcher and Pierre Pory-Papy. Having stepped down on a technicality soon after being elected, he would regain a seat in the Legislative Assembly in June of the following year, after returning to his native island for the first time in twenty-five years. In Martinique, he was acclaimed by the formerly enslaved masses, who took to calling him "Papa Bissette," and greeted as the voice of reason by the native whites, who were relieved by his conciliatory rhetoric and his insistence on a béké running mate. To the bitter disappointment of many of his own caste, Bissette would go on to conduct a vigorous and successful campaign against his rival Schœlcher.[109] For the brief duration of the Second Republic, the Antilles would be sharply divided into two political camps: *bissettistes* and *schœlchéristes*, the former dominant in Martinique (where Bissette and the progressive béké planter Auguste-François Pécoul crushed the absentee Schœlcher, gaining 95 percent of the vote) and the latter in Guadeloupe (where Schœlcher and the mulatto François-Auguste Perrinon, who had himself once shared Bissette's suspicions about the white abolitionist's views on the *classe de couleur*, returned the favor).[110] This polarization would only be ended with Louis Napoléon's coup d'état of December 2, 1851, which led to the abolition of direct parliamentary representation for the colonies; while his rival went into exile, Bissette (who happened to be in Martinique at this time) simply retired from political life, becoming a court clerk in 1853.[111] Having apparently made his peace with the new régime, he would live out the re-

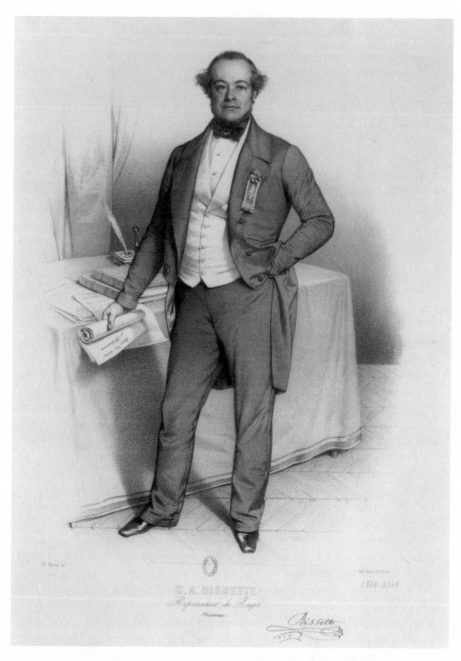

FIGURE 1. Cyrille Bissette, Représentant du peuple, "adopting whatever mask is in fashion" (Perrinon, *Explications*, p. 98). Collection of the Bibliothèque nationale, Paris.

maining few years of his life in a state of relative obscurity and ease, his faculties dulled by an attack of apoplexy—hardly the "heroic" ending that a postcolonial hagiographer might have hoped for, but in many ways an entirely appropriate one.

As a direct result of his electoral defeat in Martinique, Schœlcher produced the first of three core texts through which the second phase of the Bissette-Schœlcher exchange can be read: a lengthy tome entitled *La vérité aux ouvriers et cultivateurs de la Martinique, suivie des rapports, décrets, projets de lois et d'arrêtés concernant l'abolition immédiate de l'esclavage* (1849).[112] Much of this work is taken up with an account of his own role in the revolutionary events of 1848 and a justification of the provisory government's rapid implementation of such policies as abolition and universal suffrage, but a large chunk of it is devoted to Bissette—a man whom, Schœlcher assures the "workers and farmers" of Martinique, they have elected "by error" (p. 16). Despite the "extreme repugnance" that dealing with "a soiled individual like Monsieur Bissette" (p. 96) inspires in him, the latter's success and popularity means, as Schœlcher states in the concluding lines of the book, that he can no longer, "as in the past, silently turn the other cheek to him; I have been forced to make him known, to reveal him as he really is" (p. 460). Breaking years of "dignified" silence, Schœlcher returns to the offending passages in his own early works (the 1830 article, the 1833 brochure) and to the comments about the gens de couleur and mulattoes in the two books that inspired Bissette's 1843 and 1844 *Réfutations* (pp. 73–80), apologizing for the occasional needless generalization or inappropriate turn of phrase while insisting upon the bad faith of the attacks on him, the complete sincerity and increasing fervor of his own beliefs, and the hypocritical inconsistency of Bissette's.

Finding it convenient to ally himself with the béké elite that he had until recently excoriated, Bissette has (in Schœlcher's account) abandoned his former socially progressive pose, while continuing to use it to his own advantage in winning over the black electorate by repeatedly portraying himself as the long-suffering victim of colonial injustice and falsely emphasizing the centrality of his own role in the events of 1823–24 (a centrality Schœlcher had already subtly put into question in *Des colonies françaises* by referring to "the celebrated episode, referred to as the 'affaire des hommes de couleur,' that brought into prominence the names of Fabien and Bissette, which will have a permanent place in colonial history" [p. 376]).[113] Against Bissette's claims that he had been branded and exiled for *conspiring* against the established order in Martinique, Schœlcher exclaims: "Playacting! Playacting! The companion of Fabien and Volny is bragging; he was not a conspirator, he never conspired. He was the negative victim of a social system that had need of terror in order to maintain itself; an awful injustice elevated him to a position that he did not have the honor of seeking out. One might well call him the reluctant martyr [*le martyr malgré lui*]" (p. 65). Hardly a conspirator in 1823, this "martyr malgré lui" had in fact been an eager defender of the colonial order in the preceding year, as a member of the militia forces that in 1822 helped put down a slave revolt at Carbet (pp. 68–69).[114] Acknowledging that Bissette had gone on to do some important work for the cause of mulattoes and blacks, Schœlcher cited it (no doubt smarting from Bissette's frequent attacks on his own leisurely adoption of the call for immediate abolition) as evidence of his rival's ideological and moral decline: "the Bissette of old is still the standard by which the Bissette of today can be most severely judged!" (p. 94). In short, Schœlcher informs his *ouvriers et cultivateurs*,

you believed that you owed your freedom to the man who had been proscribed in 1823, but you will soon find that the only ones making this claim are he and the eternal enemies of your independence . . . and that he has gained your trust only in order to sow division and wreak havoc. It will all become clear to you one day, in a flash, like the bursting of an illusion, and the role of a *Papa* unworthy of you will be brought to an end; the immense power that your affection alone gives him will vanish. It is thus, after all, a good thing that he has come along: his past made him the floating wand of the fable; [look closer and] you will see that it is only a stick. Monsieur Bissette was for the Antilles one of those things [*une de ces choses*] that must be tried out and left to destroy itself. (p. 103)

Given the fact that he will later speak of slavery as an institution that turned men into *hommes-choses* (p. 214), Schœlcher's reduction here of his opponent to the status of a *chose* is revealing: the discursive struggle for mastery necessarily leads the abolitionist to "enslave" Bissette; in full command of a prophetic truth that delegitimizes the illusory power of this false father (or, might we say, this rival brother), Schœlcher does a "masterful" job in *Vérité* of wishing away this "bâton flottant"—or, to put it another way, of *imitating* the slave's polemical discourse and becoming *subject* to the very condition that he feels himself to be above.

Among the most damning of Schœlcher's charges against Bissette was that the "proscrit de 1823" had perversely formed an electoral alliance with the plantation-owning creole elite, those whom only a few years before Schœlcher had himself spoken of with relative sympathy,[115] but whom he now identified as "incorrigibles." The alliance with Pécoul amounts to "political apostasy" (p. 95), a cynical abandonment on the part of this "colonial Christ" (p. 52) of the cause he had ostensibly been promoting for decades:

Is it so strange that a good many voters, finding the editor of the *Revue des Colonies* in an alliance with the most prominent, the most persistent, enemies of abolition, should come to the conclusion that in converting to these men he had converted to their doctrines? On the one hand, they see him furiously fighting the candidature of those who have done everything to give them their freedom; on the other, they see him backing that of the people who have done everything, *up until the very last moment*, to prevent it being given to them. Hardly extraordinary, then, that they suspect him of no longer being passionately committed to keeping [their freedom] intact! (p. 93)

After his arrival in Martinique, the "Messiah of the incorrigibles" (p. 459) had even gone so far as to embrace the very man who twenty-five years before had condemned him to death: writing in his diary of their momentous meeting in 1849, Pierre Dessalles reports Bissette saying that he no longer thinks about the 1824 court verdict and that, "in any case, it made my political fortune and gave me an influence that I will now use for the good of our common homeland."[116] Such conduct for Schœlcher can only be explained by Bissette's lack of character, insatiable greed ("when the poor 'affranchis,' in the outpouring of their generosity, come to lavish him with their gifts, he accepts these, taking all that they possess—gold, silver, jewelry, barrels of sugar, poultry, game, fruit and vegetables—and shamelessly selling off at the market what he does not consume himself!" [p. 459]), and an obsessive hatred of his rival: "the friend of Monsieur Pécoul has sunk so low in his wild hatred as to wallow in the filth left by the Granier Cassagnacs and the Maynards" (p. 38).

The Maynard under discussion here, whom Schœlcher derisively describes as "nobly hurling insults at me from a distance of eighteen hundred leagues" (p. 38), is Louis's brother, Auguste Gaillard de Maynard, editor of the *Courrier de la Martinique*, the media organ of the planter class, which vigorously promoted the campaign of the "illustrious Bissette" (to cite a line from the exemplary poem that serves as the second epigraph for this section).[117] The irony of this situation is not lost on a Schœlcher who had been repeatedly charged with a lack of respect for "family values" ("les sentiments de la famille"):

The alliance between these men who accuse me of disregarding family values is a living insult to what is most sacred about the family—namely, the respect that we owe to our mother, to our brother, to the tender affection that pure souls have for the memory of those revered and beloved beings. There was once a young man, whom we knew and loved in Paris, a young man with a graceful nature, an affectionate heart, a born poet, dead in the full bloom of his youth and his talent. But here is the sort of disgusting language that the editor of the *Revue des Colonies* (January 1837, page 300) puts into his mouth: "I am going to speak of Louis Maynard de Queilhe, pay attention! I descend from the old viscounts of Quercy, *the region of France where there are the most pigs!*" Well, as it happens, Monsieur Maynard, the editor of the *Courrier de la Martinique*, who proclaims himself a friend of Monsieur Bissette and who in his newspaper accepts that man's patronage, is the brother of Louis Maynard! (pp. 38–39)

Schœlcher's critique of "Monsieur Maynard and the man who insulted his brother" (p. 62) is rhetorically effective, though in making it he once again raises questions about his own judgment of character and the extent to which his perspective remains curiously complicit with that of the man who authored *Outre-mer* in a spirit of dubious "impartiality" ("I tried my best to be impartial, I simply told a story," as Maynard puts it in the novel's preface [1.vi]). In any case, reminding readers of Bissette's "disgusting" remarks about Auguste's deceased brother confirms (for Schœlcher) not only the hypocrisy of this alliance but its unstable nature: (for Schœlcher) it can only be a temporary "coalition of hatreds" and, he augurs, "this marriage of convenience, made for reasons that have nothing to do with honor, will dissolve along with the causes that produced it in the first place; under the cloak of fraternity, theirs is an alliance based on nothing more than ambitions and grudges." "They each want to rule through the other," he concludes, "and the day of their scission is perhaps near" (p. 99). Once this "dishonorable" alliance has broken apart, the way will be clear for the "famille nègre," which has been riven by political factionalism ("When I hear that the *bissettistes* have attacked the *schœlchéristes*, it grieves me, for these conflicts only weaken you, my poor friends, as much as your unity would strengthen you. May the *bissettistes* and the *schœlchéristes* disappear, in order for there to be only brothers in your ranks" [p. 280]), to be reunited and thus assured of its continued freedom and independence.

Schœlcher's *Vérité* was soon followed by Bissette's *Réponse au factum de M. Schœlcher intitulé La vérité aux ouvriers et cultivateurs de la Martinique* (1850), also addressed to the (black) Martiniquan voting public, those "released from the hideous plague of slavery." Identifying himself as the man "to whom you have unanimously awarded, in return for my long martyrdom, a [new] name that sounds sweeter to my heart, that is more precious and dear: the name of father, that name you came upon in the sublime innocence of your loving and grateful hearts" (p. 48), Bissette provides a portrait of Schœlcher that doubles the unsavory one of himself in *Vérité*. He portrays "the author of this noxious rant" (p. 2) as a man driven by "his arrogant jealousy," and whose goal "is to dominate the colonial populations without rivals and without partners" (p. 83). Noting that in order to "nullify once and for all the old accusations of Monsieur Schœlcher" he had had to be "courageous enough to read to the very end those five hundred pages signed Schœlcher and steeped in bile, venom, pique, the spirit of revenge, and wounded self-esteem" (p. 2), Bissette explains to his constituency how it is that he has become the scapegoat of "Schœlcher, Perrinon et Compagnie" (p. 6). After his 1843 *Réfutation*, which "profoundly, irremissibly, mortally wounded the self-esteem of citizen Schœlcher" (p. 10), the French abolitionist "nursed a deadly hatred for me: he swore . . . to pursue me by all imaginable means, to harm me whenever and wherever he could. My friends become his enemies ... and since I do not have any enemies, he stamps the ground with his patent leather boot and causes a few to spring up from it, as the spirit of his revenge requires" (p. 11). The usual offending passages about the gens de couleur from Schœlcher's earlier books and articles are mentioned in passing, but the majority of the *Réponse* is taken up with fending off the many charges of moral turpitude, financial misconduct, and physical cowardice leveled at him in *Vérité* (we will be looking in detail at one such charge shortly), and redirecting many of the same charges back at his opponents. Most importantly, he defends his alliance with a plantation owner like Pécoul. Noting that his "esteemed colleague in the National Legislative Assembly . . . never pleaded the cause of slavery, was never a cruel or wicked master but, rather, one who mitigated the system of slavery on his property" (p. 97), Bissette stresses that such alliances were necessary to advance the cause of fusion ("I wanted peace and a single family" [p. 97]). Indeed, it must be said—contra Schœlcher—that these conciliatory tactics are not really inconsistent with those of the "Bissette d'autrefois," who in the very first issue of the *Revue des Colonies* had declared that the journal "is entirely dedicated to the political, intellectual, moral, and industrial interests of colonists of both colors" (I.i: 4), and who in subsequent issues would entertain the possibility of forgiving even those who had had him branded and of "forgetting the past" once slavery was finally abolished (e.g., I.iv: 35). For Bissette,

a thousand good things can come from conciliation, from a confrontational, militant politics a thousand evils. . . . It is my belief that when it comes to uniting those who were once divided something altogether different is needed than a hotheaded politics intent on creating difficulties. That is why my first words to you, upon disembarking on my native soil after twenty-five years of exile, were: CONCILIATION; FORGETTING THE PAST. (p. 103)

As with his analysis of independent Haiti, this "OUBLI DU PASSÉ" leads ideally to an emancipated, *post*-revolutionary world in which social justice has been achieved and racial factions have disappeared: statements like "in 1848, when the freedom of my brothers was proclaimed, the colonial war lost its entire raison d'être" (p. 97) and "today, blacks, mulattoes, and whites no longer exist, there are only citizens of a single homeland now!" (p. 97) abound in his *Réponse*. Given the extreme nature of such claims it is doubtful whether Bissette actually believed them to be true; as rhetorical assertions, however, it can certainly be argued that, like those in the *Déclaration des droits de l'homme*, they situate political responsibility squarely in the unresolved and unresolvable present, rather than conveniently deferring it to a revolutionary future in which this desirable state of affairs might be more truly realized.

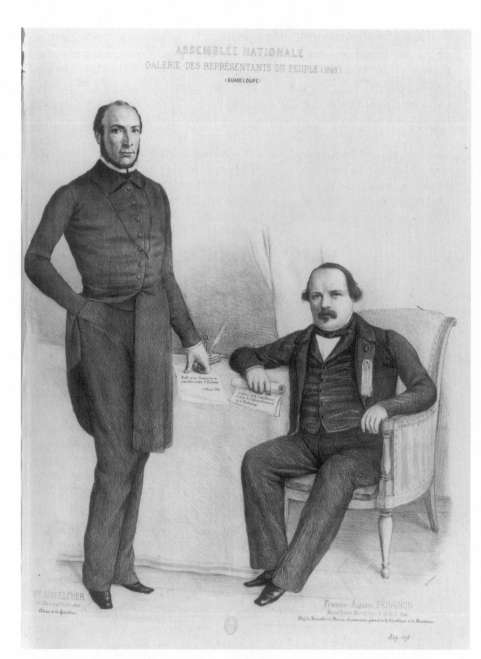

FIGURE 2. Victor Schœlcher and François-Auguste Perrinon, "Siamese twins" (Bissette, *Réponse*, p. 72). Collection of the Bibliothèque nationale, Paris.

Schœlcher himself would not reply to Bissette's *Réponse*, leaving that task to his fellow *représentant* from Guadeloupe, François-Auguste Perrinon (Fig. 2), whom Bissette had blisteringly and repeatedly attacked in the *Réponse* as Schœlcher's "understudy" (p. 89; "doublure"), his "Siamese twin" (p. 72), the "head of an artillery batallion in the Navy, decorated without ever having seen combat" (p. 11), who "one fine day dreamed that he, too, was a great politician" (p. 4). Restoring the "mask of austere virtue" that Bissette in the *Réponse* had rhetorically ripped away from Schœlcher's ally "as one must tear it away from every actor—tragedian or cabaret artist—who lies in order to slander people" (p. 20), Perrinon angrily countered with his *Explications à propos d'un récent libelle de M. Bissette* (1850). The level of abuse directed in this brochure toward the book that Bissette is said to have "vomited" (p. 87) in a futile attempt at rehabilitating himself is high indeed. Noting that "Monsieur Bissette's method is to credit his adversaries with the vices that have been observed in him," Perrinon asserts that his opponent "would like to lower everything to his level." "He balks at honesty," Perrinon declares, "loyalty is odious to him, and he dislikes—above all else, he dislikes—courage" (p. 42). Schœlcher's proxy alternately chastizes and ridicules this "slanderous," "cowardly," "ungrateful" individual for such things as not repaying his many creditors, cowardly refusing Schœlcher's repeated attempts at engaging him in a duel,[118] and stooping so low as to have circulated a manuscript in 1842 in which he "heaped foul abuse" on Louis Fabien, a year after his former "comrade in captivity" had lost his mind and was thus "powerless to defend himself" (p. 90). In short, Bissette, whom Perrinon himself sadly admits once having esteemed ("My story is one that I have in common with all [mulattoes] of my generation; it is also the story of most of those who came after us in various French schools. All of us believed in the reluctant martyr, and what was needed to dispel this error was not evidence—for that ought to have smacked us in the face long before—but the sad experience that comes with age" [p. 89]), is a self-aggrandizing opportunist and "hypocrite," a devious master of rhetoric "who adopts whatever mask is in fashion, whatever jargon is being spoken at the moment" (p. 98), and thus a fitting ally for the likes of Auguste Maynard, "whose wild and raging talk, manifesting itself in filthy abuse directed toward all respectable people, ensures that indignation wins out over the contempt and the disgust that he inspires" (p. 110).

Toward the beginning of his 1844 book on Haiti, Bissette noted that several otherwise sympathetic readers of the first *Réfutation* felt he had at times "detracted from . . . the strength of my arguments on the principal issues" by insisting on errors of "little importance" in Schœlcher's book (p. 5); Bissette maintained, though, that even the "most *insignificant facts*" (p. 6) needed to be addressed, even were it at the cost of "weakening" his own argument. It is in this spirit that, of all the accusations made against Bissette, I would like to concentrate on a particularly trivial one that both Schœlcher and Perrinon make, and that exemplifies the extent to which Bissette's method had become their own. Schœlcher's *Vérité* concluded by reprinting and commenting on two documents that, he affirms, had only just come into his hands as he was on the point of completing the book, and which he justifies reprinting because they "put the finishing touches on our portrait of the Messiah of the incorrigibles" (p. 459). It is the second of these documents that concerns us here (pp. 457–59), an ostensibly unsolicited letter dated December 7, 1849, sent to Schœlcher by a certain "A. Demerey Mana," a twenty-year-old nephew of Bissette's. The young man writes in order to draw Schœlcher's attention to "an event that I was victimized by, which happened around eight years ago": as a twelve-year-old schoolboy in Paris, tired of always wearing "the school uniform," he had with his father's permission bought "a frock coat [*redingote*] and pants made to order," as well as a pair of boots. Having been allowed out of school on a one-day pass and having spent that day with his uncle, he left his new set of clothes at Bissette's for safekeeping. Some time later, he attempted to reclaim his outfit, only to be told that everything had been "pawned for the sum of 25 francs." Despite promises that these objects would be recovered as soon as possible, the young man never saw them again: "this, Monsieur, is the trick played on a twelve-year-old child by his uncle," the young man concludes. Schœlcher then comments briefly on how this episode reflects his rival's "immoral" character: "Not content with forcing people to loan him money (as we have detailed), he pawned the holiday outfit of a child, his ward. The holiday outfit of a child! This is to add cruelty to improbity" (p. 459).

Bissette's response to Schœlcher's use of this letter excites Perrinon into reprinting the letter of "A. Demercy-Mana" in his *Explications* (pp. 84–85) and then commenting on the unsatisfactory ways in which "the uncle refutes . . . these facts that are really impossible to invent" (p. 85). Bissette, Perrinon remarks scoffingly, disposes of these facts by means of his "usual method," denying them to be true and casting aspersions on those who make them, applying the "system from which he has never departed: he thinks he can *wash himself* by besmirching others" (p. 87). Denying the calumnies, Bissette suggests that his nephew has made them in order to "'satisfy the hatred of my enemy, whose self-interested flatterer he has become,'" to which Perrinon exclaims, "but what possible interest could Monsieur Mana have in flattering Monsieur Schœlcher at his uncle's expense? What an immense influence Monsieur Schœlcher wields! Was ever a man more powerful?" (p. 85). Having posed this rhetorical question, Perrinon then cites a number of other such accusations that could only, according to Bissette's logic, have been due to their authors' desire to please

Schœlcher but that are (for Perrinon) in reality nothing more than the plain, unsolicited truth. Bissette's manner of casting aspersions on his "vain" nephew also comes under attack, the uncle having compared "'this unnatural child to Ham, betraying the guilty father to the gaze and derision of the people'"; having reproached "the young man whose frock coat he took of not having covered over the odious deed with Noah's mantle, he adopts a tragic expression and curses him, crying out that 'God will ratify the paternal curse called down upon the guilty Ham'" (p. 86). Ridiculing "these grand biblical phrases, these indecent parodies" (an indecency that for Perrinon reveals the hollowness of this "devout" man's loudly proclaimed "new faith"), Perrinon goes so far as to assert that they could not have been authored by the likes of Bissette: they can "no doubt be traced solely to Monsieur Bissette's 'ghost-writer'; it is known that this glorious representative, who borrows so many things, is not shy about borrowing other people's pens whenever he feels the need to speak something approximating French" (p. 86). With such emphatic gestures of deauthorization does the textual exchange of Bissette, Schœlcher, and his understudy Perrinon come to an inglorious end, for Bissette chose not to publish a second *Réponse*; no longer containable in writing, the mimetic violence of their textual relations would give way to the physical violence of the duel, with Bissette and Perrinon crossing swords and their white doubles, Schœlcher and Pécoul, opting for pistols (none of the men being seriously injured in these encounters).[119]

And yet we can imagine what that second, textual response might have looked like by turning back to the first and reading, more closely than Perrinon, Bissette's own interpretation (pp. 99–101) of his nephew's "puerile letter," in which Bissette claims "there is not a true word" (p. 100)—not even its signature, if we are to believe him when he says that it was authored by "the son of my sister, *Dumercy* Mana"! Attuned as he was to the potential for distortion involved in textual (re)citation—to the "*suppressio veri* and *suggestio falsi*" that results from the substitution of an "abbreviated quotation" for the "actual text"[120]—Bissette might well have pointed out a number of apparently minor instances in which Perrinon advances the same sort of "false interpretations of extremely clear texts" that he accuses Bissette of manufacturing (p. 29). For example, Perrinon oversimplifies Bissette's parodic biblical analogy: it is not merely, or even primarily, his nephew whom Bissette likens to Ham but Schœlcher himself. Entertaining the hypothesis that his rival actively solicited this document from the young man, Bissette deprecates the individual whose "poisoned breath insinuates itself into the nephew's heart, teaching him to be slanderous and ungrateful toward his uncle":

Is this not, the truth of the facts excepted, the very crime of Ham betraying the guilty father to the gaze and derision of the people? The father cursed the unnatural child. What does this nephew merit, this child whose squalid and miserable youth I protected from the indignation of his teachers and the sarcasms of his classmates? In this sorry imitation of the ancient story, is it not citizen Schœlcher—the seducer, the corrupter, the tempter of young Dumercy Mana—who is the true Ham, who ought to bear the curse of God and the contempt of men?

Overdetermining the straightforward biblical analogy by positing the existence of two Hams, situating the influential rival on the same level as the insignificant nephew, Bissette reverses the colonial hierarchies, putting *himself* in the place of Noah, the father, and the abolitionist patron in that of the son—and no less a son than Ham, supposed ancestor of the African peoples whose malediction (Genesis 9:21–25) had so often been cited by colonial mythographers as sufficient justification for the enslavement of his descendants, as both Bissette and Schœlcher were very well aware.[121]

This sly reversal of the roles of master and slave, father and son, originator and imitator, which Perrinon has evident difficulty reading, also goes unread in a second revealing example of *suppressio veri*. After noting that the uncle has denied his nephew's accusations, Perrinon points out that Bissette also refers to himself as being "condemned 'by his poverty to turn a wretched luxury item into bread with which to allay the *hunger of an old man*'" (p. 86). When one returns to Bissette's actual words, though, the apparent contradiction raised by this simultaneous denial and admission dissolves: the comments about the "misérable objet de luxe" are, in fact, part of a hypothetical speech that Bissette has put into Schœlcher's mouth. Setting his claims about Schœlcher's role in soliciting the letter aside for a moment, Bissette allows for the possibility that his nephew's "perverted instinct" had given him "access to citizen Schœlcher's heart of hearts, had allowed him to anticipate, to sniff out the manuscript lying on the writer's desk, and had spurred him on to the abominable initiative." He then suggests that Schœlcher ought to have responded to this "troubled child" in the following terms:

I am not going to make a place for this cowardly denunciation of your uncle, the brother of your mother, in my book. People would think that I put you up to it, in the interests of my hatred and my ambition; I would be brought into disrepute amongst men! I am not going to make a place in my book for your impious letter, because even had the events really taken place, I repeat, you ought to throw a mantle of silence over the cruel and painful poverty that certainly could alone have led your uncle, your adopted father, to turn a wretched luxury item, good only for satisfying the vanity of a young man like you, into bread with which to allay the hunger of an old man! (pp. 100–101)

Imitating the master's apparently transparent voice, Bissette renders it opaque by inextricably (con)fusing it with his own. The monological authority claimed by the master is translated into a ventriloquistic dialogue where it is no longer possible simply to separate the words of the one from those of the other, to undo this troubling mimetic bond and trace the words out of which it is composed back to their respective origins (as Perrinon attempts to do in identifying Bissette's imitation of Schœlcher with Bissette himself).

There is a point, to be sure, at which the subtleties of a rusing language, and the difficulties involved in reading it, (appear to) cease mattering: Salman Rushdie's various protestations to the contrary,[122] *The Satanic Verses* (1988) was (mis)read and he was judged accordingly. In the fundamentalist community's eager scapegoating of Rushdie (and the liberal community's equally zealous scapegoating of fundamentalists), the violence that is at the heart of this—and of all other—communities became horrifyingly visible, and it is an attenuated, secularized version of such violence that one can see at work on both sides of the Bissette-Schœlcher exchange. What Bissette's readings of Schœlcher's work in the early 1840s registered was the abolitionist's need for a scapegoat: committed to certain "civilized" values that he had in common with his creole hosts, Schœlcher was incapable of simply attacking them at this point in his career; instead, the violence of his (progressive) colonial discourse was partially, and only momentarily, diverted toward the anomalous class of the (mulatto) hommes de couleur, already identified by the (reactionary) colonial discourse of the planters as the primary threat to their power. Schœlcher's representations of mulattoes are mimetically indebted to those found, say, in *Outre-mer*—albeit ostensibly purged of the *desire* that was so evident in Maynard's novel and that embarrassingly signaled his complicity with the rival class from which he wanted to separate himself. Bissette ably identifies this blind spot in his two *Réfutations*; in so doing, he not only identifies himself as Schœlcher's rival, but also repeats the violence to which he is responding, scapegoating Schœlcher. If Schœlcher is blind to the reasons why he needs to portray the hommes de couleur and mulattoes in the way that he does, Bissette is much more conscious of the mimetic violence generating his critique of the white abolitionist: as he puts it in his 1844 *Réfutation*, the Frenchman should not "be surprised at my argumentation, at my persistence, at my perfidious method, if that is how he wants to call it, since I am only returning blow for blow [*je ne fais ici que rendre guerre pour guerre*], and imitating the example he has given me" (p. 111). To be sure, Bissette completes this sentence in a way that legitimizes his own war and delegitimizes Schœlcher's: his imitation differs from the original because it also contains "the historical truth, which I have adhered to in my refutation of him, by drawing on sources other than those that he thought it best to model himself after when writing the history of Haiti and of the colonies." But, as his debilitating commitment to the "mulatto legend" demonstrates, Bissette's relation to the historical truth is only partially respectful at best; even more fundamentally, his ideological commitments are themselves conditioned by a mimetic rivalry with Schœlcher that has little or nothing to do with the truth and the principles that might derive from it—as the insistently rhetorical nature of Bissette's writing, especially in the late 1840s, makes us uncomfortably aware.

In his *Mensonge romantique et vérité romanesque*, René Girard identifies the source of our discomfort with Bissette's strategies in a discussion of how the "last hundred years of French history" have confirmed Stendhal's analysis of political factionalism in *Le rouge et le noir* (1830):

The struggle between factions is the only stable element in the otherwise unstable contemporary world. It is no longer principles that create rivalry; it is metaphysical rivalry that slips into opposing principles, in the manner of those mollusks that nature has not provided with a shell and that move into the first one they happen upon, regardless of what type it is. (*MR*, p. 136)

This is the unprincipled state of affairs (a state of affairs that, as Girard's subsequent work would show, has been with us in one form or another "since the foundation of the world") that the violence of Bissette and Schœlcher's textual encounters forces us to consider (and that finds physical expression in the disorderly confrontations between bissettistes and schœlchéristes during the electoral campaigns of 1849). We become aware of the inadequacies and violence of the abolitionist's apparently benign discourse, its continued allegiance to colonial paradigms with which it ought to have broken, but Bissette cannot provide us with an adequate alternative to it; instead, he repeatedly draws our attention to the complicity of his position with Schœlcher's, notwithstanding the increasingly virulent attempts of both men at differentiating themselves from one another. Faced with this complicity, we can only ask ourselves: if the differences between political factions are not essential but simply engendered by mimetic rivalries, then how can any political action ever be justified? If those who claim to be absolutely different from one another are actually bound in a complicitous *relation*, then how can any (personal, cultural, national, racial) identity ever be secure(d)?

To ponder such questions is to gaze into an abyss from which there may be no return. Inasmuch as Bissette actively forces us to confront this abyss, he is indeed the disseminator of chaos and discord that Schœlcher makes him out to be in *Vérité*. However, inasmuch as Bissette takes on the role of the scapegoat (a role that is not only thrust upon him but that he willingly adopts), he also offers the way—or, rather, one way—out of this abyss, becoming the figure around whom a consensus can be arrived at through his exclusion from the community. It is a simple matter to "finish with" Bissette ("I cannot wait to be done with Monsieur Bissette," Perrinon notes toward the end of his *Explications* [p. 114; "j'ai hâte d'en finir avec M. Bissette"]). As Schœlcher repeatedly remarks in the *Vérité*, Bissette was *not* a "man of honor" (p. 13). He *was*, as Perrinon claims, someone "devoid of moral sense" (p. 90), and his "*perfide méthode*" consists of nothing more than, again in Perrinon's words, "crediting his adversaries with the vices that have been observed in him" (p. 42). His undoubted and prescient commitment to the abolitionist cause aside, if he actually held any political beliefs, as opposed to simply adopting rhetorical poses, then they were conservative and reinforced what Brathwaite has termed (in a discussion of the Jamaican free colored writer Edward Jordon) the "Euro-creolizing or ac/culturative process,"[123] hardly good postcolonial credentials. There is a thin line between being a conservative and a reactionary, and Bissette's conciliation with the plantation-owning classes and failure to support the well-intentioned Schœlcher, as well as his failure to speak out against the coup d'état of December 2, 1851, are sure signs that he crossed this line; his personal attacks on Schœlcher, moreover, provide evidence of a Rousseauesque paranoia. Bissette is at once "the last gasp of the ancien régime" (as the schœlchériste newspaper *La liberté* put it)[124] and dishearteningly anticipates the emergence in the second half of the nineteenth century of a colored (and eventually black) petit bourgeoisie in the French islands, of which it has been said that "those in control have incorporated [this class] into the dominant order while excluding it from the decision-making process."[125] Even more frighteningly, the electoral campaign of 1849 and the populist agitations surrounding it raise the specter of a cult of personality that renders nugatory whatever qualms we might have about the "noble white man saves easily fooled black men from evil brown man" scenario that is undoubtedly at work in Schœlcher's *Vérité*; "Papa" Bissette's racialist and paternalistic rhetoric in the *Réponse* ("whatever happens, I am you," he says to his black readers, "and you are me; the heart, the blood, and past misfortune unite us indissolubly, and the iniquitous will never succeed in dividing us, in turning the sons against the father, the father against the sons" [p. 9])[126] anticipates that of another Papa by the name of Duvalier, whose own palinodic trajectory from Negritude intellectual (as a member of *Les griots* in the 1930s) to quasi-fascist dictator seems mirrored, *in petto*, by the "political apostasy" that Schœlcher ascribes to his rival.

   To finish with Bissette in this way is a simple matter. I would hope that my discussion of him has at the very least succeeded in putting such attractively simple conclusions into question and that I have succeeded in portraying him, to (re)cite a phrase of Perrinon's, as "a man who runs away" (p. 16; "un homme qui fuit")—a man who eludes not just those to whom he was in debt or who felt sufficiently outraged by his words as to send their seconds to his place of residence but those who attempt, with malice or sympathy, to interpret him. Be that as it may, there is another sense in which one cannot "finish with" Bissette. It is his rival Schœlcher, the man who in 1848 "carefully refrained from appointing Bissette, the leading black advocate of anti-slavery under the previous regime, to the seven-person commission instituted to formulate the slave liberation process,"[127] who must have the last word, because history has so ordained. As no less an authority than C. L. R. James has affirmed, commenting on Schœlcher's *Vie de Toussaint-Louverture* (1889), "his heart is in the right place" (*BJ*, p. 319). Thus, I would like to conclude here by considering a number of passages that Nelly Schmidt quotes and discusses in the closing pages of her excellent biography of Schœlcher. The first of these comes from Aimé Césaire's enthusiastic tribute to this "great man" in his introduction to a 1948 collection of the Frenchman's works entitled *Esclavage et colonisation*; the author of *Cahier d'un retour au pays natal* there states that each word of Schœlcher's "is even now a bullet waiting to explode" and claims that he "transcends [*dépasse*] abolitionism and takes his place in the tradition [*rejoint la lignée*] of the revolutionary man: he who resolutely locates himself in reality and directs History toward its end [*oriente l'Histoire vers sa fin*]."[128] For the moment, let us take Césaire's claim at face value as evidence of how outrageously false Bissette's representation of this "grand'homme" was. Schœlcher provides Césaire with the best of models: "let us ponder a few of the most forceful of the comments of this admirable man, whose memory it would be pointless to commemorate were one not determined to imitate his politics" (p. 258). As Schmidt points out, though, Césaire's imitation of this "revolutionary" politics is not without its problems: "Schœlcher, when he was alive, and the myth that survived him, both contributed to the illusion that there exist two Frances, a republican France, that of the Revolutions of 1789 and of 1848, and another one, conservative, supporting slavery, miserly in bestowing civic rights" (p. 260); this "republican myth," less easy to expose than the "mulatto legend" in which Bissette believed but equally pernicious, would underwrite the assimilationist politics of which Schœlcher no less than Bissette was a proponent and that in practice, notwithstanding his theoretical contributions to the critique of colonialism, Césaire would himself doggedly pursue throughout his lengthy career as a deputy in the French Assembly. It is Césaire's problematically faithful imitation of his "revolutionary" models that I will be discussing at the beginning of the next chapter—a chapter in which, through a consideration of Daniel Maximin's postmodern reworking of Caribbean modernism (or "Caribbean romanticism," to recall Ménil's words), I will be interrogating the explosive rhetoric of transcendence (*dépassement*), linearity (*lignée*), and ends and/or goals (*fin*) with which Césaire justifies the emulation of his nineteenth-century model.

Given our discussion of Bissette's young nephew, I believe that a second passage cited by Schmidt speaks for itself. In a 1923 letter to France's Colonial Minister, written with the purpose of urging the government to close down the infamous prison in French Guiana, the journalist and travel-writer Albert Londres describes a statue that he had seen in the colony's capital, Cayenne:

The first thing I saw was enthroned on a pedestal. Two great tall fellows, hand in hand, one of them in a frock coat and the other completely naked. I should add that they were quite still, being in bronze. It was Schœlcher, the guy who abolished slavery. On the stone below was a blazing flourish of fine words about the Republic and Humanity. (quoted in Schmidt, p. 256)

This is monumental history at its "best" and Bissette would have had little difficulty in recognizing Londres's ironical description of it: the naked black man, his white savior, a lovely turn of phrase—all in their full and undeconstructed glory. He might well have added, by way of finishing once and for all with the unfilial insinuations of his nephew, that Dumercy (Demerey, Demercy-) Mana need look no further for his precious frock coat . . . or its rightful owner.

Coda: "Zaffai cabrite (pas) zaffai mouton"—Raphaël Confiant, Annie Le Brun, and a Not-So-Sudden Abyss

In the 1846 letter to Arago that Bissette appended to his *Réponse*, he notes with evident insincerity that if Schœlcher, "this great *apostle of liberty for blacks and the emancipation of the hommes de couleur, of the griffes and the métis, and of who knows who else!*," were ever to wish to expiate his reprehensible deeds by putting a premature end to his life, "we would enjoin your friend not to make this sacrifice, for we, poor blacks and mulattoes, who do not ask for the sinner's death but only his conversion, would ask him simply by way of penance to make an auto-da-fé of his miserable books and commit them to the flames" (p. 124). No one was more aware than Bissette of the impossibility of such a conversion: the words have been written, they demand a response, and the post/colonial dialogue is set into motion, for better and for worse. If Bissette and Schœlcher's struggle for discursive mastery is a now relatively forgotten but nonetheless key moment in this dialogue, one need only turn to the most recent debate concerning Franco-Caribbean literature and culture in order to gauge the extent to which this nineteenth-century polemic, in all its perfidiousness, continues to undergird the disputes of our own fin de siècle.[129] Written under the banner of a Créolité that Césaire is accused of having consistently occluded in his work, Raphaël Confiant's aggressive book-length critique of the father of Negritude, *Aimé Césaire: Traversée paradoxale d'un siècle*, has since its publication in 1993 elicited a great deal of indignant commentary, most notably from the French poet and literary theorist Annie Le Brun, author of a good many books written in praise of "subversives" like the Marquis de Sade (most notably, *Soudain un bloc d'abîme, Sade* [1986]; translated as *Sade: A Sudden Abyss* [1990]). Le Brun has twice taken on the responsibility of "refuting" Confiant directly (and more indirectly tarring the other authors of the *Éloge* and even Glissant himself with the same brush): she first rebuked Confiant, who only a few year's before had declared himself "forever a son of Césaire's," in her *Pour Aimé Césaire* (1994), but although she begins that pamphlet by dismissively rebutting Confiant's Oedipal criticisms ("all the pusillanimities of the rebellion against the father are of course present here")[130] most of her energies are devoted to an impassioned reading of and plea for Césaire's poetry. Since her second pamphlet, *Statue cou coupé* (1996), both repeats and expands upon her initial critique of the authors of the *Éloge* it is this text that I will briefly discuss here.

The first two-thirds of *Statue cou coupé* is taken up by a conference paper that Le Brun gave in Fort-de-France in early 1995, her first pamphlet having excited a good deal of intellectual commotion in the Antilles during the preceding year. Throughout the paper she chides those who have dared to take the "wrong" side by criticizing a revolutionary artist like Césaire, and angrily disposes of the "mind your own business, French lady" argument that Confiant and Chamoiseau among others had directed her way in the wake of *Pour Aimé Césaire*'s publication—an argument that Bissette was himself prone to making, as when he reminded Schœlcher, significantly shifting linguistic registers from French to Creole, that "zaffai cabrite pas zaffai mouton" (literally, "the concerns of a little goat are not those of a sheep").[131] Gracefully admitting that "it is not for me to tell you what is creole and what is not" (p. 31), and restricting her comments on Césaire to his work as a poet and anticolonial thinker (a rather significant limitation, given that Confiant's book is largely a reaction against what he feels have been the disastrous consequences for Martinique of Césaire's ambivalent politics, and that his discussion of Césaire's poetry is in large part simply a foil for condemning political choices that certainly do not exhibit the "force of insubordination" that she so cherishes in Césaire),[132] Le Brun pursues three main points in her attack on *Confiant et compagnie*.

First, in a highly offensive manner, she questions both the intellect and the literary talents of her adversaries, speaking of "the insignificance of their arguments and, to say the least, the mediocrity of their novelistic production" (p. 12). If the likes of Confiant and Chamoiseau have gained a readership and won literary prizes (this last being a real badge of dishonor in Le Brun's book!), then this can only be, she argues, because their ideas and novels serve the interests of the powers-that-be. Citing Milan Kundera's influential 1991 article on Caribbean literature, which paid special tribute to Chamoiseau (paving the way, in her account, for the positive reception of the Martiniquan's soon-to-be-published and eventually Prix Goncourt–winning *Texaco*), Le Brun identifies it as part of a conspiracy of French publishers in the early 1990s to launch a "new exoticism" (p. 84). The success of this media conspiracy, the resulting consecration of "mediocre" writers, and the consequent occlusion of Césaire's (in her view) less complacent francophone vision, cause Le Brun to throw up her arms in despair: "what is one to think of a certain Europe that, along with all of those whose taste it has managed to colonize, is in such a state that it prefers the sham goods of this new exoticism to the greatness of Césaire, and even worse, no longer knows how to tell the difference between them" (p. 126). Telling the difference between Césaire and these "Caribbean epigones" of Milan Kundera (p. 115), she asserts, is not "a question of taste, it's a question of heart" (p. 126), and she, like James's Schœlcher, clearly has her heart in the right place! Stripped of the insults and the paranoia (but one must keep in mind that she is only *rendant guerre pour guerre*—having been rather badly treated herself by Confiant and Chamoiseau, as she repeatedly reminds her readers),[133] this point about the theory and practice of Créolité being inseparable from a new, media-generated exoticism is not without merit. Are Chamoiseau and Confiant not playing to and entrapped by the French (and potentially United States) literary market, and to what extent can any francophone writer escape this trap and still gain some measure of success? Might not the work of these two prolific authors be a little less "mediocre" if rather than blasting out product at the rate of a book a year they spent somewhat more time crafting their oeuvre? These are legitimate questions, although they could certainly be turned against Le Brun herself, who has written many a book "quickly, very quickly," spurred on by "a strange interior haste,"[134] and who in her second pamphlet proudly claims to have written *Pour Aimé Césaire* in ten days (p. 11).

Equally valid, up to a point, is her second main criticism of Confiant and the authors of the *Éloge*: despite their rhetoric of hybridity and inclusiveness, they have in practice been very dogmatic and exclusionary when it comes to their "likes and dislikes" and their "dos and don'ts." This authoritarian tone can be at least in part accounted for by the fact that, as she put it in *Pour Aimé Césaire*, "the inventors of Créolité are imitating . . . those who champion the new American moral order" (p. 20). Le Brun reworks this claim at length in *Statue cou coupé*: in accusing Césaire of not being "créolement correct" (p. 39), Confiant and the "followers of this new sect" have transformed themselves into "witch hunters" and in so doing are

"thus imitating the rabble who are behind America's moral revival, track-
ing down everything that is not 'politically correct.'" The long-standing
ressentiment of French radicals with regard to the United States (a ressentiment, I hasten to add, with which this Canadian post/nationalist is himself
all too intimate) gets metonymically transferred onto the shoulders of these
Français d'outre-mer, whose repeated calls for her to mind her own (white
woman's) business are cited as evidence not only of their mimetic attachment to the "lies of multiculturalism" (p. 15), which ultimately promote
mindless conformity rather than true diversity (p. 121), but quite simply of
the racism and sexism of those who oppose her, which find expression not
only in their counterattacks on her (pp. 59–60) but in the antisemitic (pp.
62–68) and antimulatto (pp. 68–70) sentiments that have occasionally sur-
faced in interviews with Confiant and in his journalistic writings, causing
Le Brun to speak at several points of his *"national-créolisme"* (pp. 40, 63).
Notwithstanding Le Brun's simplistic scapegoating of "political correctness," there can be no question that Confiant and Chamoiseau have not
taken kindly to any criticisms of their work or their ideas and that they
have shown a penchant for anathematizing their opponents that has perhaps more to do with the sort of strong-man tactics that have long dogged
Caribbean political life than with the current obsessions of moralizing aca-
demics from the United States. One might well question, as Confiant and
Chamoiseau have done, what "right" the white, French, non-Creole-
speaking Le Brun has to comment on their family quarrel with Papa Césaire—a version of the same question that Bissette raised when he spoke of
Schœlcher as someone "whose abolitionist credentials still need to be verified by us blacks and mulattoes, the *only* ones competent to address the
question." On the other hand, one can equally point out that denying her
this right ("it's a black, Caribbean, creole thing, you wouldn't understand")
not only testifies to a "Stalinist" intolerance (p. 171), but is in obvious contradiction with the postidentitarian rhetoric of the authors of the *Éloge.*
(How) can one *legitimately* choose between these two positions? This is a
question that must be posed but that cannot be answered—or, rather, to
which we can, and perhaps must, respond illegitimately, in a partisan manner determined by where each of us is provisionally located on the ever-
shifting creole continuum of post/colonial theory.

The authoritarian conduct of the antiauthoritarian advocates of Créolité
is symptomatic of a larger contradiction at work in the poetics of creolization that Confiant, Chamoiseau, *and* Glissant are promoting (and this is the
third main point in her critique): Le Brun sums this contradiction up in the
phrase *"totalitarisme soft"* (p. 41). Glissant's enthusiastic advocacy of diversity—his emphasis on creolization, relationality, and chaos—serves only
to mask, according to Le Brun, the spread of a "globally generalized Club

Méditerranée" (p. 43): the author of the *Poétique*, in a more subtle and productive but no less dangerous way than disciples like Chamoiseau and Confiant, is fiddling while Rome does not so much burn as transfigure itself into a seductively soft gulag. Asserting that "it is difficult to see in this patchwork ideology, in each of these different phrases 'creolization of the world,' 'chaos-world,' or 'tout-monde,' to cite Glissant's terms, anything more than an elaborate cover that serves to camouflage the [negative] realities we are living" (p. 41), Le Brun aligns these Caribbean advocates of métissage with "reactionary" thinkers in France: "it is illuminating that their arguments about the creolization of the world coincide with those of the 'dominant thinking,' which, from Julia Kristeva to Michel Serres and all the rest of what passes for chic in Paris, without even mentioning America and its penchant for correctness, is working athwart their apologias of diversity toward a standardization of the world that could not be more catastrophic" (p. 42). For Le Brun, the thinking of "diversity" and cross-cultural "relations" ultimately amounts to a renunciation of real difference, a capitulation to "la pensée dominante," and the consecration "of a world reduced to a supermarket of changing tastes, where everyone can choose the cultural gadget appropriate for the whim of the moment" (p. 42). This vision of a compromised and compromising global supermarket, and the threat of cultural homogenization that it poses, is one with a long history: a commonplace since at least the time of the French Revolution in both conservative and revolutionary critiques of modernity, it has been equally prevalent in the countless objections that have been leveled over the past several decades against a leveling postmodernity. If Le Brun's invocation of this vision in her attack on what some (to recall Lionnet's arguments in favor of creolization [see Chapter 2]) might want to interpret as a "transcendent" post-colonial alternative to modernity is salutary, this is not because it directs us back to the subversive radicalism that she wants to privilege in opposition to Glissant's complicitous "chaos-monde," but because it reminds us that this creolized and creolizing world, in all its relational complexity, is one that simply cannot be read unilaterally (be it positively, as with the authors of the *Éloge*, or negatively, as with Le Brun).

In portraying creolization as a concept that colludes with global homogenization, in contradicting Glissant's repeated claims that "the poetics of relationality is not one that jumbles everything together, that remains neutral and fails to differentiate" (*ID*, p. 42; "la poétique de la Relation n'est pas une poétique du magma, de l'indifférencié, du neutre"), Le Brun not only draws parallels between these "diversifying" Caribbean thinkers and "reactionary" European ones but emphasizes—in a way that is reminiscent of Baudelaire's account of creole writers—the extent to which the authors of the *Éloge* are simply mimic men, slaves to (the wrong) European ideas: "it is hardly astonishing that these fabricators have as their intellectual point of reference the fashionable European values of the likes of Roland Barthes and Umberto Eco, whereas by contrast Césaire—whom they never stop denouncing for his attachment to Western values—relied on those who, from Rimbaud to Breton, by way of Schœlcher, Frobenius, Leiris or Lautréamont . . . have the most radically questioned these values." "That is to say," she adds, in case there might be any doubt as to the identity of these heroic Europeans, "those who have shown us that freedom cannot be fabricated but only invented, dangerously, and that there is no other path that can be taken if a point of view is to become a vision" (p. 45). Once again, Le Brun's sarcastic emphasis on the hypocrisy of Westernized thinkers accusing a writer like Césaire of being Westernized is extremely well taken (as, to a lesser degree, is her frequently repeated assertion that in order to be logically and morally consistent the authors of the *Éloge* ought to have published it in Creole, as opposed to issuing it in a bilingual French and English edition), but the inadequacies, and the totalitarianism, of her own thinking is equally on evidence in a passage such as this. Be like Rimbaud or else! There is no other way to transform your point of view into a vision! It is Césaire's resemblance to her heroes, and not his difference from them, that alone attracts her to him.[135] Le Brun's disdainful references to "the fabricators of ideology, their flatterers and their adherents, eager to stuff themselves with certitudes," as she put it in the first pamphlet (p. 22), are all very well and fine, but when push comes to shove she is as filled with certitudes as the next man or woman and, in her own very small way, as "homogenizing" as the dominant system she so sanctimoniously rejects: Schœlcher, Rimbaud, Frobenius(!)—all engaged in one and the same struggle! These are the good guys, who have truth on their side: men like André Breton, whose embarrassingly romanticized 1948 account of Martinique (*Martinique charmeuse de serpents*) is lovingly and naively offered up as an example of "his refusal of exoticism" (p. 132), without even the slightest nod to the possibility that it might also be infused—as it most certainly is—with risible and objectionable exoticist and colonial stereotypes; but most of all, men like the Marquis de Sade, who turns out to be virtually indistinguishable as far as Le Brun is concerned from Toussaint Louverture, whose "intellectual integrity" he shares (p. 161), and who, like the divine Marquis, was committed to "denouncing the snares of humanism" (p. 158) and combatting "the lie of Enlightenment" (p. 163). Taking up the last third of *Statue*, the chapters on Breton and "the strange objectivity whereby the Sadian exception and the black revolution of Saint-Domingue link up with one another" (pp. 151–64) are a distressing but also revealing example of the absurd lengths that some (anti)intellectuals will go in trying to establish their own subversive credentials and those of their pet interests, and readers with the slightest sensitivity to post-colonial issues will doubtless find the credibility of Le Brun's pamphlet badly damaged by their inclusion.

And yet one cannot simply "finish with" Le Brun and her critique of Confiant: the exchange certainly does not leave her unscathed (paranoid, self-important, hyperbolic, ridiculous, patronizing . . . all of these adjectives could be applied to aspects of *Statue cou coupé*), and it is impossible not to agree with Chamoiseau's laconic statement regarding Le Brun's first pamphlet that "it is certainly easier to defame than to refute."[136] However, it is equally, and painfully, obvious that *Confiant et compagnie* do not come out of this transatlantic encounter untarnished. Has the debate progressed since the days of Bissette and Schœlcher? Can we speak of progress within the context of this debate if we cannot legitimately choose between Bissette/Confiant and their mimetic rivals Schœlcher/Le Brun but must situate ourselves, unsatisfactorily and unsatisfied, somewhere between the two positions? As Gramsci wrote, and as Nadine Gordimer insisted after him, during the interregnum there arise a "great diversity of morbid symptoms": as the reactivation of the nineteenth-century Bissette-Schœlcher debate in our own vastly different, and yet disturbingly similar, late-twentieth-century circumstances testifies, we have not finished with these symptoms. That it is perhaps time to claim the interregnum as our home rather than (only) as a place of exile and to begin to learn how to live with a condition that we cannot cure is what I will be suggesting in the following chapter.

7 The (Un)exploded Volcano

DANIEL MAXIMIN'S 'SOUFRIÈRES' AND
THE APOCALYPSE OF NARRATIVE

"The Great Zombi of Modernity": Modernist Destiny, Postmodern Errancy, and the Problem of Intertextuality

> *The problem of those who are waiting.*—It requires strokes
> of luck and much that is incalculable if a higher man in
> whom the solution of a problem lies dormant is to get
> around to action in time—to "eruption," one might say.
> —Nietzsche, *Beyond Good and Evil*
>
> And in the shadow of the smoking mountain, everyone
> waited.
> —*Time* magazine, August 30, 1976

The passage from Nietzsche that serves as my first epigraph for this section can be read as raising one of the central concerns of our modernity: namely, that we live in a "problematic" time of waiting, from which solutions appear absent, and in which reaction has taken the place of action. What is called for, as a way out of this unenviable position, is a volcanic "eruption" (*Ausbruch*) that will propel us beyond the confines of the waiting world that we find ourselves humanly, all-too-humanly, inhabiting.[1] Nietzsche identifies the agent of this historical change with the individual subject, the higher man—quite possibly the artist—who may, but only if he gets around to action in time, solve the problem of our modernity. However, even as this passage urges us toward a deproblematized future, it also stresses the aleatory, contingent nature of this desired change, and in so doing emphatically puts into question the resolutely systematic and projective thinking of modernity from Hegel onward: as Alejo Carpentier would discover in attempting to write his own *Explosion*, "history turns out to be the error, the errancy inherent in all action, as opposed to theory or intention."[2] Nietzsche's description of the problem of modernity, then, while remaining attached to the idea of its eruptive solution, also confronts us with a world, let us call it the *postmodern* world, in which the revolutionary possibility of getting around to action in time has increasingly come to seem a matter of sheer chance and errancy, and perhaps even an historical aberration.

The relation between Nietzsche's modern(ist) call for an end to the problem of modernity, and his postmodern intuition that such ends cannot be willed but only happened upon by chance, is one that overlaps with that other relation—between the colonial and the post-colonial—that I have repeatedly scrutinized in this book. If a modernist writer like Aimé Césaire could, at the height of the decolonization movement in the late 1950s, assure his audience that "the writer and the artist are for their part already laying the foundations for a *good decolonization* by helping to put some order into the cultural chaos,"[3] the prospect of this "*bonne décolonisation*" and of this salvational order appear altogether unlikely under the chaotic postmodern condition(s) to which postcolonial writers respond. Post/colonialism as I have defined it is that time in which those who are waiting for the eruptive solution anticipated by decolonization, perhaps the last of modernity's great metanarratives, must face up to the prolonged absence of any such resolution and the consequent necessity of learning how to live reactively, within rather than beyond the problematic boundaries of a colonial modernity that has—since at least the age of Nietzsche and the New Imperialism—taken on the dimensions of, in Glissant's words, a "planetary adventure that does not allow us to guess where solutions to the problems that have arisen from the precipitate contact of cultures will materialize" (*PR*, p. 177).

The modernist literature associated with the period of decolonization makes ample use of Nietzsche's volcanic metaphor of eruption, and this is especially true of the Caribbean, where natural geography dictates its relevance. The volcano stands as a dominant symbol of revolutionary change and poetic innovation, for instance, in the work of Aimé Césaire, or "I who Krakatoa" as he identifies himself in the opening line of the poem "Corps perdu." One of Césaire's "privileged images,"[4] the volcano appears twice in that epic poem of Negritude, *Cahier d'un retour au pays natal*, which since its publication in book form in 1947 has consistently been read as the opening salvo of a truly original, because modern(ist), Caribbean literature. The first appearance of the word "volcano" in the *Cahier* occurs during the opening invocation of Fort-de-France, in which the poet excoriates that inert, flattened-out town ("cette ville inerte," "cette ville plate-étalée") and "the awful futility of our raison d'être" ("l'affreuse inanité de notre raison d'être"), and unleashes an apocalyptic promise that "the volcanoes will explode" (*CP*, pp. 34–35; "les volcans éclateront"). The second appearance comes at the beginning of what has been identified as the poem's third and final movement, which is "turned entirely toward the future":[5] here, the poet's earlier promise is fulfilled, as he is suddenly overwhelmed by "the fire hoarded in volcanoes and the gigantic seismic pulse which now beats the measure of a living body in my firm conflagration" ("le feu thésaurisé des volcans et le gigantesque pouls sismique qui bat maintenant la mesure d'un corps vivant en mon ferme embrasement"). No longer isolated from his surroundings but part of a new collective subject ("nous sommes debout maintenant, mon pays et moi"), he has been salvationally assailed by "the strength [that] is not in us but above us, in a voice that drills the night and the hearing like the penetrance of an apocalyptic wasp" ("la force [qui] n'est pas en nous, mais au-dessus de nous, dans une voix qui vrille la nuit et l'audience comme la pénétrance d'une guêpe apocalyptique" [pp. 76–77]). The explosive promises of this apocalyptic voice with which the literature of decolonization begins—or, rather, renews the rhetoric of an earlier Caribbean Romanticism[6]—are to be fulfilled at its end: this literature of "Revelations" would draw together the beginning and the end, suturing the middle ground that separates them.[7] As Césaire puts it in the *Cahier*:

> Il faut bien commencer.
> Commencer quoi?
> La seule chose au monde qui vaille
> la peine de commencer:
> La Fin du monde parbleu.
>
> One must begin somewhere.
> Begin what?
> The only thing in the world
> worth beginning:
> The End of the world of course.

(pp. 54–55)

Césaire, "at one and the same time a man of both 'initiations' and 'endings'" (as the authors of the *Éloge* remind us [p. 18]), gives vent here to the modern(ist) insistence on beginning anew and ending conclusively; it is precisely this imperative to begin the End of the (colonial) world, and to "found" another,[8] that I will be interrogating throughout this chapter in my analysis of the role of beginnings and endings in the emphatically postmodern novels of the Guadeloupean novelist Daniel Maximin.

The volcano functions in Césaire's work not only as a metaphor for political change but as an emblem of his poetics, as he once noted in an interview with Maximin. Elaborating upon the filiations that he feels bind the people of Martinique to its volcano, Mt. Pelée, Césaire remarks that the Martiniquans are "un peuple péléen": "I've always felt that the mountain gave birth to us. We are the sons of the volcano."[9] He sees his poetry, in turn, as mimicking this elective parent: it is "the eruption of forces long buried and occulted by debris and scoria" (p. 8). Real poetry, he continues, is the means of a "revelation"; it provides its listeners with an "access to Being . . . like an access to one's self, an access to the powers deep inside us [*aux forces profondes*]." Césaire's apocalyptic-modernist vision of poetry as a revelatory force is thus explicitly linked to the question of essence: it posits an *Être* that is identical with one's true self, that dwells under the deceptive surface of things, and that must be (re)captured by the writer ("in order for it to be valid," he once remarked, Caribbean literature "must have as its only course of action the exploration and recovery of being [*ne peut être qu'une démarche de prospection et de récupération de l'être*]").[10] Whether or not this identity can be summed up by an essentialist interpretation of what Negritude involves is, of course, a matter of some ambivalence in Césaire, who wavers back and forth between a biological and a cultural reading of the word (and it must be acknowledged, as Confiant has argued, that Césaire's obsessive use of the word "blood" in his poetry lends credence to the essentialist reading, notwithstanding the fact that it has become a critical commonplace to distantiate him from Senghor's now discredited biologism and its penchant for "rhythmic attitudes" [*AC*, pp. 42–43]).[11] What is clear, in any case, is that—like Brathwaite's nam, which organically connects past, present, and a future to which it explosively looks forward ("in its future, *nam* is capable of atomic explosion: *nam ... dynamo ... dynamite*")[12]—these "forces profondes" can be accessed simply by clearing away the debris and the scoria of a problematic colonial history.

The sort of revelatory imperatives to which Césaire gives voice here are basic to modernist aesthetics. His comments directly echo, for instance, those of Victor Segalen, the early-twentieth-century French writer whose prophetic advocacy of "le Divers" has won him an increasingly influential following amongst (francophone) postcolonial writers and theorists. Segalen's quest, which I have explored at some length in my *Exotic Memories*, was to disentangle the exotic from the colonial: *e*xoticism provided a potential way out of what he looked down upon, from Nietzschean high places, as the degraded world of the colonial Same that threatened to engulf all that was truly Other.[13] As he put it in his never-completed *Essai sur l'Exotisme*, the task of a genuine exoticism, of a literature capable of giving expression to "the purity and the intensity of 'le Divers,'"[14] was thus one of liberating the remaining spaces of alterity from the banalities to which the "pseudo-Exotes" and "colonial writers" had subjected it:

having divested it [*l'ayant dépouillée*] of its innumerable scoria, the smears, the stains, the bacilli, and the moulds deposited upon it over the years through the contact of so many mouths, so many prostituted and touristic hands . . . let us allow it

once again to take on flesh, and like a seed, this time pure, to develop freely, joy-
ously, unfettered and unaltered. (1.749)

Césaire and his avant-gardist colleagues of the 1930s and 1940s are capti-
vated by a similar language of purification and divestment (*dépouillement*,
a word that as we saw in the preceding chapter was also central to Maynard's analysis of Hugo's "revolutionary" use of language). In the same
manner that Segalen had attempted to dissociate himself from the badly
written ("scorified") works of a degraded "littérature coloniale," they
would define their liberatory enterprise by anathematizing previous generations of Caribbean authors, whom they wrote off in the pages of formative
journals like *Légitime Défense* and *Tropiques* as talentless mimic men—a
"space-clearing gesture" (in Anthony Appiah's words [*IMFH*, p. 149]) typical of modernism, which cultural critics and historians have, ever since,
found it virtually impossible to contest. When in 1941, on the opening page
of the first issue of *Tropiques*, Césaire surveys the literary scene of the native land to which he has recently returned, he sees "no poetry, not even a
seed of it, not a single sprout—or else the hideous leprosy of counterfeits."[15] This critique of the counterfeit, grounded in the same language of
medical pathology to which Segalen so often had recourse (not surprisingly,
given that he served as a doctor in the French navy), in turn induces a call
for health and authenticity: "the time for parasitizing the world is over;
what is at stake, rather, is saving it." (Ironically, decades later, the authors
of *Toward the Decolonization of African Literature* would redeploy this
language in their nativist critique of modernism: the general aim of their
work, they note, is "to help release African culture from the death-grip of
the West; and the particular aim of this anthology is to help scotch the
modernist infection, with its narrowness of themes and genres, its anemic
treatment, and its general lack of robustness and gusto.")[16]

To be sure, where the aloof Segalen's faith in a Nietzschean higher man
led to an aristocratic distaste for democracy and the masses in general, and
a consequent—and typically modernist—enshrinement of the isolated
artist as the repository of value and the most (and perhaps only) suitable
agent of social change, Césaire's own faith in the apocalypse would allow
him, though in an always ambivalent fashion given the "formal individualism" of his poetry and (in Confiant's words) "the hypertrophy of the ego
that has always characterized Césaire" (*AC*, p. 99), to rewrite Nietzsche in
terms of the collective subject, thus drawing him closer to the more systematic (Marxist) visions of decolonization that flourished in the decades following upon the publication of his *Cahier*. And yet the overlaps between
these two men are as important as their points of divergence and help account, ultimately, for Césaire's ambiguous positioning in regard to what
might be considered the more radically modernist politics of *désaliénation*

that we find at work in a subsequent generation of Martiniquan writers like Fanon and Glissant.

Since, as we have seen, Glissant's trajectory as a writer takes him from modernism to post/modernism, a further word about him, and about his relation to the modernist Césaire and the postmodern Maximin, is in order here. This relation needs to be addressed on at least two very different fronts: that of his poetics and his politics. Although it is a common tendency when speaking of Glissant to read his theoretical writings as a consistent body of work, these writings strike me as being founded upon a (no doubt fruitful, no doubt inevitable) contradiction: they are moving in the two very different directions that are required, on the one hand, by his emphasis on creolization and relationality, and, on the other, by his continued insistence on nationality and identity. It is the first direction that most obviously shapes Glissant's poetics—a poetics that explicitly rejects the explosive approach of a magisterial predecessor like Césaire and that has come to dominate his later post/nationalist theoretical writings. Glissant sees the apocalyptic style of a writer like Césaire as being no longer adequate to a transnational world of global relations—a world in which no revelation can be anything more than partial, no resolution final. Césaire, and Rimbaud before him, embody what Glissant refers to as a "poetics of the moment" ("poétique de l'instant") but this momentous emphasis—the suturing of beginning and end in a moment of and/or outside time discussed a few pages back—has now been, or ought to have been (pace Annie Le Brun), replaced by a "poetics of duration" ("poétique de la durée") better capable of registering the complexities of the planetary adventure that is drawing the world ambivalently together and ensuring the ongoing creolization, and thus relativization, of our identities. The time is over for definitive revelations of the sort metaphorically signaled by Césaire's volcano and called forth in a journal like *Légitime Défense* (e.g., "the wind that is rising up from black America will, let us hope, have done quick work of cleansing our Antilles of the aborted fruits of a superannuated culture").[17] "We no longer reveal totality in ourselves through fulgurations," Glissant notes in the *Poétique* (pp. 44–45); rather, because "in its circulation and its action poetry is no longer a matter of conjecturing (about) a specific people, but (about) the very future of the planet Earth" (p. 44), the poet's vocation has become one of "piling up" and of "an indeterminate impatience infinitely rehearsed" (p. 223; "l'entassement et l'indéfinie impatience infiniment recommencée"). The poet of the tout-monde (im)patiently accumulates visions that are rooted in the local but open to the world, in an uninterrupted process of "mise en relation" (p. 216) that is synonymous with what Glissant terms "errant" thinking, which "conceives (of) totality, but willingly renounces the pretension of summoning or possessing it" (p. 33). Like Nietzsche's problematically contingent world of waiting, Glissant's chaos-monde of errant relations is one that can be neither systematically encompassed nor divested of the "impurities" that (as Segalen lamented) make possible our modernity and the ever-escalating process of cultural métissage to which Glissant has so ably sensitized his readers.

If, however, Glissant's poetics are thus altogether *less* modernist than Césaire's in their renunciation of an explosive style, such is not the case with his politics—or at least the politics of his most influential theoretical work, *Discours antillais*. This politics would appear to be, or to have been, equally or *more* modernist than Césaire's inasmuch as it is grounded (as we saw in Chapter 4) in a continued, although increasingly frustrated and "Cassandra-like,"[18] attachment to those revolutionary dreams of decolonization and of national liberation that Césaire eloquently voiced ("*true* decolonization," he asserted, adapting André Breton's famous pronouncement about the necessary convulsiveness of beauty, "*will be revolutionary or not at all*")[19] but that his political accommodation with France—his nuanced compliance with the policy of *départementalisation*—has done so little to further, as Confiant repeatedly points out in his assertively Oedipal polemics with Césaire ("today, it is possible to be an authentic son of Césaire and of his way of thinking only by mistrusting him, by straying from the paths that he marked out" [*AC*, p. 38]). The nationalist politics of a Caribbean discourse, unlike the international poetics of relationality, continue (as I argued in Chapter 2) to "conjecturer un peuple donné"—to evoke, for instance, the promise of an independent Martinique, to view the island's inhabitants from the Fanonesque perspective of the need for their disalienation, to critique a world of theatrical appearances in the name of some more authentic identity, be that identity conceived in purely national terms (*the* Martiniquan) or the quasi-national geocultural terms of Antillanité. This tension between a creolizing (global) poetics and a (local) identity politics is basic to Glissant's oeuvre, and constitutes one of its fundamental strengths; however, in each of the following sections of this chapter, as a means of differentiating Maximin's postmodern enterprise from Glissant's in many ways still emphatically modernist one, I will be strategically isolating some of the latter's political conjectures in *Discours antillais* from the context of his work as a whole and putting them into question from the perspective of a postmodernism that can no longer credit the imperative of self-possession that undergirds them.

The postmodern vision takes as its point of departure the collapse of the heroic dreams of modernism—and of the aesthetic and political revolutions and/or resolutions that such dreams promised. In a recent interview, the exiled Haitian writer René Depestre has identified the condition of postmodernism about as succinctly, and (from a feminist perspective) revealingly, as is possible when he speaks about his failed "relationship" with radical politics and the Cuban Revolution, for which he was once such an ardent spokesman (so ardent a spokesman, indeed, that his temporary adhesion to the doctrine of social realism would provoke a stinging rebuke from Césaire—the poem "Le verbe marronner"—at the time of the latter's break with the Communist Party in the mid-1950s):

If the notion of revolution itself has failed, it would be illusory for me to continue to sleep with a phantom. The great zombi of modernity is revolution, alas. The great zombi.[20]

Leaving aside the metaphorical dimension of Depestre's "Adieu à la Révolution" (to cite the title of a recent poem of his), which in its dependence upon the figure of (a phantom) woman establishes a significant continuity between himself and Césaire (to say nothing of Segalen and the "mains prostitueuses et touristes" that so dismay the author of *Essai sur l'Exotisme*),[21] I find his comments admirably exact in their situating of the postmodern dilemma: if we have slept with a zombi, where does that leave us upon waking? Once again back in the folds of a life we renounced that we might follow "her" apocalyptic lures, or at an even further remove from that life—ourselves zombified by the encounter with the siren call of political and cultural transformation that generates the revolutionary drive forward of modernity? What happens when we have outlived the dream, finding ourselves no longer present (to recall Nietzsche's words) "in time" but at best, as it were, represented "in *Time*"—sons and daughters of the sons of the volcano, for whom such phrases as "revolution," "reformation of the world," "disalienation of man" ring hollow (as they now do for Depestre [p. 149])? What is our belated relation to the originating force that assailed modernist literature and politics and to which the author of the *Discours antillais* remains ambivalently attached? What is left in our ears of Césaire's apocalyptic "voix qui vrille dans la nuit"—a drilling that one might once have hoped would end up blasting a way out of the impasse of our modernity?

It is modernist questions such as these that are posed and (not) resolved in the novels of Daniel Maximin. As Clarisse Zimra has pointed out with regard to his first novel, *L'isolé soleil* (1981), Maximin is a writer who self-consciously "follows in the footsteps of his elders";[22] unremittingly intertextual, a "novel of and about (re)writing," *L'isolé soleil* grounds itself in words already said (notably, those of Césaire and the surrealists) and events already lived (various episodes from a pointedly revisionist history of Guadeloupe). As I will be arguing, Maximin's use of intertextuality can be read as exemplary of the creolization process, and as such it is opposed to a strictly modernist intertextuality of the sort that Simon Gikandi has rightly identified with the Jamaican Michelle Cliff's first novel: "*Abeng* finds its power in its parasitic and subversive relationship to previous texts, which it appropriates and then spits out, clearing a space for alternative systems of representation."[23] What Gikandi's portrait of *Abeng* has isolated in Cliff, I would venture, is an avatar of that "dépouillement" Segalen knew was necessary if the foundations for a truly "alternative system of representation," a purified exoticism, were ever to be laid. Previous texts (notably, those of a degraded colonial literature) are chewed over and then expunged as a means of asserting the writer's own generative power. Simultaneously, a more "appropriate" (some might say narcissistic) identification with the past is established: Segalen becomes the scribe of imperial China, Césaire—in his expulsion of the "exotic poets"—aligns himself with Rimbaud, the French surrealists, and ancestral Africa, while Cliff flatteringly connects herself back up with the maroon resistance leader, Nanny, the "activist Subject-in-History,"[24] who provides a heuristic counterpoint to the novel's as yet alienated protagonist Clare Savage, still in the process of trying to digest texts that will only serve, so (this version of) the modernist argument goes, to disempower her.

It is precisely this strong, "subversive" use of intertextuality that Maximin's novel puts into question, or *parodies* (a word whose ambivalences I will be exploring in the following section of this chapter). To appropriate another's language is necessarily, for Maximin, to absorb it; the words of others, once spoken, and they are always-already spoken, cannot be simply expelled but must, rather, be cautiously *in*habited. Nor can the (narcissistic) processes of identification that are such an essential part of modernism be considered as anything more (or less) than textual strategies that have their provisional, but always deconstructible, uses—a point that the metafictive trajectory of *L'isolé soleil*, a novel that is all about (hi)story-telling, emphasizes. This metafiction centers around the protagonist Marie-Gabriel's repeated attempts at identifying herself with the past through writing: first, by chronicling a heroic but male-dominated official history of anticolonial resistance and revolution, exemplified for her by Louis Delgrès, who in 1802, in the face of French forces intent on restoring slavery in Guadeloupe, famously blew up himself, his troops, and a good many of Napoléon's soldiers on the flanks of the island's volcano, *la Soufrière*; second, by then recuperating the less world-historic story of her own mother's life in the Paris of the 1930s and Vichy-occupied Guadeloupe in the early 1940s. As Zimra points out, this shift from a male-centered story to a female-centered one, and from historical chronicle to "écriture féminine," serves to hollow out paternal myths, but it would be a mistake to read this shift (as Zimra appears to do)[25] in terms of a definitive rupture with "the father's explosive tale." Maximin is purposefully conjoining one provisional discourse to another, parodying both with dignity, and establishing a problematic continuity—an interdependency—between these two mirror texts. In so doing, he weakens the claims of both his adopted fathers *and* mothers, while remaining ambivalently attached to what he can neither fully spit out nor wholly embrace.

The relation (in Glissant's sense of the word) of interdependency that obtains between the two main narrative sequences of his first novel gets repeated when Maximin comes to write *Soufrières*—the 1987 sequel to *L'isolé soleil* with which I will be chiefly concerned in this chapter: with this second novel, Maximin is not merely rewriting others as in his first, but rewriting himself (in a move that in many ways reads as a belated and parodic homage to the self-referential world of Glissant's novels, with their cast of recurring characters and episodes). Significantly, the action of this novel occurs *before* Marie-Gabriel has finished the manuscript of *L'isolé soleil*, a fact that situates us in a chiasmatic space between the (male-focused) beginning and the (female-focused) ending of a first novel that is thus both anterior and ulterior to its successor. Again, this ambiguous relation can be usefully compared with the one established by Cliff in her own follow-up to *Abeng*, *No Telephone to Heaven* (1987): the story of the light-skinned Clare Savage picks up directly where it left off, taking Clare from her adolescent years, when she is still deeply entrapped within the alienating logic of her "colonial education," to an adulthood that will be redeemed by the discovery of her vocation, that of historically revisionist educator and, ultimately, of freedom fighter dying for the revolutionary cause and thereby (re)enacting the resistance of Nanny and her maroons. For all its attempts at formal experimentation, Cliff's modernist novel remains steadfastly attached to what Patrick Taylor has identified, and valorized, as the "narrative of liberation" and the apocalyptic resolutions it demands: exemplified by Fanon, this narrative maintains that "only through a total spiritual transformation in which the colonized recognize their situation and take responsibility for the sociopolitical totality can there be a new beginning."[26] For Fanon, as a consequence, the storyteller is one who "'presides over a real invocation' in which a new historical movement and a new type of person are 'revealed'"[27]—and this is certainly the light in which Cliff wants her revisionary enterprise to be read.

For Maximin, by contrast, the storyteller can only preside over *unreal* invocations, apostrophes that acknowledge the (im)purely rhetorical ground of such imperatives as a "total spiritual transformation." Contemporary writers from the Antilles are in a position to be especially attuned to the hollowness of these imperatives because of the "dispossessed" political status of the islands, which have failed to gain even a nominal independence from the colonial power of the mère-patrie. As Marie-Gabriel's male coun-

terpart, Adrien, puts it in *L'isolé soleil,* Guadeloupe is a place in which "liberation"—in the strong sense of the word—has not taken place: reflecting
upon the Haitian Revolution, he asks her, "do you know that we would
have been a free people at the same time as Haiti if the Soufrière had
erupted onto Basse-Terre in 1802, to the joyful applause of an insurgent
people?" (p. 88). It is the *absence* of this volcanic explosion that predicates
their future, forming a people who "now only get together [*se retrouvent*]
to commemorate—like Mt. Pelée in 1902—acts of heroism in which neither the one nor the other have participated" (p. 88). But this absence, I am
arguing, is not merely a lamentable quirk of history distinguishing the Antilles from the rest of the "liberated" postcolonial world, but a postmodern
condition of dispossession to which the entire multinationalized and mul-
tirelationalized world is now subject, in a diversity of ways, and of which
these French départements, simultaneously a part of the Caribbean and of
the European Economic Community, are hardly on the margins but, rather,
at the very center. No longer able to participate in the aesthetic and political dreams of a revolutionary modernism, nor to credit a past-oriented essentialist (Senghor) or future-oriented nationalist (Fanon) identity politics,
forced into living reactively, the inhabitants of this creolized world find
themselves ("se retrouvent") in a place of waiting and of commemoration—in the place of the (un)exploded volcano.

It is from this place that Maximin writes, stressing the ungroundedness
of the modernist project in the wake of which he is writing, and the fictive-
ness of the identities, past and future, he is (re)constructing. As Maximin
has said, "the present always invents a past for itself out of its own desire":[28] the ancestral past and the identity that might once have accompanied it are for Maximin nothing more or less than inventions generated out
of desire, a rhetorical *inventio,* and for this reason his books have been well
characterized as an "anti-*Roots*";[29] in turn, the revolutionary future, and
the "new type of person" to which the modernist project looked forward,
has been emptied of its promise. The creolized subject finds her- or himself
in a textual and geographical space that is at a definitive, and defining, remove from any and all cultural points of departure or ideological points of
arrival: the origin and the telos can be present only as insubstantial yet
eroticized traces, in the Derridean sense of the word. In following up on,
and upon, these traces, however, they take on a material reality of their
own, becoming paths (a specifically Antillean meaning of the word *trace*)
that lead not back to but away from the obsession with origins and resolutions that characterizes both Euro- and Afrocentric thinking and toward a
place in which such "biases" will, in Wilson Harris's words, be yet further
"consumed,"[30] if never entirely disposed of for the simple reason that we
cannot avoid talking (with)in the very terms that we have outlived. Max-

imin's two novels, in their intertextual correspondence, produce a mutual transformation of the past by the present and the present by the past, and thereby create the unstable ground for a future that does not so much lie beyond as within the interstices of these two ambivalently, and ineluctably, conjoined worlds. In embracing this (con)fusion and interdependence a writer like Maximin sets himself up against a simplistic, and narcissistic, politics of "identification" with a particular race or culture-core ("identification is the enemy of identity," as one of the characters in *L'isolé soleil* puts it [p. 193]),[31] or with the eruptive ideological agendas of the modernists and their avatars—while at the same time recognizing that these hollowed out strategies often remain, in Nadine Gordimer's famous phrase, "essential gestures."

This position that Maximin occupies cannot fail to disappoint those readers and critics still in search of political or aesthetic revelations, of originality and not imitation, of active *ex*plosions rather than reactive strategies for living with(in) an ever more cross-culturalized and mutually contaminated world. It is clear that Maximin's work does not "live up to" that of the modernist predecessors whom he so insistently (re)cites; it is equally clear, from the critical silence that has surrounded his second novel, that what some might have mistaken for the literary promise of *L'isolé soleil* has not been realized in *Soufrières* (and even less so in the sequel to that sequel, *L'île et une nuit* [1995]). An astute reader of both Césaire and Glissant's work, Bernadette Cailler, for instance, has offered the following negative reaction to Maximin's first novel: "the work of a talented and knowledgeable intellectual, this work is not yet that of a Caribbean poet." She then goes on to ask,

but is it the consciousness of a Caribbean destiny that permeates [*pénètre*] the reader as he turns the pages of this sophisticated mosaic, produced [*fabriquée*] by someone in complete control, one would say, of his emotions, delighting [*jouissant*], one would say, in his acrobatics and even in his shortcomings, as if the drama, the real drama, did not exist?[32]

The terms of Cailler's critique are exceptionally revealing: according to her, there exists a sharp distinction between intellectuals and poets, which is at least in part due to the absence or presence of the consciousness of a "destiny"—a destiny that ought to *penetrate* the reader (and one thinks here of Césaire's *pénétrance*, not to mention Senghor's claims about how rhythm allows the African "to enter into [*pénétrer*] the spirituality of an object").[33] The novel is merely a "sophisticated" mosaic (and how can we fail to hear in her use of this adjective the long-standing Platonic critique of the Sophists and their reliance on mere rhetoric?);[34] it is guilty of *jouissance*; it is mere theater as opposed to "real drama" (an opposition that we will be ex-

ploring at some length in the final section of this chapter). The postmodern
text proves to be nothing but "scraps, echoes, rehearsals [*des sons à
l'essai*]." Lacking the systematic method of modernism, written in a provisional "essayistic" spirit, Maximin's novels cannot live up to the destinal
expectations of a critic like Cailler.

What are we to make of such expectations? Can we simply avoid them?
And can we actually deny the value of the need for revelations that drives
them? As Lois Zamora has emphasized in her excellent introduction to the
various uses to which apocalyptic imagery has been put in recent New
World literature, the "apocalyptic imagination" proposes "radical changes
in the organization of future world governance, in reaction to existing inadequacies and abuses"; it is "subversive in its recognition that present
forms of thought and action are inadequate, and revolutionary in its impulse to create a new synthesis out of psychic or social dislocation."[35] How
can we object to this imagination (a question that I intend in both its
senses: by what means can we do so; what could we possibly object to in
it)? This is the question, I believe, that the postmodern condition forces us
to address, and in so doing it situates us squarely within the terms of a
double bind: we cannot actually live with*out* that which we have outlived.
Part of what it means to outlive, say, modernism is to remain a prey to its
explosive dreams, which are in one form or another always also still *our*
dreams. Any rethinking of the apocalypse, any objection to it, as Derrida
has so astutely pointed out in his *D'un ton apocalyptique adopté naguère
en philosophie*, will remain enfolded within the very thing that it is supposedly intent upon unfolding. "A demystificatory desire with regard to the
apocalyptic tone" will itself become caught up in the same revelatory logic
that made possible the promises of a modernity whose end the demystifica-
tors (or deconstructors) are attempting to convey but whose coming, whose
second coming, they are always also announcing in the very gesture of
their renunciation.[36] Like Derrida, and like the later Glissant who also situates us in the ambivalent double time marked in Derrida's title by the
word "naguère" (as we saw at the very end of Chapter 4), Maximin will
remain within the folds of the logic—a different logic than Derrida's, to be
sure, with different historical and geographical pre-texts—of what he is
putting into question: in the face of his modernist precursors, he can only
repeat—(re)cite and (re)site—the very thing that he has survived and the
end of which he is announcing. In so doing, he prepares us for a simultaneously de- and reconstructive way of thinking that is perhaps best captured in the phrase "apocalypse *sans* apocalypse," which Derrida puts forward as a compromised alternative to modernity and the mystifications of
its apocalyptic ideologies. This "apocalypse *without* apocalypse" conveys
to us both modernity's promise of an ending and the ending of that

promise. This double ending, this *without* that always also remains *within* what it has come to question, and that is situated *between* the apocalypses that it ought to have come *after*, is what characterizes the complicitous relation of the postmodern to the modern, of the postcolonial to the colonial. It is this post/apocalyptic complicity that I will now attempt to describe in the following account of the beginning(s) and ending(s) of Maximin's *Soufrières*.

In the Beginning(s): (Re)sounding Apostrophes, (De)touring the Catastrophe

> The explosion will not take place today: it is too early... or too late.
>
> —Frantz Fanon, *Peau noire, masques blancs*

"L'explosion n'aura pas lieu aujourd'hui. Il est trop tôt... ou trop tard": these opening lines of Fanon's influential first book, published in 1952, invoke the image of the volcano and the promise of the apocalyptic explosion that, as we have seen, is central to the poetics and politics of Caribbean modernism. And yet they also situate the reader in a space from which that explosion is absent, in a present that has only a hypothetical connection to the once and future explosion. This ambiguous positioning can also be read in the title of Fanon's book, since it not only maps out the opposition between a single black skin and a plurality of white masks, but also a space of relation—marked by the comma—between the two: between an epidermally defined identity-reality and a bleached succession of masks-appearances. As gateways into Fanon's text, its title and opening lines pose problems that are central to any reading of his work as a whole: notably, is there, today, any place for an explosively revolutionary politics, or are we limited to a series of intermediary and irresolute gestures that inevitably situate us between past eruptions and those that we might once have projected onto a radically different future? What, moreover, is to be our attitude toward a single "black" identity, and how are we to negotiate the world of "white" masks that apparently betrays it?

As Henry Louis Gates has pointed out in a recent overview of the uses to which Fanon's oeuvre has been put in postcolonial theory, Fanon has served as a site in which "the disruptive relation between narratives of subject-formation and narratives of liberation" becomes acutely visible.[37] A certain reading of Fanon, and of postcolonial literature as a whole, would call forth the possibility of the explosive liberation that Fanon both defers and nostalgically looks back upon at the very outset of his career, but that is very much *present* in the work with which it ends, *Les damnés de la terre*

(1961)—a work, significantly enough, from which all traces of Fanon's Caribbean origins have been effaced.[38] It is this revolutionary Fanon, indeed, whom a fictionalized Angela Davis will evoke in *L'isolé soleil*: for her, Fanon is first and foremost the man who argued that "the unconscious Black-White relationship . . . can only be made to evolve through the dynamics of revolutionary rupture" (p. 275). Grounding herself in the "language of rupture,"[39] Maximin's Davis criticizes Marie-Gabriel for concentrating too much on the sort of ambivalent psychological issues that were of primary importance in Fanon's early work. But it is precisely this emphasis on ambivalence in Fanon that other postcolonial critics, such as Homi Bhabha, have privileged against the Manichean thinking that more obviously dominates a late work like *Les damnés de la terre*, the opening page of which bluntly defines decolonization as a "total, complete, absolute substitution," the replacement "without transitions" of "one species of men with another" (p. 5). While suggesting with regard to Fanon's later work that "the state of emergency from which he writes demands more insurgent answers, more immediate identifications," Bhabha sees the importance of Fanon as lying primarily not in his blunt claims about decolonization and the creation of "new men" but in his emphasis on "ambivalent, uncertain questions of colonial desire."[40] In line with this second(ary) critical direction, Maximin's work explores the dimensions of the transitional (and translational) space that has emerged with the collapse of the ends-oriented metanarratives that once appeared to justify the later Fanon's claim in *Damnés* that "the people" were readying themselves "to interrupt the dead time introduced by colonialism, to make History" (p. 32), and his belief that "struggle is what, by making the old colonial reality explode, reveals unknown facets, causes new meanings to materialize, and puts the finger on the contradictions that were camouflaged by this reality" (p. 94). As the ongoing debate between the two orientations of postcolonial criticism bears witness, however, the opposition between them is itself a constitutive feature of this ambivalent space, which thus in an attenuated fashion *includes* the very thing that is *precluded* from it: namely, the sort of volcanic explosions after which Maximin's Angela Davis longs, caught up as she is in "the rigidity of the self/other binarism governing traditional discourse on colonialism."[41]

In his use of the volcano as the central focus of *Soufrières*, a novel that takes place in 1976 and chronicles the reactions of various Guadeloupeans to an anticipated explosion of *la Soufrière*, Maximin can be read as providing an extended gloss on the statement with which Fanon's work as an author effectively begins; he is interrogating, and commemorating, the (im)possibility of an explosive identity politics of the sort posited by such modernist thinkers as Césaire, Fanon, and the leaders of the Black Power movement. *Soufrières*, in the wake of (and in imitation of) *L'isolé soleil*, insistently addresses the issue of revolutionary change, which it apostrophizes in the form of the volcano that hangs over the novel and, indeed, narrates the fourth of its six chapters. As Pérez Firmat has pointed out in his discussion of the mestizo Cuban poet Nicolás Guillen's use of this rhetorical figure, "apostrophes are performative: they bring into being the entities they invoke" (CC, p. 85).[42] This sort of performance has always been central to the construction of the historical novel—the genre that we examined in Chapter 5 and to which Maximin's novels parodically attach themselves. Sir Walter Scott's early-nineteenth-century invention of a primitive Scottish past in the face of the modernization brought about by the colonizing English has, moreover, obvious genealogical affinities with that ongoing recuperation of pre-colonial traditions by colonized intellectuals so ably analyzed by Fanon in his discussion of how one goes about constructing a "national culture,"[43] so it is worth citing here—as a way of beginning to explore the nuances of Maximin's own invocations of the past—the following description of a Highland *bhairdh* as he first appears to the eponymous protagonist of Scott's *Waverley* (1815):

He seemed to Edward, who attended to him with much interest, to recite many proper names, to lament the dead, to apostrophize the absent, to exhort, and entreat and animate those who were present. (p. 98)

Here is the original performance, the (oral) performance of origins, that is central to the telling of alternative histories with which so much of postcolonial literature is concerned. The performance is highly ambivalent: on the one hand, we realize that Edward Waverley cannot possibly understand what it is that the bhairdh is actually saying since as an Englishman he is a stranger to this culture, limited to the realm of appearances ("seemed"); on the other hand, it is equally clear that he *has* understood the role of the bhairdh in Highland culture—that, in other words, Scott's anthropological understanding of this culture speaks, ventriloquistically, through Edward's own doubtful apprehension of it. But, in a further reading of this moment, the highly metafictive nature of Scott's novelistic universe prevents us from crediting this very plausible understanding of the past. As Diane Elam has argued, the "postmodern romances" of Scott, while asserting the necessity of thinking the past they recount, also emphasize our insuperable distance from it:[44] they alert us to the rhetoricity of their own performance. Scott's bhairdh-griot is a belated invention whose presence in an historical novel only serves to emphasize his actual absence from history—the absence of what is apparently being "brought into being," the absence of a figure who is himself engaged in the task of "apostrophizing the absent" and thereby "animating the present." This self-reflexive distance from the very worlds

that they are intent upon "reciting" is what draws Scott and Maximin together, and separates them from those writers who, in Fanon's words,
naively "endeavor to renew contact with the oldest, most pre-colonial
lifeblood of their people."[45] Maximin's novelistic world is, to be sure, much
more openly preoccupied with this distance than is Scott's: with Maximin
we find ourselves at an even further remove from the reality of the native
bhairdh's performance, as evidenced by the fact that the storytellers *in* his
novels are themselves acutely aware of the temporal ironies to which only
the narrator *of* Scott's novels had access.

This further remove is also attested to in much of the novel's paratextual
material which, in typically postmodern fashion, refuses to respect the
boundaries between the actual narrative and its frame. Pursuing my discussion of the apostrophic nature of Maximin's novel and its relation to a catastrophic thinking of the apocalypse, I would like to defer for a moment
our consideration of that narrative and perform a reading of one detail
from the paratextual frame: the revealing title of the novel's fourth chapter,
"Apostroph'apocalypse." As with so much of Maximin's work, the most
obvious function of this title is to serve as a mnemonic device, furthering
the creation of what Vèvè Clark has called "Diaspora literacy": that is,
"the ability to read and comprehend the discourses of Africa, Afro-America
and the Caribbean from an informed, indigenous perspective."[46] Like the
novel's other chapter titles, this one is a reference to the title of a work by
the influential Cuban painter Wifredo Lam: in this case, a series of fourteen
aquatints made in the mid-1960s as companion pieces to a text by the Italian poet Gherasim Luca. Lam's visual art stands, of course, as an exemplary instance of the aesthetics of creolization, situated as it is—and as he
himself was, ancestrally speaking—at the crossroads of at least three cultures (African, Asian, and European), and it is for precisely this reason that
the cover of my book features his *La réunion*, a painting that Glissant has
interpreted as an allegory of global relationality.[47] Like Lam's composite
images, the phrase "Apostroph'apocalypse" is markedly hybrid, drawing
together a word with strong Euro-Christian connotations and another word
that reads less assuredly, but that, at one referential level at least, directs us
toward the realm of Afro-Caribbean nomenclature (Glissant at one point
speaks, for instance, of a certain "Apostrophe," swallower of shadows and
keeper of snakes [*DA*, p. 303]). In terms of the title's composition, moreover, a further transcultural nuance needs to be kept in mind: to whom does
the title actually "belong"? To the written words of Luca or to the visual
images of Lam that are "consigned" to it? The collaborative nature of this
text (and such collaborations were always an important aspect of Lam's
work, starting with his illustrations for, on the one hand, the surrealist André Breton's *Fata Morgana* in 1940 and, on the other, the 1942 Cuban edi-

tion of Césaire's *Cahier*) defies any simple response, and it also serves to remind us that "Diaspora literacy" is always also a learning of exile—at a distance from the indigenous perspective that it presupposes and always compelled to include material that ought to have been exogenous to it.

Cultural and historical context aside, the grammatical peculiarity of the title begs interpretation. It would appear to be a noun, but a noun created out of the compounding of what had hitherto been two separate words; this bringing together of words, which is a process that typifies Creole languages ("composition . . . [is] the most important process of lexical creation in Creole"),[48] effectively puts an end to their independent status. The explosive apocalypse referred to in this title no longer stands on its own: rather, it exists as the object of a rhetorical operation that precedes it and upon which it depends. Moreover, not only is this apocalypse preceded by a word that suggests its essentially rhetorical nature ("apostroph"), but by a graphic mark of elision ('), which doubles—in significantly different form—the first term of the title. This second apostrophe marks out an intermediary space of difference that troubles, at the same time as it joins together, the emphatically alliterative invocation of beginnings that the two alphas of the chapter title also suggest. As such, this apostrophe can be read as standing for the "relation" between Maximin's first and second novels: each is connected to the other in a way that deprives it of a separate identity. In constantly emphasizing the intertextual connections between his two novels, Maximin will force the reader to negotiate the elisive, and elusive, space between them, in which a mixed, composite identity can alone be thought, and from which the apostrophized apocalypse must remain absent. This second apostrophe in the chapter title also marks out the recursive space of intertextuality, the place where one novel incessantly reflects back upon the first, and the latter proleptically refers forward to the former. Importantly, however, this space cannot be heard in and of itself; it only exists in the (re)sounding of the two words that it has brought together and thereby modified. This is the same unrepresentable space that the intersection of the two book titles creates: rather than a synthesis of, or opposition between, singular (*L'isolé soleil*) and plural (*Soufrières*), self and others, we are faced with a chiasmus that necessitates our shuttling back and forth between these two poles, each of which has been substantially changed by its encounter with the other.

From the very first sentence of his second novel, Maximin encourages his reader to think this elision and this chiasmus: " ... and the leaf takes flight at the risk of its greenness" (" ... et la feuille prend son vol au risque de sa verdure"), the line which closed *L'isolé soleil* (p. 281), also provides *Soufrières* with its opening (p. 9). The ellipsis here at the outset, which (re)cites and (re)sites the one that occupies the middle of the opening sentence of Fanon's *Peau noire, masques blancs*, shows that his novel cannot inscribe its own beginning: the ground from which it springs is absent from this text—a perfect metaphor for the "state of exile" that George Lamming once identified with the colonial condition when he noted that "it is that mutual experience of separation from their original ground which makes both master and slave colonial."[49] The opening lines of *Soufrières* reenact this separation; the repetition of these apparently identical phrases, which establishes a continuity and provisional unity between the two novels, also cannot help marking their constitutive difference. It is this difference that the dialogical poetics of Mikhail Bakhtin so exuberantly privileges as when, for instance, the Russian critic points out that "within one and the same utterance, a sentence may be repeated (a repetition, a self-quotation, or even accidentally), but each time this is a new part of the utterance, since its place and function in the utterance as a whole is changed."[50] It is somewhere between an exiled nostalgia for the lost ground and a Bakhtinian exuberance at the dialogical possibilities of the new, between the equally unrealizable dictates of both tradition and innovation, that the poetics of creolization has its place—a place in which the differing repetitions of this opening sentence immediately situate us as readers.

The repetitive first sentence of *Soufrières*, which transforms the ending of *L'isolé soleil* into a moment of beginning ("every book beckons another in order to offer a future to its ending," as he puts it in *L'île et une nuit* [p. 48]), provides a metafictive commentary on Maximin's intertextual enterprise. In referring to the way in which the flight of the leaf, which is always also that of the page (*feuille*) on which this leaf is inscribed, occurs only at the risk of its greenness, Maximin is alluding to the risk of unoriginality that he has taken in thus extending the world of his first novel: the greenness that one might have expected of this new novel (one thinks here of Walcott's appeals to "a green world, one without metaphors" in his poem "Crusoe's Journal") is disturbed by the very unoriginality of its beginning. Furthermore, the original itself (that is, the phrase from *L'isolé soleil*) has lost, through repetition, whatever originality it might once have been thought to possess: as that which has been said before it becomes a commonplace, a "lieu commun" (a phrase that needs, as Glissant has often suggested, to be redeemed from the impasse of Flaubertian cliché by rethinking it in positive terms as marking the site of cultural convergences). Moreover, it can never again be said as it was once said: detached from its original context, it can now appear only in its own likeness, as the very absence of itself, in translation—just as the aboriginal, pre-colonial self can never be re(at)tained after the first contact of colonialism. It is the risk of this absence that Maximin consistently confronts: on the point of finishing her first novel, a novel about her paternal and maternal roots (and of which parts have *already* been included in *L'isolé soleil*), Marie-Gabriel asks, and in so asking stands in for the author of *Soufrières* himself, "at the very moment when the entire (hi)story of its roots is nearing an end, why would the leaf take flight at the risk of its greenness?" (p. 64; "alors que toute l'histoire de ses racines touche à sa fin, pourquoi la feuille prendrait-elle son vol au risque de sa verdeur?"). The creolized, and creolizing, author must always chance another work—and another self—that, even in the form of sheer repetition, finds itself at a remove from any and all points of (textual, cultural) departure. And yet if this chance must be taken, and with it the lures of a permanently fixed identity abandoned, the author—who can never wholly escape such lures—cannot help putting this chance itself into question ("pourquoi?"), duplicitously addressing, *re(an)nouncing*, the very thing that must be absent if his essentially secondary enterprise is to take flight.

It is this risk, this aleatory exploration of a middle space cut off from both the beginning and the end it cannot help calling forth that D. A. Miller (as we saw in Chapter 3) has astutely identified with the realm of "narrative," "a domain in which the absoluteness of value is *risked*, where nothing can be got whole or at once."[51] This is the risk of a present that cannot see its way back to the past nor forward to the future—a present that must, from the perspective of those who are "waiting," seem intolerable, as the following passage from Glissant's *Quatrième siècle* bears witness (a passage that the last sentence of *L'isolé soleil* and the first sentence of *Soufrières* attempt to rewrite in less "agonistic" terms). Glissant's narrator is describing the situation of a Martiniquan everyman at an unspecified point in the early to mid-twentieth century:

He rails against himself, there is still a precipice to cross over. As long as he has not crossed over, it is the past that continues, and at the moment when he will have crossed it, the future begins. There is no present. The present is a yellowed leaf on the stem of the past, branching off to the side [of the tree] where neither hand nor eye can reach it. The present falls on the other side, it is an endless death agony. A death agony [*il agonise sans fin. Il agonise*]. (p. 224)

It is this end-less agony, which will (as we have seen in Chapter 4) be reinscribed and reenvisioned in his later novel *Mahagony*, that Glissant's work insistently confronts and, at times, desperately attempts to remedy. This desire for the future well and truly to begin—a future that depends upon definitively crossing over a (Nietzschean?) abyss—empties the present of any value. Perhaps, though, one can begin to see this agony, this suspended narrative (the suspension that is narrative), from another perspective—one that accepts, as it were, the yellowing of all that was once green, and a fall that is never final.

Where the first line of *Soufrières*—or lines, since this incipit is, as we have seen, unthinkable without its double, the concluding sentence of *L'isolé soleil*—literally reactivates Maximin's first novel, the remainder of its opening section (pp. 9–12) records, in italics that visibly differentiate this lengthy remainder from its brief, elliptical beginning(s), the reawakening of Guadeloupe's volcano: "*the phreatic eruption is reactivating all the old fractures from 1956 and before*" (p. 10), we are told. (It should be noted, incidentally, that this opening section is not numbered or titled; it precedes the first clearly identified chapter, "Défilé antillais," and thus establishes a pre-narrative space that both is and is not the novel's true beginning—yet another instance of the "excès des commencements" [p. 187] that characterizes the creolized text and that I am in the process of examining here.) This initial reactivation of a fractured past proves, however, to have been nothing more than a dream of Marie-Gabriel's: as she puts it soon after, in the first chapter proper, "I dreamed that the eruption took place [*avait lieu*] and that I was left as sole survivor between the branches of my mango tree" (p. 22). This dream at, and of, the beginning will be followed by a purposefully anticlimactic story in which the anticipated eruption has only the most tenuous and attenuated of places, and in which the connection between a reactivated past and the future that it appears to prophesy can only be the work of dreams, or of language itself. It is only once the oneiric nature of this apocalyptic scenario has been exposed that the story of actually living through the series of minor phreatic (as opposed to what would have been the more devastating magmatic) explosions that did occur in 1976 can be told. The characters in *Soufrières*, who are ostensibly waiting for the volcano to erupt, are actually living in the aftermath of this eruption, in a space of survival—to use Marie-Gabriel's term (with its Derridean connotations of "living on"). But if Marie-Gabriel dreamt of herself as a lone survivor, Maximin will insist that this aftermath can and must be shared by all the inhabitants of the island, linked together in a communal solidarity founded on diversity rather than simple identity—a repeating-differing solidarity that he directs us toward in the frequently iterated phrase "c'est nous-mêmes nous-mêmes." It is toward the collective experience of a post/apocalyptic politics, a self-consciously creolized politics, that he urges his people, faced as they are with the diffident horizons that have emerged from the explosion of the nostalgically essentialist dreams of a Return to the origin and the violently eruptive dreams of a Progression toward a radically different future.

Maximin invokes this collective experience in the final beginning of *Soufrières* that will occupy us here: namely, the title of the first chapter proper, "Défilé antillais." The primary referent of this *défilé*, which also conveys a sense of the narrow passageway that the Antilles must negotiate in order to survive, is that of a carnivalesque procession, the parade of interwoven (textualized) characters that we will encounter in Maximin's pluri-focalized novel and that serves as a counter to the lone survival feared by Marie-Gabriel. The phrase not only quotes from Lam's painting of the same name but, I believe, refers us back to the *roman de nous* that Glissant has spent his life attempting to write: back to "the procession [*défilé*] of faces, gestures, and words" of which the Mathieu of *Quatrième siècle* is trying to ascertain (to master?) the history (p. 189); back to what the pessimistic narrator of *Malemort*, discussing the Martiniquan people, referred to as "this death march [*ce défilé de mort*] that one might call their history" (p. 132). In the context of our discussion about the beginning(s) of *Soufrières*, though, it is the first syllable of this word that is of special interest: the prefix *dé*, which recurs with obsessive regularity in the novel.

This prefix signals a beginning—a debut, as it were—that disruptively puts an end to the very thing it introduces: one that from the beginning undoes—and, yes, *de*constructs—the object that it is in the process of helping to create. This beginning negation takes many different yet interrelated forms in the world of Maximin's novels. To cite only three, from among the most obvious and thematically important: first, in the revelatory spirit of *décolonisation*, a negating of appearances in the name of some ulterior truth, as in such oft and (un)ironically cited words as *dévoiler* (e.g., p. 163) and *démasquer* (e.g., p. 171); second, the quasi-Barthesian privileging of drift readable in words like *dérader* (p. 71) and *dériver* (p. 120), and which is in turn linked to the sense of boundary-troubling one finds in a phrase like *déborder son identité* (*IS*, p. 149) or a verb like *déraciner*, which Maximin often, but not always, uses in a positive sense (p. 71); finally, the catastrophic undoing of some original whole, as in those *débris d'identité* (p. 197) or *débris de synthèse* (*IS*, p. 281) that Maximin would rework and rewrite in other, more positive terms, but without losing sight of the *déracinement*, in its negative sense, that produced such debris in the first place. Parading across the pages of Maximin's novels, these words, and the various ideologies they exemplify, all have one thing in common: the negation that defines them. Every stabilizing gesture, in the creolized world of Daniel Maximin, is prefixed by this negation and can only be apprehended in the wake of it; all affirmative positions are generated out of this destabilizing syllable, and can thus never take any definitive precedence over the others. The strategies that he puts into play must all be read together ("syllable": from the Greek for "to take together"), in the absence of a ground that the opening syllable of *Soufrières*'s first chapter title marks out for the reader. It is together upon this absent ground, and in this relativizing light, that we must read (to resituate the above list of three discursive strategies in a broader Caribbean context): first, Césaire's oppositional claims of kinship "with dementia praecox with the flaming madness / of persistent cannibalism" ("*démence* précoce de la folie flambante / du cannibalisme tenace") and his affirmations of a poetry that "begins with excess, with immoderation, with forbidden inquests, in the heedless beating of the great tam-tam" ("commence avec l'excès, le *démesure*, les recherches frappées d'interdit, dans le grand tam-tam aveugle"),[52] as well as the unveilings of nam in Brathwaite or the unmasking of alienation in Fanon; second, the poetics of detours and errancy in Glissant, and the complementary overflowing and uprooting of personal identity in Wilson Harris; and, lastly, the despairing vision of displacement and dissociation, the unthreading into chaos and separation, that dominates in writers like V. S. Naipaul and Orlando Patterson.

As I have just mentioned, this disturbing syllable is also vital to the work of Glissant, where it frequently signals, as it does for Maximin, a state of negation that he sees as generative of Caribbean culture. For Glissant, the post-Conquest Caribbean has, from its very beginnings, been characterized by a practice of the *détour*—camouflages, ruses, misdirections that were necessitated by the impossibility of a *retour* to the Old Worlds from which its peoples originated. "The Return," Glissant notes in *Discours antillais*, "is the obsession with the One: [the belief that] one's being must not be changed. To go back is to hallow permanence and nonrelationality" (p. 30); this obsession, the ultimate expression of which would be a physical, or at least ideological, return to a place of origin such as Africa, is inadequate to the Caribbean reality because, in the passage from one continent to the other, those who were once Africans were transformed "into another people" (p. 29)—a people whose identity will henceforth always be relational, relative, and thus irreducible to any One thing. Glissant's analysis of the Caribbean detour, which he sees as generating the area's religious syncretism and its hybrid languages, is very much in accord with the anti-essentialist (and antipatriarchal) creolizing impulses of Maximin's novels, as is especially clear in *L'isolé soleil* when Marie-Gabriel rejects "the law of the return of the prodigal fathers and children, and of everything that seeks to return to the same" (p. 19; "la loi du retour des pères et des enfants prodigues, et de tout ce qui cherche à revenir au même"), to cite just one of countless such repudiations in Maximin's novels—repudiations, one might add, that can never be final(ized), that must always turn back upon themselves at some point in the maze of doubting that his work explores.

There is, however, an important difference between Maximin and Glissant, which stems from a lingering commitment to the "apocalyptic tone" in Glissant's writings from the 1970s. Not content with the essentially reactive practice of the detour, Glissant also asserts (notably, in the sections of *Discours antillais* most concerned with a specific analysis of contemporary

Martinique and least intent upon the mapping out of a globalized cross-cultural poetics) the need for, and the possibility of, definitively transcending this state of negation at some point in the future. For (this) Glissant, the detour is only of value if it leads beyond itself, in an act of "surpassing" (*dépassement*) that will restore a missing direction to Caribbean society. "The Detour *leads nowhere*," he asserts, "when its original ruse tactics are not matched by conditions in which a 'surpassing' can be realized" (p. 34). This model of transcendence, which prolongs the desire for rupture and the anxiety of influence characteristic of modernism, is inherited most directly from Sartre, whose critique in "Orphée noir" of the poems of Étienne Léro (one of the editors of *Légitime Défense*) is worth citing here: "his poems are schoolboy exercises, they remain strictly imitations, they do not 'surpass themselves' [*ils ne se 'dépassent pas'*]; on the contrary, they close in upon themselves."[53] Just as for Sartre the sterility of an imitative poetry must be transcended in the name of a literature that is authentically innovative (Césaire's poetry is thus valorized by the author of "Orphée noir" because it is "un perpétuel dépassement" [p. 257]), to say nothing of manifestly virile, so too for (this) Glissant a real end to the Caribbean detour and the agony of its present must be thought.

This ending finds its prototype in Fanon's revolutionary passage "à l'acte" (that is, his involvement in the Algerian war of independence): to enter into this passage is, according to Glissant, to "accept fully the *radical break*." "The radical break," he affirms, "is the furthest point of the Detour" (p. 36). This "coupure radicale" is the light at the end of the tunnel, when the detour will have been surpassed and "the impossible that it skirts around tends to resolve itself into realizable 'positivities'" (p. 33). Arriving at such "positivités concrètes" is essential because only thus can be overcome what Glissant sees as an ultimately lethal state of *dépossession* (a word that crops up everywhere in the *Discours* and that has its source in Jacques Berque's well-known account of the decolonization movement, *Dépossession du monde* [1964]).[54] It is this lack of cultural and political self-possession that is, in Glissant's view, especially characteristic of such places as the Antilles or areas of Micronesia, where national and individual autonomy is increasingly difficult to envision, and where what he terms "alienation" is the nigh inevitable result of this dispossession ("loss of personality, cultural consumption not accompanied by creativity, derisory substitutes: devitalized folklore, etc." [*DA*, p. 379]).[55] The resolution of this collective neurosis, which Glissant would like to "cure" in a gesture of Fanonesque disalienation, hinges in the Antilles upon "the national problematic that will arise sooner or later [*tôt ou tard*]" (*IP*, p. 134), and that will ideally eventuate in an end to the Fránco-Caribbean detour.[56] If, as Simon Gikandi has argued, the essential feature of Caribbean modernism is "the reversion of exile from a sense of loss into the necessity from which na-tional consciousness springs,"[57] then Glissant's political vision here is effec-tively modernist insofar as it remains committed to surpassing a state of ex-ile and loss in the name of this liberated consciousness, to healing—as he put it in the late 1950s at the height of the decolonization movement—the "cultural deracination" upon which hinges the "systematic enterprise of economic exploitation" that is colonialism.[58]

Notwithstanding his emphasis on creolization, on a gradualist politics of repetition and métissage, there is a strongly revelatory tendency in (some of) Glissant's work, the urge of the prophet who wants to lead his people out of the wilderness of the detour by unveiling home truths to them. Contrasting the situation in the Antilles with "resolutions put into practice by other peo-ples" (p. 35), Glissant often lapses into a tragic pessimism, sprinkling his prose with jeremiads about his native land: "there are a few of us (in Mar-tinique) who estimate that perhaps no other community in the world is as alienated as ours, as menaced with dilution," he typically remarks in *Dis-cours antillais* (p. 63). This fear of dilution hovers over his work and draws it into epistemological complicity with, say, Matthew Arnold's nineteenth-century vision of Celtic culture "expiring on the horizon before the growing tumult of uniform civilization."[59] This fear of the "disappearing Other," which so loudly echoes the concerns of nineteenth-century exoticism analysed in my *Exotic Memories*, often drowns out the other more hybrid(izing) voices to which he is theoretically committed—voices that urge another paradigm for understanding cultural change, one that would, in Robert Young's terms, "acknowledge the extent to which cultures were not simply destroyed but rather layered on top of each other, giving rise to strug-gles that themselves only increased the imbrication of each with the other and their translation into increasingly uncertain patchwork identities."[60]

As Glissant stated in the context of a discussion of his most pessimistic novel, *Malemort*:

With every passing day it seems that for us Martiniquans the sleight of hand oblit-eration is speeding up. We just keep on disappearing, victims of worlds in friction. Packed down along the volcanoes' line of emergence. Banal example of a liquida-tion by the absurd, in the unhorrific horror of a successful colonization. What can writing do about it? It never catches up [*Elle ne rattrape jamais*]. (*DA*, p. 15)

Here is a cultural landscape from which the revolutionary potential of the volcano has been obliterated. Glissant's Martiniquans are revealed as the victims of a cultural liquidation, inhabitants of a banally horrific flattened-out world ("tassés sur la ligne d'émergence des volcans"), increasingly sub-ject to a loss of axiological points of reference that Francis Affergan, in his *L'anthropologie à la Martinique*, has termed "déréalisation."[61] The presence of this tragic (and eminently anthropological) vision in Glissant's work is inevitable, given his continued attachment to the diametrically opposed comic vision of a "coupure radicale" that would do away with the irresolute world of what I have been calling "narrative." Both this vision and the ideology that subtends it are the by-products of an ends-oriented, either/or mind-set that predominates in the writings of a modernist like Césaire,[62] and that would approach the problem of colonialism as *resoluble*, be it positively or negatively, in the form of a radical cure or the fatal liquidation that serves as its inevitable counterpoint; the one apocalyptic vision entails the other, the (good) revolution always contains within it the seeds of that *other* revolution of which Césaire spoke in 1967, "a catastrophic revolution that has given Martinique a final push into the ranks of the underdeveloped countries."[63]

As the collective narrator of the first chapter of *L'île et une nuit* puts it, "let us found projects of renewal, leaving to others that despair, so common among us, of dreams haunted by ruins and utter apocalypse" (p. 22). For Maximin, the sort of cultural cures that Glissant (or the Glissant who wrote *Discours antillais* and *Malemort*) still longs after, and the mortal illness that he fears, no longer ring true—in the Caribbean, *or elsewhere*. It is for this reason, I would argue, that he is able to explore more fully, and with greater optimism, the creolized world of the detour to which Glissant is only partially resigned and against which—even as he stringently criticizes monistic, nonrelational concepts of identity—he fulminates so often in *Discours antillais*. Glissant's tragic prophecies can never take precedence in the world of Maximin's novels (nor, I should add, do they succeed in doing so when inserted—at times intrusively—into Glissant's own multivoiced novels): the apocalyptic, ends-oriented language to which Glissant remains attached will always have a place in Maximin's creolized world, as one Caribbean discourse among many, but it will not be simply endorsed. The problematic that Maximin's postmodern vision is prepared to address at both a local and global level, and that he prepares his readers to address by insisting in his work on a multiplicity of foundationless and end-less beginnings, is that cultural and political identity has to be conceived differently in a global village where dispossession has become an inalterable fact of life. Glissant's double emphasis on either complete liquidation or radical change gives way in Maximin to an ambivalent position(ality) that is capable of coming to terms with what Benitez-Rojo has termed, from his "postmodern perspective," the Caribbean's "detour without a purpose" (*RI*, p. 11)—a detour to which neither Glissant's prophetic vision of a repossessed future nor Brathwaite's retrospective assertions of cultural essence are adequate. For Maximin, such purposeful claims must always be prefixed by a defining negation that it is precisely the aim of any resolute discourse to go beyond (Glissant's emphasis on surpassing), or to come before (Brathwaite's insistence on culture-cores and ancestral origins); as a result, these claims can only enter *parodically* into his work.

Intertextuality is, of course, one of the most basic forms of parody: one text exists "to the side of" (*para*) another text that is present in it only as a foundational absence. It is thus not surprising that the prefatory chapter of *Soufrières* explicitly raises the question of parody. Toward the end of this novel's italicized preface—its *parados*, so to speak (in Greek tragedy, the first song of the chorus after its entry on stage)—we are informed that after the volcano's explosion "it will be necessary to imagine the birth of days without parodies of real life" (p. 12). But it is precisely this aftermath that can have no place in the novel, since the explosion that has just been described is unreal, part of Marie-Gabriel's dream. What follows upon this dream, the novel proper, is not the description of a world in which the volcano has exploded but that of a world from which such explosions, and the ensuant birth of "des jours sans parodies de vraie vie," are absent. Given this absence, the imperative of a nonparodic life that is voiced at the conclusion of the novel's opening—and that generates, for instance, Glissant's calls for an end to the condition of dispossession and his despair at "the parodic culture" in which his fellow Martiniquans have supposedly become entrapped (*DA*, p. 380)—can never be fulfilled. We must learn to view this lack of fulfillment not (merely) as a cause for lamentation but (also) as the uneasy grounds upon which we can begin to explore the (im)possibilities that an incurably parodic life has to offer us and to come to a different understanding of what it means, as T. S. Eliot put it in *Four Quartets*, to "go by the way of dispossession" ("East Coker," III).

Parody itself, of course, has often been looked upon as a curative strategy for dealing with the postmodern condition and there can be little doubt that the current popularity of a catch phrase like "radical parody" stems from the need to find ways of reconciling the acknowledged weakness of that condition with the language of subversion and rupture that is our modernist legacy. In reference to Lautréamont, Césaire once spoke of "the chilling hysterical power of Parody,"[64] and we find this same need for power expressed in Fredric Jameson's notorious and unabashedly modernist distinction between parody and pastiche in his "Postmodernism, or The Cultural Logic of Late Capitalism" (1984):

Pastiche is, like parody, the imitation of a peculiar mask, speech in a dead language: but it is a neutral practice of such mimicry, without any of parody's ulterior motives, amputated of the satiric impulse, devoid of laughter and of any conviction that alongside the abnormal tongue you have momentarily borrowed, some healthy linguistic normality still exists. Pastiche is thus blank parody, a statue with blind eyeballs.[65]

The "oppositional" logic upon which Jameson bases these definitions is the same one that founds Glissant's distinction between a good and a bad detour. Jameson's parody (which would be exemplified, say, by Césaire's *Une tempête*, a straightforward revision of Shakespeare's *The Tempest*) is a mimetic ruse that leads beyond itself to a "healthy linguistic normality"; pastiche, by contrast, is an imitation that remains trapped within the world of masks within which it is inscribed. Lacking an ulterior perspective, lacking wholeness ("amputated"), pastiche is a blank and humorless monstrosity devoid of vision . . . at least from Jameson's perspective. I have been suggesting, by contrast, that we can and must learn how to "see" things, as it were, with blind eyeballs—with a lack of conviction in the "healthy" alternatives that make Jameson's "potent" distinction between parody and pastiche possible.

The imperative of a nonparodic life—the "movement of possession" that Brathwaite urges upon the Caribbean artist, the birth of the new in a dépassement of the old that Glissant, even now, at times still holds out as a promise—cannot be fulfilled in Maximin, but it does not simply disappear from his work. We cannot just do away with such directions and directives; they remain with us, but in a hollowed out, blank form. Benitez-Rojo is clearly exaggerating the case when he says "the notion of the apocalypse is not important within the culture of the Caribbean" (*RI*, p. 10); that it has been, and continues to be, a vital element of the culture, however, is less important for Maximin than the fact that it can no longer take precedence over other notions and must now be situated alongside a chorus of differing voices that parodically undermine the finality of its claims. It is but one erroneous path among many in a novelistic universe that aspires to the sort of "neutrality" that Benitez-Rojo has identified with Ortiz's *Contrapunteo cubano del tabaco y el azúcar* (1940): "a heteroclitic summa of ideologies, that is, a de-ideologized ideology" (p. 156).

If *Soufrières* aspires to this de-ideologization, it also registers the fact, though, that it is quite simply not possible to attain such neutrality. Thus, the volcano—erstwhile epicenter of explosive ideologies—does speak, or "erupt," in the novel, but in a language that has learnt how to contain itself, and that is itself contained *between* the beginning and the end that it cannot help projecting. The speech of the volcano unclimactically takes place, has its place, in the middle of *Soufrières*, and its language puts into question the authority that it might once have been thought to embody. The very first words of the volcano undercut any claims to mastery that it might, and inevitably will, make in, and for, the future:

À coups de phrases primitives et de mots copeaux échappés aux langues établies, j'aspire aujourd'hui à retourner mon pays natal. Je suis une bouche de chair en feu, mais je ne maîtrise aucune langue de dévoilement. (p. 141)

With primitive phrases and word chips that have escaped from the established languages, it is the turning over of my native land for which I am yearning today. I am a mouth of flesh on fire, but I master no language of revelation.

If the volcano will go on to repeat the authoritative language of Césaire's *Cahier*—most notably, at the very end of its monologue, when it confidently proclaims: "I say that this is right ... " (p. 167; "Et je dis que cela est bien ainsi ... ")[66]—its words have nonetheless been undermined from the outset. The languages of revelation, with which one might have chronicled the definitive explosion of the volcano and the final unveiling (*apocalypsis*) of its truth, cannot be mastered in Maximin's post/apocalyptic world. All that remains is a series of fragmentary words and gestures that rhetorically invoke the lost or hoped for cultural resolutions to which they cannot adequately give voice, and yet toward which they impossibly (re)turn—be this in the form of a turning back to the country of one's birth, to the "pays natal" without which the creolized world of the detour, of errancy and exile, cannot begin to be thought, or that of a turning over of some brand new leaf, the future birth of a self-possessed nation that could take the place left vacant since the Caribbean's "irruption into modernity" . . . since, that is, its very beginning(s).

This dissolution of the ideological certainties that in our century have supported such revolutionary projects as decolonization and avant-gardism can only provoke despair or denial in those who still seek from the figure of the volcano what the Italian futurist F. T. Marinetti had the protagonist of his *Le monoplan du Pape* discover in Mount Etna: apostrophizing the volcano, Marinetti's narrator praises it for "the mastery and the inspiration / that the blasting thunder of your voice makes manifest" (p. 43). This dream of manifest mastery that guided the Futurists, and which directly influenced the first generation of modernist writers in the Caribbean,[67] is one from which we have (never fully) awoken. The lack of such mastery and inspiration, the absence of the volcano's thunderous voice, is what confronts and continues to haunt the postcolonial and the postmodern author (and Maximin is, of course, both); how to turn this lack into a place of habitation, and how to struggle with, and against, the need to find, in the name of some more "authentic" homeland, an escape route from the detours of our post/coloniality and our post/modernity, are the questions his work engages with a careful lucidity that is best summed up, perhaps, in the following entry from the notebook of his novelistic alter ego, Adrien.

Like the leaf with which *Soufrières* begins, Adrien in the novel's penultimate chapter finds himself "en vol," on his way from Paris back to Guadeloupe:

Tu as peur de ton avion ici, peur de l'éruption là-bas, peur d'arriver trop tôt et trop tard, et tu cisèles des images d'apocalypse avec la fermeté d'âme et les certitudes

d'avenir d'un survivant unique qui prendrait à sa seule charge tous les recommence-
ments comme s'il était une fois. Apostrophant l'apocalypse, misant sur le déluge,
prêt à remodeler ton île avec le secours de ton volcan, tu as failli te faire toi aussi
prendre au piège du terrorisme par procuration. (p. 195)

You are afraid of your airplane here, afraid of the eruption there, afraid of arriving
too soon and too late, and you chisel images of the apocalypse with the firmness of
spirit and the certitudes about the future of a lone survivor who would take upon
himself all the responsibility of beginning again as if it were "once upon a time."
Apostrophizing the apocalypse, betting on the deluge, ready to remodel your island
with the help of your volcano, you too almost let yourself get caught in the trap of
terrorism by proxy.

Situated between the mainland and the island, between here and there,
afraid of arriving, in Fanon's words, "too soon and too late," Adrien momentarily gives himself over to the temptation of chiseling out apocalyptic
images—a lone survivor, filled with certitudes, aligned with the explosive
force of the volcano, ready to remodel (cure) his native land. However, he
sees that to have put himself in this place is to have worked "by proxy": to
have committed an act of terrorism on behalf of someone other than his
own volatile, creolized self—in the name, that is, of a fixed identity that
could be posited in either the past or the future but that is inadequate both
to the in-between migrant space of translation in which he presently finds
himself and to the "now" of a writing that, as Glissant himself remarked,
"ne rattrape jamais." Maximin's writing can never recover (from), nor
catch up to, the apocalypse that it would envision. It is a writing that must
(learn how to) settle for, and in, the absence of any such revelation—resigning itself to the essentially secondary nature of its enterprise, and
thereby opening itself up to the possibility of inhabiting a cross-culturalized
landscape of yellowing leaves, of (un)exploded volcanoes, in which "only
wakes and traces," as Adrien himself goes on to point out, "keep one on
the road to hope" (p. 197; "seuls les sillages et les traces font prendre la
route à l'espoir"). As I have been arguing, Maximin's Guadeloupe is situated somewhere on this (cross)road, between there (the Caribbean) and
here (the global village), in the wake of an ancestral past that can no longer
be possessed and on the trails of a liberated future that has receded from
sight. His intertextualized world of problematic traces offers a vision of
hope for those who, taking the risk of "flight" from the terroristic certitudes of ideology, prove themselves willing to negotiate with the uncertain
and constantly shifting middle ground of a creolized present that it is neither too soon nor too late for us to begin to think.

*In Lieu of an Ending: The Repeated Translations
of (the Sequels of) Being*

> What is black youth all about? Living.
> But to live truly, one has to remain oneself. The actor is the
> man who does not live truly; he makes a multitude of men
> come alive—a question of roles—but he cannot do the
> same for himself. Black youth does not want to play any
> roles; it wants to be itself.
> —Aimé Césaire

In the influential 1970 preface to a collection of his plays, "What the Twilight Says: An Overture," Derek Walcott reflected upon the attempts of his Trinidad Theatre Workshop (founded in 1959) at repeating an African scenario—namely, a play by the Nigerian writer Wole Soyinka—in a different, Caribbean context:

When we produced Soyinka's masterpiece *The Road*, one truth, like the murderous headlamps of his mammy-wagons, transfixed us, and this was that our frenzy goes by another name, that it is this naming, ironically enough, which weakens our effort at being African. We tried, in the words of his Professor, to "hold the god captive," but for us, Afro-Christians, the naming of the god estranged him. Ogun was an exotic for us, not a force. We could pretend to enter his power but he would never possess us, for our invocations were not prayer but devices.[68]

This passage emphatically alerts the reader to the problem of translation that is such an inescapable feature of post/colonial societies: instead of a one-to-one correspondence uniting original and image, in which the latter possesses and is possessed by the former, we are faced with their disjuncture and estrangement. For Walcott, the attempt to bridge the gap separating these two worlds leads only to pretense, to (rhetorical) devices rather than real, prayerful invocations. In order to be himself, the Caribbean subject must resist the "exotic" impulse and invent a language that is endogenous to the area; the "force" and "power" that the Yoruban cosmology offered Soyinka has not survived its translation onto foreign shores, and as a result, Walcott concludes of this theatrical experience, "all we could successfully enact was a dance of doubt" (p. 9).

Walcott's preface was written at the height of his vocal critique of "the new magnifiers of Africa,"[69] who at the time seemed to have gained ascendancy on the Caribbean cultural and political stage. Against Kamau Brathwaite's seemingly Africanist aesthetics (the reference to Ogun is almost certainly a coded jab at Brathwaite's poem of the same name, published in the section of *Islands* entitled, significantly enough, "Possession") and his hermeneutic credo that "the unity is submarine," Walcott asserted the imperative of paying homage to the Old World(s) not by attempting to repeat them in the New, but by acknowledging, in an elatedly Adamic language, the lack of such a unity, the "amnesiac blow" that has dislodged us from the place(s) whence we came. Walcott's critique in his "The Muse of History" of "pure black Afro-Aryanism" (p. 19), and "the fashionable incoherence of revolutionary anger" (p. 18) that so often accompanied it, is a still relevant propadeutic to the excesses of essentialist identity politics in our own day; and his insistence on the inevitably mixed nature of New World societies corresponds well with the current emphasis on creolization in postcolonial criticism. And yet his Manichean positing of a strict boundary between the authentic and the inauthentic—between "prayer" and "devices"—seems far too pat. Is (the inevitable failure of) translation really such a straightforward affair? Are we left with only these two alternatives, or are there not ways of negotiating between them? Does this estranging experience merely result in the production of exotic "devices," or might it not be the precondition for establishing a productive "relation" of (un)likeness between two differing worlds?

Maximin's *Soufrières* forces us to ask such questions, if only because it self-consciously *repeats* the same experience as Walcott describes in his preface: two of the novel's male protagonists, Adrien and Antoine, are trying to stage a local adaptation of Soyinka's *A Dance of the Forest* (a play, significantly, that was first performed as part of Nigeria's independence ceremonies in 1960), which they have entitled "*la Danse de la femme-volcan.*" Rather than seeking to bridge the gap between the original and its translation, Maximin's protagonists emphasize the differences separating them: differences of language (the original English title of Soyinka's play remains absent from the novel, present only in slightly mistranslated form as "*la Danse de la forêt*" [p. 18]); differences of context (a newly independent African state as opposed to a problematically French département); and significant differences of content (the forest, autonomous site of both the natural and of the supernatural in Soyinka's play, as opposed to the human world of the village against which it is counterpoised, has been transformed into a volcano woman, a composite figure that better corresponds to the local features of Caribbean geography). This translation is one that foregrounds its distance, spatial and temporal, from the object it imitates: we are presented with a work that does not attempt to coincide with what came before it but deliberately situates itself in the wake of an original that remains in and of itself untranslated.

Like any translation, this one is essentially *lacking*: lacking the presence of that which it represents. Anthropomorphized as female, the volcano itself (or, rather, herself) draws the reader's attention to this absence in a commentary on one of the troupe's rehearsals ("répétitions") of the play; as she listens to the actress who is representing her, the volcano—or better, the narrative voice that has identified itself as, and with, the volcano—registers the inadequacy of the director's decision to figure her as a maroon woman: "I have given refuge in the course of three centuries to so many mar-ronnages that it is really quite derisory to have me pose as a renegade black woman" (p. 156). It is not only this attempt at translation, however, that is derisory (a mere device); if she takes a certain pleasure in the play and its "words of tribute paid to what for me is only a genuine deep wound but that the poets persist in translating with letters of fire [*s'obstinent à traduire en lettres de feu*]" (p. 156), she is not "held captive" by it anymore than she is by the French authorities who are attempting to gauge if and when she will erupt and about whom she authoritatively asserts that "my wild dra-matic art will always surpass those colonial scenarios, without it ever being possible to translate into hypotheses my fatal destiny" (p. 155; "ma dra-maturgie sauvage dépassera toujours les coloniales mises en scène, sans qu'on puisse jamais traduire en hypothèses ma destinée fatale"). Neither the poets' fiery apostrophes nor the authorities' scientific hypotheses are ad-equate to the task of translating the original and capturing its "fatal des-tiny." Indeed, the (representation of the) volcano is herself subject to these same limitations, notwithstanding the fact that she would appear to be en-gaging in a definitive critique of how she is being represented (a critique grounded in the seeming authority of "testimony" that we saw Coetzee questioning in *Foe*): *this* volcano is herself but another anthropomorphized translation, a part of "le théâtre des humains" (p. 147) that she ought properly to be outside of; and all her talk of destiny, and the Manichean distinctions between "dramaturgie sauvage" and "les coloniales mises en scène," must themselves be read as further obstinate efforts at capturing something that is, from the outset, lacking in the novel.

This self-reflexive insistence upon different levels of representation, which are all at a definitive remove from the presence they invoke, reveals a fundamental problem with the representational project of translation but does not preclude a continued exploration of it. To acknowledge the sort of defining rupture that Walcott argues for does not, Maximin is suggesting, do away with the necessity of reflecting back upon the original; it merely forces us to consider more carefully the dynamics of translation, and its in-evitable misprisions (as well as its inseparability from the devices of rhetoric). That something essential is at stake in maintaining this project is especially evident in an earlier episode from the novel that I would now like to examine, which also explicitly raises the issue of (mis)translation with re-gard to the volcano.

One of Maximin's frequent strategies in *Soufrières* is to supplement his account of the ongoing drama in Guadeloupe with references to other events occurring across the world in the year 1976. One of the most notable of these, of course, was the Soweto massacre. Adrien, still in Paris, first hears about it while stopping off at the *Présence africaine* bookstore to pick up some more copies of Soyinka's play. He offers to drive a distraught South African exile from there to the airport; on their way, they listen to a tape of South African music that he has been thinking about using as the aural backdrop for some of the scenes in his and Antoine's *Danse*. The exiled man is so enthused by the songs, "and above all by the tuneful Xhosa invocations sung by the bassist" (p. 78), that he translates some of the original verses, which are never actually presented to the reader, into English for Adrien; the last of them reads, "The volcano in its crater is fire enough to cremate the ghetto's creators ... " What *follows* this somewhat awkwardly phrased translation of an absent original is a further (mis)translation into French, juxtaposed without comment to its predecessor: "Le volcan dans son cratère *a en réserve* assez de flammes pour réduire en cendres les faiseurs de ghettos ... " (my italics). Between these two sentences there is a world of difference: imperfect likenesses of one another, the latter significantly marks its difference from the explosive discourse of the former in the shift from Being ("is") to its deferral ("a en réserve"). This Caribbean volcano, at a remove from a political context in which the project of a revolutionary decolonization still retains an obvious validity, is one from which Being is absent—one that has lost, as it were, the *présence africaine* in which its South African mirror image is grounded.

This ambivalent invocation of Being is central to Maximin's poetics. If, as we saw, Césaire's apocalyptic discourse held out the possibility of a direct "access to Being" through the medium of poetry, Maximin envisions a less immediate relation to it, one that we find most concisely, and *authoritatively*, described toward the middle of the letter that concludes *L'isolé soleil*, signed by a person named Daniel who is making his first appearance in the novel: "and, having neither crossed over to the other nor turned back to the same, we know that we are present like the verb 'to be'" (p. 281; "et, ni passés à l'autre, ni revenus au même, nous savons que nous sommes présents comme le verbe être"). In this passage, "le verbe être" denotes a presence that is neither truly present nor absent, that occupies an intermediary space between the sameness of the original and the difference of what would be truly other than that original. This is the impassable space of translation, situated between two impossibly desired objects: a past that it commemorates and yet cannot capture and a future that it promises and yet must withhold, keeping it "en réserve." Being is that which remains at a haunting distance from Maximin's self-consciously postmodern world, as the trace of what has been absent from it since the very beginning—since, that is, "the bursting into modernity, the bursting out of tradition" ("l'ir-ruption dans la modernité, l'irruption hors tradition") that, as Glissant ar-gues, has since the days of Columbus always generated, in its repeated de-partures from an original (African, Amerindian, Asian, European . . .) model, cultural production in the Caribbean and, indeed, the Americas as a whole (*DA*, pp. 255–56). What proceeds out of this irruption is necessarily a sequel to what preceded it.

What is the nature of sequels? That is the central question that Max-imin's work raises. At an early point in *Soufrières*, Marie-Gabriel's propen-sity for being overcome by an isolating nihilism is described in the follow-ing terms: "life seems a fatal accident on the extremely sure road to death, an accident that one must put up with until the sequels of being have dis-appeared into nothingness" (p. 23; "la vie apparaît un accident fatal sur la route très sûre de la mort, un accident dont il faut s'accommoder jusqu'à la disparition des séquelles d'être dans le néant"). Maximin's postmodern per-spective acknowledges that Being (*l'être*) comes to us only "accidentally," in the belated form of its sequels, but refuses to embrace what for the ni-hilist might seem the logical conclusion to draw from such accidents: namely, the fatal scenario of disappearance and the certainty-safety that the "route très sûre de la mort" affords (to invoke the double meaning of "sûre" here). We *are* confined to a world of sequels, living in the risky, un-safe aftermath of a Being from which we have not fully recovered (the med-ical meaning of the word "sequel," it should be recalled, refers to a patho-logical condition that remains with the convalescent even after the official "end"—through death or a return to health—of her or his illness). While this intermediate position may be cause for despair to those who want ei-ther to return to the original or to distance themselves from it entirely, such need not be the case for those who can resign themselves to living with(in) it. As long as one holds out the *possibility* of either an essential continuity with the past or a complete discontinuity with it, as long as one remains in-tent upon defining "the good *decolonization*" as, in Césaire's words, "a *de-colonization* without aftereffects" ("une *décolonisation* sans séquelles"),[70] then one remains committed to a modernist framework that cannot seri-ously entertain the ambiguities of cultural translation—ambiguities that are, as the Italian philosopher Gianni Vattimo has argued, germane to the postmodern condition.

For Vattimo, as I have demonstrated at greater length elsewhere,[71] the poetics and politics of postmodernism revolve around a double strategy of fictive commemoration (*Andenken*) and irresolute overcoming (*Verwin-dung*). The particulars of his argument are concerned with the question of Being and the metaphysical tradition that addresses it, but its relevance to more general issues of translation is obvious, although one must always keep in mind the distortions that any such transposition of a Europhilosophical meditation onto a postcolonial context involves. On the one hand, Vattimo sees the continued necessity of thinking a relation with Being, with that out of which we beings originate; but this act of recollection, as he conceives it, is one that begins by acknowledging its foundational distance from what is being recalled, the absence of that which it is attempting to render present. For that reason it can never lead back to a determinate place: Andenken is a "going back that leads us no place, if not to our remembering of Being as that from which we have always already taken leave."[72] Along with this pious gesture of remembering what we can no longer (truly) remember, we are called upon to move forward and away from it, because the idea of Being is not just a source of strength that we need to reflect (back) upon but a debilitating force that holds us back and that it would be better to be *without*; to translate this into the terms of cultural politics, the idea of an ancestral identity can be empowering but also terribly limiting. And yet we are to some extent always circumscribed by those limits, by what Appiah has termed the "imperialism of identity";[73] as Vattimo argues, no matter how far we seem to wander from these limits, they are "something that remains in us like the traces of an illness or like a pain to which we are resigned" (p. 181). Verwindung is a form of overcoming that is never final, that never actually recovers from the illness from which it marks a recovery: it is "a convalescent, resigned (but also re-signed, marked with a new sign) acceptance, signaled by the dis-tortion, and by the errancies, of metaphysics" (p. 186). Perhaps to be what in Creole is called a *docteur-feuilles* is to know how to administer, in the absence of any radical cures, prescriptions for this double condition that results from the repeated translations of Being (or identity)—to oppose, in sum, the sort of modernist-nihilist mentality, and its scenario of disappearance, that threatens to overwhelm Marie-Gabriel in the passage cited above, and that we find, to take a random example, in the following typically apocalyptic diagnosis of a supposedly dispossessed Antilles: "the only remedy, the only treatment likely to put a stop to the slow death of these communities is for them to take their sovereignty into their own hands."[74]

Following in the medico-modernist footsteps of "the Césaire-type diagnosis of social pathology,"[75] all such radical claims base themselves upon strict distinctions between health and illness, authenticity and alienation, presence and representation, which Maximin and Vattimo repeatedly put into question—in their differing ways, to be sure (differences that for some critics, one might add, function as the grounds for a comfortingly therapeutic but entirely illegitimate distinction between the exhausted and vibrant worlds of postmodernity and postcoloniality, respectively). The scenario of disappearance that we have just been examining—what Maximin in *L'île et une nuit* refers to as "catastrophe's finishing touches" (p. 172; "les finitions de la catastrophe")—is a particularly dramatic, if extreme, way of preserving such distinctions: holding out the promise of a "slow death," as for instance when Chamoiseau speaks (significantly enough, in a tribute to Glissant) of "this anesthesia under which, even now, we will die without our knowing it,"[76] and forecasting the ultimate dissolution of mere "sequels of being" into a final state of nothingness, in fact allows one to maintain—at a rather high cost, to be sure!—a separation between *reality* and *appearances* that has been one of the leading obsessions of European thought from Plato on through to Rousseau, for whom the talent of the actor consists in "the art of counterfeiting oneself, of taking on another character than one's own, of appearing differently from what one is, of being cold-bloodedly passionate, of saying something other than what one is thinking as naturally as if one really thought it, and of forgetting finally one's own place by dint of taking that of others."[77] Rather than beginning to think about what it means to *survive* in a "disfigured" world in which the boundaries between, say, the authentic (essential reality) and the inauthentic (alienated appearances) cannot be properly discerned, the proponents of such scenarios verify the existence of the former by killing it off, thereby preserving it from a world that has, by their criteria, become dominated by the latter—a world that is, in a word, all too *theatrical*. This critique of theatricality (which, as we saw in Chapter 5, was central to Carpentier's *Kingdom of this World*) is a commonplace not only of the European literary tradition but of its various postcolonial translations, as we can see by briefly citing a few relevant instances of that critique, which will help establish the ideological bias that Maximin is contesting through his emphasis on, as it were, the representativeness of representation in a postmodern age.

In an article written almost fifty years after he and his colleagues at *Légitime Défense* had effectively launched modernism in the Antilles, the Marxist critic René Ménil engaged in a powerful attack on the role played by "*reactive* mythologies" in the Caribbean: in the face of European myths about the Other—those perpetrated by exoticism, for instance—Caribbean writers have responded, inadequately by his account, with mere "countermythologies," a "counterexotic exoticism," the most notable example of which was Césaire's Negritude. Ménil performs the same deconstruction of the myths of heroism as did Maximin in his shift away from a male-oriented story in *L'isolé soleil*: he criticizes, for instance, the way authors and politicians have reactively sought after "a lofty historical ancestry, great heroes from the past, the venerable dead whom they can borrow as a 'disguise' in order to perform on the historical stage the difficult and uncertain act of a national liberation,"[78] going on to cite their abusive recourse to such now familiar historical tropes as the maroon, Toussaint, Delgrès, and the Matouba explosion. What is wrong with this mythological tendency is that it falsifies reality: "mythology embellishes, decorates, theatricalizes reality, by raising the discursive tone" (p. 59). Fortunately, he adds, one can go beyond such theatricalizing by subscribing to the nonreactive politics of Marxism, "which wants to ground itself in truth," and in which one can find both "a method that resolves and reduces mythology and the idea of a politics without mythology" (pp. 59–60). Adopting the "language of rupture" that we commented upon in the previous section, he asserts that "the right sort of change [*la bonne rupture*] could only come about in a *nonmythological elsewhere*" (p. 56); recuperating the transcendental language of Sartre, he claims that "we must go beyond [*il faut dépasser*] counterexotic poetic expression, which is contaminated by the very thing against which it wants to rebel" (p. 24). It is this same reaction against the reactive that generates the later Fanon's political vision, which, as Patrick Taylor puts it, stresses the need for transforming the "drama of colonialism" into the "history of liberation."[79]

We also find this critique of (bad) theater in the essays of Walcott's with which this section began—not, to be sure, made in the name of a liberational politics like Marxism but in defense of his own antihistorical aesthetics. If Walcott appears to be lamenting the impermeable boundary between African original and Caribbean image that his (re)production of Soyinka's play revealed to him, this boundary actually becomes a positive criterion that allows him to distinguish—in an aggressively Eliotonian way—between worthy and worthless writing, to contrast "the great poetry of the New World" (Saint-John Perse, Césaire, Neruda, and so on) with literary "performances" that, because they refuse the Adamic imperative, do not meet the standards of his essentially modernist canon. Modernism is in part founded upon the belief that there are such things as great poets and that art really could be the equivalent of prayer: this belief allows the modernist writer to contain the "dance of doubt" with which Walcott's translational project confronted him, and to transform an experience of estrangement into one of forceful self-assertion. The doubts raised by the existence of a boundary between original and translation resolve themselves into the certitudes of the *author(itative)-critic*, who knows the difference between art and mere theater. As Walcott puts it in "The Muse of History," those infected with "the malaria of nostalgia and the delirium of revenge" can do no more than engage in "minstrel postures"; "basically, the anger of the black is entertainment, or theater, if it makes an aesthetic out of anger, and this is no different in its 'naturalness' than the legendary joy or spontaneous laughter of the minstrel" (p. 18). Instead of a "natural poetics," we have—to adapt Glissant's terms—a "forced poetics,"[80] what for Walcott can be no more than "night-club and cabaret, professional fire-eating and dancing on broken bottles"; the Ogun of Soyinka's *The Road* is, in the Caribbean context, presumably part and parcel of this theater—an impure device, unworthy of those who are "dedicated to purifying the language of the tribe."[81] This modernist imperative of purification, it must be added, is strangely at odds with the creolizing emphasis on adulteration that is equally present in these essays. The tension in Walcott's work resides in the double identity to which he lays claim: not so much the tension between his African and European ancestors, which is such an explicit part of his self-portraiture, but the tension between a creolized and a modernist authorial self, the one being necessarily implicated in a dissonant, impurely mixed world, and the other—coherent and unified, sovereign artist and eventual Nobel Laureate—purposefully cutting himself off, in the name of a high modernist aesthetics, from the sort of historical ambiguities that the project of translating Soyinka's African play onto the Caribbean stage inevitably drew to his attention.

The seemingly opposed projects of Ménil and Walcott share underlying assumptions that rise to the surface in their use of the theater as a metaphor for inauthenticity. We find these same assumptions at work in Glissant's discussions of the pressing need for a national theater in his article "Théâtre, conscience du peuple" (*DA*, pp. 396–414), a manifesto that was first published in 1971 in the journal *Acoma*. He there argues that the establishment of a theater, because it provides a stage for the unfolding of a collective consciousness, is a necessary precondition of nation-building: "in its beginning, there is no nation without theater" (p. 396). As history has demonstrated, he asserts, the birth of both nations and the theater involves the passage from "lived folklore" to "represented culture," and the consequent expression of a people's "common destiny" (p. 398). However, this passageway has not opened up in the Antilles: "our tragedy," he notes, "is not being resolved." What we get in place of such resolutions is a sterile "folklorization" (equivalent to Ménil's countermythologies), which the political and cultural elite perpetuates: "the elite, which has not contributed to the productive 'transcendence' of folklore [*au dépassement fécond du folklore*], will end up contributing to its fossilization" (p. 404). This blocked situation results in a twofold spectacle of "dispossession" (p. 405): on the one hand, we are confronted with "a folklore that is wasting away (or fossilizing)—the people are less and less sure of their own truth" ("un folklore qui dépérit [ou se fige]: le peuple est de moins en moins sûr de la vérité qu'il vit"); and on the other, we witness "the proliferation of parodies of folklore—the elites are at an ever greater distance from the dignity of folkloric expression, about which they know nothing" ("des parodies de folklore qui fleurissent: les élites sont de plus en plus loin de la dignité des expressions folkloriques, qu'elles ignorent"). On the one hand, then, a tragic process of disappearance, in which the truth and authenticity that once characterized folklore are seen as perishing, and on the other, the mounting victory of an undignified parodic culture in which, for example, a once vibrant Carnival has become "an explicit tool of alienation," ever more reducible to "parades in which we can detect the alienated performance [*la représentation aliénée*] that we have been talking about as well as the restricted, pejorative, distorted, and lifeless meaning that we can attribute to the word 'theater'" (p. 410).

It is these alienated performances-representations that must be "liquidated" (p. 406): the word "theater" must be given a new meaning that erases the memory of its deformed double and ensures that Martinique will no longer be a "country where appearances have continually taken precedence over the real" (*DA*, p. 22). The fact that the Martiniquan's *représentation* has been "amputated," Glissant argues, "only makes the opening of a theater in which he could meet up with himself all the more pressing" (p. 397). Predictably, this opening can only be effected through a recourse to *praxis*, without which, as Fanon remarked in *Damnés*, "it is all just one big song and dance" (p. 94; "il n'y a plus que carnaval et flonflons"). Glissant calls for the establishment of "performative practices [*une activité de représentation*] whereby the collectivity can really think (about) itself, critique itself, and construct itself" (p. 406)—a dynamic process that, because it hinges upon the collective itself rather than the individual parts that make up this totality, will "not ensue from a gradual approach to the problems but, rather, from the suddenness of a cultural revolution" (p. 409). As was not the case for "peoples formed long ago" (e.g., the Greeks), the passage from a lived to a represented culture—and with it a conscious awareness of (cultural, national) identity—can only result from a conscious, willed effort on the part of those who, like the peoples of the Caribbean, were forged in the cauldron of modernity: "a determined effort at becoming aware of itself is what gives rise to [*donne lieu à*] the collectivity." "The theater," Glissant proclaims, "will have to figure this place, express this effort" (p. 409). This (good) theater will (re)*place* its alienated double, creating that lieu of which Fanon spoke in the essay from *Damnés* entitled "Sur la culture nationale," where he stressed that the colonized intellectual "who wants to do authentic work" must come to grips with the "national reality" and find his way to "the tumultuous place where knowledge [of the nation] is prefigured" (p. 156). Only by entering into "this secret place of disequilibrium where the people are to be found" (p. 157), Fanon continues, can the colonial subject escape the process of alienation that is transforming him into "the incarnation of contradictions that threaten to be insurmountable" (p. 150; "le lieu vivant de contradictions qui menacent d'être insurmontables").

By contrast, it is precisely this insuperably contradictory place in which Maximin situates his readers, not by simply opposing the Fanonesque voice that dominates Glissant's "Théâtre, conscience du peuple," but by simultaneously pursuing and opposing that voice, as well as those of Walcott and Ménil. In line with Ménil, his novels offer a critique of countermythologies; they caution against the sort of naive translations that Walcott lambasts; and, as the emphasis on Adrien and Antoine's theatrical project in *Soufrières* attests, they stress the need for finding (inventing) a *place* in which the Caribbean subject might go "à la rencontre de lui-même." But, lacking the firm ideological ground upon which these other writers feel themselves to be situated, Maximin also puts such positions into question: the *place* that Glissant would like to make present, to represent, remains resolutely absent in Maximin (significantly, the *Danse* never gets past the rehearsal stage and is barely mentioned in the final third of the novel); although the rhetorical nature of all translation is acknowledged, Maximin continues to engage with that rhetoric, often dressing his characters up, as it were, in "the robes of Ogun" (p. 254), making use of devices whose relation to prayer, to that "prière virile" of which Césaire spoke more than once in his *Cahier* (e.g., CP, pp. 72–73), is not simply one of antithesis but of profound ambivalence; and, while keeping them *at a distance*, he does not rule out of his novelistic universe the sort of mythological tropes that Ménil identified—"the roar of Matouba," as Glissant once put it (*DA*, p. 131), is still, for instance, very audible in *Soufrières*, even though it only comes to us in theatricalized (and geographically exiled) form, as part of an adaptation of André Schwarz-Bart's novel *La mulâtresse Solitude* that Adrien attends in Avignon (pp. 123–24).

Maximin's novels map out a theatrical space in which the "dramaturgie sauvage" to which Glissant aspires in his nationalist manifesto is a horizon present only in its dramatic absence, and in which the colonial "mise en scène" thus continues to generate one's act(ion)s. In their discussion of the development of stage productions in the Antilles, Chamoiseau and Confiant link the emergence of the *saynète*, a form of semi-improvised community theater, to the tradition of storytelling that developed out of Caribbean plantation societies: "the storyteller firing off a tale at a wake is the beginnings of our theater," they assert.[82] As they go on to argue, the conte—at the heart of what Chamoiseau refers to as creole "oraliture," "an oral production that stands out from normal speaking by virtue of its aesthetic dimension"[83]—is characterized not by an aesthetics of rupture but by a "questioning dynamic that accepts and refuses" (p. 57): it "installs the place of marooning within the plantation," rather than attempting to situate it on the outside (p. 58). A form of *petit marronnage* as opposed to *grand marronnage*, the conte and its subsequent theatricalizations in the saynète take their duplicitous place within a system to which they are opposed but that they cannot openly contest or, in Michel de Certeau's term, "resist." As Richard D. E. Burton for one has pointed out, de Certeau's distinction between "resistance" and "opposition" is extremely relevant to the political and cultural situation of the Antilles in the late twentieth century: where the former "requires an 'elsewhere' from which the system may be perceived and grasped as a whole," the latter has "no space which it can properly call its own" and "takes place of necessity *within* the system, on ground defined by the system."[84] It is the absence of this elsewhere, I have been arguing, that postmodernism takes as its point of departure, and in this respect the tactical detours that characterized the colonial societies of the Caribbean from their outset have assumed a global relevance in our own ambivalently "oppositional" age.

The nostalgia for what de Certeau calls "resistance," for *grand marronnage*, remains an inescapable part of this postmodern world; however, one needs, Maximin suggests through his portrait in *Soufrières* of the independentist Toussaint, to engage this nostalgia with great caution. Toussaint's failure to exercise this caution makes of him the most unhappy and self-destructive character in the novel, one in whom "the fantasy of envy and violence that has been running throughout masculinist anti-imperialist discourse since Fanon" is glaringly evident.[85] Toussaint's name, of course, stands as an ironic but also pious echo of the man who facilitated the independence of Haiti, and who from that time on has been turned into the tragic protagonist of countless plays, including Glissant's one rather unsuccessful foray into the theater, *Monsieur Toussaint*. The name also repeats that of the character from *L'isolé soleil* who died during the Carnival festivities of 1943 as part of the Resistance to the government of Admiral Robert and Vichy's "National Revolution." *This* Toussaint finds himself, by contrast, in a substantially less heroic world, constantly regretting a past in which action might have been possible (notably, the 1967 riots in Pointe-à-Pitre, which for many independence-minded Guadeloupeans "seemed like the final, tragic illusion,"[86] and in which, to his shame, Toussaint failed to confront the "colonial" authorities). Living on in the aftermath of this specific event and, more generally, that of the revolutionary enthusiasms of the 1960s, this Toussaint is incapable of paying heed to his mother's advice: "my son, never go looking in the ashes for what you will have lost in the fire" (p. 112). Insistently rejecting the undramatic reality of contemporary Guadeloupe's dispossessed culture, his vision fenced in by "watchwords" (p. 50; "la clôture des mots d'ordre"), Toussaint refers to the efforts of his contemporaries at opposing (in de Certeau's sense) the system as merely

"light comic theater," a pathetic reflection of "revolutions on 'serious' continents" (p. 103). Just as Césaire's apocalyptic desire for "la Fin du monde"
in the *Cahier* is to some degree counterbalanced by his relational vision of
"my nonfence island" (pp. 46–47; "mon île non-clôture"), Toussaint is
more complex than I am making him out to be here; however, it is precisely
his own complexity, "the perplexity of living" that constitutes his hybrid
identity, to which he cannot face up and that, toward the very end of the
novel, he will attempt to erase in an act of "terroristic" self-negation.

We are told in the final pages that Toussaint has tried to leave behind "a
story [or a history] that he never wanted to read in fragments, as if he was
already sure of being at the rendezvous of his finale. And he is not the kind
of terrorist to survive his own terror [*ce n'est pas le genre de terroriste à
survivre à sa terreur*]" (p. 275). Toussaint will become a victim, as it were,
of the revolutionary genre and the ideological boundaries it enforces; he
finds himself unable to accept a world in which the "rendezvous of victory"
is not sure, to survive in a (hi)story of fragments from which the whole is
lacking. He will run his car, which contains a homemade bomb, into a con-
voy of carts loaded with sugar cane; the explosion that follows upon what
appears to have been a simple accident allows Toussaint once and for all to
free himself of the doubts that torture him, as he becomes the main player
in his own private scenario of disappearance. His death will have marked
the victory of Ogun over Eshu (p. 276), of resistance over opposition, but
it is the most hollow of victories. His death, be it accident or suicide, is simply a waste, an "act" of terrorism that is motivated merely by his own personal impatience with, and his terror of, the political impasse with which
the other characters in the novel are in the process of learning how better to
live; like the sun in *L'isolé soleil*, he mistakenly "scorns . . . everything that
takes its time and measures its outbursts," and as a result the only choice he
has left is "between warmth and coldness, pleasure or death, with nothing
in between [*sans milieu*]" (p. 42).

Toussaint is the pathos-laden avatar of the modernist hero who sacrifices
himself for the greater good of the community, like Manuel in Jacques
Roumain's *Gouverneurs de la rosée* (1944) or the Rebel in Césaire's *Et les
chiens se taisaient* (1946), a work specifically referred to at the beginning of
the paragraph that recounts Toussaint's death. Toussaint desires to put himself in the place of Césaire's Rebel and proclaim to the world:

> Je veux être celui qui refuse l'inacceptable.
> Dans votre vie de compromis, je veux bâtir,
> moi, de dacite coiffé de vent,
> le monument sans oiseaux du Refus.[87]

> I want to be the one who refuses the unacceptable.
> In your life of compromise, I want to build,

I, from dacite crowned with wind,
the birdless monument of Refusal.

The Rebel's heroic refusal of compromise, and Toussaint's futile repetition of it, are generated by a desire for a radically new order, a "national revolution," as it were. As Simon Gikandi points out, "the central texts of Caribbean modernism are dominated by a certain anxiety about endings which is also an anxiety about new cultural beginnings."[88] Maximin acknowledges this anxiety, but displaces it by making Toussaint, with his (will to) heroism, merely one character among many (and one might well contrast his isolation, for instance, with the coherence and homogeneity of the revolutionary community in Glissant's first novel, La Lézarde). Moreover, Maximin quite literally puts into question the (will to an) ending that Toussaint's death signals. For the future-tense description of that death is, in the very next paragraph, immediately rewritten in terms of the conditional: certitudes about the future give way to doubts, and "perhaps," the narrator suggests, referring to a (hypothetical?) phone call from his estranged French wife and their son, "the voice of Ariel and Manuel might, this afternoon, still be enough to stop him from abandoning his solidarity with life ... " (p. 276). What are we to make of this double ending that both asserts a death and negates it, that both negates a life and (re)asserts it?

The anti-apocalyptic desire not to end, so often gestured toward in Maximin's novels, is clearly at play in this hypothetical reversal of Toussaint's fate (a reversal that will itself be "definitively" overturned in Maximin's most recent novel, L'île et une une nuit, where Toussaint's death would appear to be no longer in question, although its exact cause remains uncertain [p. 119]). We find this desire expressed most emphatically in one of the paragraphs of the letter with which L'isolé soleil ends, where the author-surrogate Daniel suggests that there will (should?) be "no dénouement, above all no ending: still more thirst, with the fire of the heart and the volcano, the wind of hurricanes and kisses, the water of springs and of the sea" (p. 281). The imperative voiced here, and the anticlimactic nature of the first novel's final chapter (a series of disconnected letters, fragments that assertively refuse to be read as a whole), coincide exactly with what Benitez-Rojo has said of "the dramatic structure of the Caribbean text," which does not ordinarily conclude with "the phallic orgasm of climax, but rather with a kind of coda" (RI, p. 25). A resistance to totalization and closure, to the "birdless monument of Refusal" that Césaire's Rebel wished to build, indeed characterizes Maximin's postmodern novels; it is no doubt significant that the last chapter of Soufrières—narrated by Marie-Gabriel's notebook from the ambivalent perspective of that "aujourd'hui" (to cite its very first words) unhappily signaled by Fanon in the opening lines of Peau noire—should be entitled "L'oiseau du possible."

It would be simple enough to conclude with an éloge of the end-less possibilities to which Maximin's novels direct us, and that the ideological directives Toussaint continues to follow prevent him from envisioning. Writing to Marie-Gabriel, Adrien refers to "your novel that is never done with
ending [*qui n'en finit pas de finir*], on account of your desire to explore
every nook and cranny of the island and its history" (p. 71). This lack of an
ending, this nontotalizing (because always incomplete) quest for totality, is
precisely what Glissant's relational poetics privileges as "errancy." As he
says in the *Poétique*, playing off of Césaire's indictment in *Et les chiens se
taisaient* of the Great Promoter of colonialism ("My name is the Discoverer, my name is the Inventor, my name is the Unifier, the one who opens
the world to the nations!" [p. 23]), "the wanderer [*l'errant*] . . . is no longer
the traveler, nor the discoverer, nor the conqueror; he seeks to acquaint himself with the totality of the world and already knows that he will never
accomplish this—and that in this [lack of 'accomplishment'] resides the endangered beauty of the world" (p. 33). The inordinate length of the penultimate chapters of Maximin's first two novels emphasizes this errant position, sensitizing the reader to the importance of the *middle* space of narrative and risk toward which the succession of false beginnings in *Soufrières*
directed us. Maximin's writing describes the errancy of the postcolonial
subject—a wandering without end that, as Glissant argues, involves "the
negation of every pole or every metropole" (p. 31). This is the in-between
space, the milieu, wherein Marie-Gabriel's notebook will situate its author
in a graceful apostrophe: "between the exodus past and the genesis to
come" (p. 253; "entre le passé d'exode et la genèse à venir"), at an enabling
distance from both.

However, for all its seductiveness, this vision of end-less possibility must
itself be put into question, as Maximin well knows. In the previous section
of this chapter, we saw how the errancy that the excess of *beginnings* in
Soufrières made possible is always also haunted by a sense of exile from an
absent *origin* (to make use of Edward Said's distinction).[89] At novel's end,
Maximin's writing will similarly acknowledge the inevitability of closure,
of translating errancy into error, and the consequent impossibility of a pure
negation of poles and metropoles. As the notebook points out, Marie-
Gabriel would prefer to ward off this inevitability:

Depuis qu'elle a senti en elle venir ma fin—la fixation d'un style sur le chaos des années—, elle quête encore chaque occasion d'une ultime dérive: une nouvelle donne
d'histoires anciennes, un conte pour veiller, un appel de lectures, un envol de feuil-
lets, un pourvoi de désirades [a neologism alluding to *la Désirade*, a small island off
the coast of Guadeloupe], frêles esquives au risque du courant, afin de retarder la
conclusion de mon fleuve au sein de sa mer ... (p. 264)

Ever since she first felt within herself the coming of my end—the settling of a style upon the chaos of the years—she has been in search of any chance for one last drift: a new deal from the pack of old stories, a tale to stay awake and keep watch by, an invitation to further readings, a flight of pages, the petitions of desire, flimsy evasions risking the current, so as to defer the final flowing of my river into the midst of its sea ...

The final coming of this fixation, the end of the quest for its deferral, is what the notebook will take upon itself in the last chapter, thus becoming a double of the novel that contains it—a novel whose markedly monological style so differs from the dialogical exuberance of *L'isolé soleil*; no matter who talks in *Soufrières*, they all seem to be speaking with the same voice (the voice, as we will see at the very end of this chapter, of writing). The notebook accepts the necessity of narrating "the last day" (p. 244), aware that in so doing it must eventually betray the poetics of drift and errancy, which its author has been pursuing, by performing an act of closure that Marie-Gabriel wants to resist.

This betrayal will not, however, be a simple one, as the notebook establishes through repeatedly emphasizing the performative nature of its closing act. The duplicitous treatment of Toussaint's death, the process of both displaying and displacing his end, is but one instance of this emphasis in the final pages of *Soufrières*, which enact a rapid-fire series of dramatic endings to a book that has been all about waiting for the one truly explosive event that never takes place—the eruption of the volcano and all that this eruption would symbolically entail. The inclusion and hypothetical erasure of the ending of Toussaint's narrative of heroism is enclosed by two other familiar stories whose ending the notebook stages: the narratives of romance and of (national) community. I will pass over the predictable conclusion of the first plot, which involves the sexual union of the novel's central author-protagonists, Marie-Gabriel and Adrien: figured in terms of an eclipse, of a hieratic fusion of moon and sun, this self-consciously romantic moment of closure inevitably brings to mind the rather less self-conscious and implicitly sexist ending of one of the classics of European postmodernism, Italo Calvino's *Se una notte d'inverno un viaggiatore ...* (1979), which ends with a self-satisfied invocation of the marital union of the [Male] and [Female] Readers who have served as the two central protagonists of the novel's metafictive adventures. As was the case with Toussaint's death, however, this conclusive moment is followed upon by a series of commentaries that disturb, without fully erasing and thereby taking us well and truly beyond, the conventional ending demanded by the narrative of romance.[90]

It is the final and most "flamboyant" act with which *Soufrières* ends, the most profoundly unreadable moment in the entire book, that demands our close scrutiny here at the end of this chapter on Maximin's novels: what follows directly upon Toussaint's hypothetical death is a fire that, with no explanation as to its cause, burns down *les Flamboyants*, the old plantation house that was Marie-Gabriel's home and that in the final chapters of *Soufrières* serves as the "lieu commun" where virtually all the main characters in the novel have gathered. This incendiary event clearly echoes (but to what end?) not only a previous—and highly motivated—burning down of the Flamboyants in *L'isolé soleil* as part of the Napoleonic reprisals against one of the few whites to have resisted the reimposition of slavery in 1802 (p. 64), but also the explosion of "l'habitation du Matouba," in which Delgrès laid his mines and "which marked the territory of the last combat, the place of the holocaust" (p. 123). How are we to read this echo of a past history, and this invocation of what Margaret Atwood once called "the Incendiary or Burning Mansion theme"?[91] This final ending, problematically reminiscent of the tragic collapse of Thomas Sutpen's "doomed house" in *Absalom, Absalom!*,[92] or of the conflagration with which Maynard's *Outre-mer* apocalyptically ends, is more complex than those of the romantic and heroic narratives that immediately preceded it, where the displaying and the displacement of an ending were treated as two separate, serialized moments; this ending, by contrast, puts into play a simultaneous critique and assertion of the narrative of (national) community that has played such an important role in post/colonial literature, from Virginie's funeral down to the assertion of a collective subject at the end of Césaire's *Cahier*. Instead of commentaries *on* the narrative, the narrative event itself becomes the means of commenting on closure—a means that is complicitous with the end upon which it remarks.

As a critique of the narrative of community, the unexplained fire serves to disperse the place of finality around which that community had apparently been forming. Temporarily housing the novel's entire cast of characters, the Flamboyants had become a possible site of resolution, a microcosm of the nation that could serve as home to the Glissantian *nous*; with the burning down of the habitation, the possibility of thus materially *locating* a community vanishes, and the characters find themselves once again in a space of risk and drifting uncertainty from which such resolutions are absent or present only (to cite a beautiful phrase used by Glissant to describe the poetry of Saint-John Perse) as "the nostalgia of the impossible dwelling" (*DA*, p. 432; "la nostalgie de l'impossible maison"). The vision of a stable community, and the collective identity that comes with it, is one that must be rejected because, as the authors of the *Éloge* put it, "creolization is not a matter of syntheses" (p. 48). If the narrative of community promotes this dream of synthesis, the burning down of the Flamboyants cuts it short. The irony, of course, is that this critique of closure is itself imposed through an emphatic act of closure; instead of a supplemental gloss stressing ambivalence, we are faced with an event that enacts the very thing it is, in the name of a nonclosural vision of the world, contesting. Furthermore, it is entirely possible to read this ending in a completely opposite manner, as an *assertion* of the narrative of community. When the habitation burns down, so too, it might be argued, does the tarnished past it represents; as the "ensemble culturel" out of which creole society emerged, the habitation, as Chamoiseau and Confiant have argued, is characterized by "an ambiguity that will never disappear from our creole being."[93] And yet might not the physical disappearance of this place be the precondition for a truly new beginning, the tabula rasa necessary for the establishment of an authentic community in the Caribbean? To have the historic site of oppression and ambiguity burn down becomes, from this second perspective, an act that prepares the ground for a radically different future. Destroying a place, making way for a place: the two hypotheses that I have just suggested are theoretically incompatible, but inhabit the same narrative space. Confronted with this double possibility, we find ourselves no place in particular, somewhere between the two, between which we are impossibly forced to choose *and* to acknowledge the (im)possibility of that choice. The aleatory nature of this ending prevents the reader from considering it with the certainty that it equally, by virtue of its apocalyptic finality, demands.

In the burning down of the Flamboyants, in the ambivalent recognition that—to (re)cite Adorno—"the house is past,"[94] Maximin's novel thus establishes a dynamics of reading that forces us to offer up one or several hypotheses about an ending that, for all its arbitrariness, is emphatically *non*-hypothetical; what the reader must confront is both the necessity and the arbitrariness of this ending and of the meaning that it presumably conveys. The ultimate result of Maximin's complex emphasis on closure here is, I would argue, to ensure that what might be read as the novel's apolitical emphasis on supplementarity, on Barthesian dérive, Derridean deferral, Glissantian errancy, is always also translatable into a tactical positioning that temporarily puts an end to the end-less world of what I have been calling narrative. Speaking both as a supporter and a critic of Derrida's postmodern insights into deferral, staggering, serialization, and such like, Stuart Hall agrees that "signification depends upon the endless re-positioning of its differential terms," but goes on to suggest that Derrida "has permitted his profound theoretical insight to be re-appropriated into a celebration of formal 'playfulness,' which evacuates it of its political meaning." What Hall wants to stress, by contrast, is that "meaning, in any specific instance, depends on the contingent and arbitrary stop—the necessary and temporary 'break' in the infinite semiosis of language"; we need to take this meaning seriously, while ensuring that this "'cut' of identity" be seen as "an arbitrary and contingent 'ending'" rather than something "natural and permanent."[95] If this critique is no more than a strategic (mis)reading of Derrida in order to establish a polemical and at best tenuous distinction between "evacuated" postmodern and "meaningful" postcolonial deconstructive practices, it is nonetheless central to an understanding of Maximin's enterprise.

Provisional assertions of (cultural, racial, ethnic, sexual) identity, or for that matter of the various *generic* identities into which the narrato-logics of romance, revolutionary heroism, or (national) community resolve themselves, are a necessary feature of any deconstructive practice; such assertions cannot be avoided, and it is precisely their inevitability that Maximin insists upon by highlighting narrative closure at the end of his novel. Contingent and arbitary stops along the way, lacking a ground that would authorize them, these endings nonetheless have their part to play, even if they cannot be spoken of with the same assurance as of old. If the volcano that narrated the fourth chapter of *Soufrières*, and whose own lack of mastery we have already commented upon, could still parodically repeat, word for masterful word, the authoritative voice of Césaire's *Cahier* ("Et je dis que cela est bien ainsi ... "), the *cahier* that puts an end to *Soufrières* is well aware that it must translate this voice into the form of a duplicitous question: "I who am neither earth nor fire, can I say that this is right?" (p. 259). This question, which never entirely escapes the original assertion that is nonetheless in and of itself absent from its present (re)formulation, makes possible the enactment of that dance of doubt of which the modernist poet Walcott, would-be heir to Césaire's and Saint-John Perse's poetic authority, spoke with such trepidation. The ending, the endings, of Maximin's novel confronts us with this strange mixture of doubts and certainties, and it is the dynamics of this mixture that a post/colonial identity politics must always take into account. To put oneself in this place of doubt and certainty, to "live inside a repetition of a representation without end,"[96] is not to lose sight of the volcano and all that it betokens, but to see it, finally, from the perspective of a present in which it has been substantially disempowered. As Adrien and Antoine put it in their manifesto for the *Danse*, "the Soufrière does not disarm us, it forces us in all urgency to position ourselves in relation to our masks" (p. 29). The (absent) presence of the volcano does not simply disarm us, turning everything into mere "carnaval et flonflons." Rather, it signals an urgent need, in the "théâtre des humains," to distinguish between masks, to choose intelligently, and with a provisional sense of commitment, the ending(s) that one must always also not choose. Not (only) disarmed, but (also) miraculously armed with an identity that is never final, never authentic, a confusing mixture of Self and Other, original and representation, the creolized subject accepts the challenge of living in a post/colonial world of (mis)translations and deadly serious end-games. This is a world in which, as Michael Taussig has argued, "the masks of appearance do more than suffice[;] they are an absolute necessity."[97] That we must never stop speaking, and writing, the relativized truths that this absolute necessity makes possible for us is the message the creolized subject, emerging from out of the burning habitation into that space of survival to which our attention has been repeatedly drawn from beginning to end of the novel, will communicate to us on the very last page of *Soufrières*.

The novel has almost, but not quite, "come" to a close: the Flamboyants is burning, last in a series of climaxes that have situated us in a perplexingly contradictory place that demands to be read in more than one way, according to more than one "positioning" (in Stuart Hall's terms). The repeated staging of these apocalyptic endings, ironically enough, results in the creation of a textual space in excess of, albeit in no way *beyond*, the final word(s) they seductively offer. As with the concluding section of Coetzee's *Foe*, which was split into two parts that were disturbingly (un)like one another, this coda (pp. 278–79) lends itself to a double reading—a reading that refuses the authorization of any single solution to the problem of how best to live in the space of survival revealed by this brief supplement, while nonetheless insisting that such solutions *be written*.

The very last ending of *Soufrières* focuses on Marie-Gabriel's young friend Élisa, who ten years previously had lost the power of speech, after the 1967 riot in Pointe-à-Pitre in which her little brother was killed by the authorities. Élisa emerges from the burning house into the open, carrying a few hurriedly gathered-together items, which she deposits by the fountain where Marie-Gabriel has left her notebook. After a moment's thought, she takes out her pencil and "dashes off a few lines—a memory that is no longer repressed," on one of the notebook's empty pages:

L'exil s'en va ainsi portant de malhabiles grains aux oiseaux nés du temps qui jamais ne s'endorment jamais aux espaces fertiles des enfances remuées. (p. 278)

Exile thus goes bearing clumsy grains to the birds born of time which never never fall asleep in the fertile spaces of stirred up childhoods.

What Élisa has written-remembered is an ever so slightly revised version of a four-line poem entitled "Oiseaux," which comes from Aimé Césaire's *Fer-rements*, and which had already provided the title for the last chapter of Maximin's first novel ("L'exil s'en va ... "). Élisa's revision, or faulty memory, of Césaire's original text consists in three changes, which exemplify Maximin's own intertextual relation to his modernist predecessor. The poem is cited verbatim, with the exception of a prepositional phrase that has been left out after the word "ainsi": "dans la mangeoire des astres" (*CP*, pp. 274–75; "into the feeder made of stars"). Maximin's postmodern vision cannot, and does not wish to, encompass the cosmic ("astral") territory charted by his more ambitious predecessor (and here it is appropriate to recall our earlier discussion in Chapter 4 of Glissant's similar rejection of the "profondeur astrale de méduses" laid claim to by Césaire in his "Ode à la Guinée"). His characters inhabit a world that has been substantially de-mythologized and (the second change) depoeticized. Poetry, and the access to Being that it enabled (to recall Césaire's claim), can only be remembered here in the translated form of prose: the four distinct lines of Césaire's poem have been compressed into a paragraph that resembles the novelistic prose surrounding it, while remaining in certain respects distinct from it (by virtue of its italicized status and the blank spaces that separate it off from what comes before and after it). Finally, the prosaic memory that Élisa adds on to Marie-Gabriel's *cahier* differs from the poetic original in its acknowl-edgement of the inevitability of closure: not the absolute ending dreamt of in Césaire's *Cahier* but a provisional "stop" that is simply designated by the period with which Élisa's revision of "Oiseaux" concludes but that is eu-phorically absent from Césaire's open-ended poem (an absence that is the logical complement of the resolutely apocalyptic insistence on ending in the *Cahier*). Such slight but revealing changes confirm one last time the relation of (un)likeness that obtains between the modernist and the postmodern text, and their respective evaluations of a post/colonial exile that in its "go-ing" never simply *goes away* but, sequel-like, *moves on*.

The novel does not, though, simply end with this faulty (re)citation of Césaire; rather, as with *Foe*, this one ending is matched by another, which quickly follows upon it and is also italicized. Having stopped writing, Élisa finds herself "wedged between sky and earth"—between, that is, the two extremes to which the modernist poet aspired: the cosmic heights at which he aimed, and the ancestral earth into which he plunged—and closes her eyes "for the night of the ending, after having turned on her little tape recorder, from which escapes the ancient voice of grandmother Nono softly singing a creole nursery rhyme" ("pour la nuit de la fin, après avoir ouvert son petit magnétophone, d'où s'échappe la voix ancienne de la grande-mère Nono chantant une très douce comptine créole"). It is with this *comptine* that the novel finally ends:

> *Lorsque le fil des jours*
> *suit l'aiguille de l'espoir*
> *il raccommode le destin.*
>   (p. 279)
> *When the thread of days*
> *follows the needle of hope*
> *it mends destiny.*

One might well argue that Maximin has here not only given voice to the opposition between orality and writing that is such a common trope in Ca-

ribbean and postcolonial literature, but privileged the former by choosing
to end with it. The *writing* of the literary father Césaire would in this account have been made to take second place to the *voice* of a grandmother
whose presence at the very end might be thought of as posing the same
question that the aging Anastasie asks the (fictionalized) novelist Glissant in
Tout-monde: "Why is it that you all want to write books, when it's so
agreeable just to sit oneself down and have a talk, pretending to take it all
in and letting the voice spin itself out [*laissant filer la voix*]?" (p. 198). Such
an argument would, however, overlook the mirroring relationship that
Maximin has established between the two italicized passages, through
which he stresses that both the oral and the written need to be thought together, in a mix that substantially undoes the original identity of both. Just
as Césaire's poetic text has, through the transformative workings of a falli-
ble memory, lost some of its original authoritativeness, so too has the
grandmother's "comptine créole" undergone a substantial change: mechanically reproduced, her actual voice "escapes"; its original presence remains
with us only in the form of an absence, a copy. Moreover, the song itself,
while invoking elements of a traditional comptine (e.g., the phrase "filer des
aiguilles"),[98] has obviously been reworked, translated into a self-consciously
literary, and decidedly French rather than Creole,[99] language that has as
much to do with, say, the dark and foreboding nursery rhyme entitled
"Comptine" that Césaire also included in the collection *Ferrements* (*CP*,
pp. 264–65), as it does with that oraliture, those "scraps of oral memory,
scattered across the country, those snippets of story, those snatches of
comptines," to which a writer like Chamoiseau has attempted to do justice
in his exuberantly inventive novels.[100]

To do justice to this world of orality, for both Chamoiseau and Maximin, is to register—to memorialize—its absence in writing. However, if
these two exemplars of contemporary Franco-Caribbean literature are both
engaged in this same project of recalling what in *Malemort* Glissant refers
to as "notre parler impossible et quêté" (p. 151),[101] they go about it in very
different ways. The novels of Chamoiseau recall (the absence of) orality by
forcefully miming what Henry Louis Gates (with a nod to the Russian for-
malists) has referred to as the "speakerly text," "a text whose rhetorical
strategy is designed to represent an oral literary tradition, designed 'to em-
ulate the phonetic, grammatical, and lexical patterns of actual speech and
produce the "illusion of oral narration."' "[102] In a novel like *Solibo Magnifique* (1988), Chamoiseau simultaneously conjures up this strategic illusion and deconstructs it in a series of metafictive gestures that remind his
readers of the author's distance from the oral narrations that he is (re)pre-
senting (as when the *conteur* Solibo, commenting on the desire of a novelist
by the name of "Oiseau de Cham" to "capture the word in writing," points

out the impossibility of this enterprise: "I was speaking, but you, you write, letting it be known that the spoken word has been passed down to you. Across the distance, you hold out your hand to me. That's all well and good, but you've got distance on your hands ... " (pp. 52–53; "Je parlais, mais toi tu écris en annonçant que tu viens de la parole. Tu me donnes la main par-dessus la distance. C'est bien, mais tu touches la distance ... ").[103] Maximin's archly written novels touch this distance in a different manner, for it is quite simply impossible to be under any illusion that the words with which they are written are a mimesis of spoken language: with Maximin, we are manifestly always-already (to recall Walcott's argument about the Caribbean's relation to Africa) on the side of a writing that can only "feel the verb 'to be' from a distance" (S, p. 271), and it is only from this perspective that the other side can be read; and yet, as with the comptine, we are nonetheless repeatedly asked to perform this reading, in translation. Such translations, recuperating the trace of the original, direct us toward a space that is between the oral and the written, and that puts into question the (inescapable) binary thinking that would cordon them off from one another, as when Glissant distinguishes in Discours antillais between a "poétique forcée" and a "poétique naturelle" (p. 451), the former associated with writing ("the book is the tool of a forced poetics") and the latter with speech ("the oral is the bearer of a natural poetics"). Simple binary distinctions like this, or the sort of quasi-essentialist claims about being "rooted in the oral" that one finds sprinkled throughout the Éloge de la Créolité (e.g., orality is "our understanding, our reading of this world, the as yet blind groping of our complexity" [p. 34]), break down in the novels—if not the theories—of Glissant and Chamoiseau, which no less than Maximin's explore the forced, unnatural margin of opportunity, and of error, to which the post/modern Glissant directs our attention when he notes that "there is some margin for an exploration of the dialectic of orality and writing within the very framework of writing itself."[104]

   This is a weak dialectic that will not result in the conclusive "synthesis" the modernist Glissant might once have hoped for;[105] to inhabit this margin is to remain firmly within the boundaries of a writing that cannot bring the interminable detour of our modernity to an end. It is to take hold of a thread that, unlike Ariadne's, will not lead us out of the maze of doubting but that might, to merge the two primary meanings of the verb "raccommoder" that feed into Maximin's comptine, "patch up" our condition by "reconciling" us to it, hopefully "bringing back together" in this central-marginal place—Fanon's "lieu vivant de contradictions qui menacent d'être insurmontables"—those whom the various ideologies of center and margin, and the certainties upon which they depend, would keep separate. To take hold of this thread will be to realize that whatever patching up or (m)ending we may accomplish by means of it will itself come undone, and that it is we ourselves who must undo what we have done, that the responsibility of post/colonial writing is "to unravel a thread in the dense loom or economy of being . . . to unravel a thread that may sustain us to cope with an abysmal otherness whom and which we dread but which may also bring resources to alter or change the fabric of the imagination in the direction of a therapeutic, ceaselessly unfinished genesis."[106] To change "the fabric of the imagination" (in Wilson Harris's phrase) is to begin again, in lieu of the endings that we might once have accredited. Between the literary fathers and the ancestral grandmothers there is "something else besides." After the apocalypse that we desire and the conflagration that we fear come other, more limited—and yet no less essential—possibilities, and with them the hope of learning how to *in*habit, finally, the post/colonial structures that have in the past sustained us with dread and that will remain with us in the future, as resources to be drawn on in our repeated attempts at unraveling them once and for all, at bringing to an end what we can and must only amend, in further acts of translation that beckon others, offering a future to our apparently definitive endings. It is this future to which Maximin alerts us near the beginning of his third novel, *L'île et une nuit* (p. 29), when he informs us, against all expectations, against every certainty with which *Soufrières* might have armed us, might have sent us on our way along "the extremely sure road to death," that the Flamboyants "very nearly burned down in '76 during the eruption of the Soufrière, if our Élisa had not been there to sound the alarm and save the essentials in the end."

Part IV

CONCLUSION

8 The Last Frontier

MEMORIES OF THE POST-COLONIAL
FUTURE IN KERI HULME'S 'THE
BONE PEOPLE'

> If the words "tradition" and "betrayal" have the same
> origin, then what twists and turns have led to their having
> such very different, or such fundamentally—I mean to say,
> such radically—similar, meanings?
> —Jean Genet, *Les paravents*

Joseph Conrad's *Heart of Darkness* (1899) conjoins the self-satisfied rac(ial)ist sensibilities that characterized much Victorian literature and a nascent disgust with the rapidly industrializing and culturally homogenizing mass society that Conrad saw looming on the twentieth-century horizon. It is this disgust that would come to characterize the dominant strain of literary modernism in ensuing decades and generate a quest for cultural alternatives that often bore the name of "primitivism." Conrad's novella situates itself on an historical borderline, simultaneously recoiling from and, with an as yet unformulated longing, looking forward to an untouched wilderness that it can neither fully repress (as demanded by the Victorian cult of "efficient" progress) nor desire (in the manner of the full-bodied commitment to alterity that infuses D. H. Lawrence's mornings in Mexico and the existentialist high noon of Paul Bowles's sheltering sky). In Conrad's double vision of the primitive it appears as both a "natural" refuge (as in his description of those "black fellows" who "shouted, sang; their bodies stream[ing] with perspiration; they had faces like grotesque masks—these chaps; but they had bone, muscle, a wild vitality, an intense energy of movement, that was as natural and true as the surf along their coast" [p. 28]) and also as a "savage" horror ("prehistoric man" being reducible to "a burst of yells, a whirl of black limbs, a mass of hands clapping, of feet stamping, of bodies swaying, of eyes rolling, under the droop of heavy and motionless foliage" [p. 51]). This duplicity is at the heart of *Heart of Darkness*, and it is for that reason a "frontier novel" (in Wilson Harris's terms), bearing allegiances to both sides of the debate between Victorianism and modernism, and ultimately to neither.[1] On the other side of the primitivist territory that *Heart of Darkness* tentatively begins carving out, on one of modernism's last frontiers, we find a Cuban novel that purposefully echoes both the thematic concerns and narrative trajectories of Conrad's fin de siècle meditation: Alejo Carpentier's *The Lost Steps* (1953; *Los pasos perdidos*).

This frontier, which marks the end of modernist primitivism as a viable project, is not, however, immediately visible in Carpentier's novel, which often seems, in its obsession with recuperating "prehistory," intent upon ignoring the sort of historical, creolizing processes that the author of *Explosion in a Cathedral* would in a few years' time chronicle, and champion. In his apparently successful quest for an "authentic primitivism" (p. 76) in the remote jungles of South America, the anonymous narrator of *The Lost Steps* seems to be treading exactly the same modernist ground as enthusiasts like Lawrence and Bowles. Convinced of the "total bankruptcy of Western man" (p. 96), the narrator has set off in search of other worlds, taking a vacation from the overbearingly modern North American metropolis in which he has been stagnating for many years; the virtually unexplored interior of South America becomes an originary counterbalance to the "era of the Wasp-Man" (p. 13) that he is fleeing—a modern era characterized by psychic automatism, rampant theatricality, and Spenglerian decline, and one that, as the narrator repeatedly affirms, makes Sisyphuses of us all (e.g., p. 197). By his own account, this part-time organographer's voyage upriver in search of musical instruments used by "prehistoric man, our contemporary," permits him to escape the "net" (p. 254), the "labyrinth" (p. 252), of our modernity. Gradually attuning himself to the "genesial rhythm" (p. 109) of the jungle, he journeys ever further into the heart of the South American wilderness. At a tavern auspiciously named "Memories of the Future," he will meet a renegade gold miner, who has founded a town in a remote part of the jungle; following him back to this "city whose name was not to be found on maps, which was withdrawn from the horrors of the Epoch" (p. 188), the narrator resolves to become a citizen of this quasi-Adamic community. His decision to inhabit "these regions, as unknown as the blank *terrae incognitae* of the old cartographers" (p. 206), proves short-lived, however: lacking the paper upon which to write down the ambitious threnody that his encounter with the primitive has inspired him to compose, the narrator allows himself to be rescued by a helicopter team that his wife has sent out to find him. Although he vows to return to the city and to his native mistress Rosario as soon as possible, various circumstances prevent him from doing so; by the end of the novel, while continuing to affirm that "the Stone Age . . . is still within our reach" (p. 274), the narrator realizes that he has lost all chance of ever again inhabiting the primitive world of his antimodern desire. For him it can henceforth be no more than a wrenchingly exotic memory. The (re)discovered "world of Genesis" (p. 186) will, in the end, be once again effaced by his disillusioned point of departure, "the world of the Apocalypse where all seemed to await the opening of the Sixth Seal" (p. 252).

Carpentier's novel would thus appear to be a casebook example of the valorization of worlds at antipodes to the West that characterized modernist primitivism. In preferring this alternative present "to the present of the makers of the Apocalypse" (p. 273), the novel programmatically follows through on Paul Gauguin's aesthetic and existential agenda: "to reimmerse myself in virgin nature, to encounter only savages, to live their life, without being preoccupied by anything other than conveying, in the way that a child would, the ideas in my head, equipped only with the means available to primitive art, the only good ones, the only true ones."[2] It shares, moreover, the same revelatory impulse that was central to Césaire's modernist enterprise, and that one critic, speaking of Césaire's theater, has characterized as its reliance on "rituals of purification" that "precede the final initiatic trial of each Césairian hero [and that] all serve to return them to [an] original purity or nudity, this inviolable innermost core, which we can call their primitivity."[3] There can be, one must add, no doubt of Carpentier's own investment in the primitive at this point in his career: his autobiographical accounts of a trip into the interior of Venezuela, out of which *The Lost Steps* developed, feature many of the same euphoric sentiments voiced in the novel: in newspaper articles published in the late 1940s, for instance, he identifies the interior of the continent with a "virgin America," a "world of Genesis," going so far as to anticipate and refute potential critics for whom "speaking about the virginity of America is merely a cliché of some new Americanist rhetoric."[4] His earlier published works, furthermore, consistently invoked the radical otherness of non-Western cultures, from his ethnographic investigations into Afro-Cuban culture in the 1930s through to his influential concept of "lo real maravilloso," "that which we encounter in a raw state, latent, omnipresent, in everything Latin American,"[5] and that (as we saw in Chapter 1) Carpentier argued to be irretrievably absent from a modernized, secularized Europe in which all sense of wonder had been lost. *The Lost Steps* thus pursues Carpentier's modernist-primitivist dreams—dreams that lead directly back to the Romantics (as when Hugo notes, in the preface to *Cromwell*, that "in primitive times, when man awakens in a newly dawned world, poetry awakens along with him. In the presence of marvels that dazzle and intoxicate him, his first word is nothing less than a hymn").[6] However, I would argue, the novel also distances itself, though by no means explicitly, from these very dreams: alongside its insistent affirmations of the primitive, the novel also lays the groundwork for a self-consuming irony that is never openly activated, but that allows itself, uncertainly, to be read, producing the possibility that "the text is more self-aware than its narrator."[7]

The more one reads, and rereads, *The Lost Steps*, the less possible it becomes to say whether the narrator's search for the primitive is to be taken seriously, or whether he is being set up as a victim of his own inflated rhetoric and expectations. He would appear to be distressingly unaware of the extent to which his language and his desires are contaminated by the very world he is attempting to abandon. Episodes from Western literature and history, especially the colonial myth of the conquistadors' search for El Dorado, provide him with his conceptual framework for understanding the jungle. The sheer anteriority of this supposedly pre-modern space is everywhere disrupted by the traces of the world that comes after it: the founder of the "city withdrawn from the horrors of the Epoch" is, for instance, referred to as "the Adelantado"—significantly enough, a title applied to governors of frontier provinces in post-Conquest Spanish America (and one that figures prominently in Washington Irving's story "The Phantom Island: The Adalantado of the Seven Cities" [1839/1855], which chronicles a Portuguese cavalier's discovery of an island in the Atlantic that does not, as the reader realizes by the end of the tale, actually exist). The space of the Other is not the "virgin world" (p. 207) its narrator claims it to be, echoing Sir Walter Raleigh's portrait of the Guianas as a "country that hath yet its maidenhead"; rather, it is always-already penetrated and (re)named (e.g., the Adelantado has called his city Santa Mónica de los Venados). As Roberto González Echevarría puts it in his seminal study of Carpentier, the world of *The Lost Steps* is one that is "littered with texts" (*ACPH*, p. 174). The primitive has always-already been translated into other terms. As Stephen Slemon has argued of colonial discourse in general, the narrator's vision is inherently allegorical; he is doomed to read what is culturally other "by reference to an anterior set of signs that is already situated within an overarching, supposedly universal, metaphysical and political master code of recognition."[8] This allegorical reinscription of the pre-colonial within colonial terms is only one among many possible ironies that the novel offers its reader: the narrator often conflates, for instance, the scene of the primitive with the theatrical world of modernity from which he is attempting to escape, as when he likens the jungle at several points to a "real and visible stage" (e.g., p. 149). Furthermore, the Lawrentian native mistress Rosario, "a woman of the earth" (p. 179), is actually the end product of a centuries-long process of métissage. We are informed that "several races had met in this woman: Indian in the hair and cheekbones, Mediterranean in brow and nose, Negro in the heavy shoulders and the breadth of hips" (p. 83). The narrator's first encounter with this "living sum of races" clearly anticipates Esteban's "transcendental en-

counter" aboard *L'ami du peuple*,[9] and the enthusiastic account of transculturation that attaches to it, but in the context of *The Lost Steps* the figure of Rosario, and the "fusion of history and nature" she embodies,[10]
troubles and implicitly contradicts the novel's primitivist scenario, and as
The Lost Steps progresses it (or the narrator) conveniently loses sight of
her mixed identity, eventually allowing her to take on the "ancestral silhouette" of the Indians with whom she is by the end more or less assimilated (p. 172).

To complicate matters even further, near the end of the novel the narrator himself angrily denounces European modernist primitivism, viewing it
as nothing more than a manifestation of the Cartesian rationalism that it
ostensibly seeks to displace. Having returned to North America, he pauses
before a picture gallery "where dead idols were on exhibition, devoid of all
meaning for lack of worshippers"; in their "enigmatic or terrible faces," he
notes,

many contemporary painters were seeking the secret of a lost eloquence with that
same desire for instinctive energies which made many of the composers of my generation strive for the elemental power of primitive rhythms in the abuse of percussion instruments. For more than twenty years a weary culture had been seeking rejuvenation and new powers in the cult of the irrational. But now I found ridiculous
the attempt to use masks of Bandiagara, African *ibeyes*, fetishes studded with nails,
without knowing their meaning, as battering-rams against the redoubts of [Des-
cartes's] *Discourse on Method*. By labeling such things "barbarous" the labelers
were putting themselves in the thinking, the Cartesian, position, the very opposite
of the aim they were pursuing. (p. 251)

Is the narrator merely denouncing a flawed version of primitivism here, one
that has no lived experience of other worlds and thus can never know their
meaning, or is he (unwittingly) attacking *all* versions of primitivism, including his own and the "desire for instinctive energies" that led him into
the jungle? Is his every gesture no more than an ironic repetition of the very
thing he despises and from which he would detach himself? The issue is, I
believe, strictly undecidable—and it is for precisely this reason that Carpentier's novel does not inhabit the central ground of modernism, but one
of its frontiers. It both asserts and destabilizes the existence of the primitive,
as well as the power of the (specifically, Latin American) author to escape
textual (specifically, colonial and/or European) precedents. It both exults in
and questions the modernist capacity to "make it new" that characterizes
what Gustavo Pérez Firmat has called "primitive" as opposed to "critical"
criollism: where the "primitive criollist believes in aboriginal achievement[,]
thinking that he has the strength, in William Carlos Williams's phrase, to
throw away the rotted names," and "maintains that it is possible to begin
from scratch, *ab origine*," the critical criollist self-consciously "translates"

his predecessors, following them from a distance, creating a world of "relative, relational 'originality'" rather than "absolute, pristine 'aboriginality'" (*CC*, pp. 9, 12). If a later novel like *Explosion in a Cathedral*, as González Echevarría suggests, explicitly abandons the modernist commitment to the primitive, replacing "the myth of a past utopia . . . by the correlative myth of the future" (*ACPH*, p. 212)—a future to be arrived at through *either* the apocalyptic explosions of revolution *or* the dilatory processes of creolization—*The Lost Steps* inhabits an intermediary space, a way station or crossroads between these two myths, in which it has become impossible to determine the real status of the primitive.

But this last frontier of primitivism does not merely mark the boundary between a past-oriented myth and an equally modernist but revolutionary one that points obliquely forward to a time in which (to cite Benitez-Rojo's description of the direction in which Carpentier's later work tends) the problem of the "American" novel "would be resolved at some vague moment in the future, when our socio-cultural spectrum's chaotic dynamics order themselves in a 'synthesis' that can be read, interpreted, and represented textually by Latin American and Caribbean writers" (*RI*, p. 179). In crossing over this frontier, we enter not only into that creolized space to which *Explosion* alerts us, but also into that of a *post*-modernism where the foundational myths of both past and future have been decisively hollowed out: no less than the process of "mutation and adaptation" that is creolization, what some might perceive as its monstrous double, postmodernism, puts into question the postulation of spatial and temporal otherness that was at the heart of both the primitivist project (and its earlier nineteenth-century exoticizing avatars) and such teleologically minded ideologies as Marxism. Lacking the grounds for a belief in radical difference, the postmodern sensibility is unable to accredit either the integral reality of a pre-modern past, which it knows can be reached only through the mediation of written texts, or the possibility of a truly revolutionary future: it locates us in a confusing and complicitous present in which differences have become (un)likenesses. Carpentier's *Lost Steps* situates us, undecidably, at the point of interchange between a modernism in which the object of primitivist desire may still be (mis)taken as real, and a postmodern excavation of that cultural alternative, in which its existence can at best be posited only in the mode of a s(imul)acralizing nostalgia.

Forty years after the publication of Carpentier's novel, when it has become even harder to credit the continued existence of pre-modern and pre-colonial ways of life, the status of the primitive—and, by extension, of all traditional ways of life within the régime of a global modernity—nonetheless remains a pressing issue for those who feel uneasy with a situation in which "the patrimonies of different cultures and epochs are mixed in a replete present which, at the same time that it suggests a fantastic abundance, abolishes the hierarchies among historical periods."[11] For some, this mixture of cultures and the "replete present" that it makes possible is cause for celebration: this celebratory mood, which most often informs discussions of creolization, is evident—to take a random example—in Iain Chambers's paean to "the shifting, mixing, contaminating, experimenting, revisiting and recomposing that the wider horizons and the inter- and trans-cultural networks of the city both permit and encourage."[12] And yet this halcyon vision has, for others, its dark underside, which often surfaces in critical discussions of postmodernism: in her book on "primitivist discourse," Marianna Torgovnick exemplifies this second attitude toward cultural mixing when she anxiously warns against the dangers of "carnivalesque rejoicing, of celebrating the crossing and recrossing of things, of believing that contact and polyphony are inherently liberating,"[13] and wags a politically correct finger in the direction of those who extol "the postmodern mélange of us and them" (p. 41). Like Wordsworth in Book Seven of the 1805 *Prelude*, gazing with dismay at the "mighty City" of London and those who live "amid the same perpetual whirl / Of trivial objects, melted and reduced / To one identity, by differences / That have no law, no meaning, and no end,"[14] Torgovnick is horrified by this mélange—in which cultural differences, historical disjunctions, political and economic imbalances all seem under threat of erasure—and, intent on repelling the threat it poses, she (re)turns to the primitive: like Carpentier's narrator, she will debunk certain modernist visions of the primitive, demonstrating the way in which "sets of images and ideas . . . have slipped from their original metaphoric status to control perceptions of primitives" (p. 8), but will remain committed to a less "ridiculous" (in the words of Carpentier's narrator) representation of its reality. Even if we lack "a neutral, politically acceptable vocabulary" with which "to designate the kinds of societies it describes" (p. 21), she argues, we would do well to learn from the differences that primitives embody and the "full and valid alternatives to Western cultures" that they offer (p. 247). In her insistence on the reality of this difference (the primitive is not merely a trope, it had and continues to have a literal referent), Torgovnick links herself back up, ironically enough, with the modernist—to say nothing of Romantic—project, one of personal and cultural renewal through an encounter with alternative worlds, that she believes herself to be in the process of critiquing. This insistence allows her to salvage a whole lexicon of differential terms in the name of a familiar "radical" agenda—an agenda that leads at one and the same time back to the transgressive dreams of modernism and forward to a liberated post-postmodern future.

Marjorie Perloff has ably criticized Torgovnick's "would-be oppositional discourse" and its zealous attachment to "the still exotic Others" without whom this discourse would be inconceivable,[15] and one can only deplore the sort of rhetorical self-congratulation that generates a statement like "to question the carnivalesque mood is a graceless role—antisocial, overly serious, not fun" (p. 41), when in fact such puritanical questioning has become virtually de rigueur in the North American academy. For our purposes, though, what needs pointing out is that her emphasis on the "fullness" of these cultural alternatives avoids the issue of whether or not cross-cultural contact depletes the primitive: (how) can this fullness be preserved in the face of that contact? For the modernist, this question necessarily evokes either a sad acknowledgment or a robust denial of the scenario of disappearance that we discussed in the previous chapter: "speak[ing] eloquently on behalf of traditional Polynesia," an early-twentieth-century novel like Victor Segalen's *Les Immémoriaux*, as James Clifford notes, readily adopts this scenario, "fall[ing] rather too easily into an elegiac lament for the vanishing primitive."[16] In a similar spirit the anthropologist Michael Taussig has criticized "the conventional liberal trope of nostalgic despair about the eclipse and extinction of Indian societies from Alaska to Tierra del Fuego"[17]—a trope that is also at work generating Torgovnick's dystopian visions of "postmodern mélange." In countering such visions of "eclipse and extinction," Taussig argues for another, admittedly paradoxical way of reading the effects of cross-cultural contact: he analyzes Cuna society and its ethnohistory, for instance, in terms of how they "stay the same by adapting to the outside world," "becoming different while remaining the same" (p. 116); cultural identity may actually be reinforced by the myriad transformations of the original that living in (falling into, the modernists would say) the relational world of "second contact" entails. This sort of appeal to the "changing same" has become increasingly popular of late, as cultural theorists attempt to negotiate the widening gap between the extremes of a discredited essentialism and what is sometimes perceived as the over facile (and typically postmodern) malleability of cultural constructionism. This oxymoronic appeal, to be sure, may well function for some theorists simply as a covert way of salvaging quasi-essentialist arguments about cultural integrity while at the same time paying lip service to the reality of transculturation or even asserting that reality as the centerpiece of their poetics and politics,[18] but taken seriously it marks the effective *end* of those "alternative" cultures with which Torgovnick wants to "fill" our hollow postmodern world. As Taussig puts it, "modernity stimulated primitivism along with wiping out the primitive" (p. 231): to speak of the primitive under these conditions is to acknowledge its founding absence, the translation of what has been definitively "wiped out" into other cultural forms that perpetuate it only (as the epigraph from Genet suggests)[19] by also betraying—mimicking, re-presenting—its original identity; it is to acknowledge that any recuperation of cultural tradition involves, as Simon During puts it (in an argument that complicates his earlier vision of post-colonial literature's quest for "an identity uncontaminated by universalist or Eurocentric concepts and images" [see Chapter 2]), "the impossible preservation of lost auras," the resigned interrogation of "the unfixable relation between the dead past . . . and the traces of that past."[20]

The anthropologist Greg Dening has spoken of those who, exhibiting a "distrust of their processual selves," act "as if they think being Hawaiian or being Tahitian is some positive, unchanging essence that is now lost but is somehow recoverable."[21] Examples of such insecure thinking, which refuses to acknowledge the loss of auras that cannot *possibly* be preserved and the definitive end of pre-colonial traditions that might once have provided the ground for a truly post-colonial future, still abound and are, of course, especially facilitated in locations such as Africa where, as Wilson Harris points out, in contrast to the Caribbean and South America, "by and large, tradition tends towards homogeneous imperatives."[22] It would be illegitimate simply to impose a concept like creolization, which originated as a way of understanding the remarkably hybrid cultures of the Caribbean, onto other parts of the globe; nevertheless, by way of summing up my argument in this book (and returning it to the rather more general level of discussion that characterized my opening account of Coetzee's *Foe*), I would like to shift locations here at the end, briefly turning to New Zealand, to islands in which the question of (pre-colonial) tradition would appear to be altogether more relevant than in the New World societies of the Caribbean.

The antiprocessual appeal to indigenous traditions and essential identities that Dening critiques makes itself felt, to cite but one example, in Donna Awatere's call for "Maori sovereignty," which, she argues, can only be achieved by ridding New Zealand of such colonial "illusions" as capitalism, with its concomitant concepts of individualism and property, and replacing "artificial religion with natural spirituality" and the West's "'mechanical materialism with spiritual materialism rooted not in man-made artifice, but in land-based dialectic.'"[23] Such straightforward romanticized claims about a pre- and post-colonial identity are, as Nicholas Thomas has pointed out, not limited to a Maori activist like Awatere; they found their way, for instance, into the catalog for the recent *Taonga Maori* exhibition, which participated in "a cultural essentialism that construes Maoriness primarily in terms of its difference from *pakeha* (white New Zealander) identity, and thus reduces it to terms that complement white society's absences: against the alienations of modernity are 'intimate connections' that constitute 'roots, origins, and identity.'" Citing the catalogue's claim that "'to return to the *marae* from the brashness of urban life is to return to a simpler time, to a place of enduring human values,'" Thomas points out that such nostalgic arguments turn a blind eye to "the great expansion of urban *marae*" and other such hybrid phenomena through which Maori tradition has translated itself into the present;[24] they ignore the way in which "Maori identity and distinctiveness" have (in the words of another anthropologist) "always been created against a background of European technological superiority and Pakeha political and social institutions."[25]

Such arguments about "roots, origins, and identity," when voiced by museum curators, perpetuate the primitivism that was central to the modernist project and its critique of modernity; when voiced by "natives" these "memories of the future" just as obviously exemplify what Brathwaite has referred to as *"negative or regressive creolization*: a self-conscious refusal to borrow or be influenced by the Other, and a coincident desire to fall back upon, unearth, recognize elements in the maroon or ancestral culture that will preserve or apparently preserve the unique identity of the group."[26] The related projects of primitivism and nativism (equally groundless, if not, in their various manifestations, of equal value—the value of either project depending, of course, on how they are specifically formulated to address discrete sociohistorical contexts) are historical reactions to colonialism, but for that very reason they cannot be (simply) written off, as the naive antiessentialist might be tempted to do: as Thomas points out, after having provided a thorough critique of such essentializing projects, it is nonetheless dangerous, in turn, to "essentialize nativism by taking its politics to be historically uniform" (p. 188). That such a politics cannot escape the hybrid conditions at work generating it is an irony that needs to be registered, but one must also acknowledge the historical and cultural forces at work producing each differently creolized manifestation of this politics; if, as Ella Shohat puts it, "post-colonial theory's celebration of hybridity risks an antiessentialist condescension toward those communities obliged by circumstances to assert, for their very survival, a lost and even irretrievable past,"[27] then this risk must itself be factored into any discussion (such as my own) that valorizes an impure creole identity over that "unique identity" self-consciously desired—be it out of "vanity" (to recall the Girardian parameters of our discussion in Chapters 5 and 6) or out of the need for "survival"—by many a "postcolonial subject."

In the introductory chapter of this book I cited the epistemological and ethical concerns that have led me to attenuate my own argument for hybridity: we cannot simply avoid the language of "identity and difference" (Appiah), and even if we could there are still situations in which we are "obliged by circumstances" to pursue this unviable path. Mine is a sensible and obvious enough distinction that it is hardly surprising another critic should also have made it, and by way of self-critique, I would like to cite Anne Maxwell's recent and virtually identical distinction between what she terms "epistemological" and "ethico-political" considerations of identity, which she makes in the context of an attack on James Clifford's "postcultural" model of identity. For Maxwell, Clifford's position is inadequate because "modern and non-modern cultures are thought of as being equally inauthentic, both belonging to the plurality of the post-modern."[28] It might at first glance seem that here she is simply making an argument along the lines of Torgovnick, asserting the greater authenticity of certain cultures that have not yet been fully modernized-hybridized; however, if Maxwell would clearly like to make this argument, she nonetheless feels compelled to acknowledge that Clifford may have, in theory, a point. Thus, she goes on to argue that what he is ultimately guilty of is failing to distinguish between identity as an epistemological and as an ethicopolitical problem: perhaps, she admits, the postcultural model holds true as an epistemological assessment of the late twentieth century and accounts of identity that are framed in terms of "authenticity" and "integrity" do not carry the weight they might once have; but even granted this, Clifford's model is inadequate because it is incapable of acknowledging "the *political* need for difference of the Maori" (p. 79). Coming at the question from a very different direction than mine, offering "two cheers for nativism" as opposed to my "two cheers for hybridity," Maxwell's argument nonetheless converges with my own (and with Shohat's) on the "need" for identitarian arguments in a post/identitarian world. And it is a convergence, I must admit, with which I am not particularly comfortable. To acknowledge less begrudgingly than a critic like Maxwell the admixtures of the postmodern condition and the ethos of hybridization and contamination that they entail, to admit willingly the lack of an absolute foundation for any and all (racial, ethnic, national) identities, must surely be to have arrived somewhere new, to have escaped the same old claims of and for identity—to have reached, indeed, that place in which it is possible to ask and perhaps even to answer such heretical questions as: why are communities "obliged" to survive (Shohat); why do ethnic groups "need" to be different (Maxwell); why can we not, once and for all, "finish with" these groundless fictions, these ultimately *needless* biases, which have their basis (as the Girardian analysis of Chapters 5 and 6 suggests) in nothing more or less than an (anti)mimetic violence? Are there not different ethicopolitical arguments that might take us *beyond* community and identity as it has been traditionally defined; are there not ways out of the epistemological impasse that has led me back into the morass of identitarian language in a reversal of the trajectory that has seen a reluctant Maxwell dragged at least partially out of it?

Such questions situate themselves at the (apocalyptic) limits of my own project, which remains committed—no doubt erroneously—to insisting on those same differences that many a postcolonial subject remains intent on asserting, and that also underwrote the poetics and politics of modernism, especially its primitivist variant: the insular dreams of both postcolonialism and modernism can and must be pursued, but only with the relativizing and relational knowledge that they are founded upon differences that are essentially unreal, origins that are irrevocably absent, and an emancipated future that is strictly unthinkable. It is this double argument that I will be putting forward here one last time in a reading of the New Zealand writer Keri Hulme's Booker Prize–winning novel *the bone people*.[29] In *the bone people*, Hulme carefully deconstructs and simultaneously reconstructs certain literary (modernist) and cultural (Maori) traditions, treating them as disempowered but empowering origins, which can only be accessed fictively, and with a cautious awareness of their inadequacy and groundlessness. The steps which would take us back to these traditions and forward to the post-colonial future are forever lost, and yet inescapable; it is both this loss and this inescapability that shape our present in a post/colonial age. Although the international success of a novel like *the bone people*—its ability to cross national boundaries—may well sully it in the eyes of those critics for whom the idea of cultural and political authenticity still holds true, I would argue that it is cosmopolitan texts like this that in their insistence on thinking the local and the global not antithetically but, rather, as part of a single textual and geopolitical whole, best anticipate the challenge of living in a world where such boundaries are becoming at one and the same time ever more nebulous, and ever more calcified. Hulme's novel situates us on the troubling border between modernism (with its commitment to the traditional past and the revolutionary future) and a simultaneously homogenizing and hybridizing postmodernism—an ambivalent territory in which our every certainty has been revealed as a bias that we are called upon to renounce and doomed to reannounce. It is the presence of this borderland that Wilson Harris has located in a novel like *Heart of Darkness*, which he situates upon "a threshold of capacity to which Conrad pointed though he never attained that capacity himself": namely, the capacity to "confess" one's own partiality, to "consume" one's own biases, and thereby make both visible and livable "a complex wholeness inhabited by other confessing parts that may have once masqueraded themselves as monolithic absolutes or monolithic codes of behaviour in the Old Worlds from which they emigrated by choice or by force."[30] Renouncing neither the masks of the Old Worlds from which we have been exiled nor the complexities of the New World that has (not) taken their place, my own argument, like Conrad's, points to a threshold it cannot attain. This is its undoubted weakness, but also, I would suggest, its forever doubtful strength.

> When would my head shake off its echoes like a horse
> shaking off a wreath of flies? When would it stop,
> the echo in the throat, insisting, "Omeros";
> when would I enter that light beyond metaphor?
> —Derek Walcott, *Omeros*

The question of (the commodification of) ancestral identity is central to Keri Hulme's *the bone people*—indeed, not only to the novel, but to the (auto?)biographical blurbs that have prefaced it. The descriptions of Hulme in the Picador and the later Penguin edition are the scene of a revealing shift in which her European origins get erased: where, in the former, she is someone who has "Kai Tahu, Orkney Island and English ancestry," in the latter, she has become simply a "Maori writer." Regardless of the provenance of these blurbs, Hulme herself seems to endorse the latter monolithic identity at times, as when she speaks in a conference talk of "we, as a people, the Maori people,"[31] although she has also insisted that "you can't section up your Maori side and your Pakeha side because they are intimately intertwined."[32] What are readers to make of this erasure of Europe, and this identification with her "best part"—as Kerewin Holmes, the autobiographical protagonist of *the bone people*, characterizes her one-eighth Maoriness (p. 62)? Is this an exclusionary claim, along the lines of the one that has created the concept of "Afro-American" in the United States, that a single drop of Maori blood weighs heavier than seven drops of Orkney and English? Is it, by contrast, a radically inclusionary gesture, giving new meaning to an old word, paving the way for a visionary reinventing of the identity of *all* residents of New Zealand as Maoris, regardless of their biological origins? Is it an appropriative gesture on Hulme's part, the claiming of an identity to which she is not fully entitled. Or is it just some callous publisher's idea of how to sell an "exotic" novel? Perhaps the word must be made to encompass each of these possibilities, and others besides. In any case, the problematic issue of the author's, and the novel's, Maoriness has raised lengthy polemics about who is, and who can write as, (the) Other.[33] That the novel does not fit *comfortably* into traditional categories is, at the very least, clear. As one critic has pointed out, the attempt to claim *the bone people* as a "Maori novel" is seriously compromised "by the admixture of cultural beliefs and values expressed and practised" therein.[34] The title itself, to cite but one example, situates us in an ambivalent territory somewhere between the world of Maori myth and the bone-covered landscapes of T. S. Eliot's *The Waste Land*. Any reading that ignores the cen-

trality of this admixture to Hulme's novel is seriously incomplete, and it is
the dimensions of this uncomfortable, interstitial space that I will be charting in the remainder of this concluding chapter.

Hulme's novel tells the tale of a mixing together, or what might be more
forcefully described as a synthesis. Kerewin Holmes, a New Zealand painter
and self-styled "octoroon," lives in a six-floored tower that she has constructed for herself from the huge sums of money she won at a lottery; estranged from her family, she lives in what has become an increasingly unhappy and sterile isolation, amid a vast array of esoterica and exotica. This
physical and spiritual isolation is broken into by Simon, an obviously troubled child of indeterminate age who lacks the power of speech, and who
proves by turns endearing and infuriating. As Kerewin learns from Simon's
surrogate father, Joe Gillayley, the child is the lone survivor of a shipwreck,
whom Joe and his late wife Hana had adopted three years before. The three
characters, all of mixed or unknown ancestry (Joe is mostly Maori, but had
an English father; Simon is clearly "white" but otherwise of undetermined,
possibly Irish and French, origins—a point clarified in Hulme's short story
"A Drift in Dream"),[35] start spending a good deal of time together, and their
painful isolation begins to lessen. However, this promising alliance is eventually shattered. Simon is often uncontrollable, and Joe, who sometimes responds by beating him, finally goes too far—hospitalizing the child and
landing himself in jail. Kerewin, feeling a certain amount of complicity in
these events, burns down her tower and wanders around South Island in
search of death or healing. After he is released from prison, Joe, guided by
his instincts, retreats to a remote part of the islands, where he comes upon a
mysterious old Maori guarding an ancestral site and awaiting its new
watcher. In a brief and euphoric epilogue, which few critics have found ar-
tistically convincing,[36] the three main characters are united again at the end,
on the site of the old tower. The foundations for a new community have
clearly (wishfully?) been laid, in a straightforward moment of closure that
contrasts starkly with the ambivalent ending(s) of a novel like Maximin's
Soufrières.

At the level of allegory, which is such an insistent feature of much (if
not, pace Fredric Jameson, all) postcolonial literature, Kerewin and Joe can
be read as representing an imported modernism gone fallow and an indigenous tradition adrift. Hulme's novel, according to this reading, is a story
about the obstacles separating the modernist and postcolonial projects,
their attraction to each other, and the necessity for thinking them together—however paradoxical, or initially unproductive, the results of that
unlikely union may be. Each project already contains a part of the other
within it: Kerewin's bit of Maori, and Joe's bit of Pakeha problematize the
categorical boundaries that might once have separated them. This creates

the condition for a confusion of roles, a postmodern mélange, that not only threatens the idea of a single cultural identity—Maori, Pakeha—founded upon sheer difference, but ironizes the projects themselves. The sterility of Kerewin's existence at the beginning of the novel bears witness to the exhaustion of the modernist enterprise; Joe's sense that he is not a "proper Maori" (p. 61) attests to the necessity of an improper identity politics that is in potential conflict with the autarkic demands of nativism—a politics, perhaps, "in which mutable diacritics such as language and behavior (rather than the fixed diacritics of race) comprise the essence of identity."[37] And yet, despite the differences that separate these two people and their respective projects, and despite their obvious inadequacy to an ambivalent present that has displaced them both, Hulme's novelistic aim is to bridge the gap between them, piously paying tribute to traditions, be they literary or cultural, that have not *truly* survived into the present.

The presence of modernism in *the bone people* is pervasive: as Simon During puts it, the novel's "psychologisation of the characters, its symbolism and most importantly, the overarching narrative frame which tells of voyages through and beyond death to regeneration are exactly modernist."[38] The symbolic play of light and dark, of sun and moon, of fire and tides, structures the novel and gives it an overwhelmingly Yeatsian feel, which is matched by its insistent appeal to the geometrical shapes of the circle (as with the title of its prologue) and the spiral. The novel's emphatic use of the stream of consciousness technique, which promotes the idea of an inner, and somehow more authentic, voice lurking below the surface of events, is distinctly modernist, as is the exoticizing use of the Maori language, which is sprinkled throughout the novel and translated in a by no means exhaustive but, unlike those with which Glissant often ends his novels, thoroughly unironical glossary at the end of the book. Most importantly, for our purposes, the novel puts into play the notion of the individual artist as a repository of values that are absent from the degraded, and increasingly fragmented, world of modernity—an originally Romantic notion that, as I have argued elsewhere, forms one of the cornerstones of modernism.[39]

Kerewin, as a type for the modernist artist, is "self-fulfilling, delighted with the pre-eminence of her art, and the future of her knowing hands" (p. 7). She inhabits a realm apart, at a distance from the vagaries of history. She is "cyclopaedic" (p. 240), possessed of a "broad general knowledge, encompassing bits of history, psychology, ethology, religious theory and practices of many kinds" (p. 90), much of which gets displayed in the novel. She has collected all this cultural debris with the goal of reworking it into an artistic whole. As the novel begins, however, she has come face to face with the bankruptcy of this project and her inability to translate her knowledge into anything more than a patchwork; the pinnacle has become an abyss, and the individual as a result needs to be reintegrated into some sort of community. Of course, this scenario is itself central to the modernist imagination, which incessantly tries to rewrite, as Hulme's novel does, Dante's familiar progression from Limbo ("the private introductory mal-bowge" [p. 36] of the novel's first two parts) through Hell (Part Three) and on to Purgatory (Part Four) and a Paradise that, as Ezra Pound pointed out in his final Canto (120), and as the brevity of Hulme's epilogue attests, it has become increasingly hard for our modernity to write. However, if the novel repeatedly exposes the inadequacy of Kerewin's initial position, and of the modernist project itself, it is equally clear that Kerewin's cyclopaedic language and pretensions are also the author's, and that Hulme is taking a great, and at times even embarrassing, pleasure in her protagonist's artistic "pre-eminence." The happy ending is Hulme's most flagrant attempt at re-deeming the modernist conception of the heroically gifted individual, al-lowing Kerewin to become again who she once was—an artist, albeit one who has now found a different, and more satisfying, "home."

And yet our experience of the failure of this ideology throughout the novel forces us to view the positive assertions at the end in a somewhat dif-ferent light. The inadequacies, and even the dangers, of this project are man-ifest, especially as regards her relation to Maori tradition. There is, for in-stance, something suspiciously *appropriative* about her (Holmes's/Hulme's) undertaking: Kerewin's "hoard" of Maori jade (p. 33), like the collection of Maori myth with which Hulme lards the novel, signals that this project has a proprietary, indeed *colonial*, dimension of which Hulme may well be crit-ical and yet in which she cannot help engaging. This disturbing dimension is emphasized most notably toward the end, during Kerewin's recuperation, when she has a dream about a "wrecked rusting building" that will inspire her, the "digger," to rebuild an old Maori hall:

She touched the threshold, and the building sprang straight and rebuilt, and other buildings flowed out of it in a bewildering colonisation. They fit onto the land as sweet and natural as though they'd grown there. (p. 428)

Here is the dream of the modernist-primitivist artist, and the dream ex-posed: she finds herself on the threshold of another world, which she re-vives, with a Gauguinesque touch that is inseparable from a "bewildering colonisation" in which the artificial is passed off as natural ("*as though* they'd grown there," like the "colonies" of mollusks or birds referred to earlier in the novel [pp. 104, 124, 166]). There is, thus, clearly something dubious, not to mention aesthetically forced, about Kerewin's restorative project, and in emphasizing this point, Hulme keeps the reader at a dis-tance from the very dream to which she herself so clearly subscribes.

Such modernist heroics, which are likely to entice those feminist readers who feel drawn to strong women protagonists, must, by contrast, make the postcolonial critic rather uneasy inasmuch as Kerewin's relation to the tradition that she discovers and saves from ruin has such an uncomfortably appropriative dimension, one that seemingly partakes of a "cultural relationship paradigmatic of settler colonialism, namely, the fashioning of white identity via indigenous emblems and references."[40] On the surface, Joe's relation to Maori tradition seems rather more straightforward than Kerewin's simultaneous assimilation and critique of European modernism. His initial distance from, and consequent need to rediscover, his non-Western roots is a familiar motif in postcolonial literature—although this motif may itself cause uneasiness among some readers because of its potential investment in an exclusionary identity politics. At the beginning of the novel, Joe describes himself as not a "proper Maori" (p. 61); he is not "yer 100% pure" (p. 62), and it is not surprising that Kerewin, with her modernist dreams of the sheerly Other, initially wants to be spared the "contamination" that he embodies (p. 12). His violent treatment of Simon perversely echoes the "absolute violence" that Fanon theorized in *Les damnés de la terre* as being indissociable from the act of decolonization and reveals the extent to which such anticolonial theories fall short of the more complex attitudes and actions necessary for negotiating life in a post/colonial location. Like Kerewin, he has reached a dead end—one that, if we are to believe the narrative trajectory of the novel, can only be escaped through a purgatorial return to the fullness of Maori tradition.

In the chapter of Part Four devoted to him, "The Kaumatua and the Broken Man," Joe comes face to face with the cultural past from which he has been estranged. After his release from prison, Joe decides, on the basis of some unexplained intuition, to betake himself to a remote littoral of the islands. No sooner has he arrived there, than he recklessly decides to leap off a bluff in order to reach the beach, "thirty shadowed feet to the bottom" (p. 335). This symbolic leap, this return to the bottom, leaves Joe injured, but he will be healed by a mysterious Maori elder, who sports an archaic tattoo and knows "the old words." The *kaumatua* has been waiting many years for the appearance of this "stranger" to whom he can pass on the guardianship of a *mauriora*—a pierced stone, hidden in a deep pool, and still inhabited, according to the old man, by "the spirit of the islands," the spirit of Aotearoa, which once allied itself with the Maoris and now rests in this godholder. It is "the heart of this country," the kaumatua asserts (p. 364), significantly echoing the title of Conrad's most famous literary offering. Having found his successor, the old man dies, passing on the land to his heir Joe, who guards the stone until an earthquake liberates it from its hiding place. Joe then gathers the rock—out of which emanates, from "the hole in the centre, light like a glow-worm, aboriginal light" (p. 384)—and takes it back with him to the former site of Kerewin's tower, where it sinks itself "into the hard ground," thus providing the epilogue's newly constituted community with a spiritual foundation, a meeting ground (marae).

There is something very forced about this episode, which sticks out from the rest of the novel. Indeed, the New Zealand critic C. K. Stead, who has remarked that Hulme's "uses of Maori language and mythology strike me as willed, self-conscious, not inevitable, not entirely authentic," finds this section of the novel to be "almost totally spurious."[41] Stead is right, given that the emphatically modernist dimension of Hulme's work, and of the character of Kerewin, is in some basic ways incompatible with (although envious of) the postcolonial direction that Joe's character takes in this chapter. The affirmation of a biological and cultural continuity with Maori tradition can only be the work of postcolonialism, not of modernism. What is spurious from one perspective becomes absolutely necessary—even predictable—from another. And yet, as with Kerewin's modernism, Hulme is both playing along with this foundationalism, and its language of "bottoms" and "hearts," and emphasizing the problematic status of the very tradition to which the postcolonial part of her novel appeals. This doubleness is most evident in a dream sequence that, matching Kerewin's vision of a naturalized colonization, reflects back ambivalently on the straightforward affirmations surrounding it.

While recovering from his injury, Joe dreams that he is "swimming down a foul mud-coloured river" (p. 351). In fact, he is "not really swimming: the water gets so shallow that he can pull himself along, hands walking on the river bottom," which serves as a foundation for him in the midst of the foulness that is "contaminating" and "corrupting" his body. Eventually, he submerges himself in this "stinking stream" and finds to his surprise that it is sweet. He then follows it back to its source, as it becomes increasingly "sparkling and ice-clear": the stream, it turns out, flows from his dead (Maori) wife Hana's vagina, "in a steady pure rivulet" (a rivulet that, like Marlow's Congo or the river that carries the anonymous narrator of Carpentier's *Lost Steps* ever further away from the degraded world of his European father and ever closer to the primitive heart of the [Latin] America in which his mother was born, has obvious Freudian resonances).[42] Hana gives him her breast to suck, while his natural son Timote looks on; Simon then appears, and also begins to suck at her breast, but as he proceeds to suck, she turns into a moth and the dream becomes a nightmare. As the kaumatua helpfully explains when Joe awakens, with a significantly improbable nod to European literary terminology, the dream is an "allegory" (p. 354): that is, it refers to something other than itself.[43] It refers, I would venture, to the events of the chapter that have led up to it and that will en sue from it: the simple resolution of Joe's search for his origins, which the happy ending of the chapter underwrites, is here negated.

This allegory invokes the encounter with the traditional past that Joe is in the process of living, but provides it with another ending—one that acknowledges the absence of the very thing that is so urgently being invoked in the rest of the chapter. The search here ends with the loss of the source he seeks, and its transformation into an object signifying death (as moths do, according to the kaumatua). The dream alerts us to the fact that what is at stake is not simply the salvaging of a culture, but also the repetition of its death in the form of Hana and their child; Joe's encounter with an apparently living tradition is actually a (re)invocation of this tradition from the distance created by mourning—a distance that cannot help registering the dreamlike nature of the primordial source for which it longs. Perhaps Joe himself is already dimly aware of this fact, for after having taken the leap that will enable his encounter with the world of (some of) his ancestors, he looks back up at the bluff and says in (the English translation of an absent) Maori, "I shall remember it as long as I live" (p. 347); what this stranger will remember, and what *the bone people* itself insistently remembers, is not the bottom, a pure origin from which the foulness of the present has disappeared, but the distance that keeps the two worlds of the contaminated present and a desired past apart—a distance across which the post/colonial subject must *invent* traditions that can no longer be directly received but that this estranged subject nonetheless, for better and for worse, still desires.[44] Indeed, it might well be argued that this desire, and these inventions, are inseparable from any consideration of cultural identity if, as Greg Dening has suggested, "culture is a stranger's invention: it is the sense of wholeness and integration an outside-outsider or an inside-outsider develops."[45]

As we have seen, then, the uneasy pairing of Kerewin and Joe, of modernist and native traditions, is central to *the bone people*, and this coupling is by no means an arbitrary one given the fact that, as Paul Gilroy has argued, "the obsession with origins which appears all too regularly in black cultural history is itself an expression of some particularly and peculiarly modernist intellectual habits."[46] In its chronicling of the entanglement of these two characters and these two traditions, their mutual attraction and opposition to each other, the novel can, as Graham Huggan has rightly pointed out, be seen as one of countless postcolonial rewritings of Shakespeare's *The Tempest*, with Kerewin in the role of Prospero and Joe as Caliban. Stressing the obvious sea changes that both roles have undergone (notably, Kerewin's gender and what we discover to be Joe's bisexuality), Huggan is nonetheless uncomfortable with both characters. Equally suspicious of the modernist and nativist projects, he views Simon as the true hero of the novel, an Ariel figure who "acts as a catalyst for and transmitter of the

tensions involved . . . in Prospero and Caliban's increasingly uncertain allegiance with their ancestral past."[47] His stance is exemplary of recent reformist approaches to the problem of cultural identity that are in certain
respects compatible with the insights of postmodernism: the new generation of postcolonial critics rejects the radical oppositions, such as Prospero
versus Caliban, that structured revolutionary anticolonialism (a point I will
return to in the concluding pages of this book); they find their ideal protagonists, by contrast, in translational figures like Ariel or Simon who, it
might be hoped, will lead us out of the ideological impasses in which the
likes of Kerewin and Joe find themselves. For theoretical support, Huggan
cites Brathwaite's idea of creolization, which he glosses as "an interculturative process within which a series of intermediary postures are struck up
that elude or actively work against the binary structures (white/black, mas-
ter/slave) which inform colonial discourse but which have also survived in
modified or transposed forms in the aftermath of the colonial era" (p. 31).

Huggan's reading of Simon in light of Brathwaite's idea of creolization is
very convincing, up to a certain point (although one must keep in mind the
dangers of applying this term to a part of the world that is in certain respects very different from the Caribbean context in which Brathwaite first
developed it). Situated between the two adult protagonists, Simon—this
"magpie child" (p. 322) who first appears in the gap between two tiers of
bookshelves (p. 16), and who Kerewin initially views as one of the "contaminating" (p. 17)—clearly disturbs their lives and their agendas: he shows
up the gaps in each of their worlds, signaling by his very presence the need
for these distinct worlds to meet on some middle ground that necessarily
transforms, and ironizes, each of them. Huggan's reading becomes less persuasive, however, when he argues that this irony is evidence that Hulme is
simply distancing herself from the projects of Kerewin and Joe. Unable to
credit Hulme's untimely attachment to these projects, Huggan attempts to
isolate Simon as the novel's ideological hero, suggesting that through his silence and the "poetics of disturbance" he embodies, Hulme "hints at the
potential emergence of an emancipated post-colonial voice containing
within it the contradictions of and hybrid elements in post-colonial cultures
which perceive their creolized status in terms other than those of self-dep-
recatory assimilation or self-glorifying recuperation" (p. 35)—in terms,
that is, other than those of modernist aesthetics and ethnic identity politics,
respectively. For Huggan, Simon does not really occupy a middle ground,
but an avant-garde; he functions as a "dialectical" figure, who might break
the ground for a future free of the binarisms that confine the unemancipated voices of past and present. In this reading, Simon becomes a sophisticated version of, say, the "messianic boy-child" in W. E. B. Du Bois's
Dark Princess (1928), who embodies a triumphant synthesis of India and

Afro-America that Paul Gilroy has effectively critiqued in his *Black Atlantic* (pp. 140–45). Sneaking his own binary structure (emancipated/unemancipated) back into the critical scheme of things, Huggan would privilege only this one figure—and one poetics and politics—in *the bone people*, thus running the risk of misreading the novel *as a whole*.

To be sure, Simon's silence (like that of Friday in Coetzee's *Foe* or Élisa in Maximin's *Soufrières*) is a vital part of the novel, and one to which a new generation of postcolonial critics must be particularly responsive. However, if Hulme insistently notes his hisses, giggles, screams, and songs, all of which point in the direction of a distinctly new voice, she is equally careful to portray him as *already* possessed of a "voice": not only are we presented with frequent examples of Simon's writing, but of his stream of consciousness as well, which is, as one might expect, essentially no different from that of the other protagonists. Simon has, in other words, already entered the fallen domain of a language from which his silence might appear to exempt him, and his "emancipatory" potential is, as a result, substantially voided. Well aware that "any voice we can hear is by that very fact purged of its uniqueness and alterity,"[48] Hulme at one and the same time preserves Simon's silence, and with it a powerful "myth of the future," and demonstrates the questionableness of this myth by emphasizing the extent to which the unemancipated language of his elders continues to speak through him. The emancipation that Simon's silence anticipates is a lure at which critics cannot help biting, but it is only a part of the story, and a necessarily absent part at that. Because of this absence, Simon is first and foremost a "tragic presence,"[49] the sign of a cross-culturalism that is less a progression toward some Other future than a shuttling back and forth, in the Same old language, between ideological extremes that have outlived themselves but that will not simply disappear. He bears the cross, and bares the crossing, of the now groundless ideologies of modernism and nativism, without offering in and of himself a positive alternative to either. This cashes out as a refusal on Hulme's part to abandon her allegiances to either (European) literary modernism or to forgo her appeals to (Maori) ethnic tradition, despite her sensitivity to the *assimilating* nature of the former and the *simulated* nature of the latter in our increasingly creolized late-twentieth-century world.

Hulme has clearly *not* abandoned the extremes that Huggan, in his admirable argument on behalf of a creolized future, feels duty-bound to reject because of their now all-too-evident lack of a foundation. Huggan's emphasis on one particularly seductive aspect of the novel avoids a full grappling with the whole. Because he finds "the implied essentialism of projects of cultural recuperation" distasteful (p. 35), and inadequate to the realities of a hybridized future, he cannot admit that such essentialism is germane to the novel's Maori half. Furthermore, the novel does not merely ironize, as he wishfully argues, "the assimilative procedures of High Modernist art"; its other half indulges rather spectacularly in them. If, as Linda Hutcheon improbably claims, "postmodern historicism is wilfully unencumbered by nostalgia in its critical, dialogical reviewing of the forms, contexts, and values of the past,"[50] then Hulme's novel can at best be described as post/modern, drenched as it is in a nostalgia for that which it also critically puts into question. The acknowledged presence of gaps in the unilateral, synthesizing projects of modernism and nativism does not prevent Hulme from continuing to engage in these projects, with both an inescapable irony and an obvious piety, at the same time as she explores the gaps that serve both to hollow them out and bind them together. As we are told at the very beginning of the novel, it is only when Kerewin, Joe, and Simon are considered "together, all together," that they can be "the instruments of change" (p. 4). In *the bone people*, the modernist longing for a redemptive art that might promote the creation of visionary communities and the nativist desire for an authentic identity that might be disentangled from the contaminations of colonialism stand alongside, frame, the spirit of disturbance that Simon embodies, and if that spirit undermines the modernist/nativist desire, the reverse is also true: those longings undermine that which they frame. This is one lesson that a great number of contemporary critics, ever intent on asserting the novelty and subversive potential of their "strategies of resistance," have a hard time digesting, but it is surely a lesson that is present in Hulme's novel, which argues that, in a postmodern world, irony is all-encompassing but also that, in a postcolonial world, it needs to be turned back on itself, as we ourselves turn back to affirm ideological positions that we know to be no longer viable in a world where (in Bhabha's words) "the natural(ized), unifying discourse of 'nation,' 'peoples,' or authentic 'folk' tradition, those embedded myths of culture's particularity, cannot be readily referenced" (*LC*, p. 172).

Hulme's emphasis on the necessity of thinking several apparently contradictory, and patently inadequate, ideological positions together, rather than categorically opting for one position, or simplistically appealing to an emancipated future in which these positions no longer hold sway, must strike single-minded critics as an unsatisfactory, perhaps even scandalous, compromise (especially when it is a matter of showing piety toward a *Western* literary tradition such as modernism). If the compromised stance of *the bone people* nicely meshes with Walcott's argument that great writers are those who "know that by openly fighting tradition we perpetuate it, that revolutionary literature is a filial impulse, and that maturity is the assimilation of the features of every ancestor,"[51] this maturity cannot fail to irritate those in search of a single, uncompromising lineage and line of thought. Anne Maxwell, for instance, who wants to valorize the novel's nationalist line, its emphasis on a coherently unified Maori identity, can only view the modernist dimension of *the bone people* as a politically regressive error: she laments the existence of an "ideological contradiction informing, and ultimately compromising, the text's overt politics," and goes on to add, with a Fanonesque insistence on rupture (and rather less epistemological sensitivity than she would later demonstrate in the article that we looked at earlier on in this chapter), that "in order to emerge as a subversive political tool, the novel must eventually break with its acquiescent fostering of high and first-world culture."[52] To thus isolate any one of the novel's constituent parts, and to reject all form of compromise in the name of some nationalist or even creolizing agenda, is to miss Hulme's point, and the political realities of a globally hybridized age. If there is an urgent need for thinking the Maoriness of Aotearoa-New Zealand—its *Maoritanga*—there is also, as C. K. Stead has argued, a need to reaffirm the island's British and European inheritance.[53] If the two positions are in some ways deeply incommensurable and antagonistic, they must nonetheless both be thought, and be thought together, in an ever more creolized world from which any and all such traditions would appear to have been excluded, given that, as Glissant has stated, "relationality resists the well-worn paths" (*IP*, p. 22; "la relation ne consent pas aux sentes de tradition"). Assimilating a literary tradition that we can no longer fully credit, simulating an ethnicity to which we can no longer substantially lay claim, exploring the absences that compr(om)ise us as parts of an unthinkable whole: such are the imperatives that a cosmopolitan (and yet also resolutely provincial, in the best sense of the word) novel like Keri Hulme's *the bone people* addresses. Endowing her modernist-nativist work with a self-consciousness that was only implicit in Carpentier's *Lost Steps*, Hulme maps out a f(r)ictional textual and political space, of loss and desire, situated between the certainties of the past and the assumptions of a future to which those certainties gave rise—a space between, on the one hand, an ancestral identity that, like Walcott's "wreath of flies," we cannot shake off and, on the other, the unspeakably hybrid identities that with an ever greater insistence beckon us, impossibly, "beyond metaphor." Occupying an impure middle ground—the "third space" of metaphor which, in Bhabha's words, "produces hybrid realities by yoking together unlikely traditions of thought"[54]—Hulme nonetheless continues to interrogate, in a mode that is simultaneously deconstructive and (re)constructive, the purity of traditional beginnings and of revolutionary endings, directing her work back to an absent past and forward to a future that does not lie *beyond* modernity, but on its unendingly last frontiers. . . .

The lingering traces in Hulme's novel of (aspects of) the story of *The Tempest*, its attenuated evocation of the Prospero-Caliban-Ariel triangle,

are hardly surprising given the frequency with which Shakespeare's play
has been invoked by postcolonial writers over the last half of this century,
and it is with a few brief comments on the uses to which that protean colonial story has been put that I would like to draw this book to a close. The
emphasis on the mediating presence of an Ariel figure in *the bone people*—
or, at the very least, the willingness of certain critics (of whom I am one) to
read this figure in(to) the novel—puts into question the standard revolutionary (and, as we saw in Chapter 3, essentially Romantic) appropriation
of the play, which fixed upon the figure of Caliban as a straightforward anticolonial counterpoint to the arch-colonial Prospero. Typical of this approach to the play is the Cuban Roberto Fernández Retamar's claim that
the colonized in general, and Latin Americans in particular, must "assume
our condition as Caliban," which "implies rethinking our history from the
other side, from the viewpoint of the *other* protagonist," in terms of our
antithetical relation to "the foreign magician" Prospero.[55] This simple logic
of reversals and binary oppositions, perpetuated by any number of Calibanist critics in North American universities,[56] is one that—as Huggan's
interpretation of *the bone people* testifies—has over the past several decades been increasingly put into question by less "radical" writers and critics for whom (the anticolonial) Caliban "is the hero only of an apocalyptic,
unlivable, 'no exit' situation."[57] Derek Walcott, for instance, acknowledged
that Prospero and Caliban "balance easily," but chose to rewrite their balanced opposition (an opposition as present in the colonial discourse of
Shakespeare as in the anticolonial discourse of Fernández Retamar) in
terms of a productive compatibility rather than of an innate antagonism:
for Walcott, "they balance on the axis of a shared sensibility," one engendered by the fact that both Prospero and Caliban, in their own different
ways, are "walking to a New World."[58] The New World that (Walcott's)
Prospero and Caliban are verging upon logically calls forth another figure,
one who might mediate between them. In line with such a logic—a logic
that is itself, to be sure, part and parcel of our colonial legacy—this mediatory role has, in the aftermath of the decolonization years, often been assigned to Ariel (in a shift of emphasis that is not without precedent: Fernández Retamar's insistence on the importance of Caliban, after all, was itself a reaction against the attraction felt by certain early-twentieth-century
Latin American intellectuals for the figure of Ariel).

To cite but one instance of the critical turn to Ariel that Walcott's argument anticipated, Aimé Césaire's *Une tempête*, an uneasily Calibanist appropriation of Shakespeare's play from the late 1960s, would be some
twenty years later appropriated by J. Michael Dash in the name of an
antiessentialist poetics intended to liberate us from the ideological "cul de
sac" of a Negritude that Césaire embodies (and, according to Dash, cri-

tiques) in the figure of Caliban. According to Dash, Césaire's parody presents us with "a bellicose, frenetic Caliban, longing for a prelapsarian Eden, an island-paradise into which Prospero never intruded." Dash unfavorably contrasts this brutal and naive "revolutionary" figure with "Ariel's incarnation of a tainted, androgynous creature, the terrible condition of knowing in the New World"; "because of his fallenness," he continues, "Ariel is freed from aping, from longing for pure origins, [whereas] Caliban remains paralyzed by his encounter with Prospero" and "neither one can free himself from this traumatic union."[59] Dash's is clearly a strategic (mis)reading of Une tempête that refuses to take into account Césaire's obvious although by no means entirely unambivalent enthusiasm for Caliban throughout the play, but it is nonetheless exemplary of the uses to which an intermediary character like Ariel can be put by critics who stress the virtues of métissage and attempt to instill in us the fallen knowledge that (to recall Appiah's words) "we are all already contaminated by each other."

The Prospero-Caliban-Ariel triangle, of course, by no means exhausts the allegorical possibilities that Shakespeare's play exfoliates. Many a feminist critic has, of course, been drawn to the figure of Miranda. Brathwaite, more of a Calibanist than an Arielist as we have had ample occasion to see throughout this book, has also turned his attention to Caliban's mother Sycorax, in whom "resides the quality of soul grit or kernel, known as *nam*."[60] Increasingly, critics have been prone to read the play in terms not of its presences but of its absences: notably, the absence of any female equivalent to Caliban, as Sylvia Wynter for one has discussed, in her account of Miranda as (white) feminist, partially complicit with the imperial hegemony of Prospero's discourse of reason and thus necessarily at odds in all sorts of ways with Caliban's racially differentiated woman(ist).[61] If remarking upon such omissions does not amount to transcending the epistemic framework established by The Tempest—critics who would insist upon the necessity of thinking Miranda's indigenous double are, after all, simply reacting to and attempting to fill in the gaps that were always-already latent in Shakespeare's play—it nonetheless paves the way for an argument about the limits of both the play and its differing appropriations by postcolonial writers. In narrato-logical fashion, the story of postcolonial revisionism can be taken "forward" to the point when The Tempest no longer matters at all: as Rob Nixon argued a decade ago in a survey of mostly English-language appropriations of the play, a text that had seemed such an appropriate tool for understanding the decolonization process has, since the early 1970s, "been drained of the immediate, urgent value it was once found to have."[62] The echo in the throat insisting "Caliban" ("Ariel," "Miranda," and so on) *will* stop; indeed (as can be gauged from the satisfied tone with which Nixon proclaimed his findings) the entanglement of

the colonial and the postcolonial that a reflecting back on Shakespeare necessarily renders visible *must* stop.

As empirical description, Nixon's seems a valid enough argument: postcolonial authors with an eye to originality are, in any case, going to be increasingly wary about committing themselves to such well-worn parallels.
His argument is also, however, and primarily a matter of ideological pre-
scription, grounded in a desire that the detour of colonialism come to an
end, that this "sign of blindness and incapacity" (to recall my discussion of
Coetzee's *Foe*) be left behind once and for all in favor of the "green world"
of the post-colonial. Those who have had the patience to read this book
through to the end will know that such prescriptions are not shared by this
author. In insisting upon our continued attachment to old colonial stories, I
have in no way been arguing that postcolonial writers are somehow
doomed in one way or another to evoke Shakespeare, Defoe, and Conrad in
perpetuity: those particular names, and the intertextual relations that they
have generated, are simply a convenient form of shorthand, serving as an
easily recognizable reminder of the labyrinthine connections that bind us to
a colonial (and colonized) past that, with "a glow of after-memory," continues obscurely to illuminate our lives. How to live, how to relive, that past
and those complicitous relations within the terms of our own globalized present? Not, assuredly, along the lines of blind repetition, of the sort that we
saw at work, say, in the Raphaël Confiant and Annie Le Brun debate, with
its violently mimetic and morbidly symptomatic defamations and recrimina-
tions. But, rather, as a repetition that knows itself to be such, and that in the
never final possession of this knowledge veers, if ever so slightly, away from
itself, away from what cannot be simply "overpassed" but what can nevertheless be *lived through*. It is this ambivalent living through—the "trans- of
(dis)possession" that permits us to be "both here and elsewhere, rooted and
exposed"—that I have argued is at the heart of the creolization process and
of the post/colonial literature that gives a never satisfactory expression to it.

Having chosen, in a self-consciously unoriginal manner, to end this book
with yet another reflection back on Shakespeare's *Tempest*, I would like to
conclude by briefly gesturing toward one recent appropriation of this play
that strikes me as particularly helpful for understanding the ambiguities of
the creolization process and the indeterminable identities it makes possible.
I will return, then, one last time to Maximin's *Soufrières* and, specifically, to
the marginal character of Toussaint's estranged French wife, Ariel, and to
their child Manuel. The Ariel of *Soufrières* needs to be read not only—and
indeed, not even primarily—in terms of the Shakespearean echo that her
name provokes, but in terms of her relation to a rather less sympathetic
character in Maximin's first novel, who also went under the name of Ariel.
In *L'isolé soleil*, Ariel is a (white) Frenchman with whom Marie-Gabriel's

mother Siméa had a love affair in Paris during the late 1930s. Typical of many an *entre-deux-guerres* intellectual, this Ariel has a "sincere" fascination for all things exotic, having fully absorbed the transgressive lessons to be found in "the poetry of architects against nature" authored by the likes of Rimbaud (p. 119). And yet he ultimately draws back from the promise of cross-cultural fraternity that his relationship with Siméa holds forth, cowardly agreeing with members of her own family (who are hypocritically appalled at the idea of Siméa becoming an unwed mother) that the child they have conceived together be aborted. Her eyes opened to the weakness of the man she still loves, Siméa returns soon after the abortion to her native island of Guadeloupe where, during the Vichy occupation, she encounters the eventual father of Marie-Gabriel, who will be conceived in Haiti; Siméa will die giving birth to Marie-Gabriel and, as we have seen, much of the second half of the novel chronicles the daughter's attempts at following (up) the traces of her mother's story and reliving it through her writing.

The recurrence of the name Ariel in *Soufrières* thus demands to be read against the backdrop of Siméa's failed relationship in *L'isolé soleil*, which was itself counterpointed in that novel by a highly seductive story of intra-Caribbean romance and cultural solidarity, or even more precisely by the romance *of* cultural solidarity—a romance consecrated, fittingly (or predictably) enough, on the island of Haiti. But faced with this demand, the reader can only remark upon the (un)likeness of the two Ariels, for in *Soufrières* the original scenario has been in large part reversed. This time it is not Ariel but Toussaint who is "to blame," who has turned away from the complexities of an "interracial" relationship, and of *la Relation* itself, in the name of "terroristic" certitudes: just as the sincerity of the first Ariel's union with Siméa was mixed in with an exoticizing objectification, so too have Toussaint's feelings for his wife gradually been overwhelmed by his ideological commitments, which lead him to objectify her as "white," as "Western," and thus not adjunctive or incremental to the revolutionary design he has in mind; she will be "dispossessed of her beautiful Mediterranean color and covered over by him with the skin of the West" (p. 51), her reality lost from sight in the face of such comforting epidermal abstractions. All too intent upon slotting himself into the role of the "black" Caliban, this would-be architect of national liberation can, as we have seen, accept nothing less than "the very sure road to death," upon which there is no risk that he will have to survive, or grapple with the consequences of survival, of living through the aftermath of the volcano's eruption and the collapse of his revolutionary designs—designs that, as with his dispossession of Ariel, fail so dismally to do justice to the "perplexity of the living." As the further revelations of Maximin's third novel, *L'île et une nuit*, make clear, the voice of Ariel and of their son Manuel carrying from one side of

the Atlantic to the other cannot save him from the tragic certitudes that
lead him to put the catastrophic finishing touches on his life.

What this transformation of one Ariel into the other, and the opening up
of the interval between them, forces Maximin's readers to confront is the
unfoundedness of the certitudes about identity that motivate Toussaint's actions. This differing repetition of a name allows us to envision identity as
that which can and must be understood as being in translation; indeed, the
very choice of such a literary name serves to emphasize this point, given
that it so patently covers over—in a self-consciously allegorical manner—
the actual man and woman who go under this name and whose unspoken
reality it inadequately represents. This unnameable being in translation can,
of course, itself be objectified and treated as an identifiable good in and of
itself, as Maximin reminds us—and this reminder serves as both a promise
and a warning—through the name that he has chosen to give Toussaint and
Ariel's "biracial" child. Manuel is the name of that "wager lost between
two solitudes" (p. 51; "un pari perdu entre deux solitudes"), who lends
himself to being read, very much like Hulme's Simon, as the living embodiment of an interculturative process that his parents have tragically failed to
negotiate. In this "child of patience and distress, of confusion and the expectation of hope" (p. 50), Maximin indeed apostrophizes the possibility of
a human being who might bridge the respective solitudes of Toussaint and
Ariel, and make good on a seemingly lost wager. The undoubted promise of
this child must, however, be read alongside the warning that Maximin has
subtly inscribed in his name, which is a simultaneously pious and ironic literary echo, not of Shakespeare this time, but of the main protagonist of the
Haitian novelist Jacques Roumain's *Gouverneurs de la rosée*—a modernist
novel that, in its depiction of the "Black Christ" Manuel through whom the
suffering peasantry of Haiti are to be redeemed, reenvisions evangelical
narratives of salvation through a more or less Marxist lens. In the ambivalently post/revolutionary world of Maximin, salvational echoes such as
these cannot stand unquestioned, though: the expectation of hope that they
bring demands to be read in a deconstructive light of the sort, say, that an
Arielist critic like Dash brings to the Haitian text when he argues that
Roumain's all-too-heroic Manuel embodies the "tyranny of the One," the
pernicious fiction of a "self capable of installing a rational order in a world
of shadows."[63] Like the hauntingly authoritative presence of Césaire in
Maximin's novels, that of Roumain and his revolutionary (and in many respects assuredly masculinist) vision is invoked in *Soufrières* not in order
simply to affirm or disavow the "tyrannical" precursor text but to demonstrate how it might be at once re- and deconstructed in that middle space,
the creole continuum, where the particular engagements and biases attaching to the various projects and designs of Prospero and Caliban, of Miranda

and Marie-Gabriel, of Manuel and Simon (all of whom might, viewed in another light, go by the name of Ariel), confusedly and repeatedly relay one another, each the sequel to a story from which they are in one way or another endlessly departing but that none of them can draw to a final close.

With Ariel, then, despite and because of his or her indeterminable status, I have chosen to end: with a metaphor that unsatisfactorily points the way toward a (con)fusing space of cross-cultural transactions, a metaphor that resists the "imperialism of identity" and its violent and divisive territorializations, but that also remains relationally attached to, if unsatisfied with, that apocalyptic way of thinking. Certainly, an argument such as mine, which declines to posit a way out of the maze of doubting, which accedes to the idea of modernity's unending frontiers, which promotes a thinking of creolized middle spaces and a "life of compromise" rather than of revolutionary endgames played out in the hope of constructing some "birdless monument of Refusal," has by no means divested itself of the logic that it would resist. Having crossed the Alps and begun his descent from those lofty heights, Wordsworth in his *Prelude* reflected upon the diverse manifestations of sublime nature surrounding him and noted that they were "all like workings of one mind, the features / Of the same face, blossoms upon one tree, / Characters of the great Apocalypse, / The types and symbols of Eternity, / Of first, and last, and midst, and without end."[64] The thinking of "midst, and without end" cannot simply be detached from that "of first, and last": it must be traced back (as is clear from the debt this last line of Wordsworth's reverent, yet profoundly secular, description owes to Milton's *Paradise Lost*)[65] to the credal outlook that it would contest; it must be understood as the echo of a past faith that has been uneasily translated into the secular(izing) uncertainty of the present. Those who argue for that present, for the creolized relat(ivizat)ions and the hybrid realities that are becoming ever more visible in the widening gap between the pre-colonial past and the post-colonial future, remain dependent upon the homogenizing, eternalizing types and symbols that betray (and translate) the ill-defined diversity of the post/colonial times that we are living through. If we cannot avoid these types and symbols, we must, I have suggested, at the very least be vigilant in using them, armed with the doubtful knowledge that these "characters of the great Apocalypse" inadequately convey an absent referent that is so fundamentally, so radically, (un)like them (as is emphasized by the similitude with which Wordsworth prefaces his description: "all *like* workings of one mind").

What difference can this knowledge make? One answer to such a question is undoubtedly: very little *in the end*. Throughout this book I have engaged in a dialogue with the ideas of Édouard Glissant, charting the ways in which they have (not) changed over the past four decades, and it is for that reason appropriate to close here by citing a very recent comment of his that for me sums up the difficulties in which even a thinker who has been among the most eloquent and courageous advocates of the claim that "ours is a creolizing world" finds himself when trying to argue for this doubtful knowledge and the problematic difference that it makes. Justifying his claim that, globalization and transculturation notwithstanding, a sense of place is uncircumventable ("le lieu est incontournable"), and that it must be defended against any and all threats of disfigurement ("dénaturation"), Glissant blandly informs us that "blacks in the United States *naturally* need Afrocentrism in order to struggle against their condition, and one cannot ask a black homeless person in New York to rise up in the name of creolization" (*ID*, p. 105; my italics). If yet further proof were needed that, as Glissant himself once put it, there are no guarantees against the "many mistakes that resulted from the old ideological ways of thinking," then this anxiously "commonsensical" remark would supply it. Aware of the "weakness" of his argument for creolization, Glissant here defers to the "strength" of an ideology that he has spent much of his life questioning: attempting to rescue the idea of a determinate and determining lieu that is not yet, and must not be, "denatured," he ends up treating a patently essentialist position as if it were somehow "natural," and in the process not only generalizes in an untenably objectifying manner about "les Noirs" but rather condescendingly balks at offering certain among them the presumably "unnatural" option of allying themselves with less exclusionary and atavistic projects that might better accord with the complex realities of a creolizing world and the "painful mutation of human thought" these realities entail. Glissant's deference here to the "imperialism of identity" troubles and perplexes. Is it motivated by a failure of nerve? Does it signal a blind spot in his vision? Is it a calculated assertion? Or is it just empty rhetoric? There are any number of ways that one might respond to questions of this sort. Regardless of the answer(s) one chooses, it is my hope that in this book I have gone some way toward clarifying the post/colonial condition that makes such troubling assertions not only sadly inevitable but questionably necessary. And it is with a faltering belief in this questionable necessity, and a doubtlessly inadequate awareness of my own argument's complicity with the faulty post/colonial logic of Glissant's perplexing statement, that I will now end on the note of relative certitude conveyed in the two epigraphs with which this book begins : "we are all responsible for one another" (Bernardin), "we are all gathered together on one and the same shore" (Glissant). It is with such commonplaces that I find it only natural to end; it is in this common place that I have found it only natural to locate us, harmoniously at rest and restlessly wandering, at home and in exile, upon the shore of our now planetary island and in the face of this shared responsibility. . . .

Notes

For complete author names, titles, and publication data for the items cited here in short form, see the Bibliography, pp. 505–27.

CHAPTER 1

1. O. Lara, *Guadeloupe*, p. 101.

2. James, *Black Jacobins* (henceforth *BJ*), pp. 115, 325. On Lara's contradictory status as both a precursor of the Negritude movement and a "regionalist" writer committed to assimilationism, see Corzani, *Littérature*, 2.113; for a more radical vision of the revisionist dimension of his work, see D. J. G. Lara's preface to the re-edition of *La Guadeloupe dans l'histoire*, pp. vii–xlix.

3. Carpentier, *Explosion*, p. 183. Henceforth all page references to novels under discussion in this book will be given parenthetically in the body of the text.

4. Quoted in González Echevarría, *Alejo Carpentier* (henceforth *ACPH*), p. 123.

5. Carpentier, *Obras*, 13.182–83 ("Lo barroco y lo real maravilloso" [1975]). Although "creole," as we will have ample occasion to see, is the most slippery of signifiers, it is worth citing the *OED*'s primary definition of the word here at the outset of this book: "In the West Indies and other parts of America, Mauritius, etc. . . . [a] person born and naturalized in the country, but of European (usually Spanish or French) or of African Negro race: the name having no connotation of colour, and in its reference to origin being distinguished on the one hand from born in Europe (or Africa) and on the other hand from aboriginal." From this noun derives the adjective, designating those "born and naturalized in the West Indies, etc., but of European (or negro) descent." For my most detailed discussion of the various meanings of this word (a word that will only be capitalized in this book when used as a noun), see the opening section of Chapter 4.

6. Chambers, *Border Dialogues*, p. 75.

7. Glissant, *Poétique*, p. 46. All subsequent references to Glissant's novels and book-length works of criticism will be included in the body of the text. When necessary, the following abbreviations will be used to identify passages from his literary and cultural criticism: *SC* (*Soleil de la conscience* [1956]); *IP* (*L'intention poétique* [1969]); *DA* (*Le discours antillais* [1981]); *PR* (*Poétique de la Relation* [1990]); *FM* (*Faulkner, Mississippi* [1996]); *ID* (*Introduction à une Poétique du Divers* [1996]). Unless otherwise indicated, all translations from the French in this book are my own: for reasons of space, I have not retained the original French, except in cases when I wanted to emphasize a particular word or turn of phrase, or when my translations stray from the original for stylistic reasons; very occasionally, to facilitate

close reading, lengthier French passages have been given in their entirety, followed by the English translation.

8. P. Hulme, *Colonial Encounters* (henceforth *CE*), p. 155.

9. Slemon, "Post-Colonial Allegory," p. 162.

10. Gratiant, "Martinique," p. 81.

11. Confiant, *Aimé Césaire* (henceforth *AC*), p. 116. For a full discussion of Gratiant, see Corzani, *Littérature*, 3.222–35; and Jean-Louis Joubert's introduction to the 1996 anthology of his work, *Fables créoles* (pp. 17–26). The following self-portrait from Gratiant's 1948 poem *Credo des Sang-Mêlé*, in which he anticipates Carpentier's reflections on "the noble juice of the vine," is exemplary of Gratiant's attention to and enthusiasm for "the complex alchemy of centuries upon centuries of mixing" ("l'alchémie complexe des surmélanges séculaires") that went into the making of what, in a 1935 article entitled "Mulâtres . . . pour le bien et le mal," he had already identified as a "new civilization with variable modes of expression, the *creole civilization*, which unifies any number of dissimilarities, borrowing this from the blacks, and that from the whites" (*Fables*, p. 705): "A *métis* mixed seventy times over in the blood / Of Bordeaux's vineyards / As in the maternal ooze of the Niger / Made fertile by the sun and sorrow, / I affirm myself as multiple" (*Fables*, p. 623; "Métis remélangé septante fois au sang / Des vignes bordelaises / Comme aux boues maternelles du Niger / Que le soleil féconde et que la peine engrosse, / Je m'affirme multiple"). One of three Martiniquan poets included by Léopold Senghor in his influential 1948 anthology of black literature in French (along with his former student Aimé Césaire and Étienne Léro), Gratiant is best remembered for championing the use in literary texts of the spoken vernacular, "that creole speech / Invented for the retelling of an entire world / By Africa and France entwined / In the hammock of the Caribbean" (*Fables*, p. 624; "le parler créole / Inventé pour redire tout un monde inventé / Par l'Afrique et la France enlacées / Au creux du hamac des Antilles"). The anomalous presence in the 1948 *Anthologie* of Gratiant's "poems in Martiniquan patois," which Senghor himself characterizes as "the most authentic expression of the Caribbean's hybrid soul [*l'âme métisse des Antilles*]" (p. 29), serves as a useful reminder of the extent to which Senghor's vision of Negritude (so often cited as exemplifying the most naive sort of essentialism) was inseparable from a positive assessment of métissage—a point that I elaborate upon in my "Francophone Conjunctures." It is this contradictory and yet productive yoking together of two such very different "authentic" identities that I will be examining, and advocating, throughout *Islands and Exiles*.

12. As Bhabha notes, "for me the importance of hybridity is not to be able to trace two original moments from which the third emerges, rather hybridity to me is the 'third space' which enables other positions to emerge. This third space displaces the histories that constitute it, and sets up new structures of authority, new political initiatives, which are inadequately understood through received wisdom" ("Third Space," p. 211).

13. Kutzinski, *Sugar's Secrets*, p. 94.

14. Pérez Firmat, *Cuban Condition* (henceforth *CC*), p. 12.

15. As Pedro M. Barreda-Tomás argues, in Carpentier's first novel, *Écue-Yamba-Ó* (1933), "the black seems to remain outside the avatars of history, to be a

purely natural entity" (quoted in González Echevarría, *ACPH*, p. 5). While accepting this critique of Carpentier's early work, González Echevarría argues that Afro-Caribbean culture plays a very different, altogether less "natural," role in *Explosion*: see his *Celestina's Brood*, pp. 170–93.

16. For a critique of Deleuze and Guattari along these lines, see Girard, *To Double Business*, pp. 84–120; C. L. Miller, "Postidentitarian Predicament"; and my own account of Miller's argument in the second section of Chapter 4.

17. Pratt, *Imperial Eyes* (henceforth *IE*), p. 9.

18. Bongie, *Exotic Memories*, pp. 1–32; see also Pagden, *Lords*, pp. 1–10.

19. For a detailed analysis of the context in which this novel was written, see González Echevarría, *ACPH*, pp. 213–25.

20. Thomas, *Colonialism's Culture*, p. 7. Jonathan Dollimore makes similar use of the slash in his *Sexual Dissidence*: "the '/' which I shall henceforth install between 'post' and 'modern' registers the provisional aspect of each of the categories modern and post-modern, and also the confused, unresolved, but always significant dimensions of their relationship" (p. 22); for another relevant example of the many recent attempts at nuancing the concept of postcolonialism(s) via punctuational markers, see Mishra and Hodge, "What is post(-)colonialism?". In a similar manner, my use of parenthetical prefixes and suffixes—e.g., (dis)continuity and global(izing)—also gestures toward an unresolved but significant relationship between ostensibly different words by adding a second contradictory or supplementary meaning to a root word, a meaning that troubles or doubles but does not cancel out the original.

21. Lyotard, "Re-writing Modernity," p. 3.

22. C. B. Davies, *Black Women*, pp. 93, 90.

23. Shohat and Stam, *Unthinking Eurocentrism*, p. 39.

24. As Glissant has noted, the notion of modernity "is a contested one: is not every age 'modern' compared with the one that preceded it? It seems, though, that at least one of the components of 'our' modernity is the generalized awareness that we have of it. The awareness of this awareness (doubled, to the second degree) is both our treasure and our torment" (*DA*, p. 258).

25. Hall, "When was 'the post-colonial'?," pp. 252–53.

26. Lamming, *Pleasures*, p. 96.

27. Quoted in Gilroy, *Black Atlantic* (henceforth *BA*), p. 150.

28. Walcott, "Muse," p. 20.

29. Saint-Pierre, *Oeuvres*, 8.215–16.

30. Césaire, *Collected Poetry* (henceforth *CP*), pp. 256–57.

31. For one critical reading along these lines of Césaire's "toute île est veuve," see Confiant, *AC*, p. 17.

32. See Díaz-Quiñones, "Hispanic-Caribbean National Discourse," p. 105.

33. See Pérez Firmat, *CC*, pp. 1–4.

34. Cliff, "Untitled," p. 69.

35. Rousseau, *Oeuvres*, 1.1047, 1041.

36. Quoted in Chenet, *"Travailleurs,"* p. 368.

37. Trousson, "Jean-Jacques Rousseau," p. 108.

38. Kellner, "Popular Culture," p. 143.

39. Rousseau, *Oeuvres*, 1.1041.

40. Péron, *Des îles*, p. 12.

41. Rousseau, *Rêveries*, p. 62; see also *Oeuvres*, 1.1795.

42. For a thorough introduction to the field of Franco-Caribbean literature, see the essays collected in J. M. Dash, "Francophone Literature."

43. Appadurai, *Modernity*, p. 32, and passim.

44. Benitez-Rojo, *Repeating Island* (henceforth *RI*), p. 235.

45. Márquez, "Nationalism," p. 329.

46. Walcott, "Muse," p. 6.

47. Rousseau, *Oeuvres*, 1.644.

CHAPTER 2

1. David Attwell has, indeed, used this passage as the point of departure for his introduction to a recent collection of Coetzee's essays; see Coetzee, *Doubling the Point*, p. 2.

2. P. Hulme, *CE*, p. 6.

3. As Walcott puts it in his poem "Crusoe's Journal," with a bittersweet mix of admiration for and wariness toward his colonial predecessor, *Robinson Crusoe* is "our first book, our profane Genesis / whose Adam speaks that prose / which, blessing some sea-rock, startles itself / with poetry's surprise, / in a green world, one without metaphors" (*Collected Poems*, pp. 92–93).

4. Petersen, "Elaborate Dead End," p. 251.

5. For a reading of Coetzee's work that is in part based on an exhaustive critique of feminist identity politics, and Gilbert and Gubar's *Madwoman in the Attic* in particular, see Dovey, pp. 330–413.

6. Spivak, "Theory," p. 168.

7. As Iain Chambers has pointed out, "central to both the Marxist and Baudrillardian critique of the sign (fetishism, simulacrum)" is the argument "that surfaces and appearances are the deceptive, seductive and mystifying manifestations of an underlying reality: the alienation of the human condition. The reduction of the apparent to a concealed, hidden value—the value of 'authenticity' supposedly masked by false appearances—denies the ontological reality of signs, surfaces and everyday life. It denies that they, too, are sites of sense, of meaning" (*Migrancy*, p. 100).

8. Harris, *Womb*, p. 56.

9. Spivak, "Theory," p. 170.

10. See his "Oppressive Silence"; for a critique of Attridge's position, see Parry, "Speech," where she argues that in Coetzee's novels "European textual power, reinscribed in the formal syntax required of Literature, survives the attempted subversion of its dominion [through such strategies as preserving Friday's silence]" (p. 3).

11. Attwell, *J. M. Coetzee*, p. 26.

12. As Fanon long ago argued in *Les damnés de la terre*, "the colonized world is a world split in two" (p. 7); "colonialism . . . is the Manicheanist, compartmentalized organization of the world" (p. 43). That this same binary rhetoric also structures the anticolonial argument of Fanon's book is the matter of an ironical (un)likeness I will be exploring in Chapter 7.

13. As Paul Gilroy has pointed out, if images like those of Africa and mother

are central to the sort of essentialist politics and poetics promoted by the Negritude movement, that of the ship fills an altogether different function, one that has been of central importance to the formation of what he calls the Black Atlantic and its migrant imaginary: ships are those "mobile elements that stood for the shifting spaces in between the fixed places that they connected," and as such they direct us away from the world of stable identities and toward a destabilized and destabilizing field of transcultural relations (see *BA*, p. 16).

14. Quoted in Rodriguez, "Contraintes," p. 44. For an extended analysis of the role of seeing (*voir*) in anthropology and travel literature, as well as its relation to knowledge (*savoir*), see Affergan, *Exotisme*, pp. 137–76.

15. Pratt, *IE*, p. 59. By the term "anti-conquest" she refers to "the strategies of representation whereby European bourgeois subjects seek to secure their innocence in the same moment as they assert European hegemony. . . . In travel and exploration writings [from the mid-eighteenth century on] these strategies of innocence are constituted in relation to older imperial rhetorics of conquest associated with the absolutist era" (p. 7).

16. Morphet, "Two Interviews," p. 462; for a reading of this statement that differs substantially from mine, see Gallagher, *Story*, p. 171.

17. Meditating upon the ambivalences of Walter Benjamin's vision of "a fight for the history of the oppressed," Rey Chow has pointed out the extent to which this vision is itself implicated in the "discourse of imperialism": "whenever the oppressed, the native, the subaltern, and so forth are used to represent the point of 'authenticity' for our critical discourse," she argues, "they become at the same time the place of myth-making and an escape from the impure nature of political realities" (*Writing Diaspora*, p. 44).

18. Quoted in Attwell, *J. M. Coetzee*, p. 15.

19. Here, of course, Coetzee is doubling a point made in the original *Robinson Crusoe*, where the eponymous protagonist cannot begin the telling of his own story without, at the very outset, admitting to the loss, the "corruption," of his proper name, which was originally Kreutznaer; as he notes, "by the usual corruption of words in England, we are now called, nay, we call our selves and write our name, Crusoe" (p. 27).

20. See Bhabha, *Location* (henceforth *LC*), pp. 9–18. Of obvious relevance to my own argument is Bhabha's claim that "in the act of translation the 'given' content becomes alien and estranged; and that, in its turn, leaves the language of translation *Aufgabe*, always confronted by its double, the untranslatable—alien and foreign" ("DissemiNation," p. 315).

21. González Echevarría, *ACPH*, p. 212.

22. Pérez Firmat, *CC*, p. 53.

23. This poem comes from the section of his 1969 collection *Islands* entitled "Possession" (*Arrivants*, p. 236). As we will see in the following section of this chapter, despite his long-standing commitment to the creolizing process, Brathwaite is also very drawn to the claims of self-possession and of an insular identity that I have been ambivalently arguing against in my discussion of *Foe*.

24. As J. Michael Dash points out in a commentary on these lines, "the heroics of self permeate Caribbean writing, whatever its ideological persuasion, and point

to its origins in nineteenth-century Romanticism" (*Édouard Glissant*, p. 5). Reflecting on the diglossic realities of predominantly creolophone Martinique and Césaire's choice of not writing in Creole, Richard D. E. Burton notes, further, that "in presenting itself as 'la bouche des malheurs qui n'ont point de bouche,' the *je* quite simply suppresses the possibility of these calamities being articulated in the language that is theirs" ("Traversée paradoxale," p. 127).

25. During, "Postmodernism" (1987), p. 33.

26. Taussig, *Mimesis*, pp. 236–37.

27. Appiah, *In My Father's House* (henceforth *IMFH*), p. 145. "Modernity," Appiah continues, "has turned every element of the real into a sign, and the sign reads 'for sale.'"

28. Bhabha, "DissemiNation," p. 313.

29. Quoted by bell hooks in her interview with J. Dash, *Daughters*, p. 27.

30. J. Dash, *Daughters*, p. 4, and pp. 27–32 for hooks's distinction between "myth" and "documentary."

31. Bambara, "Reading," p. 129.

32. Zobel, *Rue*, p. 56, and pp. 57–58 for Médouze's evocations of Africa.

33. For an analysis of Zobel's novel along these lines, see André, *Caraïbales*, pp. 55–108.

34. Gilroy, "Route Work," p. 22.

35. Gilroy, *Small Acts*, p. 188.

36. Gilroy, *Small Acts*, pp. 185–86. As Julien puts it, "Spike Lee's opposition to miscegenation probably has a lot in common with David Duke's notion of racial purity" ("Black Is," p. 263).

37. Ngugi, *Decolonising*, pp. 26–27.

38. Césaire, *Tragédie*, p. 147.

39. During's earlier comments about New Zealand's chances of entering into a "post-colonized condition" need to be reread, for example, in the context of his later assertion that "post-colonial identity politics tend towards paradox and irresolution because, with the coming of Europeans, the narratives, signifiers and practices available to Maoris . . . to articulate their needs and wants are at once inscribed within Eurocentric modernity—and vice versa" ("Waiting," p. 30).

40. Finkielkraut, *Défaite*, pp. 71–118.

41. Chinweizu, Jemie, and Madubuike, *Toward the Decolonization*, p. 4; quoted in Appiah, *IMFH*, p. 57.

42. Nietzsche, *Beyond Good and Evil*, p. 214 (section 264).

43. Appiah notes that "the very category of the Negro is at root a European product: for the 'whites' invented the Negroes in order to dominate them. Simply put, the overdetermined course of cultural nationalism in Africa has been to make real the imaginary identities to which Europe has subjected us" (*IMFH*, p. 62).

44. Parry, "Resistance Theory," p. 177.

45. Walcott, "What the Twilight Said," p. 20; Fanon, "Antillais," p. 36.

46. Walcott, "Muse," p. 17.   47. Harris, "Engineering," p. 86.

48. Harris, "Fabric," pp. 175–76.   49. Harris, *Womb*, pp. 17–18.

50. Brathwaite, *Contradictory Omens* (henceforth *CO*), p. 58.

51. Gikandi, *Writing*, p. 9.

52. Appiah, "Race," pp. 98, 81.

53. Gilroy, *BA*, pp. 99–100. By way of elucidation, he cites Foucault's comments in *Surveiller et punir* about the *produced reality* of "the modern soul" as pointing the way toward an "anti-anti-essentialism that sees racialised subjectivity as the product of the social practices that supposedly derive from it" (p. 102); for an extended account of this position, see Gilroy's *Small Acts*, pp. 120–45. This anti-anti-essentialist argument would appear to jibe well with Christopher Miller's productive definition of ethnicity as "a sense of identity and difference among peoples, founded on a fiction of origin and descent and subject to forces of politics, commerce, language, and religious culture" (*Theories*, p. 35).

54. It should be noted that this tension between essentialism and constructionism uneasily intersects with another opposition that is vitally constitutive of postcolonial theory, namely between what Paget Henry and Paul Buhle have referred to as "semantic" and "discursive" analysis. As they remark in a useful discussion of C. L. R. James, it is now a commonplace to show that "anti-colonial discourses are anchored in the 'deep structures,' codes or grammars of imperial discourses beyond the reach of these strategies" ("Caliban," p. 114). Where the "classic anti-colonial discourses" attacked colonialism at the "semantic" level (for instance, by "(1) the discursive inverting of the colonial order of things; (2) revalorizing pre-colonial traditions; (3) renaming people, places, and events; and (4) delegitimating the arguments for colonial rule" [p. 114]), their concentration on social factors has in large part given way to a "semio-linguistic emphasis," typified by theorists like Bhabha and Spivak who read imperial and anticolonial discourses as united in their use of "similar rules and forms of epistemic violence." Where a Marxist like James stressed the need for political revolution, these theorists, enacting a "poststructuralist relocation of the zone of conflict," (can only) promote "discursive insurrections that break the codes or deep structures of imperial discourses" (p. 130). For their part, Henry and Buhle stress the need to practice these two very divergent methods of "deconstruction" together, notwithstanding the obvious incompatibilities and tensions that characterize their relations.

55. Reid, "Caught," p. 136. For other pertinent critiques of Gilroy, see Lazarus, "Is a Counterculture . . . ?"; Mercer, *Welcome*, pp. 233–58; and the essays collected in *Research in African Literatures* 27.4 (1996), especially Dayan, "Paul Gilroy's Slaves."

56. Parry, "Resistance Theory," p. 182.

57. For an overview of the linguistic concept of a creole continuum, see Rickford, *Dimensions*, pp. 15–39.

58. See Bolland, "Creolization," pp. 53–57.

59. Brathwaite, *Development* (henceforth *DCS*), p. 310.

60. For a sample critique of the relatively optimistic vision of "community" that underpins Brathwaite's portrait in *Development* of pre-Emancipation Jamaica, see Lewis, *Main Currents*, pp. 321–22.

61. P. Hulme, "Locked Heart," p. 75.

62. See Chaudenson, *Des îles*, p. 228.

63. Shohat, "Notes," p. 108.

64. Suleri, *Rhetoric*, pp. 9, 3. This Manichean rhetoric, as Stuart Hall has

pointed out, informs the recent "radical" backlash against the concept of the post-colonial: the critique offered by someone like Ella Shohat ("Notes"), as well as similar-minded ones put forward by Anne McClintock and Arif Dirlik, are laced with "a certain nostalgia . . . for a return to a clear-cut politics of binary oppositions, where clear 'lines can be drawn in the sand' between goodies and baddies" ("When was 'the post-colonial'?," p. 244).

65. As Hulme notes, "the Caribbean notion of the 'creole' [is] the local name, if you like, for what the 'general' theory calls 'hybridisation'" ("Locked Heart," p. 75). Maintaining this distinction between the local and the global is vital, but I will nonetheless perforce often be eliding these and other related terms in this book.

66. Bolland, "Creolization," p. 64.

67. Brathwaite, "Introduction," p. 5.

68. Brathwaite's use of the prism nicely complements Fernando Ortiz's appeal to the *ajiaco*, a local Cuban stew, as a more appropriate metaphor than the melting pot (*crisol*) for understanding the Caribbean's mixed societies. Whereas the latter implies homogeneity, the former preserves diversity: as Pérez Firmat notes, the ajiaco is "agglutinative but not synthetic; even if the diverse ingredients form part of a new culinary entity, they do not lose their original flavor and identity"; moreover, it is "indefinitely replenishable, since new ingredients can be added to the stew as old ones are used up." The word itself, he concludes, is a perfect example of the creolizing process inasmuch as it "combines the African name of an Amerindian condiment, the *ají* or green pepper, with a Spanish suffix, *-aco*" (CC, p. 24). As Vera Kutzinski has noted in *Sugar's Secrets*, one point that Pérez Firmat overlooks in his enthusiastic gloss on Ortiz's use of the word is the fact that *Ajiaco* was the title of a nineteenth-century burlesque comedy written by a "blackface" Cuban playwright (p. 215); Ortiz's (and Pérez Firmat's) (re)citation of this word inevitably marks a complicity between their positive vision of transculturation and earlier colonial assumptions about the dynamics of cultural mixing.

69. Brathwaite, "Caliban," p. 42.

70. Brathwaite, "Timehri," pp. 41–42.

71. Ashcroft, Griffiths, and Tiffin, *Empire*, p. 147.

72. Brathwaite, "World," p. 56.

73. Brathwaite, "History," p. 34. For another relevant analysis of Brathwaite's contradictory position, see Edmondson, "Race."

74. Brathwaite, *Roots*, p. 257.

75. Gilroy, *Small Acts*, p. 209.

76. Trinh, *Woman*, p. 96.

77. Lionnet, *Autobiographical Voices*, p. 9.

78. Bernabé, Chamoiseau, and Confiant, *Éloge*, p. 27. For more on the immediate context in which this work was written, see Burton, "Between the Particular," pp. 204–7.

79. Significantly enough, this proclamation echoes the famous lines from Simón Bolívar's 1815 "Jamaica Letter" in which, discussing the creole peoples who are in the process of liberating themselves from Spain, he states that "we are . . . neither Indian nor European, but a species midway between the legitimate proprietors of this country and the Spanish usurpers" (quoted in Bushnell, *Liberator*, p. 12).

80. Fanon, *Damnés*, p. 145.

81. Glissant, "Sur la trace," p. 59.

82. Quoted in Gerbeau, "Approche," p. 149.

83. For Senghor's article ("De la liberté de l'âme ou éloge du métissage"), see *Liberté*, pp. 98–103.

84. Burton, "*Ki moun nou ye?*," p. 23; see also J. M. Dash, *Édouard Glissant*, p. 23.

85. Said, "Representing," p. 225.

86. See J. M. Dash, *Édouard Glissant*, p. 148; and Burton, "Négritude," p. 156.

87. Commenting on the "double solidarity" that characterizes "nous, Antillais créoles"—Antillanité (geopolitical links with, say, Cuba and Barbados) and Créolité (anthropological links with, say, Mauritius and Hawaii)—the authors of the *Éloge* maintain that "as Creoles we are as close, if not closer, anthropologically speaking, to people from the Seychelles, Mauritius, Réunion, than to Puerto Ricans or Cubans" (pp. 32–33). Of course, as Richard and Sally Price have pointed out, such claims *also* testify to "the créolistes' insularity—their willful nonengagement with both the non-French Caribbean and nonfrancophonic scholarship," which in turn dangerously "colors their understandings of the Caribbean past in a number of domains" ("Shadowboxing," p. 11).

88. Wynter, "Beyond the Word," p. 647. Her comments are very much in line with Bhabha's assertion that "the frontiers of cultural difference are always belated or secondary in the sense that their hybridity is never simply a question of the admixture of pre-given identities or essences" ("DissemiNation," p. 314).

89. Quoted in Huannou, *Question*, p. 113.

90. Glissant, "Romancier," p. 30.

91. As Glissant puts it in his 1996 *Introduction à une Poétique du Divers*, "the 'beyond' of creolization would, in effect, be the nonidentitarian. But there exists the Place [*le Lieu*], which maintains us" (p. 99). As he elsewhere admits in this book, it is indeed questionable whether we can "preserve this place without preserving its exclusivity" (p. 30), but we must at the very least address this question, by repeatedly and impossibly attempting to respond to another, namely, "how to be oneself without closing oneself off to the other, and how to open oneself up to the other without losing oneself?" (p. 23).

92. C. L. Miller, *Theories*, p. 63. Miller's probing critique of Fanon and his vision of "national culture" is made in the name of an "ethnic culture" that he argues is more supple and less exclusionary: "the relation to the other," Miller asserts, "is the relation of ethnicity" (see pp. 45–67).

93. Chambers, *Migrancy*, p. 14.

94. Gilroy, *BA*, p. 15. For a comprehensive argument on the need for beginning to think the configuration of cultural forms in today's "globalized, deterritorialized world" as "fundamentally fractal" and "polythetically overlapping," see Appadurai, *Modernity*, pp. 46–47, and passim.

95. Senghor, *Liberté*, p. 99.
96. Brathwaite, *Roots*, p. 243.
97. Brathwaite, "World," p. 63.
98. Brathwaite, *Arrivants*, p. 164.
99. Barnard, "Dream Topographies," p. 44.

100. This intertextual echo is worth noting in order to give one last example of

the (un)likenesses through which the two novels are related. Having salvaged as much as he could from the wreck of his ship, Crusoe carries all his goods into the "fence or fortress" that he has constructed on the side of a hill in order to "secure his self" against either savages or wild beasts. After completing this "enclosure," Crusoe informs us, "I began to work my way into the rock, and bringing all the earth and stones that I dug down out thro' my tent, I laid 'em up within my fence in the nature of a terras, that so it raised the ground within about a foot and a half; and thus I made me a cave just behind my tent, which served me like a cellar to my house" (p. 78). The ambivalent shift from Crusoe's enclosed "terras," part and parcel of his fortified settlement, and the more open, but still walled, "terraces" of Cruso is exemplary of the never complete "redressal" (in Wilson Harris's words) of colonial structures that characterizes post/colonial literature.

CHAPTER 3

1. Rousseau, *Oeuvres*, 3.169.

2. Loxley, *Problematic Shores*, p. 3.

3. P. Hulme, "Tales," p. 176. For a brilliant reading of *Robinson Crusoe* that draws attention to the way in which Defoe, in an only partially successful attempt at historical occlusion, sutures "the divided selves of Robinson Crusoe," erasing Crusoe's role as slaveholding plantation owner on the Brazilian mainland and valorizing his identity as "the man alone, on a desert island, constructing a simple and moral economy which becomes the basis of a commonwealth presided over by a benevolent sovereign," see his *CE*, pp. 219–22.

4. See Pratt, *IE*, p. 6.

5. All references will be to Édouard Guitton's edition of the novel. Bernardin has yet to find his definitive editor (although work on a scientific edition of his *Oeuvres complètes* is apparently under way [see Roger Little's introduction to *Empsaël*, p. xxiii]). Unless otherwise stated, all other references to his writings will be to the 1825–26 revised edition of the 1818 *Oeuvres complètes*.

6. Schiller, *On the Aesthetic Education*, p. 33. On the "elegiac" affinities of Rousseau and Schiller, see Starobinski, *Jean-Jacques Rousseau*, pp. 113–16. Schiller's sense of *Kultur* as a fragmentizing process that betokens a loss of social identity, rather than as an essence reflecting that identity, corresponds with what Fredric Jameson has identified as the "hidden inner meaning" of culture: namely, that culture is "the space of the symbolic moves of groups in agonistic relation to each other," "a vehicle or a medium whereby the relationship between groups is transacted" ("On Cultural Studies," pp. 633, 629). This "unnatural" (in Jameson's words [p. 629]) relationship between groups is precisely what makes a given culture, and the sense of identity and difference that "naturally" attaches to it, possible in the first place.

7. The translator's choice of equating *entwickeln* and *herstellen* nicely captures the complicitous double temporality that I am describing here, since the former more properly means "development"; this future "unfolding" is inseparable from the restoration of the past that is conveyed by the latter word (a word that also, though, means simply to manufacture, to fabricate: every restoration of the past is,

in the final analysis, a production that has its proper place in a present from which that past is foundationally absent).

8. Césaire, "Homme," p. 121.

9. As J. Hillis Miller has pointed out in his discussion of this episode, two competing semiotic theories are at work here: for the parishioner "the sign is grounded in a nonlinguistic reality"; for the architect, "the sign is free-floating" and "its functioning depends on the absence of what it signifies," though "it still depends for its meaning and function on the existence of that [absent] signified" (*Ariadne's Thread*, pp. 192, 198). Ultimately, this second theory opens out onto the possibility that the sign actually *creates*—as in catachresis—what it signifies, "rather than merely pointing to it either close at hand [the first mimetic, representational theory of signs] or out of sight [the second theory]" (p. 198). To this third semiotic theory corresponds, I would add, a supplementary way of understanding the memory (*Andenken*) that both the parishioner and the architect in their differing ways invoke: as Gianni Vattimo has argued, it is precisely this third version of *Andenken* as a fictive (but nonetheless pious) gesture of commemoration—a gesture that is by no means entirely extricable from the other two methods of conceptualizing memory— that predominates in Heidegger's later writings; it is this version of *Andenken* that I argued for at length in *Exotic Memories* and that remains crucial to the reading of post/colonial literature that I am undertaking in this book (see especially the concluding section of Chapter 7).

10. See Chaudenson's edition of Bernardin's *Voyage* (henceforth *VF*), p. 23.

11. In the fourth *Rêverie*, for instance, Rousseau castigates himself for those moments when, "carried away by the pleasure of writing, I added embellishments of my own invention to real things"—an error, to his mind, "because to embellish the truth with fables is in fact to disfigure it" (*Oeuvres*, 1.1038). Such "dangerous supplements," of course, form the basis of a deconstructionist reading of Rousseau (Derrida, De Man) to which my own analysis of Bernardin is obviously much indebted.

12. This passage has also been cited and ably analyzed in Racault, "Système," p. 402.

13. Starobinski, *Jean-Jacques Rousseau*, p. 27.

14. Coetzee, *White Writing*, p. 9.

15. Rousseau, *Oeuvres*, 3.123.

16. Quoted in Vaughan, *Shakespeare's Caliban*, pp. 104, 103.

17. T. Richards, *Imperial Archive*, p. 7. Tracing the genealogical links between Romanticism and Victorian imperialism, Richards notes that such "differing but exhaustive projects" as "the impulse toward the universal in Shelley, the project of a complete knowledge of the world in Coleridge, the ability of Blake's visions to span the globe, the sense of a fully surveyed landscape in Wordsworth" would be carried forward in the literature of Empire that reached its apex at the end of the nineteenth century.

18. Césaire, "Noir," p. 12.

19. *Tropiques* 12 (1945): 164 ("Poésie et connaissance").

20. Senghor, *Liberté*, p. 157.

21. Quoted in Lamming, *Pleasures*, p. 31.

22. Walcott, "Muse," pp. 19, 10.

23. Racault, "Pastorale," pp. 195–96; for a seminal (1953) treatment of *Paul et Virginie*'s connections to the renascent tradition of pastoral literature in the late eighteenth century, see Fabre, *Lumières*, pp. 225–57.

24. Moretti, *Signs*, p. 265.

25. Moretti, *Way*, p. 10.

26. Schiller, *On the Aesthetic Education*, pp. 31, 57.

27. Thomas, *Colonialism's Culture*, p. 71.

28. Affergan, *Exotisme*, p. 18. According to Affergan, "in the 16th century, the Other is still marked by a secret and opaque code, even though the need for categorizing it is starting to make itself felt, given the dawning of [colonial] domination" (pp. 101–3). Grounded in earlier post/Christian confrontations with non-European peoples, Enlightenment anthropology nonetheless "drained away two key elements from the soil of this ground: on the one hand, the alterity that had marked the first discoveries with its stamp was reduced to a *combinatoire* of differences; and on the other, any written evidence that could raise doubts as to its [anthropology's] objective character was progressively erased" (p. 225). See also During, "Rousseau's Patrimony," p. 53, and passim.

29. Quoted in Pagden, "Effacement," p. 142.

30. Thomas, *Colonialism's Culture*, p. 87.

31. Didier, "Métissage," pp. 15–16.

32. In a by no means etymologically authoritative gloss on the word, Brathwaite suggests that it "appears to have originated from a combination of the two Spanish words *criar* (to create, to imagine, to establish, to found, to settle) and *colono* (a colonist, a founder, a settler) into *criollo*: a committed settler, one identified with the area of settlement, one native to the settlement though not ancestrally indigenous to it" (*DCS*, pp. xiv–xv). For a more in-depth discussion of the history and varying usages of this word, see the opening pages of Chapter 4.

33. In his *Voyage à l'Île de France*, Bernardin gently ironizes the systematizing nature of Linnaeus's enterprise: on his way back to France in 1770, he stops off at the Dutch Cape where he has a discussion with the colony's Governor, who tells him that he once sent some plants to Linnaeus in Sweden, "which proved so different from known plants that this famous naturalist wrote him: You have given me the greatest pleasure, but you have made a complete mess of my system" (2.38).

34. Said, *Orientalism*, p. 93.

35. See Bhabha, *LC*, p. 71. For an important critique of Bhabha's appeal to "colonial discourse" in the singular, see Thomas, *Colonialism's Culture*, pp. 33–65.

36. Davis, *Resisting Novels*, p. 54. The accomplished realism of much of Bernardin's work bears insisting upon, given the common tendency, as Robert Chaudenson puts it, to think of this "attentive observer" as nothing more than "a daydreamer" (*Des îles*, p. 97). In the very informative preface to his edition of the *Voyage*, Chaudenson notes that "despite my hope of catching him out in some error, I have not been able to do so and in all cases where it has been possible to check archive documents or other people's testimony it became apparent that what he had to say was exact and his judgments justified" (p. 14).

37. Davis, *Resisting Novels*, p. 59. For a nuancing of this argument about Shakespeare, see P. Hulme, *CE*, pp. 89–134.

38. Mary Louise Pratt defines "contact zones" as "social spaces where disparate cultures meet, clash, and grapple with each other, often in highly asymmetrical relations of domination and subordination" (*IE*, p. 4). Notwithstanding Pratt's insistence on the often violent asymmetries of power that make possible cross-cultural contact, Peter Mason for one has reacted scathingly to her use of this term, arguing that "'contact zone' is even more sanitised and anodyne [than a phrase like 'colonial encounter'], and its application to the Putumayo region of Colombia, for instance, where a veritable culture of terror reigned at the turn of the century, is simply callous" (p. 110).

39. See his 1846 short story "Sacatove" (*Oeuvres*, 4.285).

40. Said, *Orientalism*, p. 137.   41. Quinet, *Du génie*, p. 70.

42. Chateaubriand, *Essai*, p. 706.   43. Said, *Orientalism*, p. 42.

44. Pagden, "Effacement," pp. 146–47.

45. Given our discussion in the previous paragraph, it is worth recalling here a remarkable moment from Napoléon's *Mémoires* in which Orientalist discourse intersects with the former Emperor's improbable reflections on how to solve the race problem in the French colonies (a problem that he had so heinously exacerbated with his decision to reinstitute slavery). Noting the importance of polygamy in Asia and Africa, Napoléon attributes this to the fact that these are continents "inhabited by men of several colors." Polygamy, he argues, was legislated as the only means of preventing them from persecuting one another, given "man's propensity for hating everything that is different from him." Pursuing this line of thought, he adds, "when it comes time in our colonies to free the blacks and establish there a perfect equality, legislators had better authorize polygamy and allow [men] to have a white, a black, and a mulatto wife. From that moment on, the different colors, belonging to the same family, will be confounded in everybody's minds. Without that, one will never secure a satisfactory result" (quoted in D'Eichthal and Urbain, *Lettres*, pp. 32–33).

46. Yves Benot describes this play as "the first literary work that portrays a white (female)-black (male) couple in a positive manner" (*Révolution*, p. 255). Bernardin summarizes the play's antislavery theme thus: "I believed that nothing was more suited to showing the weakness of the arguments used by the white inhabitants of our island to justify the enslavement of blacks than to put those same arguments in the mouth of a black man from the Barbary coast, directed against some habitant of our islands who has himself been enslaved in Africa" (*Empsaël*, p. 3). In this same preface, he also emphasizes the need for the French theater to take on contemporary subject matter and to globalize its vision—suggestions that strikingly anticipate Romanticism's break with classicism, Goethe's claims for a "world literature," and the relational poetics being advocated in our own day by a writer like Glissant: "Our heroic drama almost always has as its subject the Romans and Greeks; it chains our esteem to dead or very remote peoples, some of whom caused great suffering to our ancestors, whereas there exist in our vicinity living peoples with whom it would be very useful to maintain harmonious ties. We must extend our conception of humanity [*Nous devons généraliser notre humanité*]," and

thereby leave behind "that narrow sphere of patriotism in which the Greeks and Romans shut themselves up, incurring the hatred of foreign nations that ended up destroying them. If we want all men to be interested in our own fate, then we have to be interested in theirs" (p. 7).

47. As Confiant points out, "the creolization process, to be sure, involves the nativization of peoples not born on the islands, their becoming rooted in the Americas, but it also involves that of animals and plants, which makes it an ecological process. . . . Creolization engages . . . all orders of reality, the human just as much as the animal and the vegetable" (*AC*, pp. 264–65).

48. "This form of racism," Amselle notes in *Vers un multiculturalisme français*, "finds its emblematic expression in representations of a variegated France, enriched by the multiplicity of its affiliations and its differences." Exemplified, say, by "the presence in sports teams of numerous players from the Antilles, Africa, or the Maghreb," "the *soft* racism of *métissage* as it gets displayed, for example, in the advertisements of *United Colors of Benetton* could well be in the final analysis a subtle form of [asserting] the irreducibility of differences" (pp. 17–18).

49. For a biting critique of the Créolité movement's "sharply gendered identity," see Arnold, "Gendering."

50. Chambers, *Migrancy*, p. 74.

51. Chateaubriand, *Grands écrits*, 1.213.

52. Chambers, *Migrancy*, p. 71.

53. Hoffmann, *Nègre*, p. 101.

54. Gozzano, *Man*, pp. 52–53 ("Out of the dark past I see it rise [again] / clearly, the vanished land / I never knew, the land I recognize ... ").

55. Segalen, *Oeuvres*, 1.745.   56. Carpentier, "Autor," p. 16.

57. Camus, *Essais*, p. 74.   58. Walcott, "Muse," p. 6.

59. Camus, *Essais*, p. 664. For a comprehensive account of more recent critical reactions to *Paul et Virginie*, see S. Davies, *"Paul et Virginie."*

60. Hutcheon, *Poetics*, p. 4.

61. Quoted in Guitton's "Introduction" to his edition of *Paul et Virginie*, p. 19.

62. In 1775 the island had a population of roughly 30,000 compared to barely a thousand forty years before that; by the end of the century the inhabitants would number some 75,000, 85 percent of whom were black slaves (Rivière, *Historical Dictionary*, p. 99).

63. Rodriguez, "Contraintes," p. 43.

64. This supplementary connection between Bernardin's original, predominantly negative vision of the island and his later pastoral revision of it is itself mirrored in the publishing history of *Paul et Virginie*. As Édouard Guitton has pointed out in his edition of the novel, Bernardin's "writing is a continuous rewriting" (p. 31), committed both to a deferent reincorporation of the words and thoughts of other writers (notably, Rousseau) and to an incessant reworking and supplementing of his own material (for which the *Voyage* serves as the primary matrix). Initially projected, in the rudimentary form of an "Histoire de Melle de la Tour," as the fifteenth letter of the *Voyage* itself and then later envisioned as simply an addition to that work, *Paul et Virginie* was first published in 1788 as an addendum to the second edition of his very popular *Études de la nature* (1784), in which he exhaustively

put forward the providentialist argument that "Nature has done nothing in vain." Paired in this new fourth volume of the *Études* with extended fragments from his never-completed *Arcadie*, *Paul et Virginie* would finally be published as a separate volume in the following year, 1789.

65. Racault, "De l'île," p. 91. The preoccupation with problems of copyright and of counterfeiting that crops up so frequently in his work fits in interestingly with this vision of insularity. Citing the legal rights over their creative "property" enjoyed by authors in England, for instance, he notes in *Suite des voeux* that "the English, shut up on an island, undoubtedly have the means of preventing counterfeits from crossing over there, but this is not the case in France" (11.210).

66. Sainte-Beuve, *Oeuvres*, p. 107.

67. Veyrenc, *Édition*, p. 84. On the importance of the Dioscuric motif to the novel, see Racault, "De la mythologie."

68. See Hoffmann, *Nègre*, pp. 92–93.

69. *Paul et Virginie*'s sentimentalizing depiction of slavery, to which I will return briefly in a discussion of the role that maroon culture plays in the text, is undoubtedly among its most disturbing features for the twentieth-century reader. Given Bernardin's commitment to (re)presenting a pastoral "state of nature," Domingue's and Marie's presence in the text clearly serves to "naturalize" what for us is a highly unnatural cultural practice. However, given the text's concomitant intention of situating this state of nature in an historically defined locale where slavery was the central fact of life, the inclusion of this practice in the text also has to be viewed as an inevitable by-product of *Paul et Virginie*'s "realism," one that places the text in contradiction with itself, but that also draws the reader's attention to the contradictions upon which this colonial (and creole) society is founded. There can, in any case, be no doubt that, as Renata Wasserman puts it, all sorts of "unexamined assumptions invade the ideal space" that Bernardin is attempting to (re)construct, and thereby repeatedly put that space into question, as when, for instance, it is stated of the twelve-year-old Paul's gardening activities that he "had beautified what the black Domingue merely cultivated" (*Exotic Nations*, p. 140)—a claim that paradoxically valorizes the secondary realm of "embellishment" Bernardin's "return to nature" was meant to combat and that marks, in Wasserman's words, the "reintroduction of the superfluous, which Rousseau abhorred but which Bernardin [here] depicts as the proper sphere of the gentleman" (p. 107; see also Neill, "Sentimental Novel"). It should be added that, notwithstanding the unproblematized but highly problematic status of Domingue and Marie in *Paul et Virginie*, to say nothing of Bernardin's own reliance on slaves while in the King's service on the Île de France, Bernardin consistently and vocally stressed in his writings the need to abolish the practice (see, e.g., *Voeux*, 11.121–29) and to transform "foreign slaves" into "compatriot farmers" (11.128), although here, as always, he adopted a gradualist position because "political revolutions should be periodic like those of nature" (11.126). He was also remarkably astute in identifying the connections between an oppressive racial politics abroad and a domestic class politics that would soon lead to the proletarianization of the French peasantry. Noting, for instance, the alliances that, on account of their respective riches, were forming between France's "grands seigneurs" and "les habitants de nos colonies," he points out how the latter were

gradually accustoming the former "to view the white people who provide them with food in France as destined to servitude, like the black people who work their properties in America" (11.123).

70. This first-person narrator clearly participates in the same discursive logic that generated a travelogue like the *Voyage*; within the terms of this travel-logic, the *je* coincides with the monological and monadic perspective of an impersonal, third-person narrator, the *on* who appears seven times in the description of the landscape that takes up the opening two paragraphs of *Paul et Virginie*. This identification is made explicit in the opening sentence of the third paragraph, where the *je* makes its first appearance: "*I* liked going to this place, from which *one* commands a stupendous view and where *one* can enjoy an extreme isolation" (p. 103; my italics). It is precisely an erosion of this monological perspective that the shift in narrators—and the dialogical situation that ensues from it—effects. In its own very limited way, this situation anticipates the narratorial dynamics that a writer like Conrad puts into play, and the relaying of relativized voices that structures a text like *Heart of Darkness*. It is this double process of relaying and relativizing that Edward Said has privileged in his consistently positive appraisals of Conrad's work. For Said, "Conrad's self-consciously circular narrative forms encourage us to sense if not the actuality, then the potential of a reality that has remained inaccessible to imperialism and which in the post-colonial world has erupted into presence" (Said, "Intellectuals," p. 54).

71. Benrekassa, *Fables*, p. 82.

72. Wasserman, *Exotic Nations*, p. 115.

73. In Racault's words, the onset of Virginie's *mal* "marks the passage from childhood to adolescence, from the idyllic universe of pastoral to the conflictual universe of the novel, from Edenic immobility to the violence of nature, from innocence to sensuality" ("Virginie," p. 389). The novelty of Racault's argument in this article lies in his claim that, far from attempting to equate "nature" and "virtue," Bernardin is actually treating them in consecutive order, and thus registering the fundamental incompatibility of two things that he is commonly thought to have viewed as being ideally identical to one another (pp. 400–403).

74. See, for instance, J. H. Miller, *Topographies*, pp. 316–37; and Kristeva, *Étrangers*, pp. 102–11.

75. Rousseau, *Oeuvres*, 3.174.

76. Leconte de Lisle, *Oeuvres*, 4.290.

77. Brathwaite, *CO*, p. 11.

78. As Racault points out, "the distant Indian Ocean colony appears as a sort of southern double of the metropole, from which it derives its name, a fact that thus imaginarily attaches the 'other' space of the island to the familiar geography of the Same" ("Ouverture," p. 92). For an extensive commentary on the role of place names in *Paul et Virginie*, see his "Système," especially pp. 410–11, where he elaborates on "this dialectic of Other and Same, of which the eponymic nomenclature is an attempt at resolving the contradiction."

79. Dating from the sixteenth century, the French word *calebasse* "is borrowed from the Spanish *calabaza*, 'fruit of a tree from the Americas whose dried shell is used as a container.'" The related word *calebassier* "was transposed to the West African baobab before coming above all to designate (1640) a tropical American

shrub" (see the Robert *Dictionnaire historique de la langue française* [Paris, 1992], p. 328).

80. Addressed by the first narrator as "father" at several points (pp. 103, 195), a role he also plays for Paul and Virginie (e.g., pp. 236, 284), the old man embodies the sort of positive authority that Bernardin often ascribed to God (the "Father of men" [3.352]) and King (the "father of his subjects," to cite Fénelon's words, quoted in the *Avis* to the *Études* [3.xix]). In order to enhance this authority, Bernardin took active steps when revising the manuscript to detach the old man as much as possible from the colonial context, editing out any mention of his original patronym (M. Mustel) and describing him as "without wife, children, or slaves" (p. 210), whereas in the earlier versions he was possessed of all three (see Veyrenc, *Édition*, pp. 101, 219).

81. This sequence revolves around Paul and Virginie's misguidedly philanthropic decision to return a "maroon Negress" to her "rightful" master and beg for her pardon (she is later brutally punished for her escape). In it, the children are exposed both to plantation culture ("they glimpsed a well-built house, sizeable cultivated fields [*plantations*], and a great number of slaves busy at all sorts of tasks" [p. 125]) and to its anticolonial double, the resistant culture of the island's maroons (a band of whom eventually help rescue them from the forest in which they get lost while returning home from the Black River). The episode took up no more than a few lines in an early version of the manuscript, and its greatly expanded role in the final, published version allows us to read it as a supplement explicitly putting into play historical forces that are incompatible with the state of prenarrative quiescence Bernardin is attempting to convey in the opening third of *Paul et Virginie*, but that are central to the story of exile and death that follows upon the revelation of Virginie's *mal*. Bernardin's belated insistence on colonial history and its violent narratives of oppression and resistance at this early point in the text can thus be construed as an (unconsciously?) self-critical commentary on his own pastoral intentions, which necessitated either the exclusion of such narratives or at the very least their relative marginalization (as one can see from the single mention of maroons in the early manuscript version, where they function as little more than attributes of the landscape rather than potential agents of narrative: "if at night the dogs barked at the approach of the black maroons Paul would go ahead of them with a stick in his hand as his only weapon but the blacks never did any damage to their crops, for they knew that these poor whites did no one any harm" [Veyrenc, *Édition*, p. 163]). The appalling fate of the returned maroon establishes a similar self-critical dynamic because it serves to trouble, without by any means supplanting, the naive discourse of philanthropy to which Bernardin and so many writers of his time were committed in their accounts of colonial relations. We are forced into reading the children's philanthropic activities as dangerously inadequate, since they lead not to the hoped for amelioration of her condition, but to a hypocritical renewal of the master's violence, notwithstanding his promises to the contrary (once the children have left, she is "chained at the feet to a wooden block, an iron collar with three hooks around her neck" [p. 136]); this troubling of the philanthropic (lack of a) solution has the merit of anticipating, although it can do no more than that, the formulation of more active responses to the master's hypocritical renewal of violence.

82. Wasserman, *Exotic Nations*, p. 108.

83. As Wasserman, in the wake of many other critics, has pointed out, Virginie's shame "signals the introduction of the social into nature, the consciousness of the eyes of the other upon the self" (*Exotic Nations*, p. 116). Virginie's investment in her *habits* can also be read as signaling a fall away from the "natural eloquence" that, in his 1789 foreword, Bernardin favorably contrasted with mere rhetoric: given her contact with the *supplementary* world of (European, colonial) society, "the costume of thought" must henceforth cover over "the body of thought," which "is always in fashion, like the body of all objects, to which [natural eloquence] can neither add nor subtract anything, because it is in its natural proportions" (p. 93).

84. Racault, "Pastorale," pp. 199–200. We find a similar recourse to the sacred at the end of Goethe's *Elective Affinities*, which concludes with the death of Charlotte's foster daughter, Ottilie, who has throughout the novel served as a Virginie-like "figure" of innocence (an innocence whose sheer figurality Goethe's narrative repeatedly exposes to view). During the funeral procession, Ottilie's young servant Nanni falls from a window and seems to be shattered in every limb, only to be "made whole again by touching the hallowed body" of Ottilie. Ottilie's saintly reputation grows "until at length there was no one so old or weak but he had sought refreshment and relief at this shrine [a vault in, significantly enough, the *restored* chapel]" (p. 298). Eduard, madly in love with her, dies a very quiet death, reminiscent of Paul's, and is buried beside her. "Peace," the narrator tells us in the novel's final paragraph, "hovers about their abode, smiling angelic figures (with whom too they have affinity) look down upon them from the vault above, and what a happy moment it will be when one day they awaken again together" (p. 300). The most obvious irony here is, of course, that Eduard ought more properly to be buried beside his lawful wife, rather than the woman whom he wanted desperately to become his mistress—novelistic closure, the "dépassement du romanesque" of which Racault speaks, proves possible only by consecrating a quasi-adulterous relationship. Less obviously, the recourse to the sacred has not alleviated the problem of novelistic (re)presentation, the confusion of reality and picture (*Bild*), that Goethe interrogates throughout *Elective Affinities*: it is *figures* of angels (*Engelsbilder*) that are looking down upon the graves, and it is this figural identity that establishes their "affinity" with Ottilie and Eduard—an affinity between the human and the sacred that uncomfortably levels the two, drawing them into a realm of (un)likeness in which the reality of the sacred has given way to a troubled awareness of its figurality.

85. See Mestry, *Analyse*, pp. 99–113.

86. Fabian, *Time*, p. 26.

87. D. A. Miller, *Narrative*, p. ix.

88. As Miller elaborates, "one of the unwelcome implications of the narratable" is "that it can never generate the terms for its own arrest. These must be imported from elsewhere, from a world untouched by the conditions of narratability. Yet as soon as such a world is invoked in the novels [of Austen and Eliot]—its appearance is necessarily brief—its authority is put into doubt by the system of narrative itself" (*Narrative*, p. 267).

89. For an argument that connects the gift of this portrait with Virginie's fall

into the realm of representation, see Benrekassa, *Fables*, p. 106; for a commentary on the role that clothing plays in this episode, see Goodden, *Complete Lover*, pp. 173–74.

90. Racault, "De l'île," p. 96. For a fuller elaboration of this point, which makes excellent use of René Girard's theories about the connections between sacrificial violence and the consolidation of communities, see his "*Paul et Virginie*," pp. 462–67. As Racault goes on to point out, in the nineteenth century *Paul et Virginie* played an important role in helping Mauritians define their cultural identity in the face of new colonial masters (the island having been captured by England in 1810); the search for identity, he adds, now takes the form of a "search for other roots, African or Asiatic, and the development of other foundational myths" (p. 466). For a very different reading of this episode, see Kadish, *Literature*, p. 66.

91. On the importance of this mutual implication of "Eros and Polis" to nineteenth-century Latin American and Caribbean literature, see Sommer, *Foundational Fictions*, passim, and my own comments on the romance genre scattered throughout Chapter 5.

92. Racault, "*Paul et Virginie*," p. 471.

93. Walcott, "Muse," p. 7.

94. Veyrenc, *Édition*, p. 447.

95. Clifford, "On Ethnographic Authority," pp. 113–19.

96. The most blatant example of this nostalgic rhetoric, which explicitly situates the story in terms of the island's "development," occurs when the narrator remarks that "on the island at that time, before trade [became a factor], there was so much honesty and simplicity that the doors of many of the houses did not need keys, and a lock was an object of curiosity for a number of Creoles" (p. 159). A basic tenet of nineteenth-century exoticism, this insistence on historical decline by no means precludes—perhaps it even invites—the altogether contrary belief in progress that so often surfaces in Bernardin's work, as, for instance, when he asserts in his lengthy 1806 Preamble to *Paul et Virginie* that "every people has had an imbecilic childhood, a credulous adolescence, and an unbridled youth," and notes of Europe's (Greek, Roman, and so on) past that "those ancient times, so praised for their innocence and their heroic virtues, were quite simply a period of crimes and errors that for the most part, happily for us, no longer exist" (p. 356).

97. Racault, "Système," p. 402.

98. The actual origin of the name is uncertain (see Racault, "Système," p. 401); in his *Historical Dictionary of Mauritius*, Lindsay Rivière speculates that this part of the island was named after a German, Wilhem Leckenig, "who was discovered by the first French settlers in the center of the island, leading a lonely life" (p. 95).

99. As a note in Pierre Trahard's edition of *Paul et Virginie* explains, "neither the *passe* in question nor the *cap Malheureux*, the island's northernmost point, nor the *baie du Tombeau* owe their names to the catastrophe of the *Saint-Géran*. They conjure it up . . . but are prior to it" (p. 228).

100. González Echevarría, *Celestina's Brood*, p. 181.

101. Condé, *En attendant*, p. 25.

102. See, e.g., Senghor, *Poèmes*, p. 193.

103. Sartre, "Orphée noir," p. 261.

104. Corzani, *Littérature*, 1.229.

105. Walcott, "Muse," p. 8.

106. Senghor, *Poèmes*, p. 10.

107. The *Robert* dictionary, for instance, cites Bernardin's *Voyage* as its first historical example of the word. For a slightly earlier entry (1765), see the "omitted articles" section of the *Encyclopédie* (vol. 17).

108. See his edition of the *Voyage*, pp. 462 and 397; see also his *Lexique*, 2.1073–74 (for *tam-tam*) and 1.125 (for *bòb*).

109. On this theory and its uses in literature, see Sollors, *Neither Black Nor White* (henceforth *NBNW*), pp. 49–54.

110. Taussig, *Mimesis*, p. 111.

111. Rousseau, *Oeuvres*, 3.192.

CHAPTER 4

1. See, for example, *Tropiques* 4 (1942), which includes one of Hearn's transcriptions ("Conte Colibri," pp. 13–19) and Aimé Césaire and René Ménil's preface to it, "Introduction au folklore martinquais" (pp. 7–11); and Daniel Maximin's postmodern (re)citation of this material in *L'isolé soleil* (pp. 159–62).

2. Letter of August 8, 1888, quoted in Stevenson, p. 173. Hearn also comments on Bernardin's "delicious idyl" in his *Two Years* (*Collected Works*, 4.94).

3. Antoine-François Delandine, quoted in the Guitton edition of *Paul et Virginie*, p. 371.

4. Hearn, "Study," p. 172.

5. Chamoiseau and Confiant, *Lettres*, p. 170.

6. The recourse to the idea of the family in Hearn's colonial discourse is not without significance for a critical evaluation of what Paul Gilroy has identified as "the growing centrality of the family trope within black political and academic discourse, [which] points to the emergence of a distinctive and emphatically post-national variety of racial essentialism" (*BA*, p. 99). Viewed closely, the use of this trope by contemporary politicians and academicians in the United States is as unnatural as Hearn's own discomforting use of it.

7. The centrality of this figure to the creolizing process is worth noting. Hearn goes on to cite the role of das as storytellers, who developed in the "white child intrusted to her care the power of fancy—Africanizing it, perhaps, to a degree that after-education could not totally remove—creating a love of the droll and the extraordinary" (p. 282). As Confiant points out in his book on Césaire, "in creole society, the da was a second mother, indeed, the real mother" (p. 67); he exploits this fact to argue for the importance on Césaire's formation of his da, who—like much of the population in the poet's native Basse-Pointe—was of East Indian descent. Césaire's ideological emphasis on Africa, and a *first* mother, is thus for Confiant a denial of the intercultural realities of his upbringing, "the total occlusion of what these days we call Créolité" (*AC*, p. 75).

8. See my *Exotic Memories*, pp. 152–57.

9. For the connections between a fear of mass society and the literature of exoticism, see my *Exotic Memories*, pp. 157–72; for an account of the specific epi-

sode on which Hearn based the climax of his novel, see Moitt, "Slave Resistance," pp. 151–52.

10. For one critical commentary on the label "person of color," see Carby, "Multicultural Wars," p. 13.

11. OED, 2nd ed., 4.8. The verb to "creolize," meaning "to naturalize in the West Indies or adjacent regions," dates from the early decades of the nineteenth century in both English and French (as we will see in Chapter 6).

12. Sharpe, Allegories, p. 46.

13. The following overview summarizes Chaudenson, Des îles, pp. 5–16.

14. See Chaudenson, "Mulâtres," pp. 32–33.

15. See Confiant, AC, pp. 260–66.

16. Domínguez cites the very different 1869 and 1929 French Larousse entries for the word "creole" as evidence of this shift from a "racially undifferentiated conception of Creole" to one in which "race was assigned primacy over local birth or cultural allegiance as criterion of classification" (White by Definition, pp. 14–15); over the course of the nineteenth century, this shift was matched in Louisiana by the transformation of the existing "ternary system of racial classification into a binary one" (p. 276), in accordance with the rigorously Manichean vision of the expanding empire into which it was being incorporated.

17. As Chaudenson has pointed out, "in the Antilles as in Réunion, there can be observed a rather frequent tendency to replace 'Creole' with names deriving from those of the territories where one lives (Martiniquan, Guadeloupean, Antillean, Réunionnais). The use of such terms evidently stems both from identitarian revendications and from an ecumenical will to transcend the social and/or ethnic divisions that the word 'Creole' almost everywhere implies" (Des îles, p. 12).

18. In the conclusion of this book, Brathwaite rather nostalgically argued (as we saw in Chapter 2) that "despite the inefficiency, despite debasements caused by slavery, Jamaica was a viable, creative entity" during the years 1770–1820, but regretfully went on to acknowledge that the "social and cultural integration" which might have occurred with Emancipation was never realized; "the physical and psychological barriers proved to be insurmountable," and with the eventual loss of "creole autonomy" and the formal reinstitution of colonial rule in the wake of the 1865 Morant Bay Rebellion, "the society became even more estranged from itself and from its several parts" (DCS, pp. 307–9).

19. Carlyle, "Occasional Discourse," p. 353. For a good postcolonial reading of Carlyle's pamphlet, see Gikandi, Maps, pp. 57–69.

20. See Young, Colonial Desire, pp. 5–6.

21. See Appiah, IMFH, pp. 13–14.

22. Toumson, Transgression, p. 267.

23. See Césaire, CP, pp. 304–5. Interestingly enough, Césaire's wife at the time, Suzanne, wrote a play loosely based on Hearn's Youma entitled Aurore de la liberté, which was produced in 1952 (see Leiris, Contacts, pp. 88, 158).

24. For Glissant's own (negative) assessment of Youma, see FM, pp. 114–15; and of Hearn's work in general, PR, pp. 84–85, where he states that it forms part of the "literature of deception" ("littérature de leurre") that prospered in the islands from the seventeenth century to the end of the nineteenth, and "that had its mo-

ments of both charm and old-fashioned grace. Coming from Louisiana to the Antilles, Lafcadio Hearn, a great reporter, and also a writer, passed on to us at the turn
of the [nineteenth] century a very embellished echo of all that." Commenting on
Gauguin and Hearn's adoption, after brief sojourns in Martinique, of Tahiti and Japan as their respective "millenary" homes, Glissant further notes that their search
for more exotic forms of cultural difference "was a sign that they would not have
been able to live nor to accept the pleasures and the suffering of creolization," particularly since in the Caribbean context creolization presented itself as "the result of
a history of oppression and apparent renunciation [of cultural traditions], and
seemed, in their eyes, as if it could only lead to affectation, dilapidation, and the
degradation of essence" (*FM*, p. 119).

25. Hearne, *Carifesta*, p. vii.

26. Walcott, "Muse," p. 2.

27. I am quoting here from the final version of this poem, republished in *Cadas-
tre* (1961), at the height of the decolonization movement; the 1948 original, a substantially longer poem, ends with the slightly different and more attenuated line
"Guinée / muette *au demeurant* [after all] d'une profondeur astrale de méduses"
(*Soleil cou-coupé*, p. 103; my italics).

28. Roget, "Littérature," p. 317.

29. Leiris, *Contacts*, p. 114.

30. Glissant, *FM*, p. 343; see also *ID*, p. 95.

31. See the untitled note on the Institut in *Acoma* 1 (1971): 136–38.

32. The acts of several conferences devoted entirely to Glissant's work
("Édouard Glissant: The New Discourse of the Caribbean" [1989], and "Horizons
d'Édouard Glissant" [1990]) are also good places to start in terms of gaining an
overview of his work: for the proceedings, see *World Literature Today* 63.4 (1989),
and Favre and Ferreira de Brito, *Horizons*.

33. Case, *Crisis*, p. 79.

34. Ménil, *Tracées*, p. 192.

35. Condé, *Roman*, 1.12–13; see also Cudjoe, *Resistance*, p. 177. For a recent
argument valorizing Glissant's "popular opacity," see Hitchcock, "Antillanité."

36. Quoted in Damato, "Édouard Glissant," p. 253.

37. See, for instance, Confiant's 1981 review of *Discours antillais*, where he critiques Glissant's generalizing views on language in general and Creole in particular:
"We are bombarded with lovely concepts such as 'forced poetics,' 'counter-poetics,'
etc. . . . without ever getting to see, or even glimpse, their content" ("Remarques,"
p. 37).

38. Chamoiseau and Confiant, *Lettres*, p. 186.

39. *Caribbean Discourse*, J. Michael Dash's very effective translation of *Discours antillais*, nonetheless plays to non-Caribbean audiences in its selection of
texts: the arguments of most "universal" application are included, whilst many of
the detailed analyses of Martinique are excluded, thus distorting an essential aspect
of the text's dynamic, which strategically alternates between a globalizing and an
insular vision. In a different but related translation strategy, as Paul Gilroy has
pointed out in *Black Atlantic*, Dash has excised Glissant's references to Deleuze and
Guattari, "presumably because to acknowledge this exchange would somehow vio-

late the aura of Caribbean authenticity that is a desirable frame around the work" (p. 31).

40. Quoted in Baudot, *Bibliographie*, p. 464.

41. Condé, "Order," p. 121.

42. Minh-ha, "Cotton and Iron," p. 335.

43. Leiris, *Contacts*, p. 113.

44. In a disturbingly enthusiastic (at least in retrospect) 1959 article on the Guinean dictator Sékou Touré, for instance, Césaire writes, "it is a fact that, at the very moment it was being born into modern history, Black Africa was lucky enough to find an effective class of administrators, by which I mean, leaders who, as with a machete, knew what it took to clear a path for Africa through the thicket of events [*ont su dans la broussaille des évenements, frayer à l'Afrique, sa voie*]" ("Pensée," p. 65).

45. See Pérez Firmat, *CC*, p. 21.

46. Case, *Crisis*, 61. For a good standard reading of this novel, see Ormerod, *Introduction*, pp. 36-55.

47. Quoted in Baudot, *Bibliographie*, p. 39.

48. Glissant, "Romancier," p. 30.

49. Fanon, *Peau*, p. 182.

50. *Tropiques* 10 (1944): 7 ("Panorama").

51. Burton, "Comment peut-on . . . ?," p. 308; see also Ormerod, "Discourse."

52. *Acoma* 3 (1972): 7.

53. For a thorough analysis of the pessimistic vision that generates *Malemort*, see Corzani, *Littérature*, 6.254-63. One need only compare Glissant's views at this point in his career with those of Italy's Pier Paolo Pasolini in the early 1970s to grasp the extent to which his apparently plausible portrait of Martiniquan society is filtered through the well-worn clichés of a critique of modernity that has been ongoing in Europe for several centuries and that has made a bad habit of reducing complex realities into simple jeremiads—as Paul Gilroy points out, for instance, when he comments on how the process of "consumption" has been simplified and demonized in critiques of "consumer society" (see *BA*, pp. 103-8). For a relevant account of Pasolini's increasingly desperate critique of modernity, see my *Exotic Memories*, pp. 188-228.

54. Case, *Crisis*, p. 62.

55. See Césaire, "Discours," pp. 500-501.

56. Wynter, "Beyond the Word," pp. 637-38. For an application of the "blocking" metaphor to post/colonial literature in general, see Harris, *Womb*, pp. 15-26.

57. Béji, *Désenchantement*, p. 110.   58. See J. M. Dash, "Roman."

59. Césaire, "Introduction," p. 15.   60. Finkielkraut, *Défaite*, p. 96.

61. Case, *Crisis*, pp. 83-84.

62. Brossat and Maragnes, *Antilles*, p. 93.

63. Burton, "Comment peut-on . . . ?," p. 311.

64. Béji, *Désenchantement*, p. 16.

65. J. M. Dash, "Introduction," p. 7.

66. Fanon, *Damnés*, pp. 7, 9.

67. Quoted in Baudot, *Bibliographie*, p. 69.

68. Burton, "Comment peut-on . . . ?," p. 304.

69. As Jacques André has pointed out, this basic dualism can also be read in terms of a gendered distinction between masculine heights and feminine lowlands: from this critical perspective, the "relentless doubling" in these early novels serves as one way of expelling a troubling ambivalence, testifying to a "never-ending attempt at distancing, at spewing out onto the other, the femininity that is inside oneself" (*Caraïbales*, p. 149). As Carole Boyce Davies has pointed out, "nationalism thus far seems to exist primarily as a male activity with women distinctly left out or peripheralized in the various national constructs" (*Black Women*, p. 12); Glissant's early work is especially marked by this masculinist drive toward nation- and/or self-hood.

70. André, *Caraïbales*, pp. 134, 117.

71. Wynter, "Beyond the Word," pp. 642-43. For a comprehensive historical account of maroons and the role they play in Glissant's work, see Cailler, *Conquérants*, pp. 67-89.

72. Burton, "*Débrouya*," p. 473. Burton has recently expanded upon this portrait in his admirable *Le roman marron* (pp. 65-103).

73. André, *Inceste*, p. 251. According to one historian, *marronnages* in Martinique—"heroic stereotypes notwithstanding"—were more typically initiated by island-born rather than by African-born slaves (*bossales*) (Prudent, "Africanité," p. 162). Regardless of the truth or falsity of this claim, it is undoubtedly significant that in a later work like *Mahagony* Glissant seems intent on emphasizing the creole identity of his maroons (see Yerro, "Trace," p. 110), thereby distancing himself from the potentially foundationalist position of his earlier novels. On foundationalism and the Rousseauesque problematic of origins in Glissant's early novels, see André, *Caraïbales*, pp. 109-69.

74. In his *Contradictory Omens*, Brathwaite significantly limits the scope of the creolization process by rigorously differentiating it from another type of "culturation" on the islands that he refers to as "maronage," which he claims was experienced by certain groups—the maroons, many poor whites, isolated individuals such as fishermen—who "for one reason or another were outside or had opted out of the System" (p. 66).

75. Césaire, *Tempête*, p. 92.

76. Marin, "Archipels," p. 86.

77. Harris, *Womb*, p. 48.

78. Cliff's ironclad distinction between Nanny and Sekesu cashes out, for instance, in another of her novels, *No Telephone to Heaven*, in the following resolutely uncomplicated definition of the word "quashee": "betrayer; from the slave Quashee" (p. 211). By contrast, one of the primary sources for her work, Orlando Patterson, defines "the Quashee personality trait" in much more complex terms as being possessed of an "evasive, indefinable, somewhat disguised and ambiguous quality" (quoted in Brathwaite, *DCS*, p. 201). Patterson's description could very well be applied to Césaire's Ariel, who is significantly absent from the starkly oppositional and male-dominated ending of *Une tempête*; this ending, which Césaire would appear to be valorizing, and which has struck at least one reader as exemplifying a "homoerotic standoff" that glaringly fails to take the question of gender into account (Kutzinski, *Sugar's Secrets*, p. 246), unintentionally substantiates the claim

that one of the main characteristics of colonial societies in the Caribbean was "a monopoly of weaponry and technical tools shared by white and black men, and that ensured many male slaves material and symbolic advantages, as well as the maintenance at the social level of their superiority over the women" (Gautier, *Soeurs*, p. 265).

79. Affergan, *Anthropologie*, p. 235.

80. André, *Caraïbales*, p. 153.

81. Quoted in Antoine, *Littérature*, p. 354.

82. Constant, *Retraite*, p. 229.

83. Burton, "Comment peut-on . . . ?," p. 306

84. Silenieks, "Maroon," p. 124.

85. Cailler, "Édouard Glissant," p. 590; Silenieks, "Pays," p. 635.

86. Chamoiseau, "Secrets," p. 37.

87. Chamoiseau and Confiant, *Lettres*, p. 64. As Chamoiseau has recently put it, "the fascination exercised by the maroon has erased from our minds the nocturnal resistance—more subtle, more indirect—of the storyteller, who deployed his words in the very heart of the slave-owner's plantation" ("Que faire . . . ?," pp. 154–55).

88. Quoted in Gilroy, *BA*, p. 59.

89. Saint-Pierre, *Oeuvres*, 3.88; for the epigraph, see 4.381.

90. Said, *Culture*, p. 96.

91. Glissant both invokes and puts into question the anticolonial appropriation of the decapitation motif when, at the very beginning of *Tout-monde*, he notes that "our history is a body without a head," and then goes on to liken this headless body to the recently (1991) vandalized statue in Fort-de-France of Napoléon's creole wife, the Empress Joséphine, "decapitated by some intrepid souls in pursuit of a (hi)story and who for that reason had it in for History [*en quête d'histoire et qui par là même en voulaient à l'Histoire*]." They must have done this, he suggests, "out of a determination to have their (hi)story told," but, intuitively recognizing that "the unhinged head of Josephine could in no way, not even by way of antithesis, help 'head' them toward their own (hi)story [*en aucune façon ne leur fournirait un chef d'histoire*], they dumped it somewhere, this head, in some cache or bog. The authorities are still looking for it" (pp. 17–18). Although his opening statement contributes to a (predictable, given his earlier work) vision of Martinique's history as "headless," the example that follows puts into question the logic of de- and recapitation that led to Josephine's beheading, and that underwrites his own apparently authoritative statement about "our history." (For a very different, straightforwardly "revolutionary" reading of Josephine's decapitation, see Le Brun, *Statue*, pp. 170–71.)

92. Hearn, *Trois fois*, p. 119. For a discussion of the role of trees in *Mahagony*, see Madou, *Édouard Glissant*, pp. 80–96.

93. Nora, "Entre mémoire," p. xix.

94. "The less memory is lived collectively, the more it needs particular individuals who turn themselves into 'memory-men' [*des hommes-mémoire*]. They are like an interior voice that would say to Corsicans, 'You need to be Corsican,' and to Bretons, 'One must be a Breton!'" ("Entre mémoire," p. xxx). It is precisely this cate-

gorical imperative, which was at the heart of his earlier writings, that Glissant puts into question in *Mahagony* by metafictively ironizing the (autobiographical) figure of the "homme-mémoire."

95. Terdiman, *Present Past*, p. 44.

96. See my *Exotic Memories*, pp. 22–23.

97. Baudrillard, *Simulacres*, p. 23.

98. See Glissant, *DA*, pp. 254–58. Glissant argues that this literature of the "other America," or of what he elsewhere refers to as "*Neo-America*" (*ID*, p. 13), is marked by an "irruptive" relation to modernity that distinguishes it both from the "consecutive, evolved" relation one finds in most European literature and the dream of perpetuating and inheriting the European tradition that characterizes many canonical United States writers like James and Fitzgerald who—unlike, say, Faulkner—are thus not (for Glissant) American writers in this broader sense.

99. As Glissant puts it, "the most terrifying thing that ethnographic thinking engenders is the will to include one's object of study in a temporal enclosure where the entanglements of lived experience are effaced in favor of [what is supposedly] a pure abiding. In this way, one ends up asserting generalizing, notional categories that do not do justice to the network of relays that makes up the real [*le lacis des relais réels*]" (*DA*, p. 28).

100. This distinction is basic to Chamoiseau and Confiant's account of Franco-Caribbean writing in *Lettres créoles*: "To the side of the colonial roads [*routes*], which lead straight ahead and are intended for some predatory use, one finds an endless number of little footpaths called 'tracées.' The work of Maroons, slaves, [C]reoles, passing through the forests and the mornes of the country, these tracées point in another direction. They bear witness to a collective spiral that the colonial project had not foreseen" (p. 12).

101. André, *Caraïbales*, p. 163.

102. Crosta, *Marronnage*, p. 13. For a more thematically oriented discussion of the shift from *Quatrième siècle* to *Malemort*, see C. Maximin, who argues that the "épico-initiatique" system of the former is subverted in the latter by the "picaro-carnivalesque" (*Littératures*, p. 325).

103. Wing, "Ecriture," p. 299.

104. Cailler, "Édouard Glissant," p. 592.

105. Glissant himself says of *Mahagony* that "my major concern was [to chart] the passage from the oral to the written, to give expression to that which can be done for a community when it masters the writing of its own story [*l'écriture de son conte*]" (quoted in Baudot, *Bibliographie*, p. 523).

106. See Hutcheon, "Circling the Downspout," p. 168.

107. These titles read like an allegorical commentary on the progression of Glissant's novelistic oeuvre: where Le Trou-à-Roches evokes the sort of vertiginous descent into the past that characterized the modernism of *Quatrième siècle*, Malendure clearly echoes the pessimistic *Malemort*, while Le Tout-Monde just as clearly looks forward to the post/pessimistic future he will envision in *Tout-monde*. On this point, see also J. M. Dash, *Édouard Glissant*, p. 168.

108. As Cailler has remarked, "from being a master figure, the Negator progressively yields his leadership position to the many unstable, impure, 'poetic' fig-

ures of resistance or endurance, sometimes even figures of betrayal and often of mere survival" ("Édouard Glissant," p. 592).

109. The fictional newspaper extract from the *Quotidien des Antilles* that serves as preface to *La case du commandeur* does feature several "eye-witness" accounts of Marie Celat's descent into madness; however, these first-person accounts are clearly being offered up as tokens of a "parodic culture" (*DA*, p. 380) from which the rest of the novel attempts to distance itself but within which it is framed (as we noted in the previous section, the novel also ends with an extract from the *Quotidien*). In a further irony, the degraded journalistic *nous* who presents and comments on these accounts for the readers of the *Quotidien* ("another neighbor, Madame P. L. ... , mother of five children, confided to us that . . . " [p. 12]) cannot be simply dissociated from the positive collective subject that the rest of the novel aspires to create: they resemble one another, if only by name, and it is precisely this sort of ironic mirroring, I am arguing, that will become the ethical cornerstone of Glissant's subsequent novels. For an extended discussion of the relation between the *je* and the *nous* in Glissant's novels, see Cailler, *Conquérants*, pp. 156–69.

110. Corzani, *Littérature*, 5.236.

111. The double meaning of *concourir*, which renders its translation problematic, is central to the agon of author and character in *Mahagony*, who are simultaneously rival and relaying voices (an antagonistic rivalry and a supplementary relaying that is itself multiplied manyfold by the presence of other narratorial actors in the novel, who are "grafted" [Mayaux, "Structure," p. 359] onto its metafictive core). Because of the extreme duplicity-multiplicity of Glissant's language, any attempt to translate-interpret him will always be marked by the same sort of partial success, and hence partial failure, that his own novelistic characters keep coming up against in their attempts at (re)presentation (as in, say, Mathieu's archival attempts at translating the past into the present).

112. The question of identity will later be figured in exactly the same terms when Mathieu speaks of "écorces d'identité" (p. 77), and likens the mahogany tree—which, in Bernardinesque fashion, stands as the novel's primary metonym for the island's identity—to "a stylized figure in which I thought I recognized those carved pieces of bark on which rough sketches of maroons used to be made [*ces écorces gravées qui jadis avaient représenté à gros traits les nègres marrons*] and that seemed such stupid imitations of African masks. Our non-identity cards." If Mathieu desires to go *beyond* "representation" and "non-identity," to envision the tree and its "Being" as a whole rather than in parts, then the novel itself—in its deconstruction of Mathieu's organizing-organicizing language—urges upon us the responsibility of also reading these partial, superficial "cartes de non-identité" in and of themselves, as well as with a sense of their "stupidly" mimetic (un)likeness to the originals they call to mind (originals that are themselves masks, belonging to the realm of appearance rather than being).

113. Deleuze and Guattari, *Mille plateaux*, p. 9.

114. C. L. Miller, "Postidentitarian," p. 12.

115. Spivak, "Can the Subaltern Speak?," p. 80; see also Kaplan, *Questions*, pp. 85–100.

116. Gilroy, *Small Acts*, p. 105.

117. These complexities are only deepened, I might add, by the fact that Glissant's contaminatory misspelling of the word "mahogany" in his title, if not in the text itself, actually returns us, approximately, to its more original and ideologically loaded spelling: an English word of uncertain (possibly Carib) etymology, it was, the *OED* tells us, "adopted into botanical Latin by Linnaeus (1762) as *mahagoni*, and is prob[ably] the source of the continental forms" (and it is this spelling of the notoriously polymorphic word that we find, for instance, in Littré). Conjoined with a productive postcolonial disordering of conventional language, this ghostly, but never more than approximate, return of the global systematizer Linnaeus and the colonial order(ing) that his name so emphatically connotes nicely figures, I would venture, the differing complicity of the colonial and the postcolonial, the modern and the postmodern, that I am examining in this book.

CHAPTER 5

1. Chinweizu, Jemie, and Madubuike, *Toward the Decolonization*, p. 256.

2. This modernist insight into the impossibility of "unmixing" in Faulkner is, of course, matched by the blindness to it of his nineteenth-century protagonists, who repeatedly attempt to deny the existence of the "something else besides" that always threatens to undermine their Manichean worldview. Centered around the verb "démêler," the following passage from Jules Levilloux's 1835 Martiniquan novel entitled *Les créoles, ou La vie aux Antilles* both exemplifies and to some extent interrogates the belief that such a worldview is sustainable. The protagonist, a young white Creole named Briolan, is being educated in France and has become friends with a certain Estève, whom he does not yet know is a métis. In the novel's second chapter, entitled "Révélation," Briolan receives a letter from his plantation-owning father (the year is 1789), which contains a lengthy warning to be on the lookout for "young people of color who have been sent to Europe by their white [guardians]." Counseling his son to avoid contracting any "dangerous friendships," he also alerts Briolan to the fact that he must not simply limit himself to "external signs" when interrogating the racial "origins" of the Creoles he befriends. Troubled by this paternal admonition, Briolan assures himself that "Estève is of the same blood as I; his features, his color, everything ... " He then questions his own sense of unease, asking himself: "Whence comes it that my mind fastens on to this question the more I linger over it? Whence comes it that I feel haunted by an insurmountable need to clear up [*éclaircir*] these vague and miserable fantasies? Whence comes it that I think I am getting to the bottom of some truth [*que je crois démêler quelque vérité*] that, up until now, was right next to me but went unnoticed?" (p. 24). The truth of Estève's mixed origins is soon revealed to Briolan, causing a brief lapse in their friendship; however, imbued with the new revolutionary principles of equality and brotherhood, Briolan soon overcomes his prejudices and commits himself even more fully to his friendship with Estève, going so far as to deceive his now widowed mother and his younger sister Léa about his friend's racial status and actively to promote Léa's marriage to an Estève who is passing as a (white) Creole. However, the possibility of an interracial romance between his sister and Estève, which would further entangle what the father believed could and ought to be kept separate, is raised

by the novel only to be violently averted: on their wedding day, Estève's origins are revealed by his former da, the diabolical Iviane, and the marriage party itself is interrupted by a murderous band of maroons led by her son Bala. Levilloux's nineteenth-century romance embraces in theory the mixing together of Estève and Léa, of métis and Creole, but remains pathetically constrained by the "clear" categories that the novel would confuse and yet upon which it also depends.

3. J. M. Dash, *Édouard Glissant*, p. 75.

4. See Bhabha, *LC*, p. 40.

5. Langford, *Faulkner's Revision*, p. 255.

6. Snead, *Figures*, p. 113.

7. Frederick Karl, among others, has remarked upon the emphatically Conradian tone of the Haitian episode (*William Faulkner*, p. 565).

8. Carlyle, "Occasional Discourse," p. 376.

9. Committed to such solutions, a "radical" critic like Marianna Torgovnick can only cite with disapproval the subtle distinctions of someone like Christopher Miller, whom she chastizes for reading Conrad as having constructed "'allegories of Africanism,' rather than writing from within the tropes of Africanist discourse" (*Gone Primitive*, p. 271).

10. Torgovnick, *Gone Primitive*, p. 158.

11. See, e.g., McClintock, *Imperial Leather*, pp. 65–66.

12. Ladd, "Direction," p. 537; this paragraph is retained virtually verbatim in her *Nationalism* (p. 142), the only substantive change coming in the last sentence where "still a logical destination for a West Indian creole at this time" has become "still a logical destination for a West Indian Creole (especially a white one) at this time."

13. Jehlen, *Class*, p. 66 (also cited in R. Saldívar, "Looking," p. 120).

14. Significantly, if understandably, C. L. R. James glosses over this twenty-year period of "colonial" domination in the first edition of *Black Jacobins*, noting simply that "the Spaniards in San Domingo had driven out the French in 1809, and restored the colony to Spain. But in 1845 they revolted for independence. Hayti helped them, and to-day Spanish San Domingo is an independent republic" (p. 312). In subsequent editions, James simply leaves out any discussion of the fate of "Spanish San Domingo."

15. Nicholls, *From Dessalines to Duvalier* (henceforth *FDD*), p. 69.

16. A year after its proclamation in Haiti, an anonymous English translation of the Code was published as *The Rural Code of Haïti; in French and English* (London, 1827). Writing in the interests of "the fixed Capitalist" (p. xviii), the translator in his prefatory letter addressed to Earl Bathurst, one of Britain's "principal secretaries of state," cites the existence of the Code as ironic proof that the British ought to resist attempts at overturning the system of slavery in their own colonies. The creation of this rigorous Code, the translator argues, bears witness to the awareness of Haiti's leaders that in an emancipated country like their own only a "military despotism" (p. xvi) could possibly maintain the conditions necessary for efficient large-scale production of goods; the Code is an open acknowledgment that "it was necessary to render a return to compulsory labour," for all that this return has been couched in a language "palatable to a people accustomed to little restraint

upon their exertions for more than thirty-six years" (p. vi). Repeatedly drawing attention to the fact that parts of this Code of Laws appear to be "copied in spirit, and almost literally translated in language, from the Consolidated Slave Law of Jamaica passed in 1816" (p. ix), the translator notes that for all intents and purposes it reinscribes the principle of slavery, albeit with great "ingenuity" avoiding any use of the word itself: "I must not call it slavery; the word is objectionable," the translator notes, "but few of the ingredients of slavery seem to be wanting" (p. xii). The Code, he continues, could "only have been framed by a legislature composed of proprietors of land, having at their command a considerable military power, *of which themselves were leaders,* for a population whom it was necessary to compel to labour, but whose prejudices against particular modes of expression, it was advisable not to offend" (p. vi). The translator concludes by skeptically putting into question any direct link between language and the reality that it purports to name, arguing that "it matters little, under what name compulsory labour be procured, whether under the name of 'slavery' or under the periphrase of 'Cultivateurs, travaillants au quart' [workers receiving one quarter of the gross produce of their labour]" (p. xvii). While one must question the political motivations that led him to make this statement, the anonymous translator's remarks nonetheless render visible the troubling genealogy of the modern contract, and the violence that subtends it— violence that Jean-Pierre Peter and Jeanne Favret, describing the evolution of peasant society in early-nineteenth-century France in one of the essays included in the Michel Foucault-edited *Moi, Pierre Rivière*..., comment on in the following terms: "The order of the new liberal society located its control mechanisms in ... the contract, the taste for property, and the incentives to work that these afford, maintaining and perpetuating thereby hierarchies and inequalities but this time with the pretence that they were 'freely' consented to. It is here that power now operates, in secret" (pp. 298–99).

17. Watt, *Rise*, p. 64.

18. Parker, *Absalom*, p. 107; see also his "Chronology," p. 193.

19. Richard Godden has recently supplied a compelling answer to this question, arguing that Haiti functions in the novel, or at least in Sutpen's narrative, as the place where he can perform "an impossible counter-revolution," separating his "primary fire" once and for all from that of an insurgent blackness by physically mastering it and thereby freeing himself from the "dependency upon the sustaining but 'unessential consciousness' of the bound man" that Hegel identified as the inescapable foundation of master-slave relations and of which Sutpen became dimly aware when he was turned away from the front door of the Virginia plantation house for which his father worked; given Hegel's analysis, such freedom can only be illusory, and the distorted memory of Haiti, through which Sutpen tries to forget "the fact that mastery is made by bound labor," actually serves as a telling reminder of his inability to repress this fact and of his consequent failure to become—or at the very least to convince himself that he has become—the self-sufficient master his design demands that he be (*"Absalom,"* pp. 713, 695, 712).

20. R. Saldívar, "Looking," pp. 104–5.

21. See Nicholls, *FDD*, p. 35.

22. James, "Appendix," p. 391.

23. Schœlcher, *Colonies*, p. 242. "The republic," he adds, "has come to a stop [*s'est arrêtée*] amidst the ruins left by the war of independence." As we will see in the following chapter, Schœlcher's dismal vision of independent Haiti can be read as having its source in a highly contentious but widely accepted (then as now) antimulatto bias.

24. In a discussion of the Haitian novelist Marie Chauvet's novel *Amour Colère Folie* (1968) that is of (indirect) relevance to my own argument here, Ronnie Scharfman has noted the importance of the oxymoron in Chauvet's violent discursive reaction to the violence of the Duvalier régime: "the oxymoron is the textualization of a profound truth in the Haitian context, which is that of the contamination of terms, and which hides, in turn, that of the contamination of races. I would even suggest," she adds, "that the violence of Chauvet's text is governed on the level of the unconscious by that unnameable oxymoron that is repressed by the appellation 'mulâtre,' and that would be 'white nigger'" ("Theorizing," p. 232).

25. Baudrillard, *Simulacres*, p. 67. In an argument that meshes nicely with my own, and that refuses to comply with Baudrillard's pessimism regarding this aporetic condition while nonetheless sharing his sensitivity to its existence, Simon Gikandi has defined "the postimperial aporia" as that state of crisis and undecidability "in which the culture of colonialism continues to resonate in what was supposed to be its negation," and argues as a consequence that "it is still within the incomplete colonial project that the postcolonial moment must be located and interrogated" (*Maps*, pp. 14, 49).

26. The novelistic territory that Defoe's *Robinson Crusoe* begins to map out in the early eighteenth century can only be discovered once the father's law has been transgressed. Crusoe speaks of the "excellent advice of my father, the opposition to which was, as I may call it, my original sin" (p. 198): this original sin is the fault that makes possible the traditional (male, bourgeois) novel, and it is one that Crusoe greatly regrets and for which he persistently attempts to atone but that a century later Rastignac, Julien Sorel, and other such protagonists of the classic Bildungsroman will positively embrace. Quentin's tentative distancing of himself from his own father and from Southern patriarchy takes place only at the level of discourse as opposed to that of the story; in this way, modernism recuperates a seemingly discredited nineteenth-century novelistic tradition and attempts to "go on" in the face of the perceived collapse of the values (such as Bildung) that this tradition once conveyed.

27. I am alluding here to Bhabha's comment that "blasphemy is not merely a misrepresentation of the sacred by the secular; it is a moment when the subject-matter or the content of a cultural tradition is being overwhelmed, or alienated, in the act of translation" (*LC*, p. 225).

28. As Sommer argues, "after the wars of Independence and the civil wars that followed in many Latin American countries, insisting on pure categories became literally self-destructive. If nations were to survive and to prosper they had to mitigate racial and regional antagonisms and to coordinate the most diverse national sectors through the hegemony of an enlightened elite: that is, through mutual consent rather than coercion. Even the most elitist and racist founding fathers understood that their project of national consolidation under a civil government needed racial

hybridization." For nineteenth-century Latin American writers, "the conciliatory genre of romance" was the ideal symbolic form for achieving this necessary consolidation and for promoting this (often admittedly limited) hybridization: "instead of keeping race, class, gender, and cultural differences pure, the 'historical' romances that came to be considered national novels in their respective countries married hero to heroine across those former barriers" (*Foundational Fictions*, pp. 123–24). Needless to say, other less conciliatory and "impure" fictions were at the foundations of both Southern and Yankee national culture.

29. Britton, "*Discours*," p. 162.

30. To cite but one example of this critical approach that is of particular relevance to postcolonial theory, Asha Varadharajan has recently attempted to "'redeem' [Gayatri] Spivak's oeuvre" from "the limits of her 'perilous' and 'interrogative' (deconstructive) epistemology" (*Exotic Parodies*, p. 84) by drawing it back into the "materialist" framework of Adorno's philosophy, which according to her "adopts for its premise deconstruction's conclusion." For Adorno, the fact that "'philosophy can always go astray . . . is the sole reason why it can go forward'" (p. 79), and it is this insistence on going forward in the face of error that separates his negative dialectics from the sort of "tropological deconstructions" that Varadharajan views as the least helpful aspect of Spivak's labor. Her nuanced critique, which "tries to come to terms with what Spivak does before faulting her for what she fails to do" (p. 84), perhaps ends up saying little more than Spivak has herself repeatedly said, but its insistence on realigning the deconstructive insights of postmodernism, and of a certain postcolonialism, with the political imperatives of a modernist philosophy that remains alert to the "heterogeneity of the material" is nonetheless remarkably close to what I am arguing is Faulkner's own epistemological stance, which rigorously attends to the "material" while emphasizing the extent to which language must betray it, the extent to which it must homogenize the heterogeneous in a faulty (re)presentation that nonetheless bears an "attenuated" (to use a favorite Faulknerian word) relation to what it cannot identify with certainty.

31. Quoted in North, *Dialect*, pp. 162–63. For an excellent account of Toomer's pioneering efforts at giving expression to this "spiritual fusion," see Hutchinson's "Jean Toomer," which rigorously critiques the consensus view that Toomer's *Cane* is a "black" text, arguing that this view is complicitous with the dualistic "American racial discourse" that Toomer spent his entire life putting into question (to the dismay of a critic like Henry Louis Gates, who has asserted, in an embarrassingly revealing fashion, that "Toomer's was a gesture of racial castration, which, if not silencing his voice literally, then at best transformed his deep black bass into a false soprano" [quoted p. 228]).

32. Karl, *William Faulkner*, p. 558. Or, as Glissant puts it in *Faulkner, Mississippi*, "Faulkner's oeuvre is a putting into question, or into vertigo, of the very thing which he kept on upholding and reinforcing in his 'civil' life: the absolute legitimacy of the South's foundation" (p. 31).

33. Walcott, *Collected Poetry*, p. 474 ("Midsummer," VII).

34. Langford, *Faulkner's Revision*, p. 255.

35. Ragan, *William Faulkner's Absalom*, p. 207.

36. L. Johnson, "*Romance*," p. 227.

No

37. In Du Bois's play, Pauline has a marginal but structurally necessary role, serving as the supercilious French counterpoint to the heroine Odette, a sincere and passionate woman who has lived virtually her entire life in Europe and whom every-body, including herself, believes to be white. Pauline and Leclerc, along with Odette and her vile husband, take up residence in the plantation house of Odette's dead fa-ther, one of the few left standing at this point in the war, and it is there that Odette eventually learns of her "true" identity: she is actually the daughter of the planta-tion owner's dead wife, Marguerite, who was herself an "octoroon" passing for white, and one of his former house slaves, Jacques. Let in on the secret by Jacques, the revolutionary leader Henri Christophe himself tells Odette, insinuating the "truth" about her racial identity that he has sworn not to reveal to her, that "an in-stinct, greater than yourself" is at work in her, generating her otherwise inexplica-ble sympathy for the revolutionaries (p. 44). Eventually made aware of the fact that—in Christophe's words—she is "one of us" (p. 11), Odette chooses at the end of the play to stay in independent Haiti, "facing her future unafraid," rather than return to France with the remnants of the defeated army and her French lover Du-val, who is killed off by Christophe's triumphant forces while on the point of mak-ing one last attempt at convincing her to flee with him back to France. In its inter-weaving of Haitian history, (heterosexual) romance, and ridiculous appeals to blood "instinct," Du Bois's play awkwardly combines the three "modes of interpreting and dramatizing historical events" that Vèvè Clark has identified in other plays about the Haitian Revolution: "representation" (mimesis of Haitian history); "mis-representation" (distortion of Haitian history: due, in this case, to a reliance on ro-mance motifs); and "re-presentation" (reworking of history: here, on behalf of twentieth-century Pan-Africanist ideology and racialist appeals to biological "in-stinct"). See Clark, "Haiti's Tragic Overture," pp. 240–43.

38. See González Echevarría, *ACPH*, p. 232.

39. Lukács, *Historical Novel*, p. 23.

40. Hoffmann, *Nègre*, pp. 135, 168.

41. Georges, by the way, is sprung from jail at the last moment and successfully escapes from the island accompanied by his forbidden love, a white plantation owner's daughter; the interracial romance that, as we will see, is so loudly invoked only to be repeatedly denied in works like Kleist's "Betrothal in San Domingo," Hugo's *Bug-Jargal*, and Maynard's *Outre-mer* is given a more optimistic ending in Dumas's novel (not surprisingly, given his autobiographical investment in Georges). Our last sight of Georges and Sara is aboard his brother's pirate ship (which also serves, ironically enough, as a clandestine slaver), bound for destinations unknown: the "conciliatory" goal of romance has been met in Dumas's novel, but only at the cost of completely divorcing the interracial love story from the narratives of social liberation and nation-building with which it had been hitherto entangled.

42. Régis Antoine has gone so far as to speculate that Carpentier may have de-rived the name Esteban from Levilloux's métis protagonist (*Littérature*, p. 101).

43. Levilloux, "Antilles," p. 20. In this article from the journal *France maritime* (published from 1834–37), Levilloux reinforces his adulatory portrait of Dugom-mier, pairing off this "republican Creole" with the "African Spartacus" Toussaint Louverture and identifying them as the "two superior men born in the Caribbean"

and who "will above all survive in history" (p. 20). Levilloux himself has certainly
not survived, leaving barely a trace in the historical record. Translator in 1830 of an
English novel by Caroline Sheridan (better known as Caroline Norton) entitled
Carwell; or Crime and Sorrow, author of several articles in *France maritime* that
are apparently related to "an unpublished work on the Caribbean," he put out
Les créoles in early 1835 (March 14), some three months before the June 27 publication of Maynard's *Outre-mer* (see *Bibliographie de la France*). General consensus about the novel has been that it is somewhat better than Maynard's, although it
clearly degenerates from "an often exact portrait of 'creole' life in the Antilles" into
a rather ludicrous *roman noir* once bloodthirsty maroons and black poisoners become central to the plot (Corzani, *Littérature*, 1.331). A brief, positive review in *La
France littéraire* (March-April 1835) stresses its energetic portrayal of the landscape, which is linked in turn to the author of *Paul et Virginie*: "reading this book,
which transports us to the Antilles, made it clear to us that Bernardin had not said
everything there was to say about this American nature, so lush and still so young"
(p. 417). Given the virtually total absence of information about this writer (he is
identified on the novel's title page simply as "de la Martinique"), critics have even
gone so far as to speculate about his "race," especially given the novel's in certain
respects positive treatment of the mulatto caste: for instance, in his multivolume history of Franco-Caribbean literature Jack Corzani stated that "everything leads one
to think that it was perhaps [authored by] an 'homme de couleur,' since his plea
rings with too much conviction for it to be only a sign of sympathetic understanding," adding that a white liberal would have been unlikely to have "systematically
limited his plea to mulattoes, while otherwise giving vent to such an obvious racism
with regard to blacks" (*Littérature*, 1.327); Régis Antoine recently identified him as
a Guadeloupean "de couleur" (*Littérature*, p. 26)—a slip of the pen by his own admission ("I had in mind his understanding of the 'gens de couleur,' nothing more"
[pers. comm.]). Étienne Léro once wrote dismissively, in the pages of *Légitime
Défense*, about Franco-Caribbean poets who "make it a point of honor that a white
person can read one of their books without guessing the pigmentation of its author"
("Misère," p. 10), and the debates surrounding Levilloux's identity nicely call to
mind (the absurdity of) questions surrounding "écriture féminine," "écriture nègre," and so on. It is safe to say, however, that Levilloux was a white Martiniquan.
Corzani has recently come to this conclusion (though it is not clear on the basis of
what new evidence), referring to him as "a white Creole in favor of slavery" ("Littérature," p. 26), and the fact that Levilloux signed his (hitherto overlooked) *France
maritime* articles "Levilloux, *créole*" would appear decisive, given the semantic stability of the word in his novel (where it always refers to the béké class). A brief unsigned review of *Les créoles* in the *Revue des Colonies* (May 1835) leaves no doubt
about Levilloux's identity: having spoken approvingly of the novel and its "portrait
of creole customs in the first years of the French Revolution," and noted that "the
style is pleasing and readable, impassioned in places, lush, 'leafy' so to speak,
sparkling in some of its descriptions," the reviewer (almost certainly the *Revue*'s
"colored" editor, Cyrille Bissette, whom I will be discussing in detail in the following chapter) asserts that "this work of a young writer whose talent can only grow is
thus noteworthy on more than one account." Showing evident familiarity with the

author, the reviewer continues: "It is good to see a Creole, born into the privileged class, tackling serious social questions that are of general concern to people these days. This philosophical and humanitarian labor can only work in favor of progress" (Volume I, Number xi: 47–48). Aside from confirming the "racial" or "class" identity of the novelist, this review also testifies to the often exceedingly narrow outlook of the hommes de couleur at this time, and more particularly of the island's mulattoes, since the novel's treatment of the black slaves and maroons can hardly be qualified as humanitarian or progressive; such blind spots, and the fault lines separating/uniting (the categories of) "black," "mulatto," and "homme de couleur" in Martinique during the 1830s and 1840s, will occupy us in the following chapter.

44. Quoted in Bouche, *Histoire*, p. 101.

45. Lukács, *Historical Novel*, p. 26.

46. Chateaubriand, *Grands écrits*, 1.215.

47. For an overview of critical interpretations of this story, see Perraudin, "Babekan's 'Brille'"; for a commentary on the role race plays in it, see Burwick, "Issues."

48. In an earlier published version of the story (July 1811), "kreolischen" appears in place of the "Creolischen" that would find its way into the second volume (August 1811) of Kleist's collected *Erzählungen*; see *Verlobung*, p. 32. This oscillation between lowercase and capital letters—one that can only be resolved (as should be evident to any reader of this book) through arbitrary and patently inadequate rules of thumb—points toward an identity that is (to appropriate Deleuze and Guattari's well-known distinction) neither "minor" (creole) nor "major" (Creole) but, rather, an unsettling mixture of the two, a mixture that is both and neither, and whose complexity (in Trinh T. Minh-ha's words) "can hardly be conveyed through such typographic conventions as I, i, or I/i" (*Woman*, p. 94).

49. Quoted in Guillén, "National Identity," p. 39, and (differently translated) Sommer, *Foundational Fictions*, p. 357.

50. See Baudot, *Bibliographie*, p. 495.

51. Hugo, *Oeuvres*, 3.51.

52. On this literature, see Benot, *Démence*, pp. 183–210.

53. Antoine, *Écrivains*, p. 181.

54. I am here borrowing Doris Sommer's description of what the heroic mulatto protagonist in Gertrudis Gómez de Avellaneda's 1841 Cuban novel *Sab* represents (*Foundational Fictions*, p. 118).

55. On Hugo's rereading of *Paul et Virginie*, see Debien, "Roman," p. 308.

56. On the recently crowned Charles X's ordinance of April 17, 1825, in which Franco-Haitian relations were officialized at great cost to the Haitians, who agreed to pay France massive indemnities for loss of property and to reduce customs charges to French vessels, see Hoffmann, *Nègre*, pp. 161–63.

57. See Toumson, "Présentation," pp. 69–72. Toumson's lengthy preface to his edition of *Bug-Jargal*, combined with the account of that novel in his *Transgression des couleurs* (pp. 206–18), provides the most thorough introduction to it.

58. On Hugo's evolving politics at this time, see Gewecke, "Victor Hugo," especially pp. 62–65.

59. Toumson, "Présentation," pp. 23–24. For one particularly fine reading of *Bug-Jargal* in terms of Hugo's ongoing "novelistic identity crisis," see Laforgue, "*Bug-Jargal*."

60. Baudelaire, *Oeuvres*, p. 702.

61. On Hugo's use of sources, see Étienne, *Sources*; Cauna, "Sources"; and Antoine, *Écrivains*, pp. 179–88.

62. Moreau, *Description*, 1.88. For good summaries of the various points of fissure in Moreau's classificatory system, see Bonniol, *Couleur*, pp. 66–72; Dayan, "Codes," pp. 60–64; and Sollors, *NBNW*, pp. 112–41.

63. Moreau goes on to note that when skin color proved an insufficient index for determining the racial category to which an individual belonged, recourse would often be made to "the features as a whole." "This index," he cautions, "in which it would be perhaps more dangerous to believe than one might think, is only visible to the eye of prejudice, and if this same eye were to journey across all of Europe, it would—using this system—find the material upon which to base a colored nomenclature; for who has not noticed while traveling in this part of the world some very dark complexions and features that seem to belong to Africa? There are certainly some quadroons who are twice as white as a Spaniard or an Italian" (*Description*, p. 87). Moreau may well have had good reason to insist on such cautions, since it would appear that he himself was one of those "supposedly 'white' *créoles* [who] were really of mixed blood, but had secured acceptance as whites" (see Nicholls, *FDD*, p. 73). Such ambiguities, though, are of no interest to Hugo who, significantly, stops plagiarizing Pamphile de Lacroix at precisely the moment when the latter begins elaborating on the difficulties posed by the individual who has only a few drops of white or black blood. For Lacroix, such limit-cases mark the end of racial difference, "for a great many people from the south of Europe, in Spain, Provence, Italy, Turkey, and Hungary, have in their blood more than one one-hundred-and-sixty-fourth drop of black blood" (*Mémoires*, p. xiv). Indeed, Lacroix goes on to argue that Moreau's system helps us understand "the nullity of hereditary pride": ignoring the ceaseless "recomposition" of the species achieved through the various generic combinations, this "orgueil héréditaire" makes us believe that we "retain the pure blood of our ancestors from sixteen generations back, whereas we only possess a small part of it. It is a good or an evil that has been divided up ad infinitum to form part of the existing community of our species" (p. xv). In the place of such rather metaphysical considerations, Hugo decisively cuts discussion short with his authoritative appeal to the "ineffable traces" of the origin of even the most light-skinned of mulattoes.

64. Moreau, *Description*, 1.76. Generalizations of this sort can, of course, be used to very different but equally racist ends, as certain nineteenth-century Haitian ideologists would discover; the mulatto writer Léon Laroche argued in 1885, to cite but one example, that "because Haiti is composed of blacks and mulattoes, the ideal president would be a *griffe* who, being 'black in skin but mulatto in origin,' would symbolise the unity of the nation" (Nicholls, *FDD*, p. 121).

65. See Toumson's edition of *Bug-Jargal*, p. 412.

66. If this error *is* unintended, its source most probably lies in the fact that in the early days of the Massiac Club the mulatto Vincent Ogé was allowed to give a

speech there, in which—"unaware of the counterrevolutionary principles of the club" (Garran, *Rapport*, 2.43)—he futilely urged solidarity between white and colored property owners to a far from sympathetic audience; leader soon thereafter of an aborted revolt in the North (October 1790) that marked the entry of the *hommes de couleur* into a civil war that had hitherto been mostly limited to the *grands* and *petits blancs*, and tortured to death the following year (February 1791), Ogé makes several posthumous appearances in Hugo's novel, the most "representative" of which will be analyzed shortly.

67. Elam, *Romancing*, pp. 61, 68.

68. Toumson, "Présentation," pp. 77, 78; and his *Transgression*, pp. 206–11. While admitting that a character like Habibrah "appears as a failed union of opposites, one from which nothing good or beautiful can ensue," Kathryn Grossman contests Toumson's claim that Hugo's Manicheanism "is impervious to the union of opposites," valiantly but, I think, inappropriately attempting to read the character of Bug-Jargal as the embodiment of a "radically utopian vision" (*Early Novels*, pp. 89, 102): an "African, European, and American all at once, a marriage of what is best—humanity's past, its present, and its future" (p. 101). For a recent (1997) discussion of the role of hybridity in *Bug-Jargal*, see Gaitet, "Hybrid Creatures."

69. As one of Hugo's authoritative footnotes maliciously puts it, in the early years of the revolt Toussaint "had been schooled by Biassou" (p. 151), and Hugo, in turn, models Biassou in several instances after Toussaint: for instance, as Governor-General of Saint-Domingue, Toussaint is reputed to have informed certain candidates "unsuited for public office" that a knowledge of Latin was a requirement for the job (see Price-Mars, *De Saint-Domingue*, p. 88), and Biassou uses this same tactic with a would-be black officer (see pp. 145–47). In Glissant's play *Monsieur Toussaint*, the maroon leaders Macaya and Macandal rise from the dead to confront Toussaint, who is languishing in the French prison cell where he will eventually die, with the fact that in the early years of the Revolution he betrayed the Spanish and Biassou, "your brother-in-arms, a man of your color." Toussaint responds: "When I went up into the hills, I saw disorder and assassination. I fought against Biassou, he was acting like a slave by pillaging without making war. I make war, point by point. This patience of work, when the worker is free; I want us to learn that!" (pp. 41–42). Throughout the play, Glissant provides a double portrait of Toussaint: he is at once Toussaint Abréda, the former slave, and Toussaint Louverture, the "general of the rebels"; in this passage, Toussaint's desire for order and consequent distrust of Biassou's rapacity are attributable not to one side or the other of his split identity but, ambivalently, to both.

70. The novel was also turned into a melodrama by A. J. N. de Béraud and L. F. G. Rosny in 1798; see Étienne, *Sources*, pp. 74–78, for its possible influence on Hugo.

71. As Gobineau put it in his *Essai sur l'inégalité* (1853–55), what the black man wants "is to eat, to eat to excess, in a fury; there is no disgusting carcass that is unworthy of being stuffed into his stomach" (p. 340).

72. Ogé is mentioned once in the conte when Bug, revealing his own family history to Delmar, notes that his father, the former king of Gamboa, was killed "on the wheel" along with Ogé, whom the reader might very well assume was also black

(p. 245). This passage is retained in the 1826 version but takes on a new meaning, given the explicit and insistent identification of Ogé with a negatively portrayed mulatto caste (pp. 70, 108, 136): the black slave's anachronistic presence alongside Ogé and the other leaders of the mulatto revolt now has the effect of partially ennobling and legitimizing that revolt, just as Bug's participation in the events of August 1791 justifies and redeems, albeit with great ambivalence, the butchery perpetrated by the likes of the ignoble sacatra Biassou.

73. Girard, *Mensonge* (henceforth *MR*), p. 28.

74. Prendergast, *Order*, p. 18.

75. As Descourtilz put it in his 1809 *Voyages d'un naturaliste*, "these brigands, with their gift for mimicry [*par un génie imitateur*], were to Saint-Domingue what the Jacobins were in France" (3.178).

76. Grossman, *Early Novels*, p. 87 (and, more generally, pp. 81–89).

77. This last example, of course, is one that will necessarily give pause to a postcolonial reader, who in at least this one instance will share the colonial author's skepticism—and perhaps even contempt—for such revealingly ill-chosen names. Noting in his *Black Jacobins* that "Jean François entitled himself (in the fashion of European colonial governors to this day) Admiral, Generalissimo and Chevalier of the Order of St Louis, while Biassou, after a quarrel with Jean François, assumed the title of 'Viceroy of the Conquered Territories'" (p. 73), C. L. R. James speaks of such acts of self-representation as "absurdities," to be contrasted with the approach of a Toussaint Louverture, whose writings, James claims, were always characterized by "neither bombast nor rhetoric but the simple and sober truth" (p. 163). Biassou thus produces a similar anxiety in Hugo and James, both of whom attempt to put an end to the distressing "absurdities" of rhetoric, its mimetic figurations, in the name of their differing "truths."

78. Haranguing his troops, Biassou puts forward an argument that notably anticipates Glissant's Pan-Caribbean vision: "Liberty for all men! This cry, launched from *Quisqueya* ["the former name of Saint-Domingue," as Hugo's footnote tells us], reverberates in all the islands, from Tobago to Cuba, awakening them. It is the leader of one hundred and twenty five maroons from the Blue Mountains, a black man from Jamaica, Boukman, who has raised the banner of revolt among us. A victory was his first act of fraternity with the blacks of Saint-Domingue" (pp. 114–15).

79. For a comprehensive account of the "bluish tinge in the halfmoon" motif that Hugo here helps popularize, see Sollors, *NBNW*, pp. 142–61.

80. Tarbé, *Rapport*, pp. 8, 12.

81. James cites this letter as an example of the fact that "political treachery is not a monopoly of the white race, and this abominable betrayal so soon after the insurrections shows that political leadership is a matter of programme, strategy and tactics, and not the colour of those who lead it, their oneness of origin with their masses, nor the services they have rendered" (p. 83). For James, the colonists' rebuffal of the slave leaders' offer was a crucial turning point for another of the letter's cosignatories, Biassou's aide-de-camp Toussaint, who would henceforth refuse to involve himself in such vile compromises: "then and only then," James asserts, with a dramatic simplicity that reminds one of the extent to which *The Black Ja-*

cobins, too, is a sort of historical novel, "did Toussaint come to an unalterable decision from which he never wavered and for which he died" (p. 85).

82. Compare Lacroix, *Mémoires*, 1.253, 252. For further commentary on this pastiche, see Étienne, *Sources*, pp. 121–23; and Mouralis, "Histoire," pp. 56–57.

83. On the use of different languages in *Bug-Jargal*, see Kadish and Massardier-Kenney, *Translating*, pp. 178–81.

84. Thornton, "African Soldiers," p. 73.

85. Addressing the French National Assembly in early 1793, Charles Tarbé noted the importance of this disquieting confederation in the early days of the slave revolt: "a great number of hommes de couleur had joined with the rebels and were guiding the manoeuvres and the operations of the Negroes, who are always less dangerous when left to their own brutal and impetuous lack of experience" (p. 3). Comments such as these undoubtedly fed into Hugo's decision to "mulatto-ify" the slave revolt—a decision that would cause him to omit any mention of the fact that, as Tarbé himself pointed out, by the end of 1791 in the North, "virtually all the hommes de couleur who had joined with the rebels [had] yielded to entreaties and rallied round the banner of the law, which they have not deserted since that time" (p. 22).

86. On the intertextual link between the *pavillons* of Marie and Virginie, see the relevant editorial note in *Oeuvres complètes*, 2.590.

87. Although here is not the place to develop this point, it is worth keeping in mind the extent to which Hugo's anxieties about race in *Bug-Jargal* are also anxieties about gender. In a novel that revels in racial categories, the absence of any mention of those *mulâtresses* so familiar to nineteenth-century French readers as the bearers of a dangerously seductive and eminently Antillean sensuality is, to say the least, glaring. The threatening, theatrical masculinity of a mulatto like Biassou is matched by the "demonic" (p. 102) and thoroughly Africanized femaleness of the *négresses* who briefly take center stage in the novel before d'Auverney is led to Biassou's cave. A group of women form a circle near d'Auverney, who has been tied to a tree by his black captors; he recognizes them as being *griotes*, wives of the griots, those "Negroes gifted with some kind of crude talent for poetry and improvisation that resembles madness" and that one finds "among the blacks of various regions of Africa" (p. 100). (Hugo's source for this information, incidentally, is the Abbé Grégoire's 1808 *De la littérature des Nègres* [pp. 185–86], which he plagiarizes shamelessly, while at the same time transforming the negrophile abbé's positive portrait of black creativity into a negative one that emphasizes its "demonic," "parodic," and sexualized nature: we learn, for instance, that the griotes are in the habit of accompanying their husband's "barbaric songs" with "lewd dances," which offer "a grotesque parody of the bayadères of Hindustan and the Egyptian almas" [p. 100], whereas Grégoire simply notes that these women "ply more or less the same trade as the Almas in Egypt and the Bayadères in India.") The griotes have gathered together to cast spells but their "strange invocations" and "burlesque grimaces" cause d'Auverney to break out into "uncontrollable laughter" ("le fou rire"). Offended, "all the Negresses" jump up and run menacingly toward him ("I have never seen a gathering of more diversely hideous figures," d'Auverney states, "than all those furious black faces with their white teeth and their white eyes filled with

bloody-red veins" [p. 101]). Divesting themselves of the few clothes they are wearing, the griotes then begin to perform "that lascivious dance that the blacks call *la
chica*," as a prelude to ripping him apart. Saved at the last moment, d'Auverney is
then led away to his interview with Biassou, where the psychosexual anxieties that
briefly flare to the surface in this episode are submerged in, and yet no doubt continue to overdetermine, the ideological anxieties generating Hugo's aggressively negative portrayal of mulattoes.

88. The theatrical name Pierrot, one should add, was also that of a rebel leader
who came to prominence in 1793 and about whom Hugo would have read in
Lacroix's *Mémoires* (see, e.g., 1.245–46); it is, moreover, also inscribed in the name
of the fort Crête-à-Pierrot that was besieged by Leclerc in 1802 and defended by
Dessalines in "one of the most remarkable feats of arms in the history of the
Napoleonic wars" (James, *BJ*, p. 266; described in great detail by Lacroix, 2.147–
76, and Descourtilz, *Voyages*, 3.352–73).

89. Senghor, *Liberté*, p. 126.

90. Toumson, "Présentation," p. 45.

91. Moreau's description of the griffe emphasizes an erotic dimension that has
been completely sublimated in Hugo's portrait of Habibrah: for Moreau, the griffe
"is so favored by nature that it is very rare to see one who does not have an agreeable countenance [*figure*] and pleasing features as a whole. He has all the advantages of the mulatto, but none of the other combinations generated by colonial couplings [*par les mélanges coloniaux*] (and this holds true of both sexes) results in
progeny that is so given over to amorous impulses." With a mixture of fascination
and distress, Moreau goes on to note that "continency in an individual of this shade
is a very rare thing indeed—perhaps even unheard of—and, doubtless as a consequence of this impossible-to-contain [sexual] disposition, the regrets that accompany pleasure are even more bitter when they are procured by this class." Perhaps
fearing that he has made the griffe sound all too seductive, Moreau concludes his
account in a very curt manner, remarking that "it can also be noted that in general
Griffes are often liable to offend one's nostrils" (*Description*, p. 80).

92. Toumson, "Présentation," pp. 76–77.

93. See Prendergast, *Order*, p. 11.

94. Sainte-Beuve, *Pour la critique*, pp. 141–42 ("Quelques vérités sur la situation en littérature" [1843]). The final sentence of my epigraph from Sainte-Beuve,
"the portrait fills in that gap," is a translation of "le portrait y supplée."

95. Taking the story forward from the nineteenth century to our own postmodern fin de siècle, in which ethnic and racial tags still add as much "value" to (or
subtract it from) human experience as they did in the days of Moreau de Saint-
Méry, we can note that "griffe" has since the 1950s acquired a new, and in the context of my discussion highly ironic, meaning in French: namely, designer label (see
Friedman, "Narcissism," pp. 349–53).

CHAPTER 6

1. Garran, 2.325–26.

2. See P. Hulme, "Locked Heart," for a brilliant analysis of the ways in which

Rhys's highly autobiographical novel reworks and yet remains entangled in the family histories and ideological squabbles of her nineteenth-century creole ancestors.

3. To be an *électeur* (eligible to vote) one had to be at least twenty-five years old, pay 300 francs worth of direct taxes or "give proof of possessing in the colony movable or immovable property worth some 30,000 francs"; double these amounts were necessary in order to be an *éligible* (qualified for election). The first elections in Martinique involved the participation of only twenty-five colored électeurs (out of a total of 750) and a dozen éligibles (out of 371 total), higher numbers but lower percentages than for the Guadeloupe elections (ten électeurs out of eighty-two; three éligibles out of thirty-five). The total population of Martinique in 1831 was 119,078 (9,362 whites, 23,417 free coloreds, 86,299 slaves) and of Guadeloupe 112,131 (10,596 whites, 10,772 free coloreds, 90,763 slaves); by 1848, the number of free people of color had risen dramatically (reaching over 36,000 in Martinique) while the white population remained stable. See Élisabeth, "Domination," p. 396; Bouche, *Histoire*, pp. 101-2; and Forster and Forster, *Sugar*, p. 24.

4. After using it as the epigraph to her 1981 novel *July's People*, Gordimer elaborated on Gramsci's remark in her essay "Living in the Interregnum" (1982): "the interregnum is not only between two social orders but also between two identities, one known and discarded, the other unknown and undetermined" (*Essential Gesture*, pp. 269-70).

5. Adolphe Granier de Cassagnac, "Colonies françaises: De l'esclavage et de l'émancipation," *Revue de Paris* (September 1835): 106.

6. Quoted in Bonniol, *Couleur*, p. 88.

7. Tomich, *Slavery*, p. 108.

8. Antoine, *Écrivains*, p. 219.

9. Antoine, *Écrivains*, p. 214.

10. D'Eichthal and Urbain, *Lettres*, p. 60.

11. On the *Revue des Colonies*, see Antoine, *Écrivains*, pp. 214-16; and Pâme, "*Revue*." Pâme is also the author of a lengthy dissertation on Bissette—*Cyrille Bissette, 1795-1858* (Thèse de 3ᵉ cycle, Paris I, 1978)—that I have been unable to consult; based on inquiries made there in September 1996, the Sorbonne's copy would appear to be either lost or misfiled.

12. *De la situation*, pp. 6-7.

13. For more details on the "affaire Bissette," see Élisabeth, "Domination," pp. 389-91; Mesnard, "Mouvements"; Nicolas, *Histoire*, 1.320-27; and Pâme, "Affaire"; for an account of their punishments, see Bissette's 1843 *Réfutation*, pp. 19-21.

14. For details on these legal proceedings, see Bissette and Fabian, *Dénonciation*.

15. Responding some twenty years later to the confiscation by colonial authorities of a number of "incendiary" brochures including his own *Lettre à M. Agénor de Gasparin* (an abolitionist member of the Chamber of Deputies), and referring to this seizure as "a pale parody of the politico-judicial drama acted out by the colonists of Martinique some twenty years ago," Bissette would stress the ironic results of such acts of colonial censorship: when the authorities condemned *De la situation*, forbidding any black or mulatto to read it, "this famous brochure, which up until then had only been read by a very small number of people (as I can attest from

personal experience), was distributed in the thousands throughout the colony, despite its being condemned, despite the injunctions and the prohibitions of the AU-THORITIES. . . . There was not one black man, not one mulatto, who did not hold it an honor to have in his possession a copy of the document that had been burned by the executioners. There was not one black man, not one mulatto, who did not want to read it at the time and pass it on to his friends!" (*Liberté*, pp. 12, 6, 7).

16. Bouche, *Histoire*, p. 102.

17. The following passage from a letter to the Ministre de la Marine sent by the colonial delegate Fleuriau in 1831 provides a good example of the entanglements Bissette's discursive strategy created: "A letter from Monsieur Bissette, addressed to Your Excellency, has just been passed on to me. This letter would no doubt not deserve a refutation were it not for the fact that it has been sent to the printer's; it will then be distributed to the Deputies, and the slanders that it contains, the audacity with which it distorts well-known facts, leave me no choice but to deny everything in it that has to do with Martinique" (*Lettre*, p. 5).

18. Jennings, "Cyrille Bissette," p. 50, as well as pp. 57–60.

19. In a review of two 1993 studies of Césaire, Confiant's *Traversée paradoxale* and Roger Toumson and Simonne Henry-Valmore's *Aimé Césaire: Le Nègre inconsolé*, Richard D. E. Burton ably identifies the way this rhetoric shapes both works. On the one hand, the pro-Negritude, anti-Créolité biography of Toumson and Henry-Valmore has as its subtext the question, "How can a twisted-up *chabin* [a type of métis] like Confiant understand the pure, authentic *mot nègre* of a pure, authentic *Nègre* like Césaire?" ("Two Views," pp. 142–43). On the other hand, "the whole of *Traversée paradoxale* exudes an almost demential hatred of 'la mulâtraille' who, along with 'les dix familles békées,' are said to have a stranglehold on the local political scene thanks to 'le puissant réseau de solidarité qu'elles entretiennent' ['the powerful network of solidarity they maintain'] (p. 82), and so on. Not since Souquet-Basiège's (white) racist 'classic,' *Le préjugé de couleur aux Antilles* (1883), has work by a Martinican author—himself, ironically, of mixed race—been so full of hatred for 'mulattos,' whether socially or biologically defined" (pp. 145–46). See also Le Brun, *Statue*, pp. 68–70.

20. Gilroy, "Route Work," p. 21.

21. Bissette, *Examen*, pp. 8, 12.

22. Indeed, a short story by the New Orleans–born Victor Séjour entitled "Le mulâtre" (III.ix: 376–92; reprinted in the *Revue de Louisiane* [1972], and translated for publication in the *Norton Anthology of African American Literature* [1997]) has been recently identified as "the first published short story by an author of African ancestry born in the United States" (Sollors, *NBNW*, p. 165).

23. Jennings, "Cyrille Bissette," p. 54. As Jennings notes, "the authorities did everything possible to impede [the *Revue*'s] circulation, while in France itself its subscribers numbered a mere 250 in 1840."

24. This particular article from the *Revue* ends with an admission of failure, by pointing toward the possibility of a literature of the future that would transcend the "ineloquent" limits of its own workmanlike prose: "Ah! if one day an eloquent pen, tearing away the funereal veil that covers our colonies, were to relate the story [*retraçait l'histoire*] of these traders in flesh and their domination, were to conjure up

from the depth of the grave the sorry victims that are each day piled up there, no other country defiled by tyranny would offer such horrific reading. Everything we read about Mezentius, Caligula, Louis XI, everything that our hearts refuse to believe because it is too degrading for humanity, finds itself surpassed in the nineteenth century by Frenchmen living overseas" (p. 13). This future literature, in order to come into being, would have to transcend the "exteriority" built into such historical analogies (Etruscan tyrants, Roman emperors, and so on) and discover a way of rendering the Caribbean on and in its own terms, of giving expression to that "interior vision" of which the authors of the *Éloge* speak (p. 23). If, as we will see, *parodic (re)citation* is the most obviously postcolonial aspect of Bissette's style, there are nonetheless many anticipatory traces in his work of a more identifiably Martiniquan vision. Nowhere is this more evident than in his striking references to the "cemetery of Grosse-Roche," where military tribunals and law courts "have dispatched twenty or thirty corpses at a time" (I.iii: 10). Reminding his readers in a footnote that this cemetery "reserved for victims of torture is at the foot of a morne, on the sand, at the edge of the sea that laps against it and that has often unearthed newly buried corpses from their shallow graves," he returns to this image later, asserting that "to arrive at our goal, as indiscreet as the waves of the sea, we will prize open the graves of Grosse-Roche; we will dig around in this satanic archive. Each issue of the *Revue des Colonies* will examine a judicial decision from Martinique or Guadeloupe; [like Hercules] we will drag the new *Cacus* from his lair, and we will expose him to the public, which will be the instrument of our revenge" (pp. 12–13; "pour parvenir à notre but, aussi indiscrets que les flots de la mer, nous ouvrirons les tombeaux de la Grosse-Roche; nous fouillerons dans ce greffe satanique; chaque numéro de la *Revue des Colonies* examinera un arrêt de la Martinique ou de la Guadeloupe; nous arracherons de leur antre ces nouveaux *Cacus*, et nous les jetterons à la publicité, chargée de nous venger"). Notwithstanding the continued recourse to an external rhetoric (Satan, Cacus), it is impossible not to read this as an early example of Glissant's call to "live the landscape with passion. Free it from what is indistinct, dig around in it [*le fouiller*], kindle it in our midst. Find out what it signifies in us" (*IP*, p. 245).

25. In his three-volume history of the Antilles, written a decade before the 1833 charter, Eugène-Édouard Boyer-Peyreleau gives voice to this "diviser pour régner" strategy in exemplary fashion: "The number of individuals of mixed-blood is growing every day, and these individuals share in all the qualities of the two colors to which they owe their existence; sober, suited to the wear and tear of physical labor, they have nothing to fear from the influence of the climate into which they were born. Their demonstrated attachment to the native soil can only be real, what could they hope for elsewhere? Friends of the whites as much by inclination as out of self-esteem, they act as a barrier separating [the whites] from the blacks, whose natural adversaries they are. Why not take advantage of this whole situation and earn some points by getting a head start on the future, through regulating their fate by means of wise and provident laws?" (*Antilles*, 1.123–24). These laws, he adds, are all the more timely given the fact that in Saint-Domingue, Mexico, and "in all the areas adjoining the Caribbean, people of color are heads of state, or share in all political rights" (1.126), and all the more necessary given that "only offensive treatment and

persecution can provoke them into uniting with the Negroes against the whites" (1.127).

26. To cite only one example of a debunking of stereotypes, which demonstrates a commitment to archival research that is on frequent display in Bissette's work: ridiculous claims like those made by Granier de Cassagnac in the *Revue de Paris* (September 1835) that "there is probably no example of a mulatto born from a white woman and a black man" (p. 123) are countered by documentation gleaned from the birth registers of Grand'anse. "All that remains for us to do," he concludes, "is to apostrophize the white aristocrats in our usual manner: 'We are the result of the violence and seduction exercised upon young black slave girls, or of the whims and infidelity of white women; if there were some disgrace for us in these tainted origins [*dans ces souillures de notre origine*], we would throw it all back upon the responsible parties; but we are no more afflicted by such origins than are the colonists by their status as the descendants of pirates who turned themselves into noblemen" (VII.iii: 98).

27. Orr, *Headless History*, p. 11.

28. Schœlcher, *Des colonies*, p. 187.

29. Aside from its strongly abolitionist argument, *DCF* is most often remembered for its suggestion that the Caribbean might one day become the site of "little independent republics . . . which would be joined in a confederation by a common interest and would have their own navy, industry, arts, and literature" (p. 213). This visionary glimpse of the "secret and distant destinies of the Caribbean sea" (p. 214), which anticipates the perspective of Antillanité, is itself inseparable from a vision of métissage apparently at odds with the *anti*mulatto perspective that Bissette, as we will see, attributes to Schœlcher. Expanding on the idea voiced in his 1840 *Abolition* that "the mixing of races should end up laying to rest forever all the antipathies based on color" (p. 177), Schœlcher notes that "the confederated islands of the West Indies will have a mixed population; for the slave trade having been halted for good, the race that today remains there will, as the centuries progress, end up blending into the mixed blood race through its continual alliances with it, as will the white race, which despite new waves of emigration will always be too few in number to remain a species apart." Evoking the sort of transcendent argument for métissage that we saw to be absent in Bissette, Schœlcher continues: "if the white man and the black man form a duality, if (as it has been bizarrely claimed) [they] are the male and the female of humanity, who must through their union and the harmony of their respective qualities, create a genus partaking of the merits of its two progenitors [Schœlcher is referring here to the theories of Gustave d'Eichthal, secretary of the Société Ethnologique, founded in 1841], then one can expect to see emerging from the West Indies new marvels that will astonish the world" (p. 214).

30. While readily acknowledging the existence of antiblack prejudices and actions on the part of individual mulattoes, Bissette refuses to generalize them in the manner of Schœlcher: "Far be it from us to deny that among the mulattoes there are not some who merit the anathema that Monsieur Schœlcher casts down upon the mass of them, and who keep their distance from blacks. One unfortunately finds such types in each of our four colonies [Martinique, Guadeloupe, Cayenne, Bour-

bon]. Yes, a few wretches forget themselves to the point of being ashamed of their black origins! But let us hasten to add, to the honor of humanity, to the honor of Negroes and mulattoes themselves, that this is a very small part of the mulatto population" (pp. 72–73).

31. See *Réponse*, pp. 22–25.

32. Quoted in Bonniol, *Couleur*, p. 89. A few years later, by which time he had come to view the planters as absolute "incorrigibles," Schœlcher himself would accuse the colonial minister Mackau of having become "créolisé" (see *Histoire*, p. 161).

33. Nicholls, *FDD*, p. 79.

34. Quoted in Nicholls, *FDD*, p. 79.

35. On these debates, see Nicholls, *FDD*, pp. 87–102.

36. Bissette's commentary on Ogé's purchase of this cross provides an interesting gloss on Hugo's scornful treatment of it: "As for that error of Ogé's, to have attached, in 1790, more importance to a cross than it was worth, this is a weakness that this unfortunate man shared with a lot of people, who would even now imitate him if they could; for, despite the prejudice that these days attaches to those superficial honors, despite the jibes of the *Charivari*, the *Corsaire*, and the *Caricature*, there are still very few people who, after having had a good laugh over the caricatures in these witty journals, find it in themselves to ... refuse a cross if it is conferred on them. I know some friends of Monsieur Schœlcher's who, not so long ago, were going to be decked out in one and received it with tears ... of joy—and on a railway track no less! When everything is said and done, what does it all prove? Was Ogé—a *pariah* from the Antilles—wrong or right, in 1790, to share a prejudice that still prevails today among the ablest public figures in Europe?" (pp. 39–40). Bissette then pursues a possibility that Hugo's text itself uneasily raises in other contexts—namely, that one can to a certain extent control the inauthenticity that in turn controls one: "Perhaps Ogé, in *decking himself out* with these superficial decorations, the *embroidered uniform* and the *Limburg cross*, appraised these baubles at their intrinsic and moral worth. But, having to act on the masses, might he not have wished, perhaps, to impress them, to dazzle their senses? Men are not easily cured of their prejudices. What great harm if, in 1790, in order to destroy prejudices, Ogé resorted to using the very same means suggested by Monsieur Schœlcher in 1839 to eradicate them [Bissette here provides a vague footnote reference to *Abolition de l'esclavage*]?" (p. 40). Bissette further cites the early historian of the Revolution, Garran de Coulon, who noted that while it was altogether possible that Ogé had bought "a diploma from the Prince of Limburg" in order to gain credit among his cross-loving compatriots, "the one produced by the colonists during the debates [after the insurrection], rather than having been taken from Ogé, as they wanted people to believe, would appear to have been sent to the colony, along with his portrait, by the Massiac Club [on June 19, 1790], which had held up the original at the chancellery of the Prince of Limburg before it had been sent off." Garran de Coulon continues: "These critical observations may seem excessive to some people, but they should keep in mind the fact that all we know about the Ogé affair comes to us through the accounts of his mortal enemies, and that it is entirely their fault if, due to the secrecy of their procedures and their rulings against freedom

of the press, they deprived truth's scrutineers of the means of obtaining any certain knowledge about it. Leaving aside the most outrageous proofs of immorality with which one can too often reproach the agents of the colonial assemblies in France, everything indicates that, in this unfortunate case in particular, they engaged in the most criminal sort of manoeuvres in order to defeat the defenders of the hommes de couleur" (quoted pp. 64–65; see Garran, *Rapport*, 2.69–70).

37. Arguing from the perspective of a landowner who wants to be part of the Massiac Club's deliberations and find ways "to ward off the disaster that threatens us," Ogé (whom Garran de Coulon affirms was "perhaps the only colonist at the beginning of the Revolution who deigned to cast a pitying eye upon the black slaves" [*Rapport*, 4.20]) nonetheless explicitly advocated liberty for hommes de couleur and slaves alike: "This Freedom, the greatest, the foremost of possessions, is it meant for all men? I believe so. Should one give it to all men? I believe so also" (Ogé, *Motion*, p. 5).

38. Quoted in *Réponse*, p. 121. (Angered by Bissette and his political allies' constant references to this article, Schœlcher eventually reprinted it in his 1849 book-length assault on Bissette [*Vérité* (1849), pp. 288–97] and patiently explained away the offending passages, as we will see toward the end of this chapter.)

39. As he put it in his first *Réfutation*, Schœlcher "wants to pass himself off as the *patron* of the black and yellow races; a patronage that all of us reject, for we want friends and defenders of our cause, and not *patrons*" (p. 62).

40. Bissette, *Réponse*, p. 122.

41. Valesio, *Novantiqua*, p. 57.

42. In a similar vein, the escape from Martinique to Sainte-Lucie of sixteen slaves belonging to "Monsieur de Meynard de Queilhe, father of that illustrious young man who wrote a two-volume novel that nobody has every read," is attributed to the possibility that "Monsieur Louis de Meynard de Queilhe, nobleman of Quercy, wanted to make them read *Outre-mer*" (II.xi: 484).

43. I have gleaned these details from the Vauclin parish records (Archives de la Martinique). Maynard is generally assumed to have been rather older: the index note on him in Hugo's *Correspondence familiale*, for instance, gives his date of birth as 1800 (p. 929). Régis Antoine's comprehensive *Les écrivains français et les Antilles* contains a brief and highly misleading biographical entry on him (p. 191).

44. Letter of August 21, 1833, quoted in Hugo, *Oeuvres*, 4.1108; for details of the controversy, see Juin, *Victor Hugo*, pp. 704–6. Maynard's comments regarding Sainte-Beuve are worth quoting here, since they are doubtless the most influential words he would ever write: "Monsieur Sainte-Beuve lacks constancy in his affections and perseverance in his ideas; he lets himself be seduced by whatever is fashionable, he is swayed by whatever rumors are floating about. One day an enthusiast of Ronsard and the next day a devotee of Monsieur de Sénancour, he is always irresolute, wondering why contemporary criticism lacks a central point of view, when he, one of its leading lights, flickers with the slightest breath of wind!" (July 26, 1833: 257). Maynard's other contributions to *L'Europe littéraire* include a series of ten intelligent and wide-ranging articles on French painting and the 1833 Salon— even if, as Sainte-Beuve noted, his preference for Horace Vernet over Ingres, "who will not last" (April 8, 1833: 69), seems rather unfortunate! Among his other arti-

cles are a laudatory assessment of Hugo in "Sur la préface de Marie Tudor" (November 28, 1834: 245–48), as well as a number of stories, including "Un goût de femme" (September 26, 1833: 285–92) and several others to which I will refer in passing during my discussion of Maynard. He also published extensively in the *Revue de Paris*, most notably a lengthy article entitled "Du théâtre et des théâtres" (July 1834: 230–56, and August 1834: 5–43) where he proclaimed that "up to this point, when it comes to our theater only one man has counted, Monsieur Victor Hugo" (p. 35): accompanied by a critique of Alexandre Dumas, this claim contributed substantially to an increase in tensions between Hugo and Dumas. Noteworthy among other articles published in the *Revue de Paris* are his reviews of Hugo's *Claude Gueux* (August 1834: 283–84) and Musset's *Un spectacle dans un fauteuil* (September 1834: 273–86), and a biting political allegory entitled "Notre ami le juste-milieu" (August 1835: 84–110).

45. Hugo, *Oeuvres*, 5.1120. As evidence of Hugo's appreciation of Maynard's character and talents, the entirety of this letter's effusive opening paragraph is worth citing here: "We still await you. Your letter, so kind and charming, promised your imminent return; we were all eagerly looking forward to it, and you did not come! And yet, we really could have used you here: we could have used you for our own sake, because we love you, and, as for me, your generous and loyal friendship was one of the real joys of my life; we could have used you, moreover, for your own sake, because here you would produce, I am certain of it, some fine book and because an expansive mind like yours needs an expansive spectacle like ours, and Paris with its hustle and bustle is the natural vortex for planets of your order. We could have used your presence: for the ideas that you would advance, for the style that you would edify, for the criticism that you would put right, for art (which has so few men like you), for everything. And, may I say it one more time, because a noble and sincere figure like yourself, standing upright in the midst of so many bowed and sidelong glances, comforts the eye and consoles the heart. Believe me when I say that we really love you here" (pp. 1119–20).

46. Letter to Adèle Hugo, September 4, 1837, *Correspondence*, p. 464. See also Auguste Vacquerie's letter of July 18, 1837 (*Correspondence*, pp. 387–91), where Vacquerie paraphrases, in a poem, a despondent conversation that Hugo had with him soon after the author of *Bug-Jargal* had been told of Maynard's death.

47. Maynard, "Scènes," p. 266. Reprinted in *La France maritime*, this story was originally published as "Les trois nuits de la Martinique," *Europe littéraire* (June 7, 10, 1833).

48. See especially the opening of his short story "Mademoiselle Lafayolle: Tradition des Antilles," *Europe littéraire* (March 13, 1833): 26.

49. "His critical articles," Maynard notes, "cannot fail to garner acclaim, generously and rigorously thought out, as is always the case with him. Devoted particularly to *philanthropy*, he has managed to give an entirely new and honorable meaning to the name 'philanthropist.' The Negroes owe him at the very least a statue in ebony-wood; Monsieur Schœlcher would doubtless refuse one of marble" (*Europe littéraire*, August 15, 1833: 14). Almost a decade later, Schœlcher, having noted of his creole hosts that "the word *philanthropist* has for them become the ultimate term of abuse" (*DCF*, p. 243), will preface his account of Maynard's death

with an affectionate allusion to this passage: "Who knows? Perhaps the whites will be thankful to us one day for the freeing of the slaves, which will have restored their wealth, put an end to poisonings, and guaranteed their peace of mind; perhaps they will want to raise ebony-wood statues honoring the abolitionists, as the unfortunate Louis Maynard once put it, with a gentle mockery" (p. 255).

50. *Revue de Paris* (August 1834): 12.

51. In his incisive account of Rousseau's attitude toward theatrical spectacles, Maynard depicts the Genevan philosopher "digging around in his philosopher's knapsack" and pulling out of it "whatever was at hand, first, the charms of nature, which are so much better than artificial pleasures, nightingales, brooks, the setting and the rising sun, soft foliage and tender contemplations, in short, all that senti-mental and rustic baggage, which would later be taken up by the Delilles and the Bernardin de Saint-Pierres, to their misfortune and ours" (*Revue de Paris* [July 1834]: 236–37).

52. Quoted in H. A. Lara, *Contribution*, pp. 35–36.

53. To provide only a few examples of such troubled assertions from the short story "Scènes nocturnes": the metaphoric slippage of black eyes into black skin that Poirié's poem ever so slightly evokes is rendered explicit when the narrator notes of creole women, "in whom are admirably joined and mixed together the two types of the French and of the Spanish woman," that "their hair is as black as the face of their slaves" (p. 265). In the story itself, a young creole woman by the name of Vir-ginie disguises herself as a mulatress in order to consult with an old black sorceress; part of her disguise, inevitably, is a madras, "an article of clothing so charming and lascivious that it could only have been invented by slave women" (p. 267). To be sure, the reader (who at this point in the story does not realize that Virginie and the "mulâtresse" are one and the same person) is quickly assured that "the madras cov-ering her neck did not advertise itself with that immodesty and that eager impurity to which mulatresses have accustomed us" (p. 267), but such cautions only partially address the problematic of an "impure" desire that cannot properly distinguish, as the native variant of creolist discourse demands, between the "ivory," "gold," and "ebony," and that at times, indeed, as in the following description of the mulatress Flora in *Outre-mer*, threatens to overturn the hierarchies upon which this discourse depends: "Whoever saw her at those moments when, while making up a bouquet, she took to daydreaming, one hand supporting her head, the other hanging down at her side and filled with our marvelous flowers, would have exclaimed that he saw the very picture of America! Short but thick and shining curls slipped out of the madras that was pressing down her hair" (1.35).

54. "Un souper aux colonies" (June 1835): 127–39. For the most extensive crit-ical reading of the novel, see Corzani, *Littérature*, 1.334–44.

55. Adolphe Guéroult, "Lettre à un ami de la province sur quelques livres nou-veaux," *Revue de Paris* (August 1835): 186.

56. See "Moeurs créoles: La relâche du pirate," *France maritime*, 2.229–34.

57. See Jameson, *Political Unconscious*, p. 202.

58. In his preface to *Les créoles*, by contrast, Levilloux notes that he found it nec-essary to "retain the singular superstitions and the naive thoughts of the blacks, as well as the—barbarous, yes, but expressive—patois of these men-children" (p. 15).

59. Dessalles, *Correspondance*, p. 187.

60. Bissette, *Réponse*, p. 114; for the original, see *DCF*, pp. 192–93.

61. Bissette, *Réponse*, p. 68. Schœlcher would eventually apologize for having published such statements, admitting with regard to this particular passage that he regretted the word "toutes" (*Vérité*, p. 78), while pointing out that Bissette's (re)citation of it had suppressed several sentences where he had made it clear that "while judging it necessary to reveal the existence of such evils, I framed my discussion with all the excuses that could, indeed that must, be legitimately given for them" (p. 79). For Schœlcher, this is yet another instance of Bissette's penchant for "disloyally falsifying texts" in order to present him "to the 'colored' class as having deliberately insulted it" (p. 79); "do not people who distort [*dénaturent*] texts to the point of making a writer say precisely the opposite of what he wanted to say," Schœlcher questions, invoking a rather unfortunate metaphor, "merit the opprobrium [*flétrissure*] of every decent man?" (p. 62). It should be added that in reestablishing the "texte véritable" Schœlcher here attenuates his original statement by adding a "presque" before the offending "toutes" (p. 77; cf. *DCF*, p. 192).

62. Jameson, *Political Unconscious*, p. 202. As Jameson reminds us, for Nietzsche, "'the slave uprising in ethics begins when *ressentiment* becomes creative and brings forth its own values: the *ressentiment* of those to whom the only authentic way of reaction—that of deeds—is unavailable, and who preserve themselves from harm through the exercise of imaginary vengeance'" (p. 201).

63. Girard, *Bouc*, pp. 35, 36.

64. As Werner Sollors suggests in his magisterial 1997 survey of "interracial literature," *Neither Black Nor White Yet Both*, the topos of the "tragic mulatto" may well have emerged in the nineteenth century—and been consolidated in our own—as a scapegoat mechanism that enabled both white and black authors to ward off an awareness of the arbitrariness of their supposedly fixed identities (and this holds equally true of the prominence given the topos of "passing"): "since the Mulatto character may deflect from the assumption that race is a matter of 'either/or,' denouncing the figure may have become a new consensus stereotype that helps to stabilize racial boundaries and may be functional in sustaining racial dualism" (p. 241). See also Sundquist, *To Wake the Nations*, pp. 258–60.

65. Prendergast, *Order*, p. 93.

66. Maynard, of course, has no need for Jews in order to consolidate his own threatened creole identity (although there are perhaps traces of an antisemitic discourse in his unflattering portrait of Flora's father and owner, the *petit blanc* Monsieur Nicole, "merchant and usurer" (2.302), a "European adventurer . . . who did not consider it unworthy of him to speculate on the beauty of his own daughter" (1.33). As Annie Le Brun has pointed out, however, over the past decade in Martinique certain affirmations of Créolité have been unexpectedly and absurdly tinged with an antisemitism masquerading as anti-Zionism, which has gone hand in hand with an aggressively populist critique of mulattoes ("'The mulatto spirit must be destroyed with napalm. Créolité is an anti-mulatto ideology,'" as Confiant puts it; see *Statue*, pp. 68–69, and pp. 59–71 passim). No affirmation of identity—even a supposedly transculturalized or postidentitarian one—is immune to the violent reaction against indifferentiation that we find in Maynard's novel; rather than sancti-

moniously proclaiming our "difference" from such obviously hate-full reactions, might it not be more productive, and more honest, to interrogate our own investment in this violence (a violence that I have been designating with the slash that separates the euphoria of the "post" from the obvious inadequacy of the "colonial")?

67. Brooks, *Body Work*, p. 62.

68. "Romantic pride," Girard notes, "readily condemns the mediator's presence when it comes to *Others* in order to establish its own autonomy on the ruins of rival pretensions. Novelistic genius can be found when the truth of *Others* becomes the hero's truth, that is to say, that of the novelist himself" (*MR*, p. 44). As we will see at the very end of this section, the concluding paragraphs of *Madame Bovary* mark the failure of Flaubert's novelistic genius, its capitulation to the world of Romantic lies; in his ironic denunciation of the bourgeois Homais, Flaubert proudly asserts his fundamental difference from the fallen world in which Homais triumphs. As I will be suggesting, if Flaubert's irony maintains its appeal for modern readers, this is because it is directed at perhaps the one remaining Other, the bourgeois, in whom we cannot bear to see our own likeness and from whom we have all tried to differentiate ourselves in a myriad of ways that all bear a family resemblance to the hate-full scapegoating of mulattoes through which Maynard desperately attempted, and repeatedly failed, to assert his own (white) creole identity.

69. Guéroult prefaces his negative remarks with a statement that gives some idea of the esteem in which this young Creole was held: "Monsieur Louis de Maynard is known to all the readers of the *Revue* through his very distinguished, well-conceived, and well-written critical pieces; in a word, among our contemporaries he is certainly one of the most promising young writers" (p. 186). Despite Hugo's apparent admiration for the novel, it did not receive a much better press in other journals than that given it in Bissette's *Revue* (see, e.g., Jules Chabot de Bouin's review in *Le voleur* [September 5, 1835]: 782–83), although in a note attached to "Scènes," the editors of *La France maritime*, while distancing themselves from Maynard's political views, nonetheless refer to him as a writer to whom "modern literature owes one of its finest books: *Outre-[m]er*" (p. 272). The following assessment, which emphasizes the novel's indebtedness to Levilloux's *Les créoles*, is exemplary of its reception: "*Outre-mer* perhaps ought not to have crossed the Atlantic. Monsieur L. de Maynard remembered that he was a Creole, and as the Negro, the colonist, the mulatto, the slave trade, rebellion, arson, poison—the Antilles, in short—are in fashion, Monsieur de Maynard has tried to duplicate the success of Monsieur Levilloux" (*France littéraire* [July-August 1835]: 427). This reviewer goes on to add that "there has already appeared, moreover, a book by this same title in England," referring to Longfellow's European travelogue, published anonymously in book form a few months earlier that same year (a British edition came out only weeks before the French novel's publication), though the actual source of Maynard's title is most probably to be found in the pages of Chateaubriand. The phrase itself would soon (1837) be adopted as the title of a journal devoted to colonial issues and edited by Henry Descamps, a (white) Creole from Guadeloupe who was himself an associate of Hugo's.

70. Racault, "Mimétisme," p. 150. Georges's "lack of anchoring," his "conflictual relations with the social body," Racault continues, allow one to consider the

figure of the métis as exemplary of Lukács's "definition of the novel as the alienated search after an authenticity that is impossible in a degraded world."

71. Corzani, *Littérature*, 1.337.

72. Bissette angrily refers to Schœlcher as someone who "accuses those of our [class] who were brought up in French schools of giving vent, from the moment they return to the colonies, to a disgust born of vanity when faced with their lowly station there, and of not knowing how to get along with the elite of their own kind. He accuses them of aspiring to what they ought to despise, of getting annoyed with their solitary position, and of eventually leaving the country never to return; he accuses them of abandoning the homeland along with the noble mission of rehabilitating their race, of deserting a sacred cause" (*Réponse*, p. 120). Maynard's portrait of Marius coincides with Schœlcher's in all respects, except that *his* alienated mulatto chooses to remain on the island, having conflated the sacred cause of his "dreams of social rehabilitation" (1.190) with his erotic aspirations for "what he ought to despise." To recall Jameson's remarks, the inability (as with Maynard) to distinguish between political ideals and personal motivations may well be the trademark of all counterrevolutionary fiction; one might add that the ability (as with Schœlcher) to do so may well be the bad faith at the heart of all revolutionary thinking.

73. *La France littéraire* (July-August 1835): 84.

74. The utopian conclusion of Sand's *Indiana*, which finds the heroine and Sir Ralph, her cousin and childhood companion, happily living apart from the world in a "humble Indian cottage" ("chaumière indienne," the novel's last words and a direct reference to Bernardin's 1791 short story of the same name), reaches forward (and back) to a world that has not been touched by the Romantic lies, the false (mimetic) desires, to which the innocent creole protagonist has been subjected in France by her ardent and yet calculating suitor Raymon. The pastoral ending takes us beyond "novelistic truth," asserting that what has entered the fallen realm of representation (the walls of Indiana's bedroom in France, significantly enough, are covered with "engravings that represented the pastoral love of Paul and Virginie, the mountaintops of the Île Bourbon" [p. 82]) can nonetheless be returned to presence—an unlikely assertion in light of everything that has transpired over the course of the novel but one that is at the nostalgic heart of nineteenth-century exoticism.

75. Schœlcher's citation is actually a paraphrase of what the Marquis says to the slaves during the 1831 uprising with which the novel ends: "You're rebelling, that's all very well. You can believe that you are within your rights. It's a sort of war, I understand that. All to the good" (2.382). For more on the 1831 insurrection, see Nicolas, *Histoire*, 1.343-48.

76. See Schœlcher, *DCF*, pp. 139-54. He cites, for instance, Virey's article on "L'homme" in Charles-Louis-Fleury Panckoucke's multi-volume *Dictionnaire des sciences médicales* (1810s).

77. Thomas, *Colonialism's Culture*, pp. 77-78. For an account of how the abolition of the slave trade and, eventually, of slavery itself coincided with the rapid development of racial science in the first half of the nineteenth century, see Drescher, "Ending."

78. Quoted in Mauviel, "Métissages," p. 67, and see also p. 60.

79. As Steve Pile notes in a gloss on *Colonial Desire*, the important point for Young is "that whenever inter-racial sex emerges in these theories [of race], it disrupts any possibility of the immutability of racial, sexual and cultural identity" (*Body*, p. 190).

80. Pile, *Body*, p. 180.

81. On the "carnivalesque" and its importance to both Chamoiseau's novels and Caribbean literature in general, see C. Maximin, *Littératures*, pp. 167–213.

82. Prendergast, *Order*, p. 93.   83. Girard, *Bouc*, p. 182.

84. Corzani, "Littérature," p. 26.   85. Brooks, *Body Work*, p. 62.

86. "This man, born to suffer and to fight, / Who scorned the forces gathered to destroy him, / Illustrious Bissette, this man is you! / And when slander, glory's parasite, / Seeks to libel you, to vilify your story, / Amazed, you ask it: Why?"

87. *Europe littéraire* (July 10, 1833): 229

88. *Europe littéraire* (July 15, 1833): 238. For a relatively humorous elaboration of this critique, see his short story "Notre ami le juste-milieu."

89. In a figure like Quasimodo from *Notre-Dame de Paris* (1831), Hugo has more or less succeeded in erasing the colonial genealogy, the mimetic origins, of the monstrous: the monster becomes a *sui generis* anomaly and functions as proof of the author's artistic creativity and imaginative powers. As René Girard reminds us in *Bouc émissaire*, "since the age of Romanticism, there is a tendency to conceive of the mythological monster as a veritable creation *ex nihilo*, a pure invention. The imagination is interpreted as an absolute power to imagine forms that exist nowhere in nature." However, he adds, "an examination of mythological monsters reveals nothing of the sort. It is always elements borrowed from several existing forms that are combined and mixed together in the monster and that [then] give the appearance of specificity, as with the Minotaur—a mixture of man and bull" (p. 51).

90. *Revue de Paris* (August 1834): 37.

91. Gustave Planche, *Revue des deux mondes* (April-June 1835, supplement): 358–59.

92. Baudelaire, *Oeuvres*, p. 747.

93. C. L. Miller, "Nationalism," p. 68.

94. See Chamoiseau and Confiant, *Lettres*, pp. 80–88; and Price-Mars, *Ainsi parla l'oncle*, p. 255.

95. Brathwaite, *Roots*, p. 130; and CO, p. 16.

96. Corzani, *Littérature*, 1.190.

97. René Ménil, *Tropiques* 11 (1944): 133 ("Situation de la poésie aux Antilles").

98. Kesteloot, *Écrivains*, p. 35.

99. J. M. Dash, *Literature*, p. 25.

100. J. M. Dash, *Literature*, p. 75. In 1837, for instance, the Haitian Émile Nau, arguing for a "national literature," counseled "our poets or . . . those who aspire to be such" that "the source of your inspiration is within you and among you; apart from that you have no salvation" (quoted in Nicholls, *FDD*, p. 74). See Dash, pp. 8–10, for an account of Nau's vision of Haitian society as "a creole hybrid," and pp. 1–42, for a good overview of nineteenth-century Haitian literature.

101. *Tropiques* 11 (1944): 133 ("Situation de la poésie aux Antilles").

102. Toumson, *Transgression*, p. 309.

103. Senghor, *Liberté*, p. 103.

104. See Biondi, *Senghor*, pp. 86, 54, and passim.

105. Schmidt, *Victor Schœlcher*, p. 75; see also Pâme, "*Revue*," p. 536. For general accounts of the relations between these two men, see Chauleau, *Vie*, pp. 69–71, and Schmidt, pp. 71–75.

106. Bissette, *Lettres*, pp. 190–91.

107. Bissette, *Réponse*, pp. 122, 113.

108. *Revue abolitionniste*, p. 107. See Schœlcher's *Histoire* (pp. 5–99) for an exhaustive critique of the "loi Mackau." For a detailed account of the abolitionist movement in the last years of the July Monarchy, see Drescher, "British Way"; and for Bissette's "superhuman efforts" during this time, Jennings, "Cyrille Bissette," pp. 61–65.

109. The (white) Creole Souquet-Basiège—a great admirer of Bissette and his commitment to "reconciling the past rulers with the two subject races, to extinguishing all resentments, to dissolving the colonial populations, which were once separated by laws, by institutions, by prejudices, and at that time still by memories, into the larger French family" (*Préjugé*, p. 104)—noted toward the end of the century that, "with a few honorable exceptions, the entirety of what one could call the 'mixed-blood aristocracy' disavowed Monsieur Bissette and insultingly brought forward the most slanderous accusations regarding his conduct" (p. 100). Notwithstanding its angry polemic with the "race de sang-mêlé," whom he frantically accuses of pursuing an antagonistic politics of "substitution" (that is, seeking to assume the "oligarchic" power once exercised by the whites, at the expense of both the former masters and the emancipated blacks), Souquet-Basiège's book nonetheless provides the fullest account of Bissette's later years (see pp. 93–133).

110. For the election results, see Schmidt, *Victor Schœlcher*, p. 126. The campaign songs "Papa Bissette" and "Arrivée Bissette," included by Schmidt in an appendix (pp. 388–92), give a good idea of the way the Bissette-Schœlcher electoral struggle was translated into the realm of popular culture. For an overview of nineteenth-century Martiniquan politics, and of the 1848–51 period especially, see Chauleau, *Vie*, pp. 67–90, as well as Adélaïde, "Liberté," and Burton, *Famille*, pp. 66–75. For Perrinon's initially difficult relations with Schœlcher, see *CEH*, pp. 481–86.

111. Chauleau, *Vie*, p. 71; Nicolas, *Histoire*, 2.68.

112. Page references are to the original edition, but the interested reader should consult Adélaïde and Chauleau's wonderfully annotated edition of *Vérité*.

113. This is a point that would also be made by François-André Isambert, the lawyer who had succeeded in getting the original charges against Bissette and his companions annulled in the mid-1820s: in a letter published in 1850, the founder of the *Société pour l'abolition de l'esclavage* accuses Bissette of having "distorted" ("dénaturé") his past, and having sought "to do everything possible to show himself in the best light at the expense of both his companions in misfortune and the one who cleared his name [i.e., Isambert himself]" (*Lettre*, p. 12).

114. Many years before Schœlcher's "revelation" of this fact, Bissette had publicly apologized for his participation in these events, citing it as an example of the

sort of false consciousness that colonialism makes possible: "the hommes de couleur," he concludes, "are more *black* than *white*, and they must not forget this fact" (see *Revue*, II.vii: 300–301).

115. *DCF* ends, for instance, with Schœlcher extolling the "magnanimity of the Creoles" ("le grandeur d'âme des créoles") and asserting that "the colonist's role is a truly noble one, if he deigns to accept it: that of educating the unfortunate race, whom their forefathers passed down to them in a debased state [*que leurs pères leur ont laissée toute abrutie*], whom the moral code sets free, and whom the nation begs them to regenerate" (p. 414).

116. Dessalles, *Journal*, p. 117.

117. For the poem "À M[onsieur] Bissette," see *Courrier de la Martinique*, September 26, 1849. For a sample of Maynard's critique of Schœlcher and his passionate defense of Bissette, see the articles devoted to *Vérité* in the *Courrier de la Martinique*, June 15 and 18, 1850. For biographical details on Maynard, who is confused with his brother in the 1993 *Dictionnaire encyclopédique et pratique de la Martinique* (p. 331), see Debien, *Journal*, pp. 111, 124.

118. As Perrinon informs us, "Monsieur Bissette, discredited and sullied, had the chance to rehabilitate himself a little through the duel that Monsieur Schœlcher deigned to offer him, for in France, where the prejudice of courage still reigns, a duel wipes the slate clean of many things. But the cowardice that dictated his retraction of 1843 [when Bissette first declined a duel with Schœlcher] has not abandoned him; he shrinks back once again. He does not even feel the compunction of the guilty man who is stigmatized in public [*que l'on flétrit publiquement*]; crushed under the weight of the evidence and of his own shame, he nonetheless once again basely raises his head up and hurls new insults as he runs away" (*Explications*, p. 16; for the details of Bissette's 1843 "retraction," see his *Deux mots* and *Déclaration*). If we are to believe the theory put forward with regard to the importance of duels in nineteenth-century Argentina by a character in Ricardo Piglia's highly metafictive novel *Artificial Respiration* (1980), Bissette's refusal to "rehabilitate" himself amounts to something more than mere cowardice: in those days, Piglia's character notes, "'Argentine gentlemen were Hegelians without knowing it. Freedom is only preserved at the risk of one's life; someone who is willing to face the risk of death proves himself capable of being a Master, a self-aware being. Those men killed each other, you could say, because none of them wanted to be a Slave'" (p. 49). Schœlcher would like to maintain his autonomous identity as a "self-aware being"; Bissette's refusal to duel (a refusal that, as we will see, eventually proves impossible for him to persevere in) "enslaves" the French abolitionist, rendering his identity inseparable from the awareness of others—or quite simply the Other—to whom his being is inextricably related.

119. See Adélaïde, "Liberté," p. 88.

120. Bissette, *Lettres*, p. 197.

121. Schœlcher sarcastically comments, for instance, on an 1840 brochure on slavery (*L'émancipation de la race africaine considérée sous le rapport religieux*) written by an influential member of the Martiniquan *Conseil colonial* named Huc, where the writer shows—with the help of a German scholar named Heidegger!—"that it is not only absurd, but irreligious to speak out against the servitude of the

African race, because the African race descends from Canaan, son of Ham, who was cursed by his father Noah and who, along with his children, was condemned to be the slave of his brothers Shem and Japheth" (*DCF*, p. 135); in Huc's own words "the African race is, more than us, subjected to worldly servitude, because of an act of impiety that their ancestor committed four thousand and one hundred years ago" (*Émancipation*, pp. 55–56). For a thorough survey of the "curse of Ham" theme, see Sollors, *NBNW*, pp. 78–111.

122. I am thinking here in particular of his early defense of the novel's supposedly blasphemous section: "this entire sequence happens in a dream, the fictional dream of a fictional character, an Indian movie star, and one who is losing his mind" (quoted in Asad, *Genealogies*, p. 274).

123. Brathwaite, "Caliban," p. 54. "Like Prospero," Brathwaite notes of Jordon (editor of the *Watchman*, founded in 1829), "[his] sense of possession of the island *excluded* certain people/forces; and partial possessions, to defend themselves, have to become conservative" (p. 50).

124. See the ironically titled "Vive Bissette!!!," *La liberté*, April 28, 1850.

125. Affergan, *Anthropologie*, p. 52.

126. In a far-ranging psychohistorical analysis of the role played by "familial discourse" in structuring Martiniquan society, Richard D. E. Burton comments that "*bissettiste* ideology, like the *schoelchériste* ideology that opposes it, is above all a 'familialist' ideology; it raises a father of mixed race to the place formerly occupied by the white Father, the place of the collective super-ego" (*Famille*, p. 72).

127. Jennings, "Cyrille Bissette," p. 65.

128. Quoted in Schmidt, *Victor Schœlcher*, p. 256. See also "Hommage à Victor Schœlcher," *Tropiques* 13–14 (1945): 229–35.

129. In a similar spirit, discussing "one of the more curious limitations of postcolonial theory," Simon Gikandi has recently remarked upon that theory's "historical amnesia or, rather, its failure to recognize that its attempt to unravel the relation between metropolitan and colonial identities is not an original articulation but a repetition of previous social and temporal entanglements" (*Maps*, p. 86).

130. Le Brun, *Pour Aimé Césaire*, p. 19.

131. Bissette, *Réfutation* (1843), p. 6. Bissette's use of this creole proverb (and this can only come as one last disappointment to the postcolonial reader) is a purely *rhetorical* gesture, an "inauthentic" recourse to the jargon of authenticity. He has in fact culled it from the lengthy selection of "black proverbs and phrases" that Schœlcher appended to *DCF* (p. 433). As always, Bissette is here (re)citing the master's words, putting into question the spirit of appropriation that generated Schœlcher's own efforts as an anth(rop)ologist.

132. Le Brun, *Statue*, p. 18.

133. On their sexist reaction to Le Brun, see also R. and S. Price, "Shadowboxing," pp. 18–19.

134. Le Brun, *Soudain un bloc*, p. 322.

135. As Confiant put it in a response to Le Brun's first pamphlet, "Césaire is liked because he resembles Rimbaud or Lautréamont. . . . Sorry, but to appreciate the Other because he resembles you is a colonialist attitude" ("Contre les Rimbaud bronzés," p. 30).

136. See his introduction to Confiant's "Contre les Rimbaud bronzés" (*Antilla* 575: 29).

CHAPTER 7

1. See Nietzsche, *Beyond Good and Evil*, p. 222 (section 274).
2. González Echevarría, *Celestina's Brood*, p. 178.
3. Césaire, "Homme," p. 120.
4. Arnold, *Modernism*, p. 266; see also J. M. Dash, "Cri," pp. 103–5, and Rosello, *Littérature*, pp. 134–42.
5. Arnold, *Modernism*, p. 163.
6. Writing in the midst of the Haitian Revolution, Moreau de Saint-Méry points out that even if the colony were lost once and for all to the insurrecting black population, his lengthy account of pre-revolutionary Saint-Domingue would at least allow readers to "meditate upon" its past glory and, he continues, "doubtless one can, in certain regards, gain as much nourishment from these meditations as from those generated by the shards of Herculanum, which they are going to be rescuing from the ashes that have covered it over for so many centuries" (*Description*, 1.viii). This use of the volcano as a metaphor for violent or revolutionary activity would become a commonplace trope in nineteenth-century literature from and about the Caribbean. The narrator of Hugo's *Bug-Jargal* notes, for instance, that before the slaves entered the revolutionary fray in 1791 "there already existed between the whites and the free mulattoes enough hate that this volcano, kept under lid for so long, would have devastated the entire colony at the dreaded moment when it tore itself open" (p. 43). The following two random examples from "colored" writers confirm the extent to which Césaire's quintessentially modernist rhetoric stands in a relationship not of rupture but of (dis)continuity with nineteenth-century Caribbean literature: Eugène Chapus, one of the writers who flourished in the Antilles during the 1830s, speaks (in his short story "L'amour d'une Créole") of the Caribbean as a place "where vengeance lies in the hearts of the weak like volcanic fires, kept under lid deep beneath the earth's surface, and constantly threatening to engulf those who control them" (quoted in Hoffmann, *Nègre*, p. 185); describing the reaction of the black Romulus and the mulatto Remus to the murder of their mother by the white Colonist, Émeric Bergeaud, in the first Haitian novel, *Stella* (1859), notes that "the anger shut up in their hearts has grown with the passage of time and is now going to explode, just as, with the passage of centuries, the fire that hides in the depths of the earth grows and becomes a volcano" (p. 24). One last evocation of the Caribbean volcano can be cited here, from the work of another writer of "mixed race," Gilbert Gratiant, by way of suggesting that the metaphor can be adapted to other, less violently modernist ends: addressing (in his *Crédo des Sang-mêlé*) the békés of his native island, Gratiant asserts that there can be conflict or friendship, and even love, between them and his people, but only "if our hands that join together both are pure / and our volcanoes strong enough / to forge tomorrow / in the forge where hatreds and gold are smelted" (*Fables*, p. 626; "si nos mains se joignant sont l'une et l'autre pures / Et si nos volcans sont assez forts / Pour bien forger demain / Dans la forge où fondront les haines et les ors . . . ").

7. For an analysis of Césaire's ambivalent dependency upon the Book of Revelations in a later poem, see Arnold, *Modernism*, pp. 193–204; for the role it plays in his theater, see Bailey, *Ritual Theater*, pp. 153–66.

8. Situating himself squarely within the nineteenth-century tradition of the "poète maudit," Césaire once approvingly, and revealingly, likened the role of the great poet to that of the "founder" of the New World. Real poetry, he asserted, is "damned, because in the ears of the poet now resounds the very same voice that haunted Columbus: 'I will found a new Heaven and a new Earth, such that people will no longer give any thought to what came before" *Tropiques* 8–9 (1943): 8 ("Maintenir la poésie").

9. Maximin, "Aimé Césaire," p. 10. Mt. Pelée is, Césaire noted in another interview (1973), "a mountain that has been considered extinct . . . for a very long time and that shows itself rarely, but when it shows itself it does so with violence. It is an explosion; it's the explosive type" (quoted in Arnold, *Modernism*, p. 125).

10. Quoted in André, *Caraïbales*, p. 13.

11. Defending Césaire from such charges of biologism, Haitian poet René Depestre—a longtime critic of Negritude—has taken Confiant and the other authors of the *Éloge* to task for overlooking "Césaire's creole imagination." Depestre goes on to assert that, in its day, Césaire's Negritude "dismissed the semiotic scandal that is at the origin of mythic notions such as 'Black,' 'White,' 'métis,' 'homme de couleur,' and 'mulatto,' which are a desecration of diversity and the unity of the species—[a unity that exists] across the plurality of languages and the multiplicity of [what Milan Kundera calls] 'medial contexts' in which the composite imagination of the planet's civilizations dwells" ("Aventures," p. 167).

12. Brathwaite, *X-Self*, p. 127.

13. On Segalen's relation to Nietzsche, to whom he dedicates his last poem, *Thibet*, see, e.g., Bouillier, *Victor Segalen*, pp. 545–46; for the connections between Césaire and Nietzsche, see Arnold, *Modernism*, especially pp. 53–54, and Lionnet, *Autobiographical Voices*, pp. 67–73. For an extended treatment of Segalen's simultaneously contemptuous and anxious attitude toward "colonial literature," see my *Exotic Memories*, pp. 110–18.

14. Segalen, *Oeuvres*, 1.769. It is "in homage to Victor Segalen," incidentally, that Glissant has entitled one of his most recent books *Introduction à une Poétique du Divers*; Segalen's writings have been a touchstone for Glissant throughout his career (see, e.g., *IP*, pp. 95–103; *DA*, p. 430; and *PR*, pp. 41–42).

15. *Tropiques* 1 (1941): 5. For a refreshingly polemical commentary on this passage, see Condé, "Order," pp. 123–24: breaking with the self-serving chronology of literary history established by the modernists, she asks "is it not time to somehow rehabilitate the so-called exotic poets" who preceded Césaire's generation (p. 123)? For recent translations of many of the most important articles in *Légitime Défense* and *Tropiques*, see Richardson's extremely useful collection, *Refusal of the Shadow*.

16. Chinweizu, Jemie, and Madubuike, *Toward the Decolonization*, p. 6.

17. Léro, "Misère," p. 12.

18. Brossat and Maragnes, *Antilles*, p. 51.

19. Césaire, "Homme," p. 119.

20. Dayan, "France," p. 150.

21. Césaire once astoundingly remarked that "there is perhaps something even more atrocious than the great colonial bloodbaths or the spectacular acts of violence: namely, the spectacle of mediocrity emasculating [*dévirilisant*], slowly but surely, a people. This is the lot of the Antilles. . . . " (quoted in Confiant, *AC*, pp. 21–22). As he asserts in the proem to the first issue of *Tropiques*, "it is time to gird one's loins like a valiant man" (1.5): Césaire's modernist project is inseparable from a "virile" gesture that Jean-Paul Sartre would only a few years later enviously sanction in his "Orphée noir" when he asserted that "the black man remains the great male of the earth, the sperm of the world" (p. 266). In a similar vein, Segalen's biographer Bouiller has spoken approvingly of "the virile accent of *Les Immémoriaux*," Segalen's 1907 novel about the erosion of cultural traditions in early-nineteenth-century Tahiti (*Victor Segalen*, p. 124). Segalen's project of textually salvaging the "authentic" Tahiti is inseparable from a masculinist drive that disdainfully rejects in the name of primitive origins the hybridized world that has resulted from colonial contact (as when, to cite a particularly glaring example from his biographical account of Paul Gauguin, Segalen notes disdainfully that during the painter's brief return to France from Tahiti in 1893 he took up with "a mulatress from Java who was exploring Paris"—a "sinful" betrayal on Gauguin's part of "the gentle Maori female for that colonial bitch [*chienne coloniale*]" (*Oeuvres*, 1.364). As I have argued in *Exotic Memories* (and as Glissant has recently pointed out with regard to Hearn's abandonment of the Caribbean for Japan [see Chapter 4]), French Polynesia could not ultimately satisfy the primitivist impulses of a writer like Segalen given its too thoroughly colonial and/or creolized identity. Faced with a "clan" whose "total disappearance . . . through death, infertility, interbreeding [*métissage*], and civilization" he foresaw ("Hommage à Gauguin," *Oeuvres*, 1.366), his attention would soon turn toward the ostensibly more autarkic realm of imperial China: the realism of an ethnographical novel like the *Immémoriaux* proves a dead end for Segalen, since it can lead only to an acknowledgment of his defeat at the hands of an impure (and devirilizing) colonial history; for this reason, much of his work will henceforth be increasingly characterized by a dehistoricizing formalism, in which *style* becomes the sign (as with so many modernist writers) of a valiant individuality and/or masculinity that can, in a world of (as it were) "colonial bitches," be preserved in no other way.

To point out the confluence of (Césaire and Segalen's) modernism and masculinism is not, of course, to explain it. While such explanations would take us too far afield, it is worth recalling here Roger Toumson's provocative analysis of Césaire's ambivalent relation to Creole, which for the author of the *Cahier*, Toumson argues, amounted to nothing more than a "pseudo-maternal" language (*Transgression*, p. 79). Rejecting this "impure" mother tongue, Césaire goes in search of another, a "'first' language, a lost language." This "langue perdue" that belongs to the "authentic" mother is, Toumson continues, "a sort of form without content, empty. Nowhere attested, its only expression is nostalgia. A vehicle of direct communication, . . . this language is experienced as having been a 'complete signifier,' a 'pure signified.' The nostalgia for 'Mother Africa' that one finds the Negritude authors confessing to is, for many of them, a nostalgia for the paradise of this primal word [*cette première parole*]" (p. 60). Toumson concludes that this split between primary and secondary mother tongues determines the identity of "Afro-Antillean discourse as the expression of a desire that would bear the mark of its inability [*impuissance*] to coincide with itself," and it is this sense of "impotence," one might suggest, that results in the overcompensating fetishization of (male, poetic) power that I have discussed in this note.

22. Zimra, "Tracées," p. 349.

23. Gikandi, *Writing*, p. 236.

24. L. Johnson, "A-beng," p. 139.

25. See Zimra, "Tracées," p. 367, and the "Introduction" to her English translation of the novel, *Lone Sun*, pp. lii–lvii.

26. Taylor, *Narrative*, p. 182.

27. Fanon, *Damnés*, p. 170; quoted in Taylor, *Narrative*, p. 150.

28. Quoted in Zimra, "Introduction," p. xxvii.

29. Mouralis, "*L'isolé soleil*," p. 420.

30. For Harris's use of the phrase "consumption of bias," see *Womb*, pp. 26, 54, 92–93. In his most recent work, Glissant has himself taken to speaking in terms of an opposition between a "thinking of the trace" ("la pensée de la trace") and "systematic thinking or systems of thought" ("les pensées de système ou les systèmes de pensée"); see, e.g., *ID*, p. 17.

31. Maximin elaborates on this position in a 1986 interview: "To succeed in building an identity without necessarily having to undergo an identification—that is to say, without having to abandon a part of oneself for the benefit of someone else, be that someone else African, Hindu, or European. This is the historic chance that we are faced with today" ("Entretien," p. 43).

32. Cailler, *Conquérants*, pp. 174–75.

33. Quoted in Fanon, *Peau*, p. 99.

34. For a relevant discussion of Plato's self-serving opposition between his philosophical truths and the Sophists' literary rhetoric, see Rella, *Battaglia*, pp. 15–46. The Platonic critique is directly linked to the problem of creolization and métissage inasmuch as the "rusing intelligence" known in Greek as *mètis* and often associated with the Sophists would be banished by Plato from the realm of truth, as Marcel Detienne and Jean-Pierre Vernant have argued in their groundbreaking study *Les ruses de l'intelligence: La mètis des Grecs* (1974), and thus transformed into "the other of philosophy, the non- or anti-philosophical thought associated not only with error but with deception and lie" (Klein, "Mètis," p. 3). For an extension of this argument, which praises the concept of métissage for putting into question supposedly firm boundaries not only between truth and error but between different "races," see Lionnet, *Autobiographical Voices*, pp. 14–15.

35. Zamora, *Writing*, pp. 45, 76.

36. Derrida, *D'un ton*, p. 76. For an elaboration on these remarks, see my "Between Apocalypse and Narrative."

37. Gates, "Critical Fanonism," p. 468.

38. As Jack Corzani has pointed out, "in *Les damnés de la terre*, Fanon never dealt with the Caribbean, a topic that would certainly have forced him to nuance the epic, even mystical, enthusiasm with which he sketched out generalities about the liberation struggle" (*Littérature*, 5.118).

39. I take the phrase "language of rupture" from Marjorie Perloff's *The Futurist Moment*. Both "Third World" revolutionary anticolonialism and "First World" avant-gardism are projects grounded in an explosively futurist ideology that has been substantially hollowed out in the late twentieth century. For an illuminatingly revolutionary use of the volcano metaphor by the leader of the Italian Futurists, see the second and third chapters of F. T. Marinetti's *Le monoplan du Pape* (1912).

40. Bhabha, "What does . . . ?," p. 121; for Bhabha's overall take on Fanon, see *LC*, pp. 40–65. For an interesting contextualization of Fanon's rhetoric concerning "new men," see Ross, *Fast Cars*, pp. 157–65.

41. Suleri, *Rhetoric*, p. 11.

42. See Barbara Johnson for an extended treatment of this trope, which "by means of the silvery voice of rhetoric, calls up and animates the absent, the lost, and the dead" ("Apostrophe," p. 31).

43. On Fanon's discussion of "national culture," see *Damnés*, pp. 141–75. A necessary step in the dialectical narrative of liberation, this recuperation of, and "dive into," the past must be supplanted, "tôt ou tard," by bodily struggle against the oppressors (pp. 145, 154).

44. See Elam, *Romancing*, pp. 51–79. As David Richards has similarly argued, "Scott's novels are about absent subjects; it is only when the Highlanders are constructed as *historically* invisible that they can re-emerge as textually visible and capable of bearing the burden of a historical discourse from which they are excluded as an extinct species" (*Masks*, p. 121).

45. Fanon, *Damnés*, p. 144.

46. Clark, "Developing," p. 304.

47. In "Lam, l'envol et la réunion," Glissant argues that Lam's art is engaged in a "double project." On the one hand, it seeks to "locate and celebrate the primordial forms secreted by a very palpable reality, that of his native island"; this aspect of Lam's project, which involves "the rehabilitation of African forms captured not in a cliché-like manner but in their essential vivacity," is exemplified by a "manifesto-work" like *La jungle*. On the other hand, his art at the same time signals "the *cultural passage* in which we find ourselves today"; "anthology-works" like *La réunion* are not "pierced with depths" in the manner of a contemporaneous work like *La jungle*, but are created with the intention of "accumulating signs" and disseminating them across the canvas's surface, which itself stands in for that of the tout-monde. In these anthology-works, "the given content of reality, the rehabilitated forms of the black African universe, precipitously fan out in *all directions* and complete themselves (that is to say, real-ize themselves) in the unexpected locations made possible by far-flung global relations [*dans l'inattendu de l'énorme relation mondiale*]." Glissant's characterization of this double project—in which the primordial intentions of *La jungle* and the creolizing disseminations of *La réunion* are seen as being not (only) in contradiction with, but (also) complementary to, one another—beautifully conveys the productive tensions between insularity and relationality that I have been arguing is fundamental to the creolization process and the ambivalently located identities it makes possible.

48. Valdman, "Créole," p. 154. It is this compositional process that Carpentier has his protagonist Esteban discover in the Caribbean during his voyages aboard

L'ami du peuple: "Esteban marvelled to realise how the language of these islands had made use of agglutination, verbal amalgams and metaphors to convey the formal ambiguity of things which participated in several essences at once. Just as certain trees were called 'acacia-bracelets,' 'pineapple-porcelain,' 'wood-rib,' 'ten o'-clock broom,' 'cousin clover,' 'pitcher-pine-kernel,' 'tisane-cloud,' and 'iguana-stick,' many marine creatures had received names which established verbal equivocations in order to describe them accurately [*por fijar una imagen*]" (p. 178). Such creole equivocations, one might add, are typical of the "combinatory rhetoric" that characterizes Baroque discourse (see Chevigny, "Insatiable Unease," p. 41).

49. Lamming, *Pleasures*, p. 229.

50. Quoted in Caryl Emerson's preface to his *Problems of Dostoevsky's Poetics*, p. xli.

51. D. A. Miller, *Narrative*, p. 151.

52. Césaire, *CP*, pp. 48–49 (*Cahier*); *Tropiques* 6–7 (1943): 11–12 ("Isidore Ducasse, comte de Lautréamont"). (My italics.)

53. Sartre, "Orphée," pp. 256–57.

54. Berque uses the term in both a negative and a positive sense: his work not only examines the ways in which indigenous peoples were "dispossessed of their nature" by colonialism (p. 105), but the ways in which the newly decolonized nations have reacted to the "dispossession" of their erstwhile colonial masters (*Dépossession*, p. 11). Glissant registers the ambivalences of this term in his pre-*Discours* work (see, e.g., *IP*, p. 152), but then, appropriating it for his own ends, goes on to privilege its negative sense.

55. This all-too-familiar rhetoric of alienation has been resolutely put into question by writers like Maximin and the authors of the *Éloge*. As Confiant puts it, "in the Antilles, each race inhabits the other, whether it wants to or not, whether it admits to doing so or not, which ought to bring about a rethinking of that cliché 'alienation' as it has been transmitted up until now by the most eminent Caribbean thinkers, in particular Frantz Fanon, most of whose arguments—as we must bring ourselves to recognize—no longer seem, precisely in this area, suited to the reality of today's world (and especially of today's Third World)" (*AC*, p. 267).

56. The intellectual precariousness of Glissant's vision of *dépassement* in *Discours antillais* and his—in many ways essential(ist)—commitment to the idea of the nation can be gauged by situating his abstract claims about the opposition between detours that do not lead anywhere and ones that lead to a resolution in the specific context out of which they emerged. These claims follow directly upon a discussion of the use of *joual* as a linguistic detour in French-speaking Québec: "it is not surprising that joual symbolized a moment in the Québécois resistance to the domination of English-speaking Canada, nor moreover that this symbol, as such, tended to disappear as Québec began to conceive of itself and exist as a nation-in-the-making" (p. 33). One does not have to be a Cree Indian, an anglophone resident of or recent immigrant to the province of Québec, or a francophone *de souche* who nonetheless remains committed to the Canadian nation-in-the-making, to sense the profoundly disturbing ramifications of the exclusionary vision of Québécois national identity that underpins these apparently "concrete" and "positive" remarks. Glissant's ill-considered comments here, clearly, are dependent upon a conflation of

language and nation that he elsewhere firmly rejects but that unabashedly underpins, for instance, the radical claims of a linguistic nationalist like the Réunion novelist Axel Gauvin, who has argued that, whereas two different nations can possess the same language, "two groups speaking different languages do not form part of the same nation" (*Du créole*, p. 65).

57. Gikandi, *Writing*, p. 66.

58. Glissant, "Romancier," p. 30.

59. Quoted in Young, *Colonial Desire*, p. 171.

60. Young, *Colonial Desire*, p. 174.

61. Affergan, *Anthropologie*, p. 100.

62. Discussing Césaire, Confiant speaks of his "obsession with the 'all or nothing,' with the 'tabula rasa,' and his inability to think the diffuse, the chaotic, the complexity that characterizes creole society" (*AC*, p. 151).

63. Césaire, "Discours," p. 498.

64. *Tropiques* 6–7 (1943): 11 ("Isidore Ducasse, comte de Lautréamont").

65. Jameson, "Postmodernism," p. 65. This passage has been somewhat diluted in Jameson's later book of the same title (see p. 17).

66. See Césaire, *CP*, pp. 64–65. Significantly, in Césaire's *Cahier* this line ends with a period, whereas Maximin's (re)citation of it ends with an ellipsis.

67. This influence can be seen, for instance, in Étienne Léro's recourse to Marinetti's vocabulary in his critique of the older generation of regionalist writers from Martinique and Guadeloupe and their "unrepentant conformism, their Greco-Latin academic mindset, their attachment to the past, their stuffiness [*leur passéisme, leur compasséisme*]" ("Misère," p. 11)—a critique that Sartre would in turn, ironically enough, direct against Léro. For an able criticism of this passage, see Toumson, *Transgression*, p. 313.

68. Walcott, "What the Twilight Said," p. 8. My epigraph is from a 1935 article that Césaire wrote for the journal *L'étudiant noir* and that is reprinted in Confiant, *AC*, pp. 326–28.

69. Walcott, "Muse," p. 7. For a fuller account of the context that generated Walcott's revealingly defensive position at this time, see Rohlehr, *Pathfinder*, pp. 110–14, 139–40.

70. Césaire, "Homme," p. 117.

71. See my *Exotic Memories*, pp. 24–28; for another relevant account of Vattimo's "weak thought," see Chambers, *Border Dialogues*, pp. 95–98.

72. Vattimo, *Fine*, p. 182.   73. Appiah, "Race," p. 103.

74. Armet, "Guadeloupe," p. 19.   75. Antoine, *Littérature*, p. 184.

76. Chamoiseau, "En témoignage," pp. 144–45.

77. Rousseau, *Oeuvres*, 5.72–73.

78. Ménil, *Tracées*, p. 52.

79. Taylor, *Narrative*, p. 94. For a discussion of Fanon's negative use of the word "drama," see Taylor pp. 53–54.

80. For an elaboration on this distinction, see Glissant, *DA*, pp. 236–45.

81. Walcott, "What the Twilight Said," p. 9.

82. Chamoiseau and Confiant, *Lettres*, pp. 136–37.

83. Chamoiseau, "Que faire . . . ?," p. 153.

84. Burton, "*Débrouya*," p. 468. This distinction between "resistance" and "opposition," which Burton has recently argued is key to an understanding of Caribbean history and popular culture as a whole (see his *Afro-Creole*, especially pp. 50–51), is connected to the equally relevant and increasingly cited one that de Certeau makes between *strategy*, which "postulates a place that can be marked out as a discrete entity [*comme un propre*], and that can thus be made to serve as a base for managing its relations with a distinct exteriority (competitors, adversaries, customers, 'targets,' or 'objects of study')," and *tactics*, which "have as their only place that of the other" (Rosello, *Littérature*, pp. 35–37; see also Chow, *Writing Diaspora*, p. 16).

85. Chow, *Writing Diaspora*, p. 40.

86. Corzani, *Littérature*, 6.190.

87. Césaire, *Et les chiens*, p. 59. For the influence of Césaire's Rebel on Maximin's first novel, see Zimra, "Je(ux)."

88. Gikandi, *Writing*, p. 226.

89. As Said points out in his *Beginnings*, arguing (in terms that overlap nicely with D. A. Miller's account of narrative) on behalf of a novelistic condition of "secularity," "fictional narrative is . . . an *alternative* departure, a set of misadventures that *begins* away from the Origin (a term almost theological in that it must be understood in the strictest sense possible—as pure anteriority and, paradoxically, as pure genetic power)" (p. 142).

90. For a trenchant critique of Calvino's sexual politics, see De Lauretis, *Technologies*, pp. 70–83. Maximin's use of this narrative paradigm can only take us ambivalently "beyond the ending" of the romance plot to which it remains attached: it does this most notably by supplementing the notebook's ecstatic description of their coupling with a playful line of commentary, "Soufrières: soeurs et frères mêlés" (p. 273), which emphasizes that the mixing of Marie-Gabriel and Adrien leaves remainders, and thus falls well short of a total eclipse. For the phrase "beyond the ending," and its relation to "the critique of narrative characteristic of twentieth-century writing by women," see Duplessis, *Writing*.

91. Atwood, *Survival*, pp. 228–30.

92. Commenting in the *Poétique* on the final chapter of Faulkner's novel, Glissant notes that "the tragic crisis, sumptuously and ritualistically brought to a head with the burning down of Sutpen's mansion, will not restore legitimacy but will, rather, confirm its ineluctable obliteration," thereby "destroying in an heretical fashion the sacred nature of filiation" (p. 71).

93. Chamoiseau and Confiant, *Lettres*, p. 38.

94. Quoted in Kaplan, *Questions*, p. 118.

95. Hall, "Cultural Identity," p. 228. As Bhabha points out, glossing Hall's claim, "this arbitrary closure is also the cultural space for opening up new forms of identification that may confuse the continuity of historical temporalities, confound the ordering of cultural symbols, traumatize tradition" (*LC*, p. 179).

96. Chambers, *Border Dialogues*, p. 102.

97. Taussig, *Mimesis*, p. 254.

98. See Hazaël-Massieux, *Chansons*, pp. 94–96.

99. Comptines (counting songs, nursery rhymes) have been defined as "short

traditional, oral poems—most often featuring rhyme or assonance, always rhythmic or melodic—that are commonly used by children during their games and activities" (Jean Baucomont, quoted in Hazaël-Massieux, "Des berceuses," p. 14). A great deal of debate as to what constitutes an authentically creole cultural product has centered around this and other related oral forms such as the conte. Marie-Christine Hazaël-Massieux warns her readers that "whether they be in French or in Creole or in whatever language, when I refer to creole comptines I mean those brief musical forms that the Antillean community claims as its own. Certain of these forms are obviously, and without question, *in* French, but that does not keep them from being creole comptines, for they fall within the province of this creole culture, of this society that cites them as their prerogative, and that values them as much as those others that the linguist would not hesitate to label 'creole' because they are in Creole" ("Créole," p. 38). To distinguish between comptines on the basis of the language in which they are spoken would be an aberrant practice, since whatever the language—"even admitting that this could be easily determined"—those who produce or reproduce them see both Creole and French, in this specific instance at least, as belonging "to the same cultural reserve" (*Chansons*, p. 30). Hazaël-Massieux's position is thus diametrically opposed to the claims of a Maryse Condé (in *La civilisation du bossale* [1978]) who "distinguishes between tales that she considers to be truly creole (for the unavowed reason that they would seem to be of African origin) and those that she objects to designating as such because they are only, in her eyes, local versions of European tales" (see Chaudenson, *Des îles*, p. 254).

100. Chamoiseau, "Que faire . . . ?," p. 155.

101. Certain critics, to be sure, decline to read this insuperable distance that separates writing from the orality it would (re)capture. To take but one random example: remarking upon the way in which the Guadeloupean writer Simone Schwarz-Bart inserts oral stories into her novels, one commentator makes the claim that "translated into a written medium, the nonofficial, marginal, oral history becomes the center of the narrative, and thus subverts the official function of writing" (Mudimbe-Boyi, "Poetics," p. 206). The rhetoric of marginality and subversion, fond staple of the postcolonial critic, not surprisingly winds up claiming a centrality of its own, thereby reproducing the very logic with which it is ostensibly at odds; as Vera Kutzinski has pointed out, the privileging of orality in, say, much Afro-American criticism, and the self-satisfied claims about the "subversion" of official discourse that it supposedly effects, are "based upon an argument that unwittingly maintains one of the dearest assumptions of Western thought: the primacy of speech over writing" (*Against the Grain*, p. 53). As opposed to such claims, which find ample expression in the work of a modernist poet like Césaire ("it is by his cry that one recognizes man," he asserts in an early issue of *Tropiques*, adding that life "is incarnated—without any reduction, without any renunciation, with a free and unpredictable movement—in the immediacy of the voice" [2 (1941): 37 ("Introduction à la poésie nègre américaine")]), Jean Bernabé argues the case for Schwarz-Bart's indirect use of Creole in particular, and oral culture in general, in a more subtle fashion, which forgoes the simple reversals of phonocentric criticism: rather than, in Promethean fashion, attempting to convey the fire of a purely creole literary language [*langue*], "snatched out of nowhere," Schwarz-Bart has chosen,

Bernabé argues, to "catch hold of the Antillean word [*parole*]," managing in a "rus-ing" manner and "at the end of a continual negotiation to establish the absence of Creole as a presence that acts as a catalyst for the text's principal meanings" ("Tra-vail," p. 179).

102. Gates, *Signifying Monkey*, p. 181.

103. In this passage, Chamoiseau explicitly, and palinodically, associates his own desire to "capture the word in writing" with an early play of his, *Manman Dlo contre la fée Carabosse* (1981), which engages a straightforward scenario of resis-tance (in de Certeau's sense) against colonial power that his later, more mature work itself puts into question, as Richard D. E. Burton has pointed out ("*De-brouya*," pp. 469–70).

104. Glissant, "Chaos-monde," p. 118.

105. I am thinking here of a comment by Glissant that Chamoiseau (re)cites in an epigraph to his *Solibo Magnifique*: "I am evoking a synthesis, a synthesis of writ-ten syntax and spoken rhythmics, of the 'acquired' [experience] of writing and the oral 'reflex,' of the solitariness of writing and the shared participation in a song—a synthesis that is well worth attempting, it seems to me."

106. Harris, "Fabric," p. 82.

CHAPTER 8

1. See Harris, "Frontier." For a recent, comprehensive account of Conrad's re-lation to the primitive, see Griffith, *Joseph Conrad*.

2. Quoted in Brossat and Maragnes, *Antilles*, p. 33.

3. Bailey, *Ritual Theater*, p. 27; also quoted in Confiant, *AC*, p. 136.

4. Carpentier, *Obras*, 13.276, 277, 286 ("Visión de América").

5. Carpentier, *Obras*, 13.187 ("Lo barroco y lo real maravilloso").

6. Hugo, *Oeuvres*, 3.45.

7. Silver, "After El Dorado," p. 75.

8. Slemon, "Monuments," p. 8.

9. Reviewing *The Lost Steps* in 1956, Glissant cites the descriptions of Rosario and other such passages ("I was asking myself whether perhaps the role of these lands in the history of man might not be to make possible for the first time certain symbioses of cultures" [p. 120]) as evidence of the Caribbean's "vocation de syn-thèse." "Let us not recoil," he urges his fellow islanders, "from familiarizing our-selves with and taking pride in the virtues and traditions—be they black, Indian, or European—that have come down to us, but let us not hesitate to adjust them. May this keen rediscovery of one's self not lead to a sterile and exclusive entreaty of the past. This vocation of ours is one of projection: the clash of cultures is also the dy-namic passion of cultures" (*IP*, p. 142).

10. Webb, *Myth*, p. 74.

11. García Canclini, "Memory," p. 438.

12. Chambers, *Migrancy*, p. 94.

13. Torgovnick, *Gone Primitive*, p. 40.

14. Wordsworth, *Fourteen-Book 'Prelude*,' p. 157 (7.725–28); also quoted in Williams, *Country*, p. 151.

15. Perloff, "Tolerance," pp. 340, 354.

16. Clifford, *Predicament*, p. 154.

17. Taussig, *Mimesis*, p. 129.

18. I am thinking here of Neil Lazarus's useful critique of Paul Gilroy's strangely undialectical claim that "racial slavery is not only the founding but also the overdetermining instance of black Atlantic sociality, in the present as much as in the past" ("Is a Counterculture . . . ?," p. 337); as Lazarus points out, Gilroy's insistence that "the historical experience of slavery remains materially constitutive of contemporary black Atlantic sociality" is not only reductionist but also hypocritical, inasmuch as it makes the same claims for an historically determined and *closed* "black Atlantic" identity that Gilroy chides Raymond Williams for having made with regard, say, to "the determination of contemporary Welsh sociality by its 'twenty centuries of history written visibly into the earth'" (p. 336). Gilroy understandably rejects such appeals to "rooted settlements" and historical "memory" since they potentially marginalize the black contribution to Welshness or Britishness ("'How long is long enough to become a genuine Brit?'"); however, his own appeals to the "changing sameness" of black Atlantic identity and what we might call the "diasporic (lack of) settlement" it legitimizes must be questioned, if not rejected, on those very same grounds.

19. Genet, *Paravents*, p. 192 ("Par le fait de quels cheminements les mots tradition et trahison, s'ils ont la même origine, signifient-ils des idées si différentes ou si foncièrement—je veux dire si radicalement—semblables?").

20. During, "Waiting," pp. 51, 58.

21. Dening, "Poetic," p. 369.

22. Harris, "Frontier," p. 135.

23. See Dominy, "Maori Sovereignty," p. 253.

24. Thomas, *Colonialism's Culture*, p. 185.

25. Sinclair, *"Tangi,"* p. 220.   26. Brathwaite, "Caliban," p. 54.

27. Shohat, "Notes," p. 110.   28. Maxwell, "Post Colonial," p. 70.

29. The prologue of Hulme's novel is entitled "The End at the Beginning," and the title of this concluding section might well have been "The Beginning at the End," for my reading of *the bone people*, which I drafted in the summer of 1992, is the ur-text out of which developed the rest of this book, which I completed in the early months of 1997; if, in its duplicitous argument for the differential category of tradition, be it the literary tradition of (European) modernism or the cultural tradition of Maoritanga, the following account exemplifies the position that I have been arguing for throughout *Islands and Exiles*, it is nonetheless my hope that the schematic argument unfolded here has itself already been thoroughly complicated by the detailed consideration of Franco-Caribbean literature and culture that has taken up the greater part of this book.

30. Harris, "Frontier," p. 135.

31. K. Hulme, "Myth," p. 33.

32. Alley and Williams, *In the Same Room*, p. 149, and see also pp. 143–44.

33. See Fee, "Why C. K. Stead," passim.

34. Prentice, "Re-writing," p. 71.

35. K. Hulme, *Te Kaihau*, pp. 195–209.

36. See, for instance, Fuchs, "Reading," p. 209.

37. Dominy, "Maori Sovereignty," p. 249.

38. During, "Postmodernism" (1985), p. 373.

39. See my *Exotic Memories*, pp. 110–18.

40. Thomas, "Kiss," p. 96. In his examination of Gordon Walter's use of the *koru*, the basic *kowhaiwhai* [designs usually associated with the rafters of tribal meeting houses] motif in his modernist, abstract paintings, Nicholas Thomas cites this negative formulation of what is at stake in the "indigenization" process in order to contrast it with new "bicultural" modes of settler self-fashioning, "which may make profound and wide-ranging cultural, political, and economic concessions—while finding new ways of assimilating indigenous authenticity to a renovated and localised settler actor, in a space which has become compromised rather than plainly lost or gained" (p. 119). Distinguishing absolutely between appropriative and assimilative forms of indigenization, he sensibly concludes, is neither a simple issue nor a particularly helpful approach: "a creolising or synthesising project does not necessarily have a logic of dispossession; whether it does or not would seem no easy matter to measure" (p. 115).

41. Stead, "Keri Hulme," pp. 104, 107.

42. See Benitez-Rojo, *RI*, p. 195.

43. The old man's recourse to allegory can be usefully compared to the speeches of the Tahitian Orou in Diderot's *Supplément au voyage de Bougainville* (1772/1796), which are "somewhat modeled after European" discourse, as the character A points out (*Oeuvres*, p. 992). Commenting on such disparities and the impression of "inauthenticity" to which they give rise, Tzvetan Todorov remarks that they "openly indicate that Diderot's intention is not to speak about the Tahitians faithfully, but to use their situation as an allegory in order to tackle a more general topic: namely, the necessity of submitting oneself to nature" (*Nous*, p. 310). A critic like Stephen Slemon would argue that postcolonial texts use allegory "counter-discursively in order to *expose* the investment of allegory in the colonising project and thus to identify allegorical modes of cognition as the enemy of cultural decolonisation"; according to the logic of this argument, in a writer like Hulme "indigenous or pre-contact allegorical traditions engage with, and finally overcome, the kinds of allegorical reading which a universalising european tradition would want to impose" ("Monuments," p. 12). I would argue, by contrast, that a post/colonial writer like Hulme's engagement with allegory results not in the "overcoming" of one tradition by another, but in their troubling (con)fusion.

44. For an extended analysis of the role that the "invention of tradition" plays in contemporary Pacific Island societies, see the essays collected in Linnekin and Poyer, especially Linnekin's "The Politics of Culture in the Pacific" (pp. 149–73). For a discussion of the stalled dialogue between cultural constructionists and native nationalists in the Pacific, see Tobin, "Cultural Construction." While there can be little doubt, as Tobin argues, that "the vogue for cultural construction arguments appears a hegemony-preserving reaction to decolonization movements" such as those in Hawaii (p. 162), there can be even less doubt that taking these arguments seriously into account rather than naively writing them off as do Hawaiian nationalists such as Haunani-Kay Trask makes for a more supple (to say nothing of less

narcissistic) politics of identity capable of taking into account the complexities of our ineluctably transcultural circumstances.

45. Dening, "Poetic," p. 370.

46. Gilroy, "Route Work," p. 22.

47. Huggan, "Opting," p. 30. For a relevant extension of this argument, see his "Philomela's Retold Story."

48. Attridge, "Oppressive Silence," p. 226.

49. Dale, "*the bone people*," p. 421.   50. Hutcheon, *Poetics*, p. 89.

51. Walcott, "Muse," p. 1.   52. Maxwell, "Reading," pp. 82, 72.

53. Stead, "Pakeha," p. 1398. Taking his argument seriously does not, to be sure, mean supporting Stead's at times contentious presentation of it—a presentation that led Hulme, along with three of the best known writers of the Pacific Rim and Basin (Albert Wendt, Patricia Grace, and Witi Ihimaera), to opt out of his recent edition of *The Faber Book of Contemporary South Pacific Stories*. Whether Stead is guilty, in Hulme's words, of "insulting" and "attacking" Maori and Polynesian writers, or—as he puts it in the "Note on Absences" that prefaces this anthology—of simply refusing to "patronize" such writers by not giving them "special exemption from all but favourable notice, which is what these four appear to want, and mostly to get" (pp. xv–xvi), one can certainly agree with his conclusion that the boycott itself "is a reflection of the present state of the Pacific, and indeed of the world, where the disappearance of the single great power-bloc confrontation, and the consequent lifting of that pressure, has led to fragmentation, and the reassertion of older ethnic and tribal identities and grudges" (p. xvii).

54. Bhabha, "Third Space," p. 212.

55. Fernández Retamar, *Caliban*, p. 16.

56. See, e.g., Willis, "Caliban"; or J. D. Saldívar, *Dialectics*, especially p. 133 (which bears a striking resemblance to P. Hulme, *CE*, pp. 124–25).

57. Bourjea, "Ariel," p. 54.

58. Walcott, "Muse," p. 16.

59. J. M. Dash, "World," pp. 128–29.

60. Brathwaite, "Caliban," p. 44.

61. See Wynter, "Beyond Miranda's Meanings," passim.

62. Nixon, "Caribbean," p. 577.

63. J. M. Dash, "Roman," p. 24.

64. Wordsworth, *Fourteen-Book 'Prelude,'* p. 131 (6.637–41).

65. Wordsworth is (re)citing a line—"Him first, him last, him midst, and without end" (5.165)—from the prelapsarian Adam and Eve's orisons to their Maker.

Bibliography

Adam, Ian, and Helen Tiffin, eds. *Past the Last Post: Theorizing Post-Colonialism and Post-Modernism*. Calgary, 1990.

Adélaïde, Jacques, ed. *L'historial antillais*. Vol. 3. Fort-de-France, 1981.

———. "La liberté ou l'ordre (fin 1848–1851)." In *L'historial antillais*. Vol. 4. Ed. Jacques Adélaïde. Fort-de-France, 1980. 79–98.

Affergan, Francis. *Anthropologie à la Martinique*. Paris, 1983.

———. *Exotisme et altérité: Essai sur les fondements d'une critique de l'anthropologie*. Paris, 1987.

Alley, Elizabeth, and Mark Williams, eds. *In the Same Room: Conversations with New Zealand Writers*. Auckland, 1992.

Amselle, Jean-Loup. *Vers un multiculturalisme français: L'empire de la coutume*. Paris, 1996.

André, Jacques. *Caraïbales: Études sur la littérature antillaise*. Paris, 1981.

———. *L'inceste focal dans la famille noire antillaise: Crimes, conflits, structure*. Paris, 1987.

Antoine, Régis. *Les écrivains français et les Antilles: Des premiers Pères blancs aux surréalistes noirs*. Paris, 1978.

———. *La littérature franco-antillaise: Haïti, Guadeloupe et Martinique*. Paris, 1992.

Appadurai, Arjun. *Modernity at Large: Cultural Dimensions of Globalization*. Minneapolis, 1996.

Appiah, Kwame Anthony. *In My Father's House: Africa in the Philosophy of Culture*. New York, 1992.

———. "Race, Culture, Identity: Misunderstood Connections." In Anthony Appiah and Amy Gutmann, *Color Conscious: The Political Morality of Race*. Princeton, N.J., 1996. 30–105.

Aquin, Hubert. *Trou de mémoire*. Montreal, 1993.

Armet, Auguste. "Guadeloupe et Martinique: Des sociétés 'krazé'?" *Présence africaine* 121–22 (1982): 11–19.

Arnold, A. James. "The Gendering of *Créolité*: The Erotics of Colonialism." In Condé and Cottenet-Hage. 21–40.

———. *Modernism and Negritude: The Poetry and Poetics of Aimé Césaire*. Cambridge, Mass., 1981.

Asad, Talal. *Genealogies of Religion: Discipline and Reasons of Power in Christianity and Islam*. Baltimore, 1993.

Ashcroft, Bill, Gareth Griffiths, and Helen Tiffin. *The Empire Writes Back: Theory and Practice in Post-Colonial Literatures*. London, 1989.

Attridge, Derek. "Oppressive Silence: J. M. Coetzee's *Foe* and the Politics of the

Canon." In *Decolonizing Tradition: New Views of Twentieth-Century 'British' Literary Canons*. Ed. Karen R. Lawrence. Urbana, Ill., 1992. 212–38.

Attwell, David. *J. M. Coetzee: South Africa and the Politics of Writing*. Berkeley, Calif., 1993.

Atwood, Margaret. *Survival: A Thematic Guide to Canadian Literature*. Concord, 1972.

Bailey, Marianne Wichmann. *The Ritual Theater of Aimé Césaire: Mythic Structures of the Dramatic Imagination*. Tübingen, 1992.

Bakhtin, Mikhail. *Problems of Dostoevsky's Poetics*. Trans. Caryl Emerson. Minneapolis, 1984.

Bambara, Toni Cade. "Reading the Signs, Empowering the Eye: *Daughters of the Dust* and the Black Independent Cinema Movement." In *Black American Cinema*. Ed. Manthia Diawara. New York, 1993. 118–44.

Barker, Francis, Peter Hulme, and Margaret Iversen, eds. *Colonial Discourse/Postcolonial Theory*. Manchester, 1994.

Barnard, Rita. "Dream Topographies: J. M. Coetzee and the South African Pastoral." *South Atlantic Quarterly* 93.1 (1994): 33–58.

Baudelaire, Charles. *Oeuvres complètes*. Ed. Y.-G. Le Dantec and Claude Pichois. Paris, 1961.

Baudot, Alain. *Bibliographie annotée d'Édouard Glissant*. Toronto, 1993.

Baudrillard, Jean. *Simulacres et simulation*. Paris, 1981.

Béji, Hélé. *Désenchantement national: Essai sur la décolonisation*. Paris, 1982.

Benitez-Rojo, Antonio. *The Repeating Island: The Caribbean and the Postmodern Perspective*. Trans. James Maraniss. Durham, N.C., 1992.

Ben Jalloun, Tahar. *L'enfant de sable*. Paris, 1985.

Benot, Yves. *La démence coloniale sous Napoléon*. Paris, 1992.

———. *La Révolution française et la fin des colonies*. Paris, 1987.

Benrekassa, Georges. *Fables de la personne: Pour une histoire de la subjectivité*. Paris, 1985.

Bergeaud, Émeric. *Stella*. Paris, 1859.

Bernabé, Jean. "Le travail de l'écriture chez Simone Schwarz-Bart." *Présence africaine* 121–22 (1982): 166–79.

Bernabé, Jean, Patrick Chamoiseau, and Raphaël Confiant. *Éloge de la Créolité*. Paris, 1989.

Berque, Jacques. *Dépossession du monde*. Paris, 1964.

Bhabha, Homi. "DissemiNation: Time, Narrative, and the Margins of the Modern Nation." In *Nation and Narration*. Ed. Homi Bhabha. London, 1990. 291–322.

———. *The Location of Culture*. London, 1994.

———. "The Third Space." In *Identity: Community, Culture, Difference*. Ed. Jonathan Rutherford. London, 1990. 207–21.

———. "'What Does the Black Man Want?'" *New Formations* 1 (1987): 118–24.

Biondi, Jean-Pierre. *Senghor, ou La tentation de l'universel*. Paris, 1993.

Bissette, Cyrille-Charles-Auguste. *Deux mots sur une note de M. V. Schœlcher*. Paris, 1843.

———. *Examen rapide des deux projets de loi relatifs aux colonies*. Paris, 1833.

———. *Lettres politiques sur les colonies, sur l'ésclavage et sur les questions qui s'y rattachent.* Paris, 1845.

———. *Liberté de la presse confisquée à la Martinique au profit des propriétaires d'esclaves, ou Requête à M. le Ministre de la Marine et des Colonies sur cette confiscation.* Paris, 1844.

———. *Réfutation du livre de M. Victor Schœlcher, intitulé 'Des colonies françaises'.* Paris, 1843.

———. *Réfutation du livre de M. V. Schœlcher sur Haïti.* Paris, 1844.

———. *Réponse au factum de M. Schœlcher intitulé 'La vérité aux ouvriers et cultivateurs de la Martinique'.* Paris, 1850.

Bissette, Cyrille-Charles-Auguste, and Louis Fabien. *Dénonciation contre M. le comte de Peyronnet, ancien ministre de la justice, pour détention prolongée pendant vingt-un mois, par suite de rétention frauduleuse et de mauvaise foi de pièces a lui adressées par les hommes de couleur de la Martinique, pour être transmises à la Cour de cassation.* Paris, 1828.

Bolland, O. Nigel. "Creolization and Creole Societies: A Cultural Nationalist View of Caribbean Social History." In Hennessy. 1.50–79.

Bongie, Chris. "Between Apocalypse and Narrative: Drieu la Rochelle and the Fascist Novel." *Romanic Review* 93.1 (1993): 55–76.

———. *Exotic Memories: Literature, Colonialism, and the Fin de Siècle.* Stanford, Calif., 1991.

———. "Francophone Conjunctures." *New West Indian Guide / Nieuwe West-Indische Gids* 71.3–4 (1997): 291–307.

Bonniol, Jean-Luc. *La couleur comme maléfice: Une illustration créole de la généalogie des 'Blancs' et des 'Noirs'.* Paris, 1992.

Bouche, Denise. *Histoire de la colonisation française.* Vol. 2. Paris, 1991.

Bouillier, Henry. *Victor Segalen.* 2nd ed. Paris, 1986.

Bourjea, Serge. "Ariel—Celui qui sait la mer." In Leiner. 51–60.

Boyer-Peyreleau, Eugène-Édouard. *Les Antilles françaises, particulièrement la Guadeloupe, depuis leur découverte jusqu'au 1er janvier 1823.* 3 vols. Paris, 1823.

Brathwaite, Edward Kamau. *The Arrivants: A New World Trilogy.* Oxford, 1973.

———. "Caliban, Ariel, and unProspero in the Conflict of Creolization: A Study of the Slave Revolt in Jamaica in 1831–32." In *Comparative Perspectives on Slavery in New World Plantation Societies.* Ed. Vera Rubin and Arthur Tuden. New York, 1977. 41–62.

———. *Contradictory Omens: Cultural Diversity and Integration in the Caribbean.* Kingston, 1974.

———. *The Development of Creole Society in Jamaica, 1770–1820.* Oxford, 1971.

———. "History, the Caribbean Writer and X-Self." In *Crisis and Creativity in the New Literatures in English.* Ed. G. V. Davis and H. Maes-Jelinek. Amsterdam, 1990. 23–45.

———. "Introduction." In *New Poets from Jamaica: An Anthology.* Ed. E. K. Brathwaite. *Savacou* 14–15 (1979): 3–5.

———. *Roots.* Ann Arbor, Mich., 1993.

———. "Timehri." In Coombs. 29–44.

————. "World Order Models—A Caribbean Perspective." *Caribbean Quarterly* 31.1 (1985): 53–63.

————. *X/Self*. Oxford, 1987.

Britton, Celia. "*Discours* and *Histoire*, Magical and Political Discourse in Édouard Glissant's *Le quatrième siècle*." *French Cultural Studies* 5.2 (1994): 151–62.

Brooks, Peter. *Body Work: Objects of Desire in Modern Narrative*. Cambridge, Mass., 1993.

Brossat, Alain, and Daniel Maragnes. *Les Antilles dans l'impasse?* Paris, 1981.

Burton, Richard D. E. *Afro-Creole: Power, Opposition, and Play in the Caribbean*. Ithaca, N.Y., 1997.

————. "Between the Particular and the Universal: Dilemmas of the Martinican Intellectual." In Hennessy. 2.186–210.

————. "Comment peut-on être martiniquais?: The Recent Work of Édouard Glissant." *Modern Language Review* 79.2 (1984): 301–12.

————. "*Débrouya pa peché*, or *Il y a toujours moyen de moyenner*: Patterns of Opposition in the Fiction of Patrick Chamoiseau." *Callaloo* 16.2 (1993): 466–81.

————. *La famille coloniale: La Martinique et la mère patrie*. Paris, 1994.

————. "The Idea of Difference in Contemporary French West Indian Thought: Négritude, Antillanité, Créolité." In *French and West Indian: Martinique, Guadeloupe, and French Guiana Today*. Ed. R. D. E. Burton and Fred Reno. Charlottesville, Va., 1995. 137–66.

————. "*Ki moun nou ye?*: The Idea of Difference in Contemporary French West Indian Thought." *New West Indian Guide / Nieuwe West-Indische Gids* 67.1–2 (1993): 5–32.

————. *Le roman marron: Études sur la littérature martiniquaise contemporaine*. Paris, 1997.

————. "Traversée paradoxale d'un texte: *Corps perdu* d'Aimé Césaire." *Présence francophone* 46 (1995): 123–31.

————. "Two Views of Césaire: *Négritude* and *Créolité*." *Dalhousie French Studies* 35 (1996): 135–52.

Burwick, Roswitha. "Issues of Language and Communication in Kleist's 'Die Verlobung in St. Domingo.'" *German Quarterly* 65.3–4 (1992): 318–27.

Bushnell, David, ed. *The Liberator, Simón Bolívar: Man and Image*. New York, 1970.

Cailler, Bernadette. *Conquérants de la nuit nue: Édouard Glissant et l'H(h)istoire antillaise*. Tübingen, 1988.

————. "Édouard Glissant: A Creative Critic." *World Literature Today* 63.4 (1989): 589–92.

Camus, Albert. *Essais*. Ed. R. Quilliot and L. Faucon. Paris, 1965.

Carby, Hazel. "The Multicultural Wars." *Radical History Review* 54 (1992): 7–18.

Carlyle, Thomas. "Occasional Discourse on the Nigger Question." In idem, *Critical and Miscellaneous Essays*. Vol. 4. New York, 1969. 348–83.

Carpentier, Alejo. "El autor habla de su obra." *Revolución y cultura* 131–32 (1983): 10–16.

————. *Explosion in a Cathedral*. Trans. John Sturrock. London, 1963.

——. *The Kingdom of This World*. Trans. Harriet de Onís. New York, 1989.

——. *The Lost Steps*. Trans. Harriet de Onís. London, 1956.

——. *Obras completas*. 16 vols. Madrid, 1983–94.

Case, Frederick Ivor. *The Crisis of Identity: Studies in the Guadeloupean and Martiniquan Novel*. Sherbrooke, 1985.

Cauna, Jacques. "Les sources historiques de *Bug-Jargal*: 'Hugo et la révolution haïtienne.'" *Conjonction* 166 (1985): 23–36.

Césaire, Aimé. *The Collected Poetry*. Trans. Clayton Eshleman and Annette Smith. Berkeley, Calif., 1983.

——. "Discours de clôture du IIIe Congrès du P. P. M." In idem, *Oeuvres complètes*. Vol. 3. Paris, 1976. 493–511.

——. *Et les chiens se taisaient: Tragédie*. Paris, 1956.

——. "L'homme de culture et ses responsabilités." *Présence africaine* 24–25 (1959): 116–22.

——. "Introduction." In Daniel Guérin, *Les Antilles décolonisées*. Paris, 1956. 9–21.

——. "Le noir, cet inconnu: Entretien avec Aimé Césaire." *Les nouvelles littéraires*, July 17, 1969: 12.

——. "La pensée politique de Sékou Touré." *Présence africaine* 29 (1959–60): 65–73.

——. *Soleil cou-coupé*. Nendeln, 1970.

——. *Une tempête*. Paris, 1969.

——. *La tragédie du roi Christophe*. Paris, 1970.

Chambers, Iain. *Border Dialogues: Journeys in Postmodernity*. London, 1990.

——. *Migrancy, Culture, Identity*. London, 1994.

Chambers, Iain, and Lidia Curti, eds. *The Post-Colonial Question: Common Skies, Divided Horizons*. London, 1996.

Chamoiseau, Patrick. "En témoignage d'une volupté." *Carbet* 10 (1990): 143–52.

——. "Que faire de la parole? Dans la tracée mystérieuse de l'oral à l'écrit." In Ludwig. 151–58.

——. "Les secrets de Chamoiseau." *Antilla* 278 (1988): 34–38.

——. *Solibo magnifique*. Paris, 1988.

——. *Texaco*. Paris, 1992.

Chamoiseau, Patrick, and Raphaël Confiant. *Lettres créoles: Tracées antillaises et continentales de la littérature—Haïti, Guadeloupe, Martinique, Guyane 1635–1975*. Paris, 1991.

Chateaubriand, François-René de. *Essai sur les révolutions, Génie du Christianisme*. Ed. Maurice Regard. Paris, 1978.

——. *Grands écrits politiques*. 2 vols. Ed. Jean-Paul Clément. Paris, 1993.

Chaudenson, Robert. *Des îles, des hommes, des langues: Langues créoles—cultures créoles*. Paris, 1992.

——. *La léxique du parler créole de la Réunion*. 2 vols. Paris, 1974.

——. "Mulâtres, métis, créoles ... " In *Métissages: Linguistique et anthropologie*. Ed. Jean-Luc Alber, Claudine Bavoux, and Michel Watin. Paris, 1992. 23–37.

Chauleau, Liliane. *La vie quotidienne aux Antilles françaises au temps de Victor Schœlcher—XIXe siècle*. Paris, 1979.

Chenet, Françoise. "*Les travailleurs de la mer*, ou L'écriture en archipel." In Marimoutou and Racault, *Insularité*. 365–74.

Chevigny, Bell Gale. "'Insatiable Unease': Melville and Carpentier and the Search for an American Hermeneutic." In Chevigny and Laguardia. 34–59.

Chevigny, Bell Gale, and Gari Laguardia, eds. *Reinventing the Americas: Comparative Studies of Literature of the United States and Spanish America*. Cambridge, Eng., 1986.

Chinweizu, Onwuchekwa Jemie, and Ihechukwu Madubuike. *Toward the Decolonization of African Literature*. Washington, D.C., 1983.

Chow, Rey. *Writing Diaspora: Tactics of Intervention in Contemporary Cultural Studies*. Bloomington, Ind., 1993.

Clark, Vèvè A. "Developing Diaspora Literacy: Allusion in Maryse Condé's *Hérémakhonon*." In Davies and Fido. 303–19.

———. "Haiti's Tragic Overture: (Mis)Representations of the Haitian Revolution in World Drama (1796–1975)." In *Representing the French Revolution: Literature, Historiography, and Art*. Ed. James A. W. Heffernan. Hanover, N.H., 1992. 237–60.

Cliff, Michelle. *Abeng*. New York, 1990.

———. *No Telephone to Heaven*. New York, 1989.

———. "[Untitled Conference Presentation]." In *Critical Fictions: The Politics of Imaginative Writing*. Ed. Philomena Mariani. Seattle, Wash., 1991. 66–71.

Clifford, James. "On Ethnographic Allegory." In *Writing Culture: The Poetics and Politics of Ethnography*. Ed. James Clifford and George E. Marcus. Berkeley, Calif., 1986. 98–121.

———. *The Predicament of Culture: Twentieth-Century Ethnography, Literature, and Art*. Cambridge, Mass., 1988.

Coetzee. J. M. *Doubling the Point: Essays and Interviews*. Ed. David Attwell. Cambridge, Mass., 1992.

———. *Dusklands*. Harmondsworth, 1983.

———. *Foe*. Harmondsworth, 1987.

———. *Life and Times of Michael K*. Harmondsworth, 1985.

———. *Waiting for the Barbarians*. Harmondsworth, 1982.

———. *White Writing: On the Culture of Letters in South Africa*. New Haven, Ct., 1988.

Condé, Maryse. *En attendant le bonheur (Hérémakhonon)*. Paris, 1988.

———. "Order, Disorder, Freedom, and the West Indian Writer." *Yale French Studies* 83.2 (1993): 121–35.

———. *Le roman antillais*. 2 vols. Nancy, 1977.

Condé, Maryse, and Madeleine Cottenet-Hage, eds. *Penser la Créolité*. Paris, 1995.

Confiant, Raphaël. *Aimé Césaire: Une traversée paradoxale du siècle*. Paris, 1993.

———. "Contre les Rimbaud bronzés." *Antilla* 575 (1994): 29–30.

———. "Remarques sur le *Discours antillais*." *Antilla* 5 (1981): 36–38.

Conrad, Joseph. *Heart of Darkness*. Ed. Ross C. Murfin. 2nd ed. New York, 1996.

Constant, Fred. *La retraite aux flambeaux: Société et politique en Martinique*. Paris, 1988.

Coombs, Orde, ed. *Is Massa Day Dead? Black Moods in the Caribbean*. Garden City, N.Y., 1974.

Corzani, Jack. *La littérature des Antilles-Guyane françaises*. 6 vols. Fort-de-France, 1978.

———. "La littérature face à la violence: Le cas des Antilles-Guyane." In *La deriva delle francofonie: Figures et fantasmes de la violence dans les littératures francophones de l'Afrique subsaharienne et des Antilles*. Vol. 2. Ed. Carla Fratta. Bologna, 1992. 13–38.

Crosta, Suzanne. *Le marronnage créateur: Dynamique textuelle chez Édouard Glissant*. Sainte-Foy, 1991.

Cudjoe, Selwyn. *Resistance and Caribbean Literature*. Chicago, 1980.

Dale, Judith. "*the bone people*: (Not) Having It Both Ways." *Landfall* 39.4 (1985): 413–28.

Damato, Diva. "Édouard Glissant et le manifeste *Éloge de la Créolité*." In Favre and Ferreira de Brito. 245–54.

Dash, J. Michael. "Le cri du morne: La poétique du paysage césairien et la littérature antillaise." In Leiner. 101–10.

———. *Édouard Glissant*. Cambridge, Eng., 1995.

———. "Introduction." In Édouard Glissant, *The Ripening*. Trans. J. M. Dash. London, 1985. 1–17.

———. *Literature and Ideology in Haiti, 1915–1961*. London, 1981.

———. "Le roman de nous." *Carbet* 10 (1990): 21–31.

———. "The World and the Word: French Caribbean Writing in the Twentieth Century." *Callaloo* 11.1 (1988): 112–30.

———, ed. "Francophone Literature." In *A History of Literature in the Caribbean, Volume 1: Hispanic and Francophone Regions*. Ed. James A. Arnold. Amsterdam, 1994. 307–565.

Dash, Julie. *Daughters of the Dust*. New York, 1992.

Davies, Carole Boyce. *Black Women, Writing and Identity: Migrations of the Subject*. London, 1994.

Davies, Carole Boyce, and Elaine Savory Fido, eds. *Out of the Kumbla: Caribbean Women and Literature*. Trenton, N.J., 1990.

Davies, Simon. "*Paul et Virginie* 1953–1991: The Present State of Studies." In *Studies on Voltaire and the Eighteenth Century* 317 (Oxford, 1994): 239–66.

Davis, Lennard J. *Resisting Novels: Ideology and Fiction*. London, 1987.

Dayan, Joan. "Codes of Law and Bodies of Color." In Condé and Cottenet-Hage. 41–67.

———. "France Reads Haiti: An Interview with René Depestre." *Yale French Studies* 83.2 (1993): 136–53.

———. "Paul Gilroy's Slaves, Ships, and Routes: The Middle Passage as Metaphor." *Research in African Literatures* 27.4 (1996): 7–14.

Debien, Gabriel, ed. *Journal du conseiller Garnier à la Martinique et à la Guadeloupe, 1848–1855*. Fort-de-France, 1969.

———. "Un roman colonial de Victor Hugo: 'Bug Jargal,' ses sources et ses intentions historiques." *Revue d'histoire littéraire de la France* 52.3 (1952): 298–313.

Defoe, Daniel. *The Life and Adventures of Robinson Crusoe*. Harmondsworth, 1965.

D'Eichthal, Gustave, and Ismayl Urbain. *Lettres sur la race noire et la race blanche*. Paris, 1839.

De la situation des gens de couleur libres aux Antilles françaises. Paris, 1823.

De Lauretis, Teresa. *Technologies of Gender: Essays on Theory, Film and Criticism*. Bloomington, Ind., 1987.

Deleuze, Gilles, and Félix Guattari. *Mille plateaux*. Paris, 1980.

Dening, Greg. "A Poetic for Histories: Transformations that Present the Past." In *Clio in Oceania: Toward a Historical Anthropology*. Ed. Aletta Biersack. Washington, D.C., 1991. 347–80.

Depestre, René. "Les aventures de la Créolité." In Ludwig. 159–70.

Derrida, Jacques. *D'un ton apocalyptique adopté naguère en philosophie*. Paris, 1983.

Descourtilz, M. E. *Voyages d'un naturaliste, et ses observations faites sur les trois règnes de la Nature, dans plusieurs ports de mer français, en Espagne, au continent de l'Amérique septentrionale, à Saint-Yago de Cuba, et à St.-Domingue, où l'Auteur devenu le prisonnier de 40,000 Noirs révoltés, et par suite mis en liberté par une colonne de l'armée française, donne des détails circonstanciés sur l'expédition du général Leclerc*. 3 vols. Paris, 1809.

Dessalles, Pierre. *Correspondance, 1808–1834 (La vie d'un colon à la Martinique au XIXème siècle)*. Ed. Henri de Frémont. Courbevoie, 1980.

———. *Journal, 1837–56 (La Vie d'un colon à la Martinique au XIXème siècle)*. 3 vols. Ed. Henri de Frémont and Léo Élisabeth. Courbevoie, 1984–86.

Diáz-Quiñones, Arcadio. "The Hispanic-Caribbean National Discourse: Antonio S. Pedreira and Ramiro Guerra y Sánchez." In Hennessy. 2.99–121.

Dictionnaire encyclopédique et pratique de la Martinique (MADRAS). 4th ed. Fort-de-France, 1993.

Diderot, Denis. *Oeuvres*. Ed. André Billy. Paris, 1951.

Didier, Béatrice. "Le métissage de l'*Encyclopédie* à la Révolution: De l'anthropologie à la politique." In Marimoutou and Racault, *Métissages*. 11–24.

Dollimore, Jonathan. *Sexual Dissidence: Augustine to Wilde, Freud to Foucault*. Oxford, 1991.

Domínguez, Virginia R. *White by Definition: Social Classification in Creole Louisiana*. New Brunswick, N.J., 1986.

Dominy, Michele D. "Maori Sovereignty: A Feminist Invention of Tradition." In Linnekin and Poyer. 237–57.

Dovey, Teresa. *The Novels of J. M. Coetzee: Lacanian Allegories*. Craighall, 1988.

Drescher, Seymour. "British Way, French Way: Opinion Building and Revolution in the Second French Slave Emancipation." *American Historical Review* 96.3 (1991): 709–34.

———. "The Ending of the Slave Trade and the Evolution of European Scientific Racism." *Social Science History* 14.3 (1990): 415–50.

Du Bois, W. E. B. *Haiti*. In *Federal Theatre Plays*. Ed. Federal Theatre Project (U.S.). New York, 1938.

Dumas, Alexandre. *Georges*. Paris, 1974.

Duplessis, Rachel Blau. *Writing Beyond the Ending: Narrative Strategies of Twentieth-Century Women Writers*. Bloomington, Ind., 1985.

During, Simon. "Postmodernism or Postcolonialism?" *Landfall* 39.3 (1985): 366–80.

———. "Postmodernism or Post-Colonialism Today." *Textual Practice* 1.1 (1987): 32–47.

———. "Rousseau's Patrimony: Primitivism, Romance and Becoming Other." In Barker et al. 47–71.

———. "Waiting for the Post: Some Relations Between Modernity, Colonization, and Writing." In Adam and Tiffin. 23–45.

Edmondson, Belinda. "Race, Tradition, and the Construction of the Caribbean Aesthetic." *New Literary History* 25.1 (1994): 109–20.

Elam, Diane. *Romancing the Postmodern*. London, 1992.

Élisabeth, Léo. "La domination française, de la paix d'Amiens à 1870." In *Histoire des Antilles et de la Guyane*. Ed. Pierre Pluchon. Toulouse, 1982. 379–411.

Encyclopédie, ou Dictionnaire raisonné des sciences, des arts et des métiers. 35 vols. Paris, 1751–80.

Étienne, Servais. *Les sources de 'Bug-Jargal,' avec en appendice quelques sources de 'Han d'Islande'*. Brussels, 1923.

Fabian, Johannes. *Time and the Other: How Anthropology Makes Its Object*. New York, 1983.

Fabre, Jean. *Lumières et romantisme: Énergie et nostalgie de Rousseau à Mickiewicz*. 2nd ed. Paris, 1980.

Fanon, Frantz. "Antillais et Africains." In idem, *Pour la révolution africaine: Écrits politiques*. Paris, 1964. 27–36.

———. *Les damnés de la terre*. Paris, 1968.

———. *Peau noire, masques blancs*. Paris, 1952.

Favre, Yves-Alain, and Antonio Ferreira de Brito, eds. *Horizons d'Édouard Glissant: Actes du colloque de Pau*. Biarritz, 1992.

Fee, Margery. "Why C. K. Stead Didn't Like Keri Hulme's *the bone people*: Who Can Write as Other?" *Australian and New Zealand Studies in Canada* 1 (1989): 11–32.

Fernández Retamar, Roberto. *Caliban and Other Essays*. Trans. Edward Baker. Minneapolis, 1989.

Finkielkraut, Alain. *La défaite de la pensée*. Paris, 1987.

Flaubert, Gustave. *Madame Bovary*. Paris, 1971.

Fleuriau [Délégué des colonies français]. *Lettre adressé au Ministre de la Marine par MM. les délégués de la Martinique*. Paris, 1831.

Forster, Elborg, and Robert Forster, eds. and trans. *Sugar and Slavery, Family and Race: The Letters and Diary of Pierre Dessalles, Planter in Martinique, 1808–1856*. Baltimore, 1996.

Friedman, Jonathan. "Narcissism, Roots and Postmodernity: The Constitution of Selfhood in the Global Crisis." In Lash and Friedman. 331–66.

Fuchs, Miriam. "Reading Toward the Indigenous Pacific." In Wilson and Dirlik. 206–25.

Gaitet, Pascale. "Hybrid Creatures, Hybrid Politics, in Hugo's *Bug-Jargal* and *Le*

Dernier Jour d'un condamné." *Nineteenth-Century French Studies* 25.3–4 (1997): 251–65.

Gallagher, Susan VanZanten. *A Story of South Africa: J. M. Coetzee's Fiction in Context*. Cambridge, Mass., 1991.

García Canclini, Néstor. "Memory and Innovation in the Theory of Art." *South Atlantic Quarterly* 92.3 (1993): 423–43.

Garran de Coulon, Jean-Philippe. *Rapport sur les troubles de Saint-Domingue*. 4 vols. Paris, An V-VII [1797–99].

Gates Jr., Henry Louis. "Critical Fanonism." *Critical Inquiry* 17.3 (1991): 457–70.

———. *The Signifying Monkey: A Theory of Afro-American Literary Criticism*. Oxford, 1988.

Gautier, Arlette. *Les soeurs de Solitude: La condition féminine dans l'esclavage aux Antilles du XVIIe au XIXe siècle*. Paris, 1985.

Gauvin, Axel. *Du créole opprimé au créole libre: Défense de la langue réunionnaise*. Paris, 1977.

Genet, Jean. *Les paravents*. Paris, 1976.

Gerbeau, Hubert. "Approche historique du fait créole à la Réunion." In *Îles tropicales: Insularité, 'insularisme'*. Ed. J. P. Doumenge et al. Bordeaux, 1987. 125–56.

Gewecke, Frauke. "Victor Hugo et la révolution haitienne: Jacobins et Jacobites, ou Les ambiguités du discours négrophobe dans la perspective du roman historique." In *Lectures de Victor Hugo*. Ed. Mireille Calle-Gruber and Arnold Rothe. Paris, 1986. 53–65.

Gikandi, Simon. *Maps of Englishness: Writing Identity in the Culture of Colonialism*. New York, 1996.

———. *Writing in Limbo: Modernism and Caribbean Literature*. Ithaca, N.Y., 1992.

Gilroy, Paul. *The Black Atlantic: Modernity and Double Consciousness*. Cambridge, Mass., 1993.

———. "Route Work: The Black Atlantic and the Politics of Exile." In Chambers and Curti. 17–29.

———. *Small Acts: Thoughts on the Politics of Black Culture*. London, 1993.

Girard, René. *Le bouc émissaire*. Paris, 1982.

———. "Innovation and Repetition." *SubStance* 19.2–3 (1990): 7–20.

———. *Mensonge romantique et vérité romanesque*. Paris, 1961.

———. *'To Double Business Bound': Essays on Literature, Mimesis, and Anthropology*. Baltimore, 1978.

Glissant, Édouard. *La case du commandeur*. Paris, 1981.

———. "Le chaos-monde, l'oral et l'écrit." In Ludwig. 111–29.

———. *Le discours antillais*. Paris, 1981.

———. *Faulkner, Mississippi*. Paris, 1996.

———. *L'intention poétique*. Paris, 1969.

———. *Introduction à une Poétique du Divers*. Paris, 1996.

———. "Lam, l'envol et la réunion." *CARE* 10 (1983): 14–15.

———. *La Lézarde*. Paris, 1958.

———. *Mahagony*. Paris, 1987.

———. *Malemort*. Paris, 1975.

———. *Monsieur Toussaint (version scènique)*. Paris, 1986.

———. *Poétique de la Relation*. Paris, 1990.

———. *Le quatrième siècle*. Paris, 1964.

———. "Le romancier noir et son peuple." *Présence africaine* 16 (1957): 26–31.

———. *Soleil de la conscience*. Paris, 1956.

———. "Sur la trace d'Édouard Glissant." *Le nouvel observateur* 1517 (December 2–8, 1993): 58–60.

———. *Tout-monde*. Paris, 1993.

Gobineau, Arthur de. *Oeuvres*. Vol. 1. Ed. Jean Gaulmier and Jean Boissel. Paris, 1983.

Godden, Richard. "*Absalom, Absalom!*, Haiti and Labor History: Reading Unreadable Revolutions." *ELH* 61.3 (1994): 685–720.

Goethe, Johann Wolfgang von. *Elective Affinities*. Trans. R. J. Hollingdale. Harmondsworth, 1971.

González Echevarría, Roberto. *Alejo Carpentier: The Pilgrim at Home*. 2nd ed. Austin, Tx., 1990.

———. *Celestina's Brood: Continuities of the Baroque in Spanish and Latin American Literature*. Durham, N.C., 1993.

Goodden, Angelica. *The Complete Lover: Eros, Nature, and Artifice in the Eighteenth-Century French Novel*. Oxford, 1989.

Gordimer, Nadine. *The Essential Gesture: Writing, Politics and Places*. Ed. Stephen Clingman. London, 1988.

Gozzano, Guido. *The Man I Pretend To Be: The Colloquies and Selected Poems of Guido Gozzano*. Trans. Michael Palma. Princeton, N.J., 1981.

Gratiant, Gilbert. *Fables créoles et autres écrits*. Ed. Isabelle Gratiant, Renaud Gratiant, and Jean-Louis Joubert. Paris, 1996.

———. "Martinique—Conditionnel éden." In *Les quatre samedis des Antilles*. Paris, 1946. 69–105.

Grégoire, Abbé. *De la littérature des nègres*. Paris, 1808.

Griffith, John W. *Joseph Conrad and the Anthropological Dilemma: 'Bewildered Traveller'*. Oxford, 1995.

Grossman, Kathryn M. *The Early Novels of Victor Hugo: Towards a Poetics of Harmony*. Geneva, 1986.

Guillén, Nicolás. "National Identity and Mestizaje." In Hearne. 35–40.

Hall, Stuart. "Cultural Identity and Cinematic Representation." In *Ex-iles: Essays on Caribbean Cinema*. Ed. Mbye B. Cham. Trenton, N.J., 1992. 220–36.

———. "When Was 'The Post-Colonial'? Thinking at the Limit." In Chambers and Curti. 242–60.

Harris, Wilson. "Engineering the Female Subject: Erna Brodber's *Myal*." *Kunapipi* 12.3 (1990): 86–92.

———. "The Fabric of the Imagination." *Third World Quarterly* 12.1 (1990): 175–86.

———. "The Frontier on which *Heart of Darkness* Stands." In idem, *Explorations: A Selection of Talks and Articles, 1966–1981*. Ed. Hena Maes-Jelinek. Mundelstrup, 1981. 134–41.

————. *The Womb of Space: The Cross-cultural Imagination.* Westport, Ct., 1983.

Hazaël-Massieux, Marie-Christine. *Chansons des Antilles: Comptines, Formulettes.* Paris, 1987.

————. "Le créole et le français dans quelques comptines de Guadeloupe." *Études créoles* 11.2 (1988): 35–54.

————. "Des berceuses à la 'Lanterne des magies': Regard sur le monde des comptines et refrains traditionnels en Guadeloupe." *Études créoles* 5.1–2 (1982): 13–38.

Hearn, Lafcadio. *Collected Works.* 16 vols. Boston, 1922.

————. "A Study of Half-Breed Races in the West Indies." *The Cosmopolitan* 9.2 (1890): 167–72.

————. *Trois fois bel conte.* Trans. Serge Denis. Vaduz, 1978.

Hearne, John, ed. *Carifesta Forum: An Anthology of 20 Caribbean Voices.* Kingston, 1976.

Hennessy, Alistair, ed. *Intellectuals in the Twentieth-Century Caribbean.* 2 vols. London, 1992.

Henry, Paget, and Paul Buhle. "Caliban as Deconstructionist: C. L. R. James and Post-Colonial Discourse." In *C. L. R. James's Caribbean.* Ed. P. Henry and P. Buhle. Durham, N.C., 1992. 111–42.

Hitchcock, Peter. "Antillanité and the Art of Resistance." *Research in African Literatures* 27.2 (1996): 33–50.

Hoffmann, Léon François. *Le nègre romantique: Personnage littéraire et obsession collective.* Paris, 1973.

Huannou, Adrien. *La question des littératures nationales en Afrique noire.* Abidjan, 1989.

Huc [Conseiller colonial]. *L'émancipation de la race africaine considérée sous le rapport religieux.* Paris, 1840.

Huggan, Graham. "Opting Out of the (Critical) Common Market: Creolization and the Post-Colonial Text." *Kunapipi* 11.1 (1989): 27–40.

————. "Philomela's Retold Story: Silence, Music, and the Post-Colonial Text." *Journal of Commonwealth Literature* 25.1 (1990): 12–23.

Hugo, Victor. *Bug-Jargal, suivie de la première version du roman.* Paris, 1985.

————. *Correspondance familiale et écrits intimes, 1828–1839.* Vol. 2. Ed. Jean Gaudon et al. Paris, 1991.

————. *Oeuvres complètes.* 18 vols. Ed. Jean Massin. Paris, 1967–70.

Hulme, Keri. *the bone people.* London, 1986.

————. "Myth, Omen, Ghost and Dream." In *Poetry of the Pacific Region.* Ed. Paul Sharrad. Adelaide, 1984. 31–38.

————. *Te Kaihau/The Windeater.* New York, 1987.

Hulme, Peter. *Colonial Encounters: Europe and the Native Caribbean, 1492–1797.* London, 1986.

————. "The Locked Heart: The Creole Family Romance of *Wide Sargasso Sea.*" In Barker et al. 72–88.

————. "Tales of Distinction: European Ethnography and the Caribbean." In *Implicit Understandings: Observing, Reporting, and Reflecting on the Encounters*

Between Europeans and Other Peoples in the Early Modern Period. Ed. Stuart B. Schwartz. Cambridge, Eng., 1994. 157–97.

Hutcheon, Linda. "'Circling the Downspout of Empire.'" In Adam and Tiffin. 167–89.

———. *A Poetics of Postmodernism: History, Theory, Fiction.* London, 1988.

Hutchinson, George. "Jean Toomer and American Racial Discourse." *Texas Studies in Literature and Language* 35.2 (1993): 226–50.

Isambert, François André. *Lettre de M. Isambert contenant le rétablissement de faits importants relatifs aux événements des Antilles françaises en 1824 et en 1826 et la réponse à des calomnies.* Paris, 1850.

James, C. L. R. "Appendix: From Toussaint L'Ouverture to Fidel Castro." In idem, *The Black Jacobins: Toussaint L'Ouverture and the San Domingo Revolution.* 3rd ed. London, 1980. 391–418.

———. *The Black Jacobins: Toussaint Louverture and the San Domingo Revolution.* London, 1938.

Jameson, Fredric. "On 'Cultural Studies.'" In *A Cultural Studies Reader: History, Theory, Practice.* Ed. Jessica Munns and Gita Rajan. London, 1995. 613–45.

———. *The Political Unconscious: Narrative as a Socially Symbolic Act.* Ithaca, N.Y., 1981.

———. "Postmodernism, or The Cultural Logic of Late Capitalism." *New Left Review* 146 (1984): 53–92.

———. *Postmodernism, or The Cultural Logic of Late Capitalism.* Durham, N.C., 1991.

Jehlen, Myra. *Class and Character in Faulkner's South.* New York, 1976.

Jennings, Lawrence C. "Cyrille Bissette, Radical Black French Abolitionist." *French History* 9.1 (1995): 48–66.

Johnson, Barbara. "Apostrophe, Animation, and Abortion." *Diacritics* 16.1 (1986): 29–47.

Johnson, Lemuel A. "A-beng: (Re)Calling the Body In(to) Question." In Davies and Fido. 111–42.

———. "The *Romance bárbaro* as an Agent of Disappearance: Henrique Coelho Netto's *Rei negro* and Its Conventions." In Luis. 223–48.

Juin, Hubert. *Victor Hugo, 1802–1843.* Vol. 1. Paris, 1980.

Julien, Isaac. "'Black Is, Black Ain't': Notes on De-essentializing Black Identities." In *Black Popular Culture.* Ed. Gina Dent. Seattle, Wash., 1992. 255–63.

Kadish, Doris Y. *The Literature of Images: Narrative Landscape from 'Julie' to 'Jane Eyre'.* New Brunswick, N.J., 1987.

Kadish, Doris Y., and Françoise Massardier-Kenney, eds. *Translating Slavery: Gender and Race in French Women's Writing, 1783–1823.* Kent, Ohio, 1994.

Kaplan, Caren. *Questions of Travel: Postmodern Discourses of Displacement.* Durham, N.C., 1996.

Karl, Frederick R. *William Faulkner: American Writer—A Biography.* London, 1989.

Kellner, Douglas. "Popular Culture and the Construction of Postmodern Identities." In Lash and Friedman. 141–77.

Kesteloot, Lilyan. *Les écrivains noirs de langue française: Naissance d'une littérature*. Brussels, 1963.

Klein, Richard. "The Mètis of Centaurs." *Diacritics* 16.2 (1986): 2–13.

Kleist, Heinrich von. "The Betrothal in Santo Domingo." In idem, *The Marquise of O—and Other Stories*. Trans. David Luke and Nigel Reeves. Harmondsworth, 1978. 231–69.

———. *Die Verlobung in St. Domingo (Sämtliche Werke 2.4)*. Ed. Roland Reuss. Basel, 1988.

Kristeva, Julie. *Étrangers à nous-mêmes*. Paris, 1988.

Kutzinski, Vera M. *Against the Grain: Myth and History in William Carlos Williams, Jay Wright, and Nicolás Guillén*. Baltimore, 1987.

———. *Sugar's Secrets: Race and the Erotics of Cuban Nationalism*. Charlottesville, Va., 1993.

Lacroix, Baron Pamphile de. *Mémoires pour servir à l'histoire de la révolution de Saint-Domingue*. 2 vols. Paris, 1819.

Ladd, Barbara. "'The Direction of the Howling': Nationalism and the Color Line in *Absalom, Absalom!*" *American Literature* 66.3 (1994): 525–51.

———. *Nationalism and the Color Line in George W. Cable, Mark Twain, and William Faulkner*. Baton Rouge, La., 1996.

Laforgue, Pierre. "*Bug-Jargal*, ou De la difficulté d'écrire en 'style blanc.'" *Romantisme* 69 (1990): 29–42.

Lamming, George. *The Pleasures of Exile*. Ann Arbor, Mi., 1992.

Langford, Gerald. *Faulkner's Revision of 'Absalom, Absalom!': A Collation of the Manuscript and the Published Book*. Austin, Tx., 1971.

Lara, H. Adolphe, ed. *Contribution de la Guadeloupe à la pensée française, 1635–1935*. Paris, 1936.

Lara, Oruno. *La Guadeloupe dans l'histoire*. Paris, 1979.

Lash, Scott, and Jonathan Friedman, eds. *Modernity and Identity*. Oxford, 1992.

Lazarus, Neil. "Is a Counterculture of Modernity a Theory of Modernity?" *Diaspora* 4.3 (1995): 323–39.

Le Brun, Annie. *Pour Aimé Césaire*. Paris, 1994.

———. *Soudain un bloc d'abîme, Sade*. Paris, 1986.

———. *Statue cou coupé*. Paris, 1996.

Leconte de Lisle. *Oeuvres*. 4 vols. Ed. Edgard Pich. Paris, 1976–78.

Leiner, Jacqueline, ed. *Soleil éclaté: Mélanges offerts à Aimé Césaire à l'occasion de son soixante-dixième anniversaire*. Tübingen, 1984.

Leiris, Michel. *Contacts de civilisations en Martinique et en Guadeloupe*. Paris, 1955.

Léro, Étienne. "Misère d'une poésie." In *Légitime Défense*. Paris, 1979. 10–12.

Levilloux, Jules. "Les Antilles." *La France maritime*. 2nd ed. Paris, 1853. 1.16–20.

———. *Les créoles, ou La vie aux Antilles*. In *Romans antillais du XIXᵉ siècle*. Vol. 2. Morne-Rouge, 1977. 5–269.

Lewis, Gordon K. *Main Currents in Caribbean Thought: The Historical Evolution of Caribbean Society in Its Ideological Aspects, 1492–1900*. Baltimore, 1983.

Linnekin, Jocelyn, and Lin Poyer, eds. *Cultural Identity and Ethnicity in the Pacific*. Honolulu, 1990.

Lionnet, Françoise. *Autobiographical Voices: Race, Gender, Self-Portraiture*. Ithaca, N.Y., 1989.

Loxley, Diana. *Problematic Shores: The Literature of Islands*. London, 1990.

Ludwig, Ralph, ed. *Écrire la 'parole de nuit': La nouvelle littérature antillaise*. Paris, 1994.

Luis, William, ed. *Voices from Under: Black Narrative in Latin America and the Caribbean*. Westport, Ct., 1984.

Lukács, Georg. *The Historical Novel*. Trans. Hannah and Stanley Mitchell. London, 1962.

Lyotard, Jean-François. "Re-writing Modernity." *SubStance* 16.3 (1987): 3–9.

Madou, Jean-Pol. *Édouard Glissant: De mémoire d'arbres*. Amsterdam, 1996.

Marimoutou, Jean-Claude, and Jean-Michel Racault, eds. *L'insularité: Thématique et représentations*. Paris, 1995.

———. *Métissages: Littérature-histoire*. Paris, 1992.

Marin, Louis. "Archipels." *Silex* 14 (1979): 79–87.

Marinetti, F. T. *Le monoplan du Pape*. Paris, 1912.

Márquez, Roberto. "Nationalism, Nation, and Ideology: Trends in the Emergence of a Caribbean Literature." In *The Modern Caribbean*. Ed. Franklin W. Knight and Colin A. Palmer. Chapel Hill, N.C., 1989. 293–340.

Mason, Peter. "Figures of America." *Eighteenth-Century Life* 20.3 (1996): 107–16.

Mauviel, Maurice. "Métissages biologiques et métissages culturels." In Marimoutou and Racault, *Métissages*. 59–80.

Maximin, Colette. *Littératures caribéennes comparées*. Paris, 1996.

Maximin, Daniel. "Aimé Césaire: La poésie, parole essentielle." *Présence africaine* 126 (1983): 7–23.

———. "Entretien avec Daniel Maximin." *Nouvelles du Sud* 3 (1986): 35–50.

———. *L'île et une nuit*. Paris, 1995.

———. *L'isolé soleil*. Paris, 1981.

———. *Soufrières*. Paris, 1987.

Maxwell, Anne. "Post Colonial Histories and Identities: Negotiating the Subjects of 'Social Change' and 'Postmodern Theory.'" *Literature and History*, 3rd series, 3.1 (1994): 64–82.

———. "Reading *the bone people*: Toward a Literary Postcolonial Nationalist Discourse." *Antithesis* 1.1 (1987): 63–86.

Mayaux, Catherine. "La structure romanesque de *Mahagony* d'Édouard Glissant." In Favre and Ferreira de Brito. 349–63.

Maynard, Louis de. *Outre-mer*. 2 vols. Paris, 1835.

———. "Scènes nocturnes aux Antilles." *La France maritime*. 2nd ed. Paris, 1852. 3.265–72.

———. "Voyage à la Martinique," *La France maritime*. 2nd ed. Paris, 1853. 1.360–65.

McClintock, Anne. *Imperial Leather: Race, Gender and Sexuality in the Colonial Contest*. London, 1995.

Melville, Hermann. *Typee*. Harmondsworth, 1972.

Ménil, René. *Tracées: Identité, négritude, esthétique aux Antilles*. Paris, 1981.

Mercer, Kobena. *Welcome to the Jungle: New Positions in Black Cultural Studies.* London, 1994.

Mesnard, Éric. "Les mouvements de résistance dans les colonies françaises: L'affaire Bissette (1823–1827)." In *Les abolitions de l'esclavage: De L. F. Sonthonax à V. Schœlcher—1793, 1794, 1848.* Ed. Marcel Dorigny. Paris, 1995. 293–97.

Mestry, Philip. *Une analyse des macro-structures de 'Paul et Virginie,' suivi de deux autres études.* Paris, 1990.

Miller, Christopher L. "Nationalism as Resistance and Resistance to Nationalism in the Literature of Francophone Africa." *Yale French Studies* 82 (1993): 62–100.

———. "The Postidentitarian Predicament in the Footnotes of *A Thousand Plateaus*: Nomadology, Anthropology, and Authority." *Diacritics* 23.3 (1993): 6–35.

———. *Theories of Africans: Francophone Literature and Anthropology in Africa.* Chicago, 1990.

Miller, D. A. *Narrative and Its Discontents: Problems of Closure in the Traditional Novel.* Princeton, N.J., 1981.

Miller, J. Hillis. *Ariadne's Thread: Story Lines.* New Haven, Ct., 1992.

———. *Topographies.* Stanford, Calif., 1995.

Mishra, Vijay, and Bob Hodge. "What is Post(-)colonialism?" *Textual Practice* 5.3 (1991): 399–414.

Moitt, Bernard. "Slave Resistance in Guadeloupe and Martinique, 1791–1848." *Journal of Caribbean History* 25.1–2 (1991): 136–59.

Moreau de Saint-Méry, M. L. E. *Description topographique, physique, civile, politique et historique de la partie française de l'isle Saint-Domingue.* 2 vols. Philadelphia, 1797–98.

Moretti, Franco. *Signs Taken for Wonders: Essays in the Sociology of Literary Forms.* Rev. ed. Trans. Susan Fischer et al. London, 1988.

———. *The Way of the World: The 'Bildungsroman' in European Culture.* Trans. Albert Sbragia. London, 1987.

Morphet, Tony. "Two Interviews with J. M. Coetzee." In *From South Africa: New Writing, Photographs, and Art.* Ed. David Bunn et al. Chicago, 1987. 454–64.

Mouralis, Bernard. "Histoire et culture dans *Bug-Jargal.*" *Revue des sciences humaines* 149 (1973): 47–68.

———. "*L'isolé soleil* de Daniel Maximin, ou La sortie du ventre paternel." *Présence africaine* 121–122 (1982): 418–26.

Mudimbe-Boyi, Élisabeth. "The Poetics of Exile and Errancy in *Le baobab fou* by Ken Bugul and *Ti Jean L'horizon* by Simone Schwarz-Bart." *Yale French Studies* 83 (1993): 196–212.

Neill, Anna. "The Sentimental Novel and the Republican Imaginary: Slavery in *Paul and Virginia.*" *Diacritics* 23.3 (1993): 36–47.

Ngugi wa Thiong'o. *Decolonising the Mind: The Politics of Language in African Literature.* London, 1986.

Nicholls, David. *From Dessalines to Duvalier: Race, Colour and National Independence in Haiti.* 3rd ed. London, 1996.

Nicolas, Armand. *Histoire de la Martinique.* 2 vols. Paris, 1996.

Nietzsche, Friedrich. *Beyond Good and Evil: Prelude to a Philosophy of the Future.* Trans. Walter Kaufmann. New York, 1966.

Nixon, Rob. "Caribbean and African Appropriations of *The Tempest.*" *Critical Inquiry* 13.3 (1987): 557–78.

Nora, Pierre. "Entre mémoire et histoire: La problématique des lieux." In *Les lieux de mémoire.* Vol. 1. Ed. Pierre Nora. Paris, 1984. xv–xlii.

North, Michael. *The Dialect of Modernism: Race, Language, and Twentieth-Century Literature.* New York, 1994.

Ogé, Vincent. *Motion faite par M. Vincent Ogé, jeune à l'Assemblée des colons, Habitans de S.-Domingue, à l'Hôtel de Massiac, Place des victoires.* Paris, n.d.

Ormerod, Beverley. "Discourse and Dispossession: Édouard Glissant's Image of Contemporary Martinique." *Caribbean Quarterly* 27.1 (1981): 1–12.

———. *An Introduction to the French Caribbean Novel.* London, 1985.

Orr, Linda. *Headless History: Nineteenth-Century French Historiography of the Revolution.* Ithaca, N.Y., 1990.

Pagden, Anthony. "The Effacement of Difference: Colonialism and the Origins of Nationalism in Diderot and Herder." In *After Colonialism: Imperial Histories and Postcolonial Displacements.* Ed. Gyan Prakash. Princeton, N.J., 1995. 129–52.

———. *Lords of all the World: Ideologies of Empire in Spain, Britain and France, c. 1500–c.1800.* New Haven, Ct., 1995.

Pâme, Stella. "L'affaire Bissette (1823–1830)." In Adélaïde, *Historial.* 222–39.

———. "La *Revue des Colonies.*" In Adélaïde, *Historial.* 530–36.

Parker, Robert Dale. *'Absalom, Absalom!': The Questioning of Fictions.* Boston, 1991.

———. "The Chronology and Genealogy of *Absalom, Absalom!*: The Authority of Fiction and the Fiction of Authority." *Studies in American Fiction* 14.2 (1986): 191–98.

Parry, Benita. "Resistance Theory/Theorising Resistance, or Two Cheers for Nativism." In Barker et al. 172–96.

———. "Speech and Silence in the Fictions of J. M. Coetzee." *New Formations* 21 (1993): 1–20.

Pérez Firmat, Gustavo. *The Cuban Condition: Translation and Identity in Modern Cuban Literature.* Cambridge, Eng., 1989.

Perloff, Marjorie. *The Futurist Moment: Avant-Garde, Avant Guerre, and the Language of Rupture.* Chicago, 1986.

———. "Tolerance and Taboo: Modernist Primitivisms and Postmodernist Pieties." In Elazar Barkan and Ronald Bush, eds. *Prehistories of the Future: The Primitivist Project and the Culture of Modernism.* Stanford, Calif., 1995. 339–54.

Péron, Françoise. *Des îles et des hommes: L'insularité aujourd'hui.* Rennes, 1993.

Perraudin, Michael. "Babekan's 'Brille,' and the Rejuvenation of Congo Hoango: A Reinterpretation of Kleist's Story of the Haitian Revolution." *Oxford German Studies* 20–21 (1992): 85–103.

Perrinon, F.-A. *Explications à propos d'un récent libelle de M. Bissette.* Paris, 1850.

Peter, Jean-Pierre, and Jeanne Favret. "L'animal, le fou, le mort." In *Moi, Pierre*

Rivière, ayant égorgé ma mère, ma soeur et mon frère ... : Un cas de parricide au XIXe siècle. Ed. Michel Foucault. Paris, 1994. 293–319.

Petersen, Kirsten Holst. "An Elaborate Dead End? A Feminist Reading of Coetzee's *Foe.*" In *A Shaping of Connections: Commonwealth Literature Studies—Then and Now.* Ed. H. Maes-Jelinek et al. Sydney, 1989. 242–53.

Picquenard, Jean-Baptiste. *Adonis, ou Le bon nègre: Anecdote coloniale.* Paris, 1836.

———. *Zoflora, ou La bonne négresse: Anecdote coloniale.* 2 vols. Paris, An VIII [1800].

Piglia, Ricardo. *Artificial Respiration.* Trans. Daniel Balderston. Durham, N.C., 1994.

Pile, Steve. *The Body and the City: Psychoanalysis, Space and Subjectivity.* London, 1996.

Pratt, Mary Louise. *Imperial Eyes: Travel Writing and Transculturation.* London, 1992.

Prendergast, Christopher. *The Order of Mimesis: Balzac, Stendhal, Nerval, Flaubert.* Cambridge, Eng., 1986.

Prentice, Chris. "Re-Writing Their Stories, Renaming Themselves: Post-colonialism and Feminism in the Fictions of Keri Hulme and Audrey Thomas." *SPAN* 23 (1986): 68–80.

Price, Richard, and Sally Price. "Shadowboxing in the Mangrove." *Cultural Anthropology* 12.1 (1997): 3–36.

Price-Mars, Jean. *Ainsi parla l'oncle.* Ottawa, 1973.

———. *De Saint-Domingue à Haïti: Essai sur la culture, les arts et la littérature.* Paris, 1959.

Prudent, Félix. "L'Africanité dans la genèse créole: Science et idéologie d'un lignage." *Études créoles* 9.1 (1986): 151–68.

Quinet, Edgar. *Du génie des religions.* Paris, 1842.

Racault, Jean-Michel. "De la mythologie ornementale au mythe structurant: *Paul et Virginie* et le mythe des Dioscures." In Racault, *Études.* 40–63.

———. "De l'île réelle à l'île mythique: Bernardin de Saint-Pierre et l'Île de France." In *L'île, territoire mythique.* Ed. François Moreau. Paris, 1989. 79–99.

———. "Mimétisme et métissage: Sur *Georges* d'Alexandre Dumas." In Marimoutou and Racault, *Métissages.* 141–50.

———. "Ouverture et clôture dans *Paul et Virginie*: Essai d'analyse comparative des séquences initiale et finale." In Racault, *Études.* 83–102.

———. "Pastorale et roman dans *Paul et Virginie.*" In Racault, *Études.* 177–200.

———. "*Paul et Virginie* et l'utopie: De la 'petite société' au mythe collectif." In *Studies on Voltaire and the Eighteenth Century* 242 (Oxford, 1986): 419–71.

———. "Système de la toponymie et organisation de l'espace romanesque dans *Paul et Virginie.*" In *Studies on Voltaire and the Eighteenth Century* 242 (Oxford, 1986): 377–418.

———. "Virginie entre la nature et la vertu: Cohésion narrative et contradictions idéologiques dans *Paul et Virginie.*" *Dix-huitième siècle* 18 (1986): 389–404.

———, ed. *Études sur Paul et Virginie et l'oeuvre de Bernardin de Saint-Pierre.* Saint-Denis de la Réunion, 1986.

Ragan, David Paul. *William Faulkner's 'Absalom, Absalom!': A Critical Study*. Ann Arbor, Mich., 1987.

Reid, Calvin. "Caught in Flux: Transatlantic Aesthetics in the Museum." *Transition* 65 (1995): 131–39.

Rella, Franco. *La battaglia della verità*. Milan: 1986.

Richards, David. *Masks of Difference: Cultural Representations in Literature, Anthropology and Art*. Cambridge, Eng., 1994.

Richards, Thomas. *The Imperial Archive: Knowledge and the Fantasy of Empire*. London, 1993.

Richardson, Michael, ed. *Refusal of the Shadow: Surrealism and the Caribbean*. Trans. Krzysztof Fijatkowsi and Michael Richardson. London, 1996.

Rickford, John R. *Dimensions of a Creole Continuum: History, Texts, & Linguistic Analysis of Guyanese Creole*. Stanford, Calif., 1987.

Rivière, Lindsay. *Historical Dictionary of Mauritius*. Metuchen, N.J., 1982.

Rodriguez, Pierre. "Contraintes et contradictions du récit de voyage: L'expérience de Bernardin de Saint-Pierre." *Francofonia* 11 (1986): 35–55.

Roget, Wilbert J. "Littérature, conscience nationale, écriture aux Antilles: Entretien avec Édouard Glissant." *CLA Journal* 24.3 (1981): 304–20.

Rohlehr, Gordon. *Pathfinder: Black Awakening in 'The Arrivants' of Edward Kamau Brathwaite*. Tunapuna, 1981.

Rosello, Mireille. *Littérature et identité créole aux Antilles*. Paris, 1992.

Ross, Kristin. *Fast Cars, Clean Bodies: Decolonization and the Reordering of French Culture*. Cambridge, Mass., 1996.

Rousseau, Jean-Jacques. *Oeuvres complètes*. 5 vols. Ed. Bernard Gagnebin and Marcel Raymond. Paris, 1959–95.

———. *Les rêveries du promeneur solitaire*. Ed. Henri Roddier. Paris, 1960.

Said, Edward. *Beginnings: Intention and Method*. New York, 1985.

———. *Culture and Imperialism*. New York, 1993.

———. "Intellectuals in the Post-Colonial World." *Salmagundi* 70–71 (1986): 44–64.

———. *Orientalism*. New York, 1978.

———. "Representing the Colonized: Anthropology's Interlocutors." *Critical Inquiry* 15.2 (1989): 205–25.

Saint-Pierre, Jacques-Henri-Bernardin de. *Empsaël et Zoraïde, ou Les blancs esclaves des noirs à Maroc*. Ed. Roger Little. Exeter, 1995.

———. *Oeuvres complètes*. 12 vols. Ed. L. Aimé-Martin. Paris, 1825–26.

———. *Paul et Virginie*. Ed. Édouard Guitton. Paris, 1984.

———. *Paul et Virginie*. Ed. Pierre Trahard. Paris, 1964.

———. *Voyage à l'Isle de France*. Ed. Robert Chaudenson. Port-Louis, 1986.

Sainte-Beuve, Charles-Augustin. *Oeuvres*. Vol. 2. Ed. Maxime Leroy. Paris, 1951.

———. *Pour la critique*. Ed. Annie Prassoloff and José-Luis Diaz. Paris, 1992.

Saldívar, Jose David. *The Dialectics of Our America: Genealogy, Cultural Critique, and Literary History*. Durham, N.C., 1991.

Saldívar, Ramón. "Looking for a Master Plan: Faulkner, Paredes, and the Colonial and Postcolonial Subject." In *The Cambridge Companion to William Faulkner*. Ed. Philip M. Weinstein. Cambridge, Eng., 1995. 96–120.

Sand, George. *Indiana*. Paris, 1983.

Sartre, Jean-Paul. "Orphée noir." In idem, *Situations III*. Paris, 1949. 229–86.

Scharfman, Ronnie. "Theorizing Terror: The Discourse of Violence in Marie Chauvet's *Amour Colère Folie*." In *Postcolonial Subjects: Francophone Women Writers*. Ed. Mary Jean Green et al. Minneapolis, 1996. 229–45.

Schiller, Friedrich. *On the Aesthetic Education of Man*. Trans. Elizabeth M. Wilkinson and L. A. Willoughby. Oxford, 1967.

Schmidt, Nelly, *Victor Schœlcher et l'abolition de l'esclavage*. Paris, 1994.

Schœlcher, Victor. *Abolition de l'esclavage: Examen critique du préjugé contre la couleur des Africains et des Sang-mêlés*. Paris, 1840.

———. *Colonies étrangères et Haïti: Résultats de l'Émancipation anglaise*. 2 vols. Paris, 1843.

———. *De l'esclavage des noirs, et de la législation coloniale*. Paris, 1833.

———. *Des colonies françaises: Abolition immédiate de l'esclavage*. Paris, 1842.

———. *Histoire de l'esclavage pendant les deux dernières années*. Paris, 1847.

———. *La vérité aux ouvriers et cultivateurs de la Martinique, suivie des rapports, décrets, projets de lois et d'arrêtés concernant l'abolition immédiate de l'esclavage*. Paris, 1849.

———. *La vérité aux ouvriers et cultivateurs de la Martinique, suivie des rapports, décrets, projets de lois et d'arrêtés concernant l'abolition immédiate de l'esclavage*. 2 vols. Ed. Jacques Adélaïde and Liliane Chauleau. Lausanne, 1985.

Scott, Sir Walter. *Waverley; or, 'Tis Sixty Years Since*. Ed. Claire Lamont. Oxford, 1986.

Segalen, Victor. *Oeuvres complètes*. 2 vols. Ed. Henry Bouillier. Paris, 1995.

Senghor, Léopold Sédar, ed. *Anthologie de la nouvelle poésie nègre et malgache de langue française*. Paris, 1948.

———. *Liberté I: Négritude et humanisme*. Paris, 1964.

———. *Poèmes*. Paris, 1973.

Sharpe, Jenny. *Allegories of Empire: The Figure of Woman in the Colonial Text*. Minneapolis, 1993.

Shohat, Ella. "Notes on the 'Post-Colonial.'" *Social Text* 31–32 (1992): 99–113.

Shohat, Ella, and Robert Stam. *Unthinking Eurocentrism: Multiculturalism and the Media*. London, 1994.

Silenieks, Juris. "The Maroon Figure in Caribbean Francophone Prose." In Luis. 115–25.

———. "Pays rêvé, pays réel: The Martinican Chronotope in Édouard Glissant's Oeuvre." *World Literature Today* 63.4 (1989): 632–36.

Silver, John. "After El Dorado: Alejo Carpentier's *The Lost Steps*." *New Formations* 6 (1988): 65–82.

Sinclair, Karen P. "*Tangi*: Funeral Rituals and the Construction of Maori Identity." In Linnekin and Poyer. 219–36.

Slemon, Stephen. "Monuments of Empire: Allegory/Counter-Discourse/Post-Colonial Writing." *Kunapipi* 9.3 (1987): 1–16.

———. "Post-Colonial Allegory and the Transformation of History." *Journal of Commonwealth Literature* 23.1 (1988): 157–68.

Snead, James. *Figures of Division: William Faulkner's Major Novels*. New York, 1986.

Sollors, Werner. *Neither Black Nor White Yet Both: Thematic Explorations of Interracial Literature*. Oxford, 1997.

Sommer, Doris. *Foundational Fictions: The National Romances of Latin America*. Berkeley, Calif., 1991.

Souquet-Basiège, G. *Le préjugé de race aux Antilles françaises: Étude historique*. Saint-Pierre, 1883.

Spivak, Gayatri. "Can the Subaltern Speak?" In *Colonial Discourse and Postcolonial Theory: A Reader*. Ed. Patrick Williams and Laura Chrisman. New York, 1994. 66–111.

———. "Theory in the Margin: Coetzee's *Foe* Reading Defoe's *Crusoe/Roxana*." In *Consequences of Theory*. Ed. Jonathan Arac and Barbara Johnson. Baltimore, 1991. 154–80.

Starobinski, Jean. *Jean-Jacques Rousseau: La transparence et l'obstacle, suivi de sept essais sur Rousseau*. Paris, 1971.

Stead, C. K. "Keri Hulme's 'The Bone People,' and the Pegasus Award for Maori Literature." *Ariel* 16.4 (1985): 101–8.

———. "A Note on Absences." In *The Faber Book of Contemporary South Pacific Stories*. Ed. C. K. Stead. London, 1994. xv–xvii.

———. "Pakeha Provincialism, Maori Small-Mindedness." *Times Literary Supplement* 4578 (Dec. 28, 1990–Jan. 3, 1991): 1398.

Stevenson, Elizabeth. *Lafcadio Hearn*. New York, 1961.

Sue, Eugène. *Les mystères de Paris*. Paris, 1963.

Suleri, Sara. *The Rhetoric of English India*. Chicago, 1992.

Sundquist, Eric J. *To Wake the Nations: Race in the Making of American Literature*. Cambridge, Mass., 1993.

Tarbé, Charles. *Rapport sur les troubles de Saint-Domingue, fait à l'Assemblée nationale, IIIe partie*. Paris, 1792.

Taussig, Michael. *Mimesis and Alterity: A Particular History of the Senses*. London, 1993.

Taylor, Patrick. *The Narrative of Liberation: Perspectives on Afro-Caribbean Literature, Popular Culture, and Politics*. Ithaca, N.Y., 1989.

Terdiman, Richard. *Present Past: Modernity and the Memory Crisis*. Ithaca, N.Y., 1993.

Thomas, Nicholas. *Colonialism's Culture: Anthropology, Travel and Government*. Cambridge, Eng., 1994.

———. "Kiss the Baby Goodbye: *Kowhaiwhai* and Aesthetics in Aotearoa New Zealand." *Critical Inquiry* 22.1 (1995): 90–121.

Thornton, John K. "African Soldiers in the Haitian Revolution." *Journal of Caribbean History* 25.1–2 (1991): 58–80.

Tobin, Jeffrey. "Cultural Construction and Native Nationalism." In Wilson and Dirlik. 147–69.

Todorov, Tzvetan. *Nous et les autres: La réflexion française sur la diversité humaine*. Paris, 1989.

Tomich Dale W. *Slavery in the Circuit of Sugar: Martinique and the World Economy, 1830–1848*. Baltimore, 1990.

Torgovnick, Marianna. *Gone Primitive: Savage Intellects, Modern Lives*. Chicago, 1990.

Toumson, Roger. "Présentation." In Victor Hugo, *Bug-Jargal, ou La Révolution haïtienne: Les deux versions du roman (1818 et 1826)*. Fort-de-France, 1979. 7–85.

———. *La transgression des couleurs: Littérature et langage des Antilles (XVIIIᵉ, XIXᵉ, XXᵉ siècles)*. 2 vols. Paris, 1989.

Trinh, T. Minh-ha. "Cotton and Iron." In *Out There: Marginalization and Contemporary Cultures*. Ed. Russell Ferguson et al. Cambridge, Mass., 1990. 327–36.

———. *Woman, Native, Other: Writing Postcoloniality and Feminism*. Bloomington, Ind., 1989.

Tropiques: 1941–1945, collection complète. 2 vols. Paris, 1978.

Trousson, Raymond. "Jean-Jacques Rousseau et le mythe insulaire." In Marimoutou and Racault, *Insularité*. 105–13.

Valdman, Albert. *Le Créole: Structure, statut et origine*. Paris, 1978.

Valesio, Paolo. *Novantiqua: Rhetorics as a Contemporary Theory*. Bloomington, Ind., 1980.

Varadharajan, Asha. *Exotic Parodies: Subjectivity in Adorno, Said, and Spivak*. Minneapolis, 1995.

Vattimo, Gianni. *La fine della modernità: Nichilismo ed ermeneutica nella cultura post-moderna*. Milan, 1985.

Vaughan, Alden, and Virginia Vaughan. *Shakespeare's Caliban: A Cultural History*. Cambridge, Eng., 1991.

Veyrenc, Marie-Thérèse. *Édition critique du manuscrit de 'Paul et Virginie' de Bernardin de Saint-Pierre intitulé: 'Histoire de Mᵉˡˡᵉ de la Tour'*. Paris, 1975.

Walcott, Derek. *Collected Poems, 1948–1984*. New York, 1986.

———. "The Muse of History." In Coombs. 1–27.

———. "What the Twilight Said: An Overture." In Walcott, *Dream on Monkey Mountain and Other Plays*. New York, 1970. 1–40.

Wasserman, Renata R. Mautner. *Exotic Nations: Literature and Cultural Identity in the United States and Brazil, 1830–1930*. Ithaca, N.Y., 1994.

Watt, Ian. *The Rise of the Novel: Studies in Defoe, Richardson and Fielding*. London, 1957.

Webb, Barbara. *Myth and History in Caribbean Fiction: Alejo Carpentier, Wilson Harris, and Édouard Glissant*. Amherst, Mass., 1992.

Williams, Raymond. *The Country and the City*. London, 1993.

Willis, Susan. "Caliban as Poet: Reversing the Maps of Domination." In Chevigny and Laguardia. 92–105.

Wilson, Rob, and Arif Dirlik, eds. *Asia-Pacific as Space of Cultural Production*. Durham, N.C., 1995.

Wing, Nathaniel. "Écriture et Relation dans les romans d'Édouard Glissant." In Favre and Ferreira de Brito. 295–302.

Wordsworth, William. *The Fourteen-Book 'Prelude'*. Ed. W. J. B. Owen. Ithaca, N.Y., 1985.

Wynter, Sylvia. "Beyond Miranda's Meanings: Un/silencing the 'Demonic Ground' of Caliban's 'Woman.'" In Davies and Fido. 355–72.

———. "Beyond the Word of Man: Glissant and the New Discourse of the Antilles." *World Literature Today* 63.4 (1989): 637–47.

Yerro, Philippe-Alain. "La trace de Gani: Dialectique du mythe et de l'histoire dans l'approche du marronage chez É. Glissant." *Carbet* 10 (1990): 101–15.

Young, Robert J. C. *Colonial Desire: Hybridity in Theory, Culture and Race.* London, 1995.

Zamora, Lois Parkinson. *Writing the Apocalypse: Historical Vision in Contemporary U. S. and Latin American Fiction.* Cambridge, Eng., 1989.

Zimra, Clarisse. "Introduction." In Daniel Maximin, *Lone Sun.* Trans. C. Zimra. Charlottesville, Va., 1989. xi-lix.

———. "Je(ux) d'histoire chez Daniel Maximin et Vincent Placoly." In *L'héritage de Caliban.* Ed. Maryse Condé. Pointe-à-Pitre, 1992. 265–87.

———. "Tracées césairiennes dans *L'isolé soleil.*" In *Aimé Césaire, ou L'athanor d'un alchimiste: Actes du premier colloque international sur l'oeuvre littéraire d'Aimé Césaire.* Paris, 1987. 347–67.

Zobel, Joseph. *La rue cases-nègres.* Paris, 1974.

Index

In this index an "f" after a number indicates a separate reference on the next page, and an "ff" indicates separate references on the next two pages. A continuous discussion over two or more pages is indicated by a span of page numbers, e.g., "57–59." *Passim* is used for a cluster of references in close but not consecutive sequence.

Library of Congress Cataloging-in-Publication Data

Bongie, Chris.
   Islands and exiles : the creole identities of post/colonial
literature / Chris Bongie.
      p. cm.
   Includes bibliographical references and index.
    ISBN 0-8047-3280-9 (cloth). — ISBN 0-8047-3281-7 (pbk.).
    1. Developing countries—Literatures—History and
criticism.   2. Literature, Modern—History and criticism.
3. Islands in literature.   4. Colonies in literature.
5. Creole dialects in literature.   6. Exiles in literature.
7. Postcolonialism.   I. Title.
PN849.U43B66   1998
809'.891724—dc21   98-16325
                                               CIP

♾ This book is printed on acid-free, recycled paper.

Original printing 1998
Last figure below indicates year of this printing:
07 06 05 04 03 02 01 00 99 98